REPEATED-MEASURES ANOVA

$$SS_{\text{between}} = \sum \frac{T^2}{n} - \frac{G^2}{N} \qquad df_{\text{between}} = k - 1$$

$$SS_{\text{error}} = SS_{\text{within}} - SS_{\text{subjects}} \qquad df_{\text{error}} = (N - k) - (n - 1)$$

where $SS_{\text{within}} = \sum SS_{\text{inside each treatment}}$

and $SS_{\text{subjects}} = \sum \frac{P^2}{k} - \frac{G^2}{N}$

$$F = \frac{MS_{\text{between}}}{MS_{\text{error}}} \qquad \text{where each } MS = \frac{SS}{df}$$

TWO-FACTOR ANOVA

$$SS_{\text{between}} = \sum \frac{AB^2}{n} - \frac{G^2}{N} \qquad df_{\text{between}} = ab - 1$$

$$SS_{\text{factor A}} = \sum \frac{A^2}{bn} - \frac{G^2}{N} \qquad df_{\text{factor A}} = a - 1$$

$$SS_{\text{factor B}} = \sum \frac{B^2}{an} - \frac{G^2}{N} \qquad df_{\text{factor B}} = b - 1$$

$$SS_{A \times B} = SS_{\text{between}} - SS_A - SS_B \qquad df_{A \times B} = (a - 1)(b - 1)$$

$$SS_{\text{within}} = \sum SS_{\text{inside each treatment}} \qquad df_{\text{within}} = N - ab$$

$$F_A = \frac{MS_A}{MS_{\text{within}}} \qquad F_B = \frac{MS_B}{MS_{\text{within}}} \qquad F_{A \times B} = \frac{MS_{A \times B}}{MS_{\text{within}}}$$

where each $MS = \dfrac{SS}{df}$

PEARSON CORRELATION

$$r = \frac{SP}{\sqrt{SS_X SS_Y}}$$

where $SP = \sum (X - \overline{X})(Y - \overline{Y}) = \sum XY - \dfrac{(\sum X)(\sum Y)}{n}$

REGRESSION

$$\hat{Y} = bX + a \qquad \text{where } b = \frac{SP}{SS_X} \quad \text{and} \quad a = \overline{Y} - b\overline{X}$$

$$\text{Standard error of estimate} = \sqrt{\frac{\sum (Y - \hat{Y})^2}{n - 2}} = \sqrt{\frac{(1 - r^2)SS_Y}{n - 2}}$$

CHI-SQUARE STATISTIC

$$\chi^2 = \sum \frac{(f_o - f_e)^2}{f_e}$$

MANN-WHITNEY U

$$U_A = n_A n_B + \frac{n_A(n_A + 1)}{2} - \sum R_A$$

$$U_B = n_A n_B + \frac{n_B(n_B + 1)}{2} - \sum R_B$$

SPEARMAN CORRELATION

$$r_s = 1 - \frac{6\sum D^2}{n(n^2 - 1)}$$

TO THE STUDENT:

A complete study guide has been prepared by the authors to assist you in mastering concepts presented in this text. The study guide is available from your local bookstore under the title *Study Guide to Accompany Statistics for the Behavioral Sciences third edition*. If you cannot locate it in the bookstore, ask your bookstore manager to order it for you.

STATISTICS for the BEHAVIORAL SCIENCES

A First Course for Students of Psychology and Education

THIRD EDITION

STATISTICS for the BEHAVIORAL SCIENCES
A First Course for Students of Psychology and Education

THIRD EDITION

FREDERICK J GRAVETTER
State University of New York
College at Brockport

LARRY B. WALLNAU
State University of New York
College at Brockport

WEST PUBLISHING COMPANY
St. Paul / New York / Los Angeles / San Francisco

COPYEDITING	Linda Thompson
PROBLEM CHECKING	Roxy Peck
ART	Rolin Graphics,
	Illustrious, Inc.
COMPOSITION	The Clarinda Company
INDEXING	Lois Oster
COVER ART	© 1933 M.C. Escher/Cordon Art—Baarn—Holland
COVER DESIGN	Pollock Design Group

LIBRARY OF CONGRESS
CATALOGING-IN-PUBLICATION
DATA

Gravetter, Frederick J
  Statistics for the behavioral sciences / Frederick J Gravetter,
Larry B. Wallnau.—3rd ed.
    p.   cm.
  Includes bibliographical references and index.
  ISBN 0-314-90876-5
  1. Psychology—Statistical methods.   2. Educational statistics   I. Wallnau, Larry B.
II. Title.
BF39.G72   1991
519.5'0243—dc20   91-29602
                                                   CIP

CONTENTS

PREFACE

There are three kinds of lies: Lies, damned lies, and statistics.

This quote, attributed by Mark Twain to Benjamin Disraeli, reflects a commonly held belief that statistics (or perhaps even statisticians) should not be trusted. Unfortunately, this mistrust is sometimes justified. In this book, we shall see that statistical techniques are tools that are used to organize information and to make inferences from data. Like any other tool, statistics can be misused, which may result in misleading, distorted, or incorrect conclusions. It is no small wonder that we are sometimes skeptical when a statistician presents findings. However, if we understand the correct uses of statistical techniques, then we will recognize those situations in which statistical procedures have been incorrectly applied. We can decide which statistics are more believable. Therefore, the goal of this book is to teach not only the methods of statistics but also how to apply these methods appropriately. Finally, a certain amount of mistrust is healthy. That is, we should critically examine information and data before we accept its implications. As you shall see, statistical techniques help us look at data with a critical eye.

For those of you who are familiar with previous editions of *Statistics for the Behavioral Sciences*, you will notice that some changes have been made. Many of the changes are organizational and they are summarized in the next section, "To The Instructor." In revising this text, our students have been foremost in our minds. Over the years, they have provided honest and useful feedback. Their hard work and perseverance has made our writing and teaching most rewarding. We sincerely thank them.

Our friends at West Publishing once again have made an enormous contribution. We thank our editor Clark Baxter, developmental editor Nancy Hill-Whilton, production editor Emily Autumn, and promotion manager Kathryn Grimes. They are very capable people who possess many professional and technical skills. We are most grateful to them for their contributions to this project and for their guidance and enthusiasm. We also thank our problem-checker and troubleshooter Roxy Peck. We were very fortunate to have outstanding people provide reviews and helpful comments at various stages in the development of the manuscript. We thank the following colleagues for their thoughtful assistance:

Nancy S. Anderson
*University of Maryland–
College Park*

David L. Carpenter
Saint Bonaventure University

David P. Chiszor
University of Colorado–Boulder

Elliot M. Cramer
*University of North Carolina–
Chapel Hill*

George Domino
University of Arizona

Freeman F. Elzey
San Francisco State University

Elizabeth L. Glisky
University of Arizona

James Hodgson
Middle Tennessee State University

Daniel D. Moriarty
University of San Diego

David I. Mostofsky
Boston University

Randall R. Robey
*Southern Illinois University–
Carbondale*

Robert J. Schneider
Metropolitan State College

Elliot P. Schuman
Long Island University

Lynda Tompkins
Southwest Texas State University

Marian I. Upchurch
Southwest Texas State University

Douglas Wallen
Mankato State University

Hilda Lee Williams
Drake University

Leonard J. Williams
Glassboro State College

Carolina Zingale
Rutgers University

The authors are grateful to the literary executor of the late Sir Ronald A. Fisher, F.R.S., to Dr. Frank Yates, F.R.S., and to Longman Group Ltd. (London) for permission to adapt Tables III and VI from their book *Statistical Tables for Biological, Agricultural, and Medical Research* (6th edition, 1974). We are also grateful to the people at Minitab, Inc. for their assistance with the material in Chapter 20. John E. Grove, California State Polytechnic University, San Luis Obispo, was of great assistance in producing the printouts in Appendix E.

Finally, the authors thank the following family and friends for their assistance, encouragement, and above all, patience: Debbie, Justin, Melissa, Megan, JoAnn, Naomi, and the crew and plank owners of *Anodyne*.

TO THE INSTRUCTOR

The most noticeable change in this book is organizational. We have removed estimation from the hypothesis-testing chapters and now provide coverage of estimation in a single chapter. We believe this provides a smooth and logical development of hypothesis testing, from z-scores through the t statistics. Those of you who prefer to provide parallel coverage of hypothesis testing and estimation may still do so. The estimation chapter (Chapter 12) is organized into separate sections for the different estimation situations (σ known, σ unknown, independent-measures, repeated-measures), which may be covered with the preceding hypothesis-testing chapters.

We have also returned to using a separate chapter for hypothesis testing with the binomial distribution (Chapter 18). However, we still develop the binomial distribution in the probability chapter (Chapter 6). We have added coverage for measures of relationships, and we now include additional tests (sign test, median test).

Another change is in the way we cover computers. We have included a separate chapter on Minitab (Chapter 20). The sections in this chapter can be covered individually as the course progresses to relate the software to specific topics in the book. Computer notes in the margin facilitate this approach. We also have examples of SPSS^x printouts in the appendix that are cross-referenced to examples in the text. Finally, our computer coverage also includes a MYSTAT primer in the appendix. This software is available with the text.

We have included a new section (Demonstrations) of fully worked-out problems at the end of chapters. Thus, upon completion of a chapter, students can read the hints and cautions in Focus on Problem Solving, study the Demonstration, and then proceed to the Problems. We have improved sections that were troublesome for our students, included fresh examples and analogies where appropriate, and revised the end-of-chapter problems. Finally, a revised Statistics Organizer appendix describes the application and use of statistics tests and summarizes major sections of the text. New to this edition are decision maps provided to aid students in selecting appropriate procedures. What has not changed is our approach. As with previous editions, we still take the time to explain and discuss each statistical procedure and to give the rationale behind the formulas.

TO THE STUDENT

There is a common (and usually unfair) belief that visits to the dentist will be associated with fear and pain, even though dentists perform a service of great benefit to us. Although you initially may have some fears and anxieties about this course, we could argue that a statistics course also performs a beneficial service. This is evident when one considers that our world has become information-laden and information-dependent. The media inform us of the latest findings on oat bran and your health, global warming, economic trends, aging and memory, effects of educational programs, and so on. All these data-gathering efforts provide an enormous and unmanageable amount of information; enter the statisticians, who use statistical procedures to analyze, organize, and interpret vast amounts of data. Having a basic understanding of a variety of statistical procedures will help you understand these findings and even to examine them critically.

What about the fear of taking statistics? One way to deal with the fear is to get plenty of practice. You will notice that this book provides you with a number of opportunities to repeat the techniques you will be learning, in the form of Learning Checks, Examples, Demonstrations, and end-of-chapter Problems. We encourage you to take advantage of these opportunities. Also, we encourage you to read the text, rather than just memorizing the formulas. We have taken great pains to present each statistical procedure in a conceptual context that explains why the procedure was developed and when it should be used. If you read this material and gain an understanding of the basic concepts underlying a statistical formula, you will find that learning the formula and how to use it will be much easier.

Over the years, our students in our classes have given us many helpful suggestions. We learn from them. If you have any suggestion or comments about this book, you can send a note to us at the Department of Psychology, SUNY College at Brockport, Brockport, NY 14420. We may not be able to answer every letter, but we always appreciate the feedback.

Frederick J Gravetter

Larry B. Wallnau

Supplements

Instructor's Manual with Problem Solutions and Test Bank to Accompany STATISTICS FOR THE BEHAVIORAL SCIENCES 3/E, offers:

- Approximately 25 to 30 test questions per chapter consisting of true/false, multiple choice and computational problems.
- Complete solutions to all end of chapter problems.
- Transparency masters of most figures in the text.

Westest 2.0:

- A computerized test-generating software system intended to help instructors create, edit, store, and print tests with the personal computer.

Study Guide to Accompany *Statistics for the Behavioral Sciences* 3/e, includes:

- Learning objectives
- List of New Terms and Concepts
- List of New formulas
- Hints and Cautions
- Self Test
- Reviews consisting of 10 to 15 questions and their answers

Mystat:

- General statistics software, runs on IBM PC's and compatibles (with 512K memory) or the MacIntosh Computer and is available to adopters upon their request.
- A text appendix shows students how to use MYSTAT and provides example printouts.

STATISTICS for the BEHAVIORAL SCIENCES

A First Course for Students of Psychology and Education

THIRD EDITION

CHAPTER 1

INTRODUCTION TO STATISTICS

CONTENTS

Preview

The procedure is actually quite simple. First you arrange things into different groups depending on their makeup. Of course, one pile may be sufficient, depending on how much there is to do. If you have to go somewhere else due to lack of facilities, that is the next step; otherwise you are pretty well set. It is important not to overdo any particular endeavor. That is, it is better to do too few things at once than too many. In the short run this may not seem important, but complications from doing too many can easily arise. A mistake can be expensive as well. The manipulation of the appropriate mechanisms should be self-explanatory, and we need not dwell on it here. At first the whole procedure will seem complicated. Soon, however, it will become just another facet of life. It is difficult to foresee any end to the necessity for this task in the immediate future, but then one never can tell.*

The preceding paragraph was adapted from a psychology experiment reported by Bransford and Johnson (1972). If you have not read the paragraph yet, go back and read it now.

You probably find the paragraph a little confusing, and most of you probably think it is describing some obscure statistical procedure. Actually, this paragraph describes the everyday task of doing laundry. Now that you know the topic of the paragraph, try reading it again—it should make sense now.

Why did we begin a statistics textbook with a paragraph about washing clothes? Our goal is to demonstrate the importance of context—when not in the proper context, even the simplest material can appear difficult and confusing. In the Bransford and Johnson experiment, people who knew the topic before reading the paragraph were able to recall 73% more than people who did not know that it was about doing laundry. When you have the appropriate background, it is much easier to fit new material into your memory and to recall it later. In this book we begin each chapter with a preview. The purpose of the preview is to provide the background or context for the new material in the chapter. As you read each preview section, you should gain a general overview of the chapter content. Remember, all statistical methods were developed to serve a purpose. If you understand why a new procedure is needed, you will find it much easier to learn the procedure.

The objective for this first chapter is to provide an introduction to the topic of statistics and to give you some background for the rest of the book. We will discuss the role of statistics within the general field of scientific inquiry, and we will introduce some of the vocabulary and notation that are necessary for the statistical methods that follow. In some respects, this chapter serves as a preview section for the rest of the book.

Incidently, we cannot promise that statistics will be as easy as washing clothes. But if you begin each new topic within the proper context, you should eliminate some unnecessary confusion.

---

*Bransford, J. D., and Johnson, M. K. (1972), Contextual prerequisites for understanding: Some investigations of comprehension and recall. *Journal of Verbal Learning and Verbal Behavior, 11,* 717–726. Copyright by Academic Press. Reprinted by permission of the publisher and M. K. Johnson.

1.1 STATISTICS, SCIENCE, AND OBSERVATIONS

DEFINITIONS OF STATISTICS Why study statistics? is a question countless students ask. One simple answer is that statistics have become a common part of everyday life and therefore deserve some attention. A quick glance at the newspaper yields statistics that deal with crime rates, birth rates, average income, average snowfall, and so on. By a common definition, therefore, statistics consist of facts and figures.

DEFINITION   *Statistics* are facts and figures.

These statistics generally are informative and time saving because they condense large quantities of information into a few simple figures or statements. For example, the average snowfall in Chicago during the month of January is based on many observations made over many years. Few people would be interested in seeing a complete list of day-by-day snowfall amounts for the past 50 years. Even fewer people would be able to make much sense of all those numbers at a quick glance. But nearly everyone can understand and appreciate the meaning of an average.

There is another definition of statistics that applies to many of the topics in this book. When statisticians use the word statistics, they are referring to a set of methods and procedures that help present, characterize, analyze, and interpret observations.

DEFINITION   *Statistics* consist of a set of methods and rules for organizing and interpreting observations.

These statistical procedures help ensure that the data (or observations) are presented and interpreted in an accurate and informative way. Although facts and figures can be interesting and important, this book will focus on methods and procedures of statistics (see Box 1.1).

STATISTICS AND SCIENCE

These observations should be public, in the sense that others are able to repeat the observations using the same methods to see if the same findings will be obtained.

It is frequently said that science is *empirical*. That is, scientific investigation is based on making observations. Statistical methods enable researchers to describe and analyze the observations they have made. Thus, statistical methods are tools for science. We might think of science as consisting of methods for making observations and of statistics as consisting of methods for analyzing them.

On one mission of the space shuttle Columbia, so many scientific observations were relayed to computers on earth that scientists were hard pressed to convey, in terms the public could grasp, how much information had been gathered. One individual made a few quick computations on a pocket calculator and determined that if all the data from the mission were printed on pages, they would pile up as high as the Washington Monument. Such an enormous amount of scientific observation is unmanageable in this crude form. To interpret the data, many months of work have to be done by many people to statistically analyze them. Statistical methods serve scientific investigation by organizing and interpreting data.

1.2 POPULATIONS AND SAMPLES

WHAT ARE THEY?   A *population* is the entire group of individuals that a researcher wishes to study. By entire group, we literally mean every single individual.

DEFINITION   A *population* is the collection of all individuals of interest in a particular study.

STATISTICS IN EVERYDAY LIFE

THE FOLLOWING article appeared in the *New York Times* January, 4, 1991, and provides a good example of why a basic understanding of statistics is important for everyday tasks such as reading (and understanding) a newspaper article. This article presents a variety of statistics, using both definitions of the term. First, the report includes numerous facts and figures. In addition, the article reports the results of statistical methods that were used to help organize and interpret the figures.

Although you probably can make some sense of this report, there are a few statistical terms, such as median income, that you may not understand. After you finish Chapter 3, come back and read this newspaper article again. It should be perfectly clear by then.

PURCHASE INDEX UP FOR HOMES

WASHINGTON, Jan. 3 (AP)—Falling home prices and rising incomes combined to raise the typical American family's ability to buy a home to its highest level in 13 years, a real estate trade group said today.

The National Association of Realtors said its Housing Affordability Index reached 115.6 in November, up from 113.3 in October. This was the highest level since the index hit 116 in December 1977.

The 115.6 reading means a family earning the national median income of $35,467 had 115.6 percent of the income needed to qualify for conventional financing covering 80 percent of a median-priced home costing $91,300.

The median price of an existing home dropped $1,600, from $92,900 in October, while median income rose $114, from $32,353.

Improvement in housing affordability conditions were posted in all of the regions between October and November. But the typical family still fell short of having the funds to buy a median-priced home in the Northeast and the West, areas with the highest median prices.

In the Northeast, a family earning the median income of $41,565 had 91.9 percent of the income needed to buy a median-priced home costing $133,600. A western family with the median income of $37,825 had 82.2 percent of the income needed to buy a $138,700 home.

As you can well imagine, a population can be quite large—for example, the entire set of women on the planet earth. A researcher might be more specific, limiting the population for study to women who are registered voters in the United States. Perhaps the investigator would like to study the population consisting of women who are heads of state. Populations can obviously vary in size from extremely large to very small, depending on how the investigator defines the population. The population being studied should always be identified by the researcher. In addition, the population need not consist of people—it could be a population of rats, corporations, parts produced in a factory, or anything else an investigator wants to study. In practice, populations are typically very large, such as the population of fourth-grade children in the United States or the population of small businesses.

A *sample* is a subset of a population. It is a part of the population that is selected for study. A sample should always be identified in terms of the population from which it was selected.

DEFINITION   A *sample* is a set of individuals selected from a population, usually intended to represent the population in a study.

Just as we saw with populations, samples can vary greatly in size. Imagine that you are about to conduct an opinion poll in a large city. You are going to ask people if they believe the mayor is doing a good job. Since the poll will be conducted by telephone, you define your population as people who live in the city and are listed in the telephone directory. Realizing that it would take more time than you can spend to call everyone in the phone book (the entire population), you call 100 people. Notice that it is often necessary to study a sample because the population is so large that it would be impractical to study every member of the population. If you are more ambitious, you could use a larger sample—for example, 1000 people. Later in this book we will examine the benefits of using large samples.

PARAMETERS AND STATISTICS

When describing data, it is necessary to distinguish whether the data come from a population or a sample. Any characteristic of a population, for example, its average, is called a population *parameter*. On the other hand, a characteristic of a sample is called a *statistic*. The average of the scores for a sample is a statistic. The range of scores for a sample is another type of statistic. As we shall see later, statisticians frequently use different symbols for a parameter and a statistic. By using different symbols, we can readily tell if a characteristic, such as an average, is describing a population or a sample.

DEFINITIONS

A *parameter* is a value, usually numeric, that describes a population. A parameter may be obtained from a single measurement or it may be a value derived from a set of measurements from the population.

A *statistic* is a value, usually numeric, that describes a sample. A statistic may be obtained from a single measurement or it may be a value derived from a set of measurements from the sample.

Typically, every population parameter has a corresponding sample statistic, and much of this book is concerned with the relationship between sample statistics and the corresponding population parameters. In Chapter 7, for example, we examine the relationship between the mean obtained for a sample and the mean for the population from which the sample was obtained.

DESCRIPTIVE AND INFERENTIAL STATISTICAL METHODS

There are two major types of statistical methods. The first type, *descriptive statistics*, is used to simplify and summarize data. Data typically consist of a set of scores. These scores result from measurements taken during the course of making observations. For example, they may be IQ scores, ages, blood-alcohol levels, or number of correct responses. The original measurements or values are called *raw scores*.

DEFINITIONS

Descriptive statistical methods summarize, organize, and simplify data.

Data (plural) are measurements or observations. A *data set* is a collection of measurements or observations. *Datum* (singular) is a single measurement or observation.

A *raw score* is an original measurement or observed value.

Descriptive statistics are techniques that take raw scores and summarize them in a form that is more manageable. There are many descriptive procedures, but a common technique is to compute an average. Note that even if the data set has hundreds of scores, the average of those scores provides a single descriptive value for the entire set. Other descriptive techniques, including tables and graphs, will be covered in the next several chapters.

Inferential statistics are techniques that use sample data to make general statements about a population.

DEFINITION
Inferential statistics consist of techniques that allow us to study samples and then make generalizations about the populations from which they were selected.

As we saw with the telephone survey, it is usually not practical to make observations of every member of the population of interest. Because the population is much too large to telephone every individual, a sample is selected. By analyzing the results for the sample, we hope to make general statements about the population. In this example, results from the telephone survey (a sample) can be used to draw inferences about the opinions of the general population.

One problem with using samples, however, is that a sample provides only limited information about the population. Although samples are generally *representative* of their populations, a sample is not expected to give a perfectly accurate picture of the whole population. For example, suppose that a researcher gives a standard reading achievement test to a sample of 100 third-grade students and obtains an average score of 76. This does not mean that the entire population of third-graders would also average exactly 76 on the test. There is usually some discrepancy between a sample statistic and the corresponding population parameter, called *sampling error*, and it creates another problem to be addressed by inferential statistics.

DEFINITION
Sampling error is the discrepancy, or amount of error, that exists between a sample statistic and the corresponding population parameter.

The concept of sampling error is discussed in more detail in Chapter 7, but for now you should realize that a statistic obtained from a sample generally will not be identical to the corresponding population parameter. This fact may be easier to see if you consider the extreme case where the sample consists of a single individual. If a researcher gave a reading test to a sample of one third-grade student, you would not expect the score for that student to be exactly the same as the average score for all third-graders. In general, a bigger sample (say, 100 students) should give a more accurate picture of the population, but no matter how large the sample is, there always will be some discrepancy between the sample statistics and the population parameters. Example 1.1 shows how sampling error can affect the interpretation of experimental results, and why inferential statistical methods are needed to deal with this problem.

EXAMPLE 1.1

Figure 1.1 shows an overview of a general research situation and the role that descriptive and inferential statistics play. In this example, a researcher is examining the relative effectiveness of two teaching methods: method A and method B. One sample of students is taught by method A and a second sample is taught by method B. Then, all the students are given a standard achievement test. At the end of the experiment, the researcher has two sets of data: the scores for sample A and the scores for sample B (see Figure 1.1). Now is the time to begin using statistics.

First, descriptive statistics are used to simplify the pages of data. For example, the researcher could draw a graph showing the scores for each sample or compute the average score for each sample. Note that descriptive methods provide a simplified, organized description of the scores. In this example, the students taught by method A averaged 76 on the standardized test and the students taught by method B averaged only 71.

Once the researcher has described the results, the next step is to interpret the outcome. This is the role of inferential statistics. In this example, the researcher must decide whether the 5-point difference between the two sample means reflects a real difference between the two teaching methods. Remember, sample A represents the population of students taught by method A, and sample B represents the population of students taught by method B. However, neither sample provides a perfectly accurate picture of its population. Thus, the 5-point difference between the two sample means does not necessarily mean there is a corresponding 5-point difference between the two population means. In fact, it is possible that there is actually no difference between the two teaching methods and the sample difference is simply the result of sampling error. One goal of inferencial statistics is to help the researcher interpret sample data: Does the difference between samples represent a real difference between populations, or is the sample mean difference merely the result of sampling error? (See Figure 1.1.)

Inferential statistics are a necessary part of conducting experiments. Suppose a researcher would like to test the effectiveness of a new therapy program for depression. It would be too costly and time-consuming to test the program on all depressed individuals. Therefore, the treatment is tested on a sample of depressed patients. Of course, the researcher would like to see these people overcome their misery, but keep in mind that one is not just interested in this sample of individuals. The investigator would like to generalize the findings to the entire population. If the treatment program is effective for the sample of depressed people, it would be great to be able to state with confidence that it will also work for others. It is important to note that inferential statistical methods will allow meaningful generalizations only if the individuals in the sample are representative of the population. One way to ensure that the sample is representative is to use *random sampling*, or *random selection*. Although there are several formally defined techniques for random sampling, one basic requirement is that all individuals in the population have the same chance of being selected. There will be more to say about this topic in later chapters.

Figure 1.1

The role of statistics in experimental research.

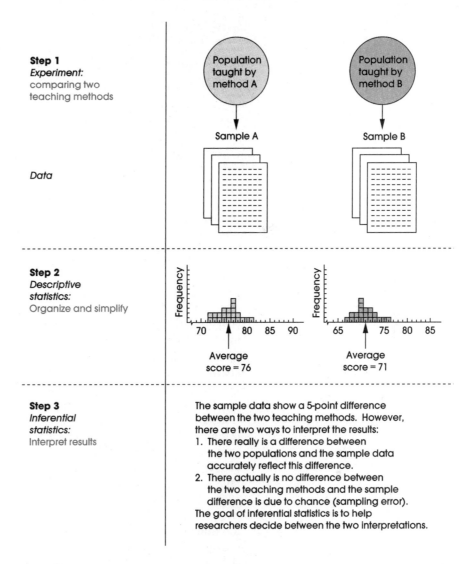

Step 1
Experiment:
comparing two
teaching methods

Data

Step 2
*Descriptive
statistics:*
Organize and simplify

Step 3
*Inferential
statistics:*
Interpret results

The sample data show a 5-point difference between the two teaching methods. However, there are two ways to interpret the results:
1. There really is a difference between the two populations and the sample data accurately reflect this difference.
2. There actually is no difference between the two teaching methods and the sample difference is due to chance (sampling error).
The goal of inferential statistics is to help researchers decide between the two interpretations.

DEFINITION

Random selection, or *random sampling,* is a process for obtaining a sample from a population that requires that every individual in the population has the same chance of being selected for the sample. A sample obtained by random selection is called a *random sample.*

LEARNING CHECK

1. Science is empirical. This means that science is based on _____.

2. Science consists of methods for making observations, and statistics are methods for _____ them.

3. A descriptive characteristic of a population is a _____. A characteristic of a sample is called a _____.

4. What are statistics?

5. What is the purpose of descriptive statistics?

6. Inferential statistics attempt to use _____ to make general statements about _____.

7. One way to ensure that a sample is representative of a population is to use _____ selection of the sample.

ANSWERS   1. observation   2. analyzing   3. parameter; statistic
4. By one definition, statistics are facts and figures. In this book, the term statistics refers to a set of methods for analyzing and interpreting data.
5. to simplify and summarize data   6. sample data; a population   7. random

1.3 THE SCIENTIFIC METHOD AND THE DESIGN OF EXPERIMENTS

OBJECTIVITY   As noted earlier, science is empirical in that knowledge is acquired by observation. Another important aspect of scientific inquiry is that it should be *objective*. That is, theoretical biases of the researcher should not be allowed to influence the findings. Usually when a study is conducted, the investigator has a hunch about how it will turn out. This hunch, actually a prediction about the outcome of the study, is typically based on a theory that the researcher has. It is important that scientists conduct their studies in a way that will prevent these hunches or biases from influencing the outcome of the research. Experimenter bias can operate very subtly. Rosenthal and Fode (1963) had student volunteers act as experimenters in a learning study. The students were given rats to train in a maze. Half of the students were led to believe that their rats were "maze-bright," and the remainder were told their rats were "maze-dull." In reality they all received the same kind of rat. Nevertheless, the data showed real differences in the rats' performance for the two groups of experimenters. Somehow the students' expectations influenced the outcome of the experiment. Apparently there were differences between the groups in how the students handled the rats, and the differences accounted for the effect. For a detailed look at experimenter bias, you might read the review by Rosenthal (1963).

RELATIONSHIPS BETWEEN VARIABLES   Science attempts to discover orderliness in the universe. Even people of ancient civilizations noted regularity in the world around them—the change of seasons, changes in the moon's phases, changes in the tides—and they were able to make many observations to document these orderly changes. Something that can change or have different values is called a *variable*.

DEFINITION   A *variable* is a characteristic or condition that changes or has different values for different individuals.

Variables are often identified by letters (usually X or Y). For example, the variable *height* could be identified by the letter X and *shoe size* could be identified by Y. It is reasonable to expect a consistent, orderly relation between these two variables: As *X* changes, *Y* also changes in a predictable way.

A value that does not change or vary is called a *constant*. For example, an instructor may adjust the exam scores for a class by adding 4 points to each student's score. Because every individual gets the same four points, this value is a constant.

DEFINITION   A *constant* is a characteristic or condition that does not vary but is the same for every individual.

A constant is often identified by its numerical value, such as 4, or by the letter *C*. Adding a constant to each score, for example, could be represented by the expression $X + C$.

Science involves a search for relationships between variables. For example, there is a relationship between the amount of rainfall and crop growth. Rainfall is one of the variables. It varies from year to year and season to season. Crop growth is the other variable. Some years the corn stalks seem short and stunted; other years they are tall and full. When there is very little rainfall, the crops are short and shriveled. When rain is ample, the crops show vigorous growth. Note that in order to document the relationship, one must make observations—that is, measurements of the amount of rainfall and size of the crops.

There are a variety of methods for obtaining observations and investigating relationships between variables. Most of these methods can be classified into three basic categories, *correlational*, *experimental*, and *quasi-experimental*, each of which is discussed in the following section.

THE CORRELATIONAL METHOD

The simplest way to look for relationships between variables is to make observations of changes in two variables. This is frequently called an *observational* or *correlational method*.

DEFINITION   In a *correlational method*, changes are observed in two variables to see if there is a relationship.

Suppose a researcher wants to examine whether or not a relationship exists between length of time in an executive position and assertiveness. A large sample of executives takes a personality test designed to measure assertiveness. Also, the investigator determines how long each person has served in an executive-level job. Suppose the investigator found that there is a relationship between the two variables—that the longer a person had an executive position, the more assertive that person tended to be. Naturally, one might jump to the conclusion that being an executive for a long time makes a person more assertive. The problem with the correlational method is that it provides no information about cause-and-effect relationships. An equally plausible explanation for the relationship is that assertive people choose to stay or survive longer in executive positions than less-assertive individuals. To determine the cause and the effect in a relationship, it is necessary to *manipulate and control* one of the variables being studied. This is accomplished by the experimental method.

THE EXPERIMENTAL METHOD

In more complex experiments, a researcher may systematically manipulate more than one variable and may observe more than one variable. Here we are considering the simplest case, where only one variable is manipulated and only one variable is observed.

The goal of the experimental method is to establish a cause-and-effect relationship between two variables. That is, the method of observing variables is intended to show that changes in one variable are *caused* by changes in the other variable. One distinguishing characteristic of the experimental method is that the researcher *manipulates* and controls one of the variables under study. Usually the manipulation is accomplished by creating two or more different treatment conditions. For example, a researcher could manipulate temperature by setting the room temperature at 70° for one condition and then changing the temperature to 90° for a second condition. The researcher would like to demonstrate that changes in temperature cause differences in performance on a memory task. The experiment would consist of observing the memory performance for a group of individuals (often called *subjects*) in the 70° room and comparing their scores with another group that is tested in the 90° room. The structure of this experiment is shown in Figure 1.2.

To be able to say that differences in memory performance are caused by temperature, the researcher must rule out any other possible explanations for the difference. To accomplish this, the experimental method has two other distinguishing characteristics. First, the experimental method requires *random assignment,* so that each subject has an equal chance of being assigned to each of the treatment conditions. Random assignment helps assure that the subjects in one treatment condition are not substantially different from the subjects in another treatment condition at the beginning of the study. For example, a researcher should not assign all the young subjects to one condition and all the old subjects to another. If this were done, the researcher could not be sure that the difference in memory performance was caused by temperature; instead, it could be caused by age differences. Second, the experimental method requires that the treatment conditions be identical except for the one variable that is being manipulated. This is accomplished by *controlling* or *holding constant* any other variables that might influence performance. For example, the researcher should test both groups of subjects at the same time of day, in the same room, with the same instructions, and so on. Again, the goal is to eliminate the contribution of all other variables,

Figure 1.2

Volunteers are randomly assigned to one of two treatment groups: 70° room or 90° room. After memorizing a list of words, subjects are tested by having them write down as many words as possible from the list. A difference between the groups in performance is attributed to the treatment—the temperature of the room.

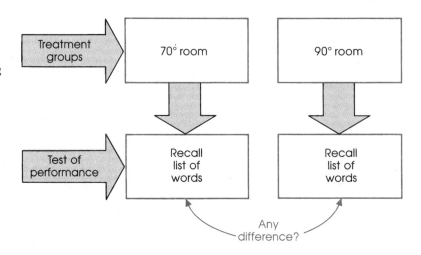

except for temperature, that might account for the difference in memory performance.

DEFINITION

In the *experimental method,* one variable is manipulated while changes are observed in another variable. To establish a cause-and-effect relationship between the two variables, an experiment attempts to eliminate or minimize the effects of all other variables by using *random assignment* and by *controlling* or *holding constant* other variables that might influence the results.

THE INDEPENDENT AND DEPENDENT VARIABLES

Specific names are used for the two variables that are studied by the experimental method. The variable that is manipulated by the experimenter is called the *independent variable.* It can be identified as the treatment conditions to which subjects are assigned. For the example in Figure 1.2, temperature is the independent variable. The variable that is observed to assess a possible effect of the manipulation is the *dependent variable.*

DEFINITIONS

The *independent variable* is the variable that is manipulated or controlled by the researcher. In behavioral research, the independent variable usually consists of the two (or more) treatment conditions to which subjects are exposed.

The *dependent variable* is the one that is observed for changes in order to assess the effect of the treatment.

In psychological research, the dependent variable is typically a measurement or score obtained for each subject. For the temperature experiment (Figure 1.2), the dependent variable is the number of words recalled on the memory test. Differences between groups in performance on the dependent variable suggest that the manipulation had an effect. That is, changes in the dependent variable *depend* on the independent variable.

Often we can identify one condition of the independent variable that receives no treatment. It is used for comparison purposes and is called the *control group.* The group that does receive the treatment is the *experimental group.*

DEFINITIONS

A *control group* is a condition of the independent variable that does not receive the experimental treatment. Typically, a control group either receives no treatment or receives a neutral, placebo treatment. The purpose of a control group is to provide a baseline for comparison with the experimental group.

An *experimental group* does receive an experimental treatment.

Note that the independent variable always consists of at least two values. (Something must have at least two different values before you can say that it is "variable.") For the temperature experiment (Figure 1.2), the independent variable is 90° versus 70° room. For an experiment with an experimental group and a control group, the independent variable would be treatment versus no treatment.

PROBLEMS THAT CAN ARISE IN EXPERIMENTS

In general, the purpose of an experiment is to show that the manipulated variable, and *only* that variable, is responsible for the changes in the second variable. Any difference that exists between the treatment conditions other than the manipulated variable is called a *confounding variable*. When a researcher allows the treatment conditions to differ with respect to some variable other than the ones being manipulated or controlled, the experiment is flawed and the researcher cannot interpret the results as demonstrating a cause-and-effect relation.

DEFINITION

A *confounding variable* is an uncontrolled variable that is unintentionally allowed to vary systematically with the independent variable.

For example, an instructor would like to assess the effectiveness of computer laboratory exercises in assisting students to grasp the fundamentals of statistics. There are two treatment conditions. One section of statistics is taught three times a week as a lecture course. A second section of students also meets three times a week, but one of these meetings is devoted to computer exercises in statistics. Professor Smith teaches the lecture, and Professor Jones teaches the second group of students. At the end of the semester, both groups receive the same final exam, and their performances are compared. The experiment is summarized in Figure 1.3.

Let's assume that a statistical analysis determined that the lecture/lab students performed better on the final exam. Can the instructors conclude that the method of instruction had an effect on learning? The answer is emphatically *no*. The independent variable, method of instruction, is not the only way the groups differ in terms of how they are treated. The instructor was allowed to vary along with the method of instruction. It is possible that

Figure 1.3

In this experiment, the effect of instructional method (the independent variable) on test performance (the dependent variable) is examined. However, any difference between groups in performance cannot be attributed to the method of instruction. In this experiment, there is a confounding variable. The instructor teaching the course varies with the independent variable, so that the treatment of the groups differs in more ways than one (instructional method and instructor vary).

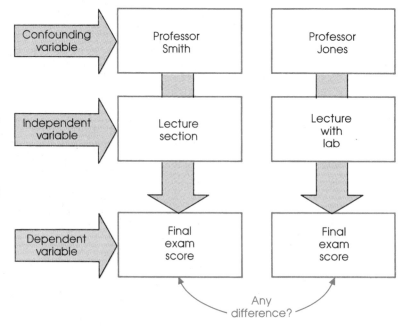

the lecture/lab group performed better because Professor Jones is a better instructor, one who motivates students and can explain concepts in understandable terms. That is, the difference between groups in performance might be due to the different instructors rather than the different treatments. One cannot be sure which interpretation is correct. When a study is confounded, it is impossible to make meaningful conclusions about the results.

THE QUASI-EXPERIMENTAL METHOD

The final research strategy that we discuss combines elements of the experimental method and the correlation method and is called the *quasi-experimental method*. The distinguishing characteristic of the quasi-experimental method is that the researcher does *not* directly manipulate the independent variable and/or the researcher does *not* randomly assign subjects to treatment conditions. Instead, this method compares preexisting groups of subject or preexisting conditions. For example, a researcher might want to compare attitude scores for men versus women. Although the researcher will have two groups of subjects (as in an experiment), the researcher does not manipulate the treatment conditions and does not assign subjects to groups—each subject assigns himself or herself to a specific group based on the subject's gender. Or, a researcher might compare anxiety levels before versus after a major earthquake. Again, the researcher does *not* manipulate the treatment conditions.

In quasi-experimental research, the variable that differentiates the groups is similar to the independent variable in an experiment and often is referred to as an independent variable. More precisely, however, it is called a *quasi-independent variable*. As in an experiment, the score obtained for each subject is called the dependent variable. In the example comparing attitude scores for men and women, gender is the quasi-independent variable, and attitude is the dependent variable.

DEFINITION

The *quasi-experimental method* examines differences between preexisting groups of subjects (for example, men versus women) or differences between preexisting conditions (before versus after an earthquake). The variable that is used to differentiate the groups is called the *quasi-independent variable,* and the score obtained for each individual is the dependent variable.

The quasi-experimental method often is used to address causal questions (for example, did the earthquake cause a change in anxiety?). However, this method does not use random assignment and cannot control for other (potentially confounding) variables. Therefore, the quasi-experimental method is essentially a correlational strategy, and the results from this research strategy cannot be used to establish unambiguous cause-and-effect relationships.

THEORIES AND HYPOTHESES

Theories are a very important part of psychological research. A psychological theory typically consists of a number of statements about the underlying mechanisms of behavior. Theories are important in that they help organize and unify many observations. They may try to account for very large areas of psychology, such as a general theory of learning. However, they may be more specific, such as a theory of the mechanisms involved in just avoidance learning. A theory is especially useful if it directs and promotes future research and provides specific predictions for the outcomes of that research.

When an investigator designs an experiment, there almost always is a specific hypothesis which is addressed. A *hypothesis* is a hunch about the result that will be obtained from the experiment.

DEFINITION

A *hypothesis* is a prediction about the outcome of an experiment. In experimental research, a hypothesis makes a prediction about how the manipulation of the independent variable will affect the dependent variable.

A theory is especially helpful if it generates many testable hypotheses. By testable we mean the hypothesis can be confirmed or disconfirmed by making observations (conducting studies).

Hypotheses are often derived from the theory that the researcher is developing. An experimenter can state the hypothesis as a prediction— specifically, as a relationship between the independent and dependent variables. Simply stated, a hypothesis is a prediction about the effect of the treatment. Therefore, we can think of an experiment as a test of a hypothesis. A very important part of inferential statistics consists of the statistical analysis of hypothesis tests. Much of the book will focus on this topic.

CONSTRUCTS AND OPERATIONAL DEFINITIONS

Theories contain hypothetical concepts, which help describe the mechanisms that underlie behavioral phenomena. These concepts are called *constructs,* and they cannot be observed because they are hypothetical. For example, intelligence, personality types, and motives are hypothetical constructs. They are used in theories to organize observations in terms of underlying mechanisms. If constructs are hypothetical and cannot be observed, then how can they possibly be studied? The answer is that we have to *define* the construct so that it can be studied. An *operational definition* defines a construct in terms of an observable and measurable response. This definition should include the process and operations involved in making the observations. For example, an operational definition for emotionality might be stated as the amount of increase in heart rate after a person is insulted. An operational definition of intelligence might be the score on the Wechsler Adult Intelligence Scale.

DEFINITIONS

Constructs are hypothetical concepts that are used in theories to organize observations in terms of underlying mechanisms.

An *operational definition* defines a construct in terms of specific operations or procedures and the measurements that result from them. Thus an operational definition consists of two components: First, it describes a set of operations or procedures for measuring a construct. Second, it defines the construct in terms of the resulting measurements.

LEARNING CHECK

1. A researcher would like to compare social interaction skills for kindergarten children who have attended a formal preschool program versus children with no preschool experience.

   a. Does this study use an experimental, correlational, or quasi-experimental strategy?

   b. What is the dependent variable for this study?

2. Cause-and-effect relationships cannot be determined by a correlational method. (True or false?)

3. In a memory experiment, subjects memorize a list of words and then must recall as many words as possible after a 6-hour retention interval. One group sleeps during the retention interval, while people in the other group remain awake and go about their daily routine. The number of words recalled is measured for each subject. The experimenter wants to determine if type of activity during the retention interval has an effect on the number of words recalled. For this study, what is the independent variable? What is the dependent variable?

4. A hypothesis can be stated as a prediction about the effect of _____ on _____.

5. An operational definition defines a construct in terms of _____.

ANSWERS

1. **a.** quasi-experimental

   b. The dependent variable is social interaction skill.

2. true

3. The independent variable is the type of activity during the retention interval; the dependent variable is the number of words recalled.

4. an independent variable (or treatment); a dependent variable

5. a measurable response

1.4 SCALES OF MEASUREMENT

WHAT IS A MEASUREMENT?

It should be obvious by now that data collection requires that we make measurements of our observations. Measurement involves either categorizing events (qualitative measurements) or using numbers to characterize the size of the event (quantitative measurement). There are several types of scales that are associated with measurements. The distinctions among the scales are important because they underscore the limitations of certain types of measurements and because certain statistical procedures are appropriate for data collected on some scales but not on others. If you were interested in people's heights, for example, you could measure a group of individuals by simply classifying them into three categories: tall, medium, and short. However, this simple classification would not tell you much about the actual heights of the individuals, and these measurements would not give you enough information to calculate an average height for the group. Although the simple classification would be adequate for some purposes, you would need more-sophisticated measurements before you could answer more-detailed questions. In this section we examine four different scales of measurement, beginning with the simplest and moving to the most sophisticated.

THE NOMINAL SCALE

A *nominal scale* of measurement labels observations so that they fall into different categories.

DEFINITION

In a *nominal scale* measurement, observations are labeled and categorized.

The word *nominal* means "having to do with names." Measurements that are made on this scale involve naming things. For example, if we wish to know the sex of a person responding to a questionnaire, it would be measured on a nominal scale consisting of two categories. A product warranty card might have you check the box that best describes your occupation, and it lists "sales," "professional," "skilled trade," "other (please specify)." Occupations are being measured in terms of categories; therefore, a nominal scale is being used. A researcher observing the behavior of a group of infant monkeys might categorize responses as playing, grooming, feeding, acting aggressive, or showing submissiveness. Again, this instance typifies a nominal scale of measurement. The nominal scale consists of qualitative distinctions. No attempt is made to measure the size of the event or response. The scales that follow do reflect an attempt to make quantitative distinctions.

THE ORDINAL SCALE

In an *ordinal scale* of measurement, observations are ranked in terms of size or magnitude. As the word *ordinal* implies, the investigator simply arranges the observations in rank order.

DEFINITION

An *ordinal scale* of measurement consists of ranking observations in terms of size or magnitude.

For example, a job supervisor is asked to rank employees in terms of how well they perform their work. The resulting data will tell us who the supervisor considers the best worker, the second best, and so on. However, the data provide no information about the amount that the workers differ in job performance. The data may reveal that Jan, who is ranked second, is viewed as doing better work than Joe, who is ranked third. However, the data do not reveal *how much* better. This is a limitation of measurements on an ordinal scale.

THE INTERVAL AND RATIO SCALES

In an *interval scale* of measurement, equal intervals between numbers reflect equal differences in magnitude. On an interval scale the 1-point difference between $X = 1$ and $X = 2$ reflects exactly the same magnitude as any other

1-point difference on the scale. On a ruler, for example, a 1-inch interval is the same size at every location on the ruler. Thus, an interval scale allows you to measure differences in the size or amount of events. However, an interval scale does not have an absolute zero point that indicates complete absence of the variable being measured, so ratios of magnitude are not meaningful. A *ratio scale* of measurement has an absolute zero point, and thus ratios of numbers on this scale do reflect ratios of magnitudes.

DEFINITIONS

In an *interval scale,* equal differences (or intervals) between numbers on the scale reflect equal differences in magnitude. However, ratios of magnitudes are not meaningful.

In a *ratio scale*, ratios of numbers do reflect ratios of magnitudes. Such a scale has an absolute zero point.

The distinction between an interval scale and a ratio scale is demonstrated in Example 1.2.

EXAMPLE 1.2

A researcher obtains measurements of height for a group of 8-year-old boys. Initially, the researcher simply records each child's height in inches, obtaining values such as 44, 51, 49, and so on. These initial measurements constitute a ratio scale. A value of zero represents no height (absolute zero). Also, it is possible to use these measurements to form ratios. For example, a child who is 80 inches tall is twice as tall as a 40-inch-tall child.

Now suppose the researcher converts the initial measurements into a new scale by calculating the difference between each child's actual height and the average height for this age group. A child who is 1 inch taller than average now gets a score of +1; a child 4 inches taller than average gets a score of +4. Similarly, a child who is 2 inches shorter than average gets a score of −2. The new scores constitute an interval scale of measurement. A score of zero no longer indicates an absence of height; now it simply means average height.

Notice that both sets of scores involve measurement in inches, and you can compute differences, or intervals, on either scale. For example, there is a 6-inch difference in height between two boys who measure 57 and 51 inches tall on the first scale. Likewise, there is a 6-inch difference between two boys who measure +9 and +3 on the second scale. However, you should also notice that ratio comparisons are not possible on the second scale. For example, a boy who measures +9 is *not* three times as tall as a boy who measures +3.

Most dependent variables we will encounter can be measured on either an interval or a ratio scale. These scales allow basic arithmetic operations that permit us to calculate differences between scores, to sum scores, and to calculate average scores. However, you should know that the distinction between different scales of measurements is often unclear when considering specific measurements. For example, the scores resulting from an IQ test are usually treated as measurements on an interval scale, but many researchers believe that IQ scores are more accurately described as ordinal data. An IQ score of 105 is clearly greater than a score of 100, but there is some question concerning *how much* difference in intelligence is reflected in the 5-point difference between these two scores.

1.5 DISCRETE AND CONTINUOUS VARIABLES

WHAT ARE THEY AND HOW DO THEY DIFFER?

The variables in a study can be characterized by the type of values that can be assigned to them. A *discrete variable* consists of separate, indivisible categories. For this type of variable there are no intermediate values between two adjacent categories. Consider the values displayed when dice are rolled. Between neighboring values—for example, seven dots and eight dots—no other values can ever be observed.

DEFINITION

A *discrete variable* consists of separate, indivisible categories. No values can exist between two neighboring categories.

A discrete variable is typically restricted to whole countable numbers—for example, the number of children in a family or the number of students attending class. If you observe class attendance from day to day, you may find 18 students one day and 19 students the next day. However, it is impossible ever to observe a value between 18 and 19. A discrete variable may also consist of observations that differ qualitatively. For example, a psychologist observing patients may classify some as having panic disorders, others as having dissociative disorders, and some as having psychotic disorders. The type of disorder is a discrete variable because there are distinct and finite categories that can be observed.

On the other hand, many variables are not discrete. Variables such as time, height, or weight are not limited to a fixed set of separate, indivisible categories. You can measure time, for example, in hours, minutes, seconds, or fractions of seconds. These variables are called *continuous* because they can be divided into an infinite number of fractional parts.

DEFINITION

For a *continuous variable*, there are an infinite number of possible values that fall between any two observed values. A continuous variable is divisible into an infinite number of fractional parts.

For example, subjects are given problems to solve, and a researcher records the amount of time it takes them to find the solutions. One person may take 31 seconds to solve the problems, whereas another may take 32 seconds. Between these two values it is possible to find any fractional amount—$31\frac{1}{2}$, $31\frac{1}{4}$, $31\frac{1}{10}$—provided the measuring instrument is sufficiently accurate. Time is a continuous variable. A continuous variable can be pictured as a number line that is continuous. That is, there are an infinite number of points on the line without any gaps or separations between neighboring points (see Figure 1.4).

Figure 1.4

When measuring time to the nearest whole second, measurements of 32.8 and 33.1 are assigned the value of 33 seconds. Any measurement in the interval between 32.5 and 33.5 will be assigned the value of 33 (part a). The boundaries that define each interval are called the real limits of the interval (part b).

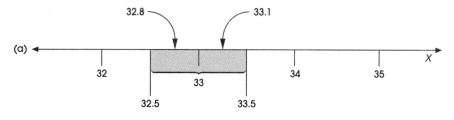

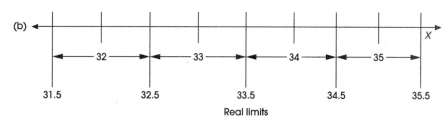

CONTINUOUS VARIABLES AND REAL LIMITS

Measurement of a continuous variable typically involves assigning an individual to an *interval* on the number line rather than a single point. For example, if you are measuring time to the nearest second, measurements of $X = 32.8$ seconds and $X = 33.1$ seconds are both rounded to scores of $X = 33$ seconds (see Figure 1.4(a)). Note that the score $X = 33$ is not a single point on the number line, but instead represents an interval on the line. In this example, a score of 33 corresponds to an interval from 32.5 to 33.5. Any measurement that falls within this interval will be assigned a value of $X = 33$ seconds. The boundaries that form the interval are called the *real limits* of the interval. For this example, 32.5 is the *lower real limit* and 33.5 is the *upper real limit* of the interval that corresponds to $X = 33$.

DEFINITION

For a continuous variable, each score actually corresponds to an interval on the scale. The boundaries that separate these intervals are called *real limits*. The real limit separating two adjacent scores is located exactly halfway between the scores. Each score has two real limits, one at the top of its interval called the *upper real limit* and one at the bottom of its interval called the *lower real limit*. Note that the upper real limit of one interval is also the lower real limit of the next higher interval.

In Figure 1.4(b), note that neighboring X values share a real limit. For example, the score $X = 33$ has an upper real limit of 33.5. The value 33.5 is also the lower real limit for $X = 34$. Thus, on a continuous number line such as in Figure 1.4, there are no gaps between adjacent intervals.

The concept of real limits applies to any measurement on a continuous variable, even when the score categories are not whole numbers. For example, if you were measuring time to the nearest tenth of a second, the measurement categories would be 31.0, 31.1, 31.2, and so on. Each of these categories represents an interval on the scale that is bounded by real limits. For example, a score of $X = 31.1$ seconds indicates that the actual measurement is in an interval bounded by a lower real limit of 31.05 and an upper real limit of 31.15. Remember, the real limits are always halfway between adjacent categories.

Later in this book, real limits are used for constructing graphs and for various calculations with continuous scales. For now, however, you should realize that real limits are a necessity whenever you make measurements of a continuous variable.

LEARNING CHECK

1. An instructor records the order in which students complete their tests— that is, the first to finish, the second to finish, and so on. A(n) _____ scale of measurement is used in this instance.

2. The Scholastic Aptitude Test (SAT) most likely measures aptitude on a(n) _____ scale.

3. In a study on perception of facial expressions, subjects must classify the emotions displayed in photographs of people as either anger, sadness, joy, disgust, fear, or surprise. Emotional expression is measured on a(n) _____ scale.

4. A researcher studies the factors that determine how many children couples decide to have. The variable, number of children, is a _____ (discrete/continuous) variable.

5. An investigator studies how concept-formation ability changes with age. Age is a _____ (discrete/continuous) variable.

6. **a.** When measuring weight to the nearest pound, what are the real limits for a score of $X = 150$ pounds?

   b. When measuring weight to the nearest ½ pound, what are the real limits for a score of $X = 144.5$ pounds?

ANSWERS   1. ordinal   **2.** interval   **3.** nominal   **4.** discrete   **5.** continuous

6. **a.** 149.5 and 150.5

   b. 144.25 and 144.75

1.6 STATISTICAL NOTATION

Measurements of behavior usually will provide data composed of numerical values. These numbers form the basis of the computations that are done for statistical analyses. There is a standardized notation system for statistical procedures, and it is used to identify terms in equations and mathematical operations. Some general mathematical operations, notation, and basic algebra are outlined in the review section of Appendix A. There is also a skills assessment exam (page A-1) to help you determine if you need the basic mathematics review. Here we will introduce some statistical notation that is used throughout this book. In subsequent chapters, additional notation will be introduced as it is needed.

SCORES

X
37
35
35
30
25
17
16

X	Y
72	165
68	151
67	160
68	146
70	160
66	133

Making observations of a dependent variable in a study will typically yield values or scores for each subject. Raw scores are the original, unchanged set of scores obtained in the study. Scores for a particular variable are represented by the letter X. For example, if performance in your statistics course is measured by tests and you obtain a 35 on the first test, then we could state that $X = 35$. A set of scores can be presented in a column that is headed by X. For example, a list of quiz scores from your class might be presented as shown in the margin.

When observations are made for two variables, there will be two scores for each subject. The data can be presented as two lists labeled X and Y for the two variables. For example, observations for people's height in inches (variable X) and weight in pounds (variable Y) can be presented as shown in the margin. Each pair X, Y represents the observations made of a single subject.

It is also useful to specify how many scores are in a set. The number of scores in a data set is represented by the letter N. For populations we will use an uppercase N, and for samples we will use a lowercase n. (Throughout the book, notational differences are used to distinguish between samples and populations.) For the height and weight data, $N = 6$ for both variables.

SUMMATION NOTATION

Many of the computations required in statistics will involve adding up a set of scores. Because this procedure is used so frequently, there is a special notation used to refer to the sum of a set of scores. The Greek letter sigma, or Σ, is used to stand for summation. The expression ΣX means to add all the scores for variable X. The summation sign Σ can be read as "the sum of." Thus ΣX is read "the sum of the scores." For the following set of quiz scores,

$$10, \quad 6, \quad 7, \quad 4$$

$\Sigma X = 27$ and $N = 4$. There are a number of rules of summation that help identify which scores are added together and which mathematical operation is performed first when several are required. These rules are summarized as follows.

1. When there are two variables X and Y, ΣX indicates the sum of the $X's$, and ΣY refers to the sum of the $Y's$. For the following data, $\Sigma X = 16$, and $\Sigma Y = 34$:

X	Y	
3	10	$\Sigma X = 3 + 1 + 7 + 3 + 2 = 16$
1	4	
7	6	$\Sigma Y = 10 + 4 + 6 + 5 + 9 = 34$
3	5	
2	9	

2. When two variables (X and Y) are multiplied together, the product is represented by the symbols XY. Note that the multiplication sign is

not written between the symbols ($X \times Y$ can cause confusion). The expression XY is understood to mean "X times Y." The table in the margin shows scores for three individuals. For each person there is a score for variable X, a score for variable Y, and the product of the two scores, XY.

The total for the X values, $\Sigma X = 9$, is obtained by adding the scores in that column, and the sum of the Y values, $\Sigma Y = 8$, is obtained by adding the Y column. The expression ΣXY means "sum the products of X and Y." The first step is to compute the product for each pair of X and Y scores. These products are displayed in the column headed by XY. In the second step, the products are added together. For this example, the sum of the products is $\Sigma XY = 23$:

$$\Sigma XY = 8 + 3 + 12 = 23$$

It is very important to note that ΣXY *does not equal* $\Sigma X \Sigma Y$. The latter expression means "the sum of X times the sum of Y." For these data, it is easy to demonstrate that the two expressions are not the same:

$$\Sigma XY \neq \Sigma X \Sigma Y$$

$$23 \neq 9(8)$$

$$23 \neq 72$$

X	Y	XY
2	4	8
3	1	3
4	3	12

3. When a constant amount C is added to each score, the expression for the resulting scores is $X + C$. In the following example, the constant equals 4. If this value is added to every score, a column headed by $X + 4$ can be made.

When a constant value is added to every score, it is necessary to use parentheses to represent the sum of these new scores, $\Sigma(X + 4)$. The calculations within the parentheses are always done first. Because the summation symbol is outside the parentheses, finding the sum is performed last. Therefore, to compute $\Sigma(X + 4)$, the constant 4 is first added to every score, creating the new $X + 4$ column of numbers. Then these new numbers are added together. For this example,

$$\Sigma(X + 4) = 5 + 8 + 10 = 23$$

X	X + 4
1	5
4	8
6	10

A word of caution is necessary. The application of a summation sign *ends* at a plus (+) or minus (−) sign. For example, in the notation $\Sigma X + 4$, the summation applies *only* to the X. To compute $\Sigma X + 4$, you first find the sum of the X values and then add 4 to this total:

$$\Sigma X + 4 = 11 + 4 = 15$$

In order for the symbol $X + 4$ to be treated as a single expression, you must use parentheses. In the notation $\Sigma(X + 4)$, the parentheses indicate that $(X + 4)$ has been created as a single variable and, therefore, the summation applies to the $(X + 4)$ values. Note that $\Sigma(X + C)$ *does not equal* $\Sigma X + C$.

Remember, when a number is squared, it is multiplied by itself. A common mistake is to multiply a number by 2 instead of squaring it.

X	X^2
3	9
1	1
4	16
2	4

4. The squared value of a score is represented by the symbol X^2. If every score in the group is squared, then a new column of squared values can be listed as shown in the margin.

The expression ΣX^2 means the sum of the squared scores. Each score is first squared, and then the sum is found for the squared values (see Box 1.2). In this example, adding the X^2 column reveals that

$$\Sigma X^2 = 9 + 1 + 16 + 4 = 30$$

Be careful! The symbol $(\Sigma X)^2$ represents a different order of operations, and the resulting value is not the same as that of ΣX^2. The operations inside the parentheses are performed first. Therefore, the sum of the X's is determined first. The exponent is outside the parentheses, so the squaring is done last. The expression $(\Sigma X)^2$ means the *squared total*. In the example, this value is

$$(\Sigma X)^2 = (10)^2 = 100$$

Therefore, $(\Sigma X)^2$ is *not the same* expression as ΣX^2. It is very important to remember the order of operations for these two expressions. Later we will have to use statistical formulas that contain both of these expressions. It is imperative that you do not confuse them for each other.

1.2 COMPUTING ΣX^2 WITH A CALCULATOR

THE SUM of squared scores, ΣX^2, is a common expression in many statistical calculations. The following steps outline the most efficient procedure for using a typical, inexpensive hand calculator to find this sum. We assume that your calculator has one memory where you can store and retrieve information. *Caution*: The following instructions work for most calculators but not for every single model. If you encounter trouble, don't panic—check your manual or talk with your instructor.

1. Clear the calculator memory. You may press the memory-clear key (usually MC) or simply turn the calculator off then back on.

2. Enter the first score.

3. Press the multiply key (×); then press the equals (=) key. The squared score should appear in the display. (Note you do not need to enter a number twice to square it. Just follow the sequence: number-times-equals.)

4. Put the squared value into the calculator memory. For most calculators, you press the key labeled M+.

5. Enter the next score, square it, and add it to memory (steps 2, 3, and 4). (Note you do not need to clear the display between scores.)

6. Continue this process for the full set of scores. Then retrieve the total (ΣX^2) from memory by pressing the memory-recall key (usually labeled MR).

Check this procedure with a simple set of scores such as: 1, 2, 3. You should find $\Sigma X^2 = 14$.

LEARNING CHECK   For the following data, find the values for the listed expressions

X	Y
3	1
3	2
1	1
2	3
4	5

1. ΣX 2. ΣX^2 3. $(\Sigma X)^2$ 4. $\Sigma(Y + 3)$ 5. $(\Sigma Y)^2$

6. $\Sigma X \Sigma Y$ 7. ΣXY 8. N for the X scores

ANSWERS   1. 13   2. 39   3. 169   4. 27   5. 144   6. 156   7. 36   8. 5

A WORD ABOUT COMPUTERS

Long before desktop computers became commonplace at home, they were routinely used in statistics. The computer can make short work of the statistical analysis of large data sets and can eliminate the tedium that goes along with complex and repetitive computations. As the use of computers became widespread, so did the availability of statistical software packages. The typical software package contains a variety of specialized programs, each one capable of performing a specific type of statistical procedure. The user enters the data to be analyzed and then specifies the analysis to be used with one or more software commands.

There are many useful and popular statistical software packages, all differing in their ease of operation, command structure, sophistication, and breadth of coverage of statistical analyses. This book covers a few of these software programs in the following manner.

1. Minitab. We have included instructional material (Chapter 20) on using this popular statistical program. Minitab is widely available on both large systems and desktop (PC compatible and MacIntosh) computers. It is easy to master—or, in computer jargon, "user-friendly." Throughout this text, we have placed computer symbols ( ) in the margins with references to sections in Chapter 20. When you see a computer symbol, turn to the cited section in the Minitab chapter. There you will find instruction on how to use Minitab to perform the statistical procedure that is discussed in the text. If your instructor is having you use Minitab in this course, then you should read Sections 20.1, 20.2, and 20.3 before proceeding to Chapter 2.

2. Mystat. Mystat statistical software was written for the desktop computer (PC compatible) and is available as an optional feature with this text in the form of a single floppy disk. For courses using this option, Appendix D provides instruction and examples for its use.

3. SPSS[X]. This software is a sophisticated package of programs capable of performing many of the statistical analyses covered in this text and much more advanced procedures as well. It is commonly used by researchers in the social and behavioral sciences. In Appendix E we provide printouts of SPSS[X] analyses performed on selected examples from chapters in this book. Here our goal is to familiarize you with reading and gleaning information from SPSS[X] printouts. Examples that have SPSS[X] printouts displayed in the appendix are noted with the symbol ⌨ followed by a page number.

While we are on the topic of computers and statistics, the authors cannot resist an editorial comment. Many students have approached us with the question: If computers are so good at doing statistical calculations, why not just teach us how to use the computer and forget about teaching us statistics? This question usually is followed with an accurate observation: If I should get a job where I need to use statistics, I probably will just use a computer anyway.

Although there are many ways to answer these comments, we will try to limit ourselves to one or two general ideas. The purpose of this book is to help you gain an understanding of statistics. Notice that we used the word *understanding*. Although computers can do statistics with incredible speed and accuracy, they are not capable of exercising any judgment or interpretation of the material that you feed into them (input) or the results that they produce (output). Too often students (and researchers) rely on computers to perform difficult calculations and have no idea of what the computer is actually doing. In some fields this lack of understanding is acceptable—we are all allowed to use the telephone even if we do not understand how it works. But in scientific research it is critical that you have a complete and accurate understanding of your data. Usually this requires an understanding of the statistical techniques used to summarize and interpret data. So use your computer and enjoy it, but do not rely on it for statistical expertise.

SUMMARY

1. By common usage, the word *statistics* means facts and figures. In this book, the general use of the word is in reference to techniques and procedures for analyzing data.

2. Science is empirical in that it provides methods for making observations. Statistics consist of methods for organizing and interpreting data.

3. A population is composed of every individual from the group one wishes to study. A sample is a subset of the population. Samples are drawn from the population for study because the population in question is usually so large that it is not feasible to study every individual in it.

4. Descriptive statistics simplify and summarize data, so that the data are more manageable. Inferential statistics are techniques that allow one to use sample data to make general statements about a population.

Meaningful generalizations are possible only if the sample is representative of the population from which it was drawn. Random sampling helps ensure that it is representative.

5. A correlational method looks for interrelationships between variables but cannot determine the cause-and-effect nature of the relationship. The experimental method is able to establish causes and effects in a relationship. The quasi-experimental method involves comparing different groups where the group differences are based on a preexisting subject variable or a preexisting condition.

6. In the experimental method, one variable (the independent variable) is intentionally manipulated and controlled by the experimenter. Then changes are noted in another variable (the dependent variable) as a result of the manipulation.

7. A hypothesis is a prediction about the effect of an independent variable on a dependent variable. Hypotheses are usually derived from theories. Experiments basically involve the test of a hypothesis.

8. Constructs are hypothetical concepts used in theories to describe the mechanisms of behavior. Because they are hypothetical, they cannot be observed. Constructs are studied by providing operational definitions for them. An operational definition defines a construct in terms of an observable and measurable response or event.

9. A nominal scale labels observations so that they fall into different categories. A nominal scale involves making qualitative distinctions. No attempt is made to measure the magnitude of the event.

10. An ordinal scale involves ranking observations in terms of size or magnitude. Although this scale will tell us which observation is larger, it will not tell us how much larger it is.

11. In an interval scale, intervals between numbers reflect differences in magnitude of observations. It is possible to determine which event is of greater magnitude and how much larger it is.

12. A ratio scale has all of the characteristics of an interval scale, and ratios of measurements on this scale reflect ratios of magnitudes. Unlike the interval scale, a ratio scale has a meaningful zero point.

13. A discrete variable is one that can have only a finite number of values between any two values. It typically consists of whole numbers that vary in countable steps. A continuous variable can have an infinite number of values between any two values.

14. For a continuous variable, each score corresponds to an interval on the scale. The boundaries that separate intervals are called real limits. The real limits are located exactly halfway between adjacent scores.

15. The letter X is used to represent scores for a variable. If a second variable is used, Y represents its scores. The letter N is used as the symbol for the number of scores in a set. The Greek letter sigma Σ is used to stand for summation. Therefore, the expression ΣX is read "the sum of the scores."

KEY TERMS

statistics	inferential statistics	dependent variable	ordinal scale
population	random selection	control group	interval scale
sample	variable	experimental group	ratio scale
population parameter	constant	quasi-independent variable	discrete variable
sample statistic	correlational method	hypothesis	continuous variable
descriptive statistics	experimental method	construct	real limits
distribution	quasi-experimental method	operational definition	upper real limit
raw score	independent variable	nominal scale	lower real limit

── *Focus on Problem Solving* ──

1. It may help to simplify summation notation if you observe that the summation sign is always followed by a symbol (or symbolic expression)—for example, ΣX or $\Sigma (X + 3)$. This symbol specifies which values you are to add. If you use the symbol as a column heading and list all the appropriate values in the column, your task is simply to add up the numbers in the column. To find $\Sigma (X + 3)$ for example, start a column headed with $(X + 3)$ next to the column of X's. List all the $(X + 3)$ values; then find the total for the column.

2. To use summation notation correctly you must be careful of two other factors:
   a. When you are determining the "symbol" that follows the summation sign, remember that everything within parentheses is part of the same symbol, for example $\Sigma (X + 3)$, and a string of multiplied values is considered to be a single symbol, for example, ΣXY.

b. Often it is necessary to use several intermediate columns before you can reach the column of values specified by a particular symbol. To compute $\Sigma (X - 1)^2$, for example, you will need three columns: first the column of original scores, X's; second, a column of $(X - 1)$ values; the third, a column of squared $(X - 1)$ values. It is the third column, headed by $(X - 1)^2$, that you should total.

Demonstration 1.1

SUMMATION NOTATION

A set of data consists of the following scores:

$$7 \quad 3 \quad 9 \quad 5 \quad 4$$

For these data find the following values:

a. ΣX **b.** $(\Sigma X)^2$ **c.** ΣX^2 **d.** $\Sigma X + 5$ **e.** $\Sigma (X - 2)$

Compute ΣX. To compute ΣX, we simply add all the scores in the group. For these data, we obtain:

$$\Sigma X = 7 + 3 + 9 + 5 + 4 = 28$$

Compute $(\Sigma X)^2$. The key to determining the value of $(\Sigma X)^2$ is the presence of parentheses. The rule is to perform the operations that are inside the paratheses first.

STEP 1 Find the sum of the scores, ΣX.

STEP 2 Square the total.

We have already determined that ΣX is 28. Squaring this total we obtain:

$$(\Sigma X)^2 = (28)^2 = 784$$

Compute ΣX^2. Calculating the sum of the squared scores, ΣX^2, involves two steps.

STEP 1 Square each score.

STEP 2 Sum the squared values.

These steps are most easily accomplished by constructing a computational table. The first column has the heading X and lists the scores. The second column is labeled X^2 and contains the squared values for each score. For this example, the table is as follows:

X	X^2
7	49
3	9
9	81
5	25
4	16

To find the value for ΣX^2, we sum the X^2 column.

$$\Sigma X^2 = 49 + 9 + 81 + 25 + 16 = 180$$

Compute $\Sigma X + 5$. In this expression, there are no parentheses. Thus, the summation sign is applied only to the X values.

STEP 1 Find the sum of X.

STEP 2 Add the constant 5 to the total from Step 1.

In part (a) we found that the sum of the scores is 28. For $\Sigma X + 5$ we obtain the following:

$$\Sigma X + 5 = 28 + 5 = 33$$

Compute $\Sigma (X - 2)$. The summation sign is followed by an expression with parentheses. In this case, $X - 2$ is treated as a single expression and the summation sign applies to the $(X - 2)$ values.

STEP 1 Subtract 2 from every score.

STEP 2 Sum these new values.

This problem can be done by using a table with two columns, headed X and $X - 2$, respectively.

X	X − 2
7	5
3	1
9	7
5	3
4	2

To determine the value for $\Sigma (X - 2)$, we sum the $X - 2$ column.

$$\Sigma (X - 2) = 5 + 1 + 7 + 3 + 2 = 18$$

───── *Demonstration 1.2* ─────

SUMMATION NOTATION WITH TWO VARIABLES

The following data consist of pairs of scores (X and Y) for four individuals.

X	Y
5	8
2	10
3	11
7	2

Determine the values for the following expressions:

a. $\Sigma X \Sigma Y$ **b.** ΣXY

Compute $\Sigma X \Sigma Y$. This expression indicates that we should multiply the sum of X by the sum of Y.

STEP 1 Find the sum of X

STEP 2 Find the sum of Y

STEP 3 Multiply the results of Steps 1 and 2.

First, we find the sum of X.

$$\Sigma X = 5 + 2 + 3 + 7 = 17$$

Next, we compute the sum of Y.

$$\Sigma Y = 8 + 10 + 11 + 2 = 31$$

Finally, we multiply these two totals.

$$\Sigma X \Sigma Y = 17(31) = 527$$

Compute ΣXY. Now we are asked to find the sum of the products of X and Y.

STEP 1 Find the XY products.

STEP 2 Sum the products.

The computations are facilitated by using a third column labeled XY.

X	Y	XY
5	8	40
2	10	20
3	11	33
7	2	14

For these data, the sum of the XY products is

$$\Sigma XY = 40 + 20 + 33 + 14 = 107$$

PROBLEMS

*1. What is the basic characteristic that distinguishes an experiment from a quasi-experimental research strategy?

_____
*Solutions for odd-numbered problems are provided in Appendix C.

2. In general, research attempts to establish and explain relationships between variables. What is the advantage of the experimental method (versus the correlational and quasi-experimental methods) for explaining relationships?

3. Describe how the experimental method is conducted.

What is the distinction between the two types of variables that are used?

4. A researcher reports that individuals on a special diet containing large amounts of oat bran had substantially lower cholesterol levels than individuals on a diet with no oat bran. For this study, identify the independent variable and the dependent variable.

5. A developmental psychologists conducts a research study comparing vocabulary skill for 5-year-old boys versus 5-year-old girls.
   a. Does this study use the experimental, correlational, or quasi-experimental method?
   b. What is the dependent variable for this study?

6. A researcher would like to examine children's preferences among three leading brands of breakfast cereal. A sample of 6-year-old children and a separate sample of 10-year-old children are obtained. Each child tastes all three cereals and selects his or her favorite from brand A, brand B, or brand C.
   a. Identify the dependent variable for this study.
   b. Is the dependent variable discrete or continuous?
   c. What scale of measurement (nominal, ordinal, interval, ratio) is used to measure the dependent variable?
   d. What is the research method (experimental, correlational, quasi-experimental) used in this study?

7. A researcher would like to determine whether or not office productivity is influenced by background music.
   a. Briefly describe how this researcher could gather data using the observational or correlational method.
   b. Briefly describe how data could be obtained using the experimental method.
   c. Identify the independent variable and the dependent variable for this experiment.

8. A questionnaire measures sex, age, occupation, and income. Identify the scale of measurement used for each of these measures.

9. A professor records the number of absences for each student in a class of $N = 20$.
   a. Is the professor measuring a discrete or a continuous variable?
   b. What scale of measurement is being used?

10. Contrast the nominal scale of measurement to the ordinal scale. What type of scale is used in a list of the order of finish in a horse race? What type of scale is used when describing the sex of the jockeys?

11. Define and differentiate a discrete variable and a continuous variable.

12. Suppose that two individuals are assigned to different categories on a scale of measurement. If the measurement scale is nominal, then the only information provided about the two individuals is that they are different.
   a. What additional information about the difference between the two individuals would by provided for if the measurement scale were ordinal instead of nominal?
   b. What additional information about the two individuals would be provided by an interval scale versus an ordinal scale?
   c. What additional information would be provided by ratio scale measurements versus interval scale measurements?

13. Define and differentiate between a construct and an operational definition.

14. What is a confounding variable, and how does it affect the interpretation of experimental results?

15. For each of the following summation expressions, state in words the sequence of operations necessary to perform the specified calculation. For example, the expression $\Sigma X + 1$ instructs you first to sum the set of scores and then add 1 to the total.
   a. $\Sigma (X + 1)$
   b. ΣX^2
   c. $\Sigma (X - 1)^2$

16. For the following scores, find the value of each expression.
   a. ΣX^2
   b. $(\Sigma X)^2$
   c. $\Sigma X + 3$
   d. $\Sigma (X + 3)$

X
4
3
5
1

17. For the following set of scores, find the value of each expression:
   a. ΣX
   b. ΣY
   c. ΣXY

X	Y
4	5
1	2
3	4

18. For a set of $N = 10$ scores, $\Sigma X = 20$.
   a. If 5 points are added to each score, what value will be obtained for the sum of the new scores? (That is, $\Sigma (X + 5) = ?$.)
   b. If each score is multiplied by 4, what value will be obtained for the sum of the new scores? (That is, $\Sigma 4X = ?$.)

19. Use summation notation to express each of the following calculations:

    a. The sum of the squared scores

    b. The square of the sum of the scores

20. Use summation notation to express each of the following calculations:

    a. Add 3 points to each score and then sum the resulting values.

    b. Sum the scores; then add 10 points to the total.

    c. Square each score and subtract 2 points from each squared value; then sum the resulting values.

21. For the following set of scores, find the value of each expression:

    a. ΣX

    b. ΣX^2

    c. $\Sigma (X + 3)$

X
3
−2
0
−1
−4

22. For the following set of scores, find the value of each expression:

    a. ΣX

    b. ΣX^2

X
0.4
1.7
0.8
0.5
1.2

23. For the following set of scores, find the value of each expression:

    a. ΣX

    b. ΣY

    c. ΣXY

    d. $\Sigma (Y - 1)^2$

X	Y
−2	4
0	5
3	2
−4	3

24. For the following set of scores, find the value of each expression:

    a. ΣX^2

    b. $(\Sigma X)^2$

    c. $\Sigma (X + 2)$

    d. $\Sigma (X + 1)^2$

X
7
4
10
3
1

25. For the following set of scores, find the value of each expression:

    a. ΣX

    b. ΣX^2

    c. $(\Sigma X)^2$

    d. $\Sigma (X - 5)^2$

X
1
7
9
5
3

CHAPTER 2

FREQUENCY DISTRIBUTIONS

TOOLS YOU WILL NEED

The following items are considered essential background material for this chapter. If you doubt your knowledge of any of these items, you should review the appropriate chapter or section before proceeding.

- Proportions (math review, Appendix A)
  - Fractions
  - Decimals
  - Percentages
- Scales of measurement (Chapter 1): Nominal, ordinal, interval, and ratio
- Continuous and discrete variables (Chapter 1)
- Real limits (Chapter 1)

CONTENTS

Reading a textbook is much different from reading a novel or a newspaper. With a textbook, your goal is to study and to learn the material, not simply to entertain yourself. As a result you must work to identify and understand the important points. You must take time to digest the material, and it helps to stop and question yourself regularly to be sure that you fully comprehend what you are reading. All this may sound like the same old "how to study" lecture that you probably have heard a hundred times by now. But it is true, and it works.

Experiments have demonstrated that reading strategy can significantly affect comphension and test performance. In 1974, John Boker presented college students with long passages (2500 words) selected from college-level texts (Boker, 1974). One group of students served as a control group and simply read straight through the material from beginning to end. For the experimental group, the passage was divided into 10 sections, each about 250 words, and the students were presented with questions at the end of each section. A week later, both groups were given a 40-question multiple-choice test covering the passage they had read. Hypothetical data similar to those obtained by Boker are shown in Table 2.1.

From looking at the data in Table 2.1, does it appear that one group did better than the other? Because these data are not organized in any systematic way, you probably find it difficult to discern any differences. This is a basic problem confronting any researcher after data are collected. To make sense of the experiment, you must organize the mass of numbers into a simpler form so that it is possible to "see" what happened. One solution is to present the scores in an organized table or a graph. Figure 2.1 shows the same data that are in Table 2.1, but now they are simplified and organized in a graph. Looking at the figure, does it appear that one group did better than the other?

It should be clear that graphing these data makes it easy to see the difference between the two groups. The students who read the passage with interspersed questions performed much better on the test—about 5 points better, which is quite a bit on a 40-question test.

There are two important points to be learned from this discussion. First, you should appreciate the value of simplifying and organizing a set of data. By structuring the data properly, it becomes possible to see at a glance what happened in an experiment. This helps researchers to decide exactly how the data should be analyzed and interpreted, and it helps others to understand the significance of the experiment. In this chapter we will examine

Table 2.1

Hypothetical Data from an Experiment Comparing Two Strategies for Studying College Textbook Material.[a]

CONTROL GROUP		EXPERIMENTAL GROUP	
25	32	28	29
27	20	25	31
28	23	31	19
17	21	29	35
24	34	30	28
22	29	24	30
24	25	33	27
21	18	34	26
19	22	29	29
30	24	27	32
26	27	30	36
24	23	22	23
23	25	32	33

[a]The experimental group had questions interspersed through the material as they were reading. The control group read through the material without seeing any questions. One week later both groups were given a 40-item multiple-choice test on the material they had read. The data given are the scores on this test.

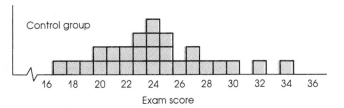

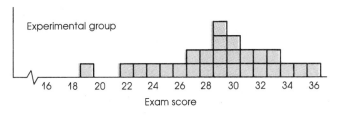

Figure 2.1

The two graphs show the same data listed in Table 2.1. In these graphs each student is represented by a block that is placed directly above his or her exam score. Notice that the experimental group generally performed better than the control group. For students in the experimental group, the exam scores pile up around $X = 29$. For the control group, the scores pile up around $X = 24$.

several statistical techniques for organizing data. The second point concerns the implications of Boker's experiment. The way you study can have a tremendous influence on what you learn. As you read through this book, you will find lots of sample problems in the examples and learning checks that appear in each chapter. Take time to work through these problems, answer the questions, and test yourself. A little extra time and effort can increase your understanding of the material, and it can improve your grade.

2.1 OVERVIEW

When a researcher finishes the data collection phase of an experiment, the results usually consist of pages of numbers. The immediate problem for the researcher is to organize the scores into some comprehensible form so that any trends in the data can be seen easily and communicated to others. This is the job of descriptive statistics: to simplify the organization and presentation of data. One of the most common procedures for organizing a set of data is to place the scores in a frequency distribution.

DEFINITION

A *frequency distribution* is an organized tabulation of the number of individuals located in each category on the scale of measurement.

A frequency distribution takes a disorganized set of scores and places them in order from highest to lowest, grouping together all individuals who have the same score. If the highest score is $X = 10$, for example, the frequency distribution groups together all the 10s, then all the 9s, then the 8s, and so on. Thus, a frequency distribution allows the researcher to see "at a glance" the entire set of scores. It shows whether the scores are generally high or low and whether they are concentrated in one area or spread out across the entire scale and generally provides an organized picture of the data. In addition to providing a picture of the entire set of scores, a frequency distribution allows you to see the location of any individual score relative to all of the other scores in the set.

Frequency distributions can be structured either as tables or graphs, but both show the original measurement scale and the frequencies associated with each category. Thus, they present a picture of how the individual scores are distributed on the measurement scale—hence the name *frequency distribution*.

2.2 FREQUENCY DISTRIBUTION TABLES

It is customary to list scores from highest to lowest, but this is an arbitrary arrangement. Many computer programs will list scores from lowest to highest.

The simplest frequency distribution table presents the measurement scale by listing the different scores (measurement categories) in a column from highest to lowest. Beside each score, we indicate the frequency, or number of times that particular measurement occurred in the data. It is customary to use an X as the column heading for the scores and an f as the column heading for the frequencies. An example of a frequency distribution table follows.

EXAMPLE 2.1

The following set of $N = 20$ scores was obtained from a 10-point statistics quiz. We will organize these scores by constructing a frequency distribution table. Scores:

8, 9, 8, 7, 10, 9, 6, 4, 9, 8

7, 8, 10, 9, 8, 6, 9, 7, 8, 8

X	f
10	2
9	5
8	7
7	3
6	2
5	0
4	1

1. The highest score is $X = 10$, and the lowest score is $X = 4$. Therefore, the first column of the table will list the scale of measurement (X values) from 10 down to 4. Notice that all of the possible values are listed in the table. For example, no one had a score of $X = 5$, but this value is included. With an ordinal, interval, or ratio scale, the X values are listed in order (usually highest to lowest). For a nominal scale, the X values can be listed in any order.

2. The frequency associated with each score is recorded in the second column. For example, two people had scores of $X = 6$, so there is a 2 in the f column beside $X = 6$.

Because the table organizes the scores, it is possible to see very quickly the general quiz results. For example, there were only two perfect scores, but most of the class had high grades (8s and 9s). With one exception (the score of $X = 4$) it appears that the class has learned the material fairly well.

Notice that the X values in a frequency distribution table represent the scale of measurement, *not* the actual set of scores. For example, the X column lists the value 10 only one time, but the frequency column indicates that there are actually two values of $X = 10$. Also, the X column lists a value of $X = 5$ but the frequency column indicates that actually there are no scores of $X = 5$.

You also should notice that the frequencies can be used to find the total number of scores in the distribution. By adding up the frequencies, you will obtain the total number of individuals:

$$\Sigma f = N$$

OBTAINING ΣX FROM A FREQUENCY DISTRIBUTION TABLE

There may be times when you need to compute the sum of the scores, ΣX, for data in a frequency distribution table. This procedure presents a problem because most students are tempted simply to add the scores listed in the X column of the table. However, this practice is incorrect because it ignores the information provided by the frequency (f) column. To calculate ΣX from a frequency distribution table, you must use both the X and f columns.

Consider the frequency distribution table for Example 2.1. It tells us that the distribution has two 10s, five 9s, and seven 8s, and so on. Therefore, you can obtain the total for X by first reconstructing the original distribution and then adding all the X values (compute ΣX): $10 + 10 + 9 + 9 + 9 + 9 + 9 + 8 + 8 + 8 + 8 + 8 + 8 + 8 + \cdots$. For the data in Example 2.1, $\Sigma X = 158$. Try it yourself.

An alternative way to get ΣX from a frequency distribution table is to multiply each X value by its frequency and then add these products. This sum may be expressed in symbols as ΣfX. The computation is summarized as follows for the data in Example 2.1:

X	f	fX	
10	2	20	
9	5	45	
8	7	56	
7	3	21	
6	2	12	
5	0	0	(There are no 5s)
4	1	4	

$$\Sigma fX = 158$$

In using either method to find ΣX, by reconstructing the distribution or by computing ΣfX, the important point is that you must use the information given in the frequency column.

PROPORTIONS AND PERCENTAGES

In addition to the two basic columns of a frequency distribution, there are other measures that describe the distribution of scores and can be incorporated into the table. The two most common are proportion and percentage.

Proportion measures the fraction of the total group that is associated with each score. In Example 2.1, there were two individuals with $X = 6$. Thus, 2 out of 20 people had $X = 6$, so the proportion would be $2/20 = 0.10$. In general, the proportion associated with each score is

$$\text{proportion} = p = \frac{f}{N}$$

Because proportions describe the frequency(f) in relation to the total number (N), they often are called *relative frequencies*. Although proportions can be expressed as fractions (for example, 2/20), they more commonly appear as decimals. A column of proportions, headed with a p, can be added to the basic frequency distribution table (see Example 2.2).

In addition to using frequencies (f) and proportions (p), researchers often describe a distribution of scores with percentages. For example, an instructor might describe the results of an exam by saying that 15% of the class earned *A*s, 23% *B*s, and so on. To compute the percentage associated with each score, you first find the proportion (p) and then multiply by 100:

$$\text{percentage} = p(100) = \frac{f}{N}(100)$$

Percentages can be included in a frequency distribution table by adding a column headed with % (see Example 2.2).

EXAMPLE 2.2   The frequency distribution table from Example 2.1 is repeated here. This time we have added columns showing the proportion (p) and the percentage (%) associated with each score.

X	f	$p = f/N$	$\% = p(100)$
10	2	$2/20 = 0.10$	10%
9	5	$5/20 = 0.25$	25%
8	7	$7/20 = 0.35$	35%
7	3	$3/20 = 0.15$	15%
6	2	$2/20 = 0.10$	10%
5	0	$0/20 = 0$	0%
4	1	$1/20 = 0.05$	5%

GROUPED FREQUENCY DISTRIBUTION TABLES

When a set of data covers a wide range of values, it is unreasonable to list all the individual scores in a frequency distribution table. For example, a set of exam scores ranges from a low of $X = 41$ to a high of $X = 96$. These scores cover a range of over 50 points.

When the X values are whole numbers, the number of rows in the list of X values can be obtained by finding the difference between the highest and lowest score and adding 1:

rows = highest − lowest + 1

If we were to list all the individual scores, it would take 56 rows to complete the frequency distribution table. Although this would organize and simplify the data, the table would be long and cumbersome. Additional simplification would be desirable. This is accomplished by dividing the range of scores into intervals and then listing these intervals in the frequency distribution table. For example, we could construct a table showing the number of students who had scores in the 90s, the number with scores in the 80s, etc. The result is called a *grouped frequency distribution table* because we are presenting groups of scores rather than individual values. The groups, or intervals, are called *class intervals*.

There are several rules that help guide you in the construction of a grouped frequency distribution table. These rules should be considered as guidelines rather than an absolute requirements, but they do help produce a simple, well-organized, and easily understood table.

RULE 1   The grouped frequency distribution table should have about 10 class intervals. If a table has many more than 10 intervals, it becomes cumbersome and defeats the purpose of a frequency distribution table. On the other hand, if you have too few intervals, you begin to lose information about the distribution of the scores. At the extreme, with only one interval, the table would not tell you anything about how the scores are distributed. Remember, the purpose for a frequency distribution is to help a researcher see the data. With too few or too many intervals, the table will not provide a clear picture. You should note that 10 intervals is a general guide. If you were constructing a table on a blackboard, for example, you probably would want only 5 or 6 intervals. If the table were to be printed in a scientific report, you may want 12 or 15 intervals. In each case your goal is to present a table that is relatively easy to see and understand.

RULE 2   The width of each interval should be a relatively simple number. For example, 2, 5, 10, or 20 would be good choices for the interval width. Notice that it is easy to count by 5s or 10s. These numbers are easy to understand and make it possible for someone to see quickly how you have divided the range.

RULE 3   The bottom score in each class interval should be a multiple of the width. If you are using a width of 10, for example, the intervals should start with 10, 20, 30, 40, etc. Again, this makes it easier for someone to understand how the table has been constructed.

RULE 4   All intervals should be the same width. They should cover the range of scores completely with no gaps and no overlaps, so that any particular score belongs in exactly one interval.

The application of these rules is demonstrated in Example 2.3.

EXAMPLE 2.3   An instructor has obtained the set of $N = 25$ exam scores shown here. To help organize these scores, we will place them in a frequency distribution table. Scores:

82, 75, 88, 93, 53, 84, 87, 58, 72, 94, 69, 84, 61,

91, 64, 87, 84, 70, 76, 89, 75, 80, 73, 78, 60

The first step is to examine the range of scores. For these data, the smallest score is $X = 53$ and the largest score is $X = 94$, so 42 rows would be needed for a table. Because it would require 42 rows to list each individual score in a frequency distribution table, we will have to group the scores into class intervals.

The best method for determining the appropriate interval width is to use Rules 1 and 2 simultaneously. According to Rule 1, we want about 10 intervals; according to Rule 2, we want the width to be a simple number. If we try a width of 2, how many intervals would it take to cover the range of scores? With each interval only 2 points wide, we would need 21 intervals to cover the range. This is too many. What about an interval width of 5? What about a width of 10? The following table shows how many intervals would be needed for each possible width:

WIDTH	NUMBER OF INTERVALS NEEDED TO COVER A RANGE OF 42 VALUES	
2	21	(too many)
5	9	(OK)
10	5	(too few)

Table 2.2

A Grouped Frequency Distribution Table Showing the Data from Example 2.3[a]

X	f
90–94	3
85–89	4
80–84	5
75–79	4
70–74	3
65–69	1
60–64	3
55–59	1
50–54	1

[a]The original scores range from a high of $X = 94$ to a low of $X = 53$. This range has been divided into nine intervals with each interval exactly five points wide. The frequency column (f) lists the number of individuals with scores in each of the class intervals.

Notice that an interval width of 5 will result in about 10 intervals, which is exactly what we want.

The next step is to actually identify the intervals. The lowest score for these data is $X = 53$, so the lowest interval should contain this value. Because the interval should have a multiple of 5 as its bottom score, the interval would be 50 to 54. Notice that this interval contains five values (50, 51, 52, 53, 54), so it does have a width of 5. The next interval would start at 55 and go to 59. The complete frequency distribution table showing all of the class intervals in presented in Table 2.2.

Once the class intervals are listed, you complete the table by adding a column of frequencies or proportions or percentages. The values in the frequency column indicate the number of individuals whose scores are located in that class interval. For this example, there were three students with scores in the 60–64 interval, so the frequency for this class interval is $f = 3$ (see Table 2.2).

REAL LIMITS AND FREQUENCY DISTRIBUTIONS

You should recall from Chapter 1 that a continuous variable has an infinite number of possible values and can be represented by a number line that is continuous and contains an infinite number of points. However, when a continuous variable is measured, the resulting measurements correspond to *intervals* on the number line rather than single points. For example, a score of $X = 8$ for a continuous variable actually represents an interval bounded by the real limits 7.5 and 8.5. Thus, a frequency distribution table showing a frequency of $f = 3$ individuals all assigned a score of $X = 8$ does not mean that all three individuals had exactly the same measurement. Instead, you should realize that the three measurements are simply located in the same interval between 7.5 and 8.5.

The concept of real limits also applies to the class intervals of a grouped frequency distribution table. For example, a class interval of 40−49 contains scores from $X = 40$ to $X = 49$. These values are called the *apparent limits* of the interval because it appears that they form the upper and lower boundaries for the class interval. But $X = 40$ is actually an interval from 39.5 to 40.5. Similarly, $X = 49$ is an interval from 48.5 to 49.5. Therefore, the real limits of the interval are 39.5 (the lower real limit) and 49.5 (the upper real limit). Notice that the next higher class interval would be 50−59, which as a lower real limit of 49.5. Thus, the two intervals meet at the real limit 49.5, so there are no gaps in the scale. You also should notice that the width of each class interval becomes easier to understand when you consider the real limits of an interval. For example, the interval 50−54 has real limits of 49.5 and 54.5. The distance between these two real limits (5 points) is the width of the interval.

LEARNING CHECK

1. Place the following scores in a frequency distribution table showing proportion and percentage as well as the frequency for each score. Scores: 2, 3, 1, 2, 5, 4, 5, 5, 1, 4, 2, 2, 5, 5, 4, 2, 3, 1, 5, 4.

2. A set of scores ranges from a high of $X = 142$ to a low of $X = 65$. If these scores are to be placed in a grouped frequency distribution table, then

   a. What interval width should be used?
   b. What are the apparent limits of the bottom interval?
   c. What are the real limits of the bottom interval?

3. Explain why you should avoid having too many rows in a frequency distribution table. What is the problem with having too few rows?

ANSWERS

1.

X	f	p	%
5	6	0.30	30%
4	4	0.20	20%
3	2	0.10	10%
2	5	0.25	25%
1	3	0.15	15%

2. **a.** The range would require 78 rows for a frequency distribution table. With an interval width of 5 points, you would need 16 intervals to cover the range. With an interval width of 10, you would need 8 intervals. For most purposes, a width of 10 points probably is best.

   b. With a width of 10, the bottom interval would have apparent limits of 60−69.

   c. The real limits of the bottom interval would be 59.5 and 69.5.

3. With too many rows the table is not simple and, therefore, fails to meet the goal of descriptive statistics. With too few rows, you lose information about the distribution.

2.3 FREQUENCY DISTRIBUTION GRAPHS

A frequency distribution graph is basically a picture of the information available in a frequency distribution table. We will consider several different types of graphs, but all start with two perpendicular lines called axes. The horizontal line is called the *X*-axis, or the abscissa. The vertical line is called the *Y*-axis, or the ordinate. The scores are listed along the *X*-axis in increasing value from left to right. The frequencies are listed on the *Y*-axis in increasing value from bottom to top. As a general rule, the point where the two axes intersect should have a value of zero for both the scores and the frequencies. A final general rule is that the graph should be constructed so that its height (*Y*-axis) is approximately three-quarters of its length (*X*-axis). Violating these guidelines can result in graphs that give a misleading picture of the data (see Box 2.1).

HISTOGRAMS AND BAR GRAPHS

The first type of graph we will consider is called either a histogram or a bar graph. For this type of graph, you simply draw a bar above each score so that the height of the bar corresponds to the frequency of the score. As you will see, the choice between using a histogram or a bar graph is determined by the scale of measurement.

When a frequency distribution graph is showing data from an interval or ratio scale, the bars are drawn so that adjacent bars touch each other. The touching bars produce a continuous figure which emphasizes the continuity of the variable. This type of frequency distribution graph is called a histogram. An example of a histogram is presented in Figure 2.2.

 Creating histograms with Minitab is shown in Section 20.4.

 SPSS^X A-77

DEFINITION

For a *histogram*, vertical bars are drawn above each score so that
1. The height of the bar corresponds to the frequency, and 2. The width of the bar extends to the real limits of the score. A histogram is used when the data are measured on an interval or ratio scale.

Figure 2.2

An example of a frequency distribution histogram. The same set of data is presented in a frequency distribution table and in a histogram.

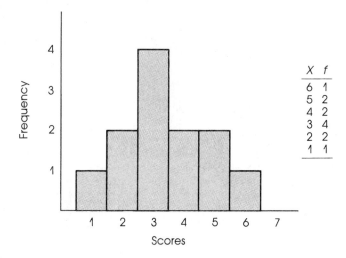

Figure 2.3

An example of a frequency distribution histogram for grouped data. The same set of data is presented in a grouped frequency distribution table and in a histogram.

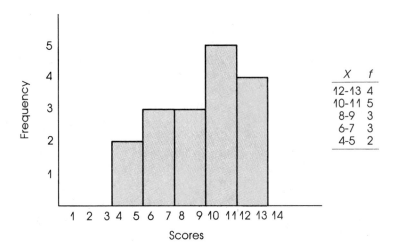

X	f
12-13	4
10-11	5
8-9	3
6-7	3
4-5	2

When data have been grouped into class intervals, you can construct a frequency distribution histogram by drawing a bar above each interval so that the width of the bar extends to the real limits of the interval. This process is demonstrated in Figure 2.3.

When you are presenting the frequency distribution for data from a nominal or ordinal scale, the graph is constructed so that there is some space between the bars. In this case the separate bars emphasize that the scale consists of separate, distinct categories. The resulting graph is called a bar graph. An example of a frequency distribution bar graph is given in Figure 2.4.

DEFINITION   For a *bar graph,* a vertical bar is drawn above each score (or category) so that 1. The height of the bar corresponds to the frequency, and 2. There is a space separating each bar from the next. A bar graph is used when the data are measured on a nominal or ordinal scale.

Figure 2.4

A bar graph showing the distribution of personality types in a sample of college students. Because personality type is a discrete variable measured on a nominal scale, the graph is drawn with space between the bars.

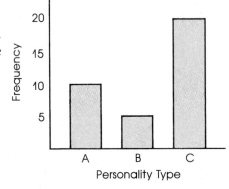

FREQUENCY DISTRIBUTION POLYGONS

Instead of a histogram, many researchers prefer to display a frequency distribution using a polygon.

DEFINITION

In a *frequency distribution polygon,* a single dot is drawn above each score so that

1. The dot is centered above the score.
2. The height of the dot corresponds to the frequency.

A continuous line is then drawn connecting these dots. The graph is completed by drawing a line down to the *X*-axis (zero frequency) at each end of the range of scores.

As with a histogram, the frequency distribution polygon is intended for use with interval or ratio scales. An example of a polygon is shown in Figure 2.5. A polygon also can be used with data that have been grouped into class intervals. In this case, you position the dots directly above the midpoint of each class interval. The midpoint can be found by averaging the apparent limits of the interval or by averaging the real limits of the interval. For example, a class interval of 40−49 would have a midpoint of 44.5.

$$\text{apparent limits:} \quad \frac{40 + 49}{2} = \frac{89}{2} = 44.5$$

$$\text{real limits:} \quad \frac{39.5 + 49.5}{2} = \frac{89}{2} = 44.5$$

An example of a frequency distribution polygon with grouped data is shown in Figure 2.6.

Figure 2.5

An example of a frequency distribution polygon. The same set of data is presented in a frequency distribution table and in a polygon. Note that these data are shown in a histogram in Figure 2.2.

X	f
6	1
5	2
4	2
3	4
2	2
1	1

Figure 2.6

An example of a frequency distribution polygon for grouped data. The same set of data is presented in a grouped frequency distribution table and in a polygon. Note that these data are shown in a histogram in Figure 2.3.

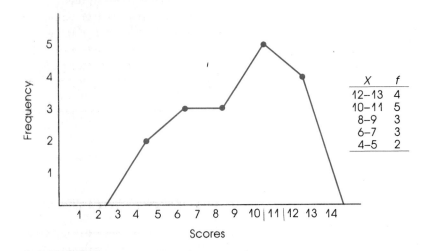

X	f
12–13	4
10–11	5
8–9	3
6–7	3
4–5	2

RELATIVE FREQUENCIES AND SMOOTH CURVES

Often it is impossible to construct a frequency distribution for a population because there are simply too many individuals for a researcher to obtain measurements and frequencies for the entire group. In this case, it is customary to draw a frequency distribution graph showing *relative frequencies* (proportions) on the vertical axis. For example, a researcher may know that a particular species of animal has three times as many females as males in the population. This fact could be displayed in a bar graph by simply making the bar above "female" three times as tall as the bar above "male." Notice that the actual frequencies are unknown but that the relative frequency of males and females can still be presented in a graph.

It also is possible to use a polygon to show relative frequencies for scores in a population. In this case, it is customary to draw a smooth curve instead of the series of straight lines that normally appears in a polygon. The smooth curve indicates that you are not connecting a series of dots (real frequencies) but rather are showing a distribution that is not limited to one specific set of data. One commonly occurring population distribution is the normal curve. The word *normal* refers to a specific shape that can be precisely defined by an equation. Less precisely, we can describe a normal distribution as being symmetrical, with the greatest frequency in the middle and relatively smaller frequencies as you move toward either extreme. A good example of a normal distribution is the population distribution for IQ scores shown in Figure 2.7. Because normal shaped distributions occur commonly and because this shape is mathematically guaranteed in certain situations, it will receive extensive attention throughout this book.

In the future we will be referring to *distributions of scores*. Whenever the term *distribution* appears, you should conjure up an image of a frequency distribution graph. The graph provides a picture showing exactly where the individual scores are located. To make this concept more concrete, you might find it useful to think of the graph as showing a pile of individuals. In Figure 2.7, for example, the pile is highest at an IQ score of around 100 because most people have "average" IQs. There are only a few individuals piled up at an IQ score of 130; it must be lonely at the top.

Figure 2.7

The population distribution of IQ scores: an example of a normal distribution.

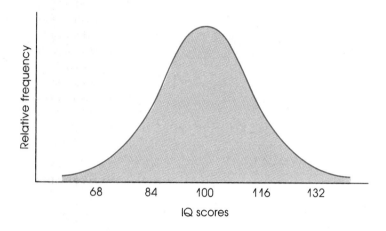

2.4 THE SHAPE OF A FREQUENCY DISTRIBUTION

Rather than drawing a complete frequency distribution graph, researchers often simply describe a distribution by listing its characteristics. There are three characteristics that completely describe any distribution: shape, central tendency, and variability. In simple terms, central tendency measures where the center of the distribution is located. Variability tells whether the scores are spread over a wide range or are clustered together. Central tendency and variability are covered in detail in Chapters 3 and 4. Technically, the shape of a distribution is defined by an equation that prescribes the exact relation between each X and Y value on the graph. However, we will rely on a few less-precise terms that will serve to describe the shape of most distributions.

Nearly all distributions can be classified as being either symmetrical or skewed.

DEFINITIONS   In a *symmetrical distribution* it is possible to draw a vertical line through the middle so that one side of the distribution is an exact mirror image of the other (see Figure 2.8).

In a *skewed distribution* the scores tend to pile up toward one end of the scale and taper off gradually at the other end (see Figure 2.8).

The section where the scores taper off toward one end of a distribution is called the *tail* of the distribution.

A skewed distribution with the tail to the right-hand side is said to be *positively skewed* because the tail points toward the positive (above-zero) end of the X-axis. If the tail points to the left, the distribution is said to be *negatively skewed* (see Figure 2.8).

For a very difficult exam, most scores will tend to be low, with only a few individuals earning high scores. This will produce a positively skewed distribution. Similarly, a very easy exam will tend to produce a negatively skewed distribution, with most of the students earning high scores and only a few with low values.

Figure 2.8

Examples of different shapes for distributions.

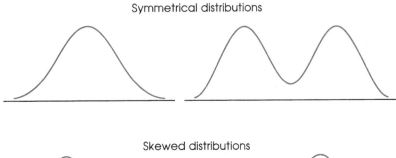

Symmetrical distributions

Skewed distributions

Positive skew   Negative skew

LEARNING CHECK

1. Sketch a frequency distribution histogram and a frequency distribution polygon for the data in the following table:

X	f
5	4
4	6
3	3
2	1
1	1

2. Describe the shape of the distribution in Exercise 1.

3. What type of graph would be appropriate to show the number of gold medals, silver medals, and bronze medals won by the United States during the 1984 Olympics?

4. What shape would you expect for the distribution of salaries for all employees of a major industry?

ANSWERS

1. The graphs are shown in Figure 2.9.

Figure 2.9

Answers to Learning Check Exercise 1.

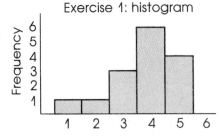

Exercise 1: histogram

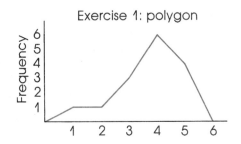

Exercise 1: polygon

2. The distribution is negatively skewed.

3. A bar graph is appropriate for ordinal data.

4. The distribution probably would be positively skewed, with most employees earning an average salary and a relatively small number of top executives with vary large salaries.

2.5 OTHER TYPES OF GRAPHS

In addition to displaying frequency distributions, graphs can be used to show relationships between variables. Perhaps the most common use is to show the results of an experiment by graphing the relation between the independent variable and the dependent variable. You should recall that the dependent variable is the score obtained for each subject and that the independent variable distinguishes the different treatment conditions or groups used in the experiment. For example, a researcher testing a new diet drug might compare several different dosages by measuring the amount of food that animals consume at each dose level. Figure 2.10 shows a *line graph* displaying hypothetical data from this experiment. Notice that the four dose levels (the independent variable) are on the *X*-axis and that food consumption (the dependent variable) is shown on the *Y*-axis. The points in the graph represent the average food consumption for the group at each dose level. Because the independent variable (on the *X*-axis) is continuous, the points are connected with a continuous line.

Figure 2.11 shows results from another experiment where the independent variable is discrete. This graph, which is another example of a bar graph, uses separate bars for each position on the *X*-axis to indicate that we are comparing separate, discrete, categories. In general, line graphs are used to display data when the independent variable (*X*-axis) is classified on an interval or ratio scale, usually a continuous variable. A bar graph is used when the independent variable consists of a nominal or ordinal scale, usually a discrete variable.

Note that values for the independent variable (or quasi-independent variable) are placed on the *X*-axis and the dependent variable (average score) is placed on the *Y*-axis.

Figure 2.10

The relationship between an independent variable (drug dose) and a dependent variable (food consumption). Because drug dose is a continuous variable, a continuous line is used to connect the different dose levels.

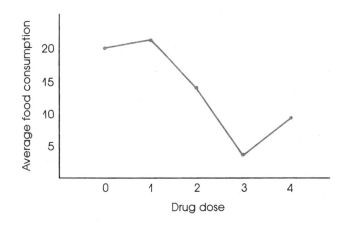

Figure 2.11

The relationship between an independent variable (brand of pain reliever) and a dependent variable (pain tolerance). The graph uses separate bars because the brand of pain reliever is measured on a nominal scale.

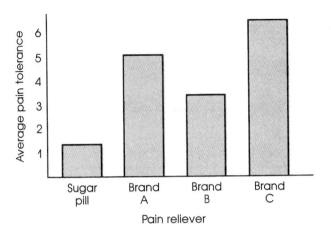

When constructing graphs of any type, you should recall the basic rules we mentioned earlier:

1. The height of a graph should be approximately three-quarters of its length.
2. Normally, you start numbering both the *X*-axis and the *Y*-axis with zero at the point where the two axes intersect.

More importantly, you should remember that the purpose of a graph is to give an accurate representation of the information in a set of data. Box 2.1 demonstrates what can happen when these basic principles are ignored.

LEARNING CHECK

1. In a study on stress, a researcher exposed groups of rats to either signaled shock, unsignaled shock, or no shock. The average size (in millimeters) of ulcers for each group was then determined. Construct a graph of the following data.

Treatment Group

	NO SHOCK	SIGNALED SHOCK	UNSIGNALED SHOCK
Average size of ulcers	0	3	7

2. A psychologist studied the effect of sleep deprivation on mood. Groups of clinically depressed subjects were deprived of sleep for either 0, 1, 2, or 3 nights. After deprivation, the amount of depression was measured with a depression inventory. Construct a graph of the following data.

NIGHTS OF DEPRIVATION	AVERAGE DEPRESSION SCORE
0	22
1	17
2	9
3	7

THE USE AND MISUSE OF GRAPHS

ALTHOUGH GRAPHS are intended to provide an accurate picture of a set of data, they can be used to exaggerate or misrepresent a set of scores. These misrepresentations generally result from failing to follow the basic rules for graph construction. The following example demonstrates how the same set of data can be presented in two entirely different ways by manipulating the structure of a graph.

For the past several years, the city has kept records of the number of major felonies. The data are summarized as follows:

YEAR	NUMBER OF MAJOR FELONIES
1982	218
1983	225
1984	229

These same data are shown in two different graphs in Figure 2.12. In the first graph we have exaggerated the height, and we started numbering the Y-axis at 210 rather than at zero. As a result, the graph seems to indicate a rapid rise in the crime rate over the 3-year period. In the second graph, we have stretched out the X-axis and used zero as the starting point for the Y-axis. The result is a graph that shows no change in the crime rate over the 3-year period.

Which graph is correct? The answer is that neither one is very good. Remember that the purpose of a graph is to provide an accurate display of the data. The first graph in Figure 2.12 exaggerates the differences between years, and the second graph conceals the differences. Some compromise is needed. You also should note that in some cases a graph may not be the best way to display information. For these data, for example, showing the numbers in a table would be better than either graph.

Figure 2.12

Two graphs showing the number of major felonies in a city over a 3-year period. Both graphs are showing exactly the same data. However, the first graph gives the appearance that the crime rate is high and rising rapidly. The second graph gives the impression that the crime rate is low and has not changed over the 3-year period.

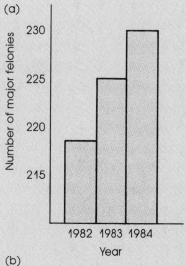
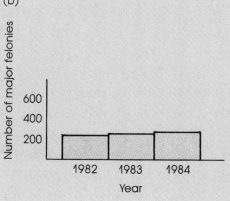

ANSWERS 1., 2. The graphs are shown in Figure 2.13.

Figure 2.13

Answers to Learning Check Exercises 1 and 2.

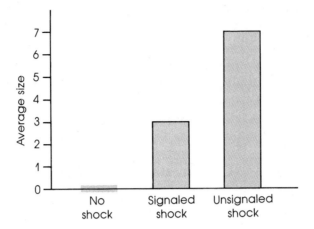

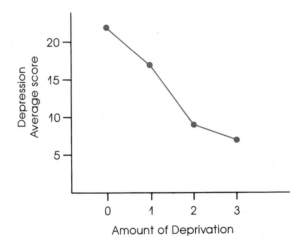

2.6 PERCENTILES, PERCENTILE RANKS, AND INTERPOLATION

Although the primary purpose of a frequency distribution is to provide a description of an entire set of scores, it also can be used to describe the position of an individual within the set. Individual scores, or X values, are called raw scores. By themselves, raw scores do not provide much information. For example, if you are told that your score on an exam is $X = 43$, you cannot tell how well you did. To evaluate your score, you need more information such as the average score or the number of people who had scores above and below you. With this additional information you would be able to determine your relative position in the class. Because raw scores do not provide much information, it is desirable to transform them into a more meaningful form. One transformation that we will consider changes raw scores into percentiles.

DEFINITIONS

The *rank* or *percentile rank* of a particular score is defined as the percentage of individuals in the distribution with scores at or below the particular value.

When a score is identified by its percentile rank, the score is called a *percentile*.

Suppose, for example, that you have a score of $X = 43$ on an exam and that you know that exactly 60% of the class had scores of 43 or lower. Then your score $X = 43$ has a percentile rank of 60%, and your score would be called the 60th percentile. Notice that *percentile rank* refers to a percentage and that *percentile* refers to a score. Also notice that your rank or percentile describes your exact position within the distribution.

CUMULATIVE FREQUENCY AND CUMULATIVE PERCENTAGE

The first step in determining percentiles is to find the number of individuals who are located at or below each point in the distribution. This can be done most easily with a frequency distribution table by simply counting the number who are in or below each category on the scale. The resulting values are called *cumulative frequencies* because they represent the accumulation of individuals as you move up the scale.

EXAMPLE 2.4

In the following frequency distribution table we have included a cumulative frequency column headed by *cf*. For each row the cumulative frequency value is obtained by adding up the frequencies in that category or lower. For example, the score $X = 3$ has a cumulative frequency of 14 because exactly 14 individuals had scores in this category or in a lower category.

X	f	cf
5	1	20
4	5	19
3	8	14
2	4	6
1	2	2

The cumulative frequencies show the number of individuals located at or below each score. To find percentiles, we must convert these frequencies into percentages. The resulting values are called *cumulative percentages* because they show the percent of individuals who are accumulated as you move up the scale.

E X A M P L E   2 . 5   This time we have added a cumulative percentage column (c%) to the frequency distribution table from Example 2.4. The values in this column represent the percent of the individuals who are located in each category or lower. For example, 70% of the individuals (14 out of 20) had scores of $X = 3$ or lower. Cumulative percentages can be computed by

$$c\% = \frac{cf}{N}(100\%)$$

X	f	cf	c%
5	1	20	100%
4	5	19	95%
3	8	14	70%
2	4	6	30%
1	2	2	10%

The cumulative percentages in a frequency distribution table give the percent of individuals with scores at or below each X value. However, you must remember that the X values in the table are not points on the scale but rather intervals. A score of $X = 2$, for example, means that the measurement was somewhere between the real limits of 1.5 and 2.5. Thus, when a table shows that a score of $X = 2$ has a cumulative percentage of 30%, you should interpret this as meaning that 30% of the individuals have been accumulated by the time you reach the top of the interval for $X = 2$. Notice that each cumulative percentage value is associated with the upper real limit of its interval. This point is demonstrated in Figure 2.14, which shows the same data that were used in Example 2.5. Figure 2.14 shows that two people, or 10%, had scores of $X = 1$; that is, two people had scores between 0.5 and 1.5.

Figure 2.14

The relationship between cumulative frequencies (*cf* values) and upper real limits. Notice that two people had scores of $X = 1$. These two individuals are located between the real limits of 0.5 and 1.5. Although their exact locations are not known, you can be certain that both had scores below the upper real limit of 1.5.

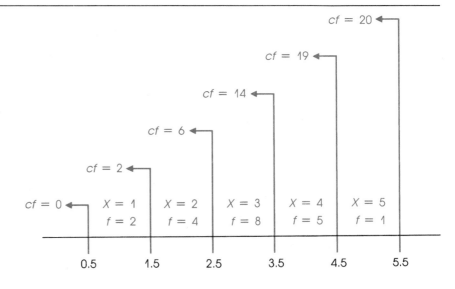

You cannot be sure that both individuals have been accumulated until you reach 1.5, the upper real limit of the interval. Similarly, a cumulative percentage of 30% is reached at 2.5 on the scale, a percentage of 70% is reached at 3.5, and so on.

INTERPOLATION It is possible to determine some percentiles and percentile ranks directly from a frequency distribution table provided that the percentiles are upper real limits and that the ranks are percentages that appear in the table. Using the table in Example 2.5, for example, you should be able to answer the following questions:

1. What is the 95th percentile? (Answer: $X = 4.5$.)
2. What is the percentile rank for $X = 3.5$? (Answer: 70%.)

However, there are many values that do not appear directly in the table, and it is impossible to determine these values precisely. Referring to the table in Example 2.5 again,

1. What is the 50th percentile?
2. What is the percentile rank for $X = 4$?

Because these values are not specifically reported in the table, you cannot answer the questions. However, it is possible to obtain estimates of these intermediate values by using a standard procedure known as interpolation.

Before we apply the process of interpolation to percentiles and percentile ranks, we will use a simple, commonsense example to introduce this method. Suppose you hear the weather report at 8 A.M. and again at noon. At 8:00 the temperature was 60°, and at noon it was 68°. What is your estimate of the temperature at 9:00? To make your task a bit easier, we shall sketch a table showing the time and temperature relations:

TIME	TEMPERATURE
8:00	60
12:00	68

If you estimated the temperature to be 62° at 9:00, you have done interpolation. You probably went through the following logical steps:

1. The total time from 8:00 to 12:00 is 4 hours.
2. During this time, the temperature changed 8°.
3. 9:00 represents 1 hour, or one-fourth of the total time.
4. Assuming that the temperature went up at a constant rate, it should have increased by 2° during the hour because 2° equals one-fourth of the temperature change.

The process of interpolation is pictured in Figure 2.15. Using the figure, try answering the following questions about other times and temperatures:

1. At what time did the temperature reach 64°?
2. What was the temperature at 11:00?

Figure 2.15

A graphic representation of the process of interpolation. The same interval is shown on two separate scales, temperature and time. Only the endpoints of the scales are known—at 8:00 the temperature is 60° and at 12:00 the temperature is 68°. Interpolation allows you to estimate values within the interval by assuming that fractional portions of one scale correspond to the same fractional portions of the other. For example, it is assumed that halfway through the temperature scale corresponds to halfway through the time scale.

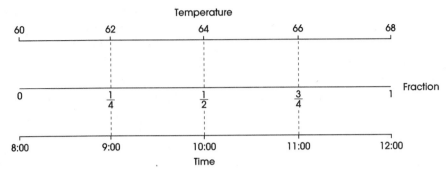

If you got answers of 10:00 and 66°, you have mastered the process of interpolation.

Notice that interpolation provides a method for finding intermediate values, that is, values that are located between two specified numbers. This is exactly the problem we faced with percentiles and percentile ranks. Some values are given in the table, but others are not. Also notice that interpolation only *estimates* the intermediate values. In the time and temperature example we do not know what the temperature was at 10:00. It may have soared to 80° between 8:00 and noon. The basic assumption underlying interpolation is that the change from one end of the interval to the other is a regular, linear change. We assumed, for example, that the temperature went up consistently at 2° per hour throughout the time period. Because interpolation is based on this assumption, the values we calculate are only estimates. The general process of interpolation can be summarized as follows:

1. A single interval is measured on two separate scales (for example, time and temperature). The endpoints of the interval are known for each scale.

2. You are given an intermediate value on one of the scales. The problem is to find the corresponding intermediate value on the other scale.

3. The interpolation process requires four steps:

   a. Find the width of the interval on both scales.

   b. Locate the position of the intermediate value in the interval. This position corresponds to a fraction of the whole interval:

   $$\text{fraction} = \frac{\text{distance from the top of the interval}}{\text{interval width}}$$

   c. Use this fraction to determine the distance from the top of the interval on the other scale:

   $$\text{distance} = (\text{fraction}) \times (\text{width})$$

d. Use the distance from the top to determine the position on the other scale.

The following examples demonstrate the process of interpolation as it is applied to percentiles and percentile ranks. The key to successfully working these problems is that each cumulative percentage in the table is associated with the upper real limit of its score interval.

You may notice that in each of these problems we use interpolation working from the *top* of the interval. However, this choice is arbitrary, and you should realize that interpolation can be done just as easily working from the bottom of the interval.

EXAMPLE 2.6 Using the following distribution of scores, we will find the percentile rank corresponding to $X = 7.0$:

X	f	cf	c%
10	2	25	100%
9	8	23	92%
8	4	15	60%
7	6	11	44%
6	4	5	20%
5	1	1	4%

Note that $X = 7.0$ is located in the interval bounded by real limits of 6.5 and 7.5. The cumulative percentages corresponding to these real limits are 20% and 44%, respectively. These values are shown in the following table:

For interpolation problems, it is always helpful to sketch a table showing the range on both scales.

SCORES (X)	PERCENTAGES
7.5	44%
7.0---------------?	
6.5	20%

STEP 1 For the scores, the width of the interval is 1 point. For the percentages, the width is 24 points.

STEP 2 Our particular score is located 0.5 point from the top of the interval. This is exactly halfway down in the interval.

STEP 3 Halfway down on the percentage scale would be

$$\frac{1}{2}(24 \text{ points}) = 12 \text{ points}$$

STEP 4 For the percentages, the top of the interval is 44%, so 12 points down would be

$$44\% - 12\% = 32\%$$

This is the answer. A score of $X = 7.0$ corresponds to a percentile rank of 32%.

This same interpolation procedure can be used with data that have been grouped into class intervals. Once again, you must remember that the cumulative percentage values are associated with the upper real limits of each interval. The following example demonstrates the calculation of percentiles and percentile ranks using data in a grouped frequency distribution.

EXAMPLE 2.7 Using the following distribution of scores, we will use interpolation to find the 50th percentile:

X	f	cf	c%
20–24	2	20	100%
15–19	3	18	90%
10–14	3	15	75%
5–9	10	12	60%
0–4	2	2	10%

A percentage value of 50% is not given in the table; however, it is located between 10% and 60%, which are given. These two percentage values are associated with the upper real limits of 4.5 and 9.5, respectively. These values are shown in the following table:

SCORES (X)	PERCENTAGES
9.5	60%
? ------------	50%
4.5	10%

STEP 1 For the scores, the width of the interval is 5 points. For the percentages, the width is 50 points.

STEP 2 The value of 50% is located 10 points from the top of the percentage interval. As a fraction of the whole interval, this is 10 out of 50, or $\frac{1}{5}$ of the total interval.

STEP 3 Using this same fraction for the scores, we obtain a distance of

$$\frac{1}{5}(5 \text{ points}) = 1 \text{ point}$$

The location we want is 1 point down from the top of the score interval.

STEP 4 Because the top of the interval is 9.5, the position we want is

$$9.5 - 1 = 8.5$$

This is the answer. The 50th percentile is $X = 8.5$.

LEARNING CHECK   1. On a statistics exam, would you rather score at the 80th percentile or at the 40th percentile?

2. For the distribution of scores presented in the following table,
   a. Find the 60th percentile.
   b. Find the percentile rank for $X = 39.5$.

X	f	cf	c%
40–49	4	25	100%
30–39	6	21	84%
20–29	10	15	60%
10–19	3	5	20%
0–9	2	2	8%

3. Use the distribution of scores from Exercise 2, and interpolation.
   a. Find the 40th percentile.
   b. Find the percentile rank for $X = 32$.

ANSWERS   1. The 80th percentile is the higher score.

2. a. $X = 29.5$ is the 60th percentile.
   b. $X = 39.5$ has a rank of 84%.

3. a. Because 40% is between the values of 20% and 60% in the table, you must use interpolation. The score corresponding to a rank of 40% is $X = 24.5$.
   b. Because $X = 32$ is between the real limits of 29.5 and 39.5, you must use interpolation. The percentile rank for $X = 32$ is 66%.

2.7 STEM AND LEAF DISPLAYS

The general term display *is used because a stem and leaf display combines the elements of a table and a graph.*

In 1977 J. W. Tukey presented a technique for organizing data that provides a simple alternative to a frequency distribution table or graph (Tukey, 1977). This technique, called a *stem and leaf display*, requires that each score be separated into two parts: the first digit (or digits) is called the *stem*, and the last digit (or digits) is called the *leaf*. For example, $X = 85$ would be separated into a stem of 8 and a leaf of 5. Similarly, $X = 42$ would have a stem of 4 and a leaf of 2. To construct a stem and leaf display for a set of data, the first step is to list all the stems in a column. For the data in Table 2.3, for example, the lowest scores are in the 30s and the highest scores are in the 90s, so the list of stems would be

Minitab can be used to create stem and leaf displays (Section 20.4).

STEMS
3
4
5
6
7
8
9

The next step is to go through the data, one score at a time, and write the leaf for each score beside its stem. For the data in Table 2.3, the first score is $X = 83$, so you would write 3 (the leaf) beside the 8 in the column of stems. This process is continued for the entire set of scores. The complete stem and leaf display is shown with the original data in Table 2.3.

COMPARING STEM AND LEAF DISPLAYS WITH FREQUENCY DISTRIBUTIONS

You should notice that the stem and leaf display is very similar to a grouped frequency distribution. Each of the stem values corresponds to a class interval. For example, the stem 3 represents all scores in the 30s, that is, all scores in the interval 30–39. The number of leaves in the display show the frequency associated with each stem. It also should be clear that the stem and leaf display has several advantages over a traditional frequency distribution:

1. The stem and leaf display is very easy to construct. By going through the data only one time, you can construct a complete display.

2. The stem and leaf display allows you to identify every individual score in the data. In the display shown in Table 2.3, for example, you know that there were three scores in the 60s, and you know that the specific values were 62, 68, and 63. A frequency distribution would tell you only the frequency, not the specific values.

3. The stem and leaf display provides both a listing of the scores and a picture of the distribution. If a stem and leaf display is viewed from the side, it is essentially the same as a frequency distribution histogram (see Figure 2.16).

4. Because the stem and leaf display presents the actual value for each score, it is easy to modify a display if you want a more-detailed pic-

Table 2.3

A set of $N = 24$ scores presented as raw data and organized in a stem and leaf display

DATA			STEM AND LEAF DISPLAY	
83	82	63	3	23
62	93	78	4	26
71	68	33	5	6279
76	52	97	6	283
85	42	46	7	1643846
32	57	59	8	3521
56	73	74	9	37
74	81	76		

Figure 2.16

A grouped frequency distribution histogram and a stem and leaf display showing the distribution of scores from Table 2.3. The stem and leaf display is placed on its side to demonstrate that the display gives the same information that is provided in the histogram.

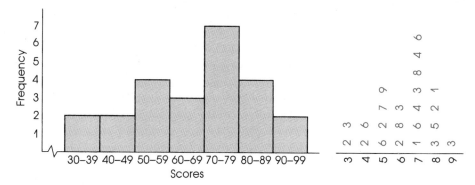

ture of a distribution. The modification simply requires that each stem be split into two (or more) parts. For example, Table 2.4 shows the same data that were presented in Table 2.3, but now we have split each stem in half. Notice that each stem value is now listed twice in the display. The first half of each stem is associated with the lower leaves (values 0–4), and the second half is associated with the upper leaves (values 5–9). In essence, we have regrouped the distribution using an interval width of 5 points instead of a width of 10 points in the original display.

Although stem and leaf displays are quite useful, you should be warned that they are considered to be a preliminary means for organizing data. Typically, a researcher would use a stem and leaf display to get a first look at experimental data. The final, published report normally would present the distribution of scores in a traditional frequency distribution table or graph.

Table 2.4

A stem and leaf display with each stem split into two parts[a]

3	23
3	
4	2
4	6
5	2
5	679
6	23
6	8
7	1434
7	686
8	321
8	5
9	3
9	7

[a]Note that each stem value is listed twice: The first occurrence is associated with the lower leaf values (0–4), and the second occurrence is associated with the upper leaf values (5–9). The data shown in this display are taken from Table 2.3.

1. Use a stem and leaf display to organize the following set of scores: 86, 114, 94, 107, 96, 100, 98, 118, 107, 132, 106, 127, 124, 108, 112, 119, 125, 115

2. Explain how a stem and leaf display contains more information than a grouped frequency distribution.

A N S W E R S   1. The stem and leaf display for these data would be

8	6
9	468
10	70768
11	48295
12	745
13	2

2. A grouped frequency distribution table tells only the number of scores in each interval; it does not identify the exact value for each score. The stem and leaf display gives the individual scores as well as the number in each interval.

SUMMARY

1. The goal of descriptive statistics is to simplify the organization and presentation of data. One descriptive technique is to place data in a frequency distribution table or graph that shows how the scores are distributed across the measurement scale.

2. A frequency distribution table lists scores (from highest down to lowest) in one column and the frequency of occurrence for each score in a second column. The table may include a proportion column showing the relative frequency for each score:

$$\text{proportion} = p = \frac{f}{N}$$

And the table may include a percentage column showing the percentage associated with each score:

$$\text{percentage} = \% = \frac{f}{N}(100)$$

3. When the scores cover a range that is too broad to list each individual value, it is customary to divide the range into sections called class intervals. These intervals are then listed in the frequency distribution table along with the frequency or number of individuals with scores in each interval. The result is called a

grouped frequency distribution. The guidelines for constructing a grouped frequency distribution table are as follows:
a. There should be about 10 intervals.
b. The width of each interval should be a simple number (e.g., 2, 5, or 10).
c. The bottom score in each interval should be a multiple of the width.
d. All intervals should be the same width, and they should cover the range of scores with no gaps.

4. A frequency distribution graph lists scores on the horizontal axis and frequencies on the vertical axis. The type of graph used to display a distribution depends on the scale of measurement used. For interval or ratio scales, you should use a histogram or a polygon. For a histogram, a bar is drawn above each score so that the height of the bar corresponds to the frequency. Each bar extends to the real limits of the score so that adjacent bars touch. For a polygon, a dot is placed above the midpoint of each score or class interval so that the height of the dot corresponds to the frequency; then lines are drawn to connect the dots. Bar graphs are used with nominal or ordinal scales. Bar graphs are similar to histograms except that gaps are left between adjacent bars.

5. Shape is one of the basic characteristics used to describe a distribution of scores. Most distributions can be classified as either symmetrical or skewed. A skewed distribution that tails off to the right is said to be positively skewed. If it tails off to the left, it is negatively skewed.

6. Cumulative percentage is the percentage of individuals with scores at or below a particular point in the distribution. The cumulative percentage values are associated with the upper real limits of the corresponding score or interval.

7. Percentiles and percentile ranks are used to describe the position of individual scores within a distribution. Percentile rank gives a cumulative percentage associated with a particular score. A score that is identified by its rank is called a percentile.

8. When a desired percentile or percentile rank is located between two known values, it is possible to estimate the desired value using the process of interpolation. Interpolation assumes a regular linear change between the two known values.

9. A stem and leaf display is an alternative procedure for organizing data. Each score is separated into a stem (the first digit or digits) and a leaf (the last digit or digits). The display consists of the stems listed in a column with the leaf for each score written beside its stem. A stem and leaf display combines the characteristics of a table and a graph and produces a concise, well-organized picture of the data.

KEY TERMS

frequency distribution	lower real limit	symmetrical distribution	percentile rank
grouped frequency distribution	apparent limits	positively skewed distribution	cumulative frequency (*cf*)
range	histogram	negatively skewed distribution	cumulative percentage (*c%*)
class interval	bar graph	tail(s) of a distribution	interpolation
upper real limit	polygon	percentile	stem and leaf display

──── *Focus on Problem Solving* ────

1. The reason for constructing frequency distributions is to transform a disorganized set of raw data into a comprehensible, organized format. Because several different types of frequency distribution tables and graphs are available, one problem is deciding which type should be used. Tables have the advantage of being easier to construct, but graphs generally give a better picture of the data and are easier to understand.

    To help you decide exactly which type of frequency distribution is best, consider the following points:

    a. What is the range of scores? With a wide range, you will need to group the scores into class intervals.
    b. What is the scale of measurement? With an interval or ratio scale you can use a polygon or a histogram. With a nominal or ordinal scale, you must use a bar graph.

2. In setting up class intervals, a common mistake is to determine the interval width by finding the difference between the apparent limits. This is incorrect! To determine the interval width, you must take the difference for the *real lim-*

its. For example, the width for the interval 70–79 is 10 because its real limits are 69.5 and 79.5, and

$$\text{width} = \text{upper real limit} - \text{lower real limit}$$

$$= 79.5 - 69.5 = 10$$

Resist the temptation to state the width is 9. You must use the real limits.

3. Percentiles and percentile ranks are intended to identify specific locations within a distribution of scores. When solving percentile problems, especially with interpolation, it is helpful to sketch a frequency distribution graph. Use the graph to make a preliminary estimate of the answer before you begin any calculations. For example, to find the 60th percentile, you would want to draw a vertical line through the graph so that slightly more than half (60%) of the distribution is on the left-hand side of the line. Locating this position in your sketch will give you a rough estimate of what the final answer should be. When doing interpolation problems, there are several points you should keep in mind:

   a. Remember that the cumulative percentage values correspond to the upper real limits of each score or interval.
   b. You should always identify the interval with which you are working. The easiest way to do this is to sketch a table showing the endpoints on both scales (scores and cumulative percentages). This is illustrated in Example 2.6 on page 55.
   c. The word *interpolation* means *between two poles*. Remember, your goal is to find an intermediate value between the two ends of the interval. Check your answer to be sure that it is located between the two endpoints. If not, then check your calculations.

——— *Demonstration 2.1* ———
A GROUPED FREQUENCY DISTRIBUTION TABLE

For the following set of $N = 20$ scores, construct a grouped frequency distribution table. Use an interval width of 5 points and include columns for f and p.

data: 14   8   27   16   10   22   9   13   16   12
        10   9   15   17   6   14   11   18   14   11

STEP 1   Set up the class intervals.
         The largest score in this distribution is $X = 27$ and the lowest is $X = 6$. Therefore, a frequency distribution table for these data would have 22 rows and would be too large. A grouped frequency distribution table would be better. We have asked specifically for an internal width of 5 points, and the resulting table will have five rows:

X
25–29
20–24
15–19
10–14
5–9

Remember, the interval width is determined by the real limits of the interval. For example, the class interval 25−29 has an upper real limit of 29.5 and a lower real limit of 24.5. The difference between these two values is the width of the interval, namely 5.

STEP 2 Determine the frequencies for each interval.

Examine the scores and count how many fall into the class interval of 25−29. Cross out each score that you have already counted. Record the frequency for this class interval. Now repeat this process for the remaining intervals. The result is the following table:

X	f	
25−29	1	(the score $X = 27$)
20−24	1	($X = 22$)
15−19	5	(the scores $X = 16, 16, 15, 17,$ and 18)
10−14	9	($X = 14, 10, 13, 12, 10, 14, 11, 14,$ and 11)
5−9	4	($X = 8, 9, 9,$ and 6)

STEP 3 Compute the proportions.

The proportion (p) of scores contained in an interval is determined by dividing the frequency (f) of that interval by the number of scores (N) in the distribution. Thus, for each interval, we must compute the following:

$$p = \frac{f}{N}$$

This is demonstrated in the following table.

X	f	p
25−29	1	$f/N = 1/20 = 0.05$
20−24	1	$f/N = 1/20 = 0.05$
15−19	5	$f/N = 5/20 = 0.25$
10−14	9	$f/N = 9/20 = 0.45$
5−9	4	$f/N = 4/20 = 0.20$

Demonstration 2.2

USING INTERPOLATION TO FIND PERCENTILES AND PERCENTILE RANKS

Find the 50th percentile for the set of scores in the grouped frequency distribution table that was constructed in Demonstration 2.1.

STEP 1 Find cumulative frequency (*cf*) and cumulative percentage values and add these values to the basic frequency distribution table.

Cumulative frequencies indicate the number of individuals located in each category (class interval) or lower. To find these frequencies, begin with the bottom interval and then accumulate the frequencies as you move up the scale. For this example, there are four individuals who are in the 5–9 interval or lower ($cf = 4$). Moving up the scale, the 10–14 interval contains an additional 9 people, so the cumulative value for this interval is $9 + 4 = 13$ (simply add the 9 individuals in the interval plus the 4 individuals below). Continue moving up the scale, cumulating frequencies for each interval.

Cumulative percentages are determined from the cumulative frequencies by the relationship:

$$c\% = \left(\frac{cf}{N}\right) 100\%$$

For example, the cf column shows that 4 individuals (out of the total set of $N = 20$) have scores in the 5–9 interval or lower. The corresponding cumulative percentage is

$$c\% = (\tfrac{4}{20})100\% = (\tfrac{1}{5})100\% = 20\%$$

The complete set of cumulative frequencies and cumulative percentages are shown in the following table:

X	f	cf	c%
25–29	1	20	100%
20–24	1	19	95%
15–19	5	18	90%
10–14	9	13	65%
5–9	4	4	20%

STEP 2   Locate the interval that contains the value that you want to calculate.

We are looking for the 50th percentile, which is located between the values of 20% and 65% in the table. The scores (upper real limits) corresponding to these two percentages are 9.5 and 14.5, respectively. The interval, measured in terms of scores and percentages, is shown in the following table:

X	c%
14.5	65%
?? - - - - - -	50%
9.5	20%

STEP 3   Locate the intermediate value as a fraction of the total interval.

Our intermediate value is 50%, which is located in the interval between 65% and 20%. The total width of the interval is 45 points ($65 - 20 = 45$), and the value of 50% is located 15 points down from the top of the interval. As a fraction, the 50th percentile is located $\tfrac{15}{45} = \tfrac{1}{3}$ down from the top of the interval.

STEP 4   Use the fraction to determine the corresponding location on the other scale.

Our intermediate value, 50%, is located $\tfrac{1}{3}$ of the way down from the top of the interval. Our goal is to find the score, the X value, that also is located $\tfrac{1}{3}$ of the way down from the top of the interval.

On the score (X) side of the interval, the top value is 14.5 and the bottom value is 9.5, so the total interval width is 5 points ($14.5 - 9.5 = 5$). The position we are seeking is ⅓ of the way from the top of the interval. One-third of the total interval is

$$(⅓)5 = ⅗ = 1.67 \text{ points}$$

To find this location, begin at the top of the interval and come down 1.67 points:

$$14.5 - 1.67 = 12.83$$

This is our answer. The 50th percentile is $X = 12.83$.

PROBLEMS

1. Place the following scores in a frequency distribution table. Include columns for proportion (p) and percentage (%) in your table.

scores: 3, 1, 1, 2, 5, 4, 4, 5, 3,
         3, 2, 3, 4, 3, 3, 4, 3, 2,
         5, 3

2. Sketch a histogram and a polygon showing the distribution of scores presented in the following table.

X	f
5	4
4	6
3	5
2	3
1	2

3. Find N, ΣX, and ΣX^2 for the set of scores in the following frequency distribution table.

X	f
5	1
4	3
3	5
2	2
1	2

4. Under what circumstances should you use a bar graph instead of a histogram to display a frequency distribution?

5. Under what circumstances should you use a grouped frequency distribution instead of a regular frequency distribution?

6. A set of scores covers a range of 15 points. Should these scores be presented in a regular table or a grouped table? Explain the advantages and disadvantages of each.

7. A set of $N = 7$ scores ranges from a high of $X = 96$ to a low of $X = 61$. Explain why it would *not* be a good idea to display this set of data in a frequency distribution table.

8. Place the following set of scores in a frequency distribution table and draw a polygon showing the distribution of scores.

Scores: 7, 5, 4, 6, 4, 3, 3, 4, 2, 5

9. For the set of scores shown in the following frequency distribution table,
   a. How many scores are in the distribution? ($N = ?$)
   b. Find ΣX for this set of scores.

X	f
4	2
3	4
2	5
1	3

10. For the following set of scores,
   a. Construct a frequency distribution table to organize the scores.
   b. Draw a frequency distribution histogram for these data.

3, 5, 4, 6, 2, 3, 4, 1, 4, 3

7, 7, 3, 4, 5, 8, 2, 4, 7, 10

11. Place the following 28 scores in a grouped frequency distribution table using
    a. An interval width of 2
    b. An interval width of 5

    23, 12, 16, 16, 17, 19, 28

    20, 14, 21, 18, 24, 29, 24

    18, 21, 22, 27, 21, 25, 19

    22, 23, 21, 30, 27, 23, 18

12. A psychologist would like to examine the effects of diet on intelligence. Two groups of rats are selected with 12 rats in each group. One group is fed the regular diet of Rat Chow, whereas the second group has special vitamins and minerals added to their food. After 6 months each rat is tested on a discrimination problem. The psychologist records the number of errors each animal makes before it solves the problem. The data from this experiment are as follows:

    regular diet scores: 13, 11, 12, 13, 11,   9
                          12, 10, 12, 14, 10, 12

    special diet scores: 9,   8,   7,   8,   9, 10
                           7,   8,   9,   6,   8, 10

    a. Identify the independent variable and the dependent variable for this experiment.
    b. Sketch a frequency distribution polygon for the group of rats with the regular diet. On the same graph (in a different color), sketch the distribution for the rats with the special diet.
    c. From looking at your graphs, would you say that the special diet had any effect on intelligence? Explain your answer.

13. Sketch a frequency distribution histogram for the following data.

X	f
15	2
14	5
13	6
12	3
11	2
10	1

14. Three sets of data are described by identifying the lowest score and the highest score for each set. De-

scribe how a grouped frequency distribution table should be constructed for each set. That is, give the interval width that you would suggest and the number of intervals needed.
    a. 3–19
    b. 51–98
    c. 270–660

15. The following data are quiz scores from two different sections of an introductory statistics course:

SECTION I			SECTION II		
9	6	8	4	7	8
10	8	3	6	3	7
7	8	8	4	6	5
7	5	10	10	3	6
9	6	7	7	4	6

    a. Organize the scores from each section in a grouped frequency distribution histogram.
    b. Describe the general differences between the two distributions.

16. A researcher evaluated the taste of four leading brands of instant coffee by having a sample of individuals taste each coffee and then rate its flavor on a scale from 1 to 5 (1 = very bad and 5 = excellent). The results from this study are summarized as follows:

COFFEE	AVERAGE RATING
Brand A	2.5
Brand B	4.1
Brand C	3.2
Brand D	3.6

    a. Identify the independent variable and the dependent variable for this study.
    b. What scale of measurement was used for the independent variable (nominal, ordinal, interval, or ratio)?
    c. If the researcher used a graph to show the obtained relationship between the independent variable and the dependent variable, what kind of graph would be appropriate (line graph, histogram, bar graph)?
    d. Sketch a graph showing the results of this experiment.

17. A researcher examined the effect of amount of relaxation training on insomnia. Four treatment groups

were used. Subjects received relaxation training for 2, 4, or 8 sessions. A control group received no training (0 sessions). Following training, the researcher measured how long it took the subjects to fall asleep. The average times for each group are presented in the following table:

TRAINING SESSIONS	AVERAGE TIME (IN MINUTES)
0	72
2	58
4	31
8	14

a. Identify the independent variable and the dependent variable for this study.
b. What scale of measurement was used for the independent variable (nominal, ordinal, interval, or ratio)?
c. If the researcher used a graph to show the obtained relationship between the independent variable and the dependent variable, what kind of graph would be appropriate (line graph, histogram, bar graph)?
d. Sketch a graph showing the results of this experiment.

18. College officials recently conducted a survey to determine student's attitudes toward extending the library hours. Four different groups of students were surveyed, representing the four major subdivisions of the college. The average score for each group was as follows:

humanities: 7.25
sciences: 5.69
professions: 6.85
fine arts: 5.90

Use a graph to present the results of this survey.

19. Add columns showing cumulative frequency (cf) and cumulative percentage ($c\%$) to the following frequency distribution table.

X	f
10	3
9	1
8	0
7	4
6	6
5	4
4	2

20. Find each of the requested values for the distribution of scores shown in the following frequency distribution table.

X	f
14–15	2
12–13	5
10–11	6
8–9	7
6–7	4
4–5	1

a. What is the 20th percentile?
b. What is the percentile rank for $X = 11.5$?
c. Use interpolation to find the 60th percentile.
d. Use interpolation to find the percentile rank for $X = 6$.

21. Complete the cumulative frequency column and the cumulative percentage column for the following table:

X	f	cf	c%
5	7		
4	8		
3	5		
2	3		
1	2		

22. Complete the following frequency distribution table and find each of the percentiles and percentile ranks requested:

X	f	cf	c%
10	2		
9	3		
8	5		
7	6		
6	2		
5	2		

a. What is the percentile rank for $X = 6.5$?
b. What is the percentile rank for $X = 9.5$?
c. What is the 50th percentile?
d. What score is needed to be in the top 10% of this distribution?

23. Using the following frequency distribution, find each of the percentiles and percentile ranks requested:

X	f	cf	c%
6	2	20	100%
5	2	18	90%
4	4	16	80%
3	6	12	60%
2	4	6	30%
1	2	2	10%

   a. What is the 60th percentile?
   b. What is the percentile rank for $X = 5.5$?
   c. Use interpolation to find the 20th percentile.
   d. Use interpolation to find the percentile rank for $X = 5$.
   e. What is the minimum score needed to be in the top 25% of this distribution? That is, find the 75th percentile.

24. Find each value requested for the frequency distribution presented in the following table:

X	f	cf	c%
20–24	10	50	100%
15–19	10	40	80%
10–14	15	30	60%
5–9	10	15	30%
0–4	5	5	10%

   a. Find the percentile rank for $X = 7$.
   b. What is the 75th percentile?
   c. Find the percentile rank for $X = 20$.

25. For the set of data shown in the following stem and leaf display:

```
8 | 271
7 | 4586
6 | 302
5 | 4169
4 | 3
3 | 26
2 | 5
```

   a. Construct a grouped frequency distribution table using an interval width of 10 to display the data.
   b. Place the same data in a frequency distribution histogram, again using an interval width of 10 points.
   c. Notice that you can use the information from a stem and leaf display to construct a frequency distribution. If you had started with the frequency distribution, would it provide enough information for you to construct a stem and leaf display? Explain why or why not.

26. Use a stem and leaf display to organize the following scores:

43, 56, 35, 47, 48, 52, 66, 57, 46

39, 43, 47, 61, 55, 50, 49, 39, 40

27. The following data are attitude scores for a sample of 25 students. A high score indicates a positive attitude, and a low score indicates a negative attitude.

ATTITUDE SCORES				
9	73	62	52	14
31	26	74	61	13
79	58	16	62	7
77	9	30	18	23
42	78	10	66	82

   a. Construct a stem and leaf display to organize these data.
   b. Using your stem and leaf display, construct a grouped frequency distribution table for these scores.
   c. Looking at the distribution of scores, which of the following descriptions best fit these data?
      1. This group has a generally positive attitude.
      2. This group has a generally negative attitude.
      3. This group is sharply split with attitudes at both extremes.

CHAPTER 3

CENTRAL TENDENCY

TOOLS YOU WILL NEED

The following items are considered essential background material for this chapter. If you doubt your knowledge of any of these items, you should review the appropriate chapter or section before proceeding.

- Summation notation (Chapter 1)
- Frequency distributions (Chapter 2)

CONTENTS

PREVIEW

In a classic study examing the relation between heredity and intelligence, Tryon (1940) used a selective breeding program to develop separate strains of "smart" and "dumb" rats. Starting with a large sampe of rats, Tryon tested each animal on a maze-learning problem. Based on their error scores for the maze, the brightest rats and the dullest rats were selected from this sample. The brightest males were mated with the brightest females. Similarly, the dullest rats were interbred. This process of testing and selectively breeding was continued for several generations until Tryon had established a line of maze-bright rats and a separate line of maze-dull rats. The results obtained by Tryon are shown in Figure 3.1.

Notice that after seven generations there is an obvious difference between the two groups. As a rule, the maze-bright animals outperform the maze-dull animals. It is tempting to describe the results of this experiment by saying that the maze-bright rats are better learners than the maze-dull rats. However, you should notice that there is some overlap between the two groups; not all the bright rats are really bright, and not all the dull animals are really dull. In fact, some of the animals bred for brightness are actually poorer learners than some of the animals bred for dullness. What is needed is a simple way of describing the general difference between these two groups while still acknowledging the fact that some individuals may contradict the general trend.

The solution to this problem is to identify the typical or average rat as the representative for each group. Then the experimental results can be described by saying that the typical maze-bright rat is a faster learner than the typical maze-dull rat. On the average, the bright rats really are brighter.

In this chapter we will introduce the statistical techniques used to identify the typical or average score for a distribution. Although there are several reasons for defining the average score, the primary advantage of an average is that it provides a single number that describes an entire distribution and can be used for comparison with other distributions.

As a footnote, you should know that later research with Tryon's rats revealed that the maze-bright rats were not really more intelligent than the maze-dull rats. Although the bright rats had developed specific abilities that are useful in mazes, the dull rats proved to be just as smart when tested on a variety of other tasks.

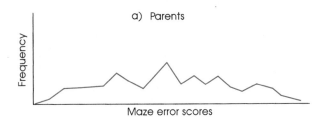

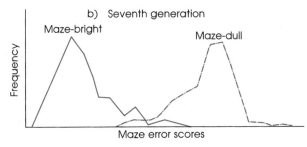

Figure 3.1

Distribution of error scores for the original sample of rats (parents, left figure) and for the two separate lines that were selectively bred for either good or poor maze performance (maze-bright and maze-dull, right figure).

Tryon R. C. (1940). "'Genetic differences in maze-learning ability in rats." *The Thirty-ninth Yearbook of the National Society for the Study of Education*, 111–119. Adapted and reprinted with permission of the National Society for the Study of Education.

3.1 OVERVIEW

The goal in measuring central tendency is to describe a group of individuals (more accurately, their scores) with a single measurement. Ideally, the value we use to describe the group will be the single value that is most representative of all the individuals.

DEFINITION   *Central tendency* is a statistical measure that identifies a single score as a representative for an entire distribution. The goal of central tendency is to find the single score that is most typical or most representative of the entire group.

Usually, we want to choose a value in the middle of the distribution because central scores are often the most representative. In everyday language, the goal of central tendency is to find the "average" or "typical" individual. This average value can then be used to provide a simple description of the entire population or sample. For example, archeological discoveries indicate that the average height for men in the ancient Roman city of Pompeii was 5 feet 7 inches. Obviously, not all the men were exactly 5 feet 7 inches, but this average value provides a general description of the population. Measures of central tendency also are useful for making comparisons between groups of individuals or between sets of figures. For example, suppose that weather data indicate that during the month of December, Seattle averages only 2 hours of sunshine per day, whereas Miami averages over 6 hours. The point of these examples is to demonstrate the great advantage of being able to describe a large set of data with a single, representative number. Central tendency characterizes what is typical for a large population and in doing so makes large amounts of data more digestible. Statisticians sometimes use the expression "number crunching" to illustrate this aspect of data description. That is, we take a distribution consisting of many scores and "crunch" them down to a single value that describes them all.

Unfortunately, there is no single, standard procedure for determining central tendency. The problem is that no single measure will always produce a typical, representative value in every situation. Therefore, there are three different ways to measure central tendency: the mean, the median, and the mode. They are computed differently and have different characteristics. To decide which of the three measures is best for any particular distribution, you should keep in mind that the general purpose of central tendency is to find the single most representative score. Each of the three measures we shall present has been developed to work best in a specific situation. We will examine this issue in more detail after we define the three measures.

3.2 THE MEAN

The mean, commonly known as the arithmetic average, is computed by adding all the scores in the distribution and dividing by the number of scores. The mean for a population will be identified by the Greek letter mu, μ (pronounced "myoo"), and the mean for a sample will be identified by $\overline{X}$ (read "*x*-bar").

DEFINITION   The *mean* for a distribution is the sum of the scores divided by the number of scores.

The formula for the population mean is

$$\mu = \frac{\Sigma X}{N}$$

                                                                                    (3.1)

Obtaining the mean with Minitab is demonstrated with the DESCRIBE and the LET commands (Section 20.4).

First, sum all the scores in the population and then divide by N. For a sample, the computation is done the same way, but the formula uses symbols that signify sample values:

$$\text{sample mean} = \overline{X} = \frac{\Sigma X}{n} \qquad (3.2)$$

In general, we will use Greek letters to identify characteristics of a population and letters of our own alphabet to stand for sample values. If a mean is identified with the symbol $\overline{X}$, you should realize that we are dealing with a sample. Also note that n is used as the symbol for the number of scores in the sample.

EXAMPLE   3.1   For a population of $N = 4$ scores,

$$3, \quad 7, \quad 4, \quad 6$$

the mean is

$$\mu = \frac{\Sigma X}{N} = \frac{20}{4} = 5$$

Although the procedure of adding the scores and dividing by the number provides a useful definition of the mean, there are two alternative definitions that may give you a better understanding of this important measure of central tendency.

The first alternative is to think of the mean as the amount each individual would get if the total (ΣX) were divided equally among all the individuals *(N)* in the distribution. This somewhat socialistic viewpoint is particularly useful in problems where you know the mean and must find the total. Consider the following example.

EXAMPLE   3.2   A group of six students decided to earn some extra money one weekend picking vegetables at a local farm. At the end of the weekend the students discovered that their average income was $\mu = \$30$. If they decide to pool their money for a party, how much will they have?

You don't know how much money each student earned. But you do know that the mean is $30. This is the amount that each student would have if the total were divided equally. For each of six students to have $30, you must start with $6 \times \$30 = \$180$. The total, ΣX, is $180. To check this answer, use the formula for the mean:

$$\mu = \frac{\Sigma X}{N} = \frac{\$180}{6} = \$30$$

The second alternative definition of the mean is to describe the mean as a balance point for a distribution. Consider the population consisting of $N = 4$ scores (2, 2, 6, 10). For this population, $\Sigma X = 20$ and $N = 4$, so $\mu = \frac{20}{4} = 5$.

Figure 3.2

The frequency distribution shown as a seesaw balanced at the mean.

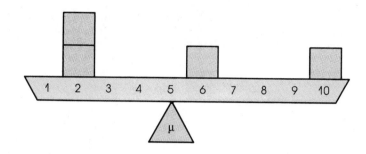

Adapted from *Statistics: An Intuitive Approach,* 4th ed. by G. Weinberg, J. Schumaker, and D. Oltman. Copyright © 1981, 1974, 1969, 1962 by Wadsworth Inc. Reprinted by permission of Brooks/Cole Publishing Co., Monterey, CA 93940.

Imagine that the frequency distribution histogram for this population is drawn so that the *X*-axis, or number line, is a seesaw, and the scores are boxes of equal weight that are placed on the seesaw (see Figure 3.2). If the seesaw is positioned so that it pivots at the value equal to the mean, it will be balanced and will rest level.

The reason the seesaw is balanced over the mean becomes clear when we measure the distance of each box (score) from the mean:

SCORE	DISTANCE FROM THE MEAN
$X = 2$	3 points below the mean
$X = 2$	3 points below the mean
$X = 6$	1 point above the mean
$X = 10$	5 points above the mean

Notice that the mean balances the distances. That is, the total distance below the mean is the same as the total distance above the mean:

3 points below + 3 points below = 6 points below

1 point above + 5 points above = 6 points above

THE WEIGHTED MEAN Often it is necessary to combine two sets of scores and then find the overall mean for the combined group. For example, an instructor teaching two sections of introductory psychology obtains an average quiz score of $\overline{X} = 6$ for the 12 students in one section and an average of $\overline{X} = 7$ for the 8 students in the other section. If the two sections are combined, what is the mean for the total group?

The solution to this problem is straightforward if you remember the definition of the mean:

$$\overline{X} = \frac{\Sigma X}{n}$$

To find the overall mean we must find two values: the total number of students (*n*) for the combined group, and the overall sum of scores for the combined group (ΣX). Finding the number of students is easy. If there are $n = 12$ in one group and $n = 8$ in the other, then there must be $n = 20$ (12 + 8) in the combined group. To find the sum of scores for the combined group, we will use the same method: First find the sum for one group, then find the sum for the other, and then add the two sums together.

We know that the first section has $n = 12$ and $\overline{X} = 6$. Using these values in the equation for the mean gives

$$\overline{X} = \frac{\Sigma X}{n}$$

$$6 = \frac{\Sigma X}{12}$$

$$12(6) = \Sigma X$$

$$72 = \Sigma X$$

The second section has $n = 8$ and $\overline{X} = 7$, so ΣX must be equal to 56. When these two groups are combined, the sum of all 20 scores will be

$$72 + 56 = 128$$

Finally, the mean for the combined group is

$$\overline{X} = \frac{\Sigma X}{n} = \frac{128}{20} = 6.4$$

Notice that this value is not obtained by simply averaging the two means. (If we had simply averaged $\overline{X} = 6$ and $\overline{X} = 7$, we would obtain a mean of 6.5.) Because the samples are not the same size, one will make a larger contribution to the total group and, therefore, will carry more weight in determining the overall mean. For this reason, the overall mean we have calculated is called the *weighted mean*. In this example, the overall mean of $\overline{X} = 6.4$ is closer to the value of $\overline{X} = 6$ (the larger sample) than it is to $\overline{X} = 7$ (the smaller sample).

COMPUTING THE MEAN FROM A FREQUENCY DISTRIBUTION TABLE

Table 3.1 shows the scores on a quiz for a section of statistics students. Instead of listing all of the individual scores, these data are organized into a frequency distribution table. To compute the mean for this sample, you must use all the information in the table, the f values as well as the X values.

Table 3.1

Statistics quiz scores for a section of $n = 8$ students

QUIZ SCORE (X)	f	fX
10	1	10
9	2	18
8	4	32
7	0	0
6	1	6

To find the mean for this sample, we will need the sum of the scores (ΣX) and the number of scores *(n)*. The number n can be found by summing the frequencies:

$$n = \Sigma f = 8$$

It is very common for people to make mistakes when determining ΣX from a frequency distribution table. Often the column labeled X is summed, while the frequency column is ignored. Be sure to use the information in the f column when determining ΣX. (See Chapter 2, p. 35.)

Note that there is one 10, two 9s, four 8s, and one 6 for a total of $n = 8$ scores. To find ΣX, you must be careful to add all eight scores:

$$\Sigma X = 10 + 9 + 9 + 8 + 8 + 8 + 8 + 6 = 66$$

This sum also can be found by multiplying each score by its frequency and then adding up the results. This is done in the third column *(fX)* in Table 3.1. Note, for example, that the two 9s contribute 18 to the total.

Once you have found ΣX and n, you compute the mean as usual:

$$\overline{X} = \frac{\Sigma X}{n} = \frac{\Sigma f X}{\Sigma f} = \frac{66}{8} = 8.25$$

LEARNING CHECK

1. Compute the mean for the sample of scores shown in the following frequency distribution table:

X	f
4	2
3	4
2	3
1	1

2. Two samples were obtained from a population. For sample A, $n = 8$ and $\overline{X} = 14$. For sample B, $n = 20$ and $\overline{X} = 6$. If the two samples are combined, will the overall mean be closer to 14 than to 6, closer to 6 than to 14, or halfway between 6 and 14? Explain your answer.

3. A sample of $n = 20$ scores has a mean of $\overline{X} = 5$. What is ΣX for this sample?

ANSWERS

1. $\overline{X} = \frac{27}{10} = 2.7$

2. The mean will be closer to 6. The larger sample will carry more weight in the combined group.

3. $\Sigma X = 100$

CHARACTERISTICS OF THE MEAN The mean has many characteristics that will be important in future discussions. In general, these characteristics result from the fact that every score in the distribution contributes to the value of the mean. Specifically, every score must be added into the total in order to compute the mean. Three of the more important characteristics will now be discussed.

1. Changing a Score or Introducing a New Score. Changing the value of any score, or adding a new score to the distribution, will change the mean. For example, the quiz scores for a psychology lab section consist of

9, 8, 7, 5, and 1

The mean for this sample is

$$\bar{X} = \frac{\Sigma X}{n} = \frac{30}{5} = 6.00$$

Suppose that the student who received the score of $X = 1$ returned a few days later and explained that she was ill on the day of the quiz. In fact, she went straight to the infirmary after class and was admitted for two days with the flu. Out of the goodness of the instructor's heart, the student was given a makeup quiz, and she received an 8. By having changed her score from 1 to 8, the distribution now consists of

9, 8, 7, 5, and 8

The new mean is

$$\bar{X} = \frac{\Sigma X}{n} = \frac{37}{5} = 7.40$$

Changing a single score in this sample has given us a different mean.

In general the mean is determined by two values: ΣX and N (or n). Whenever either of these values is changed, the mean also will be changed. In the preceding example, the value of one score was changed. This produced a change in the total (ΣX) and therefore changed the mean. If you add a new score (or take away a score), you will change both ΣX and n and must compute the new mean using the changed values. The following example demonstrates how the mean is affected when a new score is added to an existing sample.

EXAMPLE 3.3   We begin with a sample of $n = 4$ scores with a mean of $\bar{X} = 7$. A new score, $X = 12$ is added to this sample. The problem is to find the mean for the new set of scores.

To find the mean, we must first determine the values for n (the number of scores) and ΣX (the sum of the scores). Finding n is easy: We started with four scores and added one more, so the new value for n is 5 ($n = 5$).

To find the sum for the new sample, you simply begin with the total (ΣX) for the original sample and then add in the value of the new score. The original set of $n = 4$ scores had a mean of $\bar{X} = 7$; therefore, the original total must be $\Sigma X = 28$. Adding a score of $X = 12$ brings the new total to $28 + 12 = 40$.

Finally, the new mean is computed using the values for n and ΣX for the new set: $\bar{X} = \Sigma X/n = {}^{40}/_5 = 8$. The entire process can be summarized as follows:

	ORIGINAL SAMPLE	NEW SAMPLE ADDING $X = 12$
	$n = 4$	$n = 5$
	$\Sigma X = 28$	$\Sigma X = 40$
	$\overline{X} = 28/4 = 7$	$\overline{X} = 40/5 = 8$

2. Adding or Subtracting a Constant from Each Score. If a constant value is added to every score in a distribution, the same constant will be added to the mean. Similarly, if you subtract a constant from every score, the same constant will be subtracted from the mean.

EXAMPLE 3.4   Consider the feeding scores for a sample of $n = 6$ rats. See Table 3.2. These scores are the amounts of food (in grams) they ate during a 24-hour testing session. The $\Sigma X = 26$ for $n = 6$ rats, so $\overline{X} = 4.33$. On the following day, each rat is given an experimental drug that reduces appetite. Suppose that this drug has the effect of reducing the meal size by 2 grams for each rat. Note that the effect of the drug is to subtract a constant (two points) from each rat's feeding score. The new distribution is shown in Table 3.3. Now $\Sigma X = 14$ and n is still 6, so the mean amount of food consumed is $\overline{X} = 2.33$. Subtracting two points from each score has changed the mean by the same constant, from $\overline{X} = 4.33$ to $\overline{X} = 2.33$. (It is important to note that experimental effects are practically never so simple as the adding or subtracting of a constant. None-

Table 3.2

Amount of food (in grams) consumed during baseline session

RAT'S IDENTIFICATION	AMOUNT (X)	
A	6	
B	3	$\Sigma X = 26$
C	5	$n = 6$
D	3	$\overline{X} = 4.33$
E	4	
F	5	

Table 3.3

Amount of food (in grams) consumed after drug injections

RAT	BASELINE SCORE MINUS CONSTANT	DRUG SCORE (X)	
A	$6 - 2$	4	
B	$3 - 2$	1	$\Sigma X = 14$
C	$5 - 2$	3	$n = 6$
D	$3 - 2$	1	$\overline{X} = 2.33$
E	$4 - 2$	2	
F	$5 - 2$	3	

theless, the principle of this characteristic of the mean is important and will be addressed in later chapters when we are using statistics to evaluate the effects of experimental manipulations.)

3. Multiplying or Dividing Each Score by a Constant. If every score in a distribution is multiplied by (or divided by) a constant value, the mean will be changed in the same way.

EXAMPLE 3.5   Suppose a yardstick is used to measure five pieces of wood, resulting in the five scores shown in Table 3.4. Notice that each score is a measurement in yards. Now, suppose we want to convert these measurements from yards to feet. To accomplish this conversion, we simply multiply each of the original measurements by 3. Again, the resulting values are shown in Table 3.4. Notice that multiplying by 3 (changing from yards to feet) did not change any of the lengths. It simply changes the unit of measurement. Also note that the average of $\overline{X} = 30$ feet is identical in length to the original average of $\overline{X} = 10$ yards. In general, multiplying (or dividing) each score by a constant will also cause the mean to be multiplied (or divided) by the same constant.

LEARNING CHECK   **1. a.** Compute the mean for the following sample of scores:

        6,   1,   8,   0,   5

    b. Add four points to each score and then compute the mean.
    c. Multiply each of the original scores by 5 and then compute the mean.

2. After every score in a distribution is multiplied by 3, the mean is calculated to be $\overline{X} = 60$. What was the mean for the original distribution?

ANSWERS   **1. a.** $\overline{X} = \frac{20}{5} = 4$ **b.** $\overline{X} = \frac{40}{5} = 8$ **c.** $\overline{X} = \frac{100}{5} = 20$

    2. The original mean was $\overline{X} = 20$.

Table 3.4

Measurement of five pieces of wood

ORIGINAL MEASUREMENT IN YARDS	CONVERSION TO FEET (MULTIPLY BY 3)
10	30
9	27
12	36
8	24
11	33
$\Sigma X = 50$	$\Sigma X = 150$
$\overline{X} = 10$ yards	$\overline{X} = 30$ feet

3.3 THE MEDIAN

The second measure of central tendency we will consider is called the *median*. The median is the score that divides a distribution exactly in half. Exactly one-half of the scores are less than or equal to the median, and exactly one-half are greater than or equal to the median. Because exactly 50% of the scores fall at or below the median, this value is equivalent to the 50th percentile (see Chapter 2).

DEFINITION

The *median* is the score that divides a distribution exactly in half. Exactly 50% of the individuals in a distribution have scores at or below the median. The median is equivalent to the 50th percentile.

By midpoint of the distribution we mean that the area in the graph is divided into two equal parts. We are not locating the midpoint between the highest and lowest *X* values.

The goal of the median is to determine the precise midpoint of a distribution. The commonsense goal is demonstrated in the following three examples. The three examples are intended to cover all of the different types of data you are likely to encounter.

METHOD 1: WHEN *N* IS AN ODD NUMBER

With an odd number of scores, you list the scores in order (lowest to highest), and the median is the middle score in the list. Consider the following set of $N = 5$ scores, which have been listed in order:

$$3, \quad 5, \quad 8, \quad 10, \quad 11$$

The median can be determined by Minitab commands DESCRIBE and LET (Section 20.4).

The middle score is $X = 8$, so the median is equal to 8.0. In a graph, the median divides the space or area of the graph in half (Figure 3.3). The amount of area above the median consists of 2½ "boxes," the same as the area below the median (shaded portion).

METHOD 2: WHEN *N* IS AN EVEN NUMBER

With an even number of scores in the distribution, you list the scores in order (lowest to highest), and then locate the median by finding the point halfway between the middle two scores. Consider the following population:

$$3, \quad 3, \quad 4, \quad 5, \quad 7, \quad 8$$

Figure 3.3

The median divides the area in the graph exactly in half.

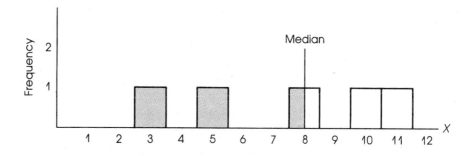

Figure 3.4

The median divides the area of the graph exactly in half.

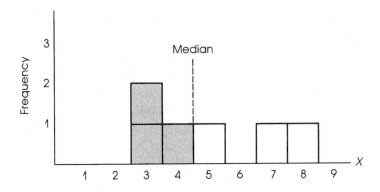

Now we select the middle pair of scores (4 and 5), add them together, and divide by 2:

$$\text{median} = \frac{4 + 5}{2} = \frac{9}{2} = 4.5$$

In terms of a graph, we see again that the median divides the area of the distribution exactly in half (Figure 3.4). There are three scores (or boxes) above the median and three below the median.

METHOD 3: WHEN THERE ARE SEVERAL SCORES WITH THE SAME VALUE IN THE MIDDLE OF THE DISTRIBUTION

In most cases, one of the two methods already outlined will provide you with a reasonable value for the median. However, when you have more than one individual at the median, these simple procedures may oversimplify the computations. Consider the following set of scores:

1, 2, 2, 3, 4, 4, 4, 4, 4, 5

There are 10 scores (an even number), so you normally would use method 2 and average the middle pair to determine the median. By this method, the median would be 4.

In many ways this is a perfectly legitimate value for the median. However, when you look closely at the distribution of scores (see Figure 3.5(a)), you probably get the clear impression that $X = 4$ is not in the middle. The problem comes from the tendency to interpret the score of 4 as meaning exactly 4.00 instead of meaning an interval from 3.5 to 4.5. The simple method of computing the median has determined that the value we want is located in this interval. To locate the median with greater precision, it is necessary to use *interpolation* to compute the 50th percentile.

Because the median can be visualized as the midpoint in a graph (dividing the graph into two equal sections), the following graphic demonstration is particularly well suited for finding the median.

The mathematical process of interpolation was introduced in Chapter 2 (see page 53). Although you can use the mathematical process to compute the 50th percentile (see Box 3.1), the following example demonstrates a simple, graphic version of the interpolation process.

E X A M P L E   3 . 6   For this example we will use the data shown in Figure 3.5(a). Notice that the figure shows a population of $N = 10$ scores, with each score

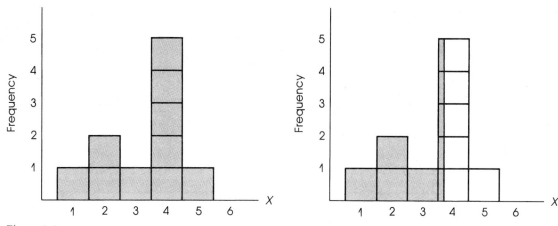

Figure 3.5

A distribution with several scores clustered at the median.

represented by a block in the histogram. To find the median, we must locate the position of a vertical line that will divide the distribution exactly in half, with 5 blocks on the left-hand side and 5 blocks on the right-hand side.

To begin the process, start at the left-hand side of the distribution and move up the scale of measurement (the X-axis), counting blocks as you go along. The vertical line corresponding to the median should be drawn at the point where you have counted exactly 5 blocks (50% of the total of 10 blocks). By the time you reach a value of 3.5 on the X-axis, you will have gathered a total of 4 blocks, so that only one more block is needed to give you exactly 50% of the distribution. The problem is that there are 5 blocks in the next interval. The solution is to take only a fraction of each of the 5 blocks so that the fractions combine to give you one more block. If you take $\frac{1}{5}$ of each block, the five fifths will combine to make one whole block. This solution is shown in Figure 3.5(b).

Notice that we have drawn a line separating each of the four blocks so that $\frac{1}{5}$ is on the left-hand side of the line and $\frac{4}{5}$ is on the right-hand side. Thus, the line should be drawn exactly $\frac{1}{5}$ of the way into the interval containing the five blocks. This interval extends from a lower real limit of 3.5 to an upper real limit of 4.5 on the X-axis and has a width of 1.00 point. One fifth of the interval would be 0.20 points ($\frac{1}{5}$ of 1.00). Therefore, the line should be drawn at the point where $X = 3.70$ (the lower real limit of 3.5 + $\frac{1}{5}$ of the interval, or 0.20). This value, $X = 3.70$, is the median and divides the distribution exactly in half.

The interpolation process demonstrated in Example 3.6 can be summarized in the following four steps which can be generalized to any situation where several scores are tied at the median.

STEP 1   Count the number of scores (boxes in the graph) below the tied value.

3.1 USING INTERPOLATION TO FIND THE MEDIAN

THE SAME data that are used in Example 3.6 (see Figure 3.5) are organized in the following frequency distribution table.

X	f	cf	c%
5	1	10	100%
4	5	9	90%
3	1	4	40%
2	2	3	30%
1	1	1	10%

The goal is to find the 50th percentile, the median, for this distribution. The score corresponding to 50% cannot be read directly from the table, so it will be necessary to use interpolation.

The intermediate value of 50% is located in the interval between cumulative percentages of 40% and 90% which correspond to the real limits 3.5 and 4.5, respectively.

X	c%
4.5	90%
??	50%
3.5	40%

On the percentage scale, the value of 50% is located 40 points from the top of the interval, or $^{40}/_{50} = ^4/_5$ of the total distance down in the interval.

On the X-scale, the total interval is 1.0 point wide, so $^4/_5$ of this total distance would be

$$(4/5)1.00 = 0.80$$

Starting at the top of the X-scale and moving down 0.80 brings us to a score of $X = 4.50 - 0.80 = 3.70$. This is the score corresponding to the 50th percentile. That is, the score $X = 3.70$ is the median. Notice that this is exactly the same answer we obtained using the graphic method of interpolation in Example 3.6.

STEP 2   Find the number of additional scores (boxes) needed to make exactly one half of the total distribution.

STEP 3   Form a fraction:

$$\frac{\text{number of boxes needed (step 2)}}{\text{number of tied boxes}}$$

STEP 4   Add the fraction (step 3) to the lower real limit of the interval containing the tied scores.

LEARNING CHECK

1. Find the median for each distribution of scores:
   a. 3, 10, 8, 4, 10, 7, 6
   b. 13, 8, 10, 11, 12, 10
   c. 3, 4, 3, 2, 1, 3, 2, 4

2. A distribution can have more than one median. (True or false?)

3. If you have a score of 52 on an 80-point exam, then you definitely scored above the median. (True or false?)

ANSWERS 1. a. The median is $X = 7$.

b. The median is $X = 10.5$.

c. The median is $X = 2.83$ (by interpolation).

2. False

3. False. The value of the median would depend on where the scores are located.

3.4 THE MODE

The final measure of central tendency that we will consider is called the mode. In its common usage, the word *mode* means "the customary fashion" or "a popular style." The statistical definition is similar in that the mode is the most common observation among a group of scores.

DEFINITION   In a frequency distribution, the *mode* is the score or category that has the greatest frequency.

The mode can be used to describe what is typical for any scale of measurement (see Chapter 1). Suppose, for example, you ask a sample of 100 students on campus to name their favorite restaurants in town. Your data might look like the results shown in Table 3.5. These are nominal data because the scale of measurement involves separate, unordered categories (restaurants). For these data, the modal response is Luigi's. This restaurant was named most frequently as a favorite place.

In a frequency distribution graph, the greatest frequency will appear as the tallest part of the figure. To find the mode, you simply identify the score located directly beneath the highest point in the distribution.

It is possible for a distribution to have more than one mode. Figure 3.6 shows the number of fish caught at various times during the day. There are two distinct peaks in this distribution, one at 6 A.M. and one at 6 P.M. Each of these values is a mode in the distribution. Note that the two modes do not have identical frequencies. Twelve fish were caught at 6 A.M., and 11 were caught at 6 P.M. Nonetheless, both of these points are called modes. The taller peak is called the *major mode*, and the shorter one is the *minor mode*. Of course, it also is possible to have a distribution with two (or more) separate

Table 3.5

Favorite restaurants named by a sample of $n = 100$ students

CAUTION: The mode is always a score or category, not a frequency. For this example, the mode is Luigi's, not $f = 42$.

RESTAURANT	f
College Grill	5
George & Harry's	16
Luigi's	42
Oasis Diner	18
Roxbury Inn	7
Sutter's Mill	12

Figure 3.6

The relationship between time of day and number of fish caught.

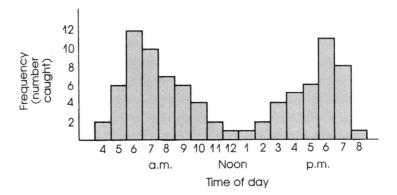

peaks that are exactly the same height. A distribution with two modes is said to be *bimodal*. When a distribution has more than two modes, it is called *multimodal*. It also is common for a distribution with several equally high points to be described as having no mode.

LEARNING CHECK

1. Find the mode for the set of scores shown in the following frequency distribution table:

X	f
5	2
4	6
3	4
2	2
1	1

2. In a recent survey comparing picture quality for three brands of color televisions, 63 people preferred brand A, 29 people preferred brand B, and 58 people preferred brand C. What is the mode for this distribution?

3. What is the reason for computing a measure of central tendency?

ANSWERS

1. The mode is $X = 4$.　　2. The mode is brand A.

3. The goal of central tendency is to identify a single value to represent an entire distribution.

3.5 SELECTING A MEASURE OF CENTRAL TENDENCY

How do you decide which measure of central tendency to use? The answer to this question depends on several factors. Before we discuss these factors, however, it should be noted that with many sets of data it is possible to compute two or even three different measures of central tendency. Often the three measures will produce similar results, but there are situations where they will be very different (see Section 3.6). Also, it should be noted that the mean is most often the preferred measure of central tendency. Because the mean uses every score in the distribution, it usually is a good representative value. Remember, the goal of central tendency is to find the single value that best represents the entire distribution. Besides being a good representative, the mean has the added advantage of being closely related to variance and standard deviation, the most common measures of variability (Chapter 4). This relationship makes the mean a valuable measure for purposes of inferential statistics. For these reasons, and others, the mean generally is considered to be the best of the three measures of central tendency. But there are specific situations where it either is impossible to compute a mean or where the mean is not particularly representative. It is in these situations that the mode and the median are used.

WHEN TO USE THE MODE

The mode has two distinct advantages over the mean. First, it is easy to compute. Second, it can be used with any scale of measurement (nominal, ordinal, interval, ratio; see Chapter 1).

It is a bit misleading to say that the mode is easy to calculate because actually no calculation is required. When the scores are arranged in a frequency distribution, you identify the mode simply by finding the score with the greatest frequency. Because the value of the mode can be determined "at a glance," it is often included as a supplementary measure along with the mean or median as a no-cost extra. The value of the mode (or modes) in this situation is to give an indication of the shape of the distribution as well as a measure of central tendency. For example, if you are told that a set of exam scores has a mean of 72 and a mode of 80, you should have a better picture of the distribution than would be available from the mean alone (see Section 3.6).

The fact that the mode can be used with any scale of measurement makes it a very flexible value. When scores are measured on a nominal scale, it is impossible or meaningless to calculate either a mean or a median, so the mode is the only way to describe central tendency. Consider the frequency distribution shown in Figure 3.7. These data were obtained by recording the academic major for each student in a psychology lab section. Notice that

Figure 3.7

Major field of study for $n = 9$ students enrolled in an experimental psychology laboratory section.

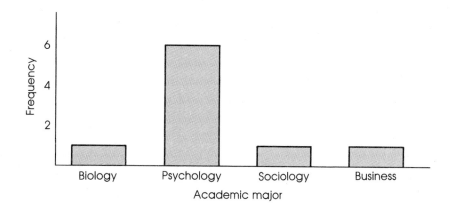

"academic major" forms a nominal scale that simply classifies individuals into discrete categories.

You cannot compute a mean for these data because it is impossible to determine ΣX. (How much is one biologist plus six psychologists?) Also note that there is no natural ordering for the four categories in this distribution. It is a purely arbitrary decision to place biology on the scale before psychology. Because it is impossible to specify any order for the scores, you cannot determine a median. The mode, on the other hand, provides a very good measure of central tendency. The mode for this sample is psychology. This category describes the typical, or most representative, academic major for the sample.

Because the mode identifies the most typical case, it often produces a more sensible measure of central tendency. The mean, for example, will generate conclusions such as "the average family has 2.4 children and a house with 5.33 rooms." Many people would feel more comfortable saying "the typical, or modal, family has 2 children and a house with 5 rooms" (see Box 3.2).

WHEN TO USE THE MEDIAN   There are four specific situations where the median serves as a valuable alternative to the mean. These occur when (1) there are a few extreme scores in the distribution, (2) some scores have undetermined values, (3) there is an open-ended distribution, and (4) when the data are measured on an ordinal scale.

Extreme scores or skewed distributions   When a distribution has a few extreme scores, scores that are very different in value from most of the others, then the mean will not be a good representative of the majority of the distribution. The problem comes from the fact that one or two extreme values can have a large influence and cause the mean to be displaced. In this situation, the fact that the mean uses all of the scores equally can be a disadvantage. For example, suppose a sample of $n = 10$ rats is tested in a T-maze for food reward. The animals must choose the correct arm of the T (right or left) to find the food in the goal box. The experimenter records the number of errors each rat makes before it solves the maze. Hypothetical data are presented in Figure 3.8.

Figure 3.8

Frequency distribution of errors committed before reaching learning criterion.

Notice that the graph in Figure 3.8 shows two *breaks* in the X-axis. Rather than listing all the scores from 0 to 100, the graph jumps directly to the first score, which is $X = 10$, and then jumps directly from $X = 15$ to $X = 100$. The breaks shown in the X-axis are the conventional way of notifying the reader that some values have been omitted.

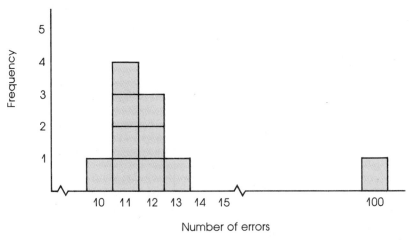

3.2 WHAT IS THE "AVERAGE"?

THE WORD *average* is used in everyday speech to describe what is typical and commonplace. Statistically, averages are measured by the mean, median, or mode. U.S. Government agencies frequently characterize demographic data, such as average income or average age, with the median. Winners of elections are determined by the mode, the most frequent choice. Scholastic Aptitude Test (SAT) scores for large groups of students usually are described with the mean. The important thing to remember about these measures of central tendency (or the "average") is that they describe and summarize a group of individuals rather than any single person. In fact, the "average person" may not actually exist. Figure 3.9 shows data which were gathered from a sample

Figure 3.10

Frequency distribution showing the age at which each infant in a sample of $n = 6$ uttered his or her first word.

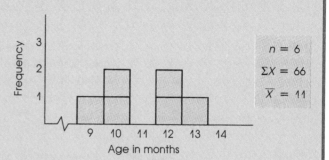

of $n = 9$ infants. The age at which each infant said his or her first word was recorded by the parents. Note that the mean for this group is $\overline{X} = 11$ months and that there are three infants who uttered their first intelligible words at this age.

Now look at the results of a different study using a sample of $n = 6$ infants (Figure 3.10). Note that the mean for this group is also $\overline{X} = 11$ months but that the "average infant" does not exist in this sample. The mean describes the group, not a single individual. It is for this reason that we find humor in statements like "the average American family has 2.4 children," fully knowing that we never will encounter this family.

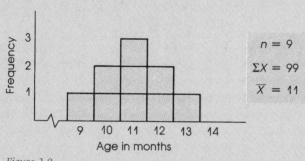

Figure 3.9

Frequency distribution showing the age at which each infant in a sample of $n = 9$ uttered his or her first word.

The mean for this sample is

$$\overline{X} = \frac{\Sigma X}{n} = \frac{203}{10} = 20.3$$

Notice that the mean is not very representative of any score in this distribution. Most of the scores are clustered between 10 and 13. The extreme score of $X = 100$ (a slow learner) inflates the value of ΣX and distorts the mean.

The median, on the other hand, is not easily affected by extreme scores. For this sample, $n = 10$, so there should be five scores on either side of the median. The median is 11.50. Notice that this is a very representative value. Also note that the median would be unchanged even if the slow learner made 1000 errors instead of only 100. The median commonly is used when

Table 3.6

Amount of time to complete puzzle

PERSON	TIME (MIN.)
1	8
2	11
3	12
4	13
5	17
6	Never finished

reporting the average value for a skewed distribution. For example, the distribution of personal incomes is very skewed, with a small segment of the population earning incomes that are astronomical. These extreme values distort the mean, so that it is not very representative of the salaries that most of us earn. As in the previous example, the median is the preferred measure of central tendency when extreme scores exist.

Undetermined values Occasionally, you will encounter a situation where an individual has an unknown or undetermined score. In psychology, this often occurs in learning experiments where you are measuring the number of errors (or amount of time) required for an individual to solve a particular problem. For example, suppose a sample of $n = 6$ people were asked to assemble a wooden puzzle as quickly as possible. The experimenter records how long (in minutes) it takes each individual to arrange all the pieces to complete the puzzle. Table 3.6 presents the outcome of this experiment.

Notice that person 6 never completed the puzzle. After an hour, this person still showed no sign of solving the puzzle, so the experimenter stopped him or her. This person has an undetermined score. (There are two important points to be noted. First, the experimenter should not throw out this individual's score. The whole purpose for using a sample is to gain a picture of the population, and this individual tells us that part of the population cannot solve the puzzle. Second, this person should not be given a score of $X = 60$ minutes. Even though the experimenter stopped the individual after 1 hour, the person did not finish the puzzle. The score that is recorded is the amount of time needed to finish. For this individual, we do not know how long this would be.)

It is impossible to compute the mean for these data because of the undetermined value. We cannot calculate the ΣX part of the formula for the mean. However, it is possible to compute the median. For these data the median is 12.5. Three scores are below the median, and three scores (including the undetermined value) are above the median.

NUMBER OF CHILDREN (X)	f
5 or more	3
4	2
3	2
2	3
1	6
0	4

Open-ended distributions A distribution is said to be *open-ended* when there is no upper limit (or lower limit) for one of the categories. The table at the left provides an example of an open-ended distribution, showing the number of children in each family for a sample of $n = 20$ households. The top category in this distribution shows that three of the families have "5 or more" children. This in an open-ended category. Notice that it is impossible to compute a mean for these data because you cannot find ΣX (the total number of children for all 20 families). However, you can find the median. For these data, the median is 1.5 (exactly 50% of the families have fewer than 1.5 children).

Ordinal scale   Many researchers believe that it is not appropriate to use the mean to describe central tendency for ordinal data. When scores are measured on an ordinal scale, the median is always appropriate and is usually the preferred measure of central tendency. The following example demonstrates that although it is possible to compute a "mean rank," the resulting value can be misleading.

EXAMPLE 3.7   Three children held a basketball competition to see who could hit the most baskets in 10 attempts. The contest was held twice; the results are shown in the following table.

	FIRST CONTEST			SECOND CONTEST	
CHILD	RANK	NUMBER OF BASKETS	CHILD	RANK	NUMBER OF BASKETS
A	1st	10	C	1st	7
B	2nd	4	B	2nd	6
C	3rd	2	A	3rd	5

According to the data, child A finished first in one contest and third in the other, for a "mean rank" of 2. Child C also finished first one time and third one time and also has a mean rank of 2. Although these two children are identical in terms of mean rank, they are different in terms of the total number of baskets: Child A hit a total of 15 baskets and child C hit only 9. The mean rank does not reflect this difference.

3.6 CENTRAL TENDENCY AND THE SHAPE OF THE DISTRIBUTION

We have identified three different measures of central tendency, and often a researcher will calculate all three for a single set of data. Because the mean, the median, and the mode are all trying to measure the same thing (central tendency), it is reasonable to expect that these three values should be related. In fact there are some consistent and predictable relationships among the three measures of central tendency. Specifically, there are situations where all three measures will have exactly the same value. On the other hand, there are situations where the three measures are guaranteed to be different. In part, the relationship between the mean, median, and mode is determined by the shape of the distribution. We will consider two general types of distributions.

SYMMETRICAL DISTRIBUTIONS   For a *symmetrical distribution,* the right-hand side of the graph will be a mirror image of the left-hand side. By definition, the median will be exactly at the center of a symmetrical distribution because exactly half of the area in the graph will be on either side of the center. The mean also will be exactly at the center of a symmetrical distribution, because each individual score in the distribution has a corresponding score on the other side (the mirror image), so that the average of these two values is exactly in the middle. Because all the scores can be paired in this way, the overall average will be exactly at the middle. For any symmetrical distribution, the mean and the median will be the same (Figure 3.11).

If a symmetrical distribution has only one mode, then it must be exactly at the center so that all three measures of central tendency will have the same value (see Figure 3.11). On the other hand, a bimodal distribution that is symmetrical [Figure 3.11(b)] will have the mean and median together in the center with the modes on each side. A rectangular distribution [Figure 3.11(c)] has no mode because all *X* values occur with the same frequency. Still, the mean and the median will be in the center of the distribution and equivalent in value.

SKEWED DISTRIBUTIONS

Distributions are not always symmetrical. In fact, quite often they are lopsided, or *skewed*. For example, Figure 3.12(a) shows a *positively skewed distribution*. In this distribution, the peak (highest frequency) is on the left-hand side. This is the position of the mode. If you examine Figure 3.12(a) carefully, it should be clear that the vertical line drawn at the mode does not divide the distribution into two equal parts. In order to have exactly 50% of the distribution on each side, the median must be located to the right of the mode. Finally, the mean will be located to the right of median because it is influenced most by extreme scores and will be displaced farthest to the right by the scores in the tail. Therefore, in a positively skewed distribution, the mean will have the largest value, followed by the median and then the mode [see Figure 3.12(a)].

Negatively skewed distributions are lopsided in the opposite direction, with the scores piling up on the right-hand side and the tail tapering off to the left. The grades on an easy exam, for example, will tend to form a negatively skewed distribution [see Figure 3.12(b)]. For a distribution with negative skew, the mode is on the right-hand side (with the peak), while the mean is displaced on the left by the extreme scores in the tail. As before, the median is located between the mean the mode. In order from highest value to lowest value, the three measures of central tendency will be the mode, the median, and the mean.

Figure 3.11

Measures of central tendency for three symmetrical distributions: normal, bimodal, and rectangular.

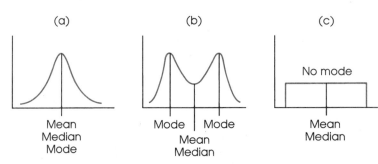

Figure 13.12

Measures of central tendency for
skewed distributions.

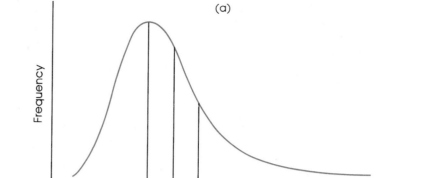

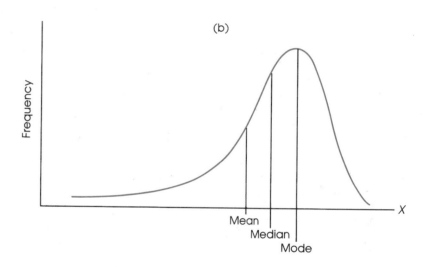

SUMMARY

1. The purpose of central tendency is to determine the
single value that best represents the entire distribution
of scores. The three standard measures of central tendency are the mode, the median, and the mean.

2. The mean is the arithmetic average. It is computed by
adding all the scores and then dividing by the number
of scores. Changing any score in the distribution will
cause the mean to be changed. When a constant
value is added to (or subtracted from) every score in a
distribution, the same constant value is added to (subtracted from) the mean. If every score is multiplied by
the same constant, the mean will be multiplied by the
same constant. In nearly all cirmunstances, the mean

is the best representative value and is the preferred
measure of central tendency.

3. The median is the value that divides a distribution
exactly in half. The median is the preferred measure
of central tendency when a distribution has a few extreme scores that displace the value of the mean. The
median also is used when there are undetermined
(infinite) scores that make it impossible to compute a
mean.

4. The mode is the most frequently occurring score in a
distribution. It is easily located by finding the peak in
a frequency distribution graph. For data measured on

a nominal scale, the mode is the appropriate measure of central tendency. It is possible for a distribution to have more than one mode.

5. For symmetrical distributions, the mean will equal the median. If there is only one mode, then it will have the same value too.

6. For skewed distributions, the mode will be located toward the side where the scores pile up, and the mean will be pulled toward the extreme scores in the tail. The median will be located between these two values.

KEY TERMS

central tendency	mode	bimodal distribution	skewed distribution
mean	major mode	multimodal distribution	positive skew
weighted mean	minor mode	symmetrical distribution	negative skew
median			

Focus on Problem Solving

1. Because there are three different measures of central tendency, your first problem is to decide which one is best for your specific set of data. Usually the mean is the preferred measure, but the median may provide a more representative value if you are working with a skewed distribution. With data measured on a nominal scale, you must use the mode.

2. Although the three measures of central tendency appear to be very simple to calculate, there is always a chance for errors. The most common sources of error are listed next.

   a. Many students find it very difficult to compute the mean for data presented in a frequency distribution table. They tend to ignore the frequencies in the table and simply average the score values listed in the X column. You must use the frequencies and the scores! Remember, the number of scores is found by $N = \Sigma f$, and the sum of all N scores is found by ΣfX.

   b. The median is the midpoint of the distribution of scores, not the midpoint of the scale of measurement. For a 100-point test, for example, many students incorrectly assume that the median must be $X = 50$. To find the median you must have the *complete set* of individual scores. The median separates the individuals into two equal-sized groups.

   c. The most common error with the mode is for students to report the highest frequency in a distribution rather than the score with the highest frequency. Remember, the purpose of central tendency is to find the most representative score. Therefore, for the following data the mode is $X = 3$, not $f = 8$.

X	f
4	3
3	8
2	5
1	2

Demonstration 3.1

COMPUTING MEASURES OF CENTRAL TENDENCY

For the following sample data, find the mean, median, and mode.

scores: 5   6   9   11   5   11   8   14   2   11

Compute the mean. Calculating the mean involves two steps:

1. Obtain the sum of the scores, ΣX
2. Divide the sum by the number of scores, n

For these data, the sum of the scores is as follows:

$$\Sigma X = 5 + 6 + 9 + 11 + 5 + 11 + 8 + 14 + 2 + 11 = 82$$

We can also observe that $n = 10$. Therefore, the mean of this sample is obtained by

$$\bar{X} = \frac{\Sigma X}{n} = \frac{82}{10} = 8.2$$

Find the median. The median divides the distribution in half, in that half of the scores are above or equal to the median and half are below or equal to it. In this demonstration, $n = 10$. Thus, the median should be a value that has 5 scores above it and 5 scores below it.

STEP 1   Arrange the scores in order.

2   5   5   6   8   9   11   11   11   14

STEP 2   With an even number of scores, locate the midpoint between the middle two scores. The middle scores are $X = 8$ and $X = 9$. The median is the midpoint between 8 and 9.

$$\text{median} = \frac{8 + 9}{2} = \frac{17}{2} = 8.5$$

Find the mode. The mode is the X value that has the highest frequency. Looking at the data, we can readily determine that $X = 11$ is the score that occurs most frequently.

—— *Demonstration 3.2* ——

COMPUTING THE MEAN FROM A FREQUENCY DISTRIBUTION TABLE

Compute the mean for the data in the following table.

X	f
6	1
5	0
4	3
3	3
2	2

To compute the mean from a frequency distribution table, you must use the information in *both* the X and f columns.

STEP 1 Multiply each X value by its frequency.
You can create a third column labeled fX. For these data,

fX
6
0
12
9
4

STEP 2 Find the sum of the fX values.

$$\Sigma fX = 6 + 0 + 12 + 9 + 4 = 31$$

STEP 3 Find n for these data.
Remember, $n = \Sigma f$.

$$n = \Sigma f = 1 + 0 + 3 + 3 + 2 = 9$$

STEP 4 Divide the sum of fX by n.

$$\overline{X} = \frac{\Sigma fX}{n} = \frac{31}{9} = 3.44$$

PROBLEMS

1. Find the mean, median, and mode for the following sample of scores: 4, 3, 4, 5, 1, 4, 3, 2, 4, 2

2. For the following set of scores: 2, 4, 8, 1, 2, 4, 3, 2, 3, 2,
   a. Sketch a frequency distribution histogram.

   b. Find the mean, median, and mode and locate these values in your graph.

3. Find the mean, median, and mode for the following set of scores: 2, 4, 3, 4, 1, 5, 4, 2.

4. A sample of $n = 6$ scores has a mean of $\overline{X} = 7$. If one of the scores, $X = 12$, is removed from the sample, what value would be obtained for the mean of the remaining scores?

5. A sample of $n = 9$ scores has a mean of $\overline{X} = 10$. If a new score, $X = 30$, is added to this sample, what value would be obtained for the mean of the new sample?

6. A population of $N = 8$ scores has a mean of $\mu = 11$. If one of the scores in this population is changed from $X = 9$ to $X = 25$, what value would be obtained for the new population mean?

7. Identify the circumstances where the median should be used instead of the mean as the preferred measure of central tendency.

8. The following frequency distribution summarizes the number of absences for each student in a class of $n = 20$.

NUMBER OF ABSENCES (X)	f
5 or more	3
4	4
3	3
2	6
1	3
0	1

  a. Find the mode for this distribution.
  b. Find the median number of absences for this class.
  c. Explain why you cannot compute the mean number of absences using the data provided in the table.

9. If you change the value of a single score in a distribution, you will sometimes change the median and sometimes leave the median unaffected. Describe the circumstances where the median would change and where the median would not change.

10. A psychologist would like to determine how many errors are made, on the average, before rats can learn a particular maze. A sample of $n = 10$ rats is obtained, and each rat is tested on the maze. The scores for the first 9 rats are as follows: 6, 2, 4, 5, 3, 7, 6, 2, 1.
  a. Calculate the mean and the median for these data. On the average, how many errors does each rat make?

  b. The tenth rat in the sample committed 100 errors before mastering the maze. When this rat is included in the sample, what happens to the mean? What happens to the median? What general conclusion can be drawn from this result?

11. In a problem-solving experiment with $n = 100$ children, 5 of the children failed to complete the problem within 10 minutes and were simply marked as "failed." If the experimenter wanted to find a measure of central tendency to describe the "average" amount of time needed to complete the problem, what measure should be used? Explain your answer.

12. Under what circumstances is the mode the preferred measure of central tendency.

13. One sample of $n = 3$ scores has a mean of $\overline{X} = 4$. A second sample of $n = 7$ scores has a mean of $\overline{X} = 10$. If these two samples are combined, what value will be obtained for the mean of the combined sample?

14. Calculate the mean, median, and mode for the following set of scores.

   scores: 1, 4, 6, 15, 8, 4, 2, 10, 4, 5

15. Find the mean, median, and mode for the set of scores in the following frequency distribution table:

X	f
6	1
5	2
4	1
3	1
2	2
1	3

16. Explain why the mean is not necessarily a good measure of central tendency for a skewed distribution.

17. Explain why the mean and the median are probably not good measures of central tendency for a symmetrical, bimodal distribution.

18. Under what circumstances will the mean, the median, and the mode all have the same value?

19. A population of $N = 50$ scores has a mean of $\mu = 26$. What is ΣX for this population?

20. A sample has a mean of $\overline{X} = 5$ and $\Sigma X = 320$. How many scores are in this sample? ($n = ?$)

21. Find the mean, median, and mode for the sample of scores presented in the following frequency distribution table.

X	f
5	1
4	2
3	3
2	5
1	1

22. Find the mean and the median for each of the following sets of scores.
   a. Scores: 1, 1, 2, 2, 5, 6, 7, 8, 9
   b. Scores: 1, 1, 1, 1, 2, 2, 3, 6

23. A distribution of exam scores has a mean of 71 and a median of 79. Is it more likely that this distribution is symmetrical, positively skewed, or negatively skewed?

24. A school psychologist has computed the average IQ for a sample of $n = 99$ children and obtained a mean of $\bar{X} = 104$. If one additional student with an IQ of 133 is included in this sample, what will the average IQ be for the entire group of 100 students?

25. A 20-point quiz is given to each of two sections of an introductory statistics class. The scores for each section are as follows:

   section I: 6, 5, 5, 7, 17, 5, 6, 5
   section II: 9, 8, 10, 7, 8, 9, 1, 0, 9, 9

   a. Sketch a histogram showing the distribution of scores for section I.
   b. Sketch a histogram showing the distribution for section II.

c. Looking at your graphs, which section would you say had better scores?
d. Calculate the mean and the median for each section. Which measure of central tendency best describes the difference between these two distributions?

26. A psychologist is collecting attitude scores for high school students as part as an experiment. Because the testing room will hold only 15 people, the students are tested in three separate groups. The data for these three groups are as follows:

   group 1: $n = 15$, $\bar{X} = 46.5$
   group 2: $n = 14$, $\bar{X} = 43.2$
   group 3: $n = 11$, $\bar{X} = 50.9$

Find the overall mean for the entire group of high school students.

27. On a standardized reading achievement test, the nationwide average for seventh grade children is $\mu = 7.0$. A seventh-grade teacher is interested in comparing class reading scores with the national average. The scores for the 16 students in this class are as follows:

   8   6   5   10   5   6   8   9
   7   6   9   5   14   4   7   6

   a. Find the mean and median reading scores for this class.
   b. If the mean is used to define the class average, how does this class compare with the national norm?
   c. If the median is used to define the class average, how does this class compare with the national norm?

CHAPTER 4   VARIABILITY

CONTENTS

PREVIEW

It's 10 A.M., and Mary L. is washing her hands for the tenth time today. Before she goes to sleep tonight, she will have washed her hands over 60 times. Is this normal?

To differentiate between normal and abnormal behavior, some psychologists have resorted to using a *statistical model*. For example, we could survey a large sample of individuals and record the number of times each person washes his/her hands during a typical day. Because people are different, the scores should be variable, and the data from this survey should produce a distribution similar to the one shown in Figure 4.1. Notice that most people will have average or moderate scores located in the central part of the distribution. Others, such as Mary L., will deviate from average. According to the statistical model, those who show substantial deviation are abnormal. Note that this model simply defines abnormal as being unusual or different from normal. The model does not imply that abnormal is necessarily negative or undesirable. Mary L. may have a compulsive personality disorder, or she may be a dentist washing her hands between patients.

The statistical model for abnormality requires two statistical concepts: a measure of the average and a measure of deviation from average. In Chapter 3 we examined the standard techniques for defining the average score for a distribution. In this chapter we will examine methods for measuring deviations. The fact that scores deviate from average means that they are variable. Variability is one of the most basic statistical concepts. As an introduction to the concept, this chapter will concentrate on defining and measuring variability. In later chapters we

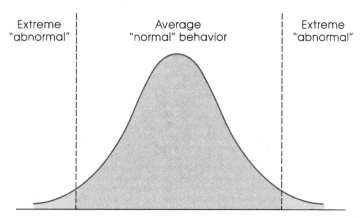

Figure 4.1

The statistical model for defining abnormal behavior. The distribution of behavior scores for the entire population is divided into three sections. Those individuals with average scores are defined as normal, and individuals who show extreme deviation from average are defined as abnormal.

will explore sources of variability and examine how variability affects the interpretation of other statistical measurements.

One additional point should be made before we proceed. You probably have noticed that central tendency and variability are closely related. Whenever one appears, the other usually is close at hand. You should watch for this association throughout the book. The better you understand the relations between central tendency and variability, the better you will understand statistics.

4.1 OVERVIEW

The term *variability* has much the same meaning in statistics as it has in everyday language; to say that things are variable means that they are not all the same. In statistics our goal is to measure the amount of variability for a particular set of scores, a distribution. In simple terms, if the scores in a distribution are all the same, then there is no variability. If there are small differences between scores, then the variability is small, and if there are big differences between scores, then the variability is large.

DEFINITION   *Variability* provides a quantitative measure of the degree to which scores in a distribution are spread out or clustered together.

The purpose of measuring variability is to determine how spread out a distribution of scores is. Are the scores all clustered together, or are they scattered over a wide range of values? A good measure of variability should provide an accurate picture of the spread of the distribution. Variability, along with central tendency and shape, is one of the three basic descriptive indices that are used to describe distributions of scores.

In addition to providing a description of the distribution, a good measure of variability serves another valuable purpose. A good measure of variability will give an indication of how well an individual score (or group of scores) represents the entire distribution. For example, there are occasions when the population mean is unknown. In these situations, a sample is selected from the population, and the sample is then used to represent the entire distribution. This is particularly important in the area of inferential statistics where relatively small samples are used to answer general questions about large populations. If the scores in a distribution are all clustered together (small variability), then any individual score will be a reasonably accurate representative of the entire distribution. But if the scores are all spread out, then a single value selected from the distribution often will not be representative of the rest of the group. This point is illustrated by the two ''games of chance'' described in Box 4.1.

In this chapter we will consider three different measures of variability: the range, the interquartile range, and the standard deviation. Of these three, the

4.1   AN EXAMPLE OF VARIABILITY

TO EXAMINE the role of variability, we will consider two games of chance.

For the first game you pay $1 to play, and you get back 90 cents every time. That's right, you pay me $1, and I give you back 90¢. Notice that this game has no variability; exactly the same thing happens every time. On the average, you lose 10¢ each time you play, and, in this case, the average gives a perfect description of the outcome of the game.

For the second game the rules are a little different. It still costs $1 to play, but this time you have a 1-out-of-10 chance of winning $9. The rest of the time you win nothing. For this second game we have added variability; the outcomes are not all the same. Notice, however, that in the long run you still lose 10¢ each time you play. In 10 games, for example, you would expect to win once ($9), but you would-have paid $10 to play. You expect to lose $1 during 10 games, for an average loss of 10¢ per game.

On the average these two games are identical. But in one case the average perfectly describes every single outcome, and in the other case the average is not at all representative of what actually happens on any single trial. The difference between these two games is the variability.

You also should notice the number of times you would need to watch each game in order to understand it. For the first game, any individual outcome (pay $1 and get back 90¢) gives a complete description of the game. After only one observation, you know the entire game. For the second game, however, you would need to watch a long time before the nature of the game became clear. In this case it would take a large sample to provide a good description of the game.

standard deviation (and the related measure of variance) is by far the most important.

4.2 THE RANGE

The range is the distance between the largest score (X_{max}) and the smallest score in the distribution (X_{min}). In determining this distance, you must also take into account the real limits of the maximum and minimum X values. The range, therefore, is computed as the difference between the upper real limit (URL) for X_{max} and the lower real limit (LRL) for X_{min}.

$$\text{range} = \text{URL } X_{max} - \text{LRL } X_{min}$$

DEFINITION   The *range* is the difference between the upper real limit for the largest (maximum) X value and the lower real limit of the smallest (minimum) X value.

For example, consider the following data:

$$3 \quad 7 \quad 12 \quad 8 \quad 5 \quad 10$$

For these data, $X_{max} = 12$ with an upper real limit of 12.5, and $X_{min} = 3$ with a lower real limit of 2.5. Thus the range equals

When the distribution consists of whole numbers, the range also can be obtained as follows: range = highest X − lowest X + 1.

$$\text{range} = \text{URL } X_{max} - \text{LRL } X_{min}$$
$$= 12.5 - 2.5 = 10$$

The range is perhaps the most obvious way of describing how spread out the scores are—simply find the distance between the maximum and minimum scores. The problem with using the range as a measure of variability is that it is completely determined by the two extreme values and ignores the other scores in the distribution. For example, the following two distributions have exactly the same range; 10 points in each case. However, the scores in the first distribution are clustered together at one end of the range, whereas the scores in the second distribution are spread out over the entire range.

distribution 1:   1,   8,   9,   9,   10,   10

distribution 2:   1,   2,   4,   6,   8,   10

If, for example, these were scores on a 10-point quiz for two different class sections, there are clear differences between the two sections. Nearly all the students in the first section have mastered the material, but there is a wide range of different abilities for students in the second section. A good measure of variability should show this difference.

Because the range does not consider all the scores in the distribution, it often does not give an accurate description of the variability for the entire distribution. For this reason, the range is considered to be a crude and unreliable measure of variability.

4.3 THE INTERQUARTILE RANGE AND SEMI-INTERQUARTILE RANGE

In Chapter 3 we defined the median as the score that divides a distribution exactly in half. In a similar way, a distribution can be divided into four equal parts using quartiles. By definition, the first quartile ($Q1$) is the score that separates the lower 25% of the distribution from the rest. The second quartile ($Q2$) is the score that has exactly two quarters, or 50%, of the distribution below it. Notice that the second quartile and the median are the same. Finally, the third quartile ($Q3$) is the score that divides the bottom three-fourths of the distribution from the top quarter. The interquartile range is defined as the distance between the first and third quartiles. The semi-interquartile range is one-half of the interquartile range. It provides a descriptive measure of the ''typical'' distance of scores from the median ($Q2$).

DEFINITIONS

The *interquartile range* is the distance between the first quartile and the third quartile:

$$\text{interquartile range} = Q3 - Q1$$

When the interquartile range is used to describe variability, it commonly is transformed into the *semi-interquartile range*. The semi-interquartile range is simply one-half of the interquartile range:

$$\text{semi-interquartile range} = \frac{(Q3 - Q1)}{2}$$

EXAMPLE 4.1

Figure 4.2 shows a frequency distribution histogram for a set of 16 scores. For this distribution the first quartile is $Q1 = 4.5$. Exactly 25% of the scores

Figure 4.2

Frequency distribution for a population of $N = 16$ scores. The first quartile is $Q1 = 4.5$. The third quartile is $Q3 = 8.0$. The interquartile range is 3.5 points. Note that the third quartile ($Q3$) divides the two boxes at $X = 8$ exactly in half, so that a total of 4 boxes are above $Q3$ and 12 boxes are below it.

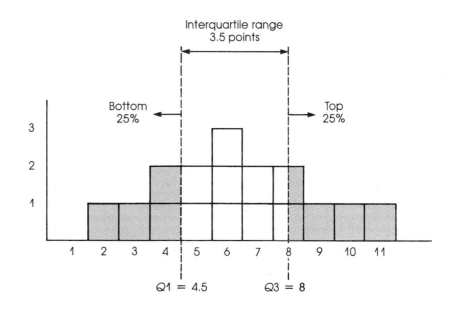

(4 out of 16) are located below $X = 4.5$. Similarly, the third quartile is $Q3 = 8.0$. Note that this value separates the bottom 75% of the distribution (12 out of 16 scores) from the top 25%. For this set of scores the interquartile range is

$$Q3 - Q1 = 8.0 - 4.5 = 3.5$$

The semi-interquartile range is simply one-half of this distance:

$$\text{semi-interquartile range} = \frac{3.5}{2} = 1.75$$

Because the semi-interquartile range focuses on the middle 50% of a distribution, it is less likely to be influenced by extreme scores and, therefore, gives a better and more stable measure of variability than the range. Nevertheless, the semi-interquartile range does not take into account the actual distances between individual scores, so it does not give a complete picture of how scattered or clustered the scores are. Like the range, the semi-interquartile range is considered to be a somewhat crude measure of variability. In chapter 6 we will introduce another method to determine the semi-interquartile range for normal distributions.

LEARNING CHECK

1. For the following data, find the range and the semi-interquartile range.

   3, 4, 5, 7, 9, 10, 11, 13

2. Consider the distribution of Exercise 1, except replace the score of 13 with a score of 100. What are the new values for the range and the semi-interquartile range? In comparing the answer to the one of the previous problem, what can you conclude about these measures of variability?

ANSWERS

1. Range = URL X_{max} − LRL X_{min} = 13.5 − 2.5 = 11; Semi-interquartile range = $(Q3 - Q1)/2$ = (10.5 − 4.5)/2 = 3.

2. Range = 98, semi-interquartile range = 3. The range is greatly affected by extreme scores in the distribution.

4.4 STANDARD DEVIATION AND VARIANCE FOR A POPULATION

The standard deviation is the most commonly used and the most important measure of variability. Standard deviation uses the mean of the distribution as a reference point and measures variability by considering the distance between each score and the mean. It determines whether the scores are generally near or far from the mean. That is, are the scores clustered together or scattered? In simple terms, the standard deviation approximates the average distance from the mean.

Although the concept of standard deviation is straightforward, the actual equations will appear complex. Therefore, we will begin by looking at the logic that leads to these equations. If you remember that our goal is to measure the standard or typical, distance from the mean, then this logic and the equations that follow should be easier to remember.

STEP 1   The first step in finding the standard distance from the mean is to determine the deviation, or distance from the mean, for each individual score. By definition, the deviation for each score is the difference between the score and the mean.

DEFINITION   *Deviation* is distance from the mean:

$$\text{deviation score} = X - \mu$$

For a distribution of scores with $\mu = 50$, if your score is $X = 53$, then your deviation score is

$$X - \mu = 53 - 50 = 3$$

If your score were $X = 45$, then your deviation score would be

$$X - \mu = 45 - 50 = -5$$

Notice that there are two parts to a deviation score: the sign ($+$ or $-$) and the number. The sign tells the direction from the mean, that is, whether the score is located above ($+$) or below ($-$) the mean. The number gives the actual distance from the mean. For example, a deviation score of -6 corresponds to score that is below the mean by six points.

STEP 2   Because our goal is to compute a measure of the standard distance from the mean, the obvious next step is to calculate the mean of the deviation scores. To compute this mean, you first add up the deviation scores and then divide by N. This process is demonstrated in the following example.

EXAMPLE 4.2   We start with the following set of $N = 4$ scores. These scores add up to $\Sigma X = 12$, so the mean is $\mu = \frac{12}{4} = 3$. For each score we have computed the deviation.

X	$X - \mu$
8	$+5$
1	-2
3	0
0	-3
	$0 = \Sigma(X - \mu)$

Remember, the mean is the balancing point for the distribution.

Notice that the deviation scores add up to zero. This should not be surprising if you remember that the mean serves as a balance point for the distribution. The distances above the mean are equal to the distances below the mean (see page 73). Logically, the deviation scores must *always* add up to zero.

Because the mean deviation is always zero, it is of no value as a measure of variability. It is zero whether the scores are grouped together or are all scattered out. The mean deviation score provides no information about variability. (You should note, however, that the constant value of zero can be useful in other ways. Whenever you are working with deviation scores, you can check your calculations by making sure that the deviation scores add up to zero.)

STEP 3   The reason that the average of the deviation scores will not work as a measure of variability is that it is always zero. Clearly, this problem results from the positive and negative values canceling each other out. The solution is to get rid of the signs (+ and −). The standard procedure for accomplishing this is to square each deviation score. Using these squared values, you then compute the mean squared deviation, which is called variance.

DEFINITION   *Population variance* = mean squared deviation. Variance is the mean of the squared deviation scores.

Note that the process of squaring deviation scores does more than simply get rid of plus and minus signs. It results in a measure of variability based on *squared* distances. Although variance is valuable for some of the *inferential* statistical methods covered later, the mean squared distance is not the best *descriptive* measure for variability.

STEP 4   Remember that our goal is to compute a measure of the standard distance from the mean. Variance, the mean squared deviation, is not exactly what we want. The final step simply makes a correction for having squared all the distances. The new measure, the standard deviation, is the square root of the variance.

DEFINITION   *Standard deviation* = $\sqrt{\text{variance}}$.

Technically, standard deviation is the square root of the mean squared deviation. But conceptually, standard deviation is easier to understand if you think of it as describing the typical distance of scores from the mean (that is, the typical $X - \mu$). As the name implies, standard deviation measures the standard, or typical, deviation score.

The concept of standard deviation (or variance) is the same for a sample as for a population. However, the details of the calculations differ slightly, depending on whether you have sample data or a complete population. Therefore, we will first consider the formulas for measures of population variability.

SUM OF SQUARED DEVIATIONS (SS)

Variance, you should recall, is defined as the mean squared deviation. This mean is computed exactly the same way you compute any mean: First find the sum; then divide by the number of scores:

$$\text{variance} = \text{mean squared deviation} = \frac{\text{sum of squared deviations}}{\text{number of scores}}$$

The value in the numerator of this equation, the sum of the squared deviations, is a basic component of variability, and we will focus on it. To simplify things, it is identified by the notation *SS* (for sum of squared deviations), and it generally is referred to as the *sum of squares*.

DEFINITION

SS, or *sum of squares*, is the sum of the squared deviation scores.

There are two formulas you will need to know in order to compute *SS*. These formulas are algebraically equivalent (they always produce the same answer), but they look different and are used in different situations.

The first of these formulas is called the definitional formula because the terms in the formula literally define the process of adding up the squared deviations:

definitional formula: $\quad SS = \Sigma (X - \mu)^2 \qquad$ **(4.1)**

Note that the formula directs you to square each deviation score $(X - \mu)^2$ and then add them. The result is the sum of the squared deviations, or *SS*. Following is an example using this formula.

EXAMPLE 4.3

We will compute *SS* for the following set of $N = 4$ scores. These scores have a sum of $\Sigma X = 8$, so the mean is $\mu = \frac{8}{4} = 2$. For each score, we have computed the deviation and the squared deviation. The squared deviations add up to $SS = 22$.

Caution: The definitional formula requires that you first square the deviations and then add them.

X	$X - \mu$	$(X - \mu)^2$	
1	−1	1	$\Sigma X = 8$
0	−2	4	$\mu = 2$
6	+4	16	
1	−1	1	
		$22 = \Sigma(X - \mu)^2$	

The second formula for *SS* is called the computational formula (or the machine formula) because it works directly with the scores (*X* values) and, therefore, is generally easier to use for calculations, especially with an electronic calculator:

computational formula: $\quad SS = \Sigma X^2 - \dfrac{(\Sigma X)^2}{N} \qquad$ **(4.2)**

4.2   **COMPUTING** *SS*
WITH A CALCULATOR

THE COMPUTATIONAL formula for *SS* is intended to simplify calculations, especially when you are using an electronic calculator. The following steps outline the most efficient procedure for using a typical, inexpensive hand calculator to find *SS*. (We assume that your calculator has one memory, where you can store and retrieve information.) The computational formula for *SS* is presented here for easy reference.

$$SS = \Sigma X^2 - \frac{(\Sigma X)^2}{N}$$

STEP 1:   The first term in the computational formula is ΣX^2. The procedure for finding this sum is described in Box 1.1 on page 23. Once you have calculated ΣX^2, write this sum on a piece of paper so you don't lose it. Leave ΣX^2 in the calculator memory and go to the next step.

STEP 2:   Now you must find the sum of the scores, ΣX. We assume that you can add a set of numbers with your calculator—just be sure to press the equals key (=) after the last score. Write this total on your paper.

   (*Note:* You may want to clear the calculator display before you begin this process. It is not necessary, but you may feel more comfortable starting with zero.)

STEP 3:   Now you are ready to plug the sums into the formula. Your calculator should still have

the sum of the scores, ΣX, in the display. If not, enter this value.

1. With ΣX in the display, you can compute $(\Sigma X)^2$ simply by pressing the multiply key (×) and then the equals key (=).

2. Now you must divide the squared sum by *N*, the number of scores. Assuming that you have counted the number of scores, just press the divide key (÷), enter *N*, and then press the equals key.

Your calculator display now shows $(\Sigma X)^2/N$. Write this number on your paper.

3. Finally, you subtract the value of your calculator display from ΣX^2, which is in the calculator memory. You can do this by simply pressing the memory subtract key (usually M−). The value for *SS* is now in memory, and you can retrieve it by pressing the memory recall key (MR).

Try the whole procedure with a simple set of scores such as 1, 2, 3. You should obtain *SS* = 2 for these scores.

   We asked you to write values at several steps during the calculation in case you make a mistake at some point. If you have written the values for ΣX^2, ΣX, and so on, you should be able to compute *SS* easily even if the contents of memory were lost.

The first part of this formula directs you to square each score and then add them up (ΣX^2). The second part requires you to add up the scores (ΣX) and then square this total and divide the result by *N* (see Box 4.2). The use of this formula is shown in Example 4.4 with the same set of scores we used for the definitional formula.

EXAMPLE 4.4   The computational formula is used to calculate *SS* for the same set of $N = 4$ scores we used in Example 4.3. First, compute ΣX. Then square each score and compute ΣX^2. These two values are used in the formula.

X	X^2	
1	1	$\Sigma X = 8$
0	0	
6	36	$\Sigma X^2 = 38$
1	1	

$$SS = \Sigma X^2 - \frac{(\Sigma X)^2}{N}$$

$$= 38 - \frac{(8)^2}{4}$$

$$= 38 - \frac{64}{4}$$

$$= 38 - 16$$

$$= 22$$

Notice that the two formulas produce exactly the same value for *SS*. Although the formulas look different, they are in fact equivalent. The definitional formula should be very easy to learn if you simply remember that *SS* stands for the sum of the squared deviations. If you use notation to write out "the sum of" (Σ) "squared deviations" $(X - \mu)^2$, then you have the definitional formula. Unfortunately, the terms in the computational formula do not translate directly into "sum of squared deviations," so you simply need to memorize this formula.

The definitional formula for *SS* is the most direct way of calculating sum of squares, but it can be awkard to use for most sets of data. In particular, if the mean is not a whole number, then the deviation scores will all be fractions or decimals, and the calculations become difficult. In addition, calculations with decimals or fractions introduce the opportunity for rounding error, which makes the results less accurate. For these reasons, the computational formula is used most of the time. If you have a small group of scores and the mean is a whole number, then the definitional formula is fine; otherwise, use the computational formula.

FORMULAS FOR POPULATION STANDARD DEVIATION AND VARIANCE

With the definition and calculation of *SS* behind you, the equations for variance and standard deviation become relatively simple. Remember, variance is defined as the mean squared deviation. The mean is the sum divided by *N*, so the equation for variance is

$$\text{population variance} = \frac{SS}{N}$$

In the same way that sum of squares, or *SS*, is used to refer to the sum of squared deviations, the term *mean square*, or *MS*, is often used to refer to variance which is the mean squared deviation.

Standard deviation is the square root of variance, so the equation for standard deviation is

$$\text{population standard deviation} = \sqrt{\frac{SS}{N}}$$

There is one final bit of notation before we work completely through an example computing *SS*, variance, and standard deviation. Like the mean (μ), variance and standard deviation are parameters of a population and will be identified by Greek letters. To identify the standard deviation, we use the

Greek letter sigma (the Greek letter *s*, standing for standard deviation). The capital letter sigma (Σ) has been used already, so we now use the lowercase sigma, σ:

$$\text{population standard deviation} = \sigma = \sqrt{\frac{SS}{N}} \qquad \text{(4.3)}$$

The symbol for population variance should help you remember the relation between standard deviation and variance. If you square the standard deviation, you will get the variance. The symbol for variance is sigma squared, σ^2:

$$\text{population variance} = \sigma^2 = \frac{SS}{N} \qquad \text{(4.4)}$$

EXAMPLE 4.5 The following population of scores will be used to demonstrate the calculation of *SS*, variance, and standard deviation:

$$1, \quad 9, \quad 5, \quad 8, \quad 7$$

These five scores add up to $\Sigma X = 30$, so the mean is $\frac{30}{5} = 6$. Before we do any other calculations, remember that the purpose of variability is to determine how spread out the scores are. Standard deviation accomplishes this by providing a measurement of the standard distance from the mean. The scores we are working with have been placed in a frequency distribution histogram in Figure 4.3 so you can see the variability more easily. Note that the score closest to the mean is $X = 5$ or $X = 7$, both of which are only 1 point away. The score farthest from the mean is $X = 1$, and it is 5 points away. For this distribution, the biggest distance from the mean is 5 points, and the smallest distance is one point. The typical, or standard, distance should be somewhere between 1 and 5. By looking quickly at a distribution in this way, you should be able to make a rough estimate of the standard deviation. In this case, the standard deviation should be between 1 and 5, probably around 3 points. Making a preliminary judgment of standard deviation can help

Figure 4.3

A frequency distribution histogram for a population of $N = 5$ scores. The mean for this population is $\mu = 6$. The smallest distance from the mean is one point, and the largest distance is 5 points. The standard distance (or standard deviation) should be between 1 and 5 points.

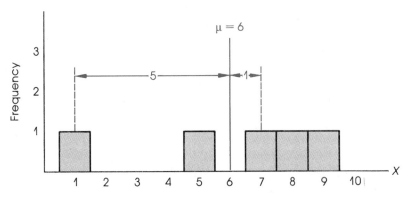

you avoid errors in calculation. If, for example, you worked through the formulas and ended up with a value of $\sigma = 12$, you should realize immediately that you have made an error. (If the biggest deviation is only 5 points, then it is impossible for the standard deviation to be 12.)

Now we will start the calculations. The first step is to find SS for this set of scores.

Because the mean is a whole number ($\mu = 6$), we can use the definitional formula for SS:

X	$X - \mu$	$(X - \mu)^2$	
1	-5	25	$\Sigma X = 30$
9	$+3$	9	$\mu = 6$
5	-1	1	
8	$+2$	4	
7	$+1$	1	
		$40 = \Sigma(X - \mu)^2 = SS$	

$$\sigma^2 = \frac{SS}{N}$$

$$= \frac{40}{5} = 8$$

$$\sigma = \sqrt{8} = 2.83$$

For this set of scores, the variance is $\sigma^2 = 8$, and the standard deviation is $\sigma = \sqrt{8} = 2.83$. Note that the value for the standard deviation is in excellent agreement with our preliminary estimate of the standard distance from the mean.

LEARNING CHECK

1. Write brief definitions of variance and standard deviation.

2. Find SS, variance, and standard deviation for the following population of scores: 10, 10, 10, 10, 10. (*Note:* You should be able to answer this question without doing any calculations.)

3. **a.** Sketch a frequency distribution histogram for the following population of scores: 1, 3, 3, 9. Using this histogram, make an estimate of the standard deviation (i.e., the standard distance from the mean.)

    b. Calculate SS, variance, the standard deviation for these scores. How well does your estimate from part a compare with the real standard deviation?

ANSWERS

1. Variance is the mean squared distance from the mean. Standard deviation is the square root of variance and provides a measure of the standard distance from the mean.

2. Because there is no variability in the population, SS, variance, and standard deviation are all equal to zero.

Figure 4.4

The graphic representation of a population with a mean of $\mu = 40$ and a standard deviation of $\sigma = 4$.

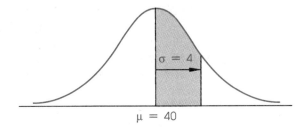

$\sigma = 4$

$\mu = 40$

3. a. Your sketch should show a mean of $\mu = 4$. The score closest to the mean is $X = 3$, and the farthest score is $X = 9$. The standard deviation should be somewhere between one point and five points.

b. For this population, $SS = 36$; the variance is $\frac{36}{4} = 9$; the standard deviation is $\sqrt{9} = 3$.

GRAPHIC REPRESENTATION OF THE MEAN AND STANDARD DEVIATION

In frequency distribution graphs we will identify the position of the mean by drawing a vertical line and labeling it with μ or $\overline{X}$ (see Figure 4.4). Because the standard deviation measures distance from the mean, it will be represented by a line drawn from the mean outward for a distance equal to the standard deviation (see Figure 4.4). For rough sketches, you can identify the mean with a vertical line in the middle of the distribution. The standard deviation line should extend approximately halfway from the mean to the most extreme score.

4.5 STANDARD DEVIATION AND VARIANCE FOR SAMPLES

The goal of inferential statistics is to use the limited information from samples to draw general conclusions about populations. The basic assumption of this process is that samples should be representative of the populations from which they come. This assumption poses a special problem for variability because samples consistently tend to be less variable then their populations. An example of this general tendency is shown in Figure 4.5. The fact that a sample tends to be less variable than its population means that sample variability gives a *biased* estimate of population variability. This bias is in the direction of underestimating the population value rather than being right on the mark. To correct for this bias, it is necessary to make an adjustment in the calculation of variability when you are working with sample data. The intent of the adjustment is to make the resulting value for sample variability a more accurate estimate of the population variability.

A sample statistic is said to be *biased* if, on the average, it consistently overestimates or underestimates the corresponding population parameter.

To compute sample variability, we begin by defining the deviation for each score in the sample. As before, deviation measures the distance from the mean, but now we are using the sample mean in place of the population mean:

$$\text{sample deviation score} = X - \overline{X} \tag{4.5}$$

Figure 4.5

The population of adult heights forms a normal distribution. If you select a sample from this population, you are most likely to obtain individuals who are near average in height. As a result, the scores in the sample will be less variable (spread out) than the scores in the population.

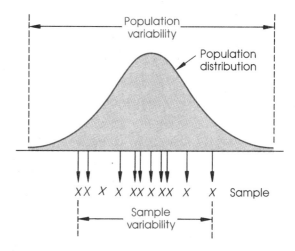

Each deviation score will have a sign and a magnitude. The sign tells the direction from the mean (+ for above, − for below), and the magnitude tells the distance from the mean. The deviation scores always add up to zero.

Variance and standard deviation for sample data have the same basic definitions as they do for populations: Variance measures the average squared distance from the mean, and standard deviation is the square root of variance. To compute the values, we first will need to find *SS*, the sum of squared deviations. The formulas we use to compute sample *SS* are essentially identical to the formulas used for populations:

$$\text{definitional formula:} \quad SS = \Sigma(X - \overline{X})^2 \tag{4.6}$$

$$\text{computational formula:} \quad SS = \Sigma X^2 - \frac{(\Sigma X)^2}{n} \tag{4.7}$$

Note that the only difference between these formulas and the population formulas is a minor change in notation. We have substituted $\overline{X}$ in place of μ and n in place of N. For all practical purposes the population and sample formulas for *SS* are interchangeable. The difference in notation will have no effect on the calculations.

After you compute *SS*, however, it becomes critical to differentiate between samples and populations. To correct for the bias in sample variability, it is necessary to make an adjustment in the formulas for sample variance and standard deviation. With this in mind, sample variance (identified by the symbol s^2) is defined as

$$\text{sample variance} = s^2 = \frac{SS}{n - 1} \tag{4.8}$$

Sample standard deviation (identified by the symbol s) is simply the square root of the variance.

$$\text{sample standard deviation} = s = \sqrt{\frac{SS}{n - 1}} \tag{4.9}$$

Remember, sample variability tends to underestimate population variability unless some correction is made.

Notice that these sample formulas use $n - 1$ instead of n. This is the adjustment that is necessary to correct for the bias in sample variability. The effect of the adjustment is to increase the value you will obtain. Dividing by a smaller number ($n - 1$ instead of n) produces a larger result and makes sample variability an accurate, or unbiased, estimator of population variability.

A complete example showing the calculation of sample variance and standard deviation will now be worked out.

EXAMPLE 4.6

We have selected a sample of $n = 7$ scores from a population. The scores are 1, 6, 4, 3, 8, 7, 6. The frequency distribution histogram for this sample is shown in Figure 4.6. Before we begin any calculations, you should be able to look at the sample distribution and make a preliminary estimate of the outcome. Remember that standard deviation measures the standard distance from the mean. For this sample the mean is $\overline{X} = 5$ ($\frac{35}{7} = 5$). The scores closest to the mean are $X = 4$ and $X = 6$, both of which are exactly 1 point away. The score farthest from the mean is $X = 1$, which is 4 points away. With the smallest distance from the mean equal to 1 and the largest distance equal to 4, we should obtain a standard distance somewhere around 2.5 (between 1 and 4).

Now let's begin the calculations. First, we will find SS for this sample. Because there are only a few scores and the mean is a whole number, the definitional formula will be easy to use. You should try this formula for practice. Meanwhile, we will work with the computational formula.

Caution: For sample variance, you use $n - 1$ after calculating SS. Do not use $n - 1$ in the formula for SS.

X	X^2	
1	1	$\Sigma X = 35$
6	36	$\Sigma X^2 = 211$
4	16	
3	9	
8	64	
7	49	
6	36	

$$SS = \Sigma X^2 - \frac{(\Sigma X)^2}{n}$$

$$= 211 - \frac{(35)^2}{7}$$

$$= 211 - \frac{1225}{7}$$

$$= 211 - 175$$

$$= 36$$

Figure 4.6

The frequency distribution histogram for a sample of $n = 7$ scores. The sample mean is $\overline{X} = 5$. The smallest distance from the mean is 1 point, and the largest distance from the mean is 4 points. The standard distance (standard deviation) should be between 1 and 4 points.

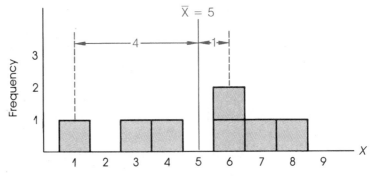

SS for this sample is 36. You should obtain exactly the same answer using the definitional formula. Continuing the calculations,

$$\text{sample variance} = s^2 = \frac{SS}{n - 1} = \frac{36}{7 - 1} = 6$$

Finally, the standard deviation is

$$s = \sqrt{s^2} = \sqrt{6} = 2.45$$

Note that the value we obtained is in excellent agreement with our preliminary prediction.

 SPSS^x A-78

The standard deviation can be computed with Minitab commands DESCRIBE or LET (Section 20.4).

Remember that the formulas for sample variance and standard deviation were constructed so that the sample variability would provide a good estimate of population variability. For this reason, sample variance is often called *estimated population variance*, and the sample standard deviation is called *estimated population standard deviation*. When you have only a sample to work with, the sample variance and standard deviation provide the best possible estimates of the population variability.

LEARNING CHECK

1. **a.** Sketch a frequency distribution histogram for the following sample of scores: 1, 1, 9, 1. Using your histogram, make an estimate of the standard deviation for this sample.

   b. Calculate *SS*, variance, and standard deviation for this sample. How well does your estimate from part a compare with the real standard deviation?

2. If the scores in the previous exercise were a population, what value would you obtain for *SS?*

3. If the scores in Exercise 1 were a population, would you obtain a larger or smaller value for the standard deviation? Explain your answer.

ANSWERS

1. **a.** Your graph should show a sample mean of $\overline{X} = 3$. The score farthest from the mean is $X = 9$, and the closest score is $X = 1$. You should estimate the standard deviation to be between two points and six points.

   b. For this sample, $SS = 48$; the sample variance is $48/3 = 16$; the sample standard deviation is $\sqrt{16} = 4$.

2. $SS = 48$ whether the data are from a sample or a population.

3. Smaller. The formulas for sample data increase the size of variance and standard deviation by dividing by $n - 1$ instead of N. The population formulas will produce smaller values.

SAMPLE VARIABILITY AND DEGREES OF FREEDOM

Although the concept of a deviation score and the calculation of *SS* are almost exactly the same for samples and populations, the minor differences in notation are really very important. When you have only a sample to work with, you must use the sample mean as the reference point for measuring deviations. Using $\overline{X}$ in place of μ places a restriction on the amount of variability in the sample. The restriction on variability comes from the fact that you must know the value of $\overline{X}$ before you can begin to compute deviations or SS. Notice that if you know the value of $\overline{X}$, then you also must know the value of ΣX. For example, if you have a sample of $n = 3$ scores and you know that $\overline{X} = 10$, then you also know that ΣX must be equal to 30 ($\overline{X} = \Sigma X/n$).

The fact that you must know $\overline{X}$ and ΣX before you can compute variability implies that not all of the scores in the sample are free to vary. Suppose, for example, that you are taking a sample of $n = 3$ scores and you know that $\Sigma X = 30$ ($\overline{X} = 10$). Once you have identified the first two scores in the sample, the value of the third score is restricted. If the first scores were $X = 0$ and $X = 5$, then the last score would have to be $X = 25$ in order for the total to be $\Sigma X = 30$. Note that the first scores in this sample could have any values but that the last score is restricted. As a result, the sample is said to have $n - 1$ degrees of freedom; that is, only $n - 1$ of the scores are free to vary.

DEFINITION   *Degrees of freedom*, or *df*, for a sample are defined as

$$df = n - 1$$

where n is the number of scores in the sample.

The $n - 1$ degrees of freedom for a sample is the same $n - 1$ that is used in the formulas for sample variance and standard deviation. Remember that variance is defined as the mean squared deviation. As always, this mean is computed by finding the sum and dividing by the number of scores:

$$\text{mean} = \frac{\text{sum}}{\text{number}}$$

To calculate sample variance (mean squared deviation), we find the sum of the squared deviations (SS) and divide by the number of scores that are free to vary. This number is $n - 1 = df$.

$$s^2 = \frac{\text{sum of squared deviations}}{\text{number of scores free to vary}} = \frac{SS}{df} = \frac{SS}{n - 1}$$

Later in this book we will use the concept of degrees of freedom in other situations. For now, you should remember that knowing the sample mean places a restriction on sample variability. Only $n - 1$ of the scores are free to vary; $df = n - 1$.

4.6 PROPERTIES OF THE STANDARD DEVIATION

Because standard deviation requires extensive calculations, there is a tendency for many students to get lost in the arithmetic and forget what standard deviation is and why it is useful. Standard deviation is primarily a descriptive measure; It describes how variable, or how spread out, the scores are in a distribution. Remember, standard deviation is a measure of *distance from the mean*. In any distribution, some individual scores will be close to the mean and others will be relatively far from the mean. Standard deviation provides a measure of the typical, or standard, distance. A small standard deviation indicates that the scores are typically close to the mean, and a large standard deviation indicates that the scores are generally far from the mean. The numerical value for standard deviation should allow you to visualize the distribution: The scores are either clustered close together or spread out over a wide range, depending on the value of the standard deviation (see Box 4.3).

Figure 4.7 shows two distributions of quiz scores. Both distributions have $\mu = 20$, but one distribution has small variability, $\sigma = 2$, and the other has larger varibility, $\sigma = 6$. For one group, the students are all very similar in terms of their quiz performance. For the second group, there are huge differences in performance from one student to the next. You also should recognize that the same score (X value) can have very different meanings in these two distributions. For example, a score of $X = 22$ is one of the highest scores in the low variability group, but it is only average in the high variability distribution.

Standard deviation also helps researchers make predictions about sample data. Referring to the two distributions in Figure 4.7, if you were to select a single score from the low-variability population, you could be very confident of obtaining a value close to $\mu = 20$. On the other hand, you have a much greater chance of obtaining an extreme score if you are picking from the high-variability distribution.

The standard deviation also is one of the critical components of inferential statistics. Remember, in inferential statistics we will be using sample data as the basis for drawing general conclusions about populations. You also should

Figure 4.7

Two hypothetical distributions of test scores for a statistics class. For both distributions, $N = 16$ and $\mu = 20$. In distribution a, where there is little variability, a score of 22 is nearly the top score. In distribution b there is more variability, and the same score occupies a more central position in the distribution.

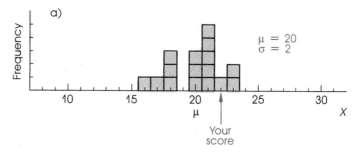

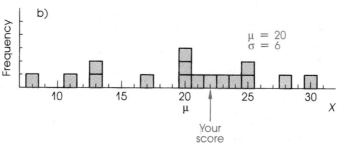

4.3 OBTAINING ROUGH ESTIMATES OF THE MEAN AND STANDARD DEVIATION FOR A DISTRIBUTION

CONCEPTUALLY, THE mean locates the midpoint, or center of a distribution. Similarly, the standard deviation measures the standard distance from the mean. When a set of scores is organized in a frequency distribution graph, you should be able to visualize the location of the mean and the size of the standard deviation, and thereby obtain rough estimates of these two statistical measures. The following example demonstrates how you can easily and quickly make commonsense estimates of the mean and standard deviation for any distribution.

Figure 4.8 shows a frequency distribution histogram for a sample of $n = 43$ scores. First, we have drawn a vertical line through the middle of this distribution at the point that "looks like" the mean. Next, we have drawn an arrow representing the standard deviation so that the arrow extends from the mean to a point that is roughly one-half of the total distance between the mean and the highest score. From this graphic representation, we can estimate that the mean is approximately 8 and the standard deviation is roughly 4 points.

We have computed the actual mean and standard deviation for this sample and obtained values of $\overline{X} = 8.35$ and $s = 3.98$. Note that our rough estimates are very close to the actual values.

Finally, notice that we have drawn two additional vertical (dashed) lines located roughly one standard deviation above the mean and one standard deviation below the mean. The vertical lines divide the total distribution into four sections, each corresponding to a distance of approximately one standard deviation. This process of dividing a distribution into four sections demonstrates another easy way to estimate standard deviation: the standard deviation is approximately one-fourth of the total range covered by a set of scores.

The process of making rough estimates of the mean and standard deviation can be very useful, and we encourage you to follow this estimation procedure for any set of data that you encounter. First, making estimates will help you develop a good conceptual understanding of the mean and standard deviation. Also, you can use your rough estimates to help identify computational errors when you actually calculate the mean and standard deviation. For example, if you calculate a value of $s = 27$ for the sample shown in Figure 4.8, you should realize instantly that this value cannot be correct.

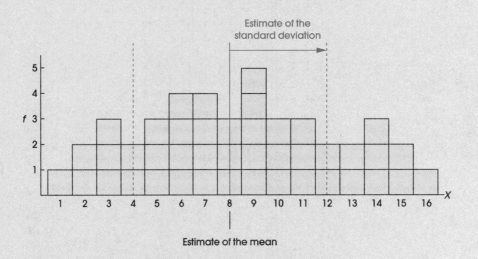

Figure 4.8

A frequency distribution histogram showing a sample of $n = 43$ scores. Rough estimates of the mean and standard deviation have been added to the figure based on the conceptual definitions of these two statistical measures.

remember that a sample generally will not provide a perfectly accurate representation of its population; there will be some discrepancy, or "error," between a sample and the population. Standard deviation provides a measure of how big this error will be. For example, suppose you randomly select a score from a population and obtain a value of $X = 47$. What value would you predict for the population mean? The answer depends on the standard deviation. With $\sigma = 4$, for example, you know that the typical distance between a score and the mean is only 4 points. Thus, you would predict that the population mean is probably within 4 points of $X = 47$. On the other hand, if the standard deviation were $\sigma = 20$, you would predict that the population mean somewhere within 20 points of $X = 47$. In general, the smaller the standard deviation, the more accurately a sample will represent its population. This topic is discussed in more detail in Chapter 7, where we will look at the precise relation between samples and populations.

In summary, you should realize that standard deviation is a valuable measure for both descriptive and inferential purposes. It appears repeatedly throughout the remainder of this book.

TRANSFORMATIONS OF SCALE

Occasionally it is convenient to transform a set of scores by adding a constant to each score or by multiplying each score by a constant value. This is done, for example, when you want to "curve" a set of exam scores by adding a fixed amount to each individual's grade or when you want to change the scale of measurement (to convert from minutes to seconds, multiply each X by 60). What happens to the standard deviation when the scores are transformed in this manner?

The easiest way to determine the effect of a transformation is to remember that the standard deviation is a measure of distance. If you select any two scores and see what happens to the distance between them, you also will find out what happens to the standard deviation.

1. Adding a constant to each score will not change the standard deviation. If you begin with a distribution that has $\mu = 40$ and $\sigma = 10$, what happens to σ if you add 5 points to every score? Consider any two scores in this distribution: Suppose, for example, that these are exam scores and that you had $X = 41$ and your friend had $X = 43$. The distance between these two scores is $43 - 41 = 2$ points. After adding the constant, 5 points, to each score, your score would be $X = 46$, and your friend would have $X = 48$. The distance between scores is still 2 points. Adding a constant to every score will not affect any of the distances and, therefore, will not change the standard deviation. This fact can be seen clearly if you imagine a frequency distribution graph. If, for example, you add 10 points to each score, then every score in the graph would be moved 10 points to the right. The result is that the entire distribution is shifted to a new position 10 points up the scale. Note that the mean moves along with the scores and is increased by 10 points. However, the variability does not change because each of the deviation scores $(X - \mu)$ does not change.

2. Multiplying each score by a constant causes the standard deviation to be multiplied by the same constant. Consider the same distribution of exam scores we looked at earlier. If $\mu = 40$ and $\sigma = 10$, what would happen to σ if each score were multiplied by 2? Again we will look at two scores, $X = 41$ and $X = 43$, with a distance between them equal to 2 points. After all the scores have been multiplied by 2, these scores would become $X = 82$ and $X = 86$. Now the distance between scores is 4 points, twice the original distance. Multiplying each score causes each distance to be multiplied, and so the standard deviation also is multiplied by the same amount.

4.7   COMPARING MEASURES OF VARIABILITY

By far the most commonly used measure of variability is standard deviation (together with the related measure of variance). Nonetheless, there are situations where the range or the semi-interquartile range may be preferred. The advantages and disadvantages of each of these three measures will be discussed.

In simple terms, there are two considerations that determine the value of any statistical measurement:

1. The measure should provide a stable and reliable description of the scores. Specifically, it should not be greatly affected by minor details in the set of data.

2. The measure should have a consistent and predictable relationship with other statistical measurements.

We will examine each of these considerations separately.

FACTORS THAT AFFECT VARIABILITY

1. Extreme Scores. Of the three measures of variability, the range is most affected by extreme scores. A single extreme value will have a large influence on the range. In fact, the range is determined exclusively by the two extremes of the distribution. Standard deviation and variance also are influenced by extreme scores. Because these measures are based on squared deviations, a single extreme value can have a disproportionate effect. For example, a score that is 10 points away from the mean will contribute $10^2 = 100$ points to the SS. For this reason, standard deviation and variance should be interpreted carefully in distributions with one or two extreme values. Because the semi-interquartile range focuses on the middle of the distribution, it is least affected by extreme values. For this reason, the semi-interquartile range often provides the best measure of variability for distributions that are very skewed or that have a few extreme scores.

2. Sample Size. As you increase the number of scores in a sample, you also tend to increase the range because each additional score has the potential to replace the current highest or lowest value in the set. Thus, the range is directly related to sample size. This relationship between sample size and variability is unacceptable. A researcher should not be able to influence variability by manipulating sample size. Standard deviation, variance, and the semi-interquartile range are relatively unaffected by sample size and, therefore, provide better measures.

3. Stability Under Sampling. If you take several different samples from the same population, you should expect the samples to be similar. Specifically, if you compute variability for each of the separate samples, you should expect to obtain similar values. Because all of the samples come from the same source, it is reasonable that there should be some "family resemblance." When standard deviation and variance are used to measure variability, the samples will tend to have similar variability. For this reason, standard deviation and variance are said to be stable under sampling. The semi-interquartile range also provides a reasonably stable measure of variability. The range, however, will change unpredictably from sample to sample and is said to be unstable under sampling.

4. Open-Ended Distributions. When a distribution does not have any specific boundary for the highest score or the lowest score, it is open-ended. This can occur when you have infinite or undetermined scores. For example, a subject who cannot solve a problem has taken an undetermined or infinite amount of time to reach the solution. In an open-ended distribution, you cannot compute the range, or the standard deviation, or the variance. In this situation, the only available measure of variability is the semi-interquartile range.

RELATIONSHIP WITH OTHER STATISTICAL MEASURES

As noted earlier, variance and standard deviation are computed from squared deviation scores. Because they are based on squared distances, these measures fit into a coherent system of mathematical relationships that underlies many of the statistical techniques we will examine in this book. Although we generally will not present the underlying mathematics you will notice that variance and standard deviation appear repeatedly. For this reason, they are valuable measures of variability. Also, you should notice that variance and standard deviation have a direct relation to the mean (they are based on deviations from the mean). Therefore, the mean and standard deviation tend to be reported together. Because the mean is the most common measure of central tendency, the standard deviation will be the most common measure of variability.

Because the median and the semi-interquartile range are both based on percentiles, they share a common foundation and tend to be associated. When the median is used to report central tendency, the semi-interquartile range is commonly used to report variability.

The range has no direct relationship to any other statistical measure. For this reason, it is rarely used in conjunction with other statistical technqiues.

SUMMARY

1. The purpose of variability is to determine how spread out the scores are in a distribution. There are four basic measures of variability: the range, the semi-interquartile range, the variance, and the standard deviation.

The range is the distance between the upper real limit of the largest X and the lower real limit of the smallest X in the distribution. The semi-interquartile range is one-half the distance between the first quartile and the third quartile. Variance is defined as the mean squared deviation. Standard deviation is the square root of the variance.

Standard deviation and variance are by far the most commonly used measures of variability.

2. The logical steps leading to the formulas for variance and standard deviation are summarized as follows. Remember that the purpose of standard deviation is to provide a measure of the standard distance from the mean.

   a. A deviation score is defined as $X - \mu$ and measures the direction and distance from the mean for each score.

   b. Because of the plus and minus signs, the sum of the deviation scores and the average of the deviation scores will always be zero.

   c. To get rid of the signs, we square each deviation and then compute the mean squared deviation, or the variance.

   d. Finally, we correct for having squared all the deviations by taking the square root of the variance. The result is the standard deviation, and it gives a measure of the standard distance from the mean.

3. To calculate either variance or standard deviation, you first need to find the sum of the squared deviations, SS. There are two formulas for SS:

   definitional formula: $SS = \Sigma(X - \mu)^2$

   computational formula: $SS = \Sigma X^2 - \dfrac{(\Sigma X)^2}{N}$

4. Variance is the mean squared deviation and is obtained by finding the sum of squared deviations and

then dividing by the number. For a population, variance is

$$\sigma^2 = \frac{SS}{N}$$

For a sample, only $n - 1$ of the scores are free to vary (degrees of freedom or $df = n - 1$), so sample variance is

$$s^2 = \frac{SS}{n - 1}$$

5. Standard deviation is the square root of the variance. For a population this is

$$\sigma = \sqrt{\frac{SS}{N}}$$

Sample standard deviation is

$$s = \sqrt{\frac{SS}{n - 1}}$$

Using $n - 1$ in the sample formulas makes sample variance and sample standard deviation accurate and unbiased estimates of the corresponding population parameters.

6. Adding a constant value to every score in a distribution will not change the standard deviation. Multiplying every score by a constant, however, will cause the standard deviation to be multiplied by the same constant.

KEY TERMS

variability	semi-interquartile range	variance	sum of squares (SS)
range	deviation score	standard deviation	degrees of freedom (df)
interquartile range			

——— *Focus on Problem Solving* ———

1. The purpose of variability is to provide a measure of how spread out the scores are in a distribution. Usually this is described by the standard deviation. Because the calculations are relatively complicated, it is wise to make a preliminary estimate of the standard deviation before you begin. Remember, standard deviation provides a measure of the typical, or standard, distance from the mean. Therefore, the standard deviation must have a value somewhere be-

tween the largest and the smallest deviation scores. As a rule of thumb, the standard deviation should be about one-fourth of the range.

2. Rather than trying to memorize all the formulas for SS, variance, and standard deviation, you should focus on the definitions of these values and the logic that relates them to each other:

> SS is the sum of squared deviations.
> Variance is the mean squared deviation.
> Standard deviation is the square root of variance.

The only formula you should need to memorize is the computational formula for SS.

3. If you heed the warnings in the following list, you may avoid some of the more common mistakes in solving variability problems.

a. Because the calculation of standard deviation requires several steps of calculation, students often get lost in the arithmetic and forget what they are trying to compute. It helps to examine the data before you begin and make a rough estimate of the mean and the standard deviation.

b. The standard deviation formulas for populations and samples are slightly different. Be sure that you know whether the data come from a sample or a population before you begin calculations.

c. A common error is to use $n - 1$ in the computational formula for SS when you have scores from a sample. Remember, the SS formula always uses n (or N). After you compute SS for a sample, you must correct for the sample bias by using $n - 1$ in the formulas for variance and standard deviation.

------- *Demonstration 4.1* -------

COMPUTING MEASURES OF VARIABILITY

For the following sample data, compute the variance and standard deviation.

> scores: 10   7   6   10   6   15

Compute sum of squares. For SS, we will use the definitional formula:

$$SS = \Sigma(X - \bar{X})^2$$

STEP 1   Calculate the sample mean for these data.

$$\bar{X} = \Sigma X/n = 54/6 = 9$$

STEP 2   Compute the deviation scores, $(X - \bar{X})$, for every X value. This is facilitated by making a table listing the scores in one column and the deviation scores in another column.

X	$X - \bar{X}$
10	$10-9=+1$
7	$7-9=-2$
6	$6-9=-3$
10	$10-9=+1$
6	$6-9=-3$
15	$15-9=+6$

STEP 3 Square the deviation scores. This is shown in a new column labeled $(X - \bar{X})^2$.

X	$X - \bar{X}$	$(X - \bar{X})^2$
10	+1	1
7	−2	4
6	−3	9
10	+1	1
6	−3	9
15	+6	36

STEP 4 Sum the squared deviation scores to obtain the value for SS.

$$SS = \Sigma(X - \bar{X})^2 = 1 + 4 + 9 + 1 + 9 + 36 = 60$$

Compute the sample variance. For sample variance, we divide SS by $n - 1$ (also known as degrees of freedom).

STEP 1 Compute degrees of freedom, $n - 1$.

$$\text{degrees of freedom} = df = n - 1 = 6 - 1 = 5$$

STEP 2 Divide SS by df.

$$s^2 = \frac{SS}{n - 1} = \frac{60}{5} = 12$$

Compute the sample standard deviation. The sample standard deviation is simply the square root of the sample variance.

$$s = \sqrt{\frac{SS}{n - 1}} = \sqrt{\frac{60}{5}} = \sqrt{12} = 3.46$$

PROBLEMS

1. In words, explain what is measured by each of the following:
   a. SS
   b. Variance
   c. Standard deviation

2. Calculate SS, variance, and standard deviation for the following population: 5, 0, 9, 3, 8, 5.

3. Calculate SS, variance, and standard deviation for the following sample: 4, 7, 3, 1, 5.

4. Calculate SS, variance, and standard deviation for the following sample: 1, 0, 4, 1

5. A population of $N = 10$ scores has a mean of $\mu =$ 30 and $SS = 200$. Find each of the following values for this population:
   a. ΣX
   b. $\Sigma(X - \mu)$
   c. $\Sigma(X - \mu)^2$

6. The standard deviation measures the standard (or typical) distance from the mean. For each of the following two populations, you should be able to use this definition to determine the standard deviation without doing any serious calculations. (*Hint:* Find the mean for each population and then look at the distances between the individual scores and the mean.)
   a. Population 1   scores: 5, 5, 5, 5
   b. Population 2   scores: 4, 6, 4, 6

7. Can *SS* ever have a value less than zero? Explain your answer.

8. A set of $n = 20$ quiz scores has a mean of $\overline{X} = 20$. One person is selected from the class to be the "mystery person." If the deviation scores for the other 19 students in the class add up to $+6$, what score did the mystery person have?

9. A population has $\mu = 100$ and $\sigma = 20$. If you select a single score from this population, on the average, how close would it be to the population mean? Explain your answer.

10. A researcher is measuring student opinions using a standard 7-point scale (1 = "strongly agree" and 7 = "strongly disagree"). For one question, the researcher reports that the student responses averaged $\overline{X} = 5.8$ with a standard deviation of $s = 8.4$. It should be obvious that the researcher has made a mistake. Explain why.

11. In general, what does it mean for a sample to have a standard deviation of zero? Describe the scores in such a sample.

12. For the following population of scores:

    scores: 1, 6, 9, 0, 4

    a. Find the mean for the population and compute the deviation score for each individual.
    b. Show that the deviation scores sum to zero.
    c. Square each deviation and find the sum of squared deviations (*SS*).
    d. Now assume that the set of scores is a sample instead of a population and repeat parts a, b, and c. How does the distinction between a sample and a population affect the calculation of *SS*?

13. For the following set of scores, calculate *SS* using the definitional formula and then using the computational formula. (You should get the same answer for each method.) Scores: 2, 6, 3, 7, 6, 1, 3

14. For the data in the following sample,

    1, 4, 3, 6, 2, 7, 18, 3, 7, 2, 4, 3

    a. Sketch a frequency distribution histogram.
    b. Compute the mean and standard deviation.
    c. Find the median and the semi-interquartile range.
    d. Which measures of central tendency and variability provide a better description of the sample? Explain your answer.

15. Compute the mean for each of the following samples and identify which formula for *SS* (definitional or computational) would be easier to use.

a. Scores: 3, 5, 0, 4, 3
b. Scores: 2, 1, 7, 2, 4

16. For the following population of scores:

    3, 4, 4, 1, 7, 3, 2, 6, 4, 2

    1, 6, 3, 4, 5, 2, 5, 4, 3, 4

    a. Sketch a frequency distribution histogram.
    b. Find the range for the population. (*Hint:* You can can use the formula for the range or you can simply count the boxes across the base of the histogram.)
    c. Find the interquartile range and the semi-interquartile range for the population.

17. For the following population of $N = 4$ scores:

    scores: 2, 0, 8, 2

    a. Use the definitional formula to compute *SS;* then find the population variance and standard deviation.
    b. Add three points to each score; then compute *SS,* variance, and standard deviation for the new population.
    c. Multiply each of the original scores by 2; then compute *SS,* variance, and standard deviation for the new poulation.
    d. When a constant is added to each score, what happens to the deviation scores? What happens to the standard deviation?
    e. When each score is multiplied by a constant, what happens to the deviation scores? What happens to the standard deviation?

18. A population of $N = 10$ scores has a standard deviation of 3.5. What is the variance for this population?

19. A sample of $n = 25$ scores has a variance of 100.
    a. Find the standard deviation for this sample.
    b. Find the value of *SS* for this sample. (Be careful to use the *sample* formula.)

20. For the following population of scores:

    8, 5, 3, 7, 5, 6, 4, 7, 2, 6

    5, 3, 6, 4, 5, 7, 8, 6, 5, 6

    a. Sketch a frequency distribution histogram.
    b. Using the procedures outlined in Box 4.3, estimate the mean and the standard deviation on your graph.
    c. Calculate the mean and standard deviation for this population and compare your estimates with the actual values.

21. Calculate the range, the semi-interquartile range, and the standard deviation for the following sample:

2, 8, 5, 9, 1, 6, 6, 3, 6, 10, 4, 12

22. Two samples are as follows:

sample A: 7, 9, 10, 8, 9, 12

sample B: 13, 5, 9, 1, 17, 9

a. Just by looking at these data, which sample has more variability? Explain your answer.
b. Compute the mean and standard deviation for each sample.
c. In which sample is the mean more representative (more "typical") of its scores? How does the standard deviation affect the interpretation of the mean?

23. The following scores are brain weights in grams for a sample of $n = 5$ fish. Calculate the mean and variance for these data. (*Hint:* Multiply each score by 100 to get rid of the decimal places. Remember to correct for this multiplication before you report your answer.) Scores: 0.08, 0.09, 0.08, 0.11, 0.09.

24. Calculate *SS*, variance, and standard deviation for the following sample of scores. (*Hint:* The calculations will be easier if you first subtract 430 from each score. For example, $431 - 430 = 1$, and $436 - 430 = 6$. (Remember, subtracting a constant will not affect these measures of variability.) Scores: 431, 432, 435, 432, 436, 431, 434.

25. People are most accurate at remembering and describing other individuals when they share some characteristics with the person being described. This fact can be very important in eye-witness testimony. A typical experiment examining this phenomenon is presented here.

Two groups of subjects are used: The first group consists of college students, all 18–20 years old. The second group consists of businesspeople aged 38–40. Each group views a short film of a bank robbery. The criminal in the film is a 40-year-old man wearing a suit and tie. After viewing the film, each subject is asked to describe the bank robber. This description includes an estimate of the robber's age. The data, showing each witness's estimate of age, are as follows:

college students: 35, 30, 55, 40, 40

50, 45, 28, 33, 50

business people: 40, 45, 40, 42, 40

40, 35, 40, 41, 38

a. Calculate the mean for each sample. Based on the two means, does it appear that one group is more accurate than the other?
b. Calculate the standard deviation for each sample. Based on these values, does it appear that one group is more accurate than the other? Explain your answer.

CHAPTER 5

z-SCORES: LOCATION OF SCORES AND STANDARDIZED DISTRIBUTIONS

TOOLS YOU WILL NEED

The following items are considered essential background material for this chapter. If you doubt your knowledge of any of these items, you should review the appropriate chapter and section before proceeding.

- The mean (Chapter 3)
- The standard deviation (Chapter 4)
- Basic algebra (math review, Appendix A)

CONTENTS

PREVIEW

A friend of mine, John, is 5 feet 10 inches tall and weighs 170 pounds. John plays football. None of this information about John is particularly remarkable, but it does allow us to make some comparisons. First, John is fairly typical in height and weight when compared with American adult males. In relation to professional football players, however, John is tiny. Most of you probably recognized that John does not play in the National Football League. Finally, when I tell you that John is only 10 years old, you should realize that he is a large boy in relation to other children his age.

The point of this example is that information about an individual can be difficult to interpret unless the individual is described in relation to some reference group. John is either average, small, or very large depending on the group in which you place him.

It is very common to describe individuals in terms of their relationships to others. Parents want to know the average age at which children begin to walk so that they can judge the developmental progress of their children.

(Is my child precocious?) Adults evaluate their salaries by comparison with other people in the same profession. (Am I underpaid?) Students want to know where their exam scores fall in the class distribution. (How did I do on the test?) In each case the goal is to describe a specific individual by his or her relative position within a larger group.

In the preceeding chapters we concentrated on methods for describing entire distributions using the basic parameters of shape, central tendency, and variability. In this chapter we will examine a procedure for describing an individual location within a distribution. The procedure we will introduce is based on the concepts of the mean and the standard deviation. We will use the mean as a reference point to determine whether the individual is above or below average. The standard deviation serves as a yardstick for measuring how much an individual differs from the group average. A good conceptual understanding of the mean and standard deviation will make this chapter much easier.

5.1 OVERVIEW

This chapter introduces the concept of z-scores, or standard scores. In this statistical technique, individual scores are converted into standardized z-scores; each resulting z-score provides a precise description of the exact location of the individual score within the distribution. Thus, each individual score has a corresponding z-score that tells where the individual is located in the distribution (in the middle, extreme right-hand tail, extreme left-hand tail, and so on).

The process of converting scores into z-scores serves both descriptive statistics and inferential statistics. As a descriptive measure, z-scores give a precise description of location in a distribution. For inferential statistics, z-scores help determine how well a particular sample represents its population. For example, a sample that is located in the middle of the distribution (according to its z-score) is considered typical or highly representative. On the other hand, an extreme sample (according to its z-score) is considered nonrepresentative.

One of the key concepts underlying z-scores involves using the standard deviation to help describe the location of scores in a distribution. Figure 5.1 shows a distribution of adult heights (measured in inches) and a distribution of adult weights (measured in pounds). Notice that these two distributions contain completely different numerical values: The distribution of heights has

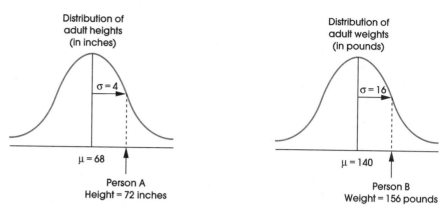

Figure 5.1

A distribution of adult heights in inches (left) with μ = 68 and σ = 4, and a distribution of adult weights in pounds (right) with μ = 140 and σ = 16.

Notice that Person A with a height of 72 inches and Person B with a weight of 156 pounds occupy identical positions within their respective distributions. Both individuals can be described as being located above the mean by exactly 1 standard deviation.

a mean of μ = 68 inches with σ = 4, and the distribution of weights has a mean of μ = 140 pounds with σ = 16. Although the distributions are different, it still is possible to identify locations within each distribution that are the same. For example, an individual who is 68 inches tall is located in the exact center of the height distribution. Similarly, a person who weighs 140 pounds is located in the exact center of the weight distribution. These two people occupy the same location, even though they have completely different scores in different distributions.

Now consider two other individuals: Person A with a height of 72 inches and Person B with a weight of 156 pounds. The locations of these two individuals are shown in their respective distributions in Figure 5.1. Once again, you should notice that the two people occupy the same location within their distributions. Person A is located exactly 1 standard deviation above the mean height, and Person B is located exactly 1 standard deviation above the mean weight. In both cases, we can describe the individual's location as being 1 standard deviation above the mean. Notice that using the standard deviation as the unit of measurement results in "standardizing" the distributions so that we obtain exactly the same location even though we begin with different numerical values.

5.2 z-SCORES AND LOCATION IN A DISTRIBUTION

WHAT IS A z-SCORE?

Suppose you received a score of X = 76 on a statistic exam. How did you do? It should be clear that you need more information to predict your grade. Your score of X = 76 could be one of the best scores in the class, or it might be the lowest score in the distribution. To find the location of your score, you must have information about the other scores in the distribution. It would be useful, for example, to know the mean for the class. If the mean were μ = 70, you would be in a much better position than if the mean were μ = 85. Obviously, your position relative to the rest of the class depends on the mean. However, the mean by itself is not sufficient to tell you the exact location of

(a)

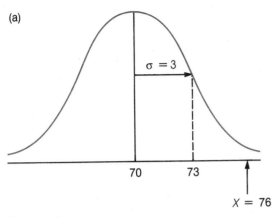

(b)

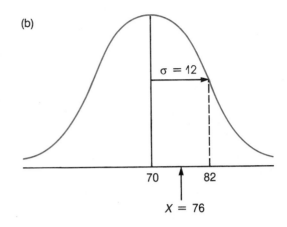

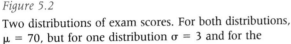

Figure 5.2

Two distributions of exam scores. For both distributions, μ = 70, but for one distribution σ = 3 and for the

other, σ = 12. The position of X = 76 is very different for these two distributions.

your score. Suppose you know that the mean for the statistics exam is μ = 70, and your score is X = 76. At this point, you know that your score is above the mean, but you still do not know exactly where it is located. You may have the highest score in the class, or you may be only slightly above average. Figure 5.2 shows two possible distributions of exam scores. Both distributions have μ = 70, but for one distribution σ = 3 and for the other σ = 12. Notice that the location of X = 76 is very different for these two distributions.

The purpose of this example is to demonstrate that a score *by itself* does not necessarily provide much information about its position within a distribution. These original, unchanged scores that are the direct result of measurement are often called *raw scores*. To make raw scores more meaningful, they are often transformed or standardized so that the resulting values contain more information. For example, IQ tests are commonly standardized so that the mean is 100 and the standard deviation is 15. Because the distribution of IQ scores is standardized, most people have a good understanding of where IQ scores such as 130 or 90 are located.

The goal of z-scores is to provide a simple procedure for standardizing *any distribution*. A z-score takes information about the population mean and standard deviation and uses this information to produce a single numerical value that specifies the location of any raw score within any distribution. The z-score accomplishes this by transforming a raw score into a signed number (+ or −) so that

1. The *sign* tells whether the score is located above (+) or below (−) the mean, and

2. The *number* tells the distance between the score and the mean in terms of the number of standard deviations.

Thus, in a distribution of standardized IQ scores with μ = 100 and σ = 15, a score of X = 130 would be transformed into z = +2.00. The z value tells that the score is located above the mean (+) by a distance of 2 standard deviations (30 points).

Figure 5.3

The relationship between *z*-score values and locations in a population distribution.

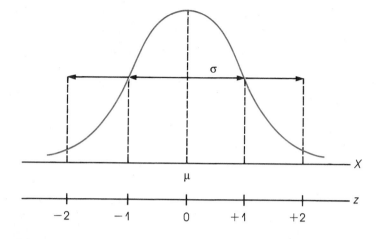

DEFINITION

A *z-score* specifies the precise location of each *X* value within a distribution. The sign of the *z*-score (+ or −) signifies whether the score is above the mean (positive) or below the mean (negative). The numerical value of the *z*-score specifies the distance from the mean by counting the number of standard deviations between *X* and μ.

Notice that a *z*-score always consists of two parts: a sign (+ or −) and a magnitude. Both parts are necessary to describe completely where a raw score is located within a distribution.

Figure 5.3 shows a population distribution with various positions identified by their *z*-score values. Notice that all *z*-scores above the mean are positive and all *z*-scores below the mean are negative. The sign of a *z*-score tells you immediately whether the score is located above or below the mean. Also, note that a *z*-score of *z* = +1.00 corresponds to a position above the mean by exactly 1 standard deviation. A *z*-score of *z* = +2.00 is always located above the mean by exactly 2 standard deviations. The numerical value of the *z*-score tells you the number of standard deviations from the mean (see Box 5.1). Now suppose that the scores from your statistics exam are reported as *z*-scores and you receive a score of *z* = −0.50. How did you do? From this single value you should be able to locate your exact position within the distribution. In this case (*z* = −0.50), you are below the mean by one-half of the standard deviation. Find this position in Figure 5.3.

The definition of a *z*-score indicates that each *X* value has a corresponding *z*-score. The following examples demonstrate the relation between *X* values and *z*-scores within a distribution.

Whenever you are working with *z*-scores you should imagine or draw a picture similar to Figure 5.3. Although you should realize that not all distributions are normal, we will use the normal shape as an example when showing *z*-scores.

EXAMPLE 5.1

A distribution of exam scores has a mean (μ) of 50 and a standard deviation (σ) of 8.

a. For this distribution, what is the *z*-score corresponding to *X* = 58? Because 58 is *above* the mean, the *z*-score has a positive sign. The score is 8 points greater than the mean. This distance is exactly 1 standard deviation (because σ = 8), so the *z*-score is

$$z = +1$$

5.1   RELATIVE POSITION WITHIN A DISTRIBUTION: THE ROLE OF STANDARD DEVIATION

WE HAVE now seen that the standard deviation is an essential part of converting any X value to a z-score. Therefore, in a general sense, the amount of variability in a distribution and the relative position of a particular score are interrelated. This can be demonstrated with a simple example of two distributions.

Suppose that in Caribou, Maine, the average snowfall per year is $\mu = 110$ inches with $\sigma = 30$. In Boston, however, let us assume that the yearly average is only $\mu = 24$ inches with $\sigma = 5$. Last year Caribou enjoyed 125 inches of snow, while Boston was blessed with 39 inches. In which city was the winter much worse than average for its residents?

We are essentially asking a question about the relative position of a raw score in its distribution. In particular, we wish to locate the relative position of last year's accumulation for each city. Thus, in the distribution of annual accumulations for Caribou, where does $X = 125$ fall? Similarly, where does $X = 39$ fall within the distribution for Boston?

If we simply consider deviation scores $(X - \mu)$, the snowfall last year was 15 inches above average for both cities. But does this tell the whole story?

In this case, it does not. The distributions for each city differ in terms of variability ($\sigma = 30$ for Caribou, $\sigma = 5$ for Boston). Again, the amount of variability affects the relative standing of a score. Therefore, it is misleading to simply look at deviation scores. When determining the position of a score in a distribution, we should measure distance of a score from the mean in terms of standard deviation units (see the definition of a z-score).

If we look at Caribou, we find that $\mu = 110$ and $\sigma = 30$. A winter with $X = 125$ inches of snow is 15 points above the mean, or 0.5 standard deviations away. For Boston, the distribution has $\mu = 24$ with $\sigma = 5$. Its winter with $X = 39$ inches is also 15 points above the mean, but this is a distance equal to 3 standard deviation units. When we consider the variability in each distribution, we see that it was not an unusual winter for Caribou. Its snowfall was only $\frac{1}{2}$ standard deviation above the mean ($z = +0.5$), close to what we would expect for that town. On the other hand, Boston had an extreme winter. Its snowfall was 3 standard deviations above the mean ($z = +3.0$), much more snow than its residents would expect.

This z-score indicates that the raw score is located 1 standard deviation above the mean.

b. What is the z-score corresponding to $X = 46$? The z-score will be negative because 46 is *below* the mean. The X value is 4 points away from the mean. This distance is exactly one-half of the standard deviation; therefore, the z-score is

$$z = -\tfrac{1}{2}$$

This z-score tells us that the X value is $\frac{1}{2}$ standard deviation below the mean.

c. For this distribution, what raw score corresponds to a z-score of $+2$? This z-score indicates that the X value is 2 standard deviations above the mean. One standard deviation is 8 points, so two standard deviations would be 16 points. Therefore, the score we are looking for is

16 points above the mean. The mean for the distribution is 50, so the X value is

$$X = 50 + 16 = 66$$

THE z-SCORE FORMULA   The relation between X values and z-scores can be expressed symbolically in a formula. The formula for transforming raw scores into z-scores is

$$z = \frac{X - \mu}{\sigma} \qquad (5.1)$$

The numerator of the equation, $X - \mu$, is a *deviation score* (Chapter 4, page 103) and measures the distance in points between X and μ and whether X is located above or below the mean. We divide this difference by σ because we want the z-score to measure distance in terms of standard deviation units. Remember, the purpose of a z-score is to specify an exact location in a distribution. The z-score formula provides a standard procedure for determining a score's location by calculating the direction and distance from the mean.

EXAMPLE 5.2   A distribution of general psychology test scores has a mean of $\mu = 60$ and a standard deviation of $\sigma = 4$. What is the z-score for a student who received a 66?

Looking at a sketch of the distribution (Figure 5.4), we see that the raw score is above the mean by at least 1 standard deviation but not quite by 2. Judging from the graph, 66 appears to be $1\frac{1}{2}$ standard deviations from the mean. The computation of the z-score with the formula confirms our estimate:

$$z = \frac{X - \mu}{\sigma} = \frac{66 - 60}{4} = \frac{+6}{4} = +1.5$$

Figure 5.4

For the population of general psychology test scores, $\mu = 60$ and $\sigma = 4$. A student whose score is 66 is 1.5σ above the mean or has a z-score of $+1.5$.

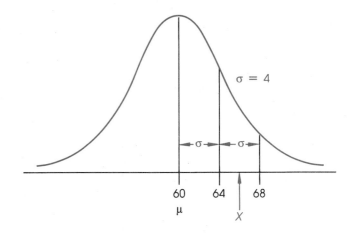

EXAMPLE 5.3 The distribution of SAT verbal scores for high school seniors has a mean of $\mu = 500$ and a standard deviation of $\sigma = 100$. Joe took the SAT and scored 430 on the verbal subtest. Locate his score in the distribution by using a z-score.

Joe's score is 70 points below the mean, so the z-score will be negative. Because 70 points is less than 1 standard deviation, the z-score should have a magnitude that is less than 1. Using the formula, his z-score is

$$z = \frac{X - \mu}{\sigma} = \frac{430 - 500}{100} = \frac{-70}{100} = -0.70$$

DETERMINING A RAW SCORE FROM A z-SCORE There may be situations in which you have an individual's z-score and would like to determine the corresponding raw score. When you start with a z-score, you can compute the X value by using a different version of the z-score formula. Before we introduce the new formula, let us look at the logic behind converting a z-score back to a raw score.

EXAMPLE 5.4 A distribution has a mean of $\mu = 40$ and a standard deviation of $\sigma = 6$.

What raw score corresponds to $z = +1.5$? The z-score indicates that the X value is located 1.5 standard deviations *above* the mean. Because 1 standard deviation is 6 points, 1.5 standard deviations equal 9 points. Therefore, the raw score is 9 points above the mean, or $X = 49$.

In Example 5.4 we used the z-score and the standard deviation to determine the deviation for an X value; that is, how much distance lies between the raw score and the mean. The deviation score was then added to or subtracted from the mean (depending on the sign of z) to yield the X value. These steps can be incorporated into a formula so that the X value can be computed directly. This formula is obtained by solving the z-score formula for X:

$$z = \frac{X - \mu}{\sigma}$$

$z\sigma = X - \mu$ (Multiply both sides by σ.)

$X - \mu = z\sigma$ (Transpose the equation.)

$X = \mu + z\sigma$ (Add μ to both sides.)   **(5.2)**

Notice that the third equation in this derivation contains the expression $X - \mu$, the definition for a deviation score (Chapter 4, page 103). Therefore, the deviation score for any raw score can also be found by multiplying the z-score by the standard deviation ($z\sigma$). Essentially, this is the method we used in Example 5.4. If $z\sigma$ provides a deviation score, then we may rewrite equation 5.2 as:

raw score = mean + deviation score

In using formula (5.2), always remember that the sign of the z-score (+ or −) will determine whether the deviation score is added to or subtracted from the mean.

EXAMPLE 5.5   A distribution has a mean of $\mu = 60$ and a standard deviation of $\sigma = 12$.

a. What raw score has $z = +0.25$?

$$X = \mu + z\sigma$$
$$= 60 + 0.25(12)$$
$$= 60 + 3$$
$$= 63$$

b. What X value corresponds to $z = -1.2$?

$$X = \mu + z\sigma$$
$$= 60 + (-1.2)(12)$$
$$= 60 - 14.4$$
$$= 45.6$$

THE CHARACTERISTICS OF A z-SCORE DISTRIBUTION

It is possible to describe the location of every raw score in the distribution by assigning z-scores to all of them. The result would be a transformation of the distribution of raw scores into a distribution of z-scores. That is, for each and every X value in the distribution of raw scores, there would be a corresponding z-score in the new distribution. This new distribution has specific characteristics—characteristics which make a *z-score transformation* a very useful tool in statistics. If every X value is transformed into a z-score, then the distribution of z-scores will have the following properties:

1. Shape. The shape of the z-score distribution will be the same as the original distribution of raw scores. If the original distribution is negatively skewed, for example, then the z-score distribution will also be negatively skewed. If the original distribution was normal, the distribution of z-scores will also be normal. Transforming raw scores into z-scores does not change anyone's location in the distribution. For example, any raw score that is above the mean by 1 standard deviation will be transformed to a z-score of $z = +1.00$, which is still above the mean by one standard deviation. Transforming a distribution from X values to z values does not move scores from

Figure 5.5

Following a z-score transformation, the *X*-axis is relabeled in z-score units. The distance that is equivalent to one standard deviation on the *X*-axis (σ = 10 points in this example) corresponds to 1 point on the z-score scale.

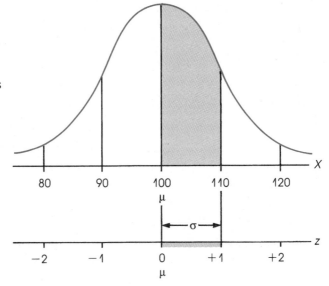

one location to another; the procedure simply relabels each score (see Figure 5.5). Because each individual score stays in its same position within the distribution, the overall shape of the distribution does not change.

2. The Mean. When raw scores are transformed into z-scores, the resulting z-score distribution will *always* have a mean of zero. This is the case regardless of the value of μ for the raw score distribution. Suppose a population of scores has μ = 100 and σ = 10. What is the z-score for the value *X* = 100? Notice that the *X* value equals the mean of the distribution, so its z-score will also be the z-score for the mean (see Figure 5.5).

$$z = \frac{X-\mu}{\sigma} = \frac{100-100}{10} = \frac{0}{10} = 0$$

The mean of the distribution has a z-score of zero. You will remember that raw scores that fall below the mean have negative z-scores (that is, z-scores *less than zero*) and that *X* values above the mean have positive z-scores (*greater than zero*). This fact makes the mean a convenient reference point.

3. The Standard Deviation. When a distribution of *X* values is transformed into a distribution of z-scores, the new distribution will have a standard deviation of 1. For example, a distribution of raw scores has μ = 100 and σ = 10. In this distribution a raw score of 110 will have a z-score of +1 (1 standard deviation above the mean). When *X* is 90, the z will be −1 (or 1 standard deviation below the mean). When *X* is 120, z is +2, and so on. The distribution in Figure 5.5 is labeled in terms of both *X* values and their corresponding z-scores. Note that 10 points on the *X* scale is the equivalent of 1 standard deviation. Furthermore, the distance of 1 standard deviation on the *X* scale corresponds to 1 point on the z-score scale. That is, the *X* scale has merely been relabeled following a z transformation, so that 1 point on the z scale corresponds to one standard deviation unit on

5.2   z-SCORE TRANSFORMATIONS: PROPERTIES OF μ AND σ

SOME OF the properties of the mean (Chapter 3) and standard deviation (Chapter 4) can help explain what happens in a z-score transformation. Consider these two situations:

1. If a constant is subtracted from every score in a distribution, then the mean of the new distribution will equal the old mean minus that constant, but the standard deviation is unchanged.

$$\mu_{new} = \mu_{old} - C$$
$$\sigma_{new} = \sigma_{old} \quad \text{(not changed)}$$

2. If every score in a distribution is divided by a constant, then the mean of the new distribution will equal the old mean divided by that constant and the standard deviation of the new distribution will equal the old standard deviation divided by that constant.

$$\mu_{new} = \frac{\mu_{old}}{C}$$

$$\sigma_{new} = \frac{\sigma_{old}}{C}$$

Now let's consider what happens in a z-score transformation. First, for *every raw score* (X) we compute a deviation score. This entails substracting μ from every score in the distribution. Note that this is basically a situation where a constant value is being subtracted from each score, but here the constant also equals μ. Next, we divide each deviation score by σ to get the z-scores. This last step amounts to nothing more than dividing by a constant value (which in this case happens to equal σ). Considering the characteristics of means and standard deviations

that we just reviewed, what will happen to a raw score distribution with μ = 100 and σ = 10 when a z-score transformation is performed? First we will look at the mean.

In this case we are first subtracting a constant of 100 from every raw score to get the deviation scores. Thus, the mean will be reduced by that constant.

$$\mu_{\text{deviation scores}} = \mu_{old} - C = 100 - 100 = 0$$

Next, every deviation score is divided by 10 to get the z-scores, so the mean will now be divided by this constant.

$$\mu_z = \frac{\mu_{\text{deviation scores}}}{C} = \frac{0}{10} = 0$$

Note that the mean for a distribution of z-scores equals zero.

The same logic also applies to the standard deviation during a z-score transformation. First the deviation scores are obtained by subtracting the constant of 100 from every raw score. However, subtracting a constant from every score does not change the standard deviation.

$$\sigma_{\text{deviation scores}} = \sigma_{old} = 10$$

Then every score is divided by 10 to obtain the z-scores. The standard deviation is also divided by 10.

$$\sigma_z = \frac{\sigma_{\text{deviation scores}}}{C} = \frac{10}{10} = 1$$

Thus, the standard deviation for a z-score distribution equals 1.

the X scale. This relabeling will give the z-score distribution a standard deviation of 1 point.

Box 5.2 examines the z-score transformation in terms of the basic properties of the mean and standard deviation that were discussed in Chapters 3 and 4. In the following section, we demonstrate the characteristics of a z-score distribution with actual data.

DEMONSTRATING THE PROPERTIES OF A z-SCORE TRANSFORMATION

By using a small population of raw scores, it is easy to demonstrate the characteristics of a distribution following a z-score transformation. A population of $N = 6$ scores consists of the following values:

$$0, \quad 6, \quad 5, \quad 2, \quad 3, \quad 2$$

The population mean is

$$\mu = \frac{\Sigma X}{N} = \frac{18}{6} = 3$$

The population standard deviation is

$$\sigma = \sqrt{\frac{SS}{N}} = \sqrt{\frac{24}{6}} = \sqrt{4} = 2$$

To demonstrate the characteristics of a z-score distribution, we must transform every raw score into a z-score using formula 5.1:

$$z = \frac{X - \mu}{\sigma}$$

Therefore, for $X = 0$,

$$z = \frac{0 - 3}{2} = -1.5$$

For $X = 6$,

$$z = \frac{6 - 3}{2} = +1.5$$

For $X = 5$,

$$z = \frac{5 - 3}{2} = +1.0$$

For $X = 2$,

$$z = \frac{2 - 3}{2} = -.5$$

For $X = 3$,

$$z = \frac{3 - 3}{2} = 0$$

For $X = 2$,

$$z = -.5 \quad \text{(already computed)}$$

The distribution now consists of $N = 6$ z-scores:

$$-1.5, \ +1.5, \ +1.0, \ -.5, \ 0, \ -.5$$

Figure 5.6

Transforming a distribution of raw scores (top) into z-scores (bottom) will not change the shape of the distribution.

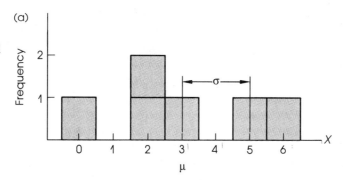

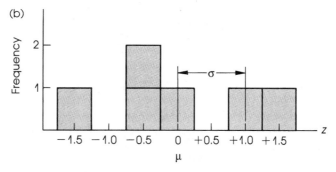

The distribution of z-scores and the original distribution of raw scores are shown in Figure 5.6. Notice that the shape of the distribution has not been changed by the z-score transformation. All individuals are in the same relative position in the distribution after the transformation to z-scores. For example, the individual with $X = 6$ and $z = +1.5$ has the highest score in both distributions. The X-axis is simply relabeled in z-score units after the transformation.

To find the mean of the z distribution, we add all the z-scores and divide by N:

$$\mu = \frac{\Sigma z}{N} = \frac{-1.5 + 1.5 + 1 + (-0.5) + 0 + (-0.5)}{6}$$

$$= \frac{-2.5 + 2.5}{6} = \frac{0}{6} = 0$$

The mean of the distribution of z-scores (μ_z) will always equal zero, regardless of the value of the mean for the raw scores.

To determine the standard deviation of the z-scores, we use the standard deviation formula but plug in z-scores in place of X values. Therefore, the sum of squares for a z-score distribution is

$$SS_z = \Sigma(z - \mu_z)^2$$

Table 5.1 summarizes the steps for the computation of SS_z. For the standard deviation of the z-score distribution (σ_z), we obtain

$$\sigma_z = \sqrt{\frac{SS_z}{N}} = \sqrt{\frac{6}{6}} = \sqrt{1} = 1$$

Computation of SS_z for a distribution of z-scores.

For a distribution of z-scores, $\mu_z = 0$. Therefore, $z = z - \mu_z$.

z	$z - \mu_z$	$(z - \mu_z)^2$
−1.5	−1.5	2.25
+1.5	+1.5	2.25
+1.0	+1.0	1.00
−.5	−.5	.25
0	0	0
−.5	−.5	.25
		$6.00 = SS_z = \Sigma(z - \mu_z)^2$

In summary, transforming raw scores to z-scores will give us a new distribution with the same shape as the original, a mean of zero, and a standard deviation equal to 1 regardless of the parameters of the distribution of raw scores.

LEARNING CHECK

1. What information does a z-score provide?

2. A population of scores has $\mu = 45$ and $\sigma = 5$. Find the z-scores for the following raw scores:

   a. $X = 47$ **b.** $X = 48$ **c.** $X = 40$ **d.** $X = 44$
   e. $X = 52$ **f.** $X = 39$ **g.** $X = 45$ **h.** $X = 56$

3. For the same population, determine the raw scores that correspond to the following z-scores:

   a. $z = +1.3$ **b.** $z = -0.4$ **c.** $z = -3.0$
   d. $z = -1.5$ **e.** $z = +2.8$ **f.** $z = 0$

4. What is the advantage of having $\mu = 0$ for a distribution of z-scores?

ANSWERS

1. A z-score identifies a precise location in a distribution. The sign indicates whether the location is above or below the mean, and the magnitude of z indicates the number of standard deviations from the mean.

2. **a.** +0.4 **b.** +0.6 **c.** −1.0 **d.** −0.2
   e. +1.4 **f.** −1.2 **g.** 0 **h.** +2.2

3. **a.** 51.5 **b.** 43 **c.** 30 **d.** 37.5 **e.** 59 **f.** 45

4. With $\mu = 0$ you know immediately that any positive value is above the mean and any negative value is below the mean.

5.3 USING z-SCORES FOR MAKING COMPARISONS

See Box 5.3 for other examples of how z-scores are useful in statistics.

The transformation of raw scores into z-scores is very useful when we want to compare scores from two different distributions. For example, Bob received a 60 on a psychology exam. For this class, the mean was 50 and $\sigma = 10$. In biology, Bob's test score was 56, and for this class $\mu = 48$ with $\sigma = 4$. In

WHY ARE *z*-SCORES IMPORTANT?

WE HAVE introduced *z*-scores as a statistical method for describing a specific location within a distribution. As you have seen, *z*-scores can be used to determine the precise location of an individual score, and *z*-scores can be used to compare the relative positions of two or more scores. The ability to describe a location in a distribution is of great value for other statistical purposes. The following is a brief outline of some of the ways that *z*-scores will be used in later chapters.

1. **Probability.** One of the basic goals for statistics is to determine the probability or likelihood of particular events. Often it is possible to use *z*-scores as a starting point for finding probabilities. In many situations, the most likely outcomes are those that are "typical," or average. In other words, observing an individual with a *z*-score near zero (in the middle of the distribution) is much more likely than observing an individual with a *z*-score of +3.00. In Chapter 6, we examine the relation between *z*-scores and probability.

2. **Evaluating Treatment Effects.** Many experiments are done to determine whether or not a particular treatment has any effect on a dependent variable. For example, a researcher testing a new stimulant drug would like to know if the drug affects heart rate. One simple test would be to look at the heart rates of individuals who have taken the drug. If these individuals have heart rates that are still average or typical (i.e.,

z-scores around zero), the researcher could conclude that drug does not seem to influence heart rate. On the other hand, if the individuals had heart rates that were extremely high (i.e., *z*-scores of +3.00 or +4.00), the researcher might conclude that the drug does increase heart rate. In general, *z*-scores provide an easy method for determining whether an individual score is average or extreme. We take a closer look at this inferential procedure in Chapters 8 and 18.

3. **Measuring Relationships.** Some statistical methods are intended to describe and measure the relationship between two variables. For example, a psychologist might be interested in the relation between physical development and mental development for 5-year-old children. Are children who are unusually large also unusually bright? In order to examine the relation, it is first necessary to find the location of each child in the distribution of heights and in the distribution of IQs. Extremely tall children will have large positive *z*-scores, those of average height will have *z*-scores near zero, and small children will have negative *z*-scores. Similarly, each child's IQ can be described as a *z*-score. The researcher can then determine whether there is a consistent relation between the *z*-scores for height and the *z*-scores for IQ. We examine statistical methods for measuring relationships in Chapter 16.

which course does Bob have a higher standing? First, you should notice that Bob's psychology score is higher than his score in biology (*X* = 60 versus *X* = 56). Also, if you look at deviation scores, Bob is 10 points above the mean in psychology and only 8 points above the mean in biology. Does this mean that he performed better in psychology than in biology? Not necessarily! The problem is that we cannot simply compare his psychology score to his biology score because these scores come from *different distributions*. Any comparisons between these two test scores would be like the proverbial comparison of apples to oranges.

To make a meaningful comparison of Bob's scores, we must standardize the distributions of both classes to make them similar. Remember, a *z*-score transformation will always produce a distribution that has $\mu = 0$ and $\sigma = 1$.

Therefore, if every raw score in the psychology and biology classes is transformed into a z-score, the resulting distributions for both classes would have $\mu = 0$ and $\sigma = 1$. All we need to do is compare Bob's z-score for psychology with his z-score for biology to determine which exam score is better. When data transformations are used to make distributions comparable, we are using *standardized distributions*. The z-scores in this instance are often called *standard scores*.

DEFINITIONS

A *standardized distribution* is composed of transformed scores that result in predetermined values for μ and σ, regardless of their values for the raw score distribution. Standardized distributions are used to make dissimilar distribution comparable.

A *standard score* is a transformed score that provides information of its location in a distribution. A z-score is an example of a standard score.

In practice it is not necessary to transform every score in a distribution to make comparisons between two scores. We need to transform only the two scores in question. In Bob's case, we must find the z-scores for his psychology and biology scores. For psychology, Bob's z-score is

Be sure to use the μ and σ values for the distribution to which X belongs.

$$z = \frac{X - \mu}{\sigma} = \frac{60 - 50}{10} = \frac{10}{10} = +1.0$$

For biology, Bob's z-score is

$$z = \frac{56 - 48}{4} = \frac{8}{4} = +2.0$$

Note that Bob's z-score for biology is +2.0, which means that his test score is 2 standard deviations above the class mean. On the other hand, his z-score is +1.0 for psychology, or 1 standard deviation above the mean. In terms of relative class standing. Bob is doing much better in the biology class. Unlike the absolute size of the raw scores, the z-scores describe *relative* positions within a distribution.

LEARNING CHECK

1. Why is it possible to compare scores from different distributions after each distribution is transformed into z-scores?

2. For distribution A, $\mu = 20$ and $\sigma = 7$. Distribution B has $\mu = 23$ and $\sigma = 2$. In which distribution will a raw score of 27 have a higher standing?

ANSWERS

1. Comparisons are possible because both distributions will have the same μ and σ ($\mu = 0$, $\sigma = 1$) following a z-score transformation.

2. For distribution A, a raw score of 27 has a z-score of +1.0. For distribution B, a score of 27 corresponds to a z-score of +2.0. Therefore, a raw score of 27 has a higher relative standing in distribution B.

5.4 OTHER STANDARDIZED DISTRIBUTIONS BASED ON z-SCORES

TRANSFORMING z-SCORES TO A PREDETERMINED μ AND σ

Although z-score distributions have distinct advantages, many people find them cumbersome because they contain negative values and decimals. For these reasons, it is common to standardize a distribution by transforming z-scores to a distribution with a predetermined mean and standard deviation that are whole round numbers. The goal is to create a new (standardized) distribution that has "simple" values for the mean and standard deviation but does not change any individual's location within the distribution. Standardized scores of this type are frequently used in psychological testing. For example, raw scores for intelligence tests are frequently converted to standard scores that have a mean of 100 and a standard deviation of 15. If the same standardized scale is used for several types of intelligence tests, then the exam scores on different tests can be more readily compared because the distributions will have the same mean and standard deviation. Basically, two steps are involved in standardizing a distribution so that it has a prespecified μ and σ: (1) Each of the raw scores is transformed into a z-score, and (2) each of the z-scores is then converted into a new X value so that a particular μ and σ are achieved. This process assures that each individual has exactly the same z-score (location) in the new distribution as in the original distribution.

EXAMPLE 5.6

An instructor gives an exam to a psychology class. For this exam, the distribution of raw scores has a mean of $\mu = 57$ with $\sigma = 14$. The instructor would like to simplify the distribution by transforming all scores into a new, standardized distribution with $\mu = 50$ and $\sigma = 10$. To demonstrate this process, we will consider what happens to two specific students: Joe, who has a raw score of $X = 64$ in the original distribution, and Maria, whose original raw score is $X = 43$.

STEP 1

Transform each of the original, raw scores into z-scores. For Joe, $X = 64$, so his z-score is

$$z = \frac{X - \mu}{\sigma} = \frac{64 - 57}{14} = +0.5$$

Remember, the values of μ and σ are for the distribution from which X was taken.

For Maria, $X = 43$, and her z-score is

$$z = \frac{X - \mu}{\sigma} = \frac{43 - 57}{14} = -1.0$$

STEP 2

Change the z-scores to the new standardized scores. The instructor wants to create a standardized distribution with $\mu = 50$ and $\sigma = 10$. Joe's z-score, $z = +0.50$, indicates that he is above the mean by exactly one-half standard deviation. In the new distribution, this position would be above the mean by 5 points ($\frac{1}{2}$ of 10), so his standardized score would be 55. Maria's score is located one standard deviation below the mean ($z = -1.00$). In the new standardized distribution, Maria is lo-

Table 5.2

	JOE	MARIA
Raw score	$X = 64$	43
Step 1: compute z-score	$z = +0.5$	−1.0
Step 2: standard score	55	40

cated 10 points ($\sigma = 10$) below the mean ($\mu = 50$), so her new score would be $X = 40$.

The results of this two-step transformation process are summarized in Table 5.2. Notice that Joe, for example, has exactly the same z-score ($z = +0.50$) in both the original, raw score distribution and the new, standardized distribution. This means that Joe's position relative to the other students in the class has not been changed. Similarly, *all* the students stay in the same position relative to the rest of the class. Thus, standardizing a distribution does not change the shape of the overall distribution and it does not move individuals around within the distribution—the process simply changes the mean and standard deviation.

A FORMULA FOR FINDING THE STANDARDIZED SCORE

Earlier in the chapter, we derived a formula (Formula 5.2) to find the raw score that corresponds to a particular z-score:

$$X = \mu + z\sigma$$

For purposes of computing the new standardized score, we can rewrite the equation:

$$\text{standard score} = \mu_{new} + z\sigma_{new} \tag{5.3}$$

The standard score equals the mean of the new standardized distribution plus its z-score times the standard deviation of the new standardized distribution. The z-score in the formula is the one computed for the original raw score (step 1). Notice that $z\sigma$ is the deviation score of the standard score. If the raw score is below the mean, then its z-score and $z\sigma$ will be negative. For scores above the mean, $z\sigma$ is positive.

EXAMPLE 5.7

A psychologist has developed a new intelligence test. For years the test has been given to a large number of people; for this population $\mu = 65$ and $\sigma = 10$. The psychologist would like to make the scores of his subjects comparable to scores on other IQ tests, which have $\mu = 100$ and $\sigma = 15$. If the test is standardized so that it is comparable (has the same μ and σ) to other tests, what would be the standardized scores for the following individuals?

PERSON	X
1	75
2	45
3	67

Table 5.3

	COMPUTATIONS	
	STEP 1: $z = \dfrac{X - \mu}{\sigma}$	STEP 2: $X = \mu + z\sigma$
Person 1	$z = \dfrac{75 - 65}{10} = +1.0$	$X = 100 + 1(15)$ $= 100 + 15 = 115$
Person 2	$z = \dfrac{45 - 65}{10} = -2.0$	$X = 100 - 2(15)$ $= 100 - 30 = 70$
Person 3	$z = \dfrac{67 - 65}{10} = +0.2$	$X = 100 + 0.2(15)$ $= 100 + 3 = 103$

		SUMMARY	
PERSON	X	z	STANDARDIZED SCORE
1	75	+1.00	115
2	45	−2.00	70
3	67	+0.20	103

STEP 1   Compute the *z*-score for each individual. Remember, the original distribution has $\mu = 65$ and $\sigma = 10$.

STEP 2   Compute the standardized score for each person. Remember that the standardized distribution will have $\mu = 100$ and $\sigma = 15$. Table 5.3 summarizes the computations for these steps and the results.

LEARNING CHECK

1. A population has $\mu = 37$ and $\sigma = 2$. If this distribution is transformed into a new distribution with $\mu = 100$ and $\sigma = 20$, what new values will be obtained for each of the following scores: 35, 36, 37, 38, 39?

2. For the following population, $\mu = 7$ and $\sigma = 4$. Scores: 2, 4, 6, 10, 13.
   a. Transform this distribution so $\mu = 50$ and $\sigma = 20$.
   b. Compute μ and σ for the new distribution. (You should obtain $\mu = 50$ and $\sigma = 20$.)

ANSWERS

1. The five scores 35, 36, 37, 38, and 39 are transformed to 80, 90, 100, 110, and 120, respectively.

2. **a.** The original scores 2, 4, 6, 10, and 13 are transformed to 25, 35, 45, 65, and 80, respectively.
   b. The new scores add up to $\Sigma X = 250$ so the mean is $\frac{250}{5} = 50$. SS for the transformed scores is 2000, the variance is 400, and the new standard deviation is 20.

SUMMARY

1. Each X value can be transformed into a z-score that specifies the exact location of X within the distribution. The sign of the z-score indicates whether the location is above (positive) or below (negative) the mean. The numerical value of the z-score specifies the number of standard deviations between X and μ.

2. The z-score formula is used to transform X values into z-scores:

$$z = \frac{X - \mu}{\sigma}$$

3. To transform z-scores back into X values, solve the z-score equation for X:

$$X = \mu + z\sigma$$

4. When an entire distribution of X values is transformed into z-scores, the result is a distribution of z-scores. The z-score distribution will have the same shape as the distribution of raw scores, and it always will have a mean of 0 and a standard deviation of 1.

5. When comparing raw scores from different distributions, it is necessary to standardize the distributions with a z-score transformation. The distributions will then be comparable because they will have the same parameters ($\mu = 0$, $\sigma = 1$). In practice, it is necessary to transform only those raw scores that are being compared.

6. In certain situations, such as in psychological testing, the z-scores are converted into standardized distributions that have a particular mean and standard deviation.

KEY TERMS

raw score   deviation score   standardized distribution   standard score

z-score   z-score transformation

―――― Focus on Problem Solving ――――

1. When you are converting an X value to a z-score (or vice versa), do not rely entirely on the formula. You can avoid careless mistakes if you use the definition of a z-score (sign and numerical value) to make a preliminary estimate of the answer before you begin computations. For example, a z-score of $z = -0.85$ identifies a score located *below* the mean by almost one standard deviation. When computing the X value for this z- score, be sure that your answer is smaller than the mean, and check that the distance between X and μ is slightly less than the standard deviation.

   A common mistake when computing z-scores is to forget to include the sign of the z-score. The sign is determined by the deviation score $(X - \mu)$ and should be carried through all steps of the computation. If, for example, the correct z-score is $z = -2.0$, then an answer of $z = 2.0$ would be wrong. In the first case, the raw score is 2 standard deviations *below* the mean. But the second (and incorrect) answer indicates that the X value is 2 standard deviation *above* the mean. These are clearly different answers, and only one can be correct. What is the best advice to avoid careless errors? Sketch the distribution, showing the mean and the raw score (or z-score) in question. This way you will have a concrete frame of reference for each problem.

2. When comparing scores from distributions that have different standard deviations, it is important to be sure that you use the correct value for σ in the z-score formula. Use the σ value for the distribution from which the raw score in question was taken.

3. Remember, a z-score specifies a relative position within the context of a spe-

cific distribution. A z-score is a relative value, not an absolute value. For example, a z-score of $z = -2.0$ does not necessarily suggest a very low raw score—it simply means that the raw score is among the lowest within that specific group.

Demonstration 5.1

TRANSFORMATION X VALUES TO z-SCORES

A distribution of scores has a mean of $\mu = 60$ with $\sigma = 12$. Find the z-score for $X = 75$.

STEP 1 Determine the sign of the z-score.
First determine whether X is above or below the mean. This will determine the sign of the z-score. For this demonstration, X is larger than (above) μ so the z-score will be positive.

STEP 2 Find the distance between X and μ.
The distance is obtained by computing a deviation score.

$$\text{deviation score} = X - \mu = 75 - 60 = 15$$

Thus, the score, $X = 75$, is 15 points above μ.

STEP 3 Convert to the distance to standard deviation units.
Converting the distance from step 2 to σ units is accomplished by dividing the distance by σ. For this demonstration,

$$\frac{15}{12} = 1.25$$

Thus, $X = 75$ is 1.25 standard deviations from the mean.

STEP 4 Combine the sign from step 1 with the number from step 2.
The raw score is above the mean, so the z-score must be positive (step 1). For these data,

$$z = +1.25$$

In using the z-score formula, the sign of the z-score will be determined by the sign of the deviation score, $X - \mu$. If X is larger than μ, then the deviation score will be positive. However, if X is smaller than μ, then the deviation score will be negative. For this demonstration, formula (5.1) is used as follows:

$$z = \frac{X-\mu}{\sigma} = \frac{75-60}{12} = \frac{+15}{12} = +1.25$$

Demonstration 5.2

CONVERTING z-SCORES TO X VALUES

For a population with $\mu = 60$ and $\sigma = 12$, what is the X value corresponding to $z = -0.50$?
Notice that in this situation we know the z-score and must find X.

STEP 1   Locate X in relation to the mean.

The sign of the z-score is negative. This tells us that the X value we are looking for is below μ.

STEP 2   Determine the distance from the mean (deviation score).

The magnitude of the z-score tells us how many standard deviations there are between X and μ. In this case, X is $\frac{1}{2}$ standard deviation from the mean. In this distribution, 1 standard deviation is 12 points ($\sigma = 12$). Therefore, X is one-half of 12 points from the mean, or

$$(0.5)(12) = 6 \text{ points}$$

STEP 3   Find the X value.

Starting with the value of the mean, use the direction (step 1) and the distance (step 2) to determine the X value. For this demonstration, we want to find the score that is 6 points below $\mu = 60$. Therefore,

$$X = 60 - 6 = 54.$$

Formula (5.2) is used to convert a z-score to an X value. For this demonstration, we obtain the following using the formula:

$$X = \mu + z\sigma$$
$$= 60 + (-0.50)(12)$$
$$= 60 + (-6) = 60 - 6$$
$$= 54$$

Notice that the sign of the z-score determines whether the deviation score is added or subtracted from the mean.

PROBLEMS

1. Describe exactly what information is provided by a z-score.

2. Describe the characteristics of a distribution following a z transformation.

3. At the beginning of the semester the instructor for developmental psychology gave the class an exam to determine how much the students already knew about the topic. The exam results were reported as z-scores, and Tom received a score of $z = +2.40$. Is Tom correct in concluding that he already knows a lot about developmental psychology? Explain your answer.

4. Suppose that two different distributions of raw scores have the same mean, $\mu = 200$. For both distributions a score of $X = 250$ is above the mean by 50 points. In which case would the score be a more ex-

treme value: in the first distribution where the variability is small, $\sigma = 20$; or in the second distribution where the variability is large, $\sigma = 100$? Explain your answer.

5. For a distribution of raw scores, the mean is $\mu = 45$. The z-score for $X = 55$ is computed and a value of $z = -2.00$ is obtained. Regardless of the value for the standard deviation, why must this z-score be incorrect?

6. For a population of scores with $\mu = 100$ and $\sigma = 16$,
   a. Find the z-scores that corresponds to each of the following X values:

   $X = 108$ $X = 104$

   $X = 132$ $X = 92$

$X = 100$ $X = 120$

$X = 124$ $X = 84$

b. Find the raw scores for each of the following z-scores:

$z = -1.00$ $z = +\frac{1}{2}$

$z = +1.50$ $z = -1.25$

$z = 0$ $x = +0.25$

$z = +2.00$ $z = -2.00$

7. A population has a mean of $\mu = 25$ with $\sigma = 5$.
a. Compute the z-scores for the following X values.

27, 31, 29, 17, 15

28, 34, 33, 19, 22

b. Compute the X values for the following z-scores.

+0.4, +1, −3, +2.8, +1.4, −0.4,

−1.4, +2

8. For a population with $\mu = 60$ and $\sigma = 8$,
a. Compute the z-scores for the following X values.

54, 40, 72, 75, 50, 66

b. Compute the X values for the following z-scores.

−1.90, +1.75, −0.80, +1.55, +0.65, +1.10

9. A population is composed of the following scores:

13, 7, 12, 15, 5, 10, 11, 11, 10, 6

a. Compute μ and σ.
b. Find the z-score for each raw score in the population.

10. A population consists of the following scores:

14, 11, 1, 4, 12, 5, 8, 7, 3, 5

a. Compute μ and σ for this population.
b. Find the z-score for each raw score in the population.

11. A population of scores has $\mu = 80$ and $\sigma = 20$. Find the z-score corresponding to each of the following X values:

85, 90, 110, 75, 60, 45

130, 82, 68, 80, 95, 30

12. A population has $\mu = 50$ and $\sigma = 6$. Find the raw score for each of the following z-scores:

2.50, 1, −3, −1.33, −1.5, +\frac{1}{2}, −2, 0, −\frac{1}{2}

13. For a population with $\mu = 50$, a raw score of 43 corresponds to a z-score of −1.00. What is the standard deviation of this population?

14. For a population with $\sigma = 40$, a score of $X = 320$ corresponds to a z-score of +2.00. What is the mean for this population?

15. The grades from a physics exam were reported in X values and in corresponding z-scores. For this exam, a raw score of 65 corresponds to a z-score of +2.00. Also, when $X = 50$, $z = -1.00$. Find the mean and standard deviation for the distribution of exam scores. (*Hint:* Sketch the distribution, and locate the positions for the two scores. How many standard deviations fall between the two X values?)

16. A distribution has $\mu = 90$ with $\sigma = 10$. Sharon's score is 9 points above the mean. Jill has a z-score of +1.2. Steve's score is $\frac{1}{2}$ standard deviation above the mean. Ramon has a score of $X = 110$. Whose score is the highest? Whose score is the lowest?

17. A population has a mean of $\mu = 115$. A raw score of $X = 145$ has a corresponding z-score of $z = +1.5$. What is the standard deviation for the population?

18. On a statistics quiz you obtain a score of 7. Would you rather be in section A where $\sigma = 2$ or in section B where $\sigma = 1$? Assume that $\mu = 6$ for both sections.

19. Answer the same question in problem 18, but assume that $\mu = 8$ for both sections. Explain your answer.

20. Suppose you have a score of $X = 60$ in a distribution with $\mu = 55$. Explain how the standard deviation could make your score appear to be either "close to" the mean or "far from" the mean.

21. In psychology, you received an exam score of 37, whereas the mean for the class is $\mu = 28$ with $\sigma = 6$. In another general psychology section, your friend received a 46. The distribution for this class has $\mu = 35$ and $\sigma = 10$. Who has a higher standing in the class?

22. A distribution of exam scores has a mean of $\mu = 75$ and a standard deviation of 8. On this exam, Mary has a score of $X = 82$, Bill has a z-score of $z = +0.75$, and Susan scored at the mean. List these three students in order from highest to lowest score.

23. The mean of a distribution after a z-score transformation is always zero because $\Sigma z = 0$. Explain why Σz must always equal zero. (*Hint:* Examine the z-score formula.)

24. The Wechsler Adult Intelligence Scale is composed of a number of subtests. Each subtest is standardized so that $\mu = 10$ and $\sigma = 3$. For one subtest, the raw scores have $\mu = 35$ and $\sigma = 6$. Following are some raw scores for this subtest. What will these scores be when standardized?

41, 32, 39, 44, 45, 24, 37, 27

25. A population of $N = 5$ scores consists of

1, 3, 5, 6, 7

a. Compute μ and σ for this population.
b. Find the z-score for each raw score in the distribution.

c. Compute the mean and standard deviation for the set of z-scores (round off all calculations to two decimal places). What is demonstrated about z- score transformations?
d. Explain the advantages of the characteristics of z transformations.

26. For a distribution, $\mu = 20$ and $\sigma = 2$. The raw scores from this distribution are as follows:

16, 17, 18, 18, 18, 20, 20, 20
21, 21, 21, 21, 21, 22, 23, 23

a. Transform this distribution so that $\mu = 50$ and $\sigma = 10$.
b. Compute the values of μ and σ for the new distribution. They should equal 50 and 10, respectively.

CHAPTER 6

PROBABILITY

TOOLS YOU WILL NEED

The following items are considered essential background material for this chapter. If you doubt your knowledge of any of these items, you should review the appropriate chapter or section before proceeding.

- Proportions (math review, Appendix A)
  - Fractions
  - Decimals
  - Percentages
- Basic algebra (math review, Appendix A)
- Upper and lower real limits (Chapters 1 and 2)
- Percentiles and percentile ranks (Chapter 2)
- Quartiles and semi-interquartile range (Chapter 4)
- z-Scores (Chapter 5)

CONTENTS

PREVIEW

If you were to read a novel or a newspaper (or this entire textbook), which of the following would you be more likely to encounter:

1. A word beginning with the letter *K*?

2. A word with a *K* as its third letter?

If you think about this question and answer honestly, you probably will decide that words beginning with a *K* are more probable.

A similar question was asked a group of subjects in an experiment reported by Tversky and Kahneman (1973). Their subjects estimated that words beginning with *K* are twice as likely as words with a *K* as the third letter. In truth, the relation is just the opposite. There are more than twice as many words with a *K* in the third position as there are words beginning with a *K*. How can people be so wrong? Do they completely misunderstand probability?

When you were deciding which type of *K* words are more likely, you probably searched your memory and tried to estimate which words are more common. How many words can you think of that start with the letter *K*? How many words can you think of that have a *K* as the third letter? Because you have had years of practice alphabetizing words according to their first letter, you should find it much easier to search your memory for words beginning with a *K* than to search for words with a *K* in the third position. Consequently, you would conclude that first-letter *K* words are more common and are therefore more likely to occur in a book.

Notice that when you use the strategy of counting words during your search, you are estimating their frequencies. From these frequencies, you estimate the proportions of these words in the population of words. Most people think of probability in this way—as a proportion based on how often an outcome occurs. As you will see in this chapter, this idea is a perfectly reasonable approach to probability. In fact, you will see that probability and proportion often are interchangeable concepts.

As for the Tversky and Kahneman study, your error in judging the relative probabilities of *K* words was not due to a misunderstanding of probability. Instead, you simply were misled by the availability of the two types of words in your memory. If you had actually searched through the words in this text (instead of those in your memory), you probably would have found more third-letter *K* words and you would have concluded (correctly) that these words are more likely.

6.1 OVERVIEW

Relations between samples and populations most often are described in terms of probability. Suppose, for example, you are selecting a sample of 1 marble from a jar that contains 50 black and 50 white marbles. Although you cannot guarantee the exact outcome of your sample, it is possible to talk about the potential outcomes in terms of probabilities. In this case, you have a fifty-fifty chance of getting either color. Now consider another jar (population) that has 90 black and only 10 white marbles. Again, you cannot specify the exact outcome of a sample, but now you know that the sample probably will be a black marble. By knowing the makeup of a population, we can determine the probability of obtaining specific samples. In this way, probability gives us a connection between populations and samples.

You may have noticed that the preceding examples begin with a population and then use probability to describe the samples that could be obtained. This is exactly backward from what we want to do with inferential statistics. Remember, the goal of inferential statistics is to begin with a sample

Figure 6.1

The role of probability in inferential statistics. The goal of inferential statistics is to use the limited information from samples to draw general conclusions about populations. The relationship between samples and populations usually is defined in terms of probability. Probability allows you to start with a population and predict what kind of sample is likely to be obtained. This forms a bridge between populations and samples. Inferential statistics uses the *probability bridge* as a basis for making conclusions about populations when you have only sample data.

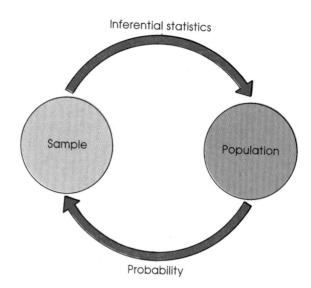

and then answer general questions about the population. We will reach this goal in a two-stage process. In the first stage, we develop probability as a bridge from population to samples. This stage involves identifying the types of samples that probably would be obtained from a specific population. Once this bridge is established, we simply reverse the probability rules to allow us to move from samples to populations (see Figure 6.1). The process of reversing the probability relation can be demonstrated by considering again the two jars of marbles we looked at earlier. (One jar has 50 black and 50 white marbles; the other jar has 90 black and only 10 white marbles.) This time, suppose that you are blindfolded when the sample is selected and that your task is to use the sample to help you to decide which jar was used. If you select a sample of $n = 4$ marbles and all are black, where did the sample come from? It should be clear that it would be relatively unlikely (low probability) to obtain this sample from jar 1; in four draws, you almost certainly would get at least 1 white marble. On the other hand, this sample would have a high probability of coming from jar 2, where nearly all the marbles are black. Your decision, therefore, is that the sample probably came from jar 2. Notice that you now are using the sample to make an inference about the population.

6.2 INTRODUCTION TO PROBABILITY

Probability is a huge topic that extends far beyond the limits of introductory statistics, and we will not attempt to examine it all here. Instead, we will concentrate on the few concepts and definitions that are needed for an introduction to inferential statistics. We begin with a relatively simple definition of probability.

DEFINITION   In a situation where several different outcomes are possible, we define the *probability* for any particular outcome as a fraction or proportion. If the possible outcomes are identified as *A, B, C, D,* etc., then

$$\text{probability of } A = \frac{\text{number of outcomes classified as } A}{\text{total number of possible outcomes}}$$

For example, when you toss a balanced coin, the outcome will be either heads or tails. Because heads is one of two possible outcomes, the probability of heads is $p = \frac{1}{2}$.

If you are selecting 1 card from a complete deck, there are 52 possible outcomes. The probability of selecting the king of hearts is $p = \frac{1}{52}$. The probability of selecting an ace is $p = \frac{4}{52}$ because there are four aces in the deck.

To simplify the discussion of probability, we will use a notation system that eliminates a lot of the words. The probability of a specific outcome will be expressed with a capital *P* (for probability) followed by the specific outcome in parentheses. For example, the probability of selecting a king from a deck of cards will be written as *P*(king). The probability of obtaining heads for a coin toss will be written as *P*(heads).

You should note that probability is defined as a proportion. This definition makes it possible to restate any probability problem as a proportion problem. For example, the probability problem "What is the probability of obtaining a king from a deck of cards?" can be restated as "Out of the whole deck, what proportion are kings?" In each case, the answer is $\frac{4}{52}$, or "four out of fifty-two." This translation from probability to proportion may seem trivial now, but it will be a great aid when the probability problems become more complex. In most situations we are concerned with the probability of obtaining a particular sample from a population. The terminology of *sample* and *population* will not change the basic definition of probability. For example, the whole deck of cards can be considered as a population, and the single card we select is the sample.

The definition we are using identifies probability as a fraction or a proportion. If you work directly from this definition, the probability values you obtain will be expressed as fractions. For example, if you are selecting a card,

$$P(\text{spade}) = \tfrac{13}{52} = \tfrac{1}{4}$$

Or if you are tossing a coin,

$$P(\text{heads}) = \tfrac{1}{2}$$

You should be aware that these fractions can be expressed equally well as either decimals or percentages:

$$p = \tfrac{1}{4} = 0.25 = 25\%$$

$$p = \tfrac{1}{2} = 0.50 = 50\%$$

By convention, probability values most often are expressed as decimal values. But you should realize that any of these three forms is acceptable.

You also should note that all the possible probability values are contained in a limited range. At one extreme, when an event never occurs, the probability is zero or 0% (see Box 6.1). At the other extreme, when an event

If you are unsure how to convert from fractions to decimals or percentages, you should review the section on proportions in the math review, Appendix A.

6.1 ZERO PROBABILITY

AN EVENT that never occurs has a probability of zero. However, the opposite of this statement is not always true: A probability of zero does not mean that the event is guaranteed never to occur. Whenever there is an extremely large number of possible events, the probability of any specific event is assigned the value zero. This is done because the probability value tends toward zero as the number of possible events gets large. Consider, for example, the series

$$\frac{1}{10} \quad \frac{1}{100} \quad \frac{1}{1000} \quad \frac{1}{10,000} \quad \frac{1}{100,000}$$

Note that the value of the fraction is getting smaller and smaller, headed toward zero. At the far extreme, when the number of possible events is so large that it cannot be specified, the probability of a single, specific event is said to be zero.

$$\frac{1}{\text{infinite number}} = 0$$

Consider, for example, the fish in the ocean. If there were only 10 fish, then the probability of selecting any particular one would be $p = \frac{1}{10}$. Note that if you add up the probabilities for all 10 fish, you get a total of 1.00. Of course, there really are billions of fish in the ocean, and the probability of catching any specific one would be 1 out of billions; for all practical purposes, $p = 0$. However, this does not mean that you are doomed to fail whenever you go fishing. The zero probability simply means that you cannot predict in advance which fish you will catch. Note that each individual fish has a probability of zero, but there are so many fish that when you add up all the zeros you still get a total of 1.00. In probability, a value of zero doesn't mean never. But, practically speaking, it does mean very, very close to never.

always occurs, the probability is 1, or 100%. For example, suppose you have a jar containing 10 white marbles. The probability of randomly selecting a black marble would be

$$P(\text{black}) = \tfrac{0}{10} = 0$$

The probability of selecting a white marble would be

$$P(\text{white}) = \tfrac{10}{10} = 1$$

Finally, you can determine a probability from a frequency distribution table by computing the proportion for the X value in question. In Chapter 2, we computed this proportion as follows:

$$P = \frac{f}{N}$$

Once again, probability and proportion are equivalent. Also note that this formula is perfectly consistent with the definition of probability. That is, the "number of outcomes classified as A" is the frequency (f) for that particular score, and the "total number of possible outcomes" is the number of scores in the entire distribution, N. Consider the following distribution of scores, which has been summarized in a frequency distribution table.

X	f
9	1
8	3
7	4
6	2

For this distribution of scores, what is the probability of selecting a score of $X = 8$? Stated as a proportion we may ask, What proportion of all scores in the distribution have a value of 8? There are 10 scores ($N = \Sigma f$) in the distribution and 3 of them are $X = 8$. Therefore,

$$P(X = 8) = \frac{f}{N} = \frac{3}{10} = 0.30$$

RANDOM SAMPLING

For the preceding definition of probability to be accurate, it is necessary that the outcomes be obtained by a process called random sampling.

DEFINITION

A *random sample* must satisfy two requirements:

1. Each individual in the population has an *equal chance* of being selected.

2. If more than one individual is to be selected for the sample, there must be *constant probability* for each and every selection.

Each of the two requirements for random sampling has some interesting consequences. The first assures that there is no bias in the selection process. For a population with N individuals, each individual must have the same probability, $p = 1/N$, of being selected. This means, for example, that you would not get a random sample of people in your city by selecting names from the yacht club membership list. Similarly, you would not get a random sample of college students by selecting individuals from your psychology classes. You also should note that the first requirement of random sampling prohibits you from applying the definition of probability to situations where the possible outcomes are not equally likely. Consider, for example, the question of whether or not there is life on Mars. There are only two possible alternatives.

1. There is life on Mars.
2. There is no life on Mars.

However, you cannot conclude that the probability of life on Mars is $p = \frac{1}{2}$.

The second requirement also is more interesting than may be apparent at first glance. Consider, for example, the selection of $n = 2$ cards from a complete deck. For the first draw, what is the probability of obtaining the jack of diamonds?

$$P(\text{jack of diamonds}) = \frac{1}{52}$$

Now, for the second draw, what is the probability of obtaining the jack of diamonds? Assuming you still are holding the first card, there are two possibilities.

$P(\text{jack of diamonds}) = \frac{1}{51}$ if the first card was not the jack of diamonds

or

$P(\text{jack of diamonds}) = 0$ if the first card was the jack of diamonds

In either case, the probability is different from its value for the first draw. This contradicts the requirement for random sampling, which says that the probability must stay constant. To keep the probabilities from changing from one selection to the next, it is necessary to replace each sample before you make the next selection. This is called *sampling with replacement*. The second requirement for random samples (constant probability) demands that you sample with replacement. (*Note:* The definition we are using defines one type of random sampling, often called a *simple random sample* or an *independent random sample*. Other types of random sampling are possible. You also should note that the requirement for replacement becomes relatively unimportant with very large populations. With large populations the probability values stay essentially constant whether or not you use replacement. For example, in a population of $N = 1,000,001$ individuals, the probability of selecting any one individual is $1/1,000,001$. If sampling with replacement is not used, then the probability of selection for the next person will be $1/1,000,000$, a negligible change in probability.)

PROBABILITY AND FREQUENCY DISTRIBUTIONS

The situations where we are concerned with probability usually will involve a population of scores that can be displayed in a frequency distribution graph. If you think of the graph as representing the entire population, then different portions of the graph will represent different portions of the population. Because probability and proportion are equivalent, a particular proportion of the graph corresponds to a particular probability in the population. Thus, whenever a population is presented in a frequency distribution graph, it will be possible to represent probabilities as proportions of the graph. The relationship between graphs and probabilities is demonstrated in the following example.

EXAMPLE   6.1

We will use a very simple population that contains only $N = 10$ scores with values 1, 1, 2, 3, 3, 4, 4, 4, 5, 6. This population is shown in the frequency distribution graph in Figure 6.2. If you are taking a random sample of $n = 1$ score from this population, what is the probability of obtaining a score greater than 4? In probability notation.

$$P(X > 4) = ?$$

Using the definition of probability, there are 2 scores that meet this criterion out of the total group of $N = 10$ scores, so the answer would be $p = \frac{2}{10}$. This answer can be obtained directly from the frequency distribution graph if you recall that probability and proportion measure the same thing. Looking at the graph (Figure 6.2), what proportion of the

Figure 6.2

A frequency distribution histogram for a population that consists of $N = 10$ scores. The shaded part of the figure indicates the portion of the whole population that corresponds to scores greater than $X = 4$. The shaded portion is two-tenths $(p = \frac{2}{10})$ of the whole distribution.

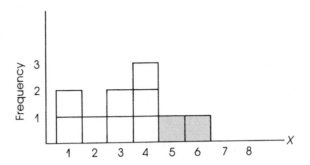

population consists of scores greater than 4? The answer is the shaded part of the distribution, that is, 2 squares out of the total of 10 squares in the distribution. Notice that we now are defining probability as proportion of *area* in the frequency distribution graph. This provides a very concrete and graphic way of representing probability.

Using the same population once again, what is the probability of selecting a score less than 5? In symbols,

$$P(X < 5) = ?$$

Going directly to the distribution in Figure 6.2, we now want to know what part of the graph is not shaded. The unshaded portion consists of 8 out of the 10 blocks ($\frac{8}{10}$ of the area of the graph), so the answer is $p = \frac{8}{10}$.

LEARNING CHECK

1. The animal colony in the psychology department contains 20 male rats and 30 female rats. Of the 20 males, 15 are white and 5 spotted. Of the 30 females, 15 are white and 15 are spotted. Suppose you randomly select 1 rat from this colony.

   a. What is the probability of obtaining a female?

   b. What is the probability of obtaining a white male?

   c. Which selection is more likely, a spotted male or a spotted female?

2. What is the purpose of sampling with replacement?

3. Suppose you are going to select a random sample of $n = 1$ score from the distribution in Figure 6.2. Find the following probabilities.

   a. $P(X > 2)$

   b. $P(X > 5)$

   c. $P(X < 3)$

ANSWERS

1. **a.** $P = 30/50 = 0.60$ **b.** $P = 15/50 = 0.30$

   c. A spotted female ($P = 0.30$) is more likely than a spotted male ($P = 0.10$).

2. Sampling with replacement is necessary to maintain constant probabilities for each and every selection.

3. **a.** $P = 7/10 = 0.70$ **b.** $P = 1/10 = 0.10$ **c.** $P = 3/10 = 0.30$

6.3 PROBABILITY AND THE NORMAL DISTRIBUTION

The normal distribution was first introduced in Chapter 2 as an example of a commonly occurring shape for population distributions. An example of a normal distribution is shown in Figure 6.3. Although the exact shape for the normal distribution is precisely defined by an equation (see Figure 6.3), we can easily describe its general characteristics: It is a symmetrical distribution, with the highest frequency in the middle (mode = mean = median) and the frequencies tapering off gradually as the scores get farther and farther from the mean. In simple terms, in a normal distribution most individuals are around average, and extreme scores are relatively rare. This shape describes many common variables such as adult heights, intelligence scores, personality scores, and so on.

The normal shape also can be defined by the proportions of area contained in each section of the distribution. For instance, all normal shaped distributions will have exactly 34.13% of their total area in the section between the mean and the point that is one standard deviation above the mean (see Figure 6.3). By this definition, a distribution is normal if and only if it has all the right proportions.

Because the normal distribution is a good model for many naturally occurring distributions and because this shape is guaranteed in some circumstances (as you will see in Chapter 7), we will devote considerable attention to this particular distribution.

The process of answering probability questions about a normal distribution is introduced in the following example.

EXAMPLE 6.2 Adult heights form a normal shaped distribution with a mean of 68 inches and a standard deviation of 6 inches. Given this information about the population, our goal is to determine the probability associated with specific samples. For example, what is the probability of randomly selecting an individual who is taller than 6 feet (6 feet = 72 inches)?

Figure 6.3

The normal distribution. The exact shape of the normal distribution is specified by an equation relating each X value (score) with each Y value (frequency). The equation is

$$Y = \frac{1}{\sqrt{2\pi\sigma^2}} e^{-(X-\mu)^2/2\sigma^2}$$

(π and e are mathematical constants.) In simpler terms, the normal distribution is symmetrical with a single mode in the middle. The frequency tapers off as you move farther from the middle in either direction.

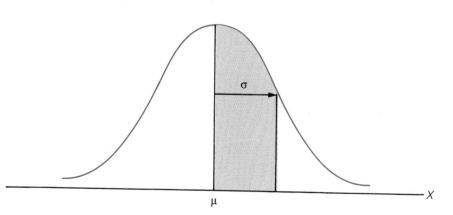

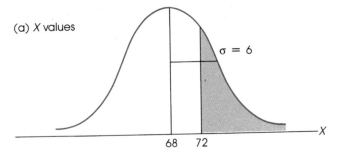

(a) X values   σ = 6

68   72   X

(b) z values

0   0.67   z

Figure 6.4

(a) The distribution of adult heights. This is a normal distribution with $\mu = 68$ and $\sigma = 6$. The portion of the distribution corresponding to scores greater than 72 has been shaded. (b) The distribution of adult heights after being transformed into z-scores.

The mean is changed to $z = 0$, and the value of $X = 72$ is transformed to $z = +0.67$. The portion of the distribution corresponding to z-scores greater than $+0.67$ has been shaded.

Restating this question in probability notation, we get

$$P(X > 72) = ?$$

We will follow a step-by-step process to find the answer to this question.

1. First, the probability question is translated to a proportion question: Out of all the possible adult heights, what proportion is greater than 72 inches?

2. You know that "all the possible adult heights" is simply the population distribution. This population is shown in Figure 6.4(a).

3. We want to find what portion of the distribution (what area) consists of values greater than 72. This part is shaded in the figure.

4. Looking at Figure 6.4(a), it appears that we have shaded in approximately 0.25 (or 25%) of the distribution. This is the answer we wanted.

THE UNIT NORMAL TABLE   Obviously, the probability answer we obtained for the preceding example was just a rough approximation. To make the answer more precise, we need a way to measure accurately the area in the normal distribution. Conceivably, you could do this by very carefully drawing the distribution on graph paper and then precisely measuring the amount of area in each section. Fortunately, this work already has been done, and the results are available in a table. The table, called the *unit normal table*, lists areas, or proportions, for all the possible sections of the normal distribution.

To use the unit normal table, you first need to transform the distribution of adult heights into a distribution of z-scores. Remember, changing from X values to z-scores will not change the shape of the distribution (it still will be normal), but it will transform the mean from $\mu = 68$ to $z = 0$ and will transform the standard deviation to 1. This is called *standardizing* the distribution. You should note that standardizing any normal distribution will produce the same result. No matter what mean or standard deviation you begin with, the standardized distribution (of z-scores) will be normal, with $\mu = 0$ and $\sigma = 1$. Because all normal distributions transform to this single standardized normal distribution, it is possible to have a single table that serves for every normal distribution.

Our distribution of adult heights is redrawn and standardized in Figure 6.4(b). Note that we have simply converted X values to z-scores. The value of $X = 72$ corresponds to a z-score of $z = \frac{4}{6}$, or 0.67. Our problem now is to determine what proportion of the normal distribution corresponds to z-scores greater than +0.67. The answer can be found in the unit normal table. This table lists the proportion of area corresponding to every possible z-score for the normal distribution.

A complete unit normal table is provided in Appendix B on page A-21, and a portion of the table is reproduced in Figure 6.5. The table lists z-score values

Figure 6.5

A portion of the unit normal table. This table lists proportions of the normal distribution corresponding to each z-score value. Column A of the table lists z-scores. Column B lists the proportion of the normal distribution that is located between the mean and the z-score value. Column C lists the proportion of the normal distribution that is located in the tail of the distribution beyond the z-score value.

(A) z	(B) Area Between Mean and z	(C) Area Beyond z
0.00	0.0000	0.5000
0.01	0.0040	0.4960
0.02	0.0080	0.4920
0.03	0.0120	0.4880
0.20	0.0793	0.4207
0.21	0.0832	0.4168
0.22	0.0871	0.4129
0.23	0.0910	0.4090
0.24	0.0948	0.4052
0.25	0.0987	0.4013
0.26	0.1026	0.3974
0.27	0.1064	0.3936
0.28	0.1103	0.3897
0.29	0.1141	0.3859
0.30	0.1179	0.3821
0.31	0.1217	0.3783
0.32	0.1255	0.3745
0.33	0.1293	0.3707
0.34	0.1331	0.3669

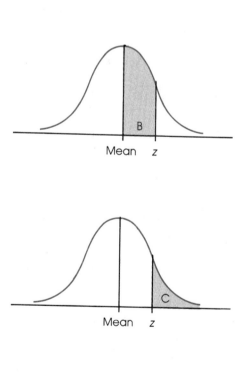

To change from a decimal value to a percentage, you multiply by 100 or simply move the decimal point two places to the right.

and two proportions associated with each z-score in the normal distribution. The z-scores are listed in column A of the table. Column B lists the proportion of the distribution that is located between the mean and each z-score. Column C lists the proportion of the distribution that lies in the tail beyond each z-score.

For a z-score of $z = 0.25$, for example, the table lists 0.0987 in column B and 0.4013 in column C. Of the entire normal distribution 0.0987 (9.87%) is located between the mean and a z-score of $+0.25$ (see Figure 6.5). Similarly, the tail of the distribution beyond $z = +0.25$ contains 0.4013 (40.13%) of the distribution (see Figure 6.5). Notice that these two values account for exactly one-half or 50% of the distribution:

$$0.0987 + 0.4013 = 0.5000$$

The following examples demonstrate several different ways the table can be used to find proportions or probabilities. Later we will return to the problem on adult heights.

EXAMPLE 6.3A   Occasionally, the answer to a proportion problem can be found directly in the table. For example, what proportion of the normal distribution corresponds to z-scores greater than $z = 1.00$? The portion we want has been shaded in the normal distribution shown in Figure 6.6(a).

In this case, the shaded portion is the tail of the distribution beyond $z = 1.00$. To find this proportion, you simply look up $z = 1.00$ in the table and read the answer directly from column C. The answer is 0.1587 (or 15.87%).

EXAMPLE 6.3B   Sometimes the table will provide only a part of the required proportion. Suppose, for example, that you want the proportion of the normal distribution corresponding to z-scores less than $z = 1.50$. This portion has been shaded in Figure 6.6(b).

In this example, the shaded area consists of two sections:

1. The section between the mean and the z-score

2. The entire left half of the distribution

Figure 6.6

Proportions of the normal distribution. (a) The portion consisting of z values greater than $+1.00$. (b) The portion consisting of z = values less than $+1.50$. (c) The portion consisting of z values less than -0.50.

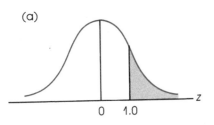
(a)

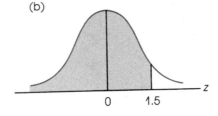
(b)

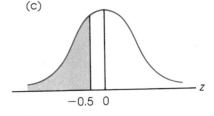
(c)

To find the area between the mean and the z-score, look up $z = 1.50$ in the table and read the proportion from column B. You should find 0.4332 in the table. The rest of the shaded area consists of the section to the left of the mean. Because the normal distribution is symmetrical, exactly one-half (0.5000, or 50%) is on each side of $z = 0$. Thus, the shaded area left of the mean is exactly 0.5000. You add the two sections to obtain the total shaded area:

$$0.5000 + 0.4332 = 0.9332$$

(*Note:* You could solve this problem by looking up $z = 1.50$ and reading the column C value of 0.0668 from the table. This proportion corresponds to the unshaded tail of the distribution—precisely the portion of the distribution that you don't want. To find the rest of the distribution, you simply subtract from 1.00: $1.0000 - 0.0668 = 0.9332$.)

EXAMPLE 6.3C Many problems will require that you find proportions for negative z-scores. For example, what proportion of the normal distribution corresponds to z-scores less than $z = -0.5$? This portion has been shaded in Figure 6.6(c).

To answer questions with negative z-scores, simply remember that the distribution is symmetrical with a z-score of zero in the middle, positive values to the right, and negative values to the left. The proportion in the left-hand tail beyond $z = -0.50$ is exactly the same as the area in the right-hand tail beyond $z = +0.50$. To find this proportion, look up $z = 0.50$ in the table and find the proportion in column C. You should get an answer of 0.3085.

As a general rule when working probability problems with the normal distribution, you should always sketch a distribution, locate the mean with a vertical line, and shade in the portion you are trying to determine. Before you start work, look at your sketch and make an estimate of the answer. (Does the shaded portion look like 20% or like 60% of the total distribution?) If you make a habit of drawing sketches and estimating answers, you will avoid careless errors.

LEARNING CHECK

To help avoid mistakes, always sketch a normal distribution and shade in the portion you want.

1. Find the proportion of a normal distribution that is located in the tail beyond each z-score listed:

   a. $z = +1.00$ **b.** $z = +0.80$ **c.** $z = -2.00$ **d.** $z = -0.33$

2. Find the proportion of a normal distribution that is located between the mean and each z-score listed:

   a. $z = -0.50$ **b.** $z = -1.50$ **c.** $z = +0.67$ **d.** $z = +2.00$

3. Find the proportion of a normal distribution that is located between the
z- score boundaries listed:
  a. Between $z = -0.50$ and $z = +0.50$
  b. Between $z = -1.00$ and $z = +1.00$
  c. Between $z = -1.96$ and $z = +1.96$

ANSWERS   **1. a.** 0.1587 (15.87%)   **b.** 0.2119 (21.19%)   **c.** 0.0228 (2.28%)
          d. 0.3707 (37.07%)

          2. a. 0.1915 (19.15%)   **b.** 0.4332 (43.32%)   **c.** 0.2486 (24.86%)
          d. 0.4772 (47.72%)

          3. a. 0.3830 (38.30%)   **b.** 0.6826 (68.26%)   **c.** 0.9500 (95.00%)

ANSWERING PROBABILITY QUESTIONS WITH THE UNIT NORMAL TABLE

The unit normal table provides a listing of proportions or probability values corresponding to every possible z-score in a normal distribution. To use this table to answer probability questions, it is necessary that you first transform the X values into z-scores (standardize the distribution) and then use the table to look up the probability value. This process is discussed in Box 6.2.

EXAMPLE 6.4

We now can use the unit normal table to get a precise answer to the probability problem we started earlier in the chapter (see Example 6.2). The goal is to find the probability of randomly selecting an individual who is taller than 6 feet (72 inches). We know that the distribution of adult heights is normal with $\mu = 68$ and $\sigma = 6$. In symbols, we want

$$P(X > 72) = ?$$

Restated as a proportion question, we want to find the proportion of the whole distribution that corresponds to values greater than 72. The whole distribution is drawn in Figure 6.4, and the part we want has been shaded (see page 158).

The first step is to change the X values to z-scores. Specifically, the score of $X = 72$ is changed to

You cannot go directly from a score to the unit normal table. You always must go by way of z-scores. (See Box 6.2.)

$$z = \frac{X - \mu}{\sigma} = \frac{72 - 68}{6} = \frac{4}{6} = 0.67$$

Next, you look up this z-score value in the unit normal table. Because we want the proportion of the distribution that is located beyond $z = 0.67$, the answer will be found in column C. A z-score of 0.67 corresponds to a proportion of 0.2514.

The probability of randomly selecting someone taller than 72 inches is 0.2514, or about 1 out of 4:

$$P(X > 72) = 0.2514 \quad (25.14\%)$$

6.2 FINDING PROBABILITIES FROM A NORMAL DISTRIBUTION

WORKING WITH probabilities for a normal distribution involves two steps: (1) using a z-score formula and (2) using the unit normal table. However, the order of the steps may vary, depending on the type of probability question you are trying to answer.

In one instance, you may start with a known X value and have to find a probability that is associated with it (as in Example 6.4). First you must convert the X value to a z-score using formula 5.1 (page 131). Then you consult the unit normal table to get the probability associated with the particular area of the graph. *Note:* You cannot go directly from the X value to the unit normal table. You must find the z-score first.

However, suppose you begin with a known probability value and want to find the X value associated with it (as in Example 6.5). In this case you use the unit normal table first, to find the z-score that corresponds with the probability value. Then you convert the z-score into an X value using formula 5.2 (page 132).

Figure 6.7 illustrates the steps you must take when moving from an X value to a probability or from a probability back to an X value. This chart, much like a map, guides you through the essential steps as you "travel" between X values and probabilities.

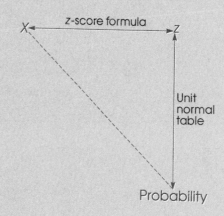

Figure 6.7

This map shows how to find a probability value that corresponds to any specific score, or how to find the score that corresponds to any specific probability value.

In the previous example we started with an X value and used the table to find the corresponding probability value. Looking at the map in Box 6.2, we started at X and moved to P. Like most maps, this one can be used to guide travel in either direction; that is, it is possible to start at P and move to X. To move in this direction means that you start with a specific probability value and then find the corresponding score. The following example demonstrates this type of problem.

EXAMPLE 6.5

Notice that this problem is asking for the 85th percentile.

Scores on the Scholastic Appitude Test (SAT) form a normal distribution with $\mu = 500$ and $\sigma = 100$. What is the minimum score necessary to be in the top 15% of the SAT distribution? This problem is shown graphically in Figure 6.8.

In this problem, we begin with a proportion (15% = 0.15) and we are looking for a score. According to the map in Box 6.2, we can move from P (proportion) to X (score) by going via z-scores. The first step is to use the unit normal table to find the z-score that corresponds to a proportion of 0.15. Because the proportion is located beyond z in the tail of the distribution, we will look in column C for a proportion of 0.1500.

Figure 6.8

The distribution of SAT scores. The problem is to locate the score that separates the top 15% from the rest of the distribution. A line is drawn to divide the distribution roughly into 15% and 85% sections.

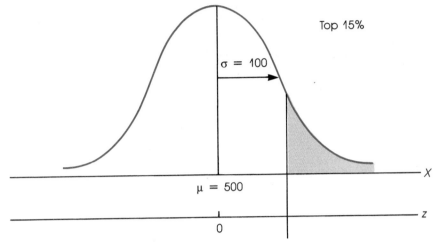

Note that you may not find 0.1500 exactly, but locate the closest value possible. In this case, the closest value in the table is 0.1492, and the z-score that corresponds to this proportion is $z = 1.04$.

The next step is to determine whether the z-score is positive or negative. Remember, the table does not specify the sign of the z-score. Looking at the graph in Figure 6.8, you should realize that the score we want is above the mean, so the z-score is positive, $z = +1.04$.

Now you are ready for the last stage of the solution, that is, changing the z-score into an X value. Using z-score formula 5.2 (page 132) and the known values of μ, σ, and z, we obtain

$$X = \mu + z\sigma$$
$$= 500 + 1.04(100)$$
$$= 500 + 104$$
$$= 604$$

The conclusion for this example is that you must have an SAT score of at least 604 to be in the top 15% of the distribution.

EXAMPLE 6.6   This example demonstrates the process of determining a probability associated with a specified range of scores in a normal distribution. Once again, we will use the distribution of SAT scores which is normal with $\mu = 500$ and $\sigma = 100$. For this distribution, what is the probability of randomly selecting an individual with a score between $X = 600$ and $X = 650$? In probability notation, the problem is to find

$$P(600 < X < 650) = ?$$

Figure 6.9 shows the distribution of SAT scores with the relevant portion shaded. Remember, finding the probability is the same as finding the proportion of the distribution located between 600 and 650.

Figure 6.9

The distribution of SAT scores. The problem is to find the proportion of this distribution located between the values $X = 600$ and $X = 650$. This portion is shaded in the figure.

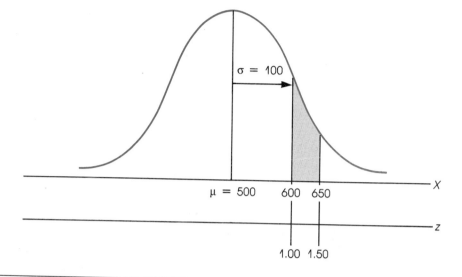

The first step is to transform each of the X values into a z-score:

For $X = 600$: $\quad z = \dfrac{X - \mu}{\sigma} = \dfrac{600 - 500}{100} = \dfrac{100}{100} = 1.00$

For $X = 650$: $\quad z = \dfrac{X - \mu}{\sigma} = \dfrac{650 - 500}{100} = \dfrac{150}{100} = 1.50$

The problem now is to find the proportion of the distribution that is located between $z = +1.00$ and $z = +1.50$. There are several different ways this problem can be solved using the information in the unit normal table. One technique is described here.

Using column C of the table, we find that the area beyond $z = 1.00$ is 0.1587. This includes the portion we want, but also includes an extra portion in the tail. This extra portion is the area beyond $z = 1.50$, and according to the table (column C), it is 0.0668 of the total distribution. Subtracting out the extra portion, we obtain a final answer of

$$P(600 < X < 650) = 0.1587 - 0.0668$$
$$= 0.0919$$

Thus, the probability of randomly selecting an individual with a SAT score between 600 and 650 is $p = 0.0919$ (9.19%).

LEARNING CHECK

1. For a normal distribution with a mean of 80 and a standard deviation of 10, find each probability value requested.

   a. $P(X > 85) = ?$ **c.** $P(X > 70) = ?$

   b. $P(X < 95) = ?$ **d.** $P(75 < X < 100) = ?$

2. For a normal distribution with a mean of 100 and a standard deviation of 20, find each value requested.

   a. What score separates the top 40% from the bottom 60% of the distribution?

b. What is the minimum score needed to be in the top 5% of this distribution?

c. What scores form the boundaries for the middle 60% of this distribution?

3. What is the probability of selecting a score greater than 45 from a positively skewed distribution with $\mu = 40$ and $\sigma = 10$?

ANSWERS 1. a. $p = 0.3085$ (30.85%)   c. $p = 0.8413$ (84.13%)

b. $p = 0.9332$ (93.32%)   d. $p = 0.6687$ (66.87%)

2. a. $z = +0.25$; $X = 105$ b. $z = +1.64$; $X = 132.8$

c. $z = \pm 0.84$; boundaries are 83.2 and 116.8

3. You cannot obtain the answer. The unit normal table cannot be used to answer this question because the distribution is not normal.

6.4 PERCENTILES AND PERCENTILE RANKS

Another useful aspect of the normal distribution is that we can determine percentiles and percentile ranks to answer questions about relative standing.

You should recall from Chapter 2 that the percentile rank of a particular score is defined as the percentage of individuals in the distribution with scores at or below that particular score. The particular score associated with a percentile rank is called a percentile. Suppose, for example, that you have a score of $X = 43$ on an exam and that you know that exactly 60% of the class had scores of 43 or lower. Then your score $X = 43$ has a percentile rank of 60% and your score would be called the 60th percentile. Remember that percentile rank refers to a percentage of the distribution, and percentile refers to a score.

FINDING PERCENTILE RANKS   Finding percentile ranks for normal distributions is straightforward if you visualize the distribution. Because a percentile rank is the percentage of the individuals that fall below a particular score, we will need to find the proportion of the distribution to the left of the score. When finding percentile ranks, we will always be concerned with the percentage on the *left-hand* side of some X value, or, in terms of symbols, $P(X < \text{some value})$.

EXAMPLE 6.7A   A population is normally distributed with $\mu = 100$ and $\sigma = 10$. What is the percentile rank for $X = 114$?

Because a percentile rank indicates one's standing relative to all lower scores, we must focus on the area of the distribution to the *left* of $X = 114$. The distribution is shown in Figure 6.10, and the area of the curve containing all scores below $X = 114$ is shaded. The proportion for this shaded area will give us the percentile rank.

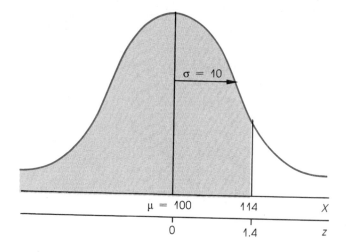

Figure 6.10

The distribution for Example 6.7A. The proportion for the shaded area provides the percentile rank for $X = 114$.

Because the distribution is normal, we can use the unit normal table to find this proportion. The first step is to compute the z-score for the X value we are considering.

$$z = \frac{X - \mu}{\sigma} = \frac{114 - 100}{10} = \frac{14}{10} = 1.40$$

The next step is to consult the unit normal table. Note that the shaded area in Figure 6.10 is made up of two sections: (1) the section below the mean and (2) the section between the mean and the z-score. The area below the mean is exactly one-half ($p = 0.5000$, or 50%) of the distribution (remember the mean equals the median in a normal distribution). The area between the mean and the z-score is represented in column B of the unit normal table. Adding the proportions for these two sections gives us the entire shaded area. For $z = 1.40$, column B indicates proportion to $p = 0.4192$. Therefore, the proportion of the distribution below $X = 114$ is

$$P = 0.5000 + 0.4192 = 0.9192$$

The percentile rank for $X = 114$ is 91.92%.

EXAMPLE 6.7B For the distribution in Example 6.7A, what is the percentile rank for $X = 92$?

This example is diagramed in Figure 6.11. The score $X = 92$ is placed in the left side of the distribution because it is below the mean. Again, percentile ranks deal with the area of the distribution below the score in question. Therefore, we have shaded the area to the left of $X = 92$.

First the X-value is transformed to a z-score:

$$z = \frac{X - \mu}{\sigma} = \frac{92 - 100}{10} = \frac{-8}{10} = -0.80$$

Figure 6.11

The distribution for Example 6.7B. The proportion for the shaded area provides the percentile rank for X = 92.

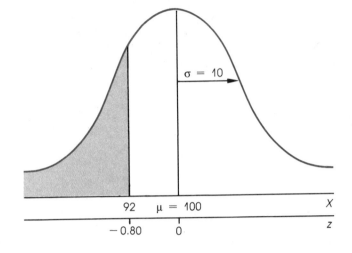

Now the unit normal table can be consulted. The proportion in the left-hand tail beyond $z = -0.80$ can be found in column C. According to the unit normal table, for $z = 0.80$ the proportion in the tail is $p = 0.2119$. This also is the area beyond $z = -0.80$. Thus the percentile rank for $X = 92$ is 21.19%. That is, a score of 92 is greater than 21.19% of the scores in the distribution.

Remember, the normal distribution is symmetrical. Therefore, the proportion in the right-hand tail beyond $z = 0.80$ is identical to that in the left-hand tail beyond $z = -0.80$.

FINDING PERCENTILES The process of finding a particular percentile is very similar to the process used in Example 6.5. You are given a percentage (this time a percentile rank) and you must find the corresponding X value (the percentile). You should recall that finding a X value from a percentage requires the intermediate step of determining the z-score for that proportion of the distribution. The following example demonstrates this process for percentiles.

EXAMPLE 6.8 A population is normally distributed with $\mu = 60$ and $\sigma = 5$. For this population, what is the 34th percentile?

In this example we are looking for an X value (percentile) that has 34% (or $p = 0.3400$) of the distribution below it. This problem is illustrated in Figure 6.12. Note that 34% is roughly equal to one-third of the distribution, so the corresponding shaded area in Figure 6.12 is located entirely on the left-hand side of the mean. In this problem, we begin with a proportion (34% = 0.3400) and we are looking for a score (the percentile). The first step in moving from a proportion to a score is to find the z-score (Box 6.2). You must look at the unit normal table to find the z-score that corresponds to a proportion of 0.3400. Because the proportion is in the tail beyond z, you must look in column C for a proportion of 0.3400. However, there is no entry in the table for the proportion of exactly 0.3400. Instead we use the closest value, which you will find to be $p = 0.3409$. The z-score corresponding to this value is $z =$

Be careful: The table does not differentiate positive and negative z-scores. You must look at your sketch of the distribution to determine the sign.

Figure 6.12

The distribution for Example 6.8.

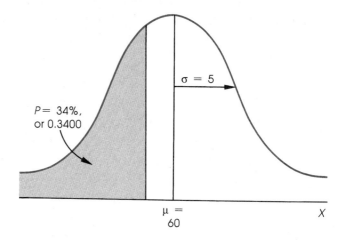

$\sigma = 5$

$P = 34\%$, or 0.3400

$\mu = 60$

X

−0.41. Note that it is a negative z-score because it is below the mean (Figure 6.12). Thus the X value for which we are looking has a z of −0.41.

The next step is to convert the z-score to an X value. Using the z-score formula solved for X, we obtain

$$X = \mu + z\sigma$$
$$= 60 + (-0.41)(5)$$
$$= 60 - 2.05$$
$$= 57.95$$

The 34th percentile for this distribution is $X = 57.95$. This answer makes sense because the 50th percentile for this example is 60 (the mean and median). Therefore, the 34th percentile has to be a value less than 60.

QUARTILES Percentiles divide the distribution into 100 equal parts, each corresponding to 1% of the distribution. The area in a distribution can also be divided into four equal parts called quartiles, each corresponding to 25%. We first looked at quartiles in Chapter 4 (page 101) in considering the semi-interquartile range. The first quartile ($Q1$) is the score that separates the lowest 25% of the distribution from the rest. Thus the first quartile is the same as the 25th percentile. Similarly, the second quartile ($Q2$) is the score that has 50% (two quarters) of the distribution below it. You should recognize the $Q2$ is the median or 50th percentile of the distribution. Finally, the third quartile ($Q3$) is the X value that has 75% (three quarters) of the distribution below it. The $Q3$ for a distribution is also the 75% percentile.

For a normal distribution, the first quartile always corresponds to $z = -0.67$, the second quartile corresponds to $z = 0$ (the mean), and the third quartile corresponds to $z = +0.67$ (Figure 6.13). These values can be found by consulting the unit normal table and are true of any normal distribution. This makes finding quartiles and the semi-interquartile range straightforward

Figure 6.13

The *z*-scores corresponding to the first, second, and third quartiles in a normal distribution.

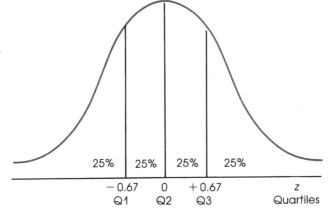

On Chapter 4 (page 101), the semi-interquartile range was defined as

| | 25% | 25% | 25% | 25% |
(This is represented in the figure above)

for normal distributions. The following example demonstrates the use of quartiles.

EXAMPLE 6.9 A population is normally distributed and has a mean of $\mu = 50$ with a standard deviation of $\sigma = 10$. Find the first, second, and third quartile, and compute the semi-interquartile range.

The first quartile, $Q1$, is the same as the 25th percentile. The 25th percentile has a corresponding *z*-score of $z = -0.67$. With $\mu = 50$ and $\sigma = 10$, we can determine the X value of $Q1$.

$$X = \mu + z\sigma$$
$$= 50 + (-0.67)(10)$$
$$= 50 - 6.7$$
$$= 43.3$$

The second quartile, $Q2$, is also the 50th percentile, or median. For a normal distribution, the median equals the mean, so $Q2$ is 50. By the formula, with a *z*-score of 0, we obtain

$$X = \mu + z\sigma$$
$$= 50 + 0(10)$$
$$= 50$$

The third quartile, $Q3$, is also the 75th percentile. It has a corresponding *z*-score of $z = +0.67$. Using the *z*-score formula solved for X, we obtain

$$X = \mu + z\sigma$$
$$= 50 + 0.67(10)$$
$$= 50 + 6.7$$
$$= 56.7$$

On Chapter 4 (page 101), the semi-interquartile range was defined as one-half the distance between the first and third quartile, or

$$\text{semi-interquartile range} = \frac{(Q3 - Q1)}{2}$$

For this example, the semi-interquartile range is

$$
\begin{aligned}
\text{semi-interquartile range} \; &= \frac{(Q3 - Q1)}{2} \\
&= \frac{(56.7 - 43.3)}{2} \\
&= \frac{13.4}{2} \\
&= 6.7
\end{aligned}
$$

Notice that $Q1$ and $Q3$ are the same distance from the mean (6.7 points in the previous example). $Q1$ and $Q3$ will always be equidistant from the mean for normal distributions because normal distributions are symmetrical. Therefore, one-half of the distance between $Q1$ and $Q3$ (the semi-interquartile range by definition) will also equal the distance of $Q3$ from mean (see Figure 6.13). The distance of $Q3$ from the mean can be obtained simply by multiplying the z-score for $Q3$ ($z = 0.67$) times the standard deviation. Using this shortcut greatly simplifies the computation. For a normal distribution.

> Remember, $z\sigma$ is a deviation score, or distance from the mean (Chapter 5).

$$\text{semi-interquartile range} = 0.67\sigma \tag{6.1}$$

Remember, this simplified formula is used *only* for normal distributions.

LEARNING CHECK
1. A population is normally distributed and has a mean of $\mu = 90$ with $\sigma = 8$. Find the following values.
   a. The percentile rank for $X = 100$
   b. The percentile rank for $X = 88$
   c. The 85th percentile
   d. The 10th percentile

2. For the population in Example 1, find $Q1$, $Q3$, and the semi-interquartile range.

ANSWERS
1. **a.** 89.44% **b.** 40.13% **c.** $X = 98.32$ **d.** $X = 79.76$
2. $Q1 = 84.64$, $Q3 = 95.36$, semi-interquartile range $= 5.36$

6.5 PROBABILITY AND THE BINOMIAL DISTRIBUTION

When a variable is measured on a scale consisting of exactly two categories, the resulting data are called binomial. The term *binomial* can be loosely translated as "two names," referring to the two categories on the measurement scale.

Binomial data can occur when a variable naturally exists with only two categories. For example, people can be classified as male or female and a coin toss results in either head or tails. It also is common for a researcher to simplify data by collapsing it into two categories. For example, a psychologist may use personality scores to classify people as either high or low in aggression.

In binomial situations, the researcher often knows the probabilities associated with each of the two categories. With a balanced coin, for example, $P(\text{heads}) = P(\text{tails}) = \frac{1}{2}$. The question of interest is the number of times each category occurs in a series of trials or in a sample of individuals. For example:

What is the probability of obtaining 15 heads in 20 tosses of a balanced coin?

What is the probability of obtaining more than 40 introverts in a sampling of 50 college freshmen?

As we shall see, the normal distribution serves as an excellent model for computing probabilities with binomial data.

THE BINOMIAL DISTRIBUTION

To answer probability questions about binomial data, we need to examine the binomial distribution. To define and describe this distribution we first introduce some notation.

1. The two categories are identified as A and B.

2. The probabilities (or proportions) associated with each category are identified as,

$$p = P(A) = \text{the probability of } A$$

$$q = P(B) = \text{the probability of } B$$

Notice that $p + q = 1.00$ because A and B are the only two possible outcomes.

3. The number of individuals or observations in the sample is identified by n.

4. The variable X refers to the number of times category A occurs in the sample.

Notice that X can have any value from 0 (none of the sample is in category A) to n (all the sample is in category A).

DEFINITION

Using the notation presented here, the *binomial distribution* shows the probability associated with each value of X from $X = 0$ to $X = n$.

A simple example of a binomial distribution is presented next.

EXAMPLE 6.10

Figure 6.14 shows the binomial distribution for the number of heads obtained in two tosses of a balanced coin. This distribution shows that it is possible to obtain as many as 2 heads or as few as 0 heads in two

Figure 6.14

The binomial distribution showing the probability for the number of heads in two tosses of a balanced coin.

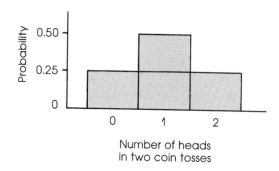

tosses. The most likely outcome (highest probability) is to obtain exactly 1 head in two tosses. The construction of this binomial distribution is discussed in detail next.

For this example, the event we are considering is a coin toss. There are two possible outcomes, heads and tails. We assume the coin is balanced, so

$$p = P(\text{heads}) = \tfrac{1}{2}$$
$$q = P(\text{tails}) = \tfrac{1}{2}$$

We are looking at a sample of $n = 2$ tosses and the variable of interest is

$$X = \text{the number of heads}$$

To construct the binomial distribution, we will look at all the possible outcomes from tossing a coin 2 times. The complete set of 4 outcomes is listed below.

1ST TOSS	2ND TOSS	
Heads	Heads	(both heads)
Heads	Tails	(each sequence has
Tails	Heads	exactly 1 head)
Tails	Tails	(no heads)

Notice that there are 4 possible outcomes when you toss a coin 2 times. Only 1 of the 4 outcomes has 2 heads, so the probability of obtaining 2 heads is $p = \tfrac{1}{4}$. Similarly, 2 of the 4 outcomes have exactly 1 head, so the probability of one head is $p = \tfrac{2}{4} = \tfrac{1}{2}$. Finally, the probability of no heads ($X = 0$) is $p = \tfrac{1}{4}$. These are the probabilities shown in Figure 6.14.

You should notice that this binomial distribution can be used to answer probability questions. For example, what is the probability of obtaining at least 1 head in 2 tosses? According to the distribution shown in Figure 6.14, the answer would be $\tfrac{3}{4}$.

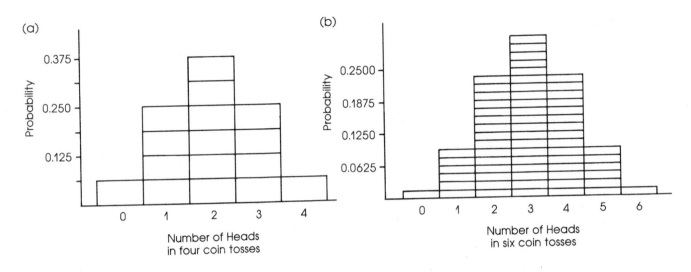

Figure 6.15

Binomial distributions showing probabilities for the number of heads in 4 tosses of a balanced coin (left) and in 6 tosses of a balanced coin (right).

Similar binomial distributions have been constructed for the number of heads in 4 tosses of a balanced coin and for 6 tosses of a coin (Figure 6.15). It should be obvious from the binomial distributions shown in Figures 6.14 and 6.15 that the binomial distribution tends toward a normal shape, especially when the sample size (*n*) is relatively large.

It should not be surprising that the binomial distribution tends to be normal. With $n = 10$ coin tosses, for example, the most likely outcome would be to obtain around $X = 5$ heads. On the other hand, values far from 5 would be very unlikely—you would not expect to get all 10 heads or all 10 tails (0 heads) in 10 tosses. Notice that we have described a normal-shaped distribution: The probabilities are highest in the middle (around $X = 5$), and they taper off as you move toward either extreme.

THE NORMAL APPROXIMATION TO THE BINOMIAL DISTRIBUTION

We have stated that the binomial distribution tends to approximate a normal distribution, particularly when *n* is large. To be more specific, the binomial distribution will be a nearly perfect normal distribution when *pn* and *qn* are both equal to or greater than 10. Under these circumstances, the binomial distribution will approximate a normal distribution with the following parameters:

Note: The value of 10 for *pn* or *qn* is a general guide, not an absolute cutoff. Values slightly less than 10 still provide a good approximation. However, with smaller values the normal approximation becomes less accurate as a substitute for the binomial distribution.

$$\text{Mean: } \mu = pn \tag{6.2}$$

$$\text{Standard Deviation: } \sigma = \sqrt{npq} \tag{6.3}$$

Within this normal distribution, each value of *X* has a corresponding *z*-score,

$$z = \frac{X - \mu}{\sigma} = \frac{X - pn}{\sqrt{npq}} \tag{6.4}$$

Figure 6.16

The relation between the binomial distribution and the normal distribution. The binomial distribution is always a discrete histogram, and the normal distribution is a continuous, smooth curve. Each *X* value is represented by a bar in the histogram or a section of the normal distribution.

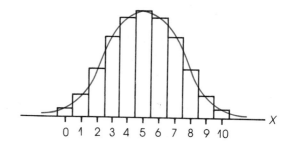

The fact that the binomial distribution tends to be normal in shape means that we can compute probability values directly from *z*-scores and the unit normal table.

It is important to remember that the normal distribution is only an approximation of a true binomial distribution. Binomial values, such as the number of heads in a series of coin tosses, are *discrete*. The normal distribution is *continuous*. However, the normal approximation provides an extremely accurate model for computing binomial probabilities in many situations. Figure 6.16 shows the difference between the discrete binomial distribution (histogram) and the normal distribution (smooth curve). Although the two distributions are slightly different, the area under the distributions is nearly equivalent. Remember, it is the area under the distribution that is used to find probabilities. To gain maximum accuracy when using the normal approximation, you must remember that each *X* value in the binomial distribution is actually an interval, not a point on the scale. In the histogram, this interval is represented by the width of the bar. In Figure 6.16, for example, *X* = 6 is actually an interval bounded by the real limits of 5.5 and 6.5. To find the probability of obtaining a score of *X* = 6, you should find the area of the normal distribution that is contained between the two real limits. If you are using the normal approximation to find the probability of obtaining a score greater than *X* = 6, you should use the area beyond the real limit boundary of 6.5. The following two examples demonstrate how the normal approximation to the binomial distribution is used to compute probability values.

EXAMPLE 6.11 Suppose you are taking a multiple-choice test where each question has four possible answers. If there are 48 questions on the test, what is the probability that you would get exactly 14 questions correct by simply guessing at the answers?

If you are just guessing, then the probability of getting a question correct is $p = \frac{1}{4}$ and the probability of guessing wrong is $q = \frac{3}{4}$. With a sample of $n = 48$ questions, this example meets the criteria for using the normal approximation to the binomial:

$$pn = \tfrac{1}{4}(48) = 12$$

$$qn = \tfrac{3}{4}(48) = 36 \qquad \text{(both greater than 10)}$$

Therefore, the distribution showing the number correct out of 48 questions will be normal with parameters:

Figure 6.17

The binomial distribution (normal approximation) for the number of answers guessed correctly (X) on a 48-question multiple-choice test. The shaded portion corresponds to the probability of guessing exactly 14 questions. Notice that the score $X = 14$ corresponds to an interval bounded by $X = 13.5$ and $X = 14.5$.

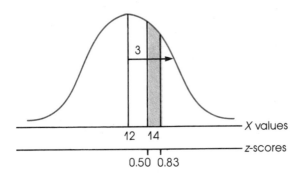

$$\mu = pn = 12$$
$$\sigma = \sqrt{npq} = \sqrt{9} = 3$$

Remember, use the real limits when determining probabilities from the normal approximation to the binomial distribution.

This distribution is shown in Figure 6.17. We want the proportion of this distribution that corresponds to $X = 14$; that is, the portion bounded by $X = 13.5$ and $X = 14.5$. This portion is shaded in Figure 6.17. To find the shaded portion, we first convert each X value into a z-score. For $X = 13.5$,

$$z = \frac{X - \mu}{\sigma} = \frac{13.5 - 12}{3} = 0.50$$

For $X = 14.5$,

$$z = \frac{X - \mu}{\sigma} = \frac{14.5 - 12}{3} = 0.83$$

Looking up these values in the unit normal table, we find

a. The area beyond $z = 0.50$ is 0.3085.

b. The area beyond $z = 0.83$ is 0.2033.

Therefore, the area between the two z-scores would be

$$0.3085 - 0.2033 = 0.1052$$

You should remember that this value is an approximation to the exact probability value. However, it is a reasonably accurate approximation. To illustrate the accuracy of the normal approximation, the exact probability of getting $X = 14$ questions correct from the binomial distribution is 0.1015. Notice that the normal approximation value of 0.1052 is very close to the exact probability of 0.1015. As we mentioned earlier, the normal distribution provides an excellent approximation for finding binomial probabilities.

EXAMPLE 6.12   Once again suppose that you are taking a multiple-choice test with 4 possible answers for each of 48 questions. If you simply guess the answer for each question, what is the probability that you would get more than 14 correct?

This is the same binomial situation that we considered in the previous example. For each question, the two categories are "correct" and "incorrect," and the probabilities are

$$p = P(\text{correct}) = \tfrac{1}{4}$$

$$q = P(\text{incorrect}) = \tfrac{3}{4}$$

Caution: If the question asked for the probability of 14 or more correct, you would use the area beyond 13.5. Read the question carefully.

The normal approximation for this binomial distribution is shown in Figure 6.17. Because we want the probability of obtaining *more than* 14 correct, we must find the area located in the tail of the distribution beyond $X = 14.5$. (Remember, a score of 14 correct corresponds to the interval from 13.5 to 14.5. We want the area beyond this interval.) The first step is to find the z-score corresponding to the boundary $X = 14.5$.

$$z = \frac{X - \mu}{\sigma} = \frac{14.5 - 12}{3} = 0.83$$

Now we can look up the probability in the unit normal table. In this case, we want the proportion in the tail of the distribution beyond $z = 0.83$.

The value from the unit normal table is 0.2033. This is the answer we want. If you are simply guessing on the exam, the probability of getting more than 14 questions correct is $p = 0.2033$, or 20.33%.

LEARNING CHECK

1. Under what circumstances is the normal distribution an accurate approximation to the binomial distribution?

2. A multiple-choice test consists of 48 questions with 4 possible answers for each question. What is the probability that you would get more than 20 questions correct just by guessing?

3. If you toss a balanced coin 36 times, you would expect, on the average to get 18 heads and 18 tails. What is the probability of obtaining exactly 18 heads in 36 tosses?

ANSWERS

1. When pn and qn are both greater than 10.

2. $p = \tfrac{1}{4}, q = \tfrac{3}{4}; P(X > 20.5) = P(z > 2.83) = 0.0023$

3. $z = \pm 0.17, p = 0.1350$

SUMMARY

1. The probability of a particular event A is defined as a fraction or proportion:

$$P(A) = \frac{\text{number of outcomes classified as A}}{\text{total number of possible outcomes}}$$

2. This definition is accurate only for a random sample. There are two requirements that must be satisfied for a random sample:

a. Every individual in the population has an equal chance of being selected.

b. When more than one individual is being selected, the probabilities must stay constant. This means there must be sampling with replacement.

3. All probability problems can be restated as proportion problems. The "probability of selecting a king from a deck of cards" is equivalent to the "proportion of the deck that consists of kings." For frequency distributions, probability questions can be answered by determining proportions of area. The "probability of selecting an individual with an IQ greater than 108" is equivalent to the "proportion of the whole population that consists of IQs above 108."

4. For normal distributions, these probabilities (proportions) can be found in the unit normal table. This table provides a listing of the proportions of a normal distribution that corresponds to each z-score value. With this table it is possible to move between X values and probabilities using a two-step procedure:
  a. The z-score formula (Chapter 5) allows you to transform X to z or to change z back to X.
  b. The unit normal table allows you to look up the probability (proportion) corresponding to each z-score or the z-score corresponding to each probability.

5. A percentile rank measures the relative standing of a score in a distribution. Expressed as a percent, it indicates the proportion of individuals with scores at or below a particular X value. For a normal distribution, you must determine the proportion (percent) of the distribution that falls to the left of the score in question. This percent of the distribution is the percentile rank of that score.

6. A percentile is the X value that is associated with a percentile rank. For example, if 80% of the scores in a distribution are less than 250, then X = 250 is the 80th percentile. Note that the 50th percentile is the median of the distribution.

7. Quartiles are the scores that divide the distribution into four areas that make up one-quarter of the distribution in each area. Thus, the first quartile (Q1) is equivalent to the 25th percentile. The second quartile (Q2) is also the 50th percentile (the median), and the third quartile is the same as the 75th percentile. For a normal distribution, the semi-interquartile range can be obtained by a special formula,

$$\text{semi-interquartile range} = 0.67\sigma$$

8. The binomial distribution is used whenever the measurement procedure simply classifies individuals into exactly two categories. The two categories are identified as A and B, with probabilities of

$$P(A) = p \quad \text{and} \quad P(B) = q$$

9. The binomial distribution gives the probability for each value of X, where X equals the number of occurrences of category A in a series of n events. For example, X equals the number of heads in $n = 10$ tosses of a coin.

10. When pn and qn are both at least 10, the binomial distribution is closely approximated by a normal distribution with

$$\mu = pn$$
$$\sigma = \sqrt{npq}$$

11. In the normal approximation to the binomial distribution, each value of X has a corresponding z-score:

$$z = \frac{X - \mu}{\sigma} = \frac{X - pn}{\sqrt{npq}}$$

With the z-score and the unit normal table, you can find probability values associated with any value of X. For maximum accuracy, however, you must remember that each X value is actually an interval bounded by real limits. Use the appropriate real limits when computing z-scores and probabilities.

KEY TERMS

probability

random sample

sampling with replacement

percentile rank

unit normal table

binomial distribution

percentile

normal approximation (binomial)

—— Focus on Problem Solving ——

1. We have defined probability as being equivalent to a proportion, which means that you can restate every probability problem as a proportion problem. This definition is particularly useful when you are working with frequency distribution graphs where the population is represented by the whole graph and probabilities (proportions) are represented by portions of the graph. When working problems with the normal distribution, you always should start with a sketch of the distribution. You should shade the portion of the graph that reflects the proportion you are looking for.

2. When using the unit normal table you must remember that the proportions in the table (columns B and C) correspond to specific portions of the distribution. This is important because you will often need to translate the proportions from a problem into specific proportions provided in the table. Also, remember that the table allows you to move back and forth between z-scores and proportions. You can look up a given z to find a proportion, or you can look up a given proportion to find the corresponding z-score. However, you cannot go directly from an X value to a probability in the unit normal table. You must first compute the z-score for X. Likewise, you cannot go directly from a probability value to a raw score. First you have to find the z-score associated with the probability (see Box 6.2).

3. Remember, the unit normal table shows only positive z-scores in column A. However, since the normal distribution is symmetrical, the probability values in columns B and C also apply to the half of the distribution that is below the mean. To be certain that you have the correct sign for z, it helps to sketch the distribution showing μ and X.

4. A common error for students to to use negative values for proportions on the left-hand side of the normal distribution. Proportions (or probabilities) are always positive: 10% is 10% whether it is in the left or right tail of the distribution.

5. The proportions in the unit normal table are accurate only for normal distributions. If a distribution is not normal, you cannot use the table.

6. When determining percentile ranks, it helps to sketch the distribution first. Remember, shade in the area to the left of the particular X value. Its percentile rank will be the proportion of the distribution in the shaded area. You will need to compute the z-score for the X value to find the proportion in the unit normal table. Percentile ranks are always expressed as a percent (%) of the distribution.

7. Percentiles are X values. When asked to find the 90th percentile, you are looking for the X value that has 90% (or 0.9000) of the distribution below (to the left of) it. The procedure of finding a percentile requires that you go from a proportion to a z-score, then from z-score to X value (Box 6.2).

8. For maximum accuracy when using the normal approximation to the binomial distribution, you must remember that each X value is an interval bounded by real limits. For example, to find the probability of obtaining an X value greater than 10, you should use the real limit 10.5 in the z-score formula. Similarly, to find the probability of obtaining an X value less than 10, you should use the real limit 9.5.

—— *Demonstration 6.1* ——

FINDING PROBABILITY FROM THE UNIT NORMAL TABLE

A population is normally distributed with a mean of $\mu = 45$ and a standard deviation of $\sigma = 4$. What is the probability of randomly selecting a score that is greater than 43? In other words, what proportion of the distribution consists of scores greater than 43?

STEP 1   Sketch the distribution.
          You should always start by sketching the distribution, identifying the mean and standard deviation ($\mu = 45$ and $\sigma = 4$ in this example). You should also find the approximate location of the specified score and draw a vertical line through the distribution at that score. The score of $X = 43$ is lower than the mean and therefore it should be placed somewhere to the left of the mean. Figure 6.18(a) shows the preliminary sketch.

STEP 2   Shade in the distribution.
          Read the problem again to determine whether you want the proportion greater than the score (to the right of your vertical line) or less than the score (to the left of the line). Then shade in the appropriate portion of the distribution. In this demonstration, we are considering scores greater than 43. Thus, we shade in the distribution to the right of this score (Figure 6.18). Notice that if the shaded area covers more than one-half of the distribution, then the probability should be greater than 0.5000.

STEP 3   Transform the X value to a z-score.
          Remember, to get a probability from the unit normal table, we must first convert the X value to a z-score.

$$z = \frac{X - \mu}{\sigma} = \frac{43 - 45}{4} = \frac{-2}{4} = -0.5$$

STEP 4   Consult the unit normal table.
          Look up the z-score (ignoring the sign) in the unit normal table. Find the two proportions in the table that are associated with the z-score and write the two proportions in the appropriate regions on the figure. Remember, column B gives the proportion of area between μ and z, and column C gives the area in the tail beyond z. Figure 6.18(c) shows the proportions for

Figure 6.18

Sketches of the distribution for Demonstration 6.1.

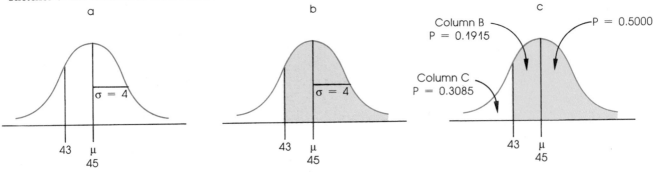

different regions of the normal distribution. For the tail beyond $z = -0.5$, $p = 0.3085$ (column C). Between z and μ the proportion is $p = 0.1915$ (column B). The entire right side of the distribution (everything above μ) makes up one-half of the distribution, or $p = 0.5000$.

STEP 5   Determine the probability.

   If one of the proportions in Step 4 corresponds exactly to the entire shaded area, then that proportion is your answer. Otherwise, you will need to do some additional arithmetic. Looking at the sketch of the distribution [Figure 6.18(c)], take note of the proportions that correspond to the shaded region of the graph and add these proportions. The result is the proportion for the entire shaded area. This is the probability we are looking for.

$$P(X > 43) = 0.1915 + 0.5000 = 0.6915$$

Demonstration 6.2

PROBABILITY AND THE BINOMIAL DISTRIBUTION

Suppose you forgot to study for a quiz and now must guess on every question. It is a true-false quiz with $n = 40$ questions. What is the probability that you will get at least 26 questions correct just by chance? Stated in symbols,

$$P(X \geq 26) = ?$$

STEP 1   Identify p and q.

   This problem is a binomial situation, where

p = probability of guessing correctly = 0.50

q = probability of guessing incorrectly = 0.50

With $n = 40$ quiz items, both pn and qn are greater than 10. Thus the criteria for the normal approximation to the binomial distribution are satisfied:

$pn = 0.50(40) = 20$

$qn = 0.50(40) = 20$

STEP 2   Identify the parameters and sketch the distribution.

   The normal approximation will have a mean and standard deviation as follows:

$\mu = pn = 0.5(40) = 20$

$\sigma = \sqrt{npq} = \sqrt{10} = 3.16$

Figure 6.19 shows the distribution. We are looking for the probability of getting $X = 26$ or more questions correct. Remember, when determining probabilities from the binomial distribution, we must use real limits. Because we are interested in scores equal to or greater than 26, we will use the real lower limit for 26 (25.5). By using the real lower limit, we include the entire interval (25.5 to 26.5) that corresponds to $X = 26$. In Figure 6.19, everything to the right of $X = 25.5$ is shaded.

Figure 6.19

The normal approximation for a binomial distribution with $\mu = 20$ and
$\sigma = 3.16$. The proportion of all scores
equal to or greater than 26 is shaded.
Notice that the real lower limit (25.5)
for $X = 26$ is used.

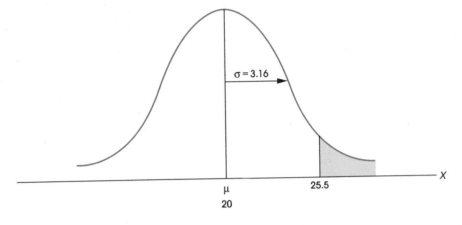

STEP 3   Compute the z-score and find the probability.
         The z-score for $X = 25.5$ is calculated as follows:

$$z = \frac{X - pn}{\sqrt{npq}} = \frac{25.5 - 20}{3.16} = +1.74$$

The shaded area in Figure 6.19 corresponds to column C of the unit normal table.
For the z-score of 1.74, the proportion of the shaded area is $P = 0.0409$. Thus, the
probability of getting at least 26 questions right just by guessing is

$$P(X \geq 26) = 0.0409, \quad \text{or} \quad 4.09\%$$

PROBLEMS

1. In a psychology class of 60 students there are 15
   males and 45 females. Of the 15 men, only 5 are
   freshmen. Of the 45 women, 20 are freshmen. If you
   randomly sample an individual from this class,
   a. What is the probability of obtaining a female?
   b. What is the probability of obtaining a freshman?
   c. What is the probability of obtaining a male fresh-
      man?

2. A jar contains 10 black marbles and 20 white marbles. If you are taking random sample of three marbles from this jar and the first two marbles are both
   white, what is the probability that the third marble
   will be black?

3. What is sampling with replacement and why is it
   used?

4. Find the proportion of the normal distribution that
   lies in the tail beyond each of the following z-scores:
   a. $z = 0.43$ c. $z = -1.35$
   b. $z = 1.68$ d. $z = -0.29$

5. Find the proportion of the normal distribution that is
   located between the following z-score boundaries:
   a. Between $z = 0.25$ and $z = 0.75$
   b. Between $z = -1.00$ and $z = +1.00$
   c. Between $z = 0$ and $z = 1.50$
   d. Between $z = -0.75$ and $z = 2.00$

6. For a normal distribution with a mean of $\mu = 80$
   and $\sigma = 12$,
   a. What is the probability of randomly selecting a
      score greater than 83?
   b. What is the probability of randomly selecting a
      score greater than 74?
   c. What is the probability of randomly selecting a
      score less than 92?
   d. What is the probability of randomly selecting a
      score less than 62?

7. One question on a multiple-choice test asked for the
   probability of selecting a score greater than $X = 50$
   from a normal population with $\mu = 60$ and $\sigma = 20$.

The answer choices were:
a. 0.1915   **b.** 0.3085   **c.** 0.6915

Sketch a distribution showing this problem, and without looking at the unit normal table, explain why answers a and b cannot be correct.

8. A normal distribution has a mean of 120 and a standard deviation of 20. For this distribution,
   a. What score separates the top 40% (highest scores) from the rest?
   b. What score corresponds to the 90th percentile?
   c. What range of scores would form the middle 60% of this distribution?

9. It takes Tom an average of $\mu = 30$ minutes to drive to work. The distribution of driving times is nearly normal with $\sigma = 10$ minutes. If Tom leaves home at 9:05, what is the probability that he will be late for a 9:30 meeting at work?

10. A normal distribution has $\mu = 75$ with $\sigma = 9$. Find the following probabilities.
   a. $P(X < 86) = ?$
   b. $P(X > 60) = ?$
   c. $P(X > 80) = ?$
   d. $P(X > 94) = ?$
   e. $P(63 < X < 88) = ?$
   f. The probability of randomly selecting a score within 3 points of the mean.

11. A normal distribution has a mean of 80 and a standard deviation of 10. For this distribution, find each of the following probability values:
   a. $P(X > 75) = ?$ **d.** $P(65 < X < 95) = ?$
   b. $P(X < 65) = ?$.   **e.** $Pl(84 < X = ?$
   c. $P(X < 100) = ?$

12. The scores on a psychology exam form a normal distribution with $\mu = 80$ and $\sigma = 8$. On this exam, Tom has a score of $X = 84$. Mary's score is located at the 60th percentile. John's score corresponds to a z-score of $z = 0.75$. If these three students are listed from highest score to lowest score, what is the correct ordering?

13. Scores on the college entrance exam are normally distributed with $\mu = 500$ and $\sigma = 100$.
   a. What is the minimum score needed to be in the top 2% on this exam?
   b. What is the 70th percentile on this exam?
   c. John has an exam score of $X = 630$. What is his percentile rank?
   d. What scores (X values) form the boundaries for the middle 95% of this distribution?
   e. Find the semi-interquartile range.

14. A positively skewed distribution has a mean of 100 and a standard deviation of 12. What is the probability of randomly selecting a score greater than 106 from this distribution? (Be careful; this is a trick problem.)

15. A normal distribution has a mean of 60 and a standard deviation of 10.
   a. Find the semi-interquartile range for this distribution.
   b. If the standard deviation were 20, what would be the value for the semi-interquartile range?
   c. In general, what is the relation between the standard deviation and the semi-interquartile range for a normal distribution?

16. A mathematics instructor teaches the same algebra course to a section of humanities students and to a section of preengineering students. The results of the final exam for each section are summarized as follows. Assume that both distributions are normal.

HUMANITIES	ENGINEERING
$\mu = 63$	$\mu = 72$
$\sigma = 12$	$\sigma = 8$

   a. Bill is in the humanities section and earned a grade of $X = 74$ on the final. What is his percentile rank in this section? What would his rank be if he were in the pre-engineering section?
   b. Tom is in the pre-engineering section. His grade on the final exam corresponds to a percentile rank of 40%. What rank would he have if he were in the humanities section?
   c. Mary scored at the 60th percentile in the humanities section, and Jane scored at the 31st percentile in the preengineering section. What are their scores?

17. All entering freshmen are required to take an English proficiency placement exam (EPPE). Based on these exam scores, the college assigns students to different sections of introductory English. The top 25% of the class goes into the advanced course, the middle 50% goes into the regular English course, the students in the bottom 25% are assigned to a remedial English course. For this year's class the distribution of EPPE scores was approximately normal with $\mu = 68$ and $\sigma = 7.5$. What scores should be used as the cutoff values for assigning students to the three English courses?

18. The scores on a civil service exam form a normal distribution with $\mu = 100$ and $\sigma = 20$. Only those

individuals scoring in the top 20% on this exam are interviewed for jobs.
  a. What is the minimum score needed to qualify for an interview?
  b. Because there was an unusually high demand for new employees this year, the civil service board offered job interviews to everyone scoring above $X = 108$. What percentage of the individuals taking the exam were offered interviews?

19. A social psychologist has developed a new test designed to measure social aggressiveness. The scores on this test form a normal distribution with $\mu = 60$ and $\sigma = 9$. Based on these test scores, the psychologist wants to classify the population into five categories of aggressiveness:

  I:　The meek (the lowest 5%)

  II:　The mild (the next 20%)

  III:　The average (the middle 50%)

  IV:　The aggressive (the next 20%)

  V:　The dangerous (the top 5%)

  What scores should be used to form the boundaries for these categories?

20. A normal distribution has $\mu = 60$ and $\sigma = 8$. Find the following.
  a. The percentile rank for $X = 70$
  b. The percentile rank for $X = 53$
  c. The percentile rank for $X = 79$

21. For the distribution in problem 20, find the following values.
  a. The 85th percentile
  b. The 60th percentile
  c. The 20th percentile

22. For the distribution in problem 20, find
  a. $Q1, Q2, Q3$
  b. The semi-interquartile range

23. A normal distribution has a mean of $\mu = 120$ with $\sigma = 15$. Find the following values.
  a. The 15th percentile
  b. The 88th percentile
  c. The percentile rank for $X = 142$
  d. The percentile rank for $X = 102$
  e. The percentile rank for $X = 120$
  f. The semi-interquartile range

24. The normal approximation to the binomial distribution is accurate only when both pn and qn are greater than 10. This requirement is violated in both of the following situations. In each case, explain why the normal distribution is not an appropriate substitute for the real binomial distribution. (*Hint:* Calculate the mean and sketch each binomial distribution.)

  Situation I:　$n = 6, p = .5,$ and $q = .5$
  Situation II:　$n = 50, p = .9,$ and $q = .1$

25. One common test for extra-sensory perception (ESP) requires subjects to predict the suit of a card that is randomly selected from a complete deck. If a subject has no ESP and is just guessing, find each of the probabilities requested
  a. What is the probability of a correct prediction on each trial?
  b. What is the probability of correctly predicting more than 18 out of 48 cards?

26. A college dormitory recently sponsored a taste comparison between two major soft drinks. Of the 64 students who participated, 39 selected brand A. If there really is no preference between the two drinks, what is the probability that 39 or more would choose Brand A just by chance?

27. A trick coin has been weighted so that the probability of heads is 0.8 and the probability of tails is 0.2.
  a. If you toss the coin 100 ties, how many heads would you expect on the average?
  b. What is the probability of obtaining more than 95 heads in 100 tosses?
  c. What is the probability of obtaining less than 95 heads in 100 tosses?
  d. What is the probability of obtaining exactly 95 heads in 100 tosses?

28. a. What is the probability of getting more than 30 heads in 50 tosses of a balanced coin?
  b. What is the probability of getting more than 60 heads in 100 tosses of a balanced coin?
  c. Parts a and b of this question both asked for the probability of getting more than 60% heads in a series of coin tosses ($\frac{30}{50} = \frac{60}{100} = 60\%$). Explain why the two probabilities are different.

29. A true-false test has 36 questions. If a passing grade on this test is $X = 24$ correct, what is the probability of obtaining a passing grade just by guessing?

CHAPTER 7

PROBABILITY AND SAMPLES: THE DISTRIBUTION OF SAMPLE MEANS

TOOLS YOU WILL NEED

The following items are considered essential background material for this chapter. If you doubt your knowledge of any of these items, you should review the appropriate chapter and section before proceeding.

- Random sampling (Chapter 6)
- Probability and the normal distribution (Chapter 6)
- z-Scores (Chapter 5)

CONTENTS

PREVIEW

Now that you have some understanding of probability, consider the following problem:

> Imagine an urn filled with balls. Two-thirds of the balls are one color, and the remaining one-third is a second color. One individual selects 5 balls from the urn and finds that 4 are red and 1 is white. Another individual selects 20 balls and finds that 12 are red and 8 are white. Which of these two individuals should feel more confident that the urn contains two-thirds red balls and one-third white balls, rather than the opposite?[*]

When Tversky and Kahneman (1974) presented this problem to a group of experimental subjects, they found that most people felt that the first sample (4 out of 5) provided much stronger evidence and therefore should give more confidence. At first glance, it may appear that this is the correct decision. After all, the first sample contained $\frac{4}{5}$ = 80% red balls, and the second sample, contained only $\frac{12}{20}$ = 60% red balls. However, you should also notice that the two samples differ in another important respect: the sample size. One sample contains only $n = 5$, and the other sample contains $n = 20$. The correct answer to the problem is that the larger sample (12 out of 20) gives a much stronger justification for concluding that the balls in the urn are predominately red. It appears that most people tend to focus on the sample proportion and pay very little attention to the sample size.

The importance of sample size may be easier to appreciate if you approach the urn problem from a different perspective. Suppose that you are the individual assigned responsibility for selecting a sample and then deciding which color is in the majority. Before you select your sample, you are offered a choice of selecting either a sample of 5 balls or a sample of 20 balls. Which would you prefer? It should be clear that the larger sample would be better. With a small number, you risk obtaining an unrepresentative sample. By chance, you could end up with 3 white balls and 2 red balls even though the reds outnumber the whites by two to one. The larger sample is much more likely to provide an accurate representation of the population. This is an example of the *law of large numbers*, which states that large samples will be representative of the population from which they are selected. One final example should help demonstrate this law. If you were tossing a coin, you probably would not be greatly surprised to obtain 3 heads in a row. However, if you obtained a series of 20 heads in a row, you almost certainly would suspect a trick coin. The large sample has more authority.

In this chapter we will examine the relation between samples and populations. More specifically, we will consider the relation between sample means and the population mean. As you will see, sample size is one of the primary considerations in determining how well a sample mean represents the population mean.

---

[*]Adapted from Tversky, A., and Kahneman, D. (1974). Judgments under uncertainty: Heuristics and biases. *Science*, 185, 1124–1131. Copyright 1974 by the AAAS.

7.1 OVERVIEW

The purpose of this chapter is to establish the set of rules that relate samples to populations. These rules, which are of great importance to later topics in inferential statistics, will be based on probabilities. In contrast to Chapter 6, in which we looked at the probability of obtaining a certain score, we will now be looking at samples of more than one score. Therefore, the focus will shift to probability questions involving sample means.

The difficulty of working with samples is that samples generally are not identical to the populations from which they come. More precisely, the statistics calculated for a sample will differ from the corresponding parameters for the population. For example, the sample mean may differ from the population mean. This difference, or *error*, is referred to as *sampling error*.

DEFINITION
Sampling error is the discrepancy, or amount of error, between a sample statistic and its corresponding population parameter.

Furthermore, samples are variable; they are not all the same. If you take two separate samples from the same population, the samples will be different. They will contain different individuals, they will have different scores, and they will have different sample means. How can you tell which sample is giving the best description of the population? Can you even predict how well a sample will describe its population? What is the probability of selecting a sample that has a certain sample mean? These questions can be answered once we establish the set of rules that relate samples to populations.

7.2 THE DISTRIBUTION OF SAMPLE MEANS

As noted, two separate samples probably will be different even though they are taken from the same population. The samples will have different individuals, different scores, different means, and the like. In most cases, it is possible to obtain thousands of different samples from one population. With all these different samples coming from the same population, it may seem hopeless to try to establish some simple rules for the relations between samples and populations. But fortunately the huge set of possible samples does fall into a relatively simple, orderly, and predictable pattern that makes it possible to accurately predict the characteristics of a sample if you know about the population it is coming from. These general characteristics are specified by the distribution of sample means.

DEFINITION
The distribution of sample means is the collection of sample means for all the possible random samples of a particular size *(n)* that can be obtained from a population.

You should notice that the distribution of sample means is different from distributions we have considered before. Until now we always have discussed distributions of scores; now the values in the distribution are not scores, they are statistics (sample means). Because statistics are obtained from samples, a distribution of statistics is referred to as a sampling distribution.

DEFINITION
A sampling distribution is a distribution of statistics obtained by selecting all the possible samples of a specific size from a population.

Thus, the distribution of sample means is an example of a sampling distribution. In fact, it often is called the sampling distribution of $\overline{X}$.

Before we consider the general rules concerning this distribution, we will look at a simple example that provides an opportunity to examine the distribution in detail.

EXAMPLE 7.1
Consider a population that consists of only four scores: 2, 4, 6, 8. This population is pictured in the frequency distribution histogram in Figure 7.1.

Figure 7.1

Frequency distribution histogram for a population of four scores: 2, 4, 6, 8.

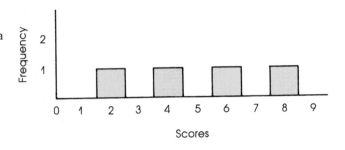

We are going to use this population as the basis for constructing the distribution of sample means for $n = 2$. Remember, this distribution is the collection of sample means from all the possible random samples of $n = 2$ from this population. We begin by looking at all the possible samples. Each of the 16 different samples is listed in Table 7.1.

Next, we compute the mean, $\overline{X}$, for each of the 16 samples (see the last column of Table 7.1). The 16 sample means form the distribution of sample means. These 16 values are organized in a frequency distribution histogram in Figure 7.2.

Remember, random sampling requires sampling with replacement.

Notice that the distribution of sample means has some predictable and some very useful characteristics:

1. The sample means tend to pile up around the population mean. For this example, the population mean is $\mu = 5$, and the sam-

Table 7.1

All the possible samples of $n = 2$ scores that can be obtained from the population presented in Figure 7.1[a].

| | SCORES | | SAMPLE MEAN |
SAMPLE	FIRST	SECOND	$\overline{X}$
1	2	2	2
2	2	4	3
3	2	6	4
4	2	8	5
5	4	2	3
6	4	4	4
7	4	6	5
8	4	8	6
9	6	2	4
10	6	4	5
11	6	6	6
12	6	8	7
13	8	2	5
14	8	4	6
15	8	6	7
16	8	8	8

[a]Notice that the table lists *random samples*. This requires sampling with replacement, so it is possible to select the same score twice. Also note that samples are listed systematically. The first four samples are all the possible samples that have $X = 2$ as the first score; the next four samples all have $X = 4$ as the first score; etc. This way we are sure to have all the possible samples listed, although the samples probably would not be selected in this order.

Figure 7.2

The distribution of sample means for $n = 2$. This distribution shows the 16 sample means from Table 7.1.

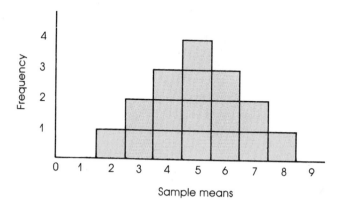

ple means are clustered around a value of 5. It should not surprise you that the sample means tend to approximate the population mean. After all, samples are supposed to be representative of the population.

2. The distribution of sample means is approximately normal in shape. This is a characteristic that will be discussed in detail later and will be extremely useful because we already know a great deal about probabilities and the normal distribution (Chapter 6).

Remember, our goal in this chapter is to answer probability questions about samples with $n > 1$.

3. Finally, you should notice that we can use the distribution of sample means to answer probability questions about sample means (see Box 7.1). For example, if you take a sample of $n = 2$ scores from the original population, what is the probability of obtaining a sample mean greater than 7? In symbols, $P(\overline{X} > 7) = ?$.

Because probability is equivalent to proportion, the probability question can be restated as follows: Of all the possible sample means, what proportion have values greater than 7? In this form the question is easily answered by looking at the distribution of sample means. All the possible sample means are pictured (Figure 7.2), and only 1 out of the 16 means has a value greater than 7. The answer, therefore, is 1 out of 16, or $p = \frac{1}{16}$.

THE CENTRAL LIMIT THEOREM

Example 7.1 demonstrates the construction of the distribution of sample means for a relatively simple, specific situation. In most cases, however, it will not be possible to list all the samples and compute all the possible sample means. Therefore, it is necessary to develop the general characteristics of the distribution of sample means that can be applied in any situation. Fortunately, these characteristics are specified in a mathematical proposition known as the *central limit theorem*. This important and useful theorem serves as a cornerstone for much of inferential statistics. Following is the essence of the theorem:

7.1   PROBABILITY AND THE DISTRIBUTION OF SAMPLE MEANS

I HAVE a bad habit of losing playing cards. This habit is compounded by the fact that I always save the old deck in hope that someday I will find the missing cards. As a result, I have a drawer filled with partial decks of playing cards. Suppose I take one of these almost-complete decks, shuffle the cards carefully, and then randomly select one card. What is the probability that I will draw a king?

You should realize that it is impossible to answer this probability question. To find the probability of selecting a king, you must know how many cards are in the deck and exactly which cards are missing. (It is crucial that you know whether or not any kings are missing.) The point of this simple example is that any probability question requires that you have complete information about the population from which the sample is being selected. In this case, you must know all the possible cards in the deck before you can find the probability for selecting any specific card.

In this chapter we are examining probability and sample means. In order to find the probability for any specific sample mean, you first must know *all the possible sample means*. Therefore, we begin by defining and describing the set of all possible sample means that can be obtained from a particular population. Once we have specified the complete set of all possible sample means (i.e., the distribution of sample means), we will be able to find the probability of selecting any specific sample mean.

DEFINITION

Central Limit Theorem: For any population with mean μ and standard deviation σ, the distribution of sample means for sample size n will approach a normal distribution with a mean of μ and a standard deviation of $\sigma/\sqrt{n}$ as n approaches infinity.

The value of this theorem comes from two simple facts. First, it describes the distribution of sample means for *any population,* no matter what shape, or mean, or standard deviation. Second, the distribution of sample means "approaches" a normal distribution very rapidly. By the time the sample size reaches $n = 30$, the distribution is almost perfectly normal.

Notice that the central limit theorem describes the distribution of sample means by identifying the three basic characteristics that describe any distribution: shape, central tendency, and variability. Each of these will be examined.

THE SHAPE OF THE DISTRIBUTION OF SAMPLE MEANS

It has been observed that the distribution of sample means tends to be a normal distribution. In fact, this distribution will be almost perfectly normal if either one of the following two conditions is satisfied.

1. The population from which the samples are selected is a normal distribution.

2. The number of scores *(n)* in each sample is relatively large, around 30 or more.

(As n gets larger, the distribution of sample means will closely approximate a normal distribution. In most situations when $n > 30$, the distribution is almost perfectly normal regardless of the shape of the original population.)

The fact that the distribution of sample means tends to be normal should not be surprising. Whenever you take a sample from a population, you expect the sample mean to be near to the population mean. When you take lots of different samples, you expect the sample means to "pile up" around μ, resulting in a normal shaped distribution. You can see this tendency emerging (although it is not yet normal) in Figure 7.2.

THE MEAN OF THE DISTRIBUTION OF SAMPLE MEANS: THE EXPECTED VALUE OF $\overline{X}$

The expected value of $\overline{X}$ is often identified by the symbol $\mu_{\overline{X}}$, signifying the "mean of the sample means." However, $\mu_{\overline{X}}$ is always equal to μ, so we will continue to use the symbol μ to refer to the mean for the population of scores and the mean for the distribution of sample means.

You probably noticed in Example 7.1 that the distribution of sample means is centered around the mean of the population from which the samples were obtained. In fact, the average value of all the sample means is exactly equal to the value of the population mean. This fact should be intuitively reasonable; the sample means are expected to be close to the population mean, and they do tend to pile up around μ. The formal statement of this phenomenon is that the mean of the distribution of sample means always will be identical to the population mean. This mean value is called the *expected value of $\overline{X}$*.

In commonsense terms, a sample mean is "expected" to be near its population mean. When all of the possible sample means are obtained, the average value will be identical to μ.

DEFINITION

The mean of the distribution of sample means will be equal to μ (the population mean) and is called the *expected value of $\overline{X}$*.

THE STANDARD ERROR OF $\overline{X}$

So far we have considered the shape and the central tendency of the distribution of sample means. To completely describe this distribution, we need one more characteristic, variability. The value we will be working with is the standard deviation for the distribution of sample means, and it is called the *standard error of $\overline{X}$*.

DEFINITION

The standard deviation of the distribution of sample means is called the *standard error of $\overline{X}$*.

Like any measure of standard deviation, the standard error defines the standard, or typical, distance from the mean. In this case, we are measuring the standard distance between a single sample mean $\overline{X}$ and the population mean μ.

The notation that is used to identify the standard error is $\sigma_{\overline{X}}$. The σ indicates that we are measuring a standard deviation or a standard distance from the mean. The subscript $\overline{x}$ indicates that we are measuring standard deviation for sample means.

$$\text{standard error} = \sigma_{\overline{X}} = \text{standard distance between } \overline{X} \text{ and } \mu$$

The standard error is an extremely valuable measure because it specifies precisely how well a sample mean estimates its population mean, that is, how much error you should expect, on the average, between $\overline{X}$ and μ. Remember, one basic reason for taking samples is to use the sample data to answer

7.2   THE ERROR BETWEEN $\overline{X}$ AND μ

CONSIDER A population consisting of $N = 3$ scores: 1, 8, 9. The mean for this population is $\mu = 6$. Using this sample, try to find a random sample of $n = 2$ scores with a sample mean ($\overline{X}$) exactly equal to the population mean. (Try selecting a few samples; record the scores and the sample mean for each of your samples.)

You may have guessed that we constructed this problem so that it is impossible to obtain a sample mean that is identical to μ. The point of this exercise is to emphasize the notion of sampling error. Samples are not identical to their populations, and a sample mean generally will not provide a perfect estimate of the population mean. The purpose of standard error is to provide a quantitative measure of the difference (or error) between sample means and the population mean. Standard error is the standard distance between $\overline{X}$ and μ.

questions about the population. Specifically, we can use the sample mean as an estimate of the population mean. Although we do not expect a sample mean to be exactly the same as the population mean, it should provide a good estimate. The standard error tells how good the estimate will be (see Box 7.2).

The numerical value of the standard error is determined by two characteristics: (1) the variability of the population from which the sample is selected and (2) the size of the sample. We will examine each of these separately.

1. Standard Deviation of the Population. The accuracy with which a sample mean represents its population mean is determined in part by the individual scores in the sample. If the sample contains extreme scores (far from μ), then the sample mean is likely to be very different from μ. On the other hand, if all the individual scores are close to μ, then the sample mean will certainly give an accurate representation of the population mean. Standard deviation measures the standard distance between an individual score (X) and the population mean (μ). When σ is small, each individual score is close to μ, and the average score ($\overline{X}$) is also close to μ. With a large standard deviation, you are likely to obtain extreme scores that can increase the distance between $\overline{X}$ and μ.

2. The Sample Size. As a general rule, the larger the sample, the more accurately the sample represents its population. This rule is also known as the *law of large numbers* (see the Preview).

DEFINITION   The *law of large numbers* states that the larger the sample size *(n)*, the more probable it is that the sample mean will be close to the population mean.

If you were assigned the job of estimating the average IQ for freshmen at your college, you would expect to get a more accurate measure from a group of $n = 100$ than from a sample of $n = 2$. The larger the sample, the smaller the standard error.

These two characteristics are combined in the formula for the standard error:

$$\text{standard error} = \sigma_{\bar{X}} = \frac{\sigma}{\sqrt{n}} \tag{7.1}$$

Notice that when the population standard deviation (σ) is small, the standard error will be small. Also, if the sample size *(n)* is increased, the standard error will get smaller.

The standard error formula also may be expressed in terms of the population variance, σ^2.

$$\sigma_{\bar{X}} = \sqrt{\frac{\sigma^2}{n}} \tag{7.2}$$

Although we will usually use the population standard deviation to determine the standard error (formula 7.1), the formula based on variance will be useful later (Chapter 10).

LEARNING CHECK

1. What is the difference between a distribution of raw scores and a sampling distribution?

2. Under what circumstances is the distribution of sample means guaranteed to be normal?

3. A population of scores is normal with $\mu = 50$ and $\sigma = 12$. Describe the distribution of sample means for samples of size $n = 16$ selected from this population. (Describe shape, central tendency, and variability for the distribution.)

4. A population of scores is normal with $\mu = 100$ and $\sigma = 16$.
   a. If you randomly select one score from this population, then, on the average, how close should the score be to the population mean?
   b. If you selected a random sample of $n = 4$ scores, how much error would you expect, on the average, between the sample mean and the population mean?
   c. If you selected a random sample of $n = 64$ scores, how much error, on the average, should there be between the sample mean and the population mean?

ANSWERS

1. A distribution of raw scores is composed of original measurements, and a sampling distribution is composed of statistics.

2. The distribution of sample means will be normal if the original population is normal or if the sample size is at least 30.

3. The distribution of sample means will be normal because the population is normal. It will have an expected value of $\mu = 50$ and a standard error of $\sigma_{\bar{X}} = 12/\sqrt{16} = 3$.

4. a. Standard deviation, $\sigma = 16$, measures standard distance from the mean.
   b. For a sample of $n = 4$ the standard error would be $16/\sqrt{4} = 8$ points.
   c. For a sample of $n = 64$ the standard error would be $16/\sqrt{64} = 2$ points.

MORE ABOUT STANDARD ERROR

The concept of standard error is probably the most important new idea in this chapter. One important aspect of this new concept is that the standard error decreases as sample size increases. The law of large numbers described this relationship in the previous section. Another important aspect of standard error is that it is derived from the population standard deviation (see formula 7.1). In fact, you might consider the population standard deviation as the "starting point" for standard error. The following example illustrates these characteristics of standard error.

EXAMPLE 7.2

Let's begin with a population of IQ scores that is normally distributed and has a standard deviation of $\sigma = 15$. Notice that we purposely did not tell you the mean of this population. Your job is to get a sample of people from this population, measure their IQs, and use the sample mean to estimate the value for μ.

Would you rather have a sample of $n = 1$, $n = 9$, or $n = 25$ people? We saw previously that sample size is a critical factor in determining how well a sample represents the population—the larger the sample, the more accurately the sample represents the population. Clearly, the larger your sample, the better you can estimate μ. The standard error tells you exactly how much better.

Figure 7.3 shows the distributions of sample means based on samples of $n = 1$, $n = 9$, and $n = 25$. Each distribution shows the collection of all possible sample means that you would obtain for that particular sample size. Notice that all three sampling distributions are normal because the population of IQ scores is a normal distribution. All three distributions have the same mean (the expected value of $\overline{X}$), which is equivalent to the unknown population mean you are trying to estimate. However, the distributions are very different with respect to variability. Let's look at each of these distributions and their standard errors.

The smallest sample size is $n = 1$. With a sample composed of a single score, the mean for a sample will equal the value of that score, $\overline{X} = X$. Thus, for all possible samples of $n = 1$, the distribution of sample means will be identical to the population of scores. In this case, the

Figure 7.3

The distribution of sample means for samples of size $n = 1$ (left), $n = 9$ (center), and $n = 25$ (right). In each case the original population is normal with $\sigma = 15$ and an unknown mean, $\mu = ?$. Notice that the standard error gets smaller as the sample size gets larger.

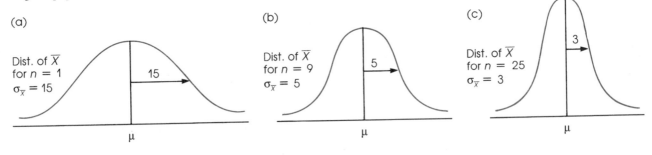

(a)

Dist. of $\overline{X}$ for $n = 1$
$\sigma_{\overline{X}} = 15$ 15

μ

(b)

Dist. of $\overline{X}$ for $n = 9$
$\sigma_{\overline{X}} = 5$ 5

μ

(c)

Dist. of $\overline{X}$ for $n = 25$
$\sigma_{\overline{X}} = 3$ 3

μ

standard error for the sampling distribution will equal the standard deviation of the population. Formula 7.1 confirms this conclusion.

$$\sigma_{\bar{X}} = \frac{\sigma}{\sqrt{n}} = \frac{15}{\sqrt{1}} = 15$$

In this sense, the population standard deviation is the starting point for standard error. Starting with the smallest possible sample ($n = 1$), the standard error equals the population standard deviation [see Figure 7.3(a)].

With larger samples, however, the standard error gets smaller. For $n = 9$ the standard error is

$$\sigma_{\bar{X}} = \frac{\sigma}{\sqrt{n}} = \frac{15}{\sqrt{9}} = \frac{15}{3} = 5$$

That is, the typical (or standard) distance between $\bar{X}$ and μ is 5 points. Figure 7.3(b) illustrates this distribution. Note that sample means in this distribution more closely approximate the population mean than in the previous distribution.

With samples of $n = 25$, the standard error is still smaller.

$$\sigma_{\bar{X}} = \frac{\sigma}{\sqrt{n}} = \frac{15}{\sqrt{25}} = \frac{15}{5} = 3$$

This is another example of the law of large numbers.

A sample of $n = 25$ scores should provide a sample mean that is a much better estimate of μ than you would obtain with a sample of $n = 9$ or $n = 1$. As shown in Figure 7.3(c), there is very little error between $\bar{X}$ and μ (you would expect a 3-point difference on average). The sample means pile up very close to μ.

In summary, this example illustrates that with the smallest possible sample ($n = 1$), the standard error and population standard deviation are the same. When sample size is increased, the standard error gets smaller and sample means will approximate μ more closely. Thus, standard error defines the relation between sample size and the accuracy with which $\bar{X}$ represents μ.

7.3 PROBABILITY AND THE DISTRIBUTION OF SAMPLE MEANS

The primary use of the distribution of sample means is to find the probability associated with any specific sample. You should recall that probability is equivalent to proportion. Because the distribution of sample means presents the entire set of all possible $\bar{X}$'s, we can use proportions of this distribution to determine probabilities. The following example demonstrates this process.

EXAMPLE 7.3 The population of scores on the SAT forms a normal distribution with $\mu = 500$ and $\sigma = 100$. If you take a random sample of $n = 25$ students,

Figure 7.4

The distribution of sample means for $n = 25$. Samples were selected from a normal population with $\mu = 500$ and $\sigma = 100$.

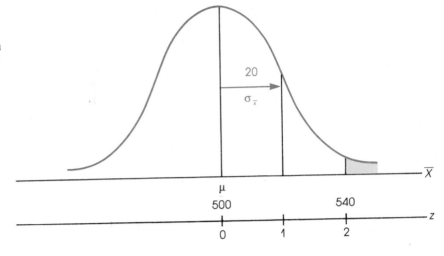

Caution: Whenever you have a probability question about a sample mean, you must use the distribution of sample means.

what is the probability that the sample mean would be greater than $\overline{X} = 540$?

First, you can restate this probability question as a proportion question: Out of all the possible sample means, what proportion have values greater than 540? You know about "all the possible sample means"; this is simply the distribution of sample means. The problem is to find a specific portion of this distribution. The parameters of this distribution are the following:

a. The distribution is normal because the population of SAT scores is normal.

b. The distribution has a mean of 500 because the population mean is $\mu = 500$.

c. The distribution has a standard error of $\sigma_{\overline{X}} = 20$:

$$\sigma_{\overline{X}} = \frac{\sigma}{\sqrt{n}} = \frac{100}{\sqrt{25}} = \frac{100}{5} = 20$$

This distribution of sample means is shown in Figure 7.4.

We are interested in sample means greater than 540 (the shaded area in Figure 7.4), so the next step is to use a z-score to locate the exact position of $\overline{X} = 540$ in the distribution. The value 540 is located above the mean by 40 points, which is exactly two standard deviations (in this case, exactly two standard errors). Thus, the z-score for $\overline{X} = 540$ is $z = +2.00$.

Because this distribution of sample means is normal, you can use the unit normal table to find the probability associated with $z = +2.00$. The table indicates that 0.0228 of the distribution is located in the tail of the distribution beyond $z = +2.00$. Our conclusion is that it is very unlikely, $p = 0.0228$ (2.28%), to obtain a random sample of $n = 25$ students with an average SAT score greater than 540.

7.3 THE DIFFERENCE BETWEEN STANDARD DEVIATION AND STANDARD ERROR

A CONSTANT source of confusion for many students is the difference between standard deviation and standard error. You should remember that standard deviation measures the standard distance between a *score* and the population mean, $X - \mu$. Whenever you are working with a distribution of scores, the standard deviation is the appropriate measure of variability. Standard error, on the other hand, measures the standard distance between a *sample mean* and the population mean, $\overline{X} - \mu$. Whenever you have a question concerning a sample, the standard error is the appropriate measure of variability.

If you still find the distinction confusing, there is a simple solution. Namely, if you always use standard error, you always will be right. Consider the formula for standard error:

$$\text{standard error} = \sigma_{\overline{X}} = \frac{\sigma}{\sqrt{n}}$$

If you are working with a single score, then $n = 1$, and the standard error becomes

$$\text{standard error} = \sigma_{\overline{X}} = \frac{\sigma}{\sqrt{n}} = \frac{\sigma}{\sqrt{1}}$$

$$= \sigma = \text{standard deviation}$$

Thus standard error always measures the standard distance from the population mean, whether you have a sample of $n = 1$ or $n = 100$.

As demonstrated in Example 7.3 it is possible to use a z-score to describe the position of any specific sample within the distribution of sample means. The z-score tells exactly where a specific sample is located in relation to all the other possible samples that could have been obtained. A z-score of $z = +2.00$, for example, indicates that the sample mean is much larger than usually would be expected: It is greater than the expected value of $\overline{X}$ by twice the standard distance. The z-score for each sample mean can be computed by using the standard z-score formula with a few minor changes. First, the value we are locating is a sample mean rather than a score, so the formula uses $\overline{X}$ in place of X. Second, the standard deviation for this distribution is measured by the standard error, so the formula uses $\sigma_{\overline{X}}$ in place of σ (see Box 7.3). The resulting formula, giving the z-score value corresponding to any sample mean, is

$$z = \frac{\overline{X} - \mu}{\sigma_{\overline{X}}} \tag{7.3}$$

Every sample mean has a z-score that describes its position in the distribution of sample means. Using z-scores and the unit normal table, it is possible to find the probability associated with any specific sample mean (as in Example 7.3). The following example demonstrates that it also is possible to make quantitative predictions about the kinds of samples that should be obtained from any population.

EXAMPLE 7.4

Suppose you simply wanted to predict the kind of value that would be expected for the mean SAT score for a random sample of $n = 25$ students. For example, what range of values would be expected for the sample mean 80% of the time? The simplest way of answering this question is to look at the distribution of sample means. Remember, this distribution is the collection of all the possible sample means, and it will show which samples are likely to be obtained and which are not.

As demonstrated in Example 7.3, the distribution of sample means for $n = 25$ will be normal, will have an expected value of $\mu = 500$, and will have a standard error of $\sigma_{\overline{X}} = 20$. Looking at this distribution, shown again in Figure 7.5, it is clear that the most likely value to expect for a sample mean is around 500. To be more precise, we can identify the range of values that would be expected 80% of the time by locating the middle 80% of the distribution. Because the distribution is normal, we can use the unit normal table. To find the middle 80%, we need exactly 40% (or 0.40) between the mean and the z-score on each side. Looking up a proportion of 0.40 in the unit normal table (column B) gives a z-score of $z = 1.28$. By definition, a z-score of 1.28 indicates that the score is 1.28 standard error units from the mean. This distance is $1.28 \times 20 = 25.6$ points. The mean is 500, so 25.6 points either direction would give a range from 474.4 to 525.6. This is the middle 80% of all the possible sample means, so you can expect any particular sample mean to be in this range 80% of the time.

Remember, when answering probability questions, it always is helpful to sketch a distribution and shade in the portion you are trying to find.

LEARNING CHECK

1. A normal population has $\mu = 80$ and $\sigma = 10$. A sample of $n = 25$ scores has a mean $\overline{X} = 83$. What is the z-score corresponding to this sample mean?

2. A random sample of $n = 9$ scores is selected from a normal population with $\mu = 40$ and $\sigma = 6$.

   a. What is the probability of obtaining a sample mean greater than 41?
   b. What is the probability of obtaining a sample mean less than 46?

Figure 7.5

The middle 80% of the distribution of sample means for $n = 25$. Samples were selected from a normal population with $\mu = 500$ and $\sigma = 100$.

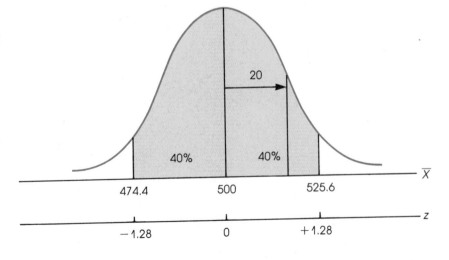

3. A skewed distribution has $\mu = 60$ and $\sigma = 8$.

    a. What is the probability of obtaining a sample mean greater than $\overline{X} = 62$ for a sample of $n = 4$? (Be careful.)

    b. What is the probability of obtaining a sample mean greater than $\overline{X} = 62$ for a sample of $n = 64$?

ANSWERS   **1.** The standard error is 2. $z = \frac{3}{2} = 1.5$.

    2. a. $\overline{X} = 41$ corresponds to $z = +0.50$. The probability is 0.3085 (30.85%).

    b. $\overline{X} = 46$ corresponds to $z = +3.0$. The probability is 0.9987 (99.87%).

    3. a. Cannot answer because the distribution of sample means is not normal.

    b. With $n = 64$ the distribution of sample means will be normal. $\overline{X} = 62$ corresponds to $z = +2.0$. The probability is 0.0228 (2.28%).

SUMMARY

1. The distribution of sample means is defined as the set of all the possible $\overline{X}$'s for a specific sample size (n) that can be obtained from a given population. The parameters of the distribution of sample means are as follows:

  a. Shape. The distribution of sample means will be normal if either one of the following two conditions is satisfied:

    (1) The population from which the samples are selected is normal.

    (2) The size of the samples is relatively large (around $n = 30$ or more).

  b. Central Tendency. The mean of the distribution of sample means will be identical to the mean of the population from which the samples are selected. The mean of the distribution of sample means is called the expected value of $\overline{X}$.

  c. Variability. The standard deviation of the distribution of sample means is called the standard error of $\overline{X}$ and is defined by the formula

$$\sigma_{\overline{X}} = \frac{\sigma}{\sqrt{n}} \quad \text{or} \quad \sigma_{\overline{X}} = \sqrt{\frac{\sigma^2}{n}}$$

Standard error measures the standard distance between a sample mean $\overline{X}$ and the population mean μ.

2. One of the most important concepts in this chapter is the standard error. The standard error is the standard deviation of the distribution of sample means. It measures the standard distance between a sample mean ($\overline{X}$) and the population mean (μ). The standard error tells how much error to expect if you are using a sample mean to estimate a population mean.

3. The location of each $\overline{X}$ in the distribution of sample means can be specified by a z score:

$$z = \frac{\overline{X} - \mu}{\sigma_{\overline{X}}}$$

Because the distribution of sample means tends to be normal, we can use these z-scores and the unit normal table to find probabilities for specific sample means. In particular, we can identify which sample means are likely and which are very unlikely to be obtained from any given population. This ability to find probabilities for samples is the basis for the inferential statistics in the chapters ahead.

KEY TERMS

sampling error

distribution of sample means

sampling distribution

central limit theorem

expected value of $\overline{X}$

standard error of $\overline{X}$

law of large numbers

Focus on Problem Solving

1. Whenever you are working probability questions about sample means, you must use the distribution of sample means. Remember, every probability question can be restated as a proportion question. Probabilities for sample means are equivalent to proportions of the distribution of sample means.

2. When computing probabilities for sample means, the most common error is to use standard deviation (σ) instead of standard error ($\sigma_{\bar{X}}$) in the z-score formula. Standard deviation measures the typical deviation (or "error") for a single score. Standard error measures the typical deviation (or error) for a sample. Remember, the larger the sample, the more accurately the sample represents the population—that is, the larger the sample, the smaller the error.

$$\text{standard error} = \sigma_{\bar{X}} = \frac{\sigma}{\sqrt{n}}$$

3. Although the distribution of sample means is often normal, it is not always a normal distribution. Check the criteria to be certain the distribution is normal before you use the unit normal table to find probabilities (see 1a of the Summary). Remember, all probability problems with the normal distribution are easier if you sketch the distribution and shade in the area of interest.

Demonstration 7.1

PROBABILITY AND THE DISTRIBUTION OF SAMPLE MEANS

For a normally distributed population with $\mu = 60$ and $\sigma = 12$, what is the probability of selecting a random sample of $n = 36$ scores with a sample mean greater than 64?

In symbols, for $n = 36$, $P(\bar{X} > 64) = ?$

Notice that we may rephrase the probability question as a proportion question. Out of all the possible sample means for $n = 36$, what proportion have values greater than 64?

STEP 1 Sketch the distribution.

We are looking for a specific proportion of *all possible sample means*. Therefore, we will have to sketch the distribution of sample means. We should include the expected value, the standard error, and the specified sample mean.

The expected value for this demonstration is $\mu = 60$. The standard error is

$$\sigma_{\bar{X}} = \frac{\sigma}{\sqrt{n}} = \frac{12}{\sqrt{36}} = \frac{12}{6} = 2$$

Remember, we must use the standard error, *not* standard deviation, because we are dealing with the distribution of sample means.

Find the approximate location of the sample mean and place a vertical line through the distribution. In this demonstration, the sample mean is 64. It is larger than the expected value of $\mu = 60$ and therefore is placed on the right side of the distribution. Figure 7.6(a) depicts the preliminary sketch.

STEP 2 Shade the appropriate area of the distribution.

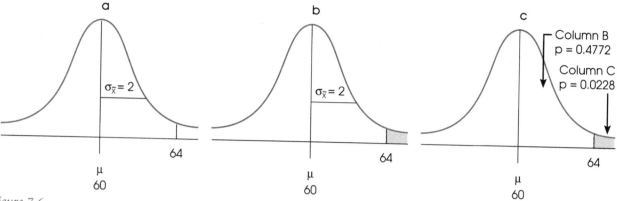

Figure 7.6

Sketches of the distribution for Demonstration 7.1.

Determine whether the problem asks for a proportion greater than (>) or less than (<) the specified sample mean. Then shade the appropriate area of the distribution. In this demonstration, we are looking for the area greater than $\bar{X} = 64$ so we shade the area on the right-hand side of the vertical line [Figure 7.6(b)].

STEP 3   Compute the z-score for the sample mean.

Use the z-score formula for sample means. Remember that it uses standard error in the denominator.

$$z = \frac{\bar{X} - \mu}{\sigma_{\bar{X}}} = \frac{64 - 60}{2} = \frac{4}{2} = 2.00$$

STEP 4   Consult the unit normal table.

Look up the z-score in the unit normal table and note the two proportions in columns B and C. Jot them down in the appropriate areas of the distribution [Figure 7.6(c)]. For this demonstration, the value in column C (the tail beyond z) corresponds exactly to the proportion we want (shaded area). Thus, for $n = 36$,

$$P(\bar{X} > 64) = P(z > +2.00) = 0.0228$$

PROBLEMS

1. Briefly define each of the following:
   a. The distribution of sample means
   b. Expected value of $\bar{X}$
   c. Standard error of $\bar{X}$

2. A population consists of exactly three scores: $X = 0$, $X = 2$, and $X = 4$.
   a. List all the possible random samples of $n = 2$

scores from this population. (You should obtain nine different samples—see Example 7.1.)
   b. Compute the sample mean for each of the nine samples, and draw a histogram showing the distribution of sample means.

3. Two samples are randomly selected from a population. One sample has $n = 5$ scores and the second

has $n = 30$. Which sample should have a mean $(\overline{X})$ that is closer to μ? Explain your answer.

4. You have a population with $\mu = 100$ and $\sigma = 30$.
   a. If you randomly select a single score from this population, then, on the average, how close would you expect the score to be to the population mean?
   b. If you randomly select a sample of $n = 100$ scores, then, on the average, how close would you expect the sample mean to be to the population mean?

5. The distribution of SAT scores is normal with $\mu = 500$ and $\sigma = 100$.
   a. If you selected a random sample of $n = 4$ scores from this population, how much error would you expect between the sample mean and the population mean?
   b. If you selected a random sample of $n = 25$ scores, how much error would you expect between the sample mean and the population mean?
   c. How much error would be expected for a sample of $n = 100$ scores?

6. A population has $\mu = 200$ and $\sigma = 50$. Find the z-score for each of the following sample means:
   a. A sample of $n = 25$ with $\overline{X} = 220$
   b. A sample of $n = 100$ with $\overline{X} = 190$
   c. A sample of $n = 4$ with $\overline{X} = 230$

7. On an immediate memory test, 10-year-old children can correctly recall an average of $\mu = 7$ digits. The distribution of recall scores is normal with $\sigma = 2$.
   a. What is the probability of randomly selecting a child with a recall score less than 6?
   b. What is the probability of randomly selecting a sample of $n = 4$ children whose average recall score is less than 6?

8. Simple reaction times for college students form a normal distribution with $\sigma = 200$ milliseconds and $\sigma = 20$.
   a. What is the probability of randomly selecting a student whose reaction time is less than 190?
   b. What is the probability of randomly selecting a sample of $n = 4$ students with an average reaction time less than 190?
   c. What is the probability of randomly selecting a sample of $n = 25$ students with an average reaction time less than 190?

9. If you select a random sample of $n = 36$ scores from a population with $\mu = 80$ and $\sigma = 24$, then
   a. What is the probability of obtaining a sample mean greater than 84?

b. What is the probability of obtaining a sample mean less than 72?

10. A sample is selected from a population with $\sigma = 10$. If the standard error for this sample is $\sigma_{\overline{X}} = 2$, how many scores are in the sample?

11. If you are taking a random sample from a normal population with $\mu = 100$ and $\sigma = 12$, which of the following outcomes is more likely?
    a. A sample mean greater than 106 for a sample of $n = 4$
    b. A sample mean greater than 103 for a sample of $n = 36$ scores

12. IQ scores form a normal distribution with $\mu = 100$ and $\sigma = 15$.
    a. What is the probability of randomly selecting a sample of $n = 9$ people so that their average IQ is different by more than one point from the population mean? (What is the probability of obtaining a sample mean greater than 101 or less than 99?)
    b. What is the probability of randomly selecting a sample of $n = 100$ individuals so that their average IQ is more than one point away from the population mean?

13. Standard error measures the standard distance between a sample mean and the population mean. For a population with $\sigma = 20$,
    a. How large a sample would be needed to obtain a standard error of less than 10 points?
    b. How large a sample would be needed to have a standard error smaller than 5 points?
    c. If you wanted your sample mean to be within 1 point of the population mean (on the average), how large a sample should you use?

14. A population is normally distributed with $\mu = 100$ and $\sigma = 20$.
    a. Find the z-score corresponding to each of the following samples:

       Sample 1: $n = 4; \overline{X} = 110$

       Sample 2: $n = 25; \overline{X} = 105$

       Sample 3: $n = 100; \overline{X} = 104$

    b. Which of the samples in part a is least likely to be obtained by random sampling?

15. The 27 freshmen in Tower Dormitory finished their first semester with a mean grade-point average of 2.61. They consider this to be a remarkable achievement because the mean GPA for the entire freshman class was only $\mu = 2.35$. If GPAs are normally dis-

tributed with $\sigma = 0.27$, what is the probability that a random sample of $n = 27$ would have an average GPA of 2.61 or higher? Are the freshmen in Tower Dorm justified in being proud?

16. The local hardware store sells screws in 1-pound bags. Because the screws are not identical, the number of screws per bag varies with $\mu = 115$ and $\sigma = 6$. A carpenter needs a total of 600 screws for a particular project. What is the probability that she will have enough screws if she buys five bags? (Assume the distribution is normal.)

17. The average age for registered voters in the county is $\mu = 39.7$ years with $\sigma = 11.8$. The distribution of ages is approximately normal. During a recent jury trial in the county courthouse, a statistician noted that the average age for the 12 jurors was $\overline{X} = 50.4$ years.
    a. How likely is it to obtain a jury this old or older by chance?
    b. Is it reasonable to conclude that this jury is not a random sample of registered voters?

18. At the beginning of this chapter we noted that the law of large numbers says that the larger the sample, the more likely that the sample mean will be close to the population mean. This law can be demonstrated using IQ scores which form a normal distribution with $\mu = 100$ and $\sigma = 16$.
    a. What is the probability of randomly selecting one individual whose IQ is within 5 points of the population mean?
    b. If you select a sample of five people, how likely is it that their average IQ will be within 5 points of the population mean?
    c. How likely is it for a sample of 10 people to have an average IQ within 5 points of the population mean?

19. A manufacturer of flashlight batteries claims that its batteries will last an average of $\mu = 34$ hours of continuous use. Of course, there is some variability in life expectancy with $\sigma = 3$ hours. During consumer testing, a sample of 30 batteries lasted an average of only $\overline{X} = 32.5$ hours. How likely is it to obtain a sample that performs this badly if the manufacturer's claim is true?

20. Error scores for laboratory rats on a standardized

discrimination problem form a normal distribution with $\mu = 85$ and $\sigma = 15$.
    a. Sketch the distribution of sample means for samples of size $n = 10$.
    b. Find the range of values corresponding to the middle 95% of this distribution. Note that 95% of all the possible samples will have a mean in this range.
    c. What is the range of sample means that would contain 99% of all the possible samples of $n = 10$ rats?

21. Boxes of sugar are filled by machine with considerable accuracy. The distribution of box weights is normal and has a mean of 32 ounces with a standard deviation of only 2 ounces. A quality control inspector takes a sample of $n = 16$ boxes and finds the sample contains on average $\overline{X} = 31$ ounces of sugar. What is the probability of obtaining a sample with this much shortchanging in its boxes? Should the inspector suspect that the filling machinery needs repair?

22. Scores on a personality questionnaire form a normal distribution with $\mu = 80$ and $\sigma = 12$. If a random sample of $n = 16$ people is selected and the average personality score is computed for this sample, then
    a. Sketch the distribution of all the possible sample means that could be obtained.
    b. Of all the possible sample means, what proportion will be greater than 85?
    c. Of all the possible sample means, what proportion will be within four points of the population mean?

23. A large grocery store chain in New York has received a shipment of 1000 cases of oranges. The shipper claims that the cases average $\mu = 40$ oranges with a standard deviation of $\sigma = 2$. To check this claim, the store manager randomly selects 4 cases and counts the number of oranges in each case. For these 4 cases, the average number of oranges is $\overline{X} = 38$.
    a. Assuming that the shipper's claim is true, what is the probability of obtaining a sample mean this small?
    b. Based on your answer for part a, does the grocery store manager have reason to suspect that he has been cheated? Explain your answer.

CHAPTER 8

INTRODUCTION TO HYPOTHESIS TESTING

TOOLS YOU WILL NEED

The following items are considered essential background material for this chapter. If you doubt your knowledge of any of these items, you should review the appropriate chapter or section before proceeding.

- z-Scores (Chapter 5)
- Distribution of sample means (Chapter 7)
  - Expected value
  - Standard error
  - Probability of sample means

CONTENTS

Psychologists have noted that stimulation during infancy can have profound effects on the development of infant rats. It has been demonstrated that stimulation (for example, increased handling) and even stress (mild electric shock) result in eyes opening sooner, more rapid brain maturation, decreases in emotionality, faster growth, and larger body weight (see Levine, 1960). Based on these data, one might theorize that increased stimulation and possibly occasional mild stress early in life can be beneficial. Suppose a researcher who is interested in this developmental theory would like to determine whether or not stimulation during infancy also has an effect on human development. This researcher might propose the following hypothesis:

For the population of human infants, extra handling early in life will have an effect on growth as measured by body weight.

Notice that the hypothesis makes a specific prediction about the relationship between an independent variable (handling) and a dependent variable (weight). Because the hypothesis identifies specific variables, it can be evaluated in an experiment. Also note that the hypothesis refers to the entire population.

Of course, it would be impossible to test the entire population of human infants in an experiment. It is reasonable, however, to test the effects of handling for a relatively small sample. Thus, a random sample of new-born infants is selected, and the researcher trains the parents to provide increased handling for their children. When each child in the sample reaches 2 years of age, his or her body weight is recorded. The researcher then uses data from the sample to evaluate the hypothesis. For this example, the researcher would determine whether or not the infants receiving extra handling weighed substantially more than normally expected at 2 years of age.

In this example, as in most scientific research, the investigator is using data from a sample to evaluate a hypothesis about a population. You should recall that the general technique of using sample data as the basis for making conclusions about a population is called inferential statistics. The process of testing hypotheses is one of the standard inferential procedures in statistics. In this chapter we introduce the logic, the notation, and the general mechanics of hypothesis testing. We also spend a lot of time discussing errors in hypothesis testing. You should realize that any inferential procedure is subject to errors. Whether you are making judgments about a person after one short meeting or making conclusions about a population based on a single sample, there is a chance that you will make the wrong decision and reach the wrong conclusion. One of the general goals in the process of hypothesis testing will be to limit or control the probability of errors.

8.1 OVERVIEW

It is usually impossible or impractical for a researcher to observe every individual in a population. Therefore, researchers usually collect data from a sample. Hypothesis testing is a statistical procedure that allows scientists to use sample data to draw inferences about the population of interest.

DEFINITION

Hypothesis testing is an inferential procedure that uses sample data to evaluate the credibility of a hypothesis about a population.

In very simple terms the logic underlying the hypothesis-testing procedure is as follows:

1. First, we state a hypothesis about a population. Usually, the hypothesis concerns the value of a population parameter. For example, we might hypothesize that the mean IQ for registered voters in the United States is $\mu = 110$.

2. Next, we obtain a random sample from the population. For example, we select a random sample of $n = 200$ registered voters.

3. Finally, we compare the sample data with the hypothesis. If the data are consistent with the hypothesis, we will conclude that the hypothesis was reasonable. But if there is a big discrepancy between the data and the hypothesis, we will decide that the hypothesis was wrong.

Although the general logic of hypothesis testing is relatively simple, there are many details involved in standardizing and quantifying the hypothesis testing procedure. In this chapter we will examine these details and develop the general technique of hypothesis testing.

8.2 THE LOGIC OF HYPOTHESIS TESTING

The hypothesis-testing procedure usually begins with an unknown population, specifically, a population with an unknown mean. Often this situation arises after a treatment is administered to a known population (see Figure 8.1). In this case, the researcher begins with an original population with known parameters. For example, suppose the original population is known to be normal with $\mu = 26$ and $\sigma = 4$. The researcher's question concerns what effect the treatment will have on this population. Will the treatment cause the scores to increase or decrease, or will the treatment have no effect whatsoever? The specific question is, What happens to the population mean after treatment? Hypothesis testing is a procedure that will help the researcher determine whether or not a treatment effect occurred. This situation is illustrated in Figure 8.1.

To simplify the hypothesis-testing situation, one basic assumption is made about the effect of the treatment: If the treatment has any effect, it is simply to add (or subtract) a constant amount to each individual's score. You should recall from Chapters 3 and 4 that adding (or subtracting) a constant will not change the shape of the population, nor will it change the standard deviation. Thus we will assume that the population after treatment has the same shape

Figure 8.1

The basic experimental situation for hypothesis testing. It is assumed that the parameter μ is known for the population before treatment. The purpose of the experiment is to determine whether or not the treatment has an effect on the population mean.

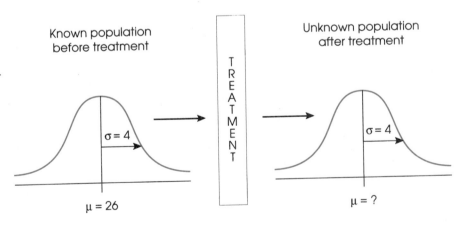

Known population before treatment

Unknown population after treatment

T R E A T M E N T

$\sigma = 4$

$\sigma = 4$

$\mu = 26$

$\mu = ?$

as the original population, and has the same standard deviation as the original population. This assumption is incorporated into the situation shown in Figure 8.1.

The first step in the hypothesis-testing procedure involves stating a hypothesis about the unknown population mean. We could, for example, hypothesize that the treatment has no effect, so that the population mean after treatment is the same as the mean for the original population. Or, we might hypothesize that the treatment will increase each individual's score by 10 points so that the mean for the treated population will be 10 points higher than the mean for the original population. Notice that the hypothesis concerns the entire population.

Next, the researcher would collect sample data. A sample of individuals is selected from the treated population. That is, the researcher obtains a sample of individuals who have received the treatment. The sample data are then used to evaluate the hypothesis. Specifically, the researcher must determine whether the sample data are consistent with the hypothesis or if the sample data contradict the hypothesis. Notice that the researcher is using the information from a sample to evaluate a hypothesis about a population. This is the basis of inferential statistics: using sample data to draw inferences about populations.

In this overview of the hypothesis-testing procedure, you can think of the researcher as a police detective gathering evidence. The sample is the evidence that the researcher uses to build a case for or against the hypothesis. Sometimes the evidence is overwhelming, and the researcher can make confident conclusions about the hypothesis. Often the evidence is not very convincing, and the researcher is uncertain about a conclusion. There is always a possibility that the evidence is misleading and the researcher will reach the wrong conclusion.

Because the process of hypothesis testing involves some uncertainty and can lead to errors, the procedure has been formalized to a standard series of operations. In this way, the researcher has a standardized method for evaluating the evidence from an experiment. Other researchers will recognize and understand exactly how the data were evaluated and how conclusions were reached. In addition, the hypothesis-testing procedure is developed so that a researcher can identify and partially control the risk of an error. Throughout this book we will present hypothesis testing as a four-step procedure. We now examine these steps in more detail, using the research example described in the Preview.

STEP 1: STATING THE HYPOTHESES

Suppose our researcher knows from national health statistics that the average weight for 2-year-olds who are not receiving any special treatment is $\mu = 26$ pounds. To determine whether increased handling has any effect, the researcher must compare the weights from the sample data with this national average. To begin this process, the researcher states two opposing hypotheses. Note that both hypotheses are stated in terms of population parameters.

The first is the *null hypothesis*, or H_0. This hypothesis states that the treatment has no effect. (The null hypothesis always says that there is no effect, no change, no difference, nothing happened—hence the name *null*.) In this example, the null hypothesis states that additional handling during

The goal of inferential statistics is to make general statements about the population by using sample data. Therefore, when testing hypotheses, we make our predictions about the population parameters.

infancy will have *no effect* on body weight for the population of infants. In symbols, this hypothesis would be

$$H_0 : \mu_{\text{infants handled}} = 26 \text{ pounds}$$

(Even with extra handling, the mean weight at 2 years is still 26 pounds.)

DEFINITION
> The *null hypothesis* (H_0) predicts that the independent variable (treatment) has no effect on the dependent variable for the population.

The second hypothesis is simply the opposite of the null hypothesis, and it is called the *scientific* or *alternative hypothesis* (H_1). This hypothesis states that the treatment will have an effect on the dependent variable. For this example, it predicts that handling does alter growth for the population. In symbols, it is represented as

$$H_1 : \mu_{\text{infants handled}} \neq 26$$

(With handling, the mean will be different from 26 pounds.)

DEFINITION
> The *alternative hypothesis* (H_1) predicts that the independent variable (treatment) will have an effect on the dependent variable for the population.

Notice that the alternative hypothesis simply states that there will be some type of change. It does not specify whether the effect will be increased or decreased growth. In some circumstances it is appropriate to specify the direction of the effect in H_1. For example, the researcher might hypothesize that increased handling will increase growth ($\mu > 26$ pounds). This type of hypothesis results in a directional hypothesis test, which will be examined in detail later in this chapter. For now we will concentrate on nondirectional tests, where the hypotheses always state that the treatment has some effect (H_1) or has no effect (H_0). A nondirectional hypothesis test is always appropriate, even when a researcher has a definite prediction that the treatment will increase (or decrease) scores. For this example, we are examining whether handling in infancy does alter growth in some way (H_1) or has no effect (H_0). You should also note that both hypotheses refer to a population whose mean is unknown—namely, the population of infants who receive extra handling early in life.

STEP 2: SETTING THE CRITERIA FOR A DECISION

The researcher will eventually use the data from the sample to evaluate the credibility of the null hypothesis. For this example, the null hypothesis states that the mean for the treated population will still be $\mu = 26$ (the same as the original population). Thus, if our sample of treated infants showed a mean weight close to 26 pounds, we could conclude that the treatment (increased handling) does not seem to have any effect. On the other hand, if our sample weighed much more (or less) than 26 pounds, we could conclude that the increased handling does seem to have an effect on development.

Notice that the final decision is based on a comparison of the sample data versus the null hypothesis. Whenever there is a big discrepancy between the data and the hypothesis, we can conclude that the hypothesis is wrong.

8.1 REJECTING THE NULL HYPOTHESIS VERSUS PROVING THE ALTERNATIVE HYPOTHESIS

IT MAY seem awkward to pay so much attention to the null hypothesis. After all, the purpose of most experiments is to show that a treatment does have an effect, and the null hypothesis states that there is no effect. The reason for focusing on the null hypothesis rather than the alternative hypothesis comes from the limitations of inferential logic. Remember, we want to use the sample data to draw conclusions, or inferences, about a population. Logically, it is much easier to demonstrate that a universal (population) hypothesis is false than to demonstrate that it is true. This principle is shown more clearly in a simple example. Suppose you make the universal statement "all dogs have four legs" and you intend to test this hypothesis by using a sample of one dog. If the dog in your sample does have four legs, have you proved

the statement? It should be clear that one four-legged dog does not prove the general statement to be true. On the other hand, suppose the dog in your sample has only three legs. In this case, you have proved the statement to be false. Again, it is much easier to show that something is false than to prove that it is true.

Hypothesis testing uses this logical principle to achieve its goals. It would be difficult to state "the treatment has an effect" as the hypothesis and then try to prove that this is true. Therefore, we state the null hypothesis, "the treatment has no effect," and try to show that it is false. The end result still is to demonstrate that the treatment does have an effect. That is, we find support for the alternative hypothesis by disproving (rejecting) the null hypothesis.

hypothesis is true. If the outcome of the experiment is consistent with this prediction, then there is no need to be suspicious about the credibility of the null hypothesis. If, on the other hand, the outcome of the experiment is very different from this prediction, then we would reject the null hypothesis because the evidence is overwhelmingly against it. In either case, it is possible that the data obtained from a single experiment can be misleading and cause a researcher to make an incorrect decision. The two possibilities are presented here and in Box 8.2.

Type I errors   It is possible to reject the null hypothesis when in reality the treatment has no effect. The outcome of the experiment could be different from what H_0 predicted just by chance. After all, unusual events do occur. For example, it is possible, although unlikely, to toss a balanced coin five times and have it turn up heads every time. In the experiment we have been considering, it is possible just by chance to select a sample of exceptional infants who display unusual (much less or much greater than normal) growth patterns even though the handling treatment has no effect. In this situation the data would lead us to reject the null hypothesis even though it is correct. This kind of mistake is called a *Type I error* (see Table 8.1), and in psychology it is very serious mistake. A Type I error results in the investigator making a false report of a treatment effect. In the handling experiment, the researcher would claim that handling during infancy alters growth when in fact no such effect exists.

DEFINITION   A *Type I error* consists of rejecting the null hypothesis when H_0 is actually true.

However, you should also notice that we are comparing a sample (the data) versus a population (the null hypothesis). You should recall from Chapter 7 that a sample generally will not be identical to its population. There will almost always be some discrepancy between a sample and its population due to sampling error. The problem for the researcher is to determine whether the difference between the sample data and the null hypothesis is the result of the treatment effect or is simply due to sampling error. When does the sample provide sufficient evidence to conclude that the treatment really does have an effect? To solve this problem, the researcher must establish criteria that define precisely how much difference must exist between the data and the null hypothesis to justify a decision that the null hypothesis is false. The procedure for establishing criteria is considered in Section 8.3. For now, you should recognize that criteria are essential for a researcher to make an objective decision about the hypotheses.

STEP 3: COLLECTING SAMPLE DATA

The next step in hypothesis testing is to obtain the sample data. A random sample of infants would be selected and parents would be trained to provide additional daily handling during the first few months of infancy. Then the body weight of the infants would be measured when they reach 2 years of age. Usually the raw data from the sample are summarized in a single statistic, such as the sample mean or a z-score. Of course, selecting a sample randomly is important because it helps ensure that the sample is representative of the population. For example, it would help avoid the selection of a group of infants that would be unusually small or large, regardless of the treatment.

You also should note that the data are collected only after the researcher has stated hypotheses and established criteria for making a decision. This sequence of events helps ensure that a researcher makes an honest, objective evaluation of the data and does not tamper with the decision criteria after the experiment outcome is known.

STEP 4: EVALUATING THE NULL HYPOTHESIS

In the final step, the researcher compares the data ($\overline{X}$) with the null hypothesis (μ) and makes a decision according to the criteria that were established in step 2. There are two possible decisions, and both are stated in terms of the null hypothesis.

One possibility is that the researcher decides to *reject the null hypothesis*. This decision is made whenever the sample data are substantially different from what the null hypothesis predicts. In this case, the data provide strong evidence that the treatment does have an effect.

The second possibility occurs when the data do not provide convincing evidence of a treatment effect. In this case the sample data are consistent with the null hypothesis, and the statistical decision is to *fail to reject the null hypothesis*. The term *fail to reject* is used because the experiment failed to produce evidence that H_0 is wrong. (See Box 8.1.)

ERRORS IN HYPOTHESIS TESTING

The problem in hypothesis testing is deciding whether or not the sample data are consistent with the null hypothesis. In the second step of the hypothesis-testing procedure, we identify the kind of data that are expected if the null

8.2   A SUMMARY OF STATISTICAL ERRORS

Definitions:

A Type I error is rejecting a true null hypothesis.
A Type II error is failing to reject a false null hypothesis.

Interpretation:

Type I error: The researcher concludes that the treatment does have an effect when, in fact, there is no treatment effect.

Type II error: The researcher concludes that there is no evidence for a treatment effect when, in fact, the treatment does have an effect.

How Does it Happen?:

Type I error: By chance, the sample consists of individuals with extreme scores. As a result, the sample looks different from what we would have expected according to H_0. Note that the treatment has not actually affected the individuals in the sample—they were different from average from the start of the experiment.

Type II error: Although there are several explanations for a type II error, the simplest is that the treatment effect was too small to have a noticeable effect on the sample. As a result, the sample does not appear to have been affected by the treatment. It is also possible that, just by chance, the sample was extreme to start with and in the opposite direction of the treatment effect. The treatment effect, in turn, restores the sample to the average that is expected by H_0. A treatment effect does not appear to have occurred even though it did.

Consequences:

Type I error: Because the sample data appear to demonstrate a treatment effect, the researcher may claim in a published report that the treatment has an effect. This is a false report and can have serious consequences. For one, other researchers may spend precious time and resources trying to replicate the findings to no avail. In addition, the false report creates a false data base upon which other workers develop theories and plan new experiments. In reality, they may be taking a journey down an experimental and theoretical dead end.

Type II error: In this case, the sample data do not provide sufficient evidence to say that the treatment has any effect—that is, the experiment has failed to detect the treatment effect. The researcher can interpret this finding in two different ways:

First, the researcher can conclude that the treatment probably does have an effect but the experiment was not good enough to find it. Perhaps an improved experiment (larger sample, better measurement, more potent treatment, etc.) would be able to demonstrate the treatment effect. The consequence is that refined experiments may be capable of detecting the effect.

Second, the researcher may believe that the statistical decision is correct. Either the treatment has no effect, or the effect is too small to be important. In this case, the experiment is abandoned. Note that this interpretation can have serious consequences. It means that the researcher is giving up a line of research that could have otherwise provided important findings.

Table 8.1

Possible outcomes of a statistical decision

		ACTUAL SITUATION	
		No Effect, H_0 True	Effect Exists, H_0 False
Experimenter's decision	Reject H_0	Type I error	Decision correct
	Retain H_0	Decision correct	Type II error

Type II errors   It also is possible for the data to be consistent with the null hypothesis even when H_0 is false. Suppose that handling has a small effect on growth so that even with early handling our sample averages slightly above 26 pounds at 2 years of age. However, the difference between the sample and the predicted (H_0) data is too small to reject H_0 confidently. Another possibility is that the sample of infants was exceptionally small at the start. Handling increases their growth but only to the extent that they reach the expected weight of 26 pounds at 2 years. In these cases, we would decide to retain a null hypothesis when in reality it is false, a *Type II error* (Table 8.1). That is, we conclude that the treatment has no effect when in fact it does.

DEFINITION   In a *Type II error,* the investigator fails to reject a null hypothesis that is really false.

Most experiments in psychology are done with the hope of rejecting the null hypothesis. Remember, the null hypothesis states that the treatment has no effect on the dependent variable. However, we face a dilemma in reaching a decision about H_0. On one hand, we would like to establish that there is a treatment effect (reject H_0). But we also would like to avoid a Type I error (rejecting H_0 when it really is true).

A similar dilemma occurs in the "hypothesis testing" that is done in the courtroom. Just as we assume H_0 is true before we collect our data, the jury is instructed to assume that the accused person is innocent of a crime—innocent until proven guilty. A Type I error would occur if the jury decides a person is guilty when in reality that person did not commit the crime (see Table 8.2). A Type I error is serious: An innocent person would be sent to prison. Just as in scientific research, it is desirable to avoid making a Type I error. This may mean that the jury will let a guilty person off the hook, a Type II error (Table 8.2). To deal with the dilemma of testing a person's innocence while avoiding a Type I error, the judge instructs the jury that the accused individual should be found guilty only if the evidence is "beyond a reasonable shadow of a doubt." This guideline will reduce the chance that the jury will commit a Type I error and punish an innocent person.

Likewise, it is important for scientists to minimize the likelihood of making a Type I error in their investigations. It is highly desirable to avoid making a

Table 8.2

Possible outcomes of a jury's decision

| | | ACTUAL SITUATION | |
		Did Not Commit Crime	Committed Crime
Jury's Verdict	Guilty	Type I error	Verdict correct
	Innocent	Verdict correct	Type II error

Adapted from *Essence of Statistics,* by G. R. Loftus and E. F. Loftus. Copyright ©1982 by Wadsworth Inc. Reprinted by permission of Brooks/Cole Publishing Company, Monterey, Calif.

false report that a treatment effect exists. To be sure a Type I error is avoided, the H_0 is rejected only when the sample data are very extreme and unlikely for H_0 to be true. That is, the evidence must be so overwhelming against H_0 that the researcher can reject the null hypothesis with the confidence that the "verdict" is correct "beyond a reasonable shadow of a doubt." How unlikely or overwhelming must the sample data be before the researcher can confidently reject H_0 and conclude there is an effect? The guideline is provided by the level of significance that the investigator uses in testing the hypothesis. We examine this guideline in Section 8.3.

LEARNING CHECK

1. What does the null hypothesis predict about a population?

2. Why do we evaluate (decide to reject or not reject) the null hypothesis instead of evaluating the alternative hypothesis?

3. What is a Type I error? A Type II error?

4. Is it possible to commit a Type II error when H_0 is rejected? Explain your answer.

5. Why do we state hypotheses in terms of population parameters?

ANSWERS

1. The null hypothesis predicts that the treatment will have no effect on the dependent variable for the population.

2. It is much easier to disprove a universal (population) statement than to prove one. Therefore, to find support for a treatment effect in the population, we must obtain sample data that suggest we should reject H_0. That is, we support the presence of a treatment effect when we disprove the null hypothesis.

3. A Type I error occurs when the experimenter rejects a null hypothesis that is actually true. An effect is reported when none exists. A Type II error occurs when the decision is "fail to reject H_0" but the null hypothesis is really false. One fails to report an effect that does exist.

4. No. A Type II error results from *failing to reject* a false H_0. Therefore, it cannot result from rejecting the null hypothesis.

5. We make predictions about the population because the goal of inferential statistics is to make general statements about the *population* based on the sample data.

8.3 EVALUATING HYPOTHESES

As previously noted, there is always the possibility for error in making an inference. As a result, we can never be absolutely positive that a hypothesis test has produced the correct decision. Although we cannot know for certain if our decision is right or wrong, we can know the probabilities for being right or wrong. Specifically, the hypothesis testing procedure is structured so that a researcher can specify and control the probability of making a Type I error. By keeping this probability small, a researcher can be confident that the risk of error is very low whenever the null hypothesis is rejected.

ALPHA LEVEL: MINIMIZING THE RISK OF A TYPE I ERROR

The final decision in a hypothesis test is based on a comparison of the sample data versus the null hypothesis. Specifically, a big discrepancy between the data ($\overline{X}$) and the null hypothesis (μ) will lead us to reject the null hypothesis. To formalize this decision process, it is necessary to determine what data are expected if H_0 is true and what data are very unlikely. This is accomplished by examining the distribution of all possible outcomes if the null hypothesis is true. Usually, this is the distribution of sample means for the sample size (n) that was used in the experiment. This distribution is then separated into two parts:

1. Those sample means that are expected (high probability) if H_0 is true—that is, sample data that are consistent with the null hypothesis.
2. Those sample means that are very unlikely (low probability) if H_0 is true— that is, sample data that are very different from the null hypothesis.

In using statistical symbols and notation for hypothesis testing, we will follow APA style as outlined in the *Publication Manual of the American Psychological Association*. The APA style does not use a leading zero in a decimal value for an alpha level. The expression $\alpha = .05$ is traditionally read "alpha equals point oh-five."

The *level of significance*, also called the *alpha level*, is simply a probability value that is used to define the term "very unlikely." By convention, alpha (α) levels are very small probabilities, commonly .05 (5%), .01 (1%), or .001 (0.1%). With an alpha level of $\alpha = .05$, for example, the extreme 5% of the distribution of sample means ("very unlikely" outcomes) would be separated from the rest of the distribution (see Figure 8.2). Thus the alpha level is used to divide the distribution of sample means into two sections: (1) sample means that are compatible with the null hypothesis (the center of the distribution), and (2) sample means that are significantly different from the null hypothesis (the very unlikely values in the extreme tails). Whenever we obtain sample data in the extreme tails of the distribution, we will conclude that there is a significant discrepancy between the data and the hypothesis, and we will reject the null hypothesis.

Figure 8.2

The alpha level separates the extreme and unlikely sample means from the rest of the distribution.

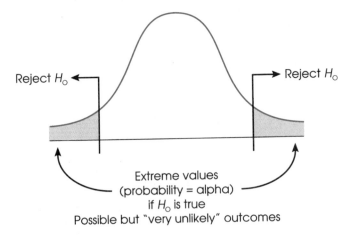

The distribution of sample means
(all possible experimental outcomes)
if the null hypothesis is true

Reject H_o ← → Reject H_o

Extreme values
(probability = alpha)
if H_o is true
Possible but "very unlikely" outcomes

Although extreme data, as defined by alpha, are very unlikely to be obtained if H_0 is true, there is still a slim probability (equal to α) that such data will be obtained. That is, when the null hypothesis is true, it is still possible to obtain extreme data that will lead us to reject the null hypothesis. Thus it is possible to reject a true null hypothesis and thereby commit a Type I error. However, the probability of this error occurring is determined by the alpha level. With $\alpha = .05$, for example, there is a 5% chance of obtaining extreme sample data that will lead us to reject H_0 even when H_0 is true. Thus, with $\alpha = .05$, there is a 5% risk of committing a Type I error.

DEFINITION

The *alpha level,* or *level of significance,* is a probability value that defines the very unlikely sample outcomes when the null hypothesis is true. Whenever an experiment produces very unlikely data (as defined by the alpha level), we will reject the null hypothesis. Thus the alpha level also defines the probability of a Type I error—that is, the probability of rejecting H_0 when it is actually true.

We will examine the role that alpha plays in the hypothesis-testing procedure by returning to the example of the effects of increased handling during infancy.

PROCEDURE AND STEPS

Recall that the study examines the effect of extra handling during infancy on growth. We will assume that the researcher intends to conduct this experiment using a sample of $n = 16$ infants. Each set of parents is instructed in how to provide additional handling during the first few months of their infant's life, and then the child's weight is measured at 2 years of age. Let us assume that weights are normally distributed with $\mu = 26$ pounds and $\sigma = 4$ for the population of untreated (did not receive additional handling) children. There are four steps to hypothesis testing: (1) state the hypotheses and select an alpha level, (2) use the alpha level to define what kind of sample data would warrant rejection of H_0, (3) analyze the sample data, and (4) make a decision about H_0. We will use these steps to assess the effect of additional handling during infancy on growth.

STEP 1

We must state the hypotheses and select an alpha level. The null hypothesis predicts that no effect will occur. That is, even with additional handling during infancy, the population mean weight for 2-year-olds will still be 26 pounds. In symbols, this hypothesis is stated as follows:

$$H_0 : \mu_{\text{handling in infancy}} = 26 \text{ pounds}$$

The alternative hypothesis states that early handling will change the mean weight for the population. In symbols, this hypothesis would state the following:

$$H_1 : \mu_{\text{handling}} \neq 26 \text{ pounds}$$

We will select an alpha level of 5%, or in terms of a proportion, $\alpha = .05$. This means that in order to reject the null hypothesis, the sample data must be extremely convincing—the data must be in the most extreme 5% of the distribution. By setting α to this level, we are limiting the probability of a Type I error to only 5%.

STEP 2   We establish criteria that define what kind of sample data would warrant rejection of the null hypothesis. We begin by looking at all the possible data that could be obtained if the null hypothesis were true. Our researcher is taking a random sample of $n = 16$. If the null hypothesis is true, it is possible to examine the distribution of all the possible sample means that could be obtained from this experiment. This distribution is the distribution of sample means based on samples of $n = 16$. It will be normal and have an expected value of $\mu = 26$ if H_0 is true. Furthermore, this distribution will have a standard error of

$$\sigma_{\bar{X}} = \frac{\sigma}{\sqrt{n}} = \frac{4}{\sqrt{16}} = \frac{4}{4} = 1$$

This distribution is shown in Figure 8.3.

If H_0 is true we expect to obtain a sample mean near the population mean, $\mu = 26$. Extreme values in the tails of the distribution would be extremely unlikely.

We have selected the value of $\alpha = .05$ for the level of significance. This proportion is divided evenly between the two tails of the distribution (see Figure 8.3). It is very unlikely that we would obtain a sample mean from this area of the distribution if H_0 is true. The area between the tails is the middle 95% of the distribution. The area contains the most likely sample means, and it is very likely that we would obtain a sample from this region if H_0 is true.

Notice that the boundaries that separate the middle 95% from the extreme 5% (2.5% in each tail) are located at the z-score values of $+1.96$ and -1.96 (from the unit normal table in Appendix B). A z-score of 1.96 indicates that the corresponding sample mean is 1.96 standard errors away from μ. For this example, the standard error is $\sigma_{\bar{X}} = 1$, so the z-score of $+1.96$ corresponds to a sample mean of 27.96 and the

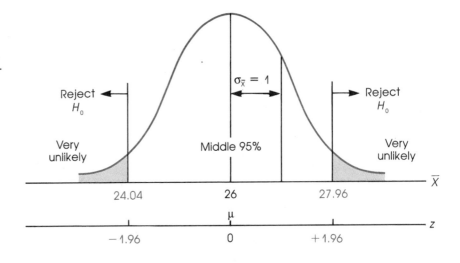

Figure 8.3

The distribution of all the possible sample means for $n = 16$ that could be obtained if H_0 is true. The boundaries separate the middle 95% from the most extreme 5% ($\alpha = .05$).

z-score of −1.96 corresponds to a sample mean of 24.04. These values mark off the boundaries between the middle 95% and the extreme tails of the distribution (see Figure 8.3).

If the treatment has no effect (H_0 is true), then we would expect to observe a sample mean near 26 pounds. Most of the time (95% to be exact) we would expect the sample to be in the middle section of the distribution. It is very improbable that we would obtain a sample mean that is out in the extreme tails of the distribution if H_0 is true. These extreme tails, the shaded areas in Figure 8.3, are called the *critical region* of the distribution. If H_0 were true, then it would be extremely unlikely to obtain a sample in the critical region. Notice that we have defined "extremely unlikely" as meaning "having a probability less than alpha." For this example, the H_0 is rejected only when the sample data are really extreme—when the probability of our sample observation is less than the alpha level ($p < .05$). In other words, H_0 is rejected when the sample data fall in the critical region. Thus it may be helpful to consider critical regions as "regions of rejection."

APA style does not use a leading zero in a probability value that refers to a level of significance.

DEFINITION

The *critical region* is composed of extreme sample values that are very unlikely to be obtained if the null hypothesis is true. The size of the critical region is determined by the alpha level. Sample data that fall in the critical region will warrant the rejection of the null hypothesis.

STEP 3

We now turn our attention to the sample data. The researcher selects a sample of $n = 16$ infants, trains each set of parents to administer extra handling, and then records each child's weight at age 2. Suppose the average weight for this sample is $\overline{X} = 31$ pounds. What can we conclude about the relationship between handling in infancy and growth?

STEP 4

We must make a decision about the null hypothesis. The result we obtained from the sample, $\overline{X} = 31$, lies in the critical region (Figure 8.3). The sample is not what we expected if the null hypothesis is true. It is an extremely unlikely outcome ($p < .05$) if H_0 is true. Therefore, we decide to reject the null hypothesis and conclude that extra handling during infancy did have a statistically significant effect on growth. With this statistical decision, we are risking a Type I error. That is, we could be rejecting a true null hypothesis. It is possible that the handling had no effect on growth and that the infants we sampled would have averaged 31 pounds anyway. However, this is very unlikely. If H_0 is true, the probability of obtaining any sample in the critical region is less than 5%, the alpha level we selected. The maximum probability of committing a Type I error is equal to alpha.

Always state your conclusion in terms of the independent variable and the dependent variable for the particular experiment being examined.

z-SCORES AND HYPOTHESIS TESTING

In the handling example, our decision to reject H_0 was based on the obtained sample mean of $\overline{X} = 31$, which falls within the critical region. We could have based this decision entirely on z-scores. For this example, the critical region consists of any z value greater than $+1.96$ or less than -1.96 (Figure 8.3). We can simply convert the obtained $\overline{X}$ value into a z-score to determine its

8.3   A RECIPE FOR A TEST STATISTIC

THE Z-SCORE formula, like any formula, can be thought of as a recipe. If you follow the instructions and use all the right ingredients, the formula will always produce a z-score. In hypothesis-testing situations, however, you do not have all the necessary ingredients. Specifically, you do not know the value for the population mean (μ), which is one component (or ingredient) in the formula.

This situation is similar to trying to follow a cake recipe where one of the ingredients is not clearly listed. For example, a cake recipe may call for flour but not specify exactly how much flour is needed. In this situation, you could proceed with the recipe and just add whatever amount of flour you think is appropriate. Your "hypothesis" about the amount of flour would be confirmed or rejected depending on the outcome of the cake. If the cake was good, you could reasonably assume that your hypothesis was correct. But if the cake was horrid, you would conclude that your hypothesis was wrong.

When using the z-score in a hypothesis test, you do not know the value for μ. Therefore, you take a hypothesized value from H_0, plug it into the z-score formula, and see how it works. If your hypothesized value produces a reasonable outcome (a z-score near zero), you conclude that the hypothesis was acceptable. But if the formula produces an extreme z value (in the critical region), you conclude that the hypothesis was wrong. This recipe concept applies not only to hypothesis tests with z-scores but also to some of the other test statistics that follow in later chapters.

location. That is, we determine whether or not it is in the critical region. For the obtained sample,

$$z = \frac{\overline{X} - \mu}{\sigma_{\overline{X}}} = \frac{31 - 26}{1} = 5.00$$

The obtained z-score is greater than +1.96 and thus lies in the critical region. The statistical decision would be the same, H_0 is rejected. Notice that the z-score is being used to test a hypothesis. In this use, the z-score is often called a *test statistic* (see Box 8.3). We examine other types of test statistics that are used in hypothesis testing in later chapters.

THE STRUCTURE OF THE z-SCORE FORMULA   It is useful to define the z-score formula

$$z = \frac{\overline{X} - \mu}{\sigma_{\overline{X}}}$$

in terms of the important steps and elements of hypothesis testing. The null hypothesis is represented in the formula by μ. The value of μ that we use in the formula is the value predicted by H_0. We test H_0 by collecting sample data, which are represented by the sample mean ($\overline{X}$) in the formula. Thus the numerator of the z formula can be rewritten as

$$\overline{X} - \mu = \text{sample data} - \text{population hypothesis}$$

You should recall that the standard error ($\sigma_{\overline{X}}$) measures the standard distance between a sample mean and the population mean. Thus standard error measures the expected difference (due to chance) between $\overline{X}$ and μ. Now we can restate the entire z-score test statistic as

$$z = \frac{\text{sample data} - \text{population hypothesis}}{\text{standard error between } \overline{X} \text{ and } \mu}$$

Notice that the difference between the sample data and the null hypothesis must be substantially larger than would be expected by chance in order to obtain a z-score that is large enough to fall in the critical region. The structure of this z-score formula will form the basis for some of the test statistics to follow in later chapters.

<table>
<tr><td>LEARNING CHECK</td><td>

1. Define alpha.

2. If H_0 is rejected when alpha is .05, will it necessarily be rejected when alpha has been set at .01?

3. What is the critical region? How is it used?

4. Experimenter 1 typically sets alpha to .10, whereas experimenter 2 always uses an alpha level of .05. In the long run, which experimenter will make more Type I errors?

</td></tr>
<tr><td>ANSWERS</td><td>

1. Alpha is the risk an investigator takes of committing a Type I error. The alpha level determines the level of significance of a statistical test.

2. Not necessarily. The data may be extreme enough to warrant rejecting H_0 at the 5% level of significance but not extreme enough for the same decision at the 1% level.

3. The critical region consists of extreme sample values that are very unlikely to be obtained (probability less than α) if the null hypothesis is true. If sample data fall in the critical region, we reject H_0.

4. Experimenter 1 is taking a greater risk (10%) of committing a Type I error.

</td></tr>
</table>

FAILURES TO REJECT THE NULL HYPOTHESIS

Using the handling example again, let us suppose that we obtained a sample of $n = 16$ infants that attained an average weight of $\overline{X} = 27.5$ pounds at 2 years. Steps 1 and 2 (stating the hypotheses and locating the critical region) remain the same. For Step 3, we can compute the z-score for this sample mean. If $\overline{X} = 27.5$, then

$$z = \frac{\overline{X} - \mu}{\sigma_{\overline{X}}} = \frac{27.5 - 26}{1} = 1.50$$

Limitations in the logic of inference make it easier to disprove a hypothesis about the population (Box 8.1).

In the final step, the statistical decision is made. The z-score for the obtained sample score is not in the critical region. This is the kind of outcome we would expect if H_0 were true. It is important to note that we have not proved that the null hypothesis is true. The sample provides only limited information about the entire population, and, in this case, we did not obtain sufficient evidence to claim that additional handling early in life does or does not have an effect on growth. For this reason, researchers avoid using the phrase "accepting the null hypothesis," opting instead for "failing to reject the null hypothesis." The latter phrase is more consistent with the logic of hypothesis testing. When the data are not overwhelmingly contrary to H_0, at best all we can say is that the data do not provide sufficient evidence to reject the null hypothesis.

Our decision to "fail to reject" H_0 means that we are risking a Type II error. For this example, a Type II error would mean that the extra handling actually did have some effect and yet we failed to discover it. A Type II error generally is not as serious a mistake as a Type I error. The consequences of a Type II error would be that a real effect is not reported. If a researcher suspects that a Type II error has occurred, there is always the option of repeating the experiment, usually with some refinements or modifications (see Box 8.4).

Unlike Type I errors, where the exact amount of risk is specified by the alpha level (α), there is no simple way to determine the probability of a Type II error. In fact, this probability is not a single value but rather depends on the size of the treatment effect. Although the exact probability of committing a Type II error is not easily calculated, it is identified by the Greek letter *beta*, β. We have more to say about Type II errors and β in Section 8.4.

α is for Type I, and β is for Type II.

REPORTING THE RESULTS OF THE STATISTICAL TEST

A special jargon and notational system are used in published reports of hypothesis tests. When you are reading a scientific journal, for example, you will not be told explicitly that the researcher evaluated the data using a *z*-score as a test statistic with an alpha level of .05. Instead, you will see a statement such as

"The treatment effect was significant, $z = 3.85$, $p < .05$".

Let us examine this statement part by part. First, what is meant by the term *significant?* In statistical tests, this word indicates that the result is different from what would be expected by chance. A significant result means that the null hypothesis has been rejected. That is, the data are in the critical region and not what we would have expected to obtain if H_0 were true.

DEFINITION

Findings are said to be *statistically significant* when the null hypothesis has been rejected. Thus, if results achieve statistical significance, the researcher concludes that a treatment effect occurred.

Next, what is the meaning of $z = 3.85$? The z indicates that the data were used to compute a *z*-score for a test statistic and that its value was 3.85. Finally, what is meant by $p < .05$? This part of the statement is the conventional way of specifying the alpha level that was used for the hypothesis test. More specifically, we are being told that the result of the experiment would occur by chance with a probability *(p)* that is less than .05.

In circumstances where the statistical decision is to fail to reject H_0, the report might state that "There was no evidence for an effect, $z = 1.30$, $p > .10$." In this case, we are saying that the obtained result, $z = 1.30$, is not unusual (not in the critical region) and is relatively likely to occur by chance (the probability is greater than .10).

8.4 PROBLEMS IN REPLICATION

WHAT CAN a researcher conclude when new experiments do not replicate an earlier finding in his or her own laboratory? This dilemma faced Dr. Neal E. Miller, a very prominent psychologist, who for years did outstanding research at Yale University and later Rockefeller University. He wanted to see if rats could learn to control their involuntary vital responses by operant conditioning and do so without the aid of voluntary movements. For example, if a rat is given a reward (pleasurable brain stimulation) for slowing down its heart rate, would it learn to control its heart and make it beat slower to get more reward? There was a "catch" to the experiment. The rats had to learn to control heart rate without voluntary movements (such as becoming very relaxed) that could slow the heart. So rats were temporarily paralyzed with a drug called curare. Sure enough, even though their muscles were paralyzed, the rats could still learn to control how fast their hearts would beat. Miller and the scientific community in general were excited by the findings and the possible applications for treating psychosomatic disorders. However, after reporting the results of the first few experiments, Miller and his coworkers found that they could no longer get the same effects. He could not replicate the conditioning of involuntary responses by use of reward.

Were the original findings actually nothing more than a Type I error? Or were the more recent findings a Type II error? Miller assumed that his original findings were correct and instead focused on the second question. He assumed that something had gone wrong in the laboratory during the later studies. Perhaps the newer batch of rats was somehow different from the previous animals? So Miller tried a different kind of rat, to no avail. Perhaps the paralyzing drug had gone bad and interfered with the conditioning of heart rates? He tried a new sample of curare, but nothing changed. Perhaps the reward was no longer as effective as before, or perhaps changes in the laboratory diet caused general physiological changes in the animals that prevent the effect? The list of possible reasons why the conditioning effect could not be replicated seems endless. As Miller and Dworkin (1974, p. 315) noted,

> The problem is that, whereas there often are millions of ways of doing something wrong, there may be only one or two ways of doing it right. Thus, one positive result can yield vastly more information than many negative ones.

Whenever a Type II error is suspected, a researcher will typically repeat the study with some modifications and improvements. Assuming a Type II error did occur, perhaps using the right combination of treatment conditions in the experiment (repeating the experiment the "one or two ways of doing it right") will result in evidence for an effect.

On the other hand, maybe Miller's assumptions were wrong. Perhaps the original finding was indeed a Type I error (there was no effect but H_0 was rejected anyway). If a great many attempts are made to replicate the original finding and they all fail to find evidence for an effect, then it would be reasonable to suspect that a Type I error occurred in the first study.

Notice that in scientific reports, the researcher does not actually state that "the null hypothesis was rejected." Instead, it is reported that the effect of the treatment was statistically significant. Likewise, when H_0 is not rejected, one simply states that the treatment effect was not statistically significant or that there was no evidence for an effect. In fact, when you read scientific reports, you will note that the terms null hypothesis and alternative hypothesis are rarely mentioned. Nevertheless, H_0 and H_1 are a part of the logic of hypothesis testing, even if they are not formally stated in a scientific report. Because of their central role in the process of hypothesis testing, you should be able to identify and state these hypotheses.

MORE ABOUT ALPHA—THE LEVEL OF SIGNIFICANCE

As you have seen, the alpha level for a hypothesis test serves two very important functions. First, alpha determines the risk of a Type I error. Second, alpha helps determine the boundaries for the critical region. As you might expect, these two functions interact with each other. When you lower the alpha level—for example, from .05 to .01—you reduce the risk of a Type I error. To gain this extra margin of safety, you must demand more evidence from the data before you are willing to reject H_0. This is accomplished by moving the boundaries for the critical region. With $\alpha = .05$ for example, the z-score boundaries are located at ± 1.96. For $\alpha = .01$, the boundaries move to $z = \pm 2.58$, and with $\alpha = .001$, the boundaries move all the way out to $z = \pm 3.30$ (see Figure 8.4). With $\alpha = .001$, it would take a huge difference between the data and the hypothesis to be significant. In general, as you lower the alpha level, the critical boundaries move farther away from the population mean, and it becomes increasingly more difficult to obtain a sample that is located in the critical region. Thus, sample data that are sufficient to reject H_0 at the .05 level of significance may not provide sufficient evidence to reject H_0 at the .01 level. If you push alpha to an extremely low level, it can become essentially impossible for an experiment ever to demonstrate a significant treatment effect.

Where do you set the critical boundaries so that your experiment has some chance of being successful and (at the same time) minimize your risk of a Type I error? Historically, the answer is to use an alpha level of .05. This value was first suggested in 1925 by a well-known statistician named Sir Ronald A. Fisher. Fisher noted that it is convenient to use the .05 level as a limit in judging whether a result is considered to be significant or not, and he suggested that researchers ignore all results that fail to reach this limit. Although Fisher selected $\alpha = .05$ as a personal, arbitrary standard, it has become recognized as the minimum level of significance that is acceptable for publication of research in many journals. In fact, some of the more prestigious journals require an alpha level of .01 for their published results. For most research an alpha level of .05 is appropriate and is generally defined as

Figure 8.4

The location of the critical region boundaries for three different levels of significance: $\alpha = .05$, $\alpha = .01$, and $\alpha = .001$.

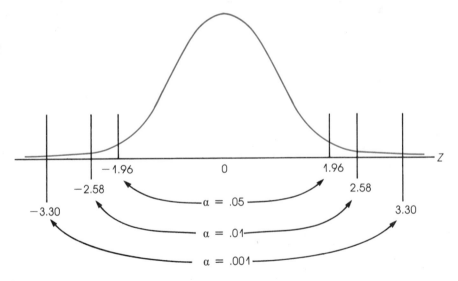

statistically significant. The .01 level of significance is used in situations where you have special reason to fear a Type I error or where you want to make an exceptionally strong demonstration of a treatment effect. The .01 alpha level is generally defined as *highly statistically significant.* (For more information on the origins of the .05 level of significance, see the excellent short article by Cowles and Davis, 1982.)

ASSUMPTIONS FOR HYPOTHESIS TESTS WITH z-SCORES

It will become evident in later chapters that certain conditions must be present for each type of hypothesis test to be an appropriate and accurate procedure. These conditions are assumed to be satisfied when the results of a hypothesis test are interpreted. However, the decisions based on the test statistic (that is, rejecting or not rejecting H_0) may be compromised if these assumptions are not satisfied. In practice, researchers are not overly concerned with the conditions of a statistical test unless they have strong suspicions that the assumptions have been violated. Nevertheless, it is crucial to keep in mind the fundamental conditions that are associated with each type of statistical test to ensure that it is being used appropriately. The assumptions for hypothesis tests with z-scores which involve one sample are summarized below.

Random sampling   It is assumed that the subjects used to obtain the sample data were selected randomly. Remember, we wish to generalize our findings from the sample to the population. This task is accomplished when we use sample data to test a hypothesis about the population. Therefore, the sample must be representative of the population from which it has been drawn. Random sampling helps to ensure that it is representative.

The value of σ is unchanged by the treatment   The general purpose of hypothesis testing is to determine whether or not a treatment (independent variable) produces a change in the population mean. The null hypothesis, the critical region, and the z-score statistic all are concerned with the treated population. In the z-score formula we use $\overline{X}$ from the treated sample, a hypothesized value of μ for the treated population and a standard error that indicates how close $\overline{X}$ should be to μ. However, you may have noticed that when we compute the standard error, we use the standard deviation from the untreated population. Thus, the z-score appears to be using values from two different populations: $\overline{X}$ and μ for the treated population and σ from the untreated population. To justify this apparent contradiction we must make an assumption. Specifically, we must assume that the value of σ is the same after treatment as it was before treatment.

Actually, this assumption is the consequence of a more general assumption that is part of many statistical procedures. This general assumption states that the effect of the treatment is to add (or subtract) a constant amount to every score in the population. You should recall that adding (or subtracting) a constant will change the mean but will have no effect on the standard deviation. You also should note that this assumption is a theoretical ideal. In actual experiments a treatment generally will not show a perfect and consistent additive effect.

Normal sampling distribution   To evaluate hypotheses with z-scores, we have used the unit normal table to identify the critical region. This table can be used only if the distribution of sample means is normal.

LEARNING CHECK   1. An instructor has been teaching large sections of general psychology for the past 10 semesters. As a group, final exam scores are normally distributed with $\mu = 42$ and $\sigma = 9$. With the current class of $n = 100$ students, the instructor tries a different teaching format. Once a week the class breaks down into smaller groups that meet with the instructor for discussion of recent lecture and reading material. At the end of the semester, the instructor notes that the mean for this section on the final exam was $\overline{X} = 46.5$. Did the teaching format have a significant effect on performance on the final exam? Test with alpha set at .05.

    a. State the hypotheses.

    b. Locate the critical region.

    c. Compute the test statistic.

    d. Make a decision regarding H_0.

    e. For this example, identify the independent and dependent variables.

ANSWERS   1. **a.** $H_0 : \mu_{\text{discussion groups}} = 42$; $H_1 : \mu_{\text{discussion groups}} \neq 42$.

    b. The critical region consists of z-score values greater than $+1.96$ or less than -1.96.

    c. $\sigma_{\overline{X}} = 0.9$; $z = +5.0$.

    d. Reject H_0 and conclude that teaching format does affect scores on the final exam. The small-group sessions improve final test performance.

    e. The independent variable is teaching format. The dependent variable is the score on the final exam.

8.4 DIRECTIONAL (ONE-TAILED) HYPOTHESIS TESTS

The hypothesis testing procedure presented in Section 8.2 was the standard, or *two-tailed*, test format. The *two-tailed* comes from the fact that the critical region is located in both tails of the distribution. This format is by far the most widely accepted procedure for hypothesis testing. Nonetheless, there is an alternative that will be discussed in this section.

Usually, a researcher begins an experiment with a specific prediction about the direction of the treatment effect. For example, a special training program is expected to *increase* student performance, or alcohol consumption is expected to *slow* reaction times. In these situations, it is possible to state the statistical hypotheses in a manner that incorporates the directional prediction into the statement of H_0 and H_1. The result is a directional test, or what commonly is called a *one-tailed test*.

DEFINITION   In a *directional hypothesis test,* or a *one-tailed test,* the statistical hypotheses (H_0 and H_1) specify either an increase or a decrease in the population mean score.

Suppose, for example, a researcher is using a sample of $n = 16$ laboratory rats to examine the effect of a new diet drug. It is known that under regular circumstances these rats eat an average of 10 grams of food each day. The distribution of food consumption is normal with $\sigma = 4$. The expected effect of the drug is to reduce food consumption. The purpose of the experiment is to determine whether or not the drug really works.

THE HYPOTHESES FOR A DIRECTIONAL TEST

Because there is a specific direction expected for the treatment effect, it is possible for the researcher to perform a directional test. The first step (and the most critical step) is to state the statistical hypotheses. Remember that the null hypothesis states that there is no treatment effect and that the alternative hypothesis says that there is an effect. For directional tests, it is easier to begin with the alternative hypothesis. In words, this hypothesis says that with the drug the mean food consumption is *less than* 10 grams per day; that is, the drug does reduce food consumption. In symbols, H_1 would say the following:

$$H_1 : \mu_{\text{with drug}} < 10 \qquad \text{(mean food consumption is reduced)}$$

The null hypothesis states that the treatment did not work (the opposite of H_1). In this case, H_0 states that the drug does not reduce food consumption. That is, even with the drug the rats still will eat at least 10 grams per day. In symbols, H_0 would say the following:

$$H_0 : \mu_{\text{with drug}} \geq 10 \qquad \text{(the mean is at least 10 grams per day)}$$

THE CRITICAL REGION FOR DIRECTIONAL TESTS

The critical region is determined by sample values that are very unlikely if the null hypothesis is true. That is, sample values that refute H_0 and provide evidence that the treatment really does work. In this example, the treatment is intended to reduce food consumption. Therefore, only sample values that are substantially less than $\mu = 10$ would indicate that the treatment worked and thereby lead to rejecting H_0. Thus the critical region is located entirely in one tail of the distribution (see Figure 8.5). This is why the directional test commonly is called one-tailed.

A complete example of a one-tailed test is presented next. Once again, the experiment examining the effect of extra handling on the physical growth of infants will be used to demonstrate the hypothesis-testing procedure.

EXAMPLE 8.1   It is known that under regular circumstances the population of 2-year-old children has an average weight of $\mu = 26$ pounds. The distribution of weights is normal with $\sigma = 4$. The researcher selects a random sample of $n = 4$ newborn infants, instructs the parents to provide each child

Figure 8.5

The distribution of sample means for $n = 16$ if H_0 is true. The null hypothesis states that the diet pill has no effect, so the population mean will be $\mu = 10$ or larger.

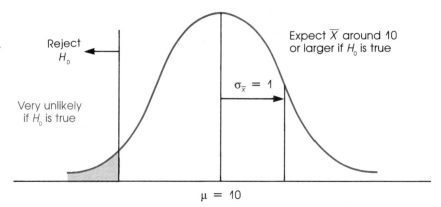

with extra handling, and then records the weight of each child at age 2 years. The average weight for the sample is $\overline{X} = 29.5$ pounds.

STEP 1 *State the hypotheses:* Because the researcher is predicting that extra handling will produce an increase in weight, it is possible to do a directional test. It usually is easier to begin with H_1, the alternative hypothesis, which states that the treatment does have an effect. In symbols,

$$H_1 : \mu > 26 \qquad \text{(there is an increase in weight)}$$

Simply because you can do a directional test does not mean that you must use a directional test. A two-tailed test is always acceptable and generally preferred.

The null hypothesis states that the treatment does not have an effect. In symbols,

$$H_0 : \mu \le 26 \qquad \text{(there is no increase)}$$

STEP 2 *Locate the critical region.* To find the critical region, we look at all the possible sample means for $n = 4$ that could be obtained if H_0 were true. This is the distribution of sample means. It will be normal (because the population is normal), it will have a standard error of $\sigma_{\overline{X}} = 4/\sqrt{4} = 2$, and it will have a mean of $\mu = 26$ if the null hypothesis is true. The distribution is shown in Figure 8.6.

Figure 8.6

Critical region for Example 8.1.

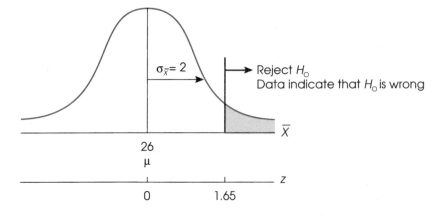

If H_0 is true and extra handling does not increase weight, we would expect the sample to average around 26 pounds or less. Only large-sample means would provide evidence that H_0 is wrong and that extra handling actually does increase weight. Therefore, it is only large values that comprise the critical region. With $\alpha = .05$, the most likely 95% of the distribution is separated from the most unlikely 5% by a z-score of $z = +1.65$ (see Figure 8.6).

STEP 3   *Obtain the sample data:* The mean for the sample is $\overline{X} = 29.5$. This value corresponds to a z-score of

$$z = \frac{\overline{X} - \mu}{\sigma_{\overline{X}}} = \frac{29.5 - 26}{2} = \frac{3.5}{2} = 1.75$$

STEP 4   *Make a statistical decision.* A z-score of $z = +1.75$ indicates that our sample mean is in the critical region. This is a very unlikely outcome if H_0 is true, so the statistical decision is to reject H_0. The conclusion is that extra handling does result in increased growth for infants.

COMPARISON OF ONE-TAILED VERSUS TWO-TAILED TESTS

The general goal of hypothesis testing is to determine whether or not a particular treatment has any effect on a population. The test is performed by selecting a sample, administering the treatment to the sample, and then comparing the result with the original population. If the treated sample is noticeably different from the original population, then we conclude that the treatment has an effect, and we reject H_0. On the other hand, if the treated sample is still similar to the original population, then we conclude that there is no evidence for a treatment effect, and we fail to reject H_0. The critical factor in this decision is the *size of the difference* between treated sample and the original population. A large difference is evidence that the treatment worked; a small difference is not sufficient to say that the treatment has any effect.

The major distinction between one-tailed and two-tailed tests is in the criteria they use for rejecting H_0. A one-tailed test allows you to reject the null hypothesis when the difference between the sample and the population is relatively small, provided the difference is in the specified direction. A two-tailed test, on the other hand, requires a relatively large difference independent of direction. This point is illustrated in the following example.

EXAMPLE 8.2   Consider again the experiment examining extra handling and infant growth (see Example 8.1). If we had used a standard two-tailed test, then the hypotheses would have been

$H_0 : \mu = 26$ pounds   (no treatment effect)

$H_1 : \mu \neq 26$ pounds   (handling does affect growth)

With $\alpha = .05$, the critical region would consist of any z-score beyond the $z = \pm 1.96$ boundaries.

If we obtained the same sample data, $\overline{X} = 29.5$ pounds, which corresponds to a z-score of $z = 1.75$, our statistical decision would be "fail to reject H_0."

Notice that with the two-tailed test (Example 8.2), the difference between the data ($\overline{X} = 29.5$) and the hypothesis ($\mu = 26$) is not big enough to conclude that the hypothesis is wrong. In this case, we are saying that the data do not provide sufficient evidence to justify rejecting H_0. However, with the one-tailed test (Example 8.1), the same data led us to reject H_0.

All researchers agree that one-tailed tests are different from two-tailed tests. However, there are several ways to interpret the difference. One group of researchers (the present authors included) contends that one-tailed tests make it too easy to reject H_0 and, therefore, too easy to make a Type I error. According to this position, a two-tailed test requires strong evidence to reject H_0 and thus provides a convincing demonstration that a treatment effect has occurred. A one-tailed test, on the other hand, can result in rejecting the null hypothesis even when the evidence is relatively weak. For this reason, you usually will find two-tailed tests used for research that is published in journal articles for scrutiny by the scientific community. In this type of research, it is important that the results be convincing, and it is important to avoid a Type I error (publishing a false report). The two-tailed (nondirectional) test satisfies these criteria.

Another group of researchers focuses on the advantages of one-tailed tests. As we have noted, one-tailed tests can lead to rejecting H_0 when the evidence is relatively weak. The statement can be rephrased by saying that one-tailed tests are more sensitive in detecting a treatment effect. If you think of a hypothesis test as a detection device that is used to seek out a treatment effect, then the advantages of a more-sensitive test should be obvious. Although a more sensitive test will generate more false alarms (Type I errors), it also is more likely to find a significant treatment effect. Thus, one-tailed tests can be very useful in situations where a researcher does not want to overlook any possible significant outcome and where a Type I error is not very damaging. A good example of this situation is in exploratory research. The intent of exploratory research is to investigate a new area or to try an approach that is new and different. Instead of producing publishable results, exploratory research is directed toward generating new research possibilities. In this atmosphere, a researcher is willing to tolerate a few false alarms (Type I errors) in exchange for the increased sensitivity of a one-tailed test.

For the reasons we have outlined, most researchers do not use one-tailed tests except in very limited situations. Even though most experiments are designed with an expectation that the treatment effect will be in a specific direction, the directional prediction is not included in the statement of the statistical hypothesis. Nevertheless, you will probably encounter one-tailed tests and you may find occasion to use them, so you should understand the rationale and the procedure for conducting directional tests.

Remember, you risk a Type I error every time H_0 is rejected.

LEARNING CHECK   1. A researcher predicts that a treatment will lower scores. If this researcher uses a one-tailed test, will the critical region be in the right- or left-hand tail of the distribution?

2. A psychologist is examining the effects of early sensory deprivation on the development of perceptual discrimination. A sample of $n = 9$ newborn kittens is obtained. These kittens are raised in a completely dark environment for 4 weeks, after which they receive normal visual stimulation. At age 6 months, the kittens are tested on a visual discrimination task. The average score for this sample is $\overline{X} = 32$. It is known that under normal circumstances cats score an average of $\mu = 40$ on this task. The distribution of scores is normal with $\sigma = 12$. The researcher is predicting that the early sensory deprivation will reduce the kittens' performance on the discrimination task. Use a one-tailed test with $\alpha = .01$ to test this hypothesis.

ANSWERS   **1.** The left-hand tail.

2. The hypotheses are $H_0 : \mu \geq 40$ and $H_1 : \mu < 40$. The critical region is determined by z-scores less than -2.33. The z-score for these sample data is $z = -2.00$. Fail to reject H_0.

8.5 STATISTICAL POWER

The purpose of a hypothesis test is to determine whether or not a particular treatment has an effect. The null hypothesis states that there is no effect, and the researcher is hoping that the sample data will provide evidence to reject this hypothesis. In previous sections, we saw that the hypothesis-testing procedure always involves some risk of reaching a wrong conclusion. Specifically, a researcher may commit a Type I error by rejecting a true null hypothesis. This risk is minimized by selecting an alpha level (usually .05 or .01) that determines the maximum probability of committing a Type I error. You should also recall that every hypothesis test has the potential for resulting in a Type II error, failing to reject a false null hypothesis. In simple terms, a Type II error means that the treatment really does have an effect but the hypothesis test failed to discover it.

In this section, we reverse our perspective on hypothesis testing. Rather than examining the potential for making an error, we examine the probability of reaching the correct decision. Remember that the researcher's goal is to demonstrate that the experimental treatment actually does have an effect. This is the purpose of conducting the experiment in the first place. If the researcher is correct and the treatment really does have an effect, then what is the probability that the hypothesis test will correctly identify it? This is a question concerning the *power* of a statistical test.

DEFINITION   The *power* of a statistical test is the probability that the test will correctly reject a false null hypothesis.

As the definition implies, the more powerful a statistical test, the more readily it will detect a treatment effect when one really exists (correctly rejecting H_0). It should be clear that the concepts of power and Type II error are closely related. *When a treatment effect exists,* the hypothesis test will have one of two results:

1. It can fail to discover the existing treatment effect (a Type II error).
2. It can correctly detect the presence of a treatment effect (rejecting a false null hypothesis).

We already have noted that the probability of a Type II error is identified by the symbol beta, β. Thus, the probability of correctly rejecting a false H_0 must be $1 - \beta$. If, for example, a hypothesis test has a probability of .20 (20% chance) of failing to detect a treatment effect (Type II error), then it must have a probability of .80 (80% chance) of successfully detecting it. Thus, the power of a statistical test is determined by

$$\text{power} = P(\text{reject a false } H_0) = 1 - \beta \qquad (8.1)$$

> Remember, the probabilities for all events must add up to 1.00 (100%).

POWER AND THE SIZE OF THE TREATMENT EFFECT

Although we have defined power, we have not attempted to compute a value for this probability. The difficulty in specifying this value comes from the fact that power depends on the size of the treatment effect. Therefore, it does not have a single value for every hypothesis test. When a treatment has a large effect, it will be easy to detect this effect and power will be high. On the other hand, when the treatment effect is very small, it will be difficult to detect and power will be low. Thus, rather than talking about power as a single value, we must examine the different values of power associated with different magnitudes of treatment effect. We can illustrate this in a set of graphs that represents different treatment effects, but first, one more reminder is necessary. Remember, the null hypothesis is rejected whenever sample data are in the critical region. With this in mind, we can restate the definition of power as follows:

DEFINITION

Power is the probability of obtaining sample data in the critical region when the null hypothesis is false.

Note: Because "data in the critical region" is equivalent to "rejecting the null hypothesis," this definition is equivalent to our original definition of power.

Consider the following situation. A researcher is interested in whether alcohol consumed by pregnant mice can affect the birth weights of their offspring. It is known that for untreated mice, the birth weights for newborn pups are normally distributed with a mean of $\mu = 200$ milligrams. Note that the null hypothesis would state

$$H_0 : \mu = 200 \qquad \text{(Even with alcohol, the average birth weight is still 200 milligrams.)}$$

Let's assume that alcohol actually has an effect and that the size of the treatment effect is 20 points (female mice that consume alcohol have newborn pups that weigh an average of 20 points less). Figure 8.7 shows two distributions of sample means:

Figure 8.7

Two distributions of sample means: when H_0 is true (null distribution, right) and when there is a 20-point treatment effect (treatment distribution, left). Statistical power is determined by the proportion of the shaded area, $1 - \beta$, in the treatment distribution.

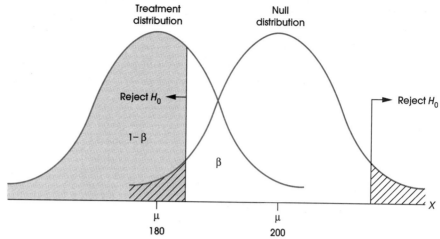

1. A null distribution (on the right, Figure 8.7) that corresponds to a situation in which H_0 is true and the treatment has no effect ($\mu = 200$).

2. A treatment distribution (on the left, Figure 8.7) that reflects the actual effect of the treatment (an average reduction in weight of 20 points).

Remember, it is the null hypothesis ($H_0 : \mu = 200$) that is being tested. Therefore, the critical region is determined by extreme, unlikely sample means in the tails of the null distribution. The treatment distribution (left) shows all the sample means that are possible, given a 20-point treatment effect. Notice that many of these sample means (shaded area) fall beyond the boundary for the critical region of the null distribution. Obtaining a sample mean from this shaded area would result in the researcher correctly rejecting H_0. The proportion for this shaded area would indicate the probability of correctly rejecting a false null hypothesis—that is, the amount of power. Thus the shaded portion of the treatment distribution represents $1 - \beta$. However, not all the sample means in the treatment distribution fall beyond the cutoff for the critical region (unshaded part of treatment distribution). Obtaining one of these sample means would result in the researcher failing to reject a false H_0, which is a Type II error. The proportion of area in this part of the treatment distribution provides the value for β, the probability of committing a Type II error.

Now let's assume that the treatment effect is only 10 points. What happens to statistical power? Figure 8.8 illustrates the null and treatment distributions, showing an average birth weight reduction of 10 points ($\mu = 190$ for newborn mice whose mother consumed alcohol). Notice that the treatment distribution for a 10-point effect is closer to the null distribution (Figure 8.8), compared with the situation when the treatment produces a 20-point effect (Figure 8.7). Thus fewer sample means from the treatment distribution fall beyond the boundary of the critical region. The shaded area is smaller and statistical power, $1 - \beta$, also is diminished (Figure 8.8). On the other hand,

Figure 8.8

Two distributions of sample means: when H_0 is true (null distribution, right) and when there is a 10-point treatment effect (treatment distribution, left). When the treatment effect is smaller, statistical power is also smaller (shaded area, $1 - \beta$).

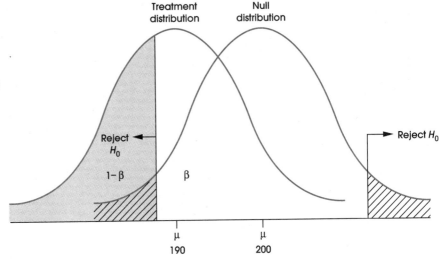

the probability of a Type II error, β, is now larger, as shown by the larger unshaded area of the treatment distribution (Figure 8.8).

Thus, when an experiment produces a large treatment effect, statistical power is large (you are more likely to correctly identify that effect). Alternatively, when an experiment produces a small treatment effect, statistical power is small (you are less likely to detect the effect).

FACTORS AFFECTING POWER

As we have seen, the size of the treatment effect is one factor that influences statistical power. Although it is an important factor, a researcher typically will not know before a study is done how much of a treatment effect, if any, exists. There are, however, three factors that affect power which are under the direct control of the experimenter. These factors are the alpha level selected, the type of test (one- vs. two-tailed), and sample size.

The alpha level Reducing the alpha level will reduce the power of a statistical test. For example, reducing α from .05 to .01 moves the critical region boundaries from $z = \pm 1.96$ to $z = \pm 2.58$. The result is that the smaller alpha level makes it harder to reject the null hypothesis. Thus, you are less likely to reject a true H_0 (a Type I error), but you also are less likely to reject a false H_0 (power). Figure 8.9 illustrates the role of alpha level in determining power using the alcohol and birth weight example. Figure 8.9(a) shows the treatment and null distributions for a 20-point effect with an alpha level of $\alpha = .05$. Figure 8.9(b) depicts the same situation, except that the alpha level is now $\alpha = .01$. Note that when alpha is .05, there are more sample means in the treatment distribution that fall beyond the boundary of the critical region. This area is shaded, and its proportion of the total distribution is $1 - \beta$, or the amount of power. When the alpha level is smaller [Figure 8.9(b)], this shaded area is smaller, indicating lower power.

Figure 8.9

Statistical power (a) when the level of significance is $\alpha = .05$ and (b) when it is $\alpha = .01$. A 20-point treatment effect is assumed in both cases. The proportion of shaded area, $1 - \beta$, is smaller in part b, indicating lower statistical power.

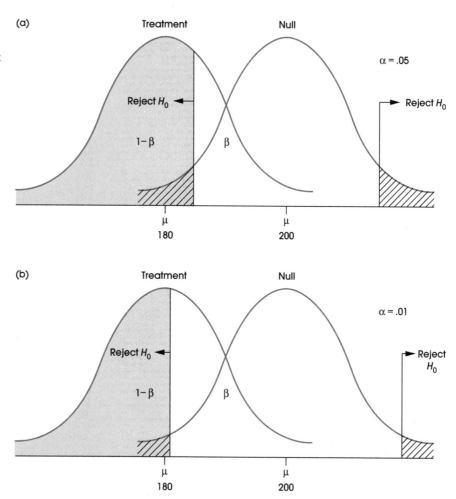

One-tailed versus two-tailed tests   Your should recall that one-tailed tests make it easier to reject the null hypothesis. Thus, one-tailed tests should increase power. Again, let's consider the experiment assessing the effects of alcohol consumption on birth weight. With $\alpha = .05$, for example, the critical boundary for a one-tailed test is located at $z = -1.65$. For a two-tailed test, the boundaries would be at $z = \pm 1.96$. Therefore, the critical region for the one-tailed test is larger, and its critical boundary is not as extreme. A greater portion of the sample means from the treatment distribution will fall beyond this boundary. Statistical power is greater.

Sample size   In general, the larger the sample, the better it will represent the population. If there actually is a treatment effect in the population, you are more likely to find it with a large sample than with a small sample. Thus, the power of a test can be increased by using larger samples. Once again, we will look at the experiment on alcohol and birth weight. For the untreated population, $\mu = 200$. We will assume that the size of the treatment effect is

Figure 8.10

Statistical power when the sample size is $n = 25$ (a) and when it is $n = 100$ (b). The treatment effect is 20 points in both figures. The proportion of the shaded area is greater in part b, reflecting greater power for larger samples.

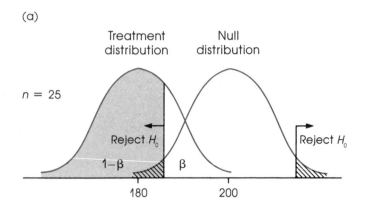

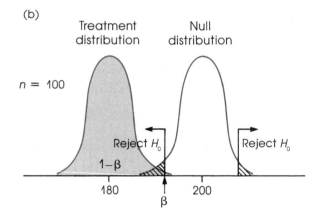

Remember, $\sigma_{\bar{x}} = \sigma/\sqrt{n}$.

20 points. Let's compare two situations: one in which the a sample of $n = 25$ mice is used and a second study where $n = 100$.

Figure 8.10 shows the set of distributions for samples of $n = 25$ and for $n = 100$. The standard error for these distributions will be larger when $n = 25$ and smaller when $n = 100$. Note that when the standard error is small (when $n = 100$), nearly all the sample means in the treatment distribution fall beyond the critical region boundary [Figure 8.10(b)]. The proportion for this shaded area is nearly 100% and the statistical power is extremely high (you are almost guaranteed to detect the treatment effect). On the other hand, when sample size is small and standard error is large, a small proportion of the sample means in the treatment distribution falls beyond the boundary of the critical region. Therefore, there is less power with the smaller sample.

LEARNING CHECK

1. For a particular hypothesis test, power, $1 - \beta$, equals .50 for a 5-point treatment effect. Will the power be greater or lower for a 10-point treatment effect?

2. As the power of a test increases, what happens to the probability of a Type II error?

3. If a researcher uses $\alpha = .01$ rather than $\alpha = .05$, then power will increase. (True or false?)

4. What is the effect of increasing sample size on power?

ANSWERS

1. The hypothesis test is more likely to detect a 10-point effect, so power will be greater.

2. As power increases, the probability of a Type II error decreases.

3. False. **4.** Power increases as sample size gets larger.

SUMMARY

1. Hypothesis testing is an inferential procedure for using the limited data from a sample to draw a general conclusion about a population. It begins with hypothesizing values for the mean of an unknown population, generally a population that has received a treatment (Figure 8.1).

2. The null hypothesis (H_0) states that the treatment has not changed the mean. That is, it is the same as the mean for a known and untreated population. At this stage we also select an alpha level, usually $\alpha = .05$ or $.01$, which sets the risk of committing a Type I error. Alpha determines the level of significance of a statistical test.

3. The second step involves locating the critical region. We examine all the possible experimental outcomes if the null hypothesis is true and then identify the most unlikely values. We define "unlikely according to H_0" as the outcomes with a probability less than alpha. Thus, the selected alpha level determines the critical z-scores that are associated with the critical region. Sample data that produce a z-score that falls within the critical region would imply that H_0 is not tenable.

4. The sample data are collected. Specifically, the sample mean $\overline{X}$ is used to test a hypothesis about μ. To determine how unlikely the obtained sample mean is, we must locate it within the distribution of sample means. This is accomplished by computing a z-score for $\overline{X}$:

$$z = \frac{\overline{X} - \mu}{\sigma_{\overline{X}}}$$

When a z-score is used in the test of a hypothesis, it is called a test statistic.

5. The z-score equation can be expressed as

$$z = \frac{\text{sample mean} - \text{hypothesized population mean}}{\text{standard error between } \overline{X} \text{ and } \mu}$$

That is, the difference between the sample mean and the hypothesized population mean (according to H_0) is compared to (divided by) the amount of error we would expect between $\overline{X}$ and μ.

6. In the fourth step, we compare the obtained data to the set of possible results that were outlined in the second step. That is, if the obtained z-score falls in the critical region, we reject H_0 because it is very unlikely that these data would be obtained if H_0 were true. We would conclude that a treatment effect occurred. If the data are not in the critical region, then there is not sufficient evidence to reject H_0. The statistical decision is "fail to reject H_0." We conclude that we failed to find sufficient evidence for an effect.

7. Whatever decision is reached in a hypothesis test, there is always a risk of making the incorrect decision. There are two types of errors that can be committed.

   A Type I error is defined as rejecting a true H_0. This is a serious error because it results in falsely reporting a treatment effect. The risk of a Type I error is determined by the alpha level and, therefore, is under the experimenter's control.

   A Type II error is defined as failing to reject a false H_0. In this case, the experiment fails to report an effect that actually occurred. The probability of a Type II error cannot be specified as a single value and depends in part on the size of the treatment effect. It is identified by the symbol β (beta).

8. When a researcher predicts that a treatment effect will be in a particular direction (increase or decrease), it is possible to do a directional or one-tailed test. The first step in this procedure is to state the alternative hypothesis (H_1). This hypothesis states that the treatment works and, for directional tests, specifies the direction of the predicted treatment effect. The null hypothesis is the opposite of H_1. To locate the critical region, you must identify the kind of experimental outcome that refutes the null hypothesis and demonstrates that the treatment works. These outcomes will be located entirely in one tail of the distribution. The entire critical region (5% or 1%, depending on α) will be in one tail.

9. Directional tests should be used with caution because they may allow the rejection of H_0 when the experimental evidence is relatively weak. Even though a researcher may have a specific directional prediction for an experiment, it is generally safer and never inappropriate to use a nondirectional (two-tailed) test.

10. The power of a hypothesis test is defined as the probability that the test will correctly reject the null hypothesis. Power is identified as

$$\text{power} = 1 - \beta$$

where β is the probability of a Type II errror.

11. To illustrate the power for a hypothesis test, you must first identify the treatment and null distribu-

tions. Also, you must specify the magnitude of the treatment effect. Next, you locate the critical region in the null distribution. The power of the hypothesis test is the portion of the treatment distribution that is located beyond the boundary (critical value) of the critical region.

12. As the size of the treatment effect increases, statistical power increases. Also, power is influenced by several factors that can be controlled by the experimenter:

a. Increasing the alpha level will increase power.

b. A one-tailed test will have greater power than a two-tailed test.

c. A large sample will result in more power than a small sample.

KEY TERMS

hypothesis testing	Type II error	critical region	directional test
null hypothesis	level of significance	test statistic	one-tailed test
alternative hypothesis	alpha level	beta	power
Type I error			

Focus on Problem Solving

1. Hypothesis testing involves a set of logical procedures and rules that enable us to make general statements about a population when all we have are sample data. This logic is reflected in the four steps that have been used throughout this chapter. Hypothesis-testing problems will become easier to tackle when you learn to follow the steps.

   STEP 1   State the hypotheses and set the alpha level.

   STEP 2   Locate the critical region.

   STEP 3   Compute the z-score for the sample data.

   STEP 4   Make a decision about H_0 based on the result of step 3.

   A nice benefit of mastering these steps is that all hypothesis tests that will follow use the same basic logic outlined in this chapter.

2. Students often ask, "What alpha level should I use?" Or a student may ask, "Why is an alpha of .05 used?" as opposed to something else. There is no single correct answer to either of these questions. Keep in mind the idea of setting an alpha level in the first place: *to reduce the risk of committing a Type I error.* Therefore, you would not want to set α to something like .20. In that case, you would be taking a 20% risk of committing a Type I error—reporting an effect when one actually does not exist. Most researchers would find this level of risk unacceptable. Instead, researchers generally agree to the convention that $\alpha = .05$ is the greatest risk one should take in making a Type I error. Thus, the .05 level of significance is frequently used and has become the "standard" alpha level. However, some researchers prefer to take even less risk and use alpha levels of .01 and smaller.

3. Take time to consider the implications of your decision about the null hypothesis. The null hypothesis states that there is no effect. Therefore, if your deci-

sion is to reject H_0, you should conclude that the sample data provide evidence for a treatment effect. However, it is an entirely different matter if your decision is to fail to reject H_0. Remember, that when you fail to reject the null hypothesis, the results are inconclusive. It is impossible to *prove* that H_0 is correct; therefore, you cannot state with certainty that "there is no effect" when H_0 is not rejected. At best, all you can state is that "there is insufficient evidence for an effect" (see Box 8.1).

4. It is very important that you understand the structure of the z-score formula (page 218). It will help you understand many of the other hypothesis tests that will be covered later.

5. When you are doing a directional hypothesis test, read the problem carefully and watch for key words (such as increase or decrease, raise or lower, and more or less) that tell you which direction the researcher is predicting. The predicted direction will determine the alternative hypothesis (H_1) and the critical region. For example, if a treatment is expected to *increase* scores, H_1 would contain a *greater than* symbol and the critical region would be in the tail associated with high scores.

Demonstration 8.1

HYPOTHESIS TEST WITH z

A researcher begins with a known population, in this case scores on a standardized test that are normally distributed with $\mu = 65$ and $\sigma = 15$. The researcher suspects that special training in reading skills will produce a change in the scores for the individuals in the population. Because it is not feasible to administer the treatment (the special training) to everyone in the population, a sample of $n = 25$ individuals is selected and the treatment is given to this sample. Following treatment, the average score for this sample is $\overline{X} = 70$. Is there evidence that the training has an effect on test scores?

STEP 1   State the hypothesis and select an alpha level.

Remember, the goal of hypothesis testing is to use sample data to make general conclusions about a population. The hypothesis always concern an unknown population. For this demonstration, the researcher does not know what would happen if the entire population were given the treatment. Nevertheless, it is possible to make hypotheses about the treated population.

Specifically, the null hypothesis says that the treatment has no effect. According to H_0, the unknown population (after treatment) is identical to the original population (before treatment). In symbols,

$H_0 : \mu = 65$ (After special training, the mean is still 65.)

The alternative hypothesis states that the treatment does have an effect which causes a change in the population mean. In symbols,

$H_1 : \mu \neq 65$ (After special training, the mean is different from 65.)

At this time you also select the alpha level. Traditionally, α is set at .05 or .01. If there is particular concern about a Type I Error, or if a researcher desires to present overwhelming evidence for a treatment effect, a smaller alpha level can be used (such as $\alpha = .001$). For this demonstration, we will set alpha to .05. Thus, we are taking a 5% risk of committing a Type I error.

STEP 2 Locate the critical region.

You should recall that the critical region is defined as the set of outcomes that is very unlikely to be obtained if the null hypothesis is true. Therefore, obtaining sample data from this region would lead us to reject the null hypothesis and conclude there is an effect. Remember, the critical region is a region of rejection.

We begin by looking at all possible outcomes that could be obtained, then use the alpha level to determine the outcomes that are unlikely. For this demonstration, we look at the distribution of sample means for samples of $n = 25$; that is, all possible sample means that could be obtained if H_0 were true. The distribution of sample means will be normal because the original population is normal. It will have an expected value of $\mu = 65$ and a standard error of

$$\sigma_{\overline{X}} = \frac{\sigma}{\sqrt{n}} = \frac{15}{\sqrt{25}} = \frac{15}{5} = 3$$

With $\alpha = .05$, we want to identify the most unlikely 5% of this distribution. The most unlikely part of a normal distribution is in the tails. Therefore, we divide our alpha level evenly between the two tails, 2.5% or $p = .0250$ per tail. In column C of the Unit Normal table, find $p = .0250$. Then find its corresponding z-score in column A. The entry is $z = 1.96$. The boundaries for the critical region are -1.96 (on the left side) and $+1.96$ (on the right side). The distribution with its critical region is shown in Figure 8.11.

STEP 3 Obtain the sample data and compute the test statistic.

For this demonstration, the researcher obtained a sample mean of $\overline{X} = 70$. This sample mean corresponds to a z-score of

$$z = \frac{\overline{X} - \mu}{\sigma_{\overline{X}}} = \frac{70 - 65}{3} = \frac{5}{3} = +1.67$$

STEP 4 Make a decision about H_0 and state the conclusion.

The z-score we obtained is not in the critical region. This indicates that our sample mean of $\overline{X} = 70$ is not an extreme or unusual value to be obtained

Figure 8.11

The critical region for Demonstration 8.1 consists of the extreme tails with boundaries of $z = -1.96$ and $z = +1.96$.

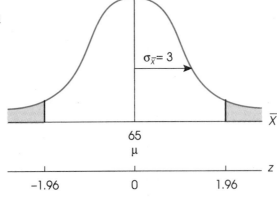

from a population with $\mu = 65$. Therefore our statistical decision is to *fail to reject* H_0. Our conclusion for the study is that the data do not provide sufficient evidence that the special training changes test scores.

PROBLEMS

1. Discuss the errors that can be made in hypothesis testing.
   a. What is a Type I error? Why might it occur?
   b. What is a Type II error? How does it happen?

2. Why do we test H_0 to establish an effect instead of H_1?

3. After several years of studying human performance in flight simulators, a psychologist knows that reaction times to an overhead emergency indicator form a normal distribution with $\mu = 200$ milliseconds and $\sigma = 20$. The psychologist would like to determine if placing the indicator in front of the person at eye level has any effect on reaction time. A random sample of $n = 25$ people is selected, they are tested in a simulator with the indicator light at eye level, and their reaction times are recorded.
   a. Identify the dependent variable and the independent variable.
   b. State the null hypothesis using a sentence that includes the dependent and independent variables.
   c. Using symbols, state the hypotheses (H_0 and H_1) that the psychologist is testing.
   d. Sketch the appropriate distribution and locate the critical region for the .05 level of significance.
   e. If the psychologist obtained an average reaction time of $\overline{X} = 195$ milliseconds for this sample, then what decision would be made about the null hypothesis?
   f. If the psychologist had used a sample of $n = 100$ subjects and obtained an average reaction time of $\overline{X} = 195$, then what decision would be made about the effects of the position of the indicator? Explain why this conclusion is different from the one in part e.

4. Suppose that scores on the Scholastic Aptitude Test form a normal distribution with $\mu = 500$ and $\sigma = 100$. A high school counselor has developed a special course designed to boost SAT scores. A random sample of $n = 16$ students is selected to take the course and then the SAT. The sample had an average score of $\overline{X} = 554$. Does the course have an effect on SAT scores?

   a. What are the dependent and independent variables for this experiment?
   b. Perform the hypothesis test using the four steps outlined in the chapter. Use $\alpha = .05$.
   c. If $\alpha = .01$ were used instead, what z-score values would be associated with the critical region?
   d. For part c, what decision should be made regarding H_0? Compare to part b and explain the difference.

5. Explain the structure of the z-score formula as it is used for hypothesis testing.
   a. What does $\overline{X} - \mu$ tell us in a hypothesis-testing situation?
   b. What does the standard error indicate?

6. Patients recovering from an appendix operation normally spend an average of $\mu = 6.3$ days is the hospital. The distribution of recovery times is normal with $\sigma = 1.2$ days. The hospital is trying a new recovery program that is designed to shorten the time patients spend in the hospital. The first 10 appendix patients in this new program were released from the hospital in an average of 5.5 days. On the basis of these data, can the hospital conclude that the new program has a significant effect on recovery time. Test at the .05 level of significance.

7. For the past 2 years the vending machine in the psychology department has charged 40¢ for a soft drink. During this time, company records indicate that an average of $\mu = 185$ cans of soft drinks were sold each week. The distribution of sales is approximately normal with $\sigma = 23$. Recently, the company increased the price to 50¢ a can. The weekly sales for the first 8 weeks after the price increase are as follows: 148, 135, 142, 181, 164, 159, 192, 173. Do these data indicate that there was a significant change in sales after the price increase? Test at the .05 level of significance.

8. IQ scores for the general population form a normal distribution with $\mu = 100$ and $\sigma = 15$. However, there are data that indicate that children's intelligence can be affected if their mothers have German measles during pregnancy. Using hospital records, a researcher obtained a sample of $n = 20$ school children whose mothers all had German measles during their pregnancies. The average IQ for this sample was $\bar{X} = 97.3$. Do these data indicate that German measles have a significant effect on IQ? Test with $\alpha = .05$.

9. In 1965 a nationwide survey revealed that U.S. grade school children spent an average of $\mu = 8.4$ hours per week doing homework. The distribution of homework times was normal with $\sigma = 3.3$. Last year a sample of $n = 200$ student was given the same survey. For this sample, the average number of homework hours was $\bar{X} = 7.1$.
   a. Do these data indicate a significant change in the amount of homework hours for American grade school children? Test at the .01 level of significance.
   b. If there had been only $n = 20$ students in the sample, would the data still indicate a significant change? Use the same sample mean, $\bar{X} = 7.1$, and use $\alpha = .01$.

10. The following sample of $n = 10$ scores was obtained from a normal population with $\sigma = 12$:

    78, 90, 54, 77, 71, 99, 85, 74, 93, 84.

    a. Use these data to test the hypothesis that the population mean is $\mu = 75$. Use $\alpha = .05$ for your test.
    b. Use these data to test the hypothesis that the population mean is $\mu = 85$. Use $\alpha = .05$ for your test.
    c. In parts a and b of this problem you should find that $\mu = 75$ and $\mu = 85$ are both acceptable hypotheses. Explain how two different values can both be acceptable.

11. A researcher is trying to assess some of the physical changes that occur in addicts during drug withdrawal. For the population, suppose the average body temperature is $\mu = 98.6°F$ with $\sigma = 0.56$. The following data consist of the body temperatures of a sample of heroin addicts during drug withdrawal: 98.6, 99.0, 99.4, 100.1, 98.7, 99.3, 99.9, 101.0, 99.6, 99.5, 99.4, 100.3. Is there a significant change in body temperature during withdrawal? Test at the .01 level of significance. Show all four steps of the hypothesis test.

12. A researcher would like to know if oxygen deprivation at the time of birth has a permanent effect on IQ. It is known that scores on a standard intelligence exam are normally distributed for the population with $\mu = 100$ and $\sigma = 15$. The researcher takes a random sample of individuals for whom complica-

tions at birth indicate moderate oxygen deprivation. The sample data are as follows: 92, 100, 106, 78, 96, 94, 98, 91, 83, 81, 86, 89, 87, 91, 89. Is there evidence for an effect?
   a. Test the hypothesis using the four-step method with alpha set at .05.
   b. What would the decision be if the .01 level of significance is used instead of the .05 level?

13. A psychologist develops a new inventory to measure depression. Using a very large standardization group of "normal" individuals, the mean score on this test is $\mu = 55$ with $\sigma = 12$, and the scores are normally distributed. To determine if the test is sensitive in detecting those individuals that are severely depressed, a random sample of patients who are described as depressed by a therapist is selected and given the test. Presumably, the higher the score on the inventory, the more depressed the patient is. The data are as follows: 59, 60, 60, 67, 65, 90, 89, 73, 74, 81, 71, 71, 83, 83, 88, 83, 84, 86, 85, 78, 79. Do patients score significantly different on the test? Test with the .01 level of significance.

14. On a vocational/interest inventory that measures interest in several categories, a very large standardization group of adults has an average score on the "literary" scale of $\mu = 22$ with $\sigma = 4$. A researcher would like to determine if scientists differ from the general population in terms of writing interests. A random sample of scientists is selected from the directory of a national scientific society. The scientists are given the inventory, and their test scores on the literary scale are as follows: 21, 20, 23, 28, 30, 24, 23, 19. Do scientists differ from the general population in their writing interests? Test at the .05 level of significance.

15. Suppose that the average birth weight for the population is $\mu = 2.9$ kilograms with $\sigma = 0.65$. An investigator would like to see if the birth weights of infants are significantly different for mothers that smoked cigarettes throughout their pregnancy. A random sample of women who smoke is selected, and the birth weight of their infants is recorded. The data (in kilograms) are as follows: 2.3, 2.0, 2.2, 2.8, 3.2, 2.2, 2.5, 2.4, 2.4, 2.1, 2.3, 2.6, 2.0, 2.3. What should the scientist conclude? Use the .01 level of significance.

16. A developmental psychologist has prepared a training program that, according to a psychological theory, should improve problem-solving ability. For the population of 6-year-olds, the average score on a standardized problem-solving test is known to be $\mu = 80$ with $\sigma = 10$. To test the effectiveness of the

training program, a random sample of $n = 18$ 6-year-old children is selected. After training, the average score for this sample is $\overline{X} = 84.44$. Can the experimenter conclude that the program has an effect? Test with alpha set at .05.

   a. Perform the hypothesis test showing all four steps. When you state the hypotheses, explain what they predict in terms of the independent and dependent variables used in this experiment.

   b. Would the same decision have been made about H_0 if a one-tailed had been used?

17. A researcher did a one-tailed hypothesis test using an alpha level of .01. For this test, H_0 was rejected. A colleague analyzed the same data but used a two-tailed test with $\alpha = .05$. In this test H_0 was *not* rejected. Can both analyses be correct? Explain your answer.

18. What happens to power as the treatment distribution gets farther from the null distribution?

19. Suppose a researcher normally uses an alpha level of .01 for hypothesis tests but this time used an alpha level of .05. What does this change in alpha level do to the amount of power? What does it do to the risk of a Type I error?

20. Explain why power for a hypothesis test can never be less than the alpha level for the test. (*Hint:* Sketch a null distribution and then add several different treatment distributions to your sketch. What happens to power as the treatment distribution gets very close to the null distribution?)

21. A researcher wants a statistical test to be powerful, yet would also like to avoid a Type I error. Which of the following approaches would achieve these goals? Explain your answer.

   a. Incease the alpha level (for example, from .05 to .10)

   b. Use a small alpha level but increase sample size

   c. Use a one-tailed test

22. A psychologist is examining the effect of chronic alcohol abuse on memory. In this experiment, a standardized memory test is used. Scores on this test for the general population form a normal distribution with $\mu = 50$ and $\sigma = 6$. A sample of $n = 22$ alcohol abusers have an average score of $\overline{X} = 47$. Is there evidence for memory impairment among alcoholics? Use $\alpha = .01$ for a one-tailed test.

23. Performance scores on a motor skills task form a normal distribution with $\mu = 20$ and $\sigma = 4$. A psychologist is using this task to determine the extent to which increased self-awareness affects performance. The prediction for this experiment is that increased self-awareness will reduce a subject's concentration and result in lower performance scores. A sample of $n = 16$ subjects is obtained, and each subject is tested on the motor skills task while seated in front of a large mirror. The purpose of the mirror is to make the subjects more self-aware. The average score for this sample is $\overline{X} = 15.5$. Use a one-tailed test with $\alpha = .05$ to test the psychologist's prediction.

24. A psychological theory predicts that individuals who grow up as an only child will have above-average IQs. A sample of $n = 64$ people from single-child families is obtained. The average IQ for this sample is $\overline{X} = 104.9$. In the general population, IQs form a normal distribution with $\mu = 100$ and $\sigma = 15$. Use a one-tailed test with $\alpha = .01$ to evaluate the theory.

25. A psychologist is interested in the long-term effects of a divorce on the children in a family. A sample is obtained of $n = 10$ children whose parents were divorced at least 5 years ago. Each child is given a personality questionnaire measuring depression. In the general population, the scores on this questionnaire form a normal distribution with $\mu = 80$ and $\sigma = 12$. The scores for this sample are as follows: 83, 81, 75, 92, 84, 107, 63, 112, 92, 88. The psychologist is predicting that children from divorced families will be more depressed than children in the general population. Use a one-tailed test with $\alpha = .05$ to test this hypothesis.

CHAPTER 9

INTRODUCTION TO THE *t* STATISTIC

TOOLS YOU WILL NEED

The following items are considered essential background material for this chapter. If you doubt your knowledge of any of these items, you should review the appropriate chapter or section before proceeding.

- Sample standard deviation (Chapter 4)
- Degrees of freedom (Chapter 4)
- Hypothesis testing (Chapter 8)

CONTENTS

Numerous accounts suggest that for many animals, including humans, a direct stare from another animal is aversive (e.g., Cook, 1977). Try it out for yourself. Make direct eye contact with a stranger in a cafeteria. Chances are the person will display avoidance by averting his or her gaze or turning away from you. Some insects, such as moths, have even developed eye-spot patterns on the wings or body to ward off predators (mostly birds) who may have a natural fear of eyes (Blest, 1957). Suppose a comparative psychologist is interested in determining whether or not the birds that feed on these insects show an avoidance of eye-spot patterns.

Using methods similar to those of Scaife (1976), the researcher performed the following experiment. A sample of $n = 16$ moth-eating birds is selected. The animals are tested in an apparatus that consists of a two-chambered box. The birds are free to roam from one side of the box to the other through a doorway in the partition that separates the two chambers. In one chamber, there are two eye-spot patterns painted on the wall. The other side of the box has plain walls. One at a time, the researcher tests each bird by placing it in the doorway between the chambers. Each subject is left in the apparatus for 60 minutes, and the amount of time spent in the plain chamber is recorded.

What kind of data should the experimenter expect if the null hypothesis is true? If the animals show no aver-

sion to the eye spots, they should spend, on average, half of the time in the plain side. Therefore, the null hypothesis would predict that

$$H_0 : \mu_{\text{plain side}} = 30 \text{ minutes}$$

Suppose the researcher collected data for the sample and found that the average amount of time spent on the plain side was $\overline{X} = 35$ minutes. The researcher now has two of the needed pieces of information to compute a z-score test statistic—the sample data ($\overline{X}$) and the hypothesized mean (according to H_0). All that is needed is the population standard deviation, so that the standard error can be computed. Note that the investigator does not have this information about the population. All that is known is that the population of animals should, on average, spend half of the 60-minute period in the plain chamber if the eye spots have no effect on behavior. Without complete information about the population, how can the comparative psychologist test the hypothesis with a z-score? The answer is simple—z cannot be used for the test statistic because the standard error cannot be computed. However, it is possible to estimate the standard error using the sample data and to compute a test statistic that is similar in structure to the z-score. This new test statistic is called the t statistic.

9.1 OVERVIEW

In the previous chapter we presented the statistical procedures that permit researchers to use a sample mean to test hypotheses about a population. These statistical procedures were based on a few basic notions, which we summarize as follows:

Remember, the expected value of the distribution of sample means is μ, the population mean.

1. A sample mean $\overline{X}$ is expected more or less to approximate its population mean μ. This permits us to use the sample mean to test a hypothesis about the population mean.

2. The standard error provides a measure of how well a sample mean approximates the population mean.

$$\sigma_{\overline{X}} = \frac{\sigma}{\sqrt{n}}$$

3. To quantify our inferences about the population, we convert each sample mean to a *z*-score using the formula

$$z = \frac{\overline{X} - \mu}{\sigma_{\overline{X}}}$$

When the *z*-scores form a normal distribution, we are able to use the unit normal table (Appendix B) to find the critical region for the hypothesis test.

The shortcoming of using the *z*-score as an inferential statistic is that the *z*-score formula requires more information than is usually available. Specifically, *z*-scores require that we know the value of the population standard deviation, which is needed to compute the standard error. Most often the standard deviation of the population is not known, and the standard error of sample means cannot be computed. Without the standard error, we have no way of quantifying the expected amount of distance (or error) between $\overline{X}$ and μ. We have no way of making precise, quantitative inferences about the population based on *z*-scores. For situations in which the population standard deviation is not known, we use the *t* statistic rather than a *z*-score.

9.2 THE *t* STATISTIC—A SUBSTITUTE FOR *z*

As previously noted, the limitation of *z*-scores in hypothesis testing is that the value for the population standard deviation must be known. However, more often than not, we have little information about the population. Fortunately, there is a relatively simple solution to the problem of not knowing the population standard deviation. When the value of σ is not known, we use the sample standard deviation in its place. In Chapter 4, the sample standard deviation was developed specifically to be an unbiased estimate of the population standard deviation. You should recall that the formula for the sample standard deviation is

$$s = \sqrt{\frac{SS}{n-1}}$$

Using this sample statistic, we can now estimate the standard error. The estimated standard error $s_{\overline{X}}$ is obtained by the formula

$$s_{\overline{X}} = \frac{s}{\sqrt{n}} \qquad (9.1)$$

Notice that we have substituted the sample standard deviation (*s*) in place of the unknown population standard deviation (σ). Also notice that the symbol for the estimated standard error is $s_{\overline{X}}$ instead of $\sigma_{\overline{X}}$, indicating that the value is computed from sample data rather than from the population parameter.

DEFINITION   *The estimated standard error* ($s_{\overline{X}}$) *is used as an estimate of* $\sigma_{\overline{X}}$ *when the value of* σ *is unknown. It is computed from the sample standard* deviation and provides an estimate of the standard distance between a sample mean $\overline{X}$ and the population mean μ

Now we can substitute the estimated standard error in the denominator of the *z*-score formula. This new test statistic is called a *t statistic:*

$$t = \frac{\overline{X} - \mu}{s_{\overline{X}}} \qquad (9.2)$$

The only difference between the *t* formula and the *z*-score formula is that the *z*-score formula uses the actual population standard deviation (σ) and the *t* statistic uses the sample standard deviation as an estimate when σ is unknown:

$$z = \frac{\overline{X} - \mu}{\sigma_{\overline{X}}} = \frac{\overline{X} - \mu}{\sigma/\sqrt{n}} \qquad t = \frac{\overline{X} - \mu}{s_{\overline{X}}} = \frac{\overline{X} - \mu}{s/\sqrt{n}}$$

Structurally, these two formulas have the same form:

$$z \text{ or } t = \frac{\text{sample mean} - \text{population mean}}{\text{(estimated) standard error}}$$

Because both *z*, and *t* formulas are used for hypothesis testing, there is one rule to remember:

RULE When you know the value of σ, use a *z*-score. If σ is unknown, use the *t* statistic.

DEFINITION The *t statistic* is used to test hypotheses about μ when the value for σ is not known. The formula for the *t* statistic is similar in structure to the *z*-score, except that the *t* statistic uses estimated standard error.

DEGREES OF FREEDOM AND THE *t* STATISTIC

In this chapter we have introduced the *t* statistic as a substitute for a *z*-score. The basic difference between these two is that the *t* statistic uses sample standard deviation (*s*), and the *z*-score uses the population standard deviation (σ). To determine how well a *t* statistic approximates a *z*-score, we must determine how well the sample standard deviation approximates the population standard deviation.

In Chapter 4 we introduced the concept of degrees of freedom. Reviewing briefly, you must know the sample mean before you can compute sample standard deviation. This places a restriction on sample variability such that only $n - 1$ scores in a sample are free to vary. The value $n - 1$ is called the *degrees of freedom* (or *df*) for the sample standard deviation.

$$\text{degrees of freedom} = df = n - 1 \qquad (9.3)$$

DEFINITION *Degrees of freedom* describe the number of scores in a sample that are free to vary. Because the sample mean places a restriction on the value of one score in the sample, there are $n - 1$ degrees of freedom for the sample (see Chapter 4).

The greater the value of *df* for a sample, the better *s* represents σ, and the better the *t* statistic approximates the *z*-score. This should make sense because the larger the sample (*n*), the better the sample represents its population. Thus, the degrees of freedom associated with *s* also describe how well *t* represents *z*.

THE *t* DISTRIBUTIONS

Every sample from a population can be used to compute a *z*-score or a *t* statistic. If you select all the possible samples of a particular size (*n*), then the entire set of resulting *z*-scores will form a *z*-score distribution. In the same way, the set of all possible *t* statistics will form a *t distribution*. As we saw in Chapter 7, the distribution of *z*-scores computed from sample means tends to be a normal distribution. For this reason, we consulted the unit normal table to find the critical region when using *z*-scores to test hypotheses about a population. The *t* distribution, on the other hand, is generally not normal. However, the *t* distribution will approximate a normal distribution in the same way that a *t* statistic approximates a *z*-score. How well a *t* distribution approximates a normal distribution is determined by degrees of freedom. In general, the greater the sample size (*n*), the larger the degrees of freedom (*n* − 1), and the better the *t* distribution approximates the normal distribution (see Figure 9.1).

THE SHAPE OF THE *t* DISTRIBUTION

The exact shape of a *t* distribution changes with degrees of freedom. In fact, statisticians speak of a "family" of *t* distributions. That is, there is a different sampling distribution of *t* (a distribution of all possible sample *t* values) for each possible number of degrees of freedom. As *df* gets very large, the *t* distribution gets closer in shape to a normal *z*-score distribution (see Box 9.1). A quick glance at Figure 9.1 reveals that distributions of *t* are bell-shaped and

Figure 9.1

Distributions of the *t* statistic for different values of degrees of freedom are compared to a normal *z*-score distribution. Like the normal distribution, *t* distributions are bell-shaped and symmetrical and have a mean of zero. However, *t* distributions have more variability, indicated by the flatter and more spread-out shape. The larger the value of *df*, the more closely the *t* distribution approximates a normal distribution.

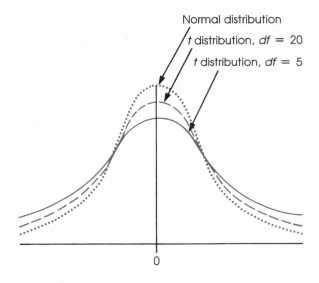

9.1 THE CRITICAL VALUES IN A NORMAL *z* DISTRIBUTION AND A *t* DISTRIBUTION: THE INFLUENCE OF DEGREES OF FREEDOM

AS PREVIOUSLY noted, a *t* distribution approximates a normal *z* distribution. How well it approximates a normal distribution depends on the value of *df*. This can be seen by simply comparing critical values for *z* with critical values of *t* at various degrees of freedom. For example, if we test a hypothesis with a *z*-score using a two-tailed test and $\alpha = .05$, the critical *z*-scores will be $+1.96$ and -1.96. However, suppose the population standard deviation were not known and we conducted this hypothesis test with a *t* statistic. For a sample of $n = 4$, the *t* statistic would have $df = 3$. For three degrees of freedom, the critical values of *t* would be $+3.182$ and -3.182 (with alpha still set at .05). When *df* is small, the *t* distribution is flatter and more spread out. Consequently, the tails have a greater area for the *t* distribution

compared to a normal distribution (see Figure 9.1). The extreme 5% of the distribution will be farther from the mean and have a larger critical value in the *t* distribution. If, however, we use a sample of $n = 31$, then $df = 30$, and the critical *t* values will be $+2.042$ and -2.042. These values are very close to the critical *z*-score values (± 1.96). If the sample is made even larger, say $n = 121$, the critical values get even closer to the *z* values. For 120 degrees of freedom, the critical values of *t* are $+1.980$ and -1.980 when $\alpha = .05$. Thus, the difference between a *t* distribution and a normal *z*-distribution becomes negligible when a sample of more than 30 individuals is used. (Note: Determining critical values for *t* is discussed on pages 247–248.)

symmetrical and have a mean of zero. However, the *t* distribution has more variability than a normal *z* distribution, especially when *df* values are small (Figure 9.1). The *t* distribution tends to be flatter and more spread out, whereas the normal *z* distribution has more of a central peak.

Why is the *t* distribution flatter and more variable than a normal *z* distribution? For a particular population, the top of the *z*-score formula, $\overline{X} - \mu$, can take on different values because $\overline{X}$ will vary from one sample to another. However, the value of the bottom of the *z*-score formula, $\sigma_{\overline{X}}$, is constant. The standard error will not vary from sample to sample because it is derived from the population standard deviation. The implication is that samples which have the same value for $\overline{X}$ should also have the same *z*-score.

On the other hand, the standard error in the *t* formula is not a constant because it is estimated. That is, $s_{\overline{X}}$ is based on the sample standard deviation, which will vary in value from sample to sample. The result is that samples can have the same value for $\overline{X}$ yet different values of *t* because the estimated error will vary from one sample to another. Therefore, a *t* distribution will have more variability than the normal *z* distribution. It will look flatter and more spread out. When the value of *df* increases, the variability in the *t* distribution decreases, and it more closely resembles the normal distribution, because with greater *df*, $s_{\overline{X}}$ will more closely estimate $\sigma_{\overline{X}}$, and when *df* is very large, they are nearly the same.

DETERMINING PROPORTIONS AND PROBABILITIES FOR *t* DISTRIBUTIONS Just as we used the unit normal table to locate proportions associated with *z*-scores, we will use a *t* distribution table to find proportions for *t* statistics. The complete *t* distribution table is presented in Appendix B, page A-24, and

Table 9.1

A portion of the *t* distribution table

			PROPORTION IN ONE TAIL			
	0.25	0.10	0.05	0.025	0.01	0.005
			PROPORTION IN TWO TAILS			
df	0.50	0.20	0.10	0.05	0.02	0.01
1	1.000	3.078	6.314	12.706	31.821	63.657
2	0.816	1.886	2.920	4.303	6.965	9.925
3	0.765	1.638	2.353	3.182	4.541	5.841
4	0.741	1.533	2.132	2.776	3.747	4.604
5	0.727	1.476	2.015	2.571	3.365	4.032
6	0.718	1.440	1.943	2.447	3.143	3.707

The numbers in the table are the values of *t* that separate the tail from the main body of the distribution. Proportions for one or two tails are listed at the top of the table and *df* values for *t* are listed in the first column.

a portion of this table is reproduced in Table 9.1. The two rows at the top of the table show proportions of the *t* distribution contained in either one or two tails, depending on which row is used. The first column of the table lists degrees of freedom for the *t* statistic. Finally, the numbers in the body of the table are the *t* values that mark the boundary between the tails and the rest of the *t* distribution.

For example, with *df* = 3, exactly 5% of the *t* distribution is located in the tail beyond *t* = 2.353 (see Figure 9.2). To find this value, you locate *df* = 3 in the first column and locate 0.05 (5%) in the one-tail proportion row. When you line up these two values in the table, you should find *t* = 2.353. Similarly, 5% of the *t* distribution is located in the tail beyond *t* = −2.353 (see Figure 9.2). Finally, you should notice that a total of 10% is contained in the two tails beyond *t* = ±2.353 (check the proportion value in the "two-tails" row at the top of the table).

Figure 9.2

The *t* distribution with *df* = 3. Note that 5% of the distribution is located in the tail beyond *t* = 2.353. Also, 5% is in the tail beyond *t* = −2.353. Thus, a total proportion of 10% (0.10) is in the two tails beyond *t* = ±2.353.

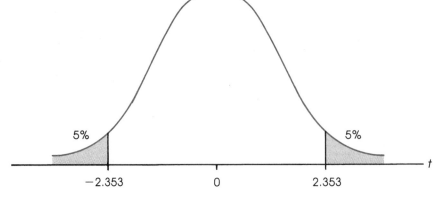

LEARNING CHECK   1. A hypothesis test with a *z*-score can be performed only when the population standard deviation is known. (True or false?)

2. To compute estimated standard error, $s_{\overline{X}}$, you must know the value for the population standard deviation. (True or false?)

3. As the value for *df* gets smaller, the *t* distribution resembles a normal distribution more and more. (True or false?)

4. As the value for *df* gets larger, *s* provides a better estimate of σ. (True or false?)

5. For *df* = 10, what *t* value(s) are associated with
   a. The top 1% of the *t* distribution?
   b. The bottom 5% of the *t* distribution?
   c. The most extreme 1% of the distribution?

ANSWERS   1. True. (With large samples, *z*-scores and *t* statistics are very similar. For this reason, some statisticians allow the use of a *z*-score instead of *t* when the sample size is at least *n* = 30. However, there is always some difference between *z* and *t*, so we recommend that you use a *z*-score only when the population standard deviation is known.)

2. false   3. false   4. true

5. a. +2.764   b. −1.812   c. +3.169 and −3.169

9.3 HYPOTHESIS TESTS WITH THE *t* STATISTIC

The *t* statistic formula is used in exactly the same way that the *z*-score formula is used to test a hypothesis about a population mean. Once again, the *t* formula and its structure are

$$t = \frac{\overline{X} - \mu}{s_{\overline{X}}} = \frac{\text{sample mean} - \text{population mean}}{\text{estimated standard error}}$$

In the hypothesis-testing situation, we have a population with an unknown mean, often a population that has received some treatment (Figure 9.3). The goal is to use a sample from the treated population as the basis for determining whether or not the treatment has any effect. As always, the null hypothesis states that the treatment has no effect. Specifically, H_0 predicts that the population mean is unchanged. The hypothesized value for the population mean is put into the *t* formula along with the sample mean (from the obtained data) and the estimated standard error (also computed from the sample data). When the resulting *t* statistic is near zero, we can conclude that the sample mean is not significantly different from the hypothesized value and the decision is "fail to reject H_0." In other words, there is no support for

Figure 9.3

The basic experimental situation for using the *t* statistic or the *z*-score is presented. It is assumed that the parameter μ is known for the population before treatment. The purpose of the experiment is to determine whether or not the treatment has an effect. We ask, Is the population mean after treatment the same as or different from the mean before treatment? A sample is selected from the treated population to help answer this question.

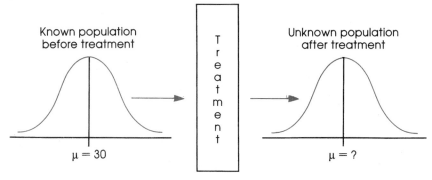

a treatment effect. If there is a substantial difference between the sample mean and the hypothesized μ, we will obtain a large value for *t* (large positive or large negative value). In this case, we would conclude that the data are not consistent with the null hypothesis and our decision would be to "reject H_0." The evidence suggests the existence of a treatment effect. The basic steps of the hypothesis-testing procedures will now be reviewed.

STEPS AND PROCEDURES   For hypothesis tests with a *t* statistic, we use the same steps that we used with *z*-scores (Chapter 8). The major difference is that we are now required to estimate standard error because σ is unknown. Consequently, we compute a *t* statistic rather than a *z*-score and consult the *t* distribution table rather than the unit normal table to find the critical region.

STEP 1   The hypotheses are stated and the alpha level is set. The experimenter states the null hypothesis, that is, what should happen if no treatment effect exists. On the other hand, the alternative hypothesis predicts the outcome if an effect does occur. These hypotheses are always stated in terms of the population parameter, μ.

STEP 2   Locate the critical region. The exact shape of the *t* distribution, and therefore the critical *t* values, vary with degrees of freedom. Thus, to find a critical region in a *t*-distribution, it is necessary to determine the value for *df*. Then the critical region can be located by consulting the *t* distribution table (Appendix B).

STEP 3   The sample data are collected and the test statistic is computed. When σ is unknown, the test statistic is a *t* statistic (formula 9.2).

STEP 4   The null hypothesis is evaluated. If the *t* statistic we obtained in step 3 falls within the critical region (exceeds the value of a critical *t*), then H_0 is rejected. It can be concluded that a treatment effect exists. However, if the obtained *t* value does not lie in the critical region, then we fail to reject H_0, and we conclude that we failed to observe evidence for an effect in our study (see Box 9.2).

9.2 COMPARING *z*-SCORES AND *t* STATISTICS AS TEST STATISTICS

CONCEPTUALLY, THE *z*-score and the *t* statistic are used similarly in hypothesis-testing situations:

$$z \text{ or } t = \frac{\text{sample data} - \text{population hypothesis}}{\text{amount of error between } \bar{X} \text{ and } \mu}$$

That is, in the numerator, we find the difference between the obtained sample data ($\bar{X}$) and the hypothesized population mean according to H_0. This discrepancy is compared to (divided by) the amount of error between $\bar{X}$ and μ that we would expect due to chance (the standard error). Thus, the discrepancy between the sample data and the null hypothesis would have to be much larger than chance (sampling error) in order to obtain a large test statistic (z or t) that falls in the critical region. The *t* statistics that follow in later chapters also have this same basic conceptual structure.

HYPOTHESIS-TESTING EXAMPLE

Let us return to the research problem posed in the Preview to demonstrate the steps and procedures of hypothesis testing. Recall that direct eye contact is avoided by many animals. Some animals, such as moths, have evolved large eye-spot patterns, presumably to ward off predators that have a natural aversion to direct gaze. The experiment will assess the effect of exposure to eye-spot patterns on the behavior of moth-eating birds, using procedures similar to Scaife's (1976) study.

EXAMPLE 9.1

 Hypothesis tests with the *t* statistic may be done with Minitab using the command TTEST (see Section 20.5).

To test the effectiveness of eye-spot patterns in deterring predation, a sample of $n = 16$ insectivorous birds is selected. The animals are tested in a box that has two separate chambers. The birds are free to roam from one chamber to another through a doorway in a partition. On the wall of one chamber, two large eye-spot patterns have been painted. The other chamber has plain walls. The birds are tested one at a time by placing them in the doorway in the center of the apparatus. Each animal is left in the box for 60 minutes, and the amount of time spent in the plain chamber is recorded. Suppose that the sample of $n = 16$ birds spent an average of $\bar{X} = 35$ minutes in the plain side, with $SS = 1215$. Can we conclude that eye-spot patterns have an effect on behavior? Note that while it is possible to predict a value for μ, we have no information about the population standard deviation.

STEP 1

State the hypotheses and select an alpha level. If the null hypothesis were true, then the eye-spot patterns would have no effect on behavior. The animals should show no preference for either side of the box. That is, they should spend half of the 60-minute test period in the plain chamber. In symbols the null hypothesis would state that

$$H_0 : \mu_{\text{plain side}} = 30 \text{ minutes}$$

Directional hypotheses could be used and would specify whether the average time on the plain side is more or less than 30 minutes.

The alternative hypothesis would state that the eye patterns have an effect on behavior. There are two possibilities: (1) The animals may avoid staying in the chamber with the eye spots as we suspect, or (2) maybe for some reason the animals may show a preference for the patterns painted on the wall. A nondirectional hypothesis (for a two-tailed test) would be represented in symbols as follows:

$$H_1 : \mu_{\text{plain side}} \neq 30 \text{ minutes}$$

We will set the level of significance at $\alpha = .05$ for two tails.

STEP 2 Locate the critical region. The test statistic is a *t* statistic because the population standard deviation is not known. The exact shape of the *t* distribution and therefore the proportions under the *t* distribution depend on the number of degrees of freedom associated with the sample. To find the critical region, *df* must be computed:

$$df = n - 1 = 16 - 1 = 15$$

For a two-tailed test at the .05 level of significance and with 15 degrees of freedom, the critical region consists of *t* values greater than $+2.131$ or less than -2.131. Figure 9.4 depicts the critical region in this *t* distribution.

STEP 3 Calculate the test statistic. To obtain the value for the *t* statistic, we first must compute s and then $s_{\overline{X}}$. The sample standard deviation is

$$s = \sqrt{\frac{SS}{n - 1}}$$
$$= \sqrt{\frac{1215}{15}}$$
$$= \sqrt{81}$$
$$= 9$$

The estimated standard error is

$$s_{\overline{X}} = \frac{s}{\sqrt{n}}$$
$$= \frac{9}{\sqrt{16}}$$
$$= 2.25$$

Finally, we can compute the *t* statistic for these sample data:

$$t = \frac{\overline{X} - \mu}{s_{\overline{X}}}$$
$$= \frac{35 - 30}{2.25}$$
$$= \frac{5}{2.25}$$
$$= 2.22$$

Figure 9.4

The critical region in the *t* distribution for α = .05 and *df* = 15.

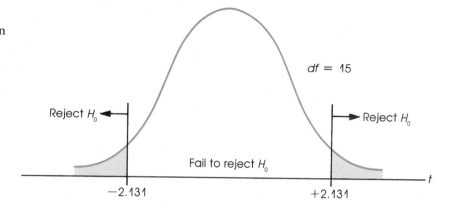

df = 15

Reject H_0 ← | → Reject H_0

Fail to reject H_0

−2.131   +2.131

t

STEP 4   Make a decision regarding H_0. The obtained *t* statistic of 2.22 falls into the critical region on the right-hand side of the *t* distribution (Figure 9.4). Our statistical decision is to reject H_0 and conclude that the presence of eye-spot patterns does influence behavior. As can be seen from the sample mean, there is a tendency for animals to avoid the eyes and spend more time on the plain side of the box. For this example, alpha was set at .05. Therefore, the probability that a Type I error has been committed is $p < .05$. It is common practice in scientific literature to report the results of the *t* test in the following manner:

> The data suggest that the birds spend significantly more time in the chamber without eye-spot patterns; $t(15) = +2.22$, $p < .05$, two-tailed.

Note that the degrees of freedom are reported in parentheses right after the symbol *t*. The value for the obtained *t* statistic follows (2.22) and next is the probability of committing a Type I error (less than 5%). Finally, the type of test (one- versus two-tailed) is noted.

DIRECTIONAL HYPOTHESES
AND ONE-TAILED TESTS

As we noted in Chapter 8, the nondirectional (two-tailed) test is commonly used for research that is intended for publication in a scientific journal. On the other hand, a directional (one-tailed) test may be used in some research situations, such as exploratory investigations or pilot studies. Although one-tailed tests are used occasionally, you should remember that the two-tailed test is preferred by most researchers. Even though a researcher may have a specific directional prediction for an experiment, it is generally safer and always appropriate to use a nondirectional (two-tailed) test. The following example demonstrates a directional hypothesis test with a *t* statistic, using the same experimental situation that was presented in Example 9.1.

EXAMPLE 9.2

The research question is whether eye-spot patterns will affect the behavior of birds placed in a special testing box. The researcher is expecting the birds to avoid the eye-spot patterns. Therefore, the researcher predicts that the birds will spend most of the hour on the plain side of the box.

STEP 1   State the hypotheses and select an alpha level. With most directional tests it is easier to begin by stating the alternative hypothesis. Remember, H_1 states that the treatment does have an effect. For this example, the eye patterns should cause the birds to spend most of their time on the plain side, In symbols,

$$H_1 : \mu_{\text{plain side}} > 30 \text{ minutes}$$

The null hypothesis states that the treatment will not have the predicted effect. In this case, H_0 says that the eye patterns will not cause the birds to spend more time on the plain side. In symbols,

$$H_0 : \mu_{\text{plain side}} \leq 30 \text{ minutes} \qquad \text{(not greater than 30 minutes)}$$

We will set the level of significance at $\alpha = .05$.

STEP 2   Locate the critical region. In this example, the researcher is predicting that the sample mean ($\overline{X}$) will be greater than 30. The null hypothesis states that the population mean is $\mu = 30$ (or less). If you examine the structure of the *t* statistic formula, it should be clear that a positive *t* statistic would support the researcher's prediction and refute the null hypothesis.

$$t = \frac{\overline{X} - \mu}{s_{\overline{X}}}$$

The problem is to determine how large a positive value is necessary to reject H_0. To find the critical value you must look in the *t* distribution table using the one-tail proportions. With a sample of $n = 16$, the *t* statistic will have $df = 15$; using $\alpha = .05$, you should find a critical *t* value of 1.753. Figure 9.5 depicts the critical region in the *t* distribution.

Figure 9.5

The critical region in the *t* distribution for $\alpha = .05$, $df = 15$, one-tailed test.

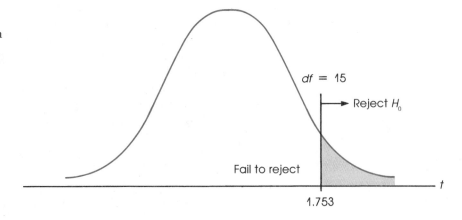

9.3 INDEPENDENT OBSERVATIONS

INDEPENDENT OBSERVATIONS are a basic requirement for nearly all hypothesis tests. The critical concern is that the observation or score obtained for one individual is not influenced by the observation or score obtained for another individual. The concept of independent observations is best demonstrated by counterexample. The following two situations demonstrate circumstances where observations are *not* independent.

1. A researcher is interested in examining television preferences for children. To obtain a sample of $n = 20$ children, the researcher selects 4 children from family A, 3 children from family B, 5 children from family C, 2 children from family D, and 6 children from family E.

    It should be obvious that the researcher does *not* have 20 independent observations. Within each family the children probably share television preference (at least they watch the same shows). Thus, the response for each child is likely to be related to the responses of his or her siblings.

2. A researcher is interested in people's ability to judge distances. A sample of 20 people is obtained. All 20 subjects are gathered together in the same room. The researcher asks the first subject to estimate the distance between New York and Miami. The second subject is asked the same question, then the third subject, fourth subject, and so on.

    Again, the observations that the researcher obtains are not independent: The response of each subject is probably influenced by the responses of the previous subjects. For example, consistently low estimates by the first few subjects could create pressure to conform and thereby increase the probability that the following subjects would also produce low estimates.

STEP 3 Calculate the test statistic. The computation of the *t* statistic is the same for either a one-tailed or a two-tailed test. Earlier (in Example 9.1), we found that the data for this experiment produce a test statistic of $t = 2.22$.

STEP 4 Make a decision. The test statistic is in the critical region, so we reject H_0. In terms of the experimental variables, we have decided that the birds spent significantly more time on the plain side of the box than on the side with eye-spot patterns.

ASSUMPTIONS OF THE *t* TEST

There are two basic assumptions necessary for hypothesis tests with the *t* statistic.

1. The values in the sample must consist of *independent* observations.

    In everyday terms, two observations are independent if there is no consistent, predictable relation between the first observation and the second. More precisely, two events (or observations) are independent if the occurance of the first event has no effect on the probability of the second event. Specific examples of independence and nonindependence are examined in Box 9.3. Usually, this assumption is satisfied by using a *random* sample, which also helps ensure that the sample is representative of the population and that the results can be generalized to the population.

2. The population sampled must be normal.

This assumption is a necessary part of the mathematics underlying the development of the *t* statistic and the *t* distribution table. However, violating this assumption has little practical effect on the results obtained for a *t* statistic, especially when the sample size is relatively large. With very small samples, a normal population is important. With larger samples, this assumption can be violated without affecting the validity of the hypothesis test. If you have reason to suspect that the population is not normal, use a large sample to be safe.

THE VERSATILITY OF THE *t* TEST

The obvious advantage of hypothesis testing with the *t* statistic (as compared to *z*-scores) is that you do not need to know the value of the population standard deviation. This means that we still can do a hypothesis test even though we have little or no information about the population. One result of this extra versatility is that it is possible to do *t* tests in circumstances where hypothesis tests with *z*-scores would not even allow for the statement of a null hypothesis.

Both the *t* statistic and *z*-score tests have been introduced as a means of determining whether or not a treatment has any effect on the dependent variable. Recall that the null hypothesis states that the treatment has no effect. That is, the population mean after treatment has the same value that it had before treatment. Notice that this experimental situation requires that we know the value of the population mean before the treatment. This requirement is often unrealistic and limits the usefulness of *z*-score tests. Although the *t* statistic often is used in this before-and-after type of experiment (Figure 9.3), the *t* test also permits hypothesis testing in situations where we do not have a "known" population to serve as a before-treatment standard. Specifically, the *t* test can be used in situations where the value for the null hypothesis can come from a theory, a prediction, or just wishful thinking. Some examples follow. Notice in each example that the hypothesis is not dependent on knowing the actual population mean before treatment and that the rest of the *t* statistic can be computed entirely from the obtained sample data.

1. A researcher would like to examine the accuracy of people's judgment of time when they are distracted. Individuals are placed in a waiting room where many distracting events occur for a period of 12 minutes. The researcher then asks each person to judge how much time has passed. The null hypothesis would state that distraction has no effect and that time judgments are accurate. That is,

$$H_0 : \mu = 12 \text{ minutes}$$

2. A local fund-raising organization has set a goal of receiving \$25 per contributor. After 1 week, a sample of contributions is selected to see if they deviate significantly from the goal. The null hypothesis would state that the contributions do not deviate from the goal of the organization. In symbols, it is

$$H_0 : \mu = \$25.00$$

3. A soft-drink company has developed a new, improved formula for its product and would like to determine how consumers respond to the new formula. A sample is obtained, and each individual is asked to taste the original soft drink and the new formula. After tasting, the subjects are required to state whether the new formula is better or worse than the original formula using a 7-point scale. A rating of 4 indicates no preference between the old and new formulas. Ratings above 4 indicate that the new formula is better (5 = slightly better, 6 = better, and 7 = much better). Similarly, ratings below 4 indicate that the new formula tastes worse than the old formula. The null hypothesis states that there is no perceived difference between the two formulas. In symbols, the new formula would receive an average rating of

$$H_0 : \mu = 4$$

LEARNING CHECK 1. A professor of philosophy hypothesizes that an introductory course in logic will help college students with their other studies. To test this hypothesis, a random sample of $n = 25$ freshmen is selected. These students are required to complete a logic course during their freshman year. At the time of graduation, the final grade point average is computed for each of these students. The mean GPA for this sample is $\bar{X} = 2.83$ with $SS = 6$. Can the professor conclude that the grades for the sample were significantly different from the rest of the graduating class, which had an average GPA of $\mu = 2.58$? Test with a two-tailed test at $\alpha = .05$.

a. State the hypotheses.

b. Determine the value for df and locate the critical region.

c. Compute the test statistic.

d. Make a decision regarding H_0.

ANSWERS 1. a. $H_0 : \mu_{\text{with logic course}} = 2.58$ (even with the logic course, the population mean GPA will still be 2.58)

$H_1 : \mu_{\text{with logic course}} \neq 2.58$ (for the population, the logic course has an effect on GPA)

b. $df = 24$; the critical region begins at t values of $+2.064$ and -2.064.

c. $s = 0.5$; $s_{\bar{X}} = 0.1$; $t = +2.5$. d. Reject H_0.

SUMMARY

1. When σ is unknown, the standard error cannot be computed, and a hypothesis test based on a z-score is impossible.

2. In order to test a hypothesis about μ when σ is un-

known, σ must first be estimated using the sample standard division s:

$$s = \sqrt{\frac{SS}{n - 1}}$$

Next, the standard error is estimated by substituting s for σ in the standard error formula. The estimated standard error ($s_{\bar{X}}$) is calculated in the following manner:

$$s_{\bar{X}} = \frac{s}{\sqrt{n}}$$

Finally, a *t* statistic is computed using the estimated standard error. The *t* statistic serves as a substitute for a *z*-score, which cannot be computed because σ is unknown.

$$t = \frac{\bar{X} - \mu}{s_{\bar{X}}}$$

3. The structure of the *t* formula is similar to that of the *z*-score in that

$$z \text{ or } t = \frac{\text{sample mean} - \text{population mean}}{\text{(estimated) standard error}}$$

4. The *t* distribution is an approximation of the normal *z* distribution. To evaluate a *t* statistic that is obtained for a sample mean, the critical region must be located in a *t* distribution. There is a family of *t* distributions, with the exact shape of a particular distribution of *t* values depending on degrees of freedom ($n - 1$). Therefore, the critical *t* values will depend on the value for *df* associated with the *t* test. As *df* increases, the shape of the *t* distribution approaches a normal distribution.

KEY TERMS

estimated standard error   *t* statistic   degrees of freedom   *t* distribution
independent observations

Focus on Problem Solving

1. The first problem we confront in analyzing data is determining the appropriate statistical test. Remember, you can use a *z*-score for the test statistic only when the value for σ is known. If the value for σ is not provided, then you must use the *t* statistic.

2. For a *t* test, students sometimes use the unit normal table to locate the critical region. This, of course, is a mistake. The critical region for a *t* test is obtained by consulting the *t* distribution table. Notice that to use this table you first must compute the value for degrees of freedom (*df*).

3. For the *t* test, the sample standard deviation is used to find the value for estimated standard error. Remember, when computing the sample standard deviation use $n - 1$ in the denominator (see Chapter 4). When computing estimated standard error, use $\sqrt{n}$ in the denominator.

Demonstration 9.1

A HYPOTHESIS TEST WITH THE *t* STATISTIC

A psychologist has prepared an "Optimism Test" that is administered yearly to graduating college seniors. The test measures how each graduating class feels about its future—the higher the score, the more optimistic the class. Last year's class had a mean score of $\mu = 15$. A sample of $n = 9$ seniors from this year's class was selected and tested. The scores for these seniors are as follows:

7   12   11   15   7   8   15   9   6

On the basis of this sample, can the psychologist conclude that this year's class has a different level of optimism than last year's class?

Note that this hypothesis test will use a t statistic because the population standard deviation (σ) is not known.

STEP 1   State the hypotheses and select an alpha level.

The statements for the null hypothesis and the alternative hypothesis follow the same form for the t statistic and the z-score test.

$H_0 : \mu = 15$ (There is no change.)

$H_1 : \mu \neq 15$ (This year's mean is different.)

For this demonstration we will use $\alpha = .05$, two tails.

STEP 2   Locate the critical region.

Remember, for hypothesis tests with the t statistic, we must now consult the t distribution table to find the critical t values. With a sample of $n = 9$ students, the t statistic will have degrees of freedom equal to

$$df = n - 1 = 9 - 1 = 8$$

For a two-tailed test with $\alpha = .05$ and $df = 8$, the critical t values are $t = \pm 2.306$. These critical t values define the boundaries of the critical region. The obtained t value must be more extreme that either of these critical values to reject H_0.

STEP 3   Obtain the sample data and compute the test statistic.

For the t formula, we need to determine the values for the following:

1. The sample mean, $\overline{X}$

2. The estimated standard error, $s_{\overline{X}}$

We will also have to compute sums of squares (SS) and the standard deviation (s) for the sample in order to get the estimated standard error.

The sample mean. For these data, the sum of the scores is

$$\Sigma X = 7 + 12 + 11 + 15 + 7 + 8 + 15 + 9 + 6 = 90$$

Therefore, the sample mean is

$$\overline{X} = \frac{\Sigma X}{n} = \frac{90}{9} = 10$$

Sum of squares. We will use the definitional formula for sum of squares,

$$SS = \Sigma (X - \overline{X})^2$$

The following table summarizes the steps in the computation of *SS*.

X	$X - \bar{X}$	$(X - \bar{X})^2$
7	$7 - 10 = -3$	9
12	$12 - 10 = +2$	4
11	$11 - 10 = +1$	1
15	$15 - 10 = +5$	25
7	$7 - 10 = -3$	9
8	$8 - 10 = -2$	4
15	$15 - 10 = +5$	25
9	$9 - 10 = -1$	1
6	$6 - 10 = -4$	16

For this demonstration problem, the sum of squares value is

$$SS = \Sigma (X - \bar{X})^2 = 9 + 4 + 1 + 25 + 9 + 4 + 25 + 1 + 16$$
$$= 94$$

Sample standard deviation. The sample standard deviation is the square root of *SS* divided by degrees of freedom.

$$s = \sqrt{\frac{SS}{n - 1}} = \sqrt{\frac{94}{8}} = \sqrt{11.75} = 3.43$$

Estimated standard error. The estimated standard error for these data is

$$s_{\bar{X}} = \frac{s}{\sqrt{n}} = \frac{3.43}{\sqrt{9}} = \frac{3.43}{3} = 1.14$$

The t statistic. Now that we have the estimated standard error and the sample mean, we can compute the *t* statistic. For this demonstration,

$$t = \frac{\bar{X} - \mu}{s_{\bar{X}}} = \frac{10 - 15}{1.14} = \frac{-5}{1.14} = -4.39$$

STEP 4   Make a decision about H_0 and a conclusion.
    The *t* statistic we obtained ($t = -4.39$) is in the critical region. Thus our sample data are unusual enough to reject the null hypothesis at the .05 level of significance. We can conclude that there is a significant difference in level of optimism between this year's and last year's graduating classes, $t(8) = -4.39$, $p < .05$, two tailed.

PROBLEMS

1. When a *t* statistic is used, why is it necessary to estimate the standard error?

2. Why is the *t* statistic more versatile for inferential statistics than the *z*-score?

3. What assumptions (or set of conditions) must be satisfied for a t test to be valid?

4. Why is a t distribution generally more variable than a normal distribution?

5. What is the relationship between the value for degrees of freedom and the shape of the t distribution? What happens to the critical value of t for a particular alpha level when df increases in value?

6. A distribution is known to be normal with $\mu = 50$ and $\sigma = 12$. A researcher would like to evaluate the effect of a particular treatment on this population. A sample of $n = 4$ individuals is selected, and the treatment is administered. After treatment, this sample yielded an average score of $\overline{X} = 64$ with $SS = 300$.
   a. Because σ is known, you can use a z-score hypothesis test. Also you could ignore the fact that σ is known and just use the sample data to compute a t statistic. Which of these two tests do you think is more likely to produce a correct decision? Explain your answer.
   b. Using the fact that $\sigma = 12$ is known, do a z-score test with $\alpha = .05$ to determine whether or not the treatment has a significant effect.
   c. Ignoring the fact that σ is known, use the sample data to compute an estimated standard error and do the t statistic test with $\alpha = .05$ to determine whether or not the treatment has a significant effect.
   (Note that the same data can lead to different conclusions, depending on which test you use.)

7. For a standard set of discrimination problems that have been used for years in primate research, it is known that monkeys require an average of $\mu = 20$ trials before they can successfully reach the criterion (five consecutive correct solutions). A psychologist hypothesizes that the animals can learn the task vicariously—that is, simply by watching other animals perform the task. To test this hypothesis, the researcher selects a random sample of $n = 4$ monkeys. These animals are placed in neighboring enclosures from which they can watch another animal learn the task. After a week of viewing other animals, the four monkeys in the sample are tested on the problem. These animals require an average of $\overline{X} = 15$ trials to solve the problem, with $SS = 300$. On the basis of these data, can the psychologist conclude that there is evidence that the animals perform significantly better after viewing others? Use a one-tailed test at the .01 level of significance

   a. State the hypotheses using symbols. Explain what they predict for this experiment.
   b. Sketch the distribution and locate the critical region.
   c. Calculate the test statistic.
   d. Make a decision regarding H_0 and state your conclusion.

8. A group of students recently complained that all of the statistics classes are offered early in the morning. They claim that they "think better" later in the day and therefore would do better in the course had it been offered in the afternoon. To test this claim, the instructor scheduled the course this past semester for 3 P.M. The afternoon class was given the same final exam that has been used in previous semesters. The instructor knows that for previous students the scores are normally distributed with a mean of 70. The afternoon class with 16 students had an average score on the final of $\overline{X} = 76$ with $SS = 960$. Do the students perform significantly better in the afternoon section?
   a. Test with alpha set at .05 and with a one-tailed test.
   b. Identify the independent and dependent variables.

9. A recent national survey reports that the general population gives the president an average rating of $\mu = 62$ on a scale of 1 to 100. A researcher suspects that college students are likely to be more critical of the president than people in the general population. To test these suspicions, a random sample of college students is selected and asked to rate the president. The data for this sample are as follows: 44, 52, 24, 45, 39, 57, 20, 38, 78, 74, 61, 56, 49, 66, 53, 49, 47, 88, 38, 51, 65, 47, 35, 59, 23, 41, 50, 19. On the basis of this sample, can the researcher conclude that college students rate the president differently? Test at the .01 level of significance, two tails.

10. A fund raiser for a charitable organization has set a goal of averaging $20 per donation. To see if the goal is being met, a random sample of recent donations is selected. The data from this sample are as follows: 20, 5, 10, 15, 25, 5, 8, 10, 30, 10, 15, 24, 50, 10, 7, 15, 10, 5, 5, 15.
   a. Do the contributions differ significantly from the goal of the fund raiser? Test at the .05 level of significance.
   b. Would you reach the same conclusion had the .01 level of significance been used?

11. A researcher would like to examine the effect of labor unions on the average pay of workers. The in-

vestigator obtains information from the National Carpenters Union, which states that the average pay for union carpenters is $\mu = \$7.80$ per hour. The researcher then obtains a random sample of eight carpenters who do not belong to a union and records the pay for each. The data from this sample are as follows: 6.25, 7.50, 6.75, 6.90, 7.10, 7.15, 8.00 6.15. Does the average pay of nonunion carpenters differ significantly from union members? Test at the .01 level of significance.

12. On a standardized spatial skills task, normative data reveal that people typically get $\mu = 15$ correct solutions. A psychologist tests $n = 7$ individuals who have brain injuries in the right cerebral hemisphere. For the following data, determine whether or not right-hemisphere damage results in significantly reduced performance on the spatial skills task. Test with alpha set at .05 with one tail. The data are as follows: 12, 16, 9, 8, 10, 17, 10.

13. After many studies of memory, a psychologist has determined that when a standard list of 40 words is presented at a rate of 2 words per second, college students can recall an average of $\mu = 17.5$ words from the list. The psychologist would like to determine if the rate of presentation affects memory. A random sample of $n = 15$ students is selected, and each is given the standard list of words at a rate of only 1 word per second. At the end of the presentation of the list, each student is tested for recall. The number of words recalled is as follows: 14, 21, 23, 19, 17, 20, 24, 16, 27, 17, 20, 21, 18, 20, 19.
    a. Is there evidence for an effect of presentation rate? Test at the .05 level of significance and with two tails.
    b. Would you arrive at the same conclusion had the .01 level of significance been used?

14. A researcher knows that the average weight of American men between the ages of 30 and 50 is $\mu = 166$ pounds. The researcher would like to determine if men who have heart attacks between those ages are heavier than the average male. For a random sample of heart patients, body weights are recorded. The data are as follows: 153, 176, 201, 188, 157, 182, 208, 186, 163, 187, 230, 196, 167, 193, 171, 198, 191, 193, 233, 197, 196.
    Are these patients significantly heavier than expected? Use a one-tailed test at the .01 level of significance.

15. A family therapist states that parents talk to their teenagers an average of 27 minutes per week. Surprised by that claim, a psychologist decided to collect some data on the amount of time parents spend in conversation with their teenage children. For $n = 12$ parents, the study revealed the following times (in minutes) devoted to conversation in a week:

29 22 19 25 27 28
21 22 24 26 30 22

Do the psychologist's findings differ significantly from the therapist's claim? If so, is the family expert's claim an overestimate or underestimate of actual time spent talking to children? Use the .05 level of significance with two tails.

16. A psychologist assesses the effect of distraction on time perception. Subjects are asked to judge the length of time between signals given by the experimenter. The actual interval of time is 10 minutes. During this period, the subjects are distracted by noises, conversation between the experimenter and his assistant, and questions from the assistant. The experimenter expects that the subjects' judgments will average around 10 minutes if the distraction has no effect. The data are as follows:

11   9.5   14   8
 8   14   15   15
12   7.5   15   18
15   12   11   10
20   10   9   14

Is there a significant effect? Test at the .05 level of significance. What conclusion can be made?

17. A researcher would like to determine whether humidity can have an effect on eating behavior. It is known that under regular circumstances laboratory rats eat an average of $\mu = 10$ grams of food each day. The researcher selects a random sample of $n = 15$ rats and places them in a controlled atmosphere room where the relative humidity is maintained at 90%. The daily food consumption for each of these rats is as follows:

FOOD CONSUMPTION				
9.1	8.3	7.6	10.2	8.4
6.9	9.3	10.7	11.2	9.8
8.5	12.1	8.4	7.7	9.2

On the basis of these data, can the researcher conclude that humidity affects eating behavior? Test with $\alpha = .05$.

18. A manufacturer of office furniture is designing a new computer table. Although it is known that the standard height for typing tables is 26 inches, the manufacturer is concerned that the best height for a computer might be different. A sample of $n = 18$ computer operators is obtained, and each is asked to position the height of an adjustable table at its most comfortable level. The heights for this sample are as follows:

HEIGHTS (INCHES)		
27.50	26.25	25.75
29.50	26.50	29.00
27.25	26.00	28.25
26.25	28.00	26.25
26.75	27.00	27.50
28.00	26.25	25.75

On the basis of this sample, should the company conclude that the best height for a computer table is different from 26 inches? Test with $\alpha = .05$.

19. Recently the college newspaper conducted a survey to assess student attitudes toward spending student government money to help support college athletic teams. Student responses were recorded on a scale from 0 (totally opposed) to 10 (completely in favor). A value of 5 on this scale represented a neutral point. The results from $n = 327$ students gave an average opinion score of $\overline{X} = 6.3$ with $SS = 1343$. Do these data indicate that the general student opinion is significantly different from neutral? Test with $\alpha = .01$.

20. For several years the members of the faculty in the department of psychology have been teaching small sections of the introductory statistics course because they believe that students learn better in small classes. For these small classes, the average score on the standardized final exam is $\mu = 73.5$. This year, for the first time, the department offered one large section. For the 81 students in this large class, the scores on the final exam averaged $\overline{X} = 71.2$ with $SS = 9647$. The psychologist would like to use these data to determine whether there is any difference between students' performance in large versus small classes. Perform the appropriate test with $\alpha = .05$.

CHAPTER 10

HYPOTHESIS TESTS WITH TWO INDEPENDENT SAMPLES

CONTENTS

In a classic study in the area of problem solving, Katona (1940) compared the effectiveness of two methods of instruction. One group of subjects was shown the exact, step-by-step procedure for solving a problem, and then these subjects were required to memorize the solution. This method was called *learning by memorization* (later called the *expository* method). Subjects in a second group were encouraged to study the problem and find the solution on their own. Although these subjects were given helpful hints and clues, the exact solution was never explained. This method was called *learning by understanding* (later called the *discovery* method).

Katona's experiment included the problem shown in Figure 10.1. This figure shows a pattern of five squares made of matchsticks. The problem is to change the pattern into exactly four squares by moving only three matches. (All matches must be used, none can be removed, and all the squares must be the same size.) Two groups of subjects learned the solution to this problem. One group learned by understanding, and the other group learned by memorization. After 3 weeks both groups returned to be tested again. The two groups did equally well on the matchstick problem they had learned earlier. But when they were given two new problems (similar to the matchstick problem), the *understanding* group performed much better than the *memorization* group.

The outcome of Katona's experiment probably is no surprise. However, you should realize that the experimental design is different from any we have considered

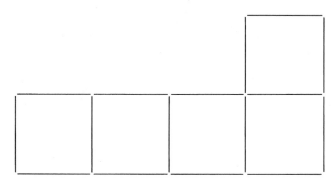

Figure 10.1

A pattern of five squares made of matchsticks. The problem is to change the pattern into exactly four squares by moving only three matchsticks.

before. This experiment involved *two separate samples*. Previously we have examined statistical techniques for evaluating the data from only one sample. In this chapter we will present the statistical procedures that allow a researcher to use two samples to evaluate the difference between two experimental treatment conditions.

Incidentally, if you still haven't discovered the solution to the matchstick problem, keep trying. According to Katona's results, it would be very poor teaching strategy for us to give you the answer.

Katona, G. (1940) *Organizing and Memorizing.* New York: Columbia University Press. Reprinted by permission.

10.1 OVERVIEW

Until this point, all the inferential statistics we have considered have involved using one sample as the basis for drawing conclusions about one population. Although these *single-sample* techniques are used occasionally in real research, most of the interesting experiments require two (or more) sets of data in order to compare two (or more) populations. For example, a social psychologist may want to compare men and women in terms of their attitudes toward abortion, or an educational psychologist may want to compare two methods for teaching mathematics. In both of these examples, the basic question concerns a mean difference between two populations or between two treatments. Is the average attitude for men any different from the average attitude for women? Do children who are taught math by method A score higher than children who are taught by method B?

Figure 10.2

Do the achievement scores for children taught by method A differ from the scores for children taught by method B? In statistical terms, are the two population means the same or different? Because neither of the two population means is known, it will be necessary to take two samples, one from each population. The first sample will provide information about the mean for the first population, and the second sample will provide information about the second population.

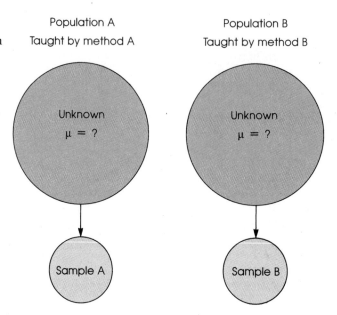

Population A
Taught by method A

Population B
Taught by method B

Unknown
$\mu = ?$

Unknown
$\mu = ?$

Sample A

Sample B

In most experimental situations, a researcher will not have prior knowledge about either of the two populations being compared. This means that the researcher has a question about two unknown populations. One way to examine two unknown populations is to take two separate samples (see Figure 10.2). In this chapter we will present the statistical techniques that permit a researcher to examine the data obtained from two separate samples. More specifically, our goal is to use the data from two samples as the basis for evaluating the mean difference between two populations.

DEFINITION

An experiment that uses a separate sample for each treatment condition (or each population) is called an *independent-measures* experimental design.

The term *independent-measures* comes from the fact that the experimental data consist of two *independent* sets of measurements, that is, two separate samples. On occasion, you will see an independent-measures experiment referred to as a *between-subjects* or a *between-groups* design. This terminology reflects the fact that an independent-measures design evaluates differences between treatments by looking at differences between the groups of subjects.

10.2 THE *t* STATISTIC FOR AN INDEPENDENT-MEASURES EXPERIMENT

Because an independent-measures experiment involves two separate samples, we will need some special notation to help specify which data go with which sample. This notation involves the use of subscripts, which are small numbers written beside each sample statistic. For example, the number of scores in the first sample would be identified by n_1; for the second sample, the number of scores would be n_2. The sample means would be identified by $\overline{X}_1$ and $\overline{X}_2$. The sums of squares would be SS_1 and SS_2.

Recall that our goal is to evaluate the mean difference between two populations (or between two treatment conditions). In symbols, the mean difference between the two populations can be written as $\mu_1 - \mu_2$. For hypothesis tests we will hypothesize a value for this mean difference. Generally, the null hypothesis says there is no difference between the two population means: $\mu_1 - \mu_2 = 0$.

The basis for the hypothesis test will be a *t* statistic. The formula for this *t* statistic will have the same general structure as the single-sample *t* formula that was introduced in Chapter 9.

$$t = \frac{\overline{X} - \mu}{s_{\overline{X}}} = \frac{\text{sample data} - \text{population parameter}}{\text{estimated standard error}}$$

However, the details of the formula must be modified to accommodate the independent-measures experimental design. Now the population parameter of interest is the difference between the two population means ($\mu_1 - \mu_2$). The corresponding sample data would be the difference between the two sample means ($\overline{X}_1 - \overline{X}_2$). The standard error in the denominator of the formula measures the standard distance between the sample data ($\overline{X}_1 - \overline{X}_2$) and the population parameter ($\mu_1 - \mu_2$). As always, standard error tells how well a sample value is expected to approximate the corresponding population value. In this case, the standard error tells how well the sample mean difference should approximate the population mean difference. The symbol for this standard error is $s_{\overline{X}_1 - \overline{X}_2}$. The *s* indicates an estimated standard distance and the subscript $\overline{X}_1 - \overline{X}_2$ simply indicates that our sample value is the difference between two sample means. Substituting these values into the general *t* formula gives

$$t = \frac{(\overline{X}_1 - \overline{X}_2) - (\mu_1 - \mu_2)}{s_{\overline{X}_1 - \overline{X}_2}}$$

This is the *t* formula that will be used with data from an independent-measures experiment. You should note that this is still a *t* statistic; it has the same basic structure as the original *t* formula that was introduced in Chapter 9. However, to distinguish between these two *t* formulas, we will occasionally refer to the original formula as the *single-sample t statistic* and this new formula as the *independent-measures t statistic*. To complete the independent-measures *t* formula, we must define more precisely the calculations needed for the standard error $s_{\overline{X}_1 - \overline{X}_2}$.

POOLED VARIANCE   The purpose of standard error is to provide a measure of how well a sample statistic represents the corresponding population parameter. In general, standard error is determined by two factors:

1. The variability of the scores
2. The size of the sample

To calculate the standard error for the independent-measures t statistic, we will begin by determining the variability of the scores.

You should recall that the original t statistic was developed to be used in situations where the population variability is unknown. The general strategy of the t statistic is to use the sample data to compute an estimate of the variability in the population. With an independent-measures experiment, we have two samples which are combined to obtain a single estimate of population variance. The result is called the *pooled variance* because it is obtained by averaging, or "pooling," the two sample variances. To compute this pooled variance, we will find the average of the two sample variances, but we will allow the bigger sample to carry more weight in determining the average. This process is demonstrated in the following example.

EXAMPLE 10.1 Suppose we have two samples from the same population. The first sample has $n = 4$ scores and $SS = 36$. For the second sample, $n = 8$ and $SS = 56$. From these data, we can compute a variance for each sample. For sample 1,

$$s^2 = \frac{SS}{n - 1} = \frac{36}{3} = 12$$

For sample 2,

$$s^2 = \frac{SS}{n - 1} = \frac{56}{7} = 8$$

Because these two samples are from the same population, each of the sample variances provides an estimate of the same population variance. Therefore, it is reasonable somehow to average these two estimates together in order to get a better estimate. Before we average the two variances, however, you should notice that one of the samples is much bigger than the other. Because bigger samples tend to give better estimates of the population, we would expect the sample variance based on $n = 8$ to be a better value than the variance based on $n = 4$. When we pool the two variances, we will let the "better" value carry more weight.

To compute the pooled variance, we will weight each of the sample variances by its degrees of freedom ($df = n - 1$). The degrees of freedom indicate how well the sample variance approximates the population variance (the bigger the sample, the bigger the df, and the better the estimate). To find the pooled variance, or the weighted mean for two sample variances, you follow two steps:

1. Multiply each s^2 by its df and then add the results together (this weights each variance).

2. Divide this total by the sum of the two df values.

The equation for this process is

$$\text{pooled variance} = s_p^2 = \frac{df_1 s_1^2 + df_2 s_2^2}{df_1 + df_2} \tag{10.1}$$

For this example, the calculation can be described in words as follows: You take 3 of the first variance ($df = 3$) and 7 of the second variance ($df = 7$). This gives you a total of 10 variances ($df_1 + df_2 = 10$). To find the average, you must divide by 10. For example,

$$\text{pooled variance} = \frac{3(12) + 7(8)}{3 + 7} = \frac{36 + 56}{10} = 9.2$$

Notice that the value we obtained is not halfway between the two sample variances. Rather it is closer to $s^2 = 8$ (the big sample) than it is to $s^2 = 12$ (the small sample), because the larger sample carried more weight in computing the average.

You may have noticed that the calculation of the pooled variance in Example 10.1 can be simplified greatly. In the numerator of the formula, each sample variance is multiplied by its *df*. When you do this, you always obtain *SS:*

$$df(s^2) = df \frac{SS}{df} = SS$$

Therefore, we can use *SS* in place of $df(s^2)$ in the formula. The simplified result is

$$\text{pooled variance} = s_p^2 = \frac{SS_1 + SS_2}{df_1 + df_2} \tag{10.2}$$

THE STANDARD ERROR FOR A SAMPLE MEAN DIFFERENCE

In general, the purpose of standard error is to provide a measure of how accurately a sample statistic approximates the population parameter. In the independent measures *t* formula, the sample statistic consists of two sample means, and the population parameter consists of two population means. We expect the sample data ($\overline{X}_1 - \overline{X}_2$) to be close to the population parameter ($\mu_1 - \mu_2$), but there will be some error. Our goal is to determine how much error. To develop the formula for this standard error, we will consider two points:

1. First, we know that each of the two sample means provides an estimate of its own population mean:

   $\overline{X}_1$ approximates μ_1 with some error.

   $\overline{X}_2$ approximates μ_2 with some error.

10.1   A CLOSER LOOK AT STANDARD ERROR

IN CHAPTER 7 we first introduced standard error as a measure of how well a sample mean ($\overline{X}$) represents its population mean (μ). Formula 7.1 (page 193) defined standard error as $\sigma_{\overline{X}} = \sigma/\sqrt{n}$. Later, in Chapter 9, we introduced the estimated standard error, $s_{\overline{X}}$, which is used with the t statistic. Estimated standard error was defined by formula (9.1) as $s_{\overline{X}} = s/\sqrt{n}$. Notice that in both equations, standard error is determined by two values:

1. The standard deviation of the scores, either σ or s

2. The sample size, n

In Chapter 7 we also noted that standard error can be expressed in terms of variance (page 193). In the independent-measures t statistic, the variance is also used to compute standard error,

$$\sqrt{\frac{s_p^2}{n}}$$

Although this equation *looks* different from the equations that use standard deviation, it actually is the same thing. This fact can be demonstrated by starting with formula (9.1) and then (1) squaring the standard error and (2) taking the square root of the squared value.

ORIGINAL STANDARD ERROR	SQUARED STANDARD ERROR	SQUARE ROOT OF SQUARED VALUE
$\dfrac{s}{\sqrt{n}}$	$\dfrac{s^2}{n}$	$\sqrt{\dfrac{s^2}{n}}$

Note that by squaring and then taking the square root, we are right back where we started. The value of the standard error is the same, but the appearance of the formula has changed. In the independent-measures t formula, standard error has a new appearance but it is really the same standard error you learned in Chapters 7 and 9, and it still provides a measure of how accurately a sample mean ($\overline{X}$) represents it population mean (μ).

Finally, you should remember that in the independent-measures formula we now have two sample means, so the formula shows two errors, one from each sample.

The amount of error from each sample is defined by the standard error of $\overline{X}$.

2. We want to know the total amount of error involved in using two sample means to approximate two population means. To do this, we will find the error from each sample separately and then add the two errors together.

The resulting formula for the independent-measures standard error is

$$s_{\overline{X}_1 - \overline{X}_2} = \sqrt{\frac{s_p^2}{n_1} + \frac{s_p^2}{n_2}}$$

(10.3)

In this formula, s_p^2/n_1 represents the error from the first sample and s_p^2/n_2 is the error from the second sample (see Box 10.1). Because we now have two sample means approximating two population means, we now have two sources of error. The formula for the standard error for the independent-measures *t* statistic simply adds together the two sources of error. Also note that the standard error formula uses the pooled variance, s_p^2, as the measure of variability for the scores.

THE FINAL FORMULA AND DEGREES OF FREEDOM

The complete equation for the independent measures *t* statistic is as follows:

$$t = \frac{(\overline{X}_1 - \overline{X}_2) - (\mu_1 - \mu_2)}{s_{\overline{X}_1 - \overline{X}_2}} = \frac{(\overline{X}_1 - \overline{X}_2) - (\mu_1 - \mu_2)}{\sqrt{\dfrac{s_p^2}{n_1} + \dfrac{s_p^2}{n_2}}} \qquad (10.4)$$

with the pooled variance s_p^2 defined by either formula 10.1 or formula 10.2.

The degrees of freedom for this *t* statistic are determined by the *df* values for the two separate samples:

Remember, we pooled the two sample variances to compute the t statistic. Now we combine the two df values to obtain the overall df for the t statistic.

$$df = df \text{ for first sample} + df \text{ for second sample} \qquad (10.5)$$
$$= df_1 + df_2$$

Occasionally, you will see degrees of freedom written in terms of the number of scores in each sample:

$$df = (n_1 - 1) + (n_2 - 1) \qquad (10.6)$$
$$= n_1 + n_2 - 2$$

This *t* formula will be used for hypothesis testing. We will use the sample data $(\overline{X}_1 - \overline{X}_2)$ as the basis for testing hypotheses about the population parameter $(\mu_1 - \mu_2)$.

LEARNING CHECK

1. Describe the general experimental situation in which an independent-measures statistic would be used.

2. Identify the two sources of error that are reflected in the standard error for the independent-measures *t* statistic.

3. Sample 1 of an experiment has dozens of subjects, and $s_1^2 = 32$. On the other hand, sample 2 has fewer than 10 subjects, and its variance is $s_2^2 = 57$. When these variances are pooled, which sample variance will s_p^2 more closely resemble?

ANSWERS

1. Independent-measures statistics are used whenever an experiment uses separate samples to represent the different treatment conditions or populations being compared.

2. The two sources of error come from the differences between the means of both

samples and their respective population means. That is, $\overline{X}_1$ approximates μ_1 with some error and $\overline{X}_2$ approximates μ_2 with some error.

3. The value for s_p^2 will be closer to $s_1^2 = 32$ because the size of sample 1 is larger.

10.3 HYPOTHESIS TESTS WITH THE INDEPENDENT-MEASURES t STATISTIC

The independent-measures t statistic can be used to test a hypothesis about the mean difference between two populations (or between two treatments). As always, the null hypothesis states that there is no difference:

$$H_0 : \mu_1 - \mu_2 = 0$$

The alternative hypothesis says that there is a mean difference:

$$H_1 : \mu_1 - \mu_2 \neq 0$$

The hypothesis test procedure will determine whether or not the data provide evidence for a mean difference between the two populations. At the conclusion of the hypothesis test, we will decide either to

a. Reject H_0: We conclude that the data indicate a significant difference between the two populations, or to

b. Fail to reject H_0: The data do not provide sufficient to evidence to conclude that a difference exists.

For hypothesis tests, the independent-measures t statistic has the same conceptual structure as the single-sample t (Chapter 9):

$$t = \frac{\text{sample data} - \text{population hypothesis}}{\text{amount of sampling error}}$$

As noted earlier, the sample data now consist of the difference between two sample means $(\overline{X}_1 - \overline{X}_2)$. The population hypothesis is the value for $\mu_1 - \mu_2$. According to the null hypothesis, this value equals zero $(\mu_1 - \mu_2 = 0)$. The amount of error between the sample data $(\overline{X}_1 - \overline{X}_2)$ and the population $(\mu_1 - \mu_2)$ is now measured by the estimated standard error for sample mean difference, $s_{\overline{X}_1 - \overline{X}_2}$. Note that when the sample data are close to the hypothesis, we should get a t statistic near zero, and our decision will be to fail to reject H_0 (see Figure 10.3). On the other hand, when the data are very different from the hypothesis, we should obtain a large value for t (large positive or large negative), and we will reject H_0.

A complete example of a hypothesis test with two independent samples follows. Notice that the hypothesis testing procedure follows the same four steps that we have used before.

Figure 10.3

The *t* distribution with *df* = 18. The critical region for $\alpha = .05$ is shown.

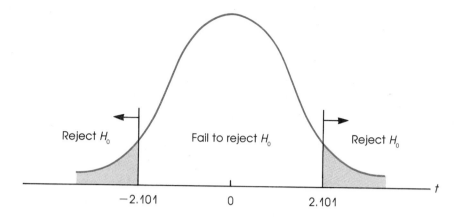

STEP 1 State the hypotheses H_0 and H_1 and select an alpha level. For the independent-measures *t* test, the hypotheses concern the difference between two population means.

STEP 2 Locate the critical region. The critical region is defined as sample data that would be extremely unlikely ($p < \alpha$) if the null hypothesis were true. In this case, we will be locating extremely unlikely *t* values.

STEP 3 Get the data and compute the test statistic. Here we compute the *t* value for our data using the value from H_0 in the formula.

STEP 4 Make a decision. If the *t* statistic we compute is in the critical region, we reject H_0. Otherwise we conclude that the data do not provide sufficient evidence that the two populations are different.

EXAMPLE 10.2 In recent years psychologists have demonstrated repeatedly that using mental images can greatly improve memory. A hypothetical experiment, designed to examine this phenomenon, is presented here.

The psychologist first prepares a list of 40 pairs of nouns (for example, dog/bicycle, grass/door, lamp/piano). Next, two groups of subjects are obtained (two separate samples). Subjects in the first group are given the list for 5 minutes and instructed to memorize the 40 noun pairs. Subjects in the second group receive the same list of words, but in addition to the regular instructions these people are told to form a mental image for each pair of nouns (imagine a dog riding a bicycle, for example). Notice that the two samples are identical except that the second group is using mental images to help learn the list.

Later each group is given a memory test, and the psychologist records the number of words correctly recalled for each individual. The data from this experiment are as follows. On the basis of these data, can the psychologist conclude that mental images affected memory?

Remember, an independent-measures design means that there are separate samples for each treatment condition.

Example 10.2 is analyzed with the Minitab command TWOSAMPLE in Section 20.5.

DATA (NUMBER OF WORDS RECALLED)			
GROUP 1 (NO IMAGES)		GROUP 2 (IMAGES)	
24	13	18	31
23	17	19	29
16	20	23	26
17	15	29	21
19	26	30	24
$n = 10$		$n = 10$	
$\overline{X} = 19$		$\overline{X} = 25$	
$SS = 160$		$SS = 200$	

STEP 1 State the hypothesis and select α.

Directional hypotheses could be used and would specify whether imagery should increase or decrease recall scores.

$H_0 : \mu_1 - \mu_2 = 0$ (No difference; imagery has no effect.)

$H_1 : \mu_1 - \mu_2 \neq 0$ (Imagery produces a difference.)

We will set $\alpha = .05$.

STEP 2 This is an independent-measures design. The t statistic for these data will have degrees of freedom determined by

$$
\begin{aligned}
df &= df_1 + df_2 \\
&= (n_1 - 1) + (n_2 - 1) \\
&= 9 + 9 \\
&= 18
\end{aligned}
$$

The t distribution for $df = 18$ is presented in Figure 10.3. For $\alpha = .05$, the critical region consists of the extreme 5% of the distribution and has boundaries of $t = +2.101$ and $t = -2.101$.

STEP 3 Obtain the data and compute the test statistic. The data are as given, so all that remains is to compute the t statistic. Because the independent measures t formula is relatively complex, the calculations can be simplified by dividing the process into three parts.

First, find the pooled variance for the two samples:

Caution: The pooled variance combines the two samples to obtain a single estimate of variance. In the formula the two samples are combined in a single fraction.

$$
\begin{aligned}
s_p^2 &= \frac{SS_1 + SS_2}{df_1 + df_2} \\
&= \frac{160 + 200}{9 + 9} \\
&= \frac{360}{18} \\
&= 20
\end{aligned}
$$

Second, use the pooled variance to compute the standard error:

Caution: The standard error adds the errors from two separate samples. In the formula these two errors are added as two separate fractions.

$$s_{\overline{X}_1 - \overline{X}_2} = \sqrt{\frac{s_p^2}{n_1} + \frac{s_p^2}{n_2}}$$

$$= \sqrt{\frac{20}{10} + \frac{20}{10}}$$

$$= \sqrt{4}$$

$$= 2$$

Third, compute the *t* statistic:

$$t = \frac{(\overline{X}_1 - \overline{X}_2) - (\mu_1 - \mu_2)}{s_{\overline{X}_1 - \overline{X}_2}} = \frac{(19 - 25) - 0}{2}$$

$$= \frac{-6}{2}$$

$$= -3.00$$

STEP 4 Make a decision. The obtained value ($t = -3.00$) is in the critical region. This result is very unlikely if H_0 is true. Therefore, we reject H_0 and conclude that using mental images produced a significant difference in memory performance. More specifically, the group using images recalled significantly more words than the group with no images.

 SPSS^X A-78

In the scientific literature it is common to report the results of a hypothesis test in a concise, standardized format. For the test described in Example 10.2, the report would state the following: $t(18) = -3.00$, $p < .05$. This statement indicates that the *t* statistic has $df = 18$, the value obtained from these sample data is $t = -3.00$, and this value is in the critical region with $\alpha = .05$.

DIRECTIONAL HYPOTHESES AND ONE-TAILED TESTS When planning an independent-measures experiment, a researcher usually has some expectation or specific prediction for the outcome. For the memory experiment described in Example 10.2, the psychologist clearly expects the group using images to have higher memory scores than the group without images. This kind of directional prediction can be incorporated into the statement of the hypotheses, resulting in a directional, or one-tailed, test. You should recall from Chapter 8 that one-tailed tests are used only in limited situations, where a researcher wants to increase the chances of finding a significant difference. In general, a nondirectional (two-tailed) test is preferred, even in research situations where there is a definite directional prediction. The following example demonstrates the procedure for stating hypotheses and locating the critical region for a one-tailed test using the independent-measures *t* statistic.

EXAMPLE 10.3 We will use the same experimental situation that was described in Example 10.2. The researcher is using an independent-measures design to examine the effect of mental images on memory. The prediction is that the imagery group will have higher memory scores.

STEP 1   State the hypotheses and select α. As always, the null hypothesis says that there is no effect, and H_1 says that there is a difference between the treatments. With a one-tailed test, it usually is easier to begin with the statement of H_1.

For this example, we will identify the no-imagery condition as treatment 1 and the imagery condition as treatment 2. Because images are expected to produce higher scores, the alternative hypothesis would be

$$H_1 : \mu_1 - \mu_2 < 0 \qquad \text{(Imagery produces higher scores.)}$$

The null hypothesis states that the treatment does not work. For this example,

$$H_0 : \mu_1 - \mu_2 \geq 0 \qquad \text{(Imagery scores are not higher.)}$$

We will set $\alpha = .05$.

STEP 2   Locate the critical region. The researcher predicts that the imagery group (sample 2) will have higher scores. If this is correct, then $\overline{X}_2$ will be greater than $\overline{X}_1$, and the data will produce a negative t statistic.

$$t = \frac{(\overline{X}_1 - \overline{X}_2) - (\mu_1 - \mu_2)}{s_{\overline{X}_1 - \overline{X}_2}}$$

Thus, a negative value for t will tend to support the researcher's prediction and refute H_0. The question is, How large a negative t value is needed to reject H_0? With $n = 10$ scores in each sample, the data will produce an independent-measures t statistic with $df = 18$. To find the critical value, look in the t distribution table with $df = 18$ and $\alpha = .05$ for a one-tailed test. You will find a critical t value of 1.734, and this value should be negative. Figure 10.4 shows the one-tailed critical region in the t distribution. The data from this example produce a test sta-

The table lists critical values without signs. You must determine whether the sign is positive or negative.

Figure 10.4

The critical region in the t distribution for $\alpha = .05$, $df = 18$, one-tailed test.

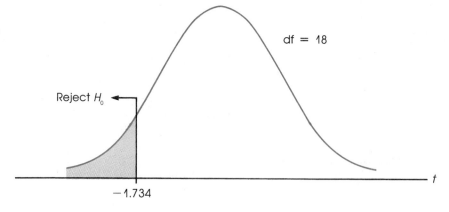

tistic of $t = -3.00$ (see Example 10.2). This value is in the critical region, so we reject H_0 and conclude that recall is significantly better in the imagery condition than in the no-imagery condition.

THE *t* STATISTIC AS A RATIO

You should note that the magnitude of the *t* statistic is determined not only by the mean difference between the two samples but also by the sample variability. The bigger the difference between the sample means (the numerator of the *t* formula), the bigger the *t* value. This relation is reasonable because a big difference between the samples is a clear indication of a difference between the two populations. However, the sample variability (in the denominator of the *t* formula) is just as important. If the variability is large, *t* will tend to be small. The role of variability becomes clearer if you consider a simplified version of the *t* formula:

$$t = \frac{\text{sample mean difference}}{\text{variability}}$$

Notice that we have left out the population mean difference because the null hypothesis says that this is zero. Also, we have used the general term *variability* in place of standard error. In this simplified form *t* becomes a ratio involving only the sample mean difference and the sample variability. It should be clear that large variability will make the *t* value smaller (or small variability will make *t* larger). Thus, variability plays an important role in determining whether or not a *t* statistic is significant. When variability is large, even a big difference between the two sample means may not be enough to make the *t* statistic significant. On the other hand, when variability is low, even a small difference between the two sample means may be enough to produce a significant *t* statistic. The importance of sample variability is demonstrated in the following example.

EXAMPLE 10.4

The following two hypothetical experiments demonstrate the influence of variability in the computation and interpretation of an independent-measures *t* statistic. Each of these experiments compares attitude scores for men versus women. Both experiments use a sample of $n = 7$ individuals from each of the populations, and both experiments obtain the sample mean values ($\overline{X} = 8$ for the men and $\overline{X} = 12$ for the women). The only difference between the two experiments is in the amount of sample variability.

The data from experiment I are pictured in Figure 10.5. In this experiment the scores in each sample are clustered around the mean, so the sample variability is relatively small. The hypothesis test using these data gives a *t* statistic of $t = 9.16$. With $df = 12$, this value is in the critical region, so we would reject H_0 and conclude that the population mean for men is different from the population mean for women.

If you look at the data in Figure 10.5, the statistical decision should be easy to understand. The two samples look like they come from different populations. By visually examining a graph of the data, you often can predict the outcome of a statistical test.

Figure 10.5

Data from experiment I comparing attitude scores for men versus women. The independent-measures *t* test for these data gives a *t* statistic of *t* = 9.16. This value is in the critical region, so we reject H_0 and conclude that the two samples come from different populations.

Now consider the data from experiment II, which are shown in Figure 10.6. Do these two samples look like they came from two separate populations? It should be clear that it is no longer easy to see a difference between the two samples. The scores completely overlap, and it appears likely that all 14 scores could have come from the same population.

The impression that the two samples do not look different is supported by the hypothesis test. The data from experiment II give a *t* statistic of *t* = 1.18. This value is not in the critical region, so we fail to reject H_0. In this case, we conclude that there is not enough evidence to say that the samples come from two different populations.

There are two general points to be made from this example. First, variability plays an important role in the independent-measures hypothesis test. In both experiments there was a 4-point difference between the two sample means. In experiment I this difference was easy to see, and it was statistically significant. In experiment II this 4-point difference gets lost in all the variability.

Figure 10.6

Data from experiment II comparing attitude scores for men versus women. The independent-measures *t* test for these data gives a *t* statistic of *t* = 1.18. This value is not in the critical region, so we fail to reject H_0 and conclude that there is not sufficient evidence to say that the two samples come from different populations.

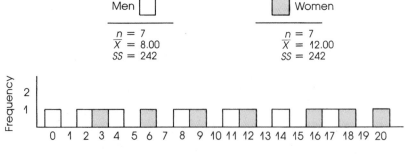

The second point is that the *t* statistic you obtain from a hypothesis test should be intuitively reasonable. In the first experiment, it looks like there are two separate populations, and the *t* statistic supports this appearance. In the second experiment, there does not appear to be any difference, and the *t* statistic says that there is no difference. The *t* value should not be a mysterious number; it simply is a precise, mathematical way of determining whether or not it "looks like" there is a difference between two samples.

LEARNING CHECK

1. A development psychologist would like to examine the difference in mathematical skills for 10-year-old boys versus 10-year-old girls. A sample of 10 boys and 10 girls is obtained, and each child is given a standardized mathematical abilities test. The data from this experiment are as follows:

BOYS	GIRLS
$\overline{X} = 37$	$\overline{X} = 31$
$SS = 150$	$SS = 210$

Do these data indicate a significant different in mathematical skills for boys versus girls? Test at the .05 level of significance.

2. A psychologist is interested in the effect of aging on memory. A sample of 10 college graduates is obtained. Five of these people are between 30 and 35 years old. The other 5 are between 60 and 65 years old. Each person is given a list of 40 words to memorize. A week later each person is asked to recall as many of the words as possible. The data from this experiment are as follows:

30-YEARS-OLDS	60-YEAR-OLDS
$\overline{X} = 21$	$\overline{X} = 16$
$SS = 130$	$SS = 190$

Do these data provide evidence for a significant change in recall ability with age? Test at the .05 level of significance.

ANSWERS

1. Pooled variance = 20; standard error = 2; $t = 3.00$. With $df = 18$, this value is in the critical region, so the decision is to reject H_0: There is a significant difference.

2. Pooled variance = 40; standard error = 4; $t = 1.25$. With $df = 8$, this value is not in the critical region, so the decision is to fail to reject H_0. These data do not provide evidence for a significant difference.

10.4 ASSUMPTIONS UNDERLYING THE INDEPENDENT-MEASURES *t* FORMULA

There are three assumptions that should be satisfied before you use the independent-measures *t* formula for hypothesis testing:

1. The observations within each sample must be independent (see page 255).
2. The two populations from which the samples are selected must be normal.
3. The two populations from which the samples are selected must have equal variances.

The first two assumptions should be familiar from the single-sample *t* hypothesis test presented in Chapter 9. As before, the normality assumption is the less important of the two, especially with large samples. When there is reason to suspect that the populations are far from normal, you should compensate by ensuring that the samples are relatively large.

The third assumption is referred to as *homogeneity of variance* and states that the two populations being compared must have the same variance. You may recall a similar assumption for both the *z*-score and the single-sample *t*. For those tests, we assumed that the effect of the treatment was to add (or subtract) a constant amount to each individual score. As a result, the population standard deviation after treatment was the same as it had been before treatment. We now are making essentially the same assumption but phrasing it in terms of variances.

You should recall that the pooled variance in the *t* statistic formula is obtained by averaging together the two sample variances. It makes sense to average these two values only if they both are estimating the same population variance—i.e., if the homogeneity of variance assumption is satisfied. If the two sample variances represent different population variances, then the average would be meaningless. (*Note:* There is no meaning to the value obtained by averaging two unrelated numbers. For example, what is the significance of the number obtained by averaging your shoe size and the last two digits of your social security number?)

The homogeneity of variance assumption is quite important because violating this assumption can negate any meaningful interpretation of the data from an independent-measures experiment. Specifically, when you compute the *t* statistic in a hypothesis test, all the numbers in the formula come from the data except for the population mean difference which you get from H_0. Thus, you are sure of all the numbers in the formula except for one. If you obtain an extreme result for the *t* statistic (a value in the critical region), you conclude that the hypothesized value was wrong. But consider what happens when you violate the homogeneity of variance assumption. In this case, you have two questionable values in the formula (the hypothesized population value and the meaningless average of the two variances). Now if you obtain an extreme *t* statistic, you do not know which of these two values is responsible. Specifically, you cannot reject the hypothesis because it may have been the pooled variance that produced the extreme *t* statistic. Without

Remember, adding (or subtracting) a constant to each score does not change the standard deviation.

The importance of the homogeneity assumption increases when there is a large discrepancy between the sample sizes. With equal (or nearly equal) sample sizes, this assumption is less critical but still important.

10.2 HARTLEY'S *F*-MAX TEST FOR HOMOGENEITY OF VARIANCE

ALTHOUGH THERE are many different statistical methods for determining whether or not the homogeneity of variance assumption has been satisfied, Hartley's *F*-max test is one of the simplest to compute and to understand. An additional advantage is that this test can be used to check homogeneity of variance with two or more independent samples. In Chapter 13 we will examine statistical methods involving several samples, and Hartley's test will be useful again.

The *F*-max test is based on the principle that a sample variance provides an unbiased estimate of the population variance. Therefore, if the population variances are the same, the sample variances should be very similar. The procedure for using the *F*-max test is as follows:

1. Compute the sample variance, $s^2 = SS/df$, for each of the separate samples.

2. Select the largest and the smallest of these sample variances and compute

$$F\text{-max} = \frac{s^2(\text{largest})}{s^2(\text{smallest})}$$

A relatively large value for *F*-max indicates a large difference between the sample variances. In this case, the data suggest that the population variances are different and that the homogeneity assumption has been violated. On the other hand, a small value of *F*-max (near 1.00) indicates that the sample variances are similar and that the homogeneity assumption is reasonable.

3. The *F*-max value computed for the sample data is compared with the critical value found in Table B3 (Appendix B). If the sample value is larger than the table value, then you conclude that the variances are different and that the homogeneity assumption is not valid.

To locate the critical value in the table, you need to know

a. k = number of separate samples. (For the independent-measures *t* test, $k = 2$.)

b. $df = n - 1$ for each sample variance. The Hartley test assumes that all samples are the same size.

c. The α level. The table provides critical values for $\alpha = .05$ and $\alpha = .01$. Generally, a test for homogeneity would use the larger alpha level.

Example: Two independent samples each have $n = 10$. The sample variances are 12.34 and 9.15. For these data,

$$F\text{-max} = \frac{s^2(\text{largest})}{s^2(\text{smallest})} = \frac{12.34}{9.15} = 1.35$$

With $\alpha = .05$, $k = 2$, and $df = n - 1 = 9$, the critical value from the table is 4.03. Because the obtained *F*-max is smaller than this critical value, you conclude that the data do not provide evidence that the homogeneity of variance assumption has been violated.

satisfying the homogeneity of variance requirement, you cannot accurately interpret a *t* statistic, and the hypothesis test becomes meaningless.

How do you know whether or not the homogeneity of variance requirement is satisfied? There are statistical tests that can be used to determine if the two population variances are the same or different (see Box 10.2), but there is a simple rule of thumb that works most of the time. If the two population variances are the same, then the two sample variances should be very similar. You can just look at the two sample variances to see whether or not they are close. For small samples ($n < 10$), if one of the sample variances is more than four times larger than the other, you probably have violated the homogeneity of variance requirement. For larger samples, there is reason for concern if one variance is more than two times larger than the other. Otherwise the two population variances are close enough to proceed with the hypothesis test.

SUMMARY

1. The independent-measures t statistic is used to draw inferences about the mean difference between two populations or between two treatment conditions. The term *independent* is used because this t statistic requires data from two separate (or independent) samples.

2. The formula for the independent measures t statistic has the same structure as the original z-score or the single-sample t:

$$t = \frac{\text{sample data} - \text{population parameter}}{\text{estimated standard error}}$$

For the independent-measures statistic, the data consist of the difference between the two sample means $(\overline{X}_1 - \overline{X}_2)$. The population parameter of interest is the difference between the two population means $(\mu_1 - \mu_2)$. The standard error is computed by combining the errors for the two sample means. The resulting formula is

$$t = \frac{(\overline{X}_1 - \overline{X}_2) - (\mu_1 - \mu_2)}{s_{\overline{X}_1 - \overline{X}_2}}$$

$$= \frac{(\overline{X}_1 - \overline{X}_2) - (\mu_1 - \mu_2)}{\sqrt{\dfrac{s_p^2}{n_1} + \dfrac{s_p^2}{n_2}}}$$

The pooled variance in the formula, s_p^2, is the weighted mean of the two sample variances:

$$s_p^2 = \frac{SS_1 + SS_2}{df_1 + df_2}$$

This t statistic has degrees of freedom determined by the sum of the df values for the two samples:

$$\begin{aligned} df &= df_1 + df_2 \\ &= (n_1 - 1) + (n_2 - 1) \end{aligned}$$

3. For hypothesis testing, the formula has the following structure:

$$t = \frac{\text{sample data} - \text{population hypothesis}}{\text{estimated standard error}}$$

The null hypothesis normally states that there is no difference between the two population means:

$$H_0 : \mu_1 = \mu_2 \quad \text{or} \quad \mu_1 - \mu_2 = 0$$

4. Appropriate use and interpretation of the t statistic requires that the data satisfy the homogeneity of variance assumption. This assumption stipulates that the two populations have equal variances. An informal test of this assumption can be made by simply comparing the two sample variances: If the two sample variances are approximately equal, the t test is justified. Hartley's F-max test provides a statistical technique for determining whether or not the data satisfy the homogeneity assumption.

KEY TERMS

independent-measures experimental design	between-subjects experimental design	pooled variance	homogeneity of variance

———— *Focus on Problem Solving* ————

1. As you learn more about different statistical methods, one basic problem will be deciding which method is appropriate for a particular set of data. Fortu-

nately, it is easy to identify situations where the independent-measures *t* statistic is used. First, the data will always consist of two separate samples (two n's, two $\bar{X}$'s, two SS's, and so on). Second, this *t* statistic always is used to answer questions about a mean difference: On the average, is one group different (better, faster, smarter) than the other group. If you examine the data and identify the type of question that a researcher is asking, you should be able to decide whether or not an independent-measures *t* is appropriate.

2. When computing an independent-measures *t* statistic from sample data, we suggest that you routinely divide the formula into separate stages rather than trying to do all the calculations at once. First, find the pooled variance. Second, compute the standard error. Third, compute the *t* statistic.

3. One of the most common errors for students involves confusing the formulas for pooled variance and standard error. When computing pooled variance, you are "pooling" the two samples together into a single variance. This variance is computed as a *single fraction*, with two SS values in the numerator and two *df* values in the denominator. When computing the standard error, you are adding the error from the first sample and the error from the second sample. These two separate errors add as *two separate fractions* under the square root symbol.

─────── *Demonstration 10.1* ───────

THE INDEPENDENT-MEASURES *t* TEST

In a study of jury behavior, two samples of subjects were provided details about a trial in which the defendant was obviously guilty. Although group 2 received the same details as group 1, the second group was also told that some evidence had been withheld from the jury by the judge. Later the subjects were asked to recommend a jail sentence. The length of term suggested by each subject is presented here. Is there a significant difference between the two groups in their responses?

group 1 scores: 4   4   3   2   5   1   1   4
group 2 scores: 3   7   8   5   4   7   6   8

There are two separate samples in this study. Therefore, the analysis will use the independent-measures *t* test.

STEP 1 State the hypothesis and select an alpha level.

$H_0 : \mu_1 - \mu_2 = 0$ (For the population, knowing evidence has been withheld has no effect on the suggested sentence.)

$H_1 : \mu_1 - \mu_2 \neq 0$ (For the population, knowledge of withheld evidence has an effect on the jury's response.)

We will set the level of significance to $\alpha = .05$, two tails.

STEP 2 Identify the critical region.

For the independent-measures *t* statistic, degrees of freedom are determined by

$$df = n_1 + n_2 - 2$$
$$= 8 + 8 - 2$$
$$= 14$$

The t distribution table is consulted, for a two-tailed test with $\alpha = .05$ and $df = 14$. The critical t values are $+2.145$ and -2.145.

S T E P 3 Compute the test statistic.

We are computing an independent-measures t statistic. To do this, we will need the mean and SS for each sample, pooled variance, and estimated standard error.

Sample means and sums of squares. The mean ($\overline{X}$) and sums of squares (SS) for the samples are computed as follows.

SAMPLE 1			SAMPLE 2	
X	X^2		X	X^2
4	16		3	9
4	16		7	49
3	9		8	64
2	4		5	25
5	25		4	16
1	1		7	49
1	1		6	36
4	16		8	64
$\Sigma X = 24$	$\Sigma X^2 = 88$		$\Sigma X = 48$	$\Sigma X^2 = 312$

$$n_1 = 8 \qquad\qquad n_2 = 8$$

$$\overline{X}_1 = \frac{\Sigma X}{n} = \frac{24}{8} = 3 \qquad \overline{X}_2 = \frac{\Sigma X}{n} = \frac{48}{8} = 6$$

$$SS_1 = \Sigma X^2 - \frac{(\Sigma X)^2}{n} \qquad SS_2 = \Sigma X^2 - \frac{(\Sigma X)^2}{n}$$

$$= 88 - \frac{(24)^2}{8} \qquad\quad = 312 - \frac{(48)^2}{8}$$

$$= 88 - \frac{576}{8} \qquad\qquad = 312 - \frac{2304}{8}$$

$$= 88 - 72 \qquad\qquad = 312 - 288$$

$$SS_1 = 16 \qquad\qquad SS_2 = 24$$

Pooled variance. For these data, the pooled variance equals

$$s_p^2 = \frac{SS_1 + SS_2}{df_1 + df_2} = \frac{16 + 24}{7 + 7} = \frac{40}{14} = 2.86$$

Estimated standard error. Now we can calculate the estimated standard error for mean differences.

$$s_{\overline{X}_1 - \overline{X}_2} = \sqrt{\frac{s_p^2}{n_1} + \frac{s_p^2}{n_2}} = \sqrt{\frac{2.86}{8} + \frac{2.86}{8}} = \sqrt{0.358 + 0.358}$$
$$= \sqrt{0.716} = 0.85$$

The t statistic. Finally, the t statistic can be computed.

$$t = \frac{(\overline{X}_1 - \overline{X}_2) - (\mu_1 - \mu_2)}{s_{\overline{X}_1 - \overline{X}_2}} = \frac{(3 - 6) - 0}{0.85} = \frac{-3}{0.85}$$
$$= -3.53$$

STEP 4 Make a decision about H_0 and state a conclusion.

The obtained t value of -3.53 falls in the critical region of the left tail (critical $t = \pm 2.145$). Therefore the null hypothesis is rejected. The subjects that were informed about the withheld evidence gave significantly longer sentences, $t(14) = -3.53$, $p < .05$, two tails.

PROBLEMS

1. For each situation described, decide whether the appropriate statistic is a single-sample t or an independent-measures t.
  a. A researcher would like to compare the average weight of 6-week-old rats with neurological damage to the known μ for the population of healthy 6-week-old rats.
  b. A researcher would like to know whether there is any difference in mathematical aptitude for 6-year-old boys versus 6-year-old girls.
  c. A researcher would like to compare subjects in a behavior-modification program versus subjects in a control group to determine how much effect behavior modification has on the eating habits of obese people.

2. What is measured by the estimated standard error that is used for the independent-measures t statistic?

3. Describe the homogeneity of variance assumption, and explain why it is important for the independent-measures hypothesis test.

4. A psychologist would like to compare the amount of information that people get from television versus newspapers. A random sample of 20 people is obtained. Ten of these people agree to get all of their news information from TV (no newspapers) for 4 weeks. The other 10 people agree to get all of their news information from newspapers. At the end of 4 weeks all 20 people are given a test on current events. The average score for the TV group was $\overline{X} = 41$ with $SS = 200$. The average for the newspaper group was $\overline{X} = 49$ with $SS = 160$. On the basis of these data, can the psychologist conclude that there is a significant difference between TV news and newspapers? Test at the .05 level of significance.

5. A local politician would like to compare the political attitudes for the older people and the younger people in his district. He develops a questionnaire which measures political attitude on a scale from 0 (very conservative) to 100 (very liberal) and administers this questionnaire to a sample of 10 young voters and a sample of 10 elderly voters. The data from these two samples are as follows:

OLD	YOUNG
$\overline{X} = 39$	$\overline{X} = 52$
$SS = 4200$	$SS = 4800$

On the basis of these data, should the politician conclude that there is a significant difference between political attitudes for younger voters and older voters? Test with $\alpha = .05$.

6. The following data are from two separate independent-measures experiments. Without doing any calculation, which experiment is more likely to demonstrate a significant difference between treatments A and B? Explain your answer. *Note:* You do not need to compute the *t* statistics; just look carefully at the data.

EXPERIMENT I		EXPERIMENT II	
TREATMENT A	TREATMENT B	TREATMENT A	TREATMENT B
$n = 10$	$n = 10$	$n = 10$	$n = 10$
$\overline{X} = 42$	$\overline{X} = 52$	$\overline{X} = 61$	$\overline{X} = 71$
$SS = 180$	$SS = 120$	$SS = 986$	$SS = 1042$

7. A researcher selects two random samples from a population with $\mu = 60$. Sample 1 is given treatment A, and sample 2 is given treatment B. The resulting data for these two samples are as follows:

SAMPLE 1	SAMPLE 2
$n = 9$	$n = 9$
$\overline{X} = 58$	$\overline{X} = 62$
$SS = 72$	$SS = 72$

a. Do the data from sample 1 indicate that the treatment A has a significant effect? Use a single-sample *t* statistic with $\alpha = .05$.
b. Do the data from sample 2 indicate that treatment B has significant effect? Use a single-sample *t* statistic with $\alpha = .05$.
c. Use an independent-measure *t* statistic to determine whether there is a significant difference between treatment A and treatment B. Test at the .05 level of significance.
d. The results from parts a and b should indicate that neither treatment has a significant effect. However, the results from the independent-measures test should show a significant difference between the two treatments. Are these results contradictory? Explain your answer.

8. In an experiment designed to examine the effect that personality can have on practical decisions, a psychologist selects a random sample of $n = 5$ people who are classified as "impulsive" and a sample of $n = 10$ people who are classified as "reflective." Each person is given a brief description of a crime and then is asked for his or her judgment of a reasonable prison sentence for the criminal. The impulsive people gave an average sentence of 14 years with $SS = 130$, and the reflective people gave an average sentence of 12.5 years with $SS = 260$. On the basis of these samples, can the psychologist con-

clude that there is a significant difference in the harshness of judgment for impulsive versus reflective people? Test with $\alpha = .01$.

9. A researcher has done a series of experiments to determine whether there is any significant difference between two treatments. The data from three of these experiments are as follows:

EXPERIMENT I	
A	B
$n = 5$	$n = 5$
$\overline{X} = 40$	$\overline{X} = 35$
$SS = 36$	$SS = 44$

EXPERIMENT II	
A	B
$n = 5$	$n = 5$
$\overline{X} = 40$	$\overline{X} = 35$
$SS = 120$	$SS = 200$

EXPERIMENT III	
A	B
$n = 5$	$n = 5$
$\overline{X} = 40$	$\overline{X} = 38$
$SS = 36$	$SS = 44$

a. Use the data from each experiment to determine whether there is any significant difference between treatment A and treatment B. Test at the .05 level of significance.
b. How do you explain the fact that the results of experiments I and II lead to different conclusions? Notice that the sample means are identical for these two experiments.
c. How do you explain that experiments I and III lead to different conclusions? Note that the sample *SS* values are identical for these two experiments.

10. A local hospital is planning a fund-raising campaign to raise money for the expansion of their pediatrics ward. Part of the campaign will involve visits to local industries to present their case to employees and to solicit contributions. One factory is selected as a test site to compare two different campaign strategies. Within this factory the employees are randomly

divided into two groups. The individuals in one group are presented the "hard facts" (number of people served, costs, and the like) about the hospital. The individuals in the second group receive an "emotional appeal" that describes in detail the personal histories of two children recently treated at the hospital. The average contribution for the 20 employees in the hard-facts group was $21.50 with $SS = 970$. The average for the 20 employees in the emotional group was $29.80 with $SS = 550$.
a. On the basis of these sample data, should the hospital conclude that one strategy is significantly better than the other? Test at the .05 level of significance.
b. Use Hartley's F-max test to determine whether these data satisfy the homogeneity of variance assumption.

11. A psychologist would like to examine the effects of fatigue on mental alertness. An attention test is prepared which requires subjects to sit in front of a blank TV screen and press a response button each time a dot appears on the screen. A total of 110 dots are presented during a 90-minute period, and the psychologist records the number of errors for each subject. Two groups of subjects are selected. The first group ($n = 5$) is tested after they have been kept awake for 24 hours. The second group ($n = 10$) is tested in the morning after a full night's sleep. The data for these two samples are as follows:

AWAKE 24 HOURS	RESTED
$\overline{X} = 35$	$\overline{X} = 24$
$SS = 120$	$SS = 270$

On the basis of these data, can the psychologist conclude that fatigue significantly increases errors on an attention task? Use a one-tailed test with $\alpha = .05$.

12. A school psychologist would like to examine cheating behavior for 10-year-old children. A standardized achievement test is used. One sample of $n = 8$ children is given the test under unsupervised conditions where cheating is possible. A second sample of 8 children receives the same test under very strict supervision. The test scores for these children are summarized as follows:

UNSUPERVISED	SUPERVISED
$\overline{X} = 78$	$\overline{X} = 65$
$SS = 3000$	$SS = 2600$

Can the psychologist conclude that the unsupervised (cheating?) group did significantly better than the strictly supervised group? Test at the .05 level of significance.

13. Siegel (1990) found that elderly people who owned dogs were less likely to pay visits to their doctors after upsetting events than those that did not own pets. Similarly, consider the following hypothetical data. A sample of elderly dog owners are compared to a similar group (in terms of age and health) who do not own dogs. The researcher records the number of visits to the doctor during the past year for each person. For the following data, is there a significant difference in the number of doctor visits between dog owners and control subjects? Use the .05 level of significance.

CONTROL GROUP	DOG OWNERS
12	8
10	5
6	9
9	4
15	6
12	
14	

14. A researcher examines the short-term effect of a single treatment with acupuncture on cigarette smoking. Subjects who smoke approximately a pack of cigarettes a day are assigned to one of two groups. One group receives the treatment with the acupuncture needles. A second group of subjects serve as a control group and are given relaxation instruction while on the examining table but no acupuncture treatment. The number of cigarettes smoked the next day is recorded for all subjects. For the following data, determine if there is a significant effect of acupuncture on cigarette consumption. Use an alpha level of .05.

CONTROL				ACUPUNCTURE			
23	20	24	17	17	9	0	12
30	18	10	22	3	24	14	10

15. In a test of cognitive dissonance theory, Festinger and Carlsmith (1959) had college students participate in a really boring experiment. Later these students were asked to recruit other subjects for the same experiment by pretending that it was an inter-

esting experience. Some of these students were paid $20 to recruit others, and some were paid only $1. Afterward, each student was asked to report how he or she really felt about the experiment. Hypothetical data representing these reports are as follows:

STUDENTS PAID $1				STUDENTS PAID $20			
3	3	4	6	1	2	5	2
5	5	5	7	3	5	4	5
8	5	4	8	2	3	4	4
2	6	4	4	1	2	3	3
6	7	5	5	5	1	1	3

Cognitive dissonance theory predicts that those paid only $1 would come to believe that the experiment really was interesting. It must have been, or they wouldn't have worked so hard for only $1. The students paid $20 were working for money, not for the experiment, so they should have no reason to change their opinions. Do the preceding data support this prediction? Test for a significant difference between the two groups with $\alpha = .01$.

16. A researcher would like to measure the effects of air pollution on life expectancy. Two samples of newborn rats are selected. The first sample of 10 rats is housed in cages where the atmosphere is equivalent to the air in a severely polluted city. The second sample of $n = 20$ is placed in cages with clean air. The average life span for the first group is $\overline{X} = 478$ days with $SS = 5020$ and for the second group $\overline{X} = 511$ with $SS = 10,100$. Does pollution cause a difference in life expectancy? Test with $\alpha = .01$.

17. A psychologist studying human memory would like to examine the process of forgetting. One group of subjects is required to memorize a list of words in the evening just before going to bed. Their recall is tested 10 hours later in the morning. Subjects in the second group memorize the same list of words in the morning, and then their memories are tested 10 hours later after being awake all day. The psychologist hypothesizes that there will be less forgetting during sleep than during a busy day. The recall scores for two samples of college students are as follows:

ASLEEP SCORES				AWAKE SCORES			
15	13	14	14	15	13	14	12
16	15	16	15	14	13	11	12
16	15	17	14	13	13	12	14

a. Sketch a frequency distribution polygon for the "asleep" group. On the same graph (in a different color) sketch the distribution for the "awake" group. Just by looking at these two distributions, would you predict a significant difference between the two treatment conditions?
b. Use the independent measures t statistic to determine whether there is a significant difference between the treatments. Conduct the test with $\alpha = .05$.

18. The experiment described in Problem 17 was repeated using samples of 6-year-old children. The data for this experiment are as follows:

ASLEEP SCORES				AWAKE SCORES			
15	13	8	10	6	8	5	8
7	10	6	9	4	7	12	9
14	11	5	12	3	10	13	11

a. Again, sketch a frequency distribution polygon for each group on the same graph. Does there appear to be a significant difference between the two treatments?
b. Use the independent measures t statistic to test for significance with $\alpha = .05$
c. Note that the data from Problem 17 and the data here show the same mean difference. Explain why the statistical analysis produces different conclusions for these two problems.

19. An instructor would like to evaluate the effectiveness of a new programmed learning course in statistics. The class is randomly divided in half. One group gets the regular lecture series and textbook, while the other group takes the programmed course. At the end of the semester all students take the same final exam. The scores are as follows:

REGULAR COURSE GRADES			PROGRAMMED COURSE GRADES		
82	73	93	92	82	97
61	89	99	81	80	62
73	91	84	72	74	68
71	68	81	84	81	71
75	72	69	63	65	73

Use these data to determine whether there is any significant difference between the programmed course and the regular course. Test at the .05 level.

20. Although the instructor from Problem 19 found no significant difference in grades for the two different statistics courses, it is possible that the students preferred one teaching method over the other. At the end of the course, each student was given a course-evaluation questionnaire that included a question about how much he or she enjoyed the course. The response range from 1 (not at all) to 5 (very much). The data for the two sections of students are as follows:

REGULAR COURSE				PROGRAMMED COURSE			
4	4	3	4	3	4	2	3
4	2	4	5	4	4	2	2
3	4	5	5	4	3	2	2
4	5	5		3	2	5	

Do these data indicate a significant preference between the two teaching methods? Test with $\alpha = .05$.

21. A researcher is interested in testing the opinions of college students concerning the value of their college education. She suspects that seniors will place more value on their education than will sophomores. A sample of 20 seniors and 20 sophomores is selected, and each subject is given an opinion questionnaire. The data for each sample are as follows:

SOPHOMORES				SENIORS			
18	21	24	21	25	19	23	22
20	19	23	26	23	21	21	18
19	24	19	28	27	18	28	21
22	17	27	18	26	25	22	16
25	22	14	17	21	29	18	20

Using a one-tailed test with $\alpha = .05$, do these data indicate that seniors have significantly higher value scores?

22. A principal for a city high school would like to determine parents' attitudes toward a proposed sex education program. A sample of 15 families is selected, and each set of parents is requested to fill out an opinion questionnaire. Part of this questionnaire requires the parents' names and occupations. Looking over the data, the principal noticed that the opinions seemed to be a lot more favorable than had been expected. The principal suspected that the parents might have felt "forced" into stating a favorable opinion because they were required to identify

themselves. They might have responded more honestly if the questionnaire had been anonymous. Therefore, a second sample of 15 families was selected, and they were requested to complete the same questionnaire without reporting their names or occupations. The data from both questionnaires are as follows:

FIRST QUESTIONNAIRE				
60	56	54	58	63
61	52	49	57	58
65	59	42	51	67

SECOND QUESTIONNAIRE				
51	50	53	48	42
62	57	47	49	50
51	43	48	53	41

Use these data to test the principal's hypothesis. Set $\alpha = .05$.

23. a. Sketch a frequency distribution polygon showing the following samples. Use a different color for each set of scores.

SAMPLE 1			SAMPLE 2		
14	18	12	15	21	16
11	18	15	22	14	12
15	17	16	19	20	18
15	18	14	20	21	17
16	14	15	22	19	20
16	17	13	20	19	18

b. By just looking at your polygon, does it appear that these two samples came from different populations or from the same population?
c. Calculate the independent-measures t statistic for these data. Does the t statistic indicate that the samples came from different populations? Set $\alpha = .05$.

24. The following data came from an independent-measures experiment comparing two different treatment conditions. The score for each subject is the amount of time (measured in minutes) required to complete a set of math problems.

TREATMENT 1 (SAMPLE 1)		TREATMENT 2 (SAMPLE 2)	
2.5	3.2	1.8	2.1
3.4	2.9	2.0	1.6
2.4	2.6	1.9	2.3
2.5	3.0	2.2	2.5
2.7	3.1	1.8	2.1

a. Use an independent-measures t statistic to determine whether or not there is a significant difference between the two treatments. Use $\alpha = .05$.

b. The experimenter would like to convert each subject's score from minutes to seconds. To do this, each value must be multiplied by 60. After each value is multiplied, what will happen to the sample means? What will happen to the sample standard deviations? What do you expect will happen to the t statistic for these data?

c. Multiply each of the original scores by 60 (i.e., change them from minutes to seconds). Now compute the independent-measures t statistic for the new scores? How does this t statistic compare with the t statistic for the original data?

CHAPTER 11

HYPOTHESIS TESTS WITH RELATED SAMPLES

TOOLS YOU WILL NEED

The following items are considered essential background material for this chapter. If you doubt your knowledge of any of these items, you should review the appropriate chapter or section before proceeding.

- Introduction to the t statistic (Chapter 9)
  - Estimated standard error
  - Degrees of freedom
  - t Distribution
  - Hypothesis tests with the t statistic
- Independent-measures design (Chapter 10)

CONTENTS

PREVIEW

Have you ever wondered what is going to happen to your mental faculties as you grow older? Many people, especially young people, are convinced that they face an inevitable decline in intellectual skills as they age. In fact many scientific studies show that average IQ scores peak around 20 years of age, dceline gradually until about age 50, and then drop sharply (Horn, 1978).

On the other hand, there is a separate group of scientific studies that show little, if any, decline in IQ between ages 20 and 50. After age 50, these studies show some drop in performance on speed-related tasks and spatial reasoning, but other intelligence skills such as general knowledge and vocabulary appear to hold constant, even up to age 85 (Horn, 1978).

How can two sets of data be so completely different? One answer lies in a closer examination of how the data were collected. The data that show IQ declining with age are generally obtained from *cross-sectional* studies that compare separate samples representing each age group. In statistical terminology, these are *independent-measures* studies. Suppose that you went out today and obtained a sample of 20-year-old, a sample of 50-year-old, and a sample of 80-year-old individuals. Beside differing in age, your three samples are probably very different in terms of educational background, work experience, and living environment. Any of these other factors could af-fect IQ scores and could be the source of the IQ differences between age groups. Using statistical terminology again, these other factors are known as *confounding variables,* and they make it impossible to conclude that age alone is responsible for the IQ differences.

The second group of studies, showing stable IQ, use a different experimental methodology. Rather than comparing different samples, these studies monitor IQ scores for the same set of people over a long period of time. This type of research is often called a *longitudinal* study. In statistical terms it is referred to as a *repeated-measures* experiment because the researcher is repeatedly measuring the same individuals. The advantages of the repeated-measures experiment should be obvious. In these studies, for example, the researcher can be certain that the 20-year-olds and the 50-year-olds grew up in the same environment and have the same educational background—after all, they are the same people. Equally obvious is the fact that this kind of research can take 20 or 30 years to complete—a tremendous disadvantage.

In this chapter we will examine the statistical methods used to evaluate data from repeated-measures experiments. In addition, we will take a closer look at the differences between independent-measures and repeated-measures experiments and discuss the advantages and disadvantages of each.

11.1 OVERVIEW

Previously we discussed inferential techniques using two separate samples to examine the mean difference between two populations. Usually, our goal was to evaluate the difference between two treatment conditions. For example, if a researcher would like to assess the effect of a new drug on depression, he or she might use two treatment conditions: a drug treatment and a no-drug treatment. With an independent-measures design (Chapter 10), one sample of patients receives the drug, and the other sample receives an ineffective placebo. Depression can be measured by the subjects' scores on a depression inventory. Differences in the severity of depression between these two samples may then be used to test the effectiveness of the new drug. This independent-measures design can be recognized by the assignment of separate, or "independent," samples of subjects for each treatment condition.

It should be obvious that there is a different experimental technique that could be used to evaluate the drug. Specifically, you could use a single sample of subjects and measure their depression scores before they receive the drug and then repeat the measurements after they have received the drug. This experimental design is called a *repeated-measures* study. By repeating measurements on a single sample of subjects, we are looking for differences *within* the same subjects from one measurement to the next. Sometimes this type of study is also called a *within-subjects* design.

DEFINITION

A *repeated-measures* study is one in which a single sample of individuals is tested more than once on the dependent variable. The same subjects are used for every treatment condition.

The main advantage of a repeated-measures experiment is that it uses exactly the same subjects in all treatment conditions. Thus, there is no risk that the subjects in one treatment are substantially different from the subjects in another. With an independent-measures design, on the other hand, there is always a risk that the results are biased by the fact that one sample was much different (smarter, faster, more extroverted, and so on) than the other.

Occasionally, researchers will try to approximate the advantages of a repeated-measures experiment by using a technique known as *matched subjects*. For example, suppose a researcher is testing the effectiveness of a special reading program. One sample of fourth graders takes the reading course, and a second sample serves as the control group. The researcher plans to compare these two groups in terms of reading comprehension. However, the researcher is concerned that there might be differences in intelligence between the two samples, which could confound the results. Therefore, the researcher matches the subjects in terms of IQ. That is, if a person assigned to the control group has an IQ of 120, the researcher assigns another individual with the same IQ to the treatment group (see Table 11.1). The result is called a *matched-subjects* experiment.

DEFINITION

In a *matched-subjects* experiment, each individual in one sample is matched with a subject in the other sample. The matching is done so that the two individuals are equivalent (or nearly equivalent) with respect to a specific variable that the researcher would like to control.

In a repeated-measures, or a matched-subjects, design all the subjects in one treatment are directly related, one-to-one, with the subjects in another

Table 11.1

Group assignment of subjects matched for IQ.

Control		Reading Program	
Subject	IQ	Subject	IQ
A	120	E	120
B	105	F	105
C	110	G	110
D	95	H	95

A matched-subjects experiment occasionally is called a *matched-samples design*. But the subjects in the samples must be matched one-to-one before you can use the statistical techniques in this chapter.

treatment. For this reason, these two experimental designs are often called *related-samples* experiments (or correlated-samples experiments). In this chapter we will focus our discussion on repeated-measures experiments because they are overwhelmingly the more common example of related-groups designs. However, you should realize that the statistical techniques used for repeated-measures experiments can be applied directly to data from a matched-subjects experiment.

Now we will examine the statistical techniques that allow a researcher to use the sample data from a repeated-measures experiment to draw inferences about the general population.

11.2 THE *t* STATISTIC FOR RELATED SAMPLES

The *t* statistic for related samples is structurally similar to the other *t* statistics we have examined. As we shall see, it is essentiallly the same as the single-sample *t* statistic covered in Chapter 9. One major distinction of the related-samples *t* is that it is based on difference scores rather than raw scores (*X* values). In this section, we examine difference scores and develop the *t* statistic for related samples.

DIFFERENCE SCORES   Table 11.2 presents hypothetical data for a drug evaluation study. The first score for each person (X_1) is the score obtained on the depression inventory before the drug treatment. The second score (X_2) was obtained after the drug treatment. Because we are interested in how much change occurs as a result of the treatment, each person's scores are summarized as a single difference score. This is accomplished by subtracting the first score (before treatment) from the second score (after treatment) for each person:

$$\text{difference score} = D = X_2 - X_1 \tag{11.1}$$

Table 11.2

Scores on a depression inventory before and after treatment.

Person	Before Treatment, X_1	After Treatment, X_2	D
A	72	64	−8
B	68	60	−8
C	60	50	−10
D	71	66	−5
E	55	56	+1

$$\Sigma D = -30$$

$$\overline{D} = \frac{\Sigma D}{n} = \frac{-30}{5} = -6$$

Figure 11.1

Because populations are usually too large to test in a study, the researcher selects a random sample from the population. The sample data are used to make inferences about the population mean μ_D. The data of interest in the repeated-measures study are difference scores (*D* scores) for each subject.

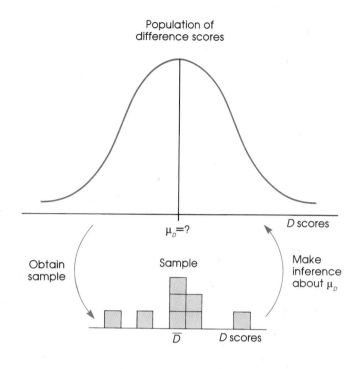

In a matched-subjects design, *D* is the difference between scores for two matched subjects.

The difference scores, or *D* values, are shown in the last column of the table. Note that the sign of each *D* score tells you the direction of change. For example, person A showed a decrease in depression, as indicated by the negative difference score.

The researcher's goal is to use this sample of difference scores to answer questions about the general population. Notice that we are interested in a population of *difference scores*. More specifically, we are interested in the mean for this population of difference scores. We will identify this population mean difference with the symbol μ_D (using the subscript letter *D* to indicate that we are dealing with *D* values rather than *X* scores). Because populations usually are too large to test in an experiment, investigators must rely on the data from samples. Do these data indicate that the drug has a significant effect (more than chance)? Our problem is to use the limited data from a sample to test hypotheses about the population. This problem is diagrammed in Figure 11.1.

Notice that the problem we are facing here is essentially identical to the situation we encountered in Chapter 9. We have a single sample of scores that must be used to test hypotheses about a single population. In Chapter 9 we introduced a *t* statistic that allowed us to use the sample mean as a basis for testing hypotheses about the population mean. This *t* statistic formula will be used again here to develop the repeated-measures *t* test.

THE *t* STATISTIC   To refresh your memory, the single-sample *t* statistic (Chapter 9) is defined by the formula

$$t = \frac{\overline{X} - \mu}{s_{\overline{X}}}$$

The sample mean $\overline{X}$ comes from the data. The standard error $s_{\overline{X}}$ (also computed from the sample data) gives a measure of the error between the sample mean and the population mean μ.

For the repeated-measures experiment, the sample data are difference scores and are identified by the letter D rather than X. Therefore, we will substitute D's in the formula in place of X's to emphasize that we are dealing with difference scores instead of X values. Also, the population mean that is of interest to us is the population mean difference (the mean amount of change for the entire population), and we identify this parameter with the symbol μ_D. With these simple changes, the *t formula for the repeated-measures design* becomes

$$t = \frac{\overline{D} - \mu_D}{s_{\overline{D}}} \tag{11.2}$$

In this formula, the estimated standard error for $\overline{D}$, $s_{\overline{D}}$, is computed exactly as it was in the original single-sample t statistic. First, we compute the standard deviation for the sample (this time a sample of D scores):

$$s = \sqrt{\frac{SS}{n - 1}}$$

Then we divide this value by the square root of the sample size:

$$s_{\overline{D}} = \frac{s}{\sqrt{n}} \tag{11.3}$$

Notice that the sample data we are using consist of the D scores. Also, there is only one D value for each subject in a repeated-measures study or for each matched pair of subjects in a matched-subjects study. Because there are only n difference scores in the sample, our t statistic will have degrees of freedom equal to

$$df = n - 1 \tag{11.4}$$

Note that this formula is identical to the *df* equation used for the single-sample t statistic (Chapter 9). However, n refers to the number of D scores, not the number of X values.

You should also note that the repeated-measures t statistic is conceptually similar to the t statistics we have previously examined:

$$t = \frac{\text{sample data} - \text{population hypothesis}}{\text{amount of error due to chance}}$$

In this case, the sample data are represented by the sample mean of the difference scores ($\overline{D}$), the population hypothesis is the value predicted by H_0 for μ_D and the amount of sampling error is measured by the standard error of sample mean differences ($s_{\overline{D}}$).

11.3 HYPOTHESIS TESTS FOR THE REPEATED-MEASURES DESIGN

In a repeated-measures experiment we are interested in whether or not any change occurs between scores in the first treatment and scores in the second treatment. In statistical terms, we are interested in the population mean difference μ_D. Is the population mean difference equal to zero (no change), or has a change occurred? As always, the null hypothesis states that there is no treatment effect. In symbols, this is

$$H_0 : \mu_D = 0$$

PROCEDURES AND STEPS

As we saw in previous tests, the level of significance defines what values are sufficiently "far away" to reject H_0

As a statistician, your job is to determine whether the sample data support or refute the null hypothesis. In simple terms, we must decide whether the sample mean difference is close to zero (indicating no change) or far from zero (indicating there is a change). The t statistic helps us determine if the sample data are "close to" or "far from" zero.

The repeated-measures t test procedure follows the same outline we have used in other situations. The basic steps for hypothesis testing are reviewed here.

STEP 1 The hypotheses are stated, and an alpha level is selected. For the repeated-measures experiment, the null hypothesis is stated symbolically as

Directional hypotheses can be used as well and would predict whether μ_D is greater or smaller than zero. A one-tailed test is used in those instances.

$$H_0 : \mu_D = 0$$

The alternative hypothesis states that there is a difference between the treatments. In symbols, this is

$$H_1 : \mu_D \neq 0$$

STEP 2 The critical region is located. As before, the critical region is defined as values that would be very unlikely (probability less than alpha) if H_0 is true. Because the repeated-measures test uses a t statistic with $df = n - 1$, we simply compute df and look up the critical values in the t distribution table.

STEP 3 Compute the test statistic, in this case, the t statistic for repeated measures. We first must find the sample mean $\overline{D}$ and SS for the set of difference scores. From SS we compute the estimated standard error $s_{\overline{D}}$. These values are then put into the t formula along with the hypothesized value of μ_D from H_0.

STEP 4 If the obtained value falls in the critical region, we reject H_0 and conclude that there is a significant treatment effect. Remember, it is very unlikely for the t value to be in the critical region if H_0 is true. On the

Table 11.3

The number of doses of medication needed for asthma attacks before and after relaxation training

PATIENT	WEEK BEFORE TRAINING	WEEK AFTER TRAINING	D	D^2
A	9	4	−5	25
B	4	1	−3	9
C	5	5	0	0
D	4	0	−4	16
E	5	1	−4	16

$$\Sigma D = -16 \qquad \Sigma D^2 = 66$$

$$\overline{D} = \frac{\Sigma D}{n} = \frac{-16}{5} = -3.2$$

$$SS = \Sigma D^2 - \frac{(\Sigma D)^2}{n} = 66 - \frac{(-16)^2}{5}$$

$$= 66 - 51.2 = 14.8$$

other hand, if the obtained t is not in the critical region, then we fail to reject H_0 and conclude that the sample data do not provide sufficient evidence for a treatment effect.

The complete hypothesis testing procedure is demonstrated in Example 11.1.

EXAMPLE 11.1

Example 11.1 is analyzed with the Minitab command TTEST in Section 20.5.

A researcher in behavioral medicine believes that stress often makes asthma symptoms worse for people who suffer from this respiratory disorder. Because of the suspected role of stress, the investigator decides to examine the effect of relaxation training on the severity of asthma symptoms. A sample of five patients is selected for the study. During the week before treatment, the investigator records the severity of their symptoms by measuring how many doses of medication are needed for asthma attacks. Then the patients receive relaxation training. For the week following training, the researcher once again records the number of doses required by each patient. Table 11.3 shows the data and summarizes the findings. Do these data indicate that relaxation training alters the severity of symptoms?

STEP 1 State hypotheses and select alpha:

$H_0 : \mu_D = 0$ (no change in symptoms)

$H_1 : \mu_D \neq 0$ (there is a change)

The level of significance is set at $\alpha = .05$ for a two-tailed test.

STEP 2 Locate the critical region. For this example, $n = 5$, so the t statistic will have $df = n - 1 = 4$. From the t distribution table, you should find that the critical values are $+2.776$ and -2.776. These values are shown in Figure 11.2.

Figure 11.2

The critical regions with $\alpha = .05$ and $df = 4$ begin at $+2.776$ and -2.776 in the t distribution. Obtained values of t that are more extreme than these values will lie in a critical region. In that case, the null hypothesis would be rejected.

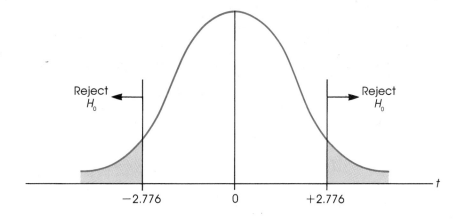

STEP 3   Calculate the t statistic. The mean for this example is $\overline{D} = -3.2$. To compute the SS for the D scores, we will use the computational formula (see Chapter 4, page 111):

$$SS = \Sigma X^2 - \frac{(\Sigma X)^2}{n}$$

Because we are using difference scores (D values) in place of X scores, this formula can be rewritten as

Remember, the computations for SS and s are based on the D scores for the subjects in the sample.

$$SS = \Sigma D^2 - \frac{(\Sigma D)^2}{n}$$

For our data, the SS is

$$SS = 66 - \frac{(-16)^2}{5}$$

$$= 66 - 51.2$$

$$= 14.8$$

Next, use the SS value to compute the sample standard deviation:

$$s = \sqrt{\frac{SS}{n-1}} = \sqrt{\frac{14.8}{4}} = \sqrt{3.7} = 1.92$$

Finally, the estimated standard error is computed:

$$s_{\overline{D}} = \frac{s}{\sqrt{n}} = \frac{1.92}{\sqrt{5}} = \frac{1.92}{2.24} = .86$$

Now these values are used to calculate the value of t:

$$t = \frac{\overline{D} - \mu_D}{s_{\overline{D}}} = \frac{-3.2 - 0}{.86} = -3.72$$

STEP 4   The t value we obtained falls in the critical region (see Figure 11.2). The investigator rejects the null hypothesis and concludes that relaxation training does affect the amount of medication needed to control the asthma symptoms. For this example, a journal report might summarize the conclusion as follows:

> Relaxation training resulted in a significant reduction in the dose of medication needed to control asthma symptoms, $t(4) = -3.72$, $p < .05$, two tails.

As is customary, the number of degrees of freedom is contained in parentheses after the t, followed by the obtained value. The probability of a Type I error (the alpha level) and the type of test (one or two tails) also are reported.

 SPSS^x A-79

DIRECTIONAL HYPOTHESES AND ONE-TAILED TESTS

In many repeated-measures and matched-subjects experiments, the researcher has a specific prediction concerning the direction of the treatment effect. For example, in the study described in Example 11.1, the researcher expects relaxation training to reduce the severity of asthma symptoms and, therefore, to reduce the amount of medication needed for asthma attacks. This kind of directional prediction can be incorporated into the statement of hypotheses, resulting in a directional, or one-tailed, hypothesis test. You should recall that directional tests should be used with caution. The standard two-tailed test usually is preferred and is always appropriate, even in situations where the researcher has a specific directional prediction. The following example demonstrates how the hypotheses and critical region are determined in a directional test.

EXAMPLE 11.2   We will reexamine the experiment presented in Example 11.1. The researcher is using a repeated-measures experiment to investigate the effect of relaxation training on the severity of asthma symptoms. The researcher predicts that people will need less medication after training than before, which will produce negative difference scores.

$$D = X_2 - X_1 = \text{after} - \text{before}$$

STEP 1   State the hypotheses and select α. With most one-tailed tests, it is easiest to incorporate the researcher's prediction directly into H_1. In this example, the researcher predicts a negative difference, so

$H_1 : \mu_D < 0$ (Medication is reduced after training.)

The null hypothesis states that the treatment does not have the predicted effect. In this example,

$H_0 : \mu_D \geq 0$ (Medication is not reduced after training.)

STEP 2   Locate the critical region. The researcher is predicting negative difference scores if the treatment works. Hence, a negative t statistic would tend to

Figure 11.3

The one-tailed critical region for $\alpha = .05$ in the t distribution with $df = 4$.

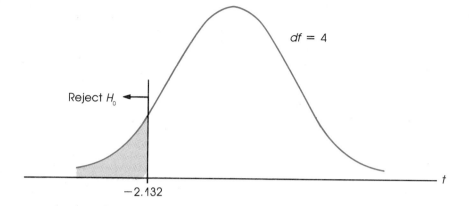

support the experimental prediction and refute H_0. With a sample of $n = 5$ subjects, the t statistic will have $df = 4$. Looking in the t distribution table for $df = 4$ and $\alpha = .05$ for a one-tailed test, we find a critical value of 2.132. Thus, a t statistic that is more extreme than -2.132 would be sufficient to reject H_0. The t distribution with the one-tailed critical region is shown in Figure 11.3. For this example, the data produce a t statistic of $t = -3.72$ (see Example 11.1). Therefore, we reject H_0 and conclude that the relaxation training did significantly reduce the amount of medication needed for asthma attacks.

LEARNING CHECK   **1.** A researcher would like to examine the effect of hypnosis on cigarette smoking. A sample of smokers ($n = 4$) is selected for the study. The number of cigarettes smoked on the day prior to treatment is recorded. The subjects are then hypnotized and given the posthypnotic suggestion that each time they light a cigarette they will experience a horrible taste and feel nauseous. The data are as follows.

The number of cigarettes smoked before and after hypnosis

SUBJECT	BEFORE TREATMENT	AFTER TREATMENT
1	19	13
2	35	37
3	20	14
4	31	25

a. Find the difference scores (D values) for this sample.

b. The difference scores have $\overline{D} = -4$ and $SS = 48$. Do these data indicate that hypnosis has a significant effect on cigarette smoking? Test with $\alpha = .05$.

ANSWER **1. a.** The difference scores are $-6, 2, -6, -6$.

b. For these data $s = 4$, $s_{\bar{D}} = 2$, and $t = -2.00$. With $\alpha = .05$, we fail to reject H_0; these data do not provide sufficient evidence to conclude that hypnosis has a significant effect on cigarette smoking.

11.4 HYPOTHESIS TESTING WITH A MATCHED-SUBJECTS DESIGN

As noted in Section 11.1, matched-subjects experiments involve two related samples. Each subject in the second sample has been matched to a subject in the first sample on some variable that the researcher wishes to control. In this way, the researcher attempts to make the groups equivalent at the start of the experiment, so that any differences observed can be attributed to the treatment (independent variable). As noted earlier, data from the matched-subjects design may be analyzed using the related-samples t test. The following example illustrates this analysis.

EXAMPLE 11.3   A psychologist studies the effectiveness of a newly developed reading program. One sample of students takes the new reading course. A second sample serves as a control group and takes the regular coursework. The groups are later tested in reading comprehension to assess the effectiveness of the new program. However, the researcher is concerned with the possibility that differences in intelligence between the two groups (rather than the new reading program) will cause differences in reading comprehension. Therefore, when assigning subjects to treatment groups, each subject in the first group is matched to one in the second group in terms of IQ score. That is, if a child in the first group has an IQ of 110,

Table 11.4

Reading comprehension scores for children in a matched-samples study of a new reading program

	CONTROL	READING PROGRAM	D	D^2
Matched pair A	6	15	+9	81
Matched pair B	5	15	+10	100
Matched pair C	11	17	+6	36
Matched pair D	6	13	+7	49

$$\Sigma \bar{D} = +32 \quad \Sigma D^2 = 266$$

$$\bar{D} = \frac{\Sigma D}{n} = \frac{+32}{4} = +8$$

$$SS = \Sigma D^2 - \frac{(\Sigma D)^2}{n} = 266 - \frac{(32)^2}{4}$$

$$= 266 - \frac{1024}{4} = 266 - 256 = 10$$

then another child with the same IQ would be assigned to the second group. Thus the study consists of matched pairs of children, with one child of each pair serving in the control group and the other participating in the reading program. The data are summarized in Table 11.4. Is there evidence for a significant effect of the new reading program?

STEP 1 State the hypotheses and select an alpha level.

$$H_0 : \mu_D = 0 \qquad \text{(no effect on reading comprehension)}$$

$$H_1 : \mu_D \neq 0 \qquad \text{(there is an effect)}$$

We will set the alpha level to .01 for a two-tailed test.

STEP 2 Locate the critical region. For this example, $df = n - 1 = 3$. The t distribution table indicates the critical values are $+5.841$ and -5.841.

STEP 3 Calculate the t statistic. This study used a matched-samples design; thus a related-samples t statistic is appropriate. The values for SS and $\overline{D}$ were calculated in Table 11.4. Now, the standard deviation is computed:

$$s = \sqrt{\frac{SS}{n - 1}} = \sqrt{\frac{10}{4 - 1}} = \sqrt{\frac{10}{3}}$$
$$= \sqrt{3.33} = 1.82$$

Next, the estimated standard error is computed:

$$s_{\overline{D}} = \frac{s}{\sqrt{n}} = \frac{1.82}{\sqrt{4}} = 0.91$$

Finally, the value for the t statistic can be determined:

$$t = \frac{\overline{D} - \mu_D}{s_{\overline{D}}} = \frac{8 - 0}{0.91} = \frac{8}{0.91} = 8.79$$

STEP 4 The obtained t value of $t = 8.79$ is more extreme than the critical value of $+5.841$. Therefore, it falls within the critical region on the right side of the t distribution. The null hypothesis can be rejected and it can be concluded that the new reading program has a significant effect on reading comprehension, $t(3) = 8.79$, $p < .01$, two tails.

11.5 USES AND ASSUMPTIONS FOR RELATED-SAMPLES *t* TESTS

USES OF RELATED-SAMPLE STUDIES The repeated-measures experiment differs from an independent-measures study in a fundamental way. In the latter type of study, a separate sample is used for each treatment. In the repeated-measures design, only one sample of subjects is used, and measurements are repeated for the same sample in each treatment. There are many situations where it is possible to examine the effect of a treatment by using either type of study. However, there are situations where one type of experimental design is more desirable or appropriate than the other. For example, if a researcher would like to study a particular type of subject (a rare species, people with an unusual illness, etc.) that is not commonly found, a repeated-measures study will be more economical in the sense that fewer subjects are needed. Rather than selecting several samples for the study (one sample per treatment), a single sample can be used for the entire experiment.

Another factor in determining the type of experimental design is the specific question being asked by the experimenter. Some questions are better studied with a repeated-measures design, especially those concerning changes in response across time. For example, a psychologist may wish to study the effect of practice on how well a person performs a task. To show that practice is improving a person's performance, the experimenter would typically measure the person's responses very early in the experiment (when there is little or no practice) and repeat the measurement later when the person has had a certain amount of practice. Most studies of skill acquisition examine practice effects by using a repeated-measures design. Another situation where a repeated-measures study is useful is in developmental psychology. By repeating observations of the same individuals at various points in time, an investigator can watch behavior unfold and obtain a better understanding of developmental processes.

Finally, there are situations where a repeated-measures design cannot be used. Specifically, when you are comparing two different populations (men versus women, firstborn versus second-born children, and the like), you must use separate samples from each population. Typically, these situations require an independent-measures design, but it is occasionally possible to match subjects with respect to a critical variable and conduct a matched-subjects experiment.

ADVANTAGES OF RELATED-SAMPLE STUDIES

There are certain statistical advantages to repeated-measures designs, particularly when you are studying a population with large differences from one individual to the next. One of the sources of variability that contributes to the standard error is due to these individual differences—that is, subjects all respond differently because they enter the experiment with different abilities, experiences, and the like. Large individual differences would produce larger standard errors, which might mask a mean difference. A repeated-measures design reduces the amount of this error variability in the analysis by using the same subjects for every treatment. The result is that the size of the standard error is reduced, and the t test will be more likely to detect the presence of a treatment effect.

It should be noted that a matched-subjects design also reduces *individual differences.* This is accomplished by matching subjects from each group with respect to some variable the researcher wants to control. If the matching variable (for example, intelligence in Example 11.3) would otherwise contribute to variability in the experiment, then using a matched-subjects design will reduce the standard error. Once again, the related-measures t test will be more sensitive in detecting a treatment effect.

CARRY-OVER EFFECTS Sometimes the outcome of a repeated-measures study is contaminated by the presence of a carry-over effect. This will occur when a subject's response in the second treatment is altered by lingering aftereffects of the first treatment. As a result, the outcome of the study may be uninterpretable. A common source of carry-over effects is fatigue that develops during treatment 1 and can cause lower performance in treatment 2. Another example is practice or experience gained in treatment 1 that could lead to improved performance in treatment 2. In either case, the obtained mean difference between treatments may be partially caused by the carry-over effect rather than the difference between treatments.

One way to deal with carry-over effects is to counterbalance the order of presentation of treatments. That is, the subjects are randomly divided into two groups, with one group receiving treatment 1 followed by treatment 2 and the other group receiving treatment 2 followed by treatment 1. When there is reason to expect strong carry-over effects, your best strategy is not to use a repeated-measures design. Instead, use independent-measures with a separate sample for each treatment condition, or use a matched-subjects design so that each individual participates in only one treatment condition.

ASSUMPTIONS OF THE RELATED-SAMPLES *t* TEST The related-samples *t* statistic requires two basic assumptions.

1. The observations within each treatment condition must be independent (see page 255).
2. The population distribution of difference scores (*D* values) must be normal.

As before, the normality assumption is not a cause for concern unless the sample size is relatively small. In the case of severe departures from normality, the validity of the *t* test may be compromised with small samples. However, with relatively large samples ($n > 30$), this assumption can be ignored.

LEARNING CHECK
1. What assumptions must be satisfied for the repeated-measures *t* tests to be valid?

2. Describe some situations for which a repeated-measures design is well suited.

3. How is a matched-subjects design similar to a repeated-measures design? How do they differ?

ANSWERS
1. The observations within a treatment are independent. The population distribution of *D* scores is assumed to be normal.

2. The repeated-measures design is suited to situations where a particular type of subject is not readily available for study. This design is helpful because it uses fewer subjects (only one sample is needed). Certain questions are addressed more adequately by a repeated-measures design—for example, anytime one would like to study changes across time in the same individuals. Also, when individual differences are large, a repeated-measures design is helpful because it reduces the amount of this type of error in the statistical analysis.

3. They are similar in that the role of individual differences in the experiment is reduced. They differ in that there are two samples in a matched-subjects design and only one in a repeated-measures study.

SUMMARY

1. In a repeated-measures experiment, a single sample of subjects is randomly selected, and measurements are repeated on this sample for each treatment condition. This type of experiment may take the form of a before-and-after study.

2. The data analysis for a repeated-measures t test is done on the basis of the difference between the first and second measurement for each subject. These difference scores (D scores) are obtained by

$$D = X_2 - X_1$$

3. The formula for the repeated-measures t statistic is

$$t = \frac{\overline{D} - \mu_D}{s_{\overline{D}}}$$

where the sample mean is

$$\overline{D} = \frac{\Sigma D}{n}$$

the estimated standard error is

$$s_{\overline{D}} = \frac{s}{\sqrt{n}}$$

and the value of degrees of freedom is obtained by

$$df = n - 1$$

4. A repeated-measures design may be more useful than an independent-measures study when one wants to observe changes in behavior in the same subjects, as in learning or developmental studies. The repeated-measures design has the advantage of reducing error variability due to individual differences.

5. A related-samples study may consist of two samples in which subjects have been matched on some variable. The repeated measures t test may be used in this situation.

KEY TERMS

repeated-measures design	matched-subjects design	repeated-measures t statistic	individual differences
within-subjects design	difference scores	estimated standard error for $\overline{D}$	

——— *Focus on Problem Solving* ———

1. Once data have been collected, we must then select the appropriate statistical analysis. How can you tell if the data call for a repeated-measures t test? Look at the experiment carefully. Is there only one sample of subjects? Are the same subjects tested a second time? If your answers are yes to both of these questions, then a repeated-measures t test should be done. There is only one situation in which the repeated-measures t can be used for data from two samples, and that is for *matched-subjects* experiments (page 302).

2. The repeated-measures t test is based on difference scores. In finding difference scores, be sure you are consistent with your method. That is, you may use either $X_2 - X_1$ or $X_1 - X_2$ to find D scores, but you must use the same method for all subjects.

Demonstration 11.1

A REPEATED-MEASURES *t* TEST

A major oil company would like to improve its tarnished image following a large oil spill. Its marketing department develops a short television commercial and tests it on a sample of $n = 7$ subjects. People's attitudes about the company are measured with a short questionnaire, both before and after viewing the commercial. The data are as follows:

PERSON	X_1 (BEFORE)	X_2 (AFTER)
A	15	15
B	11	13
C	10	18
D	11	12
E	14	16
F	10	10
G	11	19

Was there a significant change?

Note that subjects are being tested twice—once before and once after viewing the commercial. Therefore, we have a repeated-measures experiment.

STEP 1 State the hypothesis and select an alpha level.

The null hypothesis states that the commercial has no effect on people's attitude, or in symbols,

$$H_0 : \mu_D = 0 \quad \text{(the mean difference is zero)}$$

The alternative hypothesis states that the commercial does alter attitudes about the company, or

$$H_1 : \mu_D \neq 0 \quad \text{(there is a mean change in attitudes)}$$

For this demonstration we will use an alpha level of .05 for a two-tailed test.

STEP 2 Locate the critical region.

Degrees of freedom for the repeated-measures t test is obtained by the formula

$$df = n - 1$$

For these data, degrees of freedom equal

$$df = 7 - 1 = 6$$

The t distribution table is consulted for a two-tailed test with $\alpha = .05$ for $df = 6$. The critical t values for the critical region are $t = \pm 2.447$.

STEP 3 Obtain the sample data and compute the test statistic.

To compute the repeated-measures t statistics, we will have to determine the values for the difference (D) scores, $\overline{D}$, SS for the D scores, the sample standard deviation for the D scores, and the estimated standard error for $\overline{D}$.

The difference scores. The following table illustrates the computations of the D values for our sample data. Remember, $D = X_2 - X_1$.

X_1	X_2	D
15	15	$15 - 15 = 0$
11	13	$13 - 11 = +2$
10	18	$18 - 10 = +8$
11	12	$12 - 11 = +1$
14	16	$16 - 14 = +2$
10	10	$10 - 10 = 0$
11	19	$19 - 11 = +8$

The sample mean of D values. The sample mean for the difference scores is equal to the sum of the D values divided by n. For these data.

$$\Sigma D = 0 + 2 + 8 + 1 + 2 + 0 + 8 = 21$$

$$\overline{D} = \frac{\Sigma D}{n} = \frac{21}{7} = 3$$

Sum of squares for D scores. We will use the computational formula for SS. The following table summarizes the calculations.

D	D^2	
0	0	$\Sigma D = 21$
2	4	$\Sigma D^2 = 0 + 4 + 64 + 1 + 4 + 0 + 64 = 137$
8	64	
1	1	$SS = \Sigma D^2 - \dfrac{(\Sigma D)}{n} = 137 - \dfrac{(21)^2}{7}$
2	4	
0	0	$SS = 137 - \dfrac{441}{7} = 137 - 63 = 74$
8	64	

Standard deviation for D scores. The standard deviation for the sample of D values equals

$$s = \sqrt{\frac{SS}{n-1}} = \sqrt{\frac{74}{7-1}} = \sqrt{\frac{74}{6}} = \sqrt{12.33} = 3.51$$

Estimated standard error for $\overline{D}$. The estimated standard error for sample mean difference is computed as follows:

$$s_{\overline{D}} = \frac{s}{\sqrt{n}} = \frac{3.51}{\sqrt{7}} = \frac{3.51}{2.646} = 1.33$$

The repeated-measures t statistic. We now have the information required to calculate the t statistic.

$$t = \frac{\overline{D} - \mu_D}{s_{\overline{D}}} = \frac{3 - 0}{1.33} = \frac{3}{1.33} = 2.26$$

STEP 4   Make a decision about H_0 and state the conclusion.

The obtained t value is not extreme enough to fall in the critical region. Therefore, we fail to reject the null hypothesis. We conclude that there is no evidence that the commercial will change people's attitudes, $t(6) = 2.26$, $p > .05$, two tailed. (Note that we state that p is *greater than* .05 because we failed to reject H_0.)

PROBLEMS

1. For the following studies, indicate whether or not a repeated-measures t test is the appropriate analysis. Explain your answers.

   a. A researcher examines the effect of relaxation training on test anxiety. One sample of subjects receives relaxation training for 3 weeks. A second sample serves as a control group and does not receive the treatment. The researcher then measures anxiety levels for both groups in a test-taking situation.

   b. Another researcher does a similar study. Baseline levels of test anxiety are recorded for a sample of subjects. Then all subjects receive relaxation training for 3 weeks and their anxiety levels are measured again.

   c. In a test-anxiety study, two samples are used. Subjects are assigned to groups so that they are matched for self-esteem and for grade-point average. One sample receives relaxation training for 3 weeks and the second serves as a no-treatment control group. Test anxiety is measured for both groups at the end of 3 weeks.

2. What is the advantage of a matched-subjects design over an independent-measures design?

3. A psychologist would like to know if there are any changes in personality during imprisonment. She selects a random sample of $n = 25$ people who have been sentenced to at least 5 years of prison. The psychologist interviews each of these people during their first week in prison and administers a personality test which measures introversion/extroversion on a scale from 0 to 50 (low scores indicate introversion). After 1 year, the investigator returns for a second interview with the prisoners and again administers the personality test. For each person, she calculates the difference between their initial score and the score after 1 year of confinement. The average for this sample of difference scores is $\overline{D} = -5$ with $SS = 2400$.

   a. Test the hypothesis that imprisonment changes personality variables. Set alpha at .05.

   b. Would the same decision be made had alpha been set at .01?

4. A researcher arguing for stricter laws for drunk driving argues that even one can of beer an produce a significant effect on reaction time. In an attempt to prove his claim, he selects a random sample of $n = 4$ people and measures their baseline reaction times. This is accomplished by having the subjects view a stimulus display and press a button as fast as they can when a light flashes on. The subjects then consume a 12-ounce can of beer. After 30 minutes, they

are tested again on the task. The researcher computed the difference scores and determined that for this sample $\bar{D} = 32$ milliseconds. That is, on average it took the group of subjects 32 milliseconds longer to respond. Also, the sample had $SS = 1200$. Do the data support the investigator's claim? Test at the .05 level of significance.

5. For the experiment described in Problem 4, the researcher probably expects reaction times to increase following beer consumption. If a one-tailed test were performed, how would H_0 and H_1 be expressed in symbols? (Assume that difference scores are computed by $D = X_2 - X_1$.)

6. A college professor performed a study to assess the effectiveness of computerized exercises in teaching mathematics. She decides to use a *matched-subjects design*. One group of subjects is assigned to a regular lecture section of introductory mathematics. A second group must attend a computer laboratory in addition to the lecture. These students work on computerized exercises for additional practice and instruction. Both samples are matched in terms of general mathematics ability, as measured by mathematical SAT scores. At the end of the semester, both groups are given the same final exam. For $n = 16$ matched pairs of subjects, the professor found a mean improvement of $\bar{D} = 9.3$ points for the computer group. The SS for the D values was 2160. Does the computerized instruction lead to a significant improvement? Test at the .01 level of significance.

7. A researcher tested a new medication to see if it would be effective in lowering blood pressure. Two samples of subjects were matched for initial blood pressure readings and medical history. For $n = 15$ matched pairs, one member of each pair received a placebo and the remaining member got the drug. The researcher recorded their diastolic blood pressure. Subjects receiving the drug showed lower blood pressure, $\bar{D} = -12.8$, with $SS = 4536$. Did the drug produce a significant change? Use a one-tailed test with $\alpha = .01$.

8. A psychologist for NASA examines the effect of cabin temperature on reaction time. A random sample of $n = 10$ astronauts and pilots is selected. Each person's reaction time is measured in a simulator, where the cabin temperature is maintained at 70°F, and again the next day at 95°F. The subjects are run through a launch simulation. Their reaction time (in milliseconds) is measured when an emergency indicator flashes and they must quickly press the appropriate switch. The data from this experiment are as follows:

EXPERIMENT 1		
70°	95°	D
180	190	10
176	201	25
204	220	16
216	240	24
194	217	23
183	206	23
207	228	21
229	255	26
231	245	14
210	228	18

a. Using the results from this experiment, can the psychologist conclude that temperature has a significant effect on reaction time? Test at the .05 level of significance.

b. To verify the results of the first experiment, the psychologist repeats the experiment with another sample of $n = 10$. The data for the replication are as follows:

EXPERIMENT 2		
70°	95°	D
178	252	74
194	244	50
217	200	−17
186	231	45
242	218	−24
212	214	2
221	201	−20
194	236	42
187	247	60
219	207	−12

Again, test for a significant difference at the .05 level of significance.

c. Both experiments showed reaction times that were on average 20 milliseconds longer with the hotter cabin temperature. Why are the results of one experiment significant and of the other not significant? (*Hint:* Compare the two experiments in terms of the consistency of the effect for all subjects. How does the consistency (or inconsistency) of the effect affect the analysis?)

9. A high school counselor has developed a course designed to help students with the mathematics portion of the SAT. A random sample of students is selected

for the study. These students take the SAT at the end of their junior year. During the summer, they take the SAT review course. When they begin their senior year, they all take the SAT again. The data for the sample are as follows:

SAT SCORES (MATHEMATICS)	
BEFORE	AFTER
402	468
486	590
543	625
516	553
475	454
403	447
522	543
480	416
619	652
493	495
485	496
551	585
573	610
437	491
472	544
409	492

Did the students perform significantly better on the SAT after taking the special course? Use a one-tailed test with alpha at .05.

10. A researcher assessed the role of routine walking in physical fitness. In this experiment, $n = 7$ pairs of subjects were matched for age, sex, and weight. However, one member of each pair typically walked to work, whereas the other typically drove. Subjects were given a physical fitness test. Their fitness scores are summarized as follows. Is there a significant difference in fitness between walkers and drivers? Test with $\alpha = .05$, two tails.

DRIVERS	WALKERS
9	8
14	17
10	17
11	10
12	15
9	13
10	14

11. A psychologist tests a new drug for its pain-killing effects. Pain threshold is measured for a sample of subjects by determining the intensity (in milliamperes) of electric shock that causes discomfort. After the initial baseline is established, subjects receive the drug, and their thresholds are once again measured. The data are as follows:

PAIN THRESHOLDS (MILLIAMPERES)	
BEFORE	AFTER
2.1	3.2
2.3	2.9
3.0	4.6
2.7	2.7
1.9	3.1
2.1	2.9
2.9	2.9
2.7	3.4
3.2	5.3
2.5	2.5
3.1	4.9

Is there an effect of the drug treatment? Test with alpha of .05.

12. A researcher examines the effects of sensitization on cigarette smoking in habitual smokers. A random sample of $n = 12$ smokers is selected. The number of cigarettes smoked per day is first determined for these people. The subjects are then sensitized to the effects of smoking by having them view a film that graphically shows the harm caused by cigarette smoke. A week later, the subjects are asked to count the number of cigarettes they smoke that day. The data are as follows:

NUMBER OF CIGARETTES SMOKED	
BEFORE	ONE WEEK LATER
19	15
22	7
32	31
17	10
37	28
20	12
23	23
24	17
28	19
21	24
15	11
18	16

Did sensitization cause a reduction in smoking? Use the .05 level of significance.

13. A researcher studies the effect of a drug (MAO inhibitor) on the number of nightmares occurring in veterans with post-traumatic stress disorder (PTSD). A sample of PTSD clients records each incident of a nightmare for 1 month before treatment. Subjects are then given the medication for 1 month, and they continue to report each occurrence of a nightmare. For the following hypothetical data, determine if the MAO inhibitor significantly reduces nightmares. Use the .05 level of significance and a one-tailed test.

NUMBER OF NIGHTMARES	
ONE MONTH BEFORE TREATMENT	ONE MONTH DURING TREATMENT
6	1
10	2
3	0
5	5
7	2

14. A psychologist studies the effectiveness of hypnosis for weight reduction. The weights of a sample of $n = 8$ volunteers are recorded and the volunteers are placed under hypnosis. During hypnosis they are told that they will seldom get very hungry and will quickly feel full whenever they eat. The subjects' weights are measured 1 month later. For the following data, determine if this hypnosis treatment produces a significant loss of weight. Test with alpha set at .01 for one tail.

WEIGHT BEFORE TREATMENT	WEIGHT 1 MONTH LATER
210	195
175	185
193	187
184	175
209	224
199	194
203	205
211	202

15. A researcher tests the effectiveness of a drug called Ritalin on hyperkinetic children. The researcher uses a sample of $n = 12$ hyperkinetic children ranging in age from 8 to 9 years of age. The children are told several brief stories. After each story, the experimenter asks the children questions about the story. The total number of questions answered correctly for all the stories is recorded as the child's score. Because hyperkinetic children have attentional deficits, they should not perform well on this task when they are not treated. The researcher tests all of the children under two conditions: following administration of a sugar pill (placebo condition) and after receiving Ritalin. For the following data, determine if the drug treatment has an effect on performance. Use an alpha level of .01.

SUBJECT	PLACEBO	RITALIN
A	10	15
B	8	15
C	11	13
D	6	17
E	7	8
F	9	17
G	6	18
H	8	3
I	5	14
J	10	20
K	7	18
L	2	19

16. A psychologist studied cognitive ability in children whose mothers drank alcohol during pregnancy. The psychologist attempted to control several variables by matching subjects in both groups for sex, weight at birth, and socioeconomic status of parents. In each pair of subjects, one child had a mother who drank during pregnancy, whereas the other child did not. The psychologist measured the children's IQ. For $n = 18$ pairs of matched subjects, the children of nondrinkers scored on average $\overline{D} = 10.5$ points higher than the children of drinkers, with $SS = 2448$. Is there a difference between the children of drinkers and those of nondrinkers? Use the .01 level of significance and a two-tailed test.

17. A statistics instructor was unable to decide between two potential textbooks. To help with this decision, a random sample of 12 students was obtained, and each student was to rate both books using a scale from 1 (very bad) to 10 (excellent). The data from these 12 students are as follows:

STUDENT	BOOK 1	BOOK 2
1	3	5
2	6	7
3	8	7
4	7	8
5	5	6
6	3	5
7	8	6
8	6	3
9	2	5
10	5	6
11	7	5
12	4	7

Do these data indicate that students perceive a significant difference between the books? Test at the .05 level of significance.

18. Although psychologists do not completely understand the phenomenon of dreaming, it does appear that people need to dream. One experiment demonstrating this fact shows that people who are deprived of dreaming one night will tend to have extra dreams the following night, as if they were trying to make up for the lost dreams. In a typical version of this experiment, the psychologist first records the number of dreams (by monitoring rapid eye movements (REMs)) during a normal night's sleep. The next night, each subject is prevented from dreaming by being awakened as soon as he or she begins a dream. During the third night, the psychologist once again records the number of dreams. Hypothetical data from this experiment are as follows:

SUBJECT	FIRST NIGHT	NIGHT AFTER DEPRIVATION
1	4	7
2	5	5
3	4	8
4	6	7
5	4	10
6	5	7
7	4	7
8	4	6

Do these data indicate a significant increase in dreams after one night of dream deprivation? Test at the .05 level of significance.

19. A pharmaceutical company would like to test the effectiveness of a new antidepressant drug. A sample

of 15 depressed patients is obtained, and each patient is given a mood inventory questionnaire before and after receiving the drug treatment. The data for this experiment are as follows:

PATIENT	BEFORE	AFTER
1	18	23
2	21	20
3	16	17
4	19	20
5	14	13
6	23	22
7	16	18
8	14	18
9	21	21
10	18	16
11	17	19
12	14	20
13	16	15
14	14	15
15	20	21

On the basis of these data, can the company conclude that the drug has a significant effect on mood? Test with $\alpha = .01$.

20. A consumer protection agency is testing the effectiveness of a new gasoline additive that claims to improve gas mileage. A sample of 10 cars is obtained, and each car is driven over a standard 100-mile course with and without the additive. The researchers carefully record the miles per gallon for each test drive. The results of this test are as follows:

CAR	WITH ADDITIVE	WITHOUT ADDITIVE
1	23.0	21.6
2	20.2	19.8
3	17.4	17.5
4	19.6	20.7
5	22.8	23.1
6	20.4	19.8
7	26.8	26.4
8	23.7	24.0
9	17.2	15.9
10	18.5	18.3

Does the new gasoline additive have a significant effect on gas mileage? Test at the .05 level of significance.

CONTENTS

Suppose we asked you to describe the "typical" college student in the United States. For example, what is the mean age of this population? On the average, how many hours per week do members of this population study? What is the mean amount of money students spend on "junk food" each year? On average, how many hours of sleep do they get each night? Notice we are asking questions about values for population parameters (mean age, mean money spent, and so on).

When you attempt to describe the typical college student, you probably will take a look at the students you know on your campus. From this group you can begin to describe what the population of college students might be like. Notice that you are starting with a sample (the students you know) and then you are making some general statements about the population (for example, the mean age is around 21, the mean hours per week study-ing is 18, and so on). The process of using sample data to estimate the values for population parameters is called *estimation*. It is used to make inferences about unknown populations and often serves as a follow-up to hypothesis tests.

As the term *estimation* implies, the sample data provide values that are only approximations (estimates) of population parameters. Many factors can influence these estimates. One obvious factor is sample size. Suppose you knew only two other students. How might this affect your estimate? Another factor is the type of estimate used. For example, why limit our estimate to a single value? Instead of estimating the population mean age of students at precisely 21, why not estimate it to be somewhere in an interval between 20 and 23 years? In this chapter we address these and many other questions as we closely examine the process of estimation.

12.1 OVERVIEW

In Chapter 8 we introduced hypothesis testing as a statistical procedure that allows researchers to use sample data to draw inferences about populations. Hypothesis testing is probably the most frequently used inferential technique, but it is not the only one. In this chapter we will examine the process of estimation, which provides researchers with an additional method for using samples as the basis for drawing general conclusions about populations.

The basic principle underlying all of inferential statistics is that samples are representative of the populations from which they come. The most direct application of this principle is the use of sample values as estimators of the corresponding population values; that is, using statistics to estimate parameters. This process is called estimation.

DEFINITION   The inferential process of using sample data to estimate population parameters is called *estimation*.

The use of samples to estimate populations is quite common. For example, you often hear news reports such as "Sixty percent of the general public approves of the president's new budget plan." Clearly, the percentage that is reported was obtained from a sample (they don't ask everyone's opinion), and this sample statistic is being used as an estimate of the population parameter.

We already have encountered estimation in earlier sections of this book. For example, the formula for sample standard deviation (Chapter 4) was developed so that the sample value would give an accurate and unbiased estimate of the population. Now we will examine the process of using sample means as the basis for estimating population means.

PRECISION AND CONFIDENCE IN ESTIMATION

Before we begin the actual process of estimation, there are a few general points that should be kept in mind. First, a sample will not give a perfect picture of the whole population. A sample is expected to be representative of the population, but there always will be some differences between the sample and the entire population. These differences are referred to as *sampling error*. Second, there are two distinct ways of making estimates. Suppose, for example, you are asked to estimate the weight of this book. You could pick a single value (say, 2 pounds), or you could choose a range of values (say, between 1.5 pounds and 2.5 pounds). The first estimate, using a single number, is called a *point estimate*. Point estimates have the advantage of being very precise; they specify a particular value. On the other hand, you generally do not have much confidence that a point estimate is correct. You would not bet on it, for example.

DEFINITION

For a *point estimate*, you use a single number as your estimate of an unknown quantity.

The second type of estimate, using a range of values, is called an *interval estimate*. Interval estimates do not have the precision of point estimates, but they do give you more confidence. You would feel more comfortable, for example, saying that this book weighs "around 2 pounds." At the extreme, you would be very confident in estimating that this book weighs between 0.5 and 10 pounds. Notice that there is a trade-off between precision and confidence. As the interval gets wider and wider, your confidence grows. But, at the same time, the precision of the estimate gets worse. We will be using samples to make both point and interval estimates of a population mean. Because the interval estimates are associated with confidence, they usually are called *confidence intervals*.

DEFINITIONS

For an *interval estimate*, you use a range of values as your estimate of an unknown quantity.

When an interval estimate is accompanied with a specific level of confidence (or probability), it is called a *confidence interval*.

Estimation is used in the same general situations in which we have already used hypothesis testing. In fact, there is an estimation procedure that accompanies each of the hypothesis tests we presented in the preceding four chapters. Although the details of the estimation process will differ from one experiment to the next, the general experimental situation is shown in Figure 12.1. The figure shows a population with an unknown mean (the population after treatment). A sample is selected from the unknown population. The goal of estimation is to use the sample data to obtain an estimate of the unknown population mean.

COMPARISON OF HYPOTHESIS TESTS AND ESTIMATION

You should recognize that the situation shown in Figure 12.1 is the same situation in which we have used hypothesis tests in the past. In many ways hypothesis testing and estimation are similar. They both make use of sample data and either z-scores or t statistics to find out about unknown populations. But these two inferential procedures are designed to answer different

Figure 12.1

The basic experimental situation for estimation. The purpose is to use the sample data to obtain an estimate of the population mean after treatment.

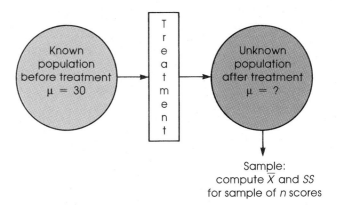

questions. Using the situation shown in Figure 12.1 as an example, we could use a hypothesis test to evaluate the effect of the treatment. The test would determine whether or not the treatment has any effect. Notice that this is a yes-no question. The null hypothesis says, "No, there is no treatment effect." The alternative hypothesis says, "Yes, there is a treatment effect."

The goal of estimation, on the other hand, is to determine the value of the population mean after treatment. Essentially, estimation will determine *how much* effect the treatment has (see Box 12.1). If, for example, we obtained a

HYPOTHESIS TESTING VERSUS ESTIMATION: STATISTICAL SIGNIFICANCE AND PRACTICAL APPLICATIONS

AS WE already noted, hypothesis tests tend to involve a yes-no decision. Either we decide to reject H_0 or we fail to reject H_0. The language of hypothesis testing reflects this process. The outcome of the hypothesis test is one of two conclusions:

There is no evidence for a treatment effect
(fail to reject H_0)
or
There is a statistically significant effect.
(H_0 is rejected).

For example, a researcher studies the effect of a new drug on people with high cholesterol. In hypothesis testing, the question is whether or not the drug has a significant effect on cholesterol levels. Suppose the hypothesis test revealed that the drug did produce a significant decrease in cholesterol. The next question might be, How much of a reduction occurs? This question calls for estimation, in which the size of a treatment effect for the population is estimated.

Estimation can be of great practical importance, because the presence of a "statistically significant"

effect does not necessarily mean the results are significant for application purposes. Consider the following possibility: Before drug treatment, the sample of patients had a mean cholesterol level of 225. After drug treatment, their cholesterol reading was 210. When analyzed, this 15-point change reached statistical significance (H_0 was rejected). Although the hypothesis test revealed that the drug produced a *statistically significant* change, it may not be *clinically significant*. That is, a cholesterol level of 210 is still quite high. In estimation, we would estimate the population mean cholesterol level for patients who are treated with the drug. This estimated value may reveal that even though the drug does in fact reduce cholesterol levels, it does not produce a large enough change (notice we are looking at a "how-much" question) to make it of any practical value. Thus the hypothesis test might reveal that an effect occurred, but estimation indicates it is small and of little *practical significance* in real-world applications.

point estimate of $\mu = 38$ for the population after treatment, we could conclude that the effect of the treatment is to increase scores by an average of 8 points (from the original mean of $\mu = 30$ to the posttreatment mean of $\mu = 38$).

WHEN TO USE ESTIMATION

There are three situations where estimation commonly is used.

1. Estimation is used after a hypothesis test where H_0 is rejected. Remember that when H_0 is rejected, the conclusion is that the treatment does have an effect. The next logical question would be, How much effect? This is exactly the question that estimation is designed to answer.

2. Estimation is used when you already know that there is an effect and simply want to find out how much. For example, the city school board probably knows that a special reading program will help students. However, they want to be sure that the effect is big enough to justify the cost. Estimation is used to determine the size of the treatment effect.

3. Estimation is used when you simply want some basic information about an unknown population. Suppose, for example, you want to know about the political attitudes of students at your college. You could use a sample of students as the basis for estimating the population mean.

THE LOGIC OF ESTIMATION

The logic underlying the general process of estimation is as follows:

1. Each set of sample data has a corresponding z-score or t statistic. For example, the data from a single sample can be used to compute either

$$z = \frac{\overline{X} - \mu}{\sigma_{\overline{X}}} \quad or \quad t = \frac{\overline{X} - \mu}{s_{\overline{X}}}$$

Remember that the z formula is used when the population standard deviation, σ, is known. The t formula is for situations where σ is unknown.

In general, the z-score or t statistic has the structure

$$z \text{ or } t = \frac{\text{sample data} - \text{population parameter}}{\text{standard error}}$$

2. For hypothesis testing we used the z or t formula to evaluate a hypothesis about the unknown population parameter. Now, our goal is to determine the value for the unknown population parameter. Therefore, we will solve the z (or t) equation for this unknown value

$$\frac{\text{population}}{\text{parameter}} = \frac{\text{sample}}{\text{data}} - (z \text{ or } t)(\text{standard error}) \qquad \text{(12.1)}$$

This is the basic structure of the equation we will use for estimation.

3. In formula 12.1, the values for the sample mean and the standard error can be computed directly from the sample data. Only the value for the z-score (or t) cannot be computed. If we can determine this missing value, then the equation can be used to compute the unknown population parameter.

4. Although the specific value for the z-score (or t statistic) cannot be computed, you do know what the entire distribution of z-scores (or t statistics) looks like. For example, the z-scores will tend to form a normal-shaped distribution with a mean of zero, and the t statistics will form a t distribution, also with a mean of zero and with a shape that depends on the value of df for the sample data.

Remember, t is used when the value of σ is unknown.

5. You still cannot compute the specific value for the z-score (or t statistic) for the sample data, but you do know that the value is located somewhere in the entire distribution. The key to the estimation process involves *estimating* the location of the sample data in the distribution.

For a point estimate, your best bet is to predict that the sample statistic is located in the exact center of the distribution at z = 0 (or t = 0). This is the most likely location because z-scores or t statistics become increasingly unlikely as you move toward the tails of the distribution.

For an interval estimate, your best bet is to predict that the sample statistic is in the middle section of the distribution. To be 90% confident, for example, you would simply predict that the sample statistic is in the middle 90% of the distribution. The unit normal table or the t-distribution table can be used to determine the precise z-scores or t values, respectively, that correspond to the middle 90%.

Notice that in step 5 you are estimating the location of your sample data in the distribution. This estimate provides specific values for the z-score or t statistic corresponding to your sample data. Once these values are obtained, they can be used in the estimation equation (formula 12.1) along with the sample mean and the standard error to compute the value of the unknown population parameter. However, because the z-score or t statistic is based on an estimate, the value you obtain for the population parameter is also an estimate.

The details of the estimation procedure will now be demonstrated for each of the experimental situations we have considered thus far: the z-score statistic, the single-sample t, the independent-measures t, and the repeated-measures t.

12.2 ESTIMATION WITH z-SCORES

The z-score statistic is used in situations where the population standard deviation is known but the population mean is unknown. Often this is a population that has received some treatment. Suppose you are examining the effect of a special summer reading program for grade school children. Using a standard reading achievement test, you know that the scores for second-graders in the city school district form a normal distribution with $\mu = 80$ and $\sigma = 10$. It is reasonable to assume that a special reading program would increase the students' scores. The questions is, How much?

The example we are considering is shown graphically in Figure 12.2. Notice that we have assumed that the effect of the treatment (the special program) is to add a constant amount to each student's reading score. As a result, after the summer reading program the entire distribution would be shifted to a new location with a larger mean. This new mean is what we want to estimate.

If the treatment simply adds a constant to each score, the standard deviation will not be changed. Although it is common practice to assume that a treatment will add a constant amount, you should realize that in most real-life situations there is a general tendency for variability to increase when the mean increases.

Because it would not be reasonable to put all the students in the special program, we cannot measure this mean directly. However, we can get a sample and use the sample mean to estimate the population value for μ. For this example, assume that a random sample of $n = 25$ students is selected to participate in the summer program. At the end of the summer, each student takes the reading test and we compute a mean reading score of $\overline{X} = 88$. Note that this sample represents the population after the special program. The goal of estimation is to use this sample mean as the basis for estimating the unknown population mean.

The procedure for estimating μ is based on the distribution of sample means (see Chapter 7). You should recall that this distribution is the set of all the possible $\overline{X}$ values for a specified sample size (n). The parameters of this distribution are the following:

1. The mean (called expected value) is equal to the population mean.
2. The standard deviation for this distribution (called standard error) is equal to $\sigma/\sqrt{n}$.
3. The distribution of sample means will be normal if either
   a. The population is normal, or
   b. The sample size is at least $n = 30$.

For the example we are considering, the distribution of sample means for $n = 25$ will be normal (because the population is normal), it will have a standard error of $\sigma/\sqrt{n} = 10/\sqrt{25} = 10/5 = 2$, and it will have a mean that is equal to the unknown population mean ($\mu = ?$). This distribution is shown in Figure 12.3.

Our sample mean, $\overline{X} = 88$, is somewhere in this distribution; that is, we have one value out of all the possible sample means. Unfortunately, we do

Figure 12.2

A population distribution before the treatment is administered and the same population after treatment. Note that the effect of the treatment is to add a constant amount to each score. The goal of estimation is to determine how large the treatment effect is; i.e., what is the new population mean $\mu = ?$.

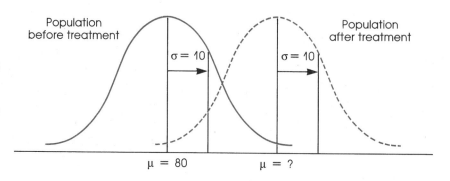

Figure 12.3

The distribution of sample means based on $n = 25$. Samples were selected from the unknown population (after treatment) shown in Figure 12.2.

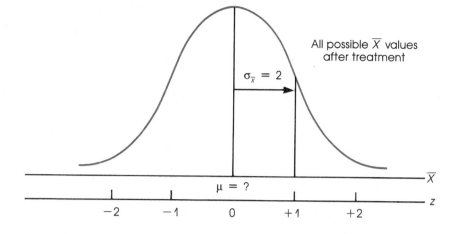

not know where our sample mean is located in the distribution. Nonetheless, we can specify different locations by using z-scores. The z-score values and their locations have been identified in Figure 12.3.

Our sample mean, $\overline{X} = 88$, has a z-score given by the formula

$$z = \frac{\overline{X} - \mu}{\sigma_{\overline{X}}}$$

Because our goal is to find the population mean (μ), we will solve this z-score equation for μ. The algebra in this process is as follows:

$z\sigma_{\overline{X}} = \overline{X} - \mu$ (Multiply both sides of the equation by $\sigma_{\overline{X}}$.)

$\mu + z\sigma_{\overline{X}} = \overline{X}$ (Add μ to both sides of the equation.)

$\mu = \overline{X} - z\sigma_{\overline{X}}$ (Subtract $z\sigma_{\overline{X}}$ from both sides of the equation.)   **(12.2)**

To use this equation, we begin with the values we know: $\overline{X} = 88$ and $\sigma_{\overline{X}} = 2$. To complete the equation we must obtain a value for z. The value we will use for z is determined by estimating the z-score for our sample mean. More precisely, we are estimating the location of our sample mean within the distribution of sample means. The estimated position will determine a z-score value which can be used in the equation to compute μ. It is important to note that the z-score value we will be using is an *estimate*; therefore, the population mean that we compute will also be an estimate.

POINT ESTIMATES   For a point estimate, you must select a single value for the z-score. It should be clear that your best bet is to select the exact middle of the distribution— that is, $z = 0$. It would be unwise to pick an extreme value such as $z = 2$ because there are relatively few samples that far away from the population mean. Most of the sample means pile up around $z = 0$, so this is your best choice. When this z-value is used in the equation, we get

$$\mu = \overline{X} - z\sigma_{\overline{X}}$$
$$\mu = 88 - 0(2)$$
$$= 88$$

This is our point estimate of the population mean. You should notice that we simply have used the sample mean $\overline{X}$ to estimate the population mean μ. The sample is the *only* information we have about the population, and you should recall from Chapter 7 that sample means tend to approximate μ (central limit theorem). Our conclusion is that the special summer program will increase reading scores from an average of $\mu = 80$ to an average of $\mu = 88$. We are estimating that the program will have an 8-point effect on reading scores.

INTERVAL ESTIMATES

To make an interval estimate, you select a range of z-score values rather than a single point. Looking again at the distribution of sample means in Figure 12.3, where would you estimate our sample mean is located? Remember, you now can pick a range of values. As before, your best bet is to predict that the sample mean is located somewhere in the center of the distribution. There is a good chance, for example, that our sample mean is located somewhere between $z = +1$ and $z = -1$. You would be almost certain that $\overline{X}$ is between $z = +3$ and $z = -3$. How do you know what range to use? Because several different ranges are possible and each range has its own degree of confidence, the first step is to determine the amount of confidence we want and then use this value to determine the range. Commonly used levels of confidence start at about 60% and go up. For this example, we will use 90%. This means that we want to be 90% confident that our interval estimate of μ is correct.

There are no strict rules for choosing a level of confidence. Researchers must decide how much precision and how much confidence are needed in each specific situation.

To be 90% confident, we simply estimate that our sample mean is somewhere in the middle 90% of the distribution of sample means. This section of the distribution is bounded by z-scores of $z = +1.65$ and $z = -1.65$ (check the unit normal table). We are 90% confident that our particular sample mean ($\overline{X} = 88$) is in this range because 90% of all the possible means are there.

The next step is to use this range of z-score values in the estimation equation. We use the two ends of the z-score range to compute the two ends of the interval estimate for μ.

At one extreme, $z = +1.65$, which gives

$$\mu = \overline{X} - z\sigma_{\overline{X}}$$
$$= 88 - 1.65(2)$$
$$= 88 - 3.30$$
$$= 84.70$$

At the other extreme, $z = -1.65$, which gives

$$\mu = \overline{X} - z\sigma_{\overline{X}}$$
$$= 88 - (-1.65)(2)$$
$$= 88 + 3.30$$
$$= 91.30$$

This confidence interval is also computed by the Minitab command ZINTERVAL in section 20.6.

The result is an interval estimate for μ. We are estimating that the population mean after the special summer program is between 84.70 and 91.30. If the mean is as small as 84.70, then the effect of the special program would be to increase reading scores by an average of 4.70 points (from $\mu = 80$ to $\mu = 84.70$). If the mean is as large as 91.30, the program would have increased score by an average of 11.30 points (from $\mu = 80$ to $\mu = 91.30$). Thus, we conclude that the special summer program will increase reading scores, and we estimate that the magnitude of the increase will be between 4.7 and 11.3 points. We are 90% confident that this estimate is correct because the only thing that was estimated was the z-score range, and we were 90% confident about that. Again, this interval estimate is called a confidence interval. In this case, it is the 90% confidence interval for μ.

Notice that the confidence interval sets up a range of values with the sample mean in the middle. As with point estimates, we are using the sample mean to estimate the population mean, but now we are saying that the value of μ should be *around* $\overline{X}$ rather than exactly equal to $\overline{X}$. Because the confidence interval is built around $\overline{X}$, adding in one direction and subtracting in the other, we will modify the estimation equation in order to simplify the arithmetic.

$$\mu = \overline{X} \pm z\sigma_{\overline{X}} \qquad\qquad (12.3)$$

To build the confidence interval, start with the sample mean and add $z\sigma_{\overline{X}}$ to get the boundary in one direction; then subtract $z\sigma_{\overline{X}}$ to get the other boundary. Translated into words, the formula says that

population mean = sample mean ± some error

The sample mean is expected to be representative of the population mean with some margin of error. Although it may seem obvious that the sample mean is used as the basis for estimating the population mean, you should not overlook the reason for this result. Sample means, on the average, provide an accurate, unbiased representation of the population mean. You should recognize this fact as one of the characteristics of the distribution of sample means: The mean (expected value) of the distribution of sample means is μ.

LEARNING CHECK   1. A cattle rancher is interested in using a newly developed hormone to increase the weight of beef cattle. Before investing in this hormone, the rancher would like to obtain some estimate of its effect. Without the hormone, the cattle weigh an average of $\mu = 1250$ pounds when they are sold at 8 months. The distribution of weights is approximately normal with $\sigma = 80$. A sample of 16 calves is selected to test the hormone. At age 8 months, the average weight for this sample is $\overline{X} = 1340$ pounds.

   a. Use these data to make a point estimate of the population mean weight if all the cattle were given the hormone.

   b. Make an interval estimate of the population mean so that you are 95% confident that the true mean is in your interval.

ANSWERS   1. a. For a point estimate, use the sample mean: $\overline{X} = 1340$ pounds.

b. For the 95% confidence interval, $z = \pm 1.96$ and $\sigma_{\bar{x}} = 20$. The interval would be

$$\mu = 1340 \pm 39.20$$

The interval ranges from 1300.80 to 1379.20 pounds.

12.3 ESTIMATION WITH THE SINGLE-SAMPLE *t* STATISTIC

The single-sample *t* statistic is used in situations where you have a population with an unknown mean ($\mu = ?$) and an unknown standard deviation ($\sigma = ?$). The goal of estimation is to use the sample data to obtain an estimate of the unknown population mean. As you will see, the process of estimation with *t* statistics is nearly identical to the process described for *z*-scores in Section 12.2. However, in situations where σ is unknown, we must use a *t* statistic instead of a *z*-score.

Because the purpose of estimation is to find the approximate value for the population mean μ, we begin with the *t* statistic.

$$t = \frac{\bar{X} - \mu}{s_{\bar{X}}}$$

Solving for μ we obtain

$$\mu = \bar{X} - ts_{\bar{X}}$$

Because *t* can have a positive or negative value in interval estimates, we can simplify the arithmetic of the formula:

$$\mu = \bar{X} \pm ts_{\bar{X}} \tag{12.4}$$

This is the basic formula for estimation using the *t* statistic. You should notice that this formula is very similar to the *z*-score formula used for estimation (formula 12.3). Also note that either formula (using *t* or *z*) can be expressed conceptually in words as

population mean = sample mean $\pm$ some error

PROCEDURES OF ESTIMATION USING A *t* STATISTIC

To obtain an estimate of μ using formula 12.4, we first find the value for the sample mean (from the sample data) and calculate the estimated standard error (also computed from the sample data). Next, we must obtain a value for *t*. Remember that you cannot calculate *t* because you do not know the population mean μ. However, you know that every sample has a corresponding *t* value, and this *t* value is located somewhere within the *t* distribution. Therefore, the next step is to estimate where your particular sample is located in the *t* distribution. For a point estimate you use the most likely value in the distribution, namely, $t = 0$. For an interval estimate you use a range of *t* values determined by the level of confidence you have selected (for example 95% or 99%). Because the *t* value in the formula is an estimate, the result we obtain is an estimate for the value of μ. The process of estimation is demonstrated in the following example.

EXAMPLE 12.1

In this example we are simply trying to estimate the value of μ. Because no particular treatment is involved here, we are not trying to determine the size of a treatment effect.

A marketing researcher for a major U.S. jeans manufacturer would like to estimate the mean age for the population of people who buy its products. This information will be valuable in making decisions about how to spend advertising dollars. For example, should the company place more advertisements in *Seventeen* magazine or in *Cosmopolitan?* These represent publications that are directed at different age groups. It would be too costly and time consuming to record the age of every person in the population of their consumers, so a random sample is taken to estimate the value of μ. A sample of $n = 30$ people is drawn from the consumers who purchase the jeans from several major clothing outlets. The mean age of this sample is $\overline{X} = 30.5$ years, with $SS = 709$. The marketing researcher wishes to make a point estimate and to determine the 95% confidence interval for μ.

Notice that nothing is known about the population parameters. Estimation of the value for μ will be based solely on the sample data. Because σ is unknown, a *t* statistic will be used for the estimation. The confidence level has been selected (95%), and the sample data have been collected. Now we can turn our attention to the computational steps of estimation.

Compute *s* and $s_{\overline{X}}$ The population standard deviation is not known; therefore, to estimate μ, it is necessary to use the estimated standard error. To obtain $s_{\overline{X}}$, we must first compute the sample standard deviation. Using the information provided, we obtain

$$
\begin{aligned}
s &= \sqrt{\frac{SS}{n-1}} \\
&= \sqrt{\frac{709}{29}} \\
&= \sqrt{24.45} \\
&= 4.94
\end{aligned}
$$

For estimated standard error we obtain

$$
\begin{aligned}
s_{\overline{X}} &= \frac{s}{\sqrt{n}} \\
&= \frac{4.94}{\sqrt{30}} \\
&= \frac{4.94}{5.48} \\
&= 0.90
\end{aligned}
$$

Compute the point estimate   The value for t that is used depends on the type of estimate being made. A single t value is used for a point estimate and an interval of values is used for the confidence interval. Just as we observed with the z-score distribution, t values are symmetrically distributed with a mean of zero. Therefore, we will use $t = 0$, the center of the distribution, as the best choice for the point estimate. Using the sample data, the estimation formula yields a point estimate of

$$\mu = \overline{X} \pm ts_{\overline{X}}$$
$$= 30.5 \pm 0(0.90)$$
$$= 30.5 \pm 0$$
$$= 30.5$$

As noted before, the sample mean is the most appropriate point estimate of the population mean.

Construct an interval estimate   For an interval estimate of μ we construct an interval around the sample mean in which the value for μ probably falls. We now use a range of t values to define this interval. For example, there is a good chance that the sample has a t value somewhere between $t = +2$ and $t = -2$ and even a much better chance it is between $t = +4$ and $t = -4$. The level of confidence (percent confidence) will determine the t values that mark off the boundaries of this interval. However, unlike the normal z distribution, there is a family of t distributions in which the exact shape of the distribution depends on the value of degrees of freedom. Therefore, the value of df that is associated with the sample is another determining factor of the t values to be used in the interval estimate. For this example,

$$df = n - 1 = 30 - 1 = 29$$

The marketing researcher selected the 95% confidence interval. Figure 12.4 depicts the t distribution for $df = 29$. To obtain the t values associ-

We do not know the actual t value associated with the $\overline{X}$ we obtained. For that information, we would need the value for μ—which we are trying to estimate. So we use values of t, just as we did with z, to define an interval around $\overline{X}$ that probably contains the value of μ.

Figure 12.4

The 95% confidence interval for $df = 29$ will have boundaries that range from $t = -2.045$ to $+2.045$. Because the t distribution table presents proportions in both tails of the distribution, for the 95% confidence interval you find the t values under $p = 0.05$ (proportions of t-scores in two tails) for $df = 29$.

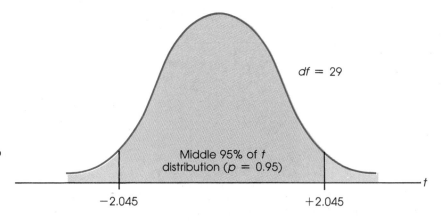

ated with the 95% confidence interval, we must consult the *t* distribution table. We look under the heading of proportions in *two tails*. If the middle 95% of the distribution is of interest to us, then both tails outside of the interval together will contain 5% of the *t* values. Therefore, to find the *t* values associated with the 95% confidence interval, we look for the entry under $p = .05$, two tails, for $df = 29$. The values of *t* used for the boundaries of this confidence interval are -2.045 and $+2.045$ (Figure 12.4). Using these values in the formula for μ, we obtain, for one end of the confidence interval,

$$\mu = \overline{X} - ts_{\overline{X}}$$
$$= 30.5 - 2.045(.90)$$
$$= 30.5 - 1.84$$
$$= 28.66$$

For the other end of the interval

$$\mu = \overline{X} + ts_{\overline{X}}$$
$$= 30.5 + 2.045(0.90)$$
$$= 30.5 + 1.84$$
$$= 32.34$$

For computing a confidence interval with the single-sample *t* statistic, the Minitab command TINTERVAL is used (see Section 20.6).

Therefore, the marketing researcher can be 95% confident that the population mean age for consumers of his product is between 28.66 and 32.34 years. The confidence level (%) determines the range of *t* values used in constructing the interval. As long as the obtained sample really does have a *t* value that falls within the estimated range of *t* values, the population mean will be included in the confidence interval.

LEARNING CHECK

1. A professor of philosophy hypothesizes that an introductory course in logic will help college students with their other studies. To test this hypothesis, a random sample of $n = 25$ freshmen is selected. These students are required to complete a logic course during their freshman year. At the time of graduation, the final grade point average is computed for each of these students. The mean GPA for this sample is $\overline{X} = 2.83$ with $SS = 6$. Using the sample data, make a point estimate and an interval estimate for the mean GPA of the population of students that take the course. Use a confidence level of 99%.

2. Suppose the same data consisted of $\overline{X} = 2.83$, $SS = 6$, and $n = 16$. Make a point estimate and construct the 99% confidence interval.

ANSWERS

1. Point estimate: $\mu = 2.83$. 99% confidence interval: μ is between 3.11 and 2.55.

2. Point estimate: $\mu = 2.83$. 99% confidence interval: $s = 0.63$; $s_{\overline{X}} = 0.16$; μ is between 3.30 and 2.36.

12.4 ESTIMATION WITH THE INDEPENDENT-MEASURES *t* STATISTIC

The independent-measures *t* statistic can be used for estimation as well as for hypothesis testing. In either case, the *t* statistic provides a means for using sample data to draw inferences about the difference between two population means. For the hypothesis test, the goal is to answer a yes-no question: Is there any mean difference between the two populations? For estimation, the goal is to determine *how much* difference.

Recall that the basic structure of the independent-measures *t* formula is the same as we observed for the initial *z*-score or single-sample *t*:

$$t = \frac{\text{sample data} - \text{population parameter}}{\text{estimated standard error}}$$

Because we are interested in finding the population parameter, we will rewrite this equation as follows:

$$\text{population parameter} = \text{sample data} \pm t(\text{estimated standard error})$$

This is the basic formula for estimation. With an independent-measures experimental design, we must solve formula 10.4 for $\mu_1 - \mu_2$. The formula we obtain for estimation is

$$\mu_1 - \mu_2 = (\overline{X}_1 - \overline{X}_2) \pm ts_{\overline{X}_1 - \overline{X}_2} \tag{12.5}$$

In words, we are using the sample mean difference, plus or minus some error, to estimate the population mean difference. To use this equation to estimate $\mu_1 - \mu_2$ requires two steps:

1. Use the sample data to compute the sample mean difference $(\overline{X}_1 - \overline{X}_2)$ and the standard error $(s_{\overline{X}_1 - \overline{X}_2})$.
2. Estimate the *t* value that is associated with the sample data. This is accomplished by selecting a *t* value that is appropriate for the type of estimate we are using. That is, we can either make a point estimate, in which case $t = 0$, or we select a level of confidence and use a range of *t* values for the estimate. With 90% confidence, for example, you would estimate that the *t* statistic for $\overline{X}_1 - \overline{X}_2$ is located somewhere in the middle 90% of the *t* distribution.

*Remember, we are not simply choosing a *t* value but are estimating the location of our sample data within the *t* distribution.*

At this point you have all the values on the right-hand side of the equation (formula 12.5), and you can compute the value for $\mu_1 - \mu_2$. If you have used a single number to estimate the location of *t*, you will get a single, point estimate for $\mu_1 - \mu_2$. If you have used a range of values for *t*, you will compute a confidence interval for $\mu_1 - \mu_2$. A complete example of this estimation procedure follows.

EXAMPLE 12.2   Recent studies have allowed psychologists to establish definite links between specific foods and specific brain functions. For example, lecithin (found in soybeans, eggs, liver) has been shown to increase the concentration of certain brain chemicals that help regulate memory and motor coordination. This experiment is designed to demonstrate the importance of this particular food substance.

The experiment involves two separate samples of newborn rats (an independent-measures experiment). The 10 rats in the first sample are given a normal diet containing standard amounts of lecithin. The 5 rats in the other sample are fed a special diet, which contains almost no lecithin. After 6 months, each of the rats is tested on a specially designed learning problem that requires both memory and motor coordination. The purpose of the experiment is to demonstrate the deficit in performance that results from lecithin deprivation. The score for each animal is the number of errors before the learning problem was solved. The data from this experiment are as follows:

REGULAR DIET	NO-LECITHIN DIET
$n = 10$	$n = 5$
$\overline{X} = 25$	$\overline{X} = 33$
$SS = 250$	$SS = 140$

Because we fully expect that there will be a significant difference between these two treatments, we will not do the hypothesis test (although you should be able to do it). We want to use these data to obtain an estimate of the size of the difference between the two population means; that is, how much does lecithin affect learning performance? We will use a point estimate and the 80% confidence interval.

The basic equation for estimation with an independent measures experiment is

$$\mu_1 - \mu_2 = (\overline{X}_1 - \overline{X}_2) \pm ts_{\overline{X}_1 - \overline{X}_2}$$

The first step is to obtain the known values from the sample data. The sample mean difference is easy; one group averaged $\overline{X} = 25$, and the other averaged $\overline{X} = 33$, so there is an 8-point difference. Notice that it is not important whether we call this a +8 or a −8 difference. In either case the size of the difference is 8 points, and the regular diet group scored lower. Because it is easier to do arithmetic with positive numbers, we will use

$$\overline{X}_1 - \overline{X}_2 = 8$$

Compute the standard error To find the standard error, we first must pool the two variances:

$$s_p^2 = \frac{SS_1 + SS_2}{df_1 + df_2} = \frac{250 + 140}{9 + 4}$$
$$= \frac{390}{13}$$
$$= 30$$

Next, the pooled variance is used to compute the standard error:

$$s_{\overline{X}_1 - \overline{X}_2} = \sqrt{\frac{s_p^2}{n_1} + \frac{s_p^2}{n_2}} = \sqrt{\frac{30}{10} + \frac{30}{5}} = \sqrt{3 + 6} = \sqrt{9} = 3$$

You should recall that this standard error combines the error from the first sample and the error from the second sample. Because the first sample is much larger, $n = 10$, it should have less error. This difference shows up in the formula. The larger sample contributes an error of 3 points, and the smaller sample contributes 6 points, which combine for a total error of 9 points under the square root.

The final value needed on the right-hand side of the equation is t. The data from this experiment would produce a t statistic with $df = 13$. With 13 degrees of freedom, we can sketch the distribution of all the possible t values. This distribution is shown in Figure 12.5. The t statistic for our data is somewhere in this distribution. The problem is to estimate where. For a point estimate, the best bet is to use $t = 0$. This is the most likely value, located exactly in the middle of the distribution. To gain more confidence in the estimate, you can select a range of t values. For 80% confidence, for example, you would estimate that the t statistic is somewhere in the middle 80% of the distribution. Checking the table, you find that the middle 80% is bounded by values of $t = +1.350$ and $t = -1.350$.

Using these t values and the sample values computed earlier, we now can estimate the magnitude of the performance deficit caused by lecithin deprivation.

Compute the point estimate   For a point estimate, use the single-value (point) estimate of $t = 0$:

$$\mu_1 - \mu_2 = (\overline{X}_1 - \overline{X}_2) \pm ts_{\overline{X}_1 - \overline{X}_2}$$
$$= 8 \pm 0(3)$$
$$= 8$$

> Sample 1 had $df = 9$, and sample 2 has $df = 4$. The t statistic has $df = 9 + 4 = 13$.

Figure 12.5

The distribution of t values with $df = 13$. Note that t values pile up around zero and that 80% of the values are between $+1.350$ and -1.350.

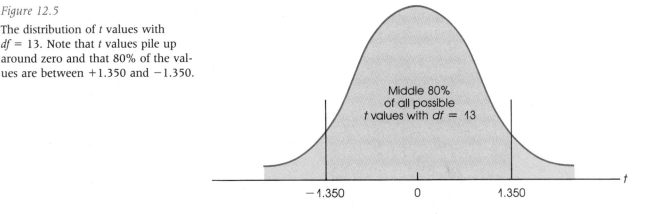

Middle 80%
of all possible
t values with $df = 13$

-1.350 0   1.350 t

Notice that the result simply uses the sample mean difference to estimate the population mean difference. The conclusion is that lecithin deprivation produces an average of 8 more errors on the learning task. (Based on the fact that the normal animals averaged around 25 errors, an 8-point increase would mean a performance deficit of approximately 30%.)

Construct the interval estimate   For an interval estimate, or confidence interval, use the range of *t* values. With 80% confidence, at one extreme,

$$\mu_1 - \mu_2 = (\bar{X}_1 - \bar{X}_2) + ts_{\bar{X}_1 - \bar{X}_2}$$
$$= 8 + 1.350(3)$$
$$= 8 + 4.05$$
$$= 12.05$$

and at the other extreme,

$$\mu_1 - \mu_2 = (\bar{X}_1 - \bar{X}_2) - ts_{\bar{X}_1 - \bar{X}_2}$$
$$= 8 - 1.350(3)$$
$$= 8 - 4.05$$
$$= 3.95$$

Confidence intervals with the independent-measures *t* statistic are provided by the Minitab command TWOSAMPLE (see Section 20.6).

This time we are concluding that the effect of lecithin deprivation is to increase errors with an average increase somewhere between 3.95 and 12.05 errors. We are 80% confident of this estimate because the only thing estimated was the location of the *t* statistic, and we used the middle 80% of all the possible *t* values.

Note that the result of the point estimate is to say that lecithin deprivation will increase errors by exactly 8. To gain confidence, you must lose precision and say that errors will increase by around 8 (for 80% confidence, we say that the average increase will be 8 ± 4.05).

LEARNING CHECK   1. In families with several children, the first-born children tend to be more reserved and serious, whereas the last-born children tend to be more outgoing and happy-go-lucky. A psychologist is using a standardized personality inventory to measure the magnitude of this difference. A sample of eight firstborn and eight last-born children is obtained. Each child is given the personality test. The results of this test are as follows:

FIRSTBORN	LAST-BORN
$\bar{X} = 11.4$	$\bar{X} = 13.9$
$SS = 26$	$SS = 30$

a. Use these sample data to make a point estimate of the population mean difference in personality for firstborn versus last-born children.

b. Make an interval estimate of the population mean difference so that you are 80% confident that the true mean difference is in your interval.

ANSWERS   **1. a.** For a point estimate, use the sample mean difference: $\overline{X}_1 - \overline{X}_2 = 2.5$ points.

b. With $df = 14$, the middle 80% of all possible t statistics is bounded by $t = +1.345$ and $t = -1.345$. For these data the pooled variance is 4, and the standard error is 1. The 80% confidence interval is 1.155 to 3.845.

12.5 ESTIMATION WITH THE REPEATED-MEASURES t STATISTIC

In a repeated-measures experiment, a single sample of subjects is measured in two different treatment conditions. For each subject a difference score is computed by subtracting the first score (treatment 1) from the second score (treatment 2).

$$D = X_2 - X_1$$

The resulting sample of difference scores can be used to draw inferences about the mean difference for the general population, μ_D. The repeated-measures t statistic allows researchers to use the sample mean difference, $\overline{D}$, to estimate the value of μ_D. Once again, the repeated-measures t formula is

$$t = \frac{\overline{D} - \mu_D}{s_{\overline{D}}}$$

Because we want to estimate the value of the population mean difference, this formula is solved for μ_D:

$$\mu_D = \overline{D} \pm ts_{\overline{D}} \tag{12.6}$$

In words, this formula may be stated as

population mean difference = sample mean difference ± some error

That is, to estimate the mean difference for the population, we use the sample mean difference plus or minus some error.

PROCEDURE FOR ESTIMATION OF μ_D The process of estimation with the repeated-measures t statistic follows the same steps that were used for estimation with the single-sample t statistic. First you calculate the sample mean ($\overline{D}$) and the estimated standard error ($s_{\overline{D}}$) using the sample of difference scores. Next, you determine the appropriate values for t ($t = 0$ for a point estimate or a range of values from the t distribution for an interval estimate). Finally, these values are used in the estimation formula (12.6) to compute an estimate of μ_D. The following example demonstrates this process.

EXAMPLE 12.3

A school psychologist has determined that a remedial reading course increases scores on a reading comprehension test. The psychologist now would like to estimate how much improvement might be expected for the whole population of students in his city. A random sample of $n = 16$ children is obtained. These children are first tested for level of reading comprehension and then enrolled in the course. At the completion of the remedial reading course, the students are tested again, and the difference between the second score and the first score is recorded for each child. For this sample, the average difference was $\overline{D} = +21$, and the *SS* for the difference scores was $SS = 1215$. The psychologist would like to use these data to make a point estimate and a 90% confidence interval estimate of μ_D.

The formula for estimation requires that we know the values of $\overline{D}$, $s_{\overline{D}}$, and *t*. We know that $\overline{D} = +21$ points for this sample, so all that remains is to compute $s_{\overline{D}}$ and look up the value of *t* in the *t* distribution table.

Compute the standard error   To find the standard error, we first must compute the sample standard deviation:

$$s = \sqrt{\frac{SS}{n-1}} = \sqrt{\frac{1215}{15}} = \sqrt{81} = 9$$

Now the estimated standard error is

$$s_{\overline{D}} = \frac{s}{\sqrt{n}} = \frac{9}{\sqrt{16}} = \frac{9}{4} = 2.25$$

To complete the estimate of μ_D, we must identify the value of *t*. We will consider the point estimate and the interval estimate separately.

Compute the point estimate   To obtain a point estimate, a single value of *t* is selected to approximate the location of $\overline{D}$. Remember that the *t* distribution is symmetrical and bell-shaped with a mean of zero (see Figure 12.6). Because $t = 0$ is the most frequently occurring value

Figure 12.6

The *t* values for the 90% confidence interval are obtained by consulting the *t* table for *df* = 15, *p* = 0.10.

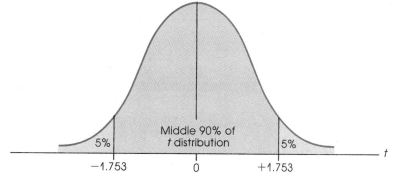

in the distribution, this is the t value that is used for the point estimate. Using this value in the estimation formula gives

$$\mu_D = \overline{D} \pm ts_{\overline{D}}$$
$$= 21 \pm 0(2.25)$$
$$= 21$$

As noted several times before, the sample mean, $\overline{D} = 21$, provides the best point estimate of μ_D.

Construct the interval estimate   The psychologist also wanted to make an interval estimate in order to be 90% confident that the interval contains the value of μ_D. To get the interval, it is necessary to determine what t values form the boundaries of the middle 90% of the t distribution. To use the t distribution table, we first must determine the proportion associated with the tails of this distribution. With 90% in the middle, the remaining area in both tails must be 10%, or $p = .10$. Also note that our sample has $n = 16$ scores, so the t statistic will have $df = n - 1 = 15$. Using $df = 15$ and $p = 0.10$ for two tails, you should find the values $+1.753$ and -1.753 in the t table. These values form the boundaries for the middle 90% of the t distribution. (See Figure 12.6.) We are confident that the t value for our sample is in this range because 90% of all the possible t values are there. Using these values in the estimation formula, we obtain the following: On one end of the interval,

$$\mu_D = \overline{D} - ts_{\overline{D}}$$
$$= 21 - 1.753(2.25)$$
$$= 21 - 3.94$$
$$= 17.06$$

and on the other end of the interval,

The Minitab command TINTERVAL is used on difference scores to obtain a confidence interval for repeated-measures designs (see Section 20.6).

$$\mu_D = 21 + 1.753(2.25)$$
$$= 21 + 3.94$$
$$= 24.94$$

Therefore, the school psychologist can be 90% confident that the average amount of improvement in reading comprehension for the population (μ_D) will be somewhere between 17.06 and 24.94 points.

LEARNING CHECK   1. A government researcher believes that driving and automotive tips will result in energy-saving habits. A sample of nine subjects is given a brochure containing energy-saving tips and is asked to follow this advice. Before and after using the tips, the subjects maintain gasoline consumption records for their automobiles. For this sample, the average improvement in gasoline mileage (in miles per gallon) was $\overline{D} = 6.50$ with

$SS = 72$. A repeated-measures t test indicated that the mean change was statistically significant. However, before the government prints millions of copies of the brochure, the researcher is requested to estimate how much mean change can be expected for the population of drivers. The investigator decides to report the 95% confidence interval. What will this interval be?

ANSWER 1. For this sample $s = 3$ and $s_{\overline{D}} = 1$. For the 95% confidence interval with $df = 8$, $t = \pm 2.306$; the 95% confidence interval for μ_D is from 4.194 to 8.806.

12.6 FACTORS AFFECTING THE WIDTH OF A CONFIDENCE INTERVAL

There are two characteristics of the confidence interval that should be noted. First, notice what happens to the width of the interval when you change the level of confidence (the percent confidence). To gain more confidence in your estimate, you must increase the width of the interval. Conversely, to have a smaller interval, you must give up confidence. This is the basic trade-off between precision and confidence that was discussed earlier. In the estimation formula, the percent confidence influences the width of the interval by way of the z-score or t value. The larger the level of confidence (the percentage), the larger the z or t value, and the larger the interval. This relationship can be seen in Figure 12.6. In the figure we have identified the middle 90% of the t distribution in order to find a 90% confidence interval. It should be obvious that if we were to increase the confidence level to 95%, it would be necessary to increase the range of t values and thereby increase the width of the interval.

Second, notice what would happen to the interval width if you had a different sample size. This time, the basic rule is as follows: The bigger the sample (n), the smaller the interval. This relation is straightforward if you consider the sample size as a measure of the amount of information. A bigger sample gives you more information about the population and allows you to make a more precise estimate (a narrower interval). The sample size controls the magnitude of the standard error in the estimation formula. As the sample size increases, the standard error decreases, and the interval gets smaller.

With t statistics, the sample size has an additional effect on the width of a confidence interval. Remember that the exact shape of the t distribution depends on degrees of freedom. As the sample size gets larger, df also get larger, and the t values associated with any specific percentage of confidence get smaller. This fact simply enhances the general relation that the larger a sample, the smaller a confidence interval.

SUMMARY

1. Estimation is a procedure that uses sample data to obtain an estimate of a population mean. The estimate can be either a point estimate (single value) or an interval estimate (range of values). Point estimates have the advantage of precision, but they do not give much confidence. Interval estimates provide confidence, but you lose precision as the interval grows wider.

2. Estimation and hypothesis testing are similar processes: Both use sample data to answer questions about populations. However, these two procedures are designed to answer different questions. Hypothesis testing will tell you whether or not a treatment effect exists (yes or no). Estimation will tell you how much treatment effect there is.

3. The z-score or t formula can be used to estimate a population mean using the data from a single sample. The z-score formula is used when the population standard deviation is known and the t formula is used when σ is unknown. The two formulas are

$$\mu = \bar{X} \pm z\sigma_{\bar{X}} \quad \text{and} \quad \mu = \bar{X} \pm ts_{\bar{X}}$$

To use either formula, first calculate the sample mean and the standard error ($\sigma_{\bar{X}}$ or $s_{\bar{X}}$) from the sample data. Next, obtain an estimate of the value of z or t by estimating the location of the sample data within the appropriate distribution. For a point estimate, use $z = 0$ or $t = 0$. For an interval estimate, first select a level of confidence (percentage) and then look up the range of z-scores or t values in the appropriate table.

4. For an independent-measures experiment, the formula for estimation is

$$\mu_1 - \mu_2 = (\bar{X}_1 - \bar{X}_2) \pm ts_{\bar{X}_1 - \bar{X}_2}$$

To use this formula, you first decide on a degree of precision and a level of confidence desired for the estimate. If your primary concern is precision, use $t = 0$ to make a point estimate of the mean difference. Otherwise you select a level of confidence (percent confidence) that determines a range of t values to be used in the formula.

5. For a repeated-measures experiment, estimation of the amount of mean change for the population is accomplished by solving the t statistic formula for μ_D:

$$\mu_D = \bar{D} \pm ts_{\bar{D}}$$

For a point estimate, a t value of zero is used. A range of t values is used to construct an interval around $\bar{D}$. As in previous estimation problems, the t values that mark the interval boundaries are determined by the confidence level that is selected and by degrees of freedom.

6. The width of a confidence interval is an indication of its precision: A narrow interval is more precise than a wide interval. The interval width is influenced by sample size and the level of confidence.
   a. As sample size (n) gets larger, the interval width gets smaller (greater precision).
   b. As the percent confidence increases, the interval-width gets greater (less precision).

KEY TERMS

estimation   point estimate   interval estimate   confidence interval

Focus on Problem Solving

1. Although hypothesis tests and estimation are similar in some respects, you should remember that they are separate statistical techniques. A hypothesis test is used to determine whether or not there is evidence for a treatment effect. Estimation is used to determine how much effect a treatment has.

2. When students perform a hypothesis test and estimation with the same set of data, a common error is to take the *z*-score or *t* statistic from the hypothesis test and use it in the estimation formula. For estimation the *z*-score or *t* value is determined by the level of confidence and must be looked up in the appropriate table.

3. Now that you are familiar with several different formulas for hypothesis tests and estimation, one problem will be determining which formula is appropriate for each set of data. When the data consist of a single sample selected from a single population, the appropriate statistic will be either *z* or the single-sample *t*, depending on whether σ is known or unknown, respectively. For an independent-measures design you will always have two separate samples. In a repeated-measures design there is only one sample, but each individual is measured twice so that difference scores can be computed.

Demonstration 12.1

ESTIMATION WITH A SINGLE-SAMPLE *t* STATISTIC

A sample of $n = 16$ is randomly selected from a population with unknown parameters. For the following sample data, estimate the value of μ using a point estimate and a 90% confidence interval.

$$\text{sample data:} \quad 13 \quad 10 \quad 8 \quad 13 \quad 9 \quad 14 \quad 12 \quad 10$$
$$11 \quad 10 \quad 15 \quad 13 \quad 7 \quad 6 \quad 15 \quad 10$$

Note that we have a single sample and we do not know the value for σ. Thus, the single-sample *t* statistic should be used for these data. The formula for estimation is

$$\mu = \overline{X} \pm t s_{\overline{X}}$$

STEP 1   Compute the sample mean.

The sample mean is the basis for our estimate of μ. For these data,

$$\Sigma X = 13 + 10 + 8 + 13 + 9 + 14 + 12 + 10 +$$
$$11 + 10 + 15 + 13 + 7 + 6 + 15 + 10$$
$$= 176$$

$$\overline{X} = \frac{\Sigma X}{n} = \frac{176}{16} = 11$$

STEP   2   Compute the estimated standard error, $s_{\overline{X}}$.

To compute the estimated standard error, we must first find the value for *SS* and the sample standard deviation.

Sum of squares. We will use the definitional formula for *SS*. The following table demonstrates the computations.

X	$X - \bar{X}$	$(X - \bar{X})^2$
13	$13-11=+2$	4
10	$10-11=-1$	1
8	$8-11=-3$	9
13	$13-11=+2$	4
9	$9-11=-2$	4
14	$14-11=+3$	9
12	$12-11=+1$	1
10	$10-11=-1$	1
11	$11-11=\ 0$	0
10	$10-11=-1$	1
15	$15-11=+4$	16
13	$13-11=+2$	4
7	$7-11=-4$	16
6	$6-11=-5$	25
15	$15-11=+4$	16
10	$10-11=-1$	1

To obtain *SS*, we sum the squared deviation scores in the last column.

$$SS = \Sigma(X - \bar{X})^2 = 112$$

Standard deviation. The sample standard deviation is computed for these data.

$$s = \sqrt{\frac{SS}{n-1}} = \sqrt{\frac{112}{16-1}} = \sqrt{\frac{112}{15}} = \sqrt{7.47} = 2.73$$

Estimated standard error. The estimated standard error can now be determined.

$$s_{\bar{X}} = \frac{s}{\sqrt{n}} = \frac{2.73}{\sqrt{16}} = \frac{2.73}{4} = 0.68$$

STEP 3   Point estimate for μ.

For a point estimate, we use $t = 0$. Using the estimation formula, we obtain

$$\mu = \bar{X} \pm ts_{\bar{X}}$$
$$= 11 \pm 0(0.68)$$
$$= 11 \pm 0 = 11$$

The point estimate for the population mean is $\mu = 11$.

STEP 4   Confidence interval for μ.

For these data, we want the 90% confidence interval. Therefore, we will use a range of *t* values that form the middle 90% of the distribution. For this demonstration degrees of freedom is

$$df = n - 1 = 16 - 1 = 15$$

If we are looking for the middle 90% of the distribution, then 10% ($p = 0.10$) would lie in both tails outside of the interval. To find the *t* values, we look up $p = 0.10$, two tails, for $df = 15$ in the *t* distribution table. The *t* values for the 90% confidence interval are $t = \pm 1.753$.

Using the estimation formula, one end of the confidence interval is

$$\mu = \overline{X} - ts_{\overline{X}}$$
$$= 11 - 1.753(0.68)$$
$$= 11 - 1.19 = 9.81$$

For the other end of the confidence interval, we obtain

$$\mu = \overline{X} + ts_{\overline{X}}$$
$$= 11 + 1.753(0.68)$$
$$= 11 + 1.19 = 12.19$$

Thus, the 90% confidence interval for μ is from 9.81 to 12.19.

—— *Demonstration 12.2* ——

ESTIMATION WITH THE INDEPENDENT-MEASURES *t* STATISTIC

Samples are taken from two school districts and knowledge of American history is tested with a short questionnaire. For the following sample data, estimate the amount of mean difference between the students of these two districts. Specifically, provide a point estimate and a 95% confidence interval for $\mu_1 - \mu_2$.

District A scores: 18   15   24   15
District B scores: 9   12   13   6

STEP 1   Compute the sample means.
The estimate of population mean difference ($\mu_1 - \mu_2$) is based of the sample mean difference ($\overline{X}_1 - \overline{X}_2$).
For district A,

$$\Sigma X = 18 + 15 + 24 + 15 = 72$$

$$\overline{X}_1 = \frac{\Sigma X}{n} = \frac{72}{4} = 18$$

For district B,

$$\Sigma X = 9 + 12 + 13 + 6 = 40$$

$$\overline{X}_2 = \frac{\Sigma X}{n} = \frac{40}{4} = 10$$

STEP 2   Calculate the estimated standard error for mean difference, $s_{\overline{X}_1 - \overline{X}_2}$.
To compute the estimated standard error, we first need to determine the values of *SS* for both samples and pooled variance.

Sum of squares. The computations for sum of squares, using the definitional formula, are shown for both samples in the following tables.

	DISTRICT A	
X	$X - \bar{X}$	$(X - \bar{X})^2$
18	$18 - 18 = 0$	0
15	$15 - 18 = -3$	9
24	$24 - 18 = +6$	36
15	$15 - 18 = -3$	9

	DISTRICT B	
X	$X - \bar{X}$	$(X - \bar{X})^2$
9	$9 - 10 = -1$	1
12	$12 - 10 = +2$	4
13	$13 - 10 = +3$	9
6	$6 - 10 = -4$	16

For district A,

$$SS_1 = \Sigma(X - \bar{X})^2 = 0 + 9 + 36 + 9 = 54$$

For district B,

$$SS_2 = \Sigma(X - \bar{X})^2 = 1 + 4 + 9 + 16 = 30$$

Pooled variance. For pooled variance, we use the SS and df values from both samples. For District A, $df_1 = n_1 - 1 = 3$. For District B, $df_2 = n_2 - 1 = 3$. Pooled variance is

$$s_p^2 = \frac{SS_1 + SS_2}{df_1 + df_2} = \frac{54 + 30}{3 + 3} = \frac{84}{6} = 14$$

Estimated standard error. The estimated standard error for mean difference can now be calculated.

$$s_{\bar{X}_1 - \bar{X}_2} = \sqrt{\frac{s_p^2}{n_1} + \frac{s_p^2}{n_2}} = \sqrt{\frac{14}{4} + \frac{14}{4}} = \sqrt{3.5 + 3.5}$$
$$= \sqrt{7} = 2.65$$

STEP 3 Point estimate for $\mu_1 - \mu_2$.

For the point estimate, we use a t value of zero. Using the sample means and estimated standard error from previous steps, we obtain

$$\mu_1 - \mu_2 = (\bar{X}_1 - \bar{X}_2) \pm ts_{\bar{X}_1 - \bar{X}_2}$$
$$= (18 - 10) \pm 0(2.65)$$
$$= 8 \pm 0 = 8$$

STEP 4 Confidence interval for $\mu_1 - \mu_2$.

For the independent measures t statistic, degrees of freedom are determined by

$$df = n_1 + n_2 - 2$$

For these data df is

$$df = 4 + 4 - 2 = 6$$

With a 95% level of confidence, 5% of the distribution falls in the tails outside the interval. Therefore, we consult the t distribution table for $p = 0.05$, two tails, with $df = 6$. The t values from the table are $t = \pm 2.447$. On one end of the confidence interval, $\mu_1 - \mu_2$ is

$$\mu_1 - \mu_2 = (\overline{X}_1 - \overline{X}_2) - ts_{\overline{X}_1 - \overline{X}_2}$$
$$= (18 - 10) - 2.447(2.65)$$
$$= 8 - 6.48$$
$$= 1.52$$

On the other end of the confidence interval, the population mean difference is

$$\mu_1 - \mu_2 = (\overline{X}_1 - \overline{X}_2) + ts_{\overline{X}_1 - \overline{X}_2}$$
$$= (18 - 10) + 2.447(2.65)$$
$$= 8 + 6.48$$
$$= 14.48$$

Thus, the 95% confidence interval for population mean difference is from 1.52 to 14.48.

PROBLEMS

1. An extensive survey in 1970 revealed that preschool children spend an average of $\mu = 6.3$ hours per day watching television. The distribution of TV times is normal with $\sigma = 2$. Last year a sample of $n = 100$ preschool children gave a mean of $\overline{X} = 5.8$ hours of television per day.
   a. Use these sample data to make a point estimate of the population mean for last year.
   b. Based on your point estimate, how much change has occurred in children's television habits since 1970?
   c. Make an interval estimate of last year's population mean so you are 80% confident that the true mean is in your interval.

2. A researcher has constructed a 90% confidence interval of 87 ± 10, based on a sample of $n = 25$ scores. Note that this interval is 20 points wide (from 77 to 97). How large a sample would be needed to produce a 90% interval that is only 10 points wide?

3. Performance scores on a motor skills task form a normal distribution with $\mu = 20$ and $\sigma = 4$. A psychologist is using this task to determine the extent to which increased self-awareness affects performance. The prediction for this experiment is that increased self-awareness will reduce a subject's concentration and result in lower performance scores. A sample of $n = 16$ subjects is obtained, and each subject is

tested on the motor skills task while seated in front of a large mirror. The purpose of the mirror is to make the subjects more self-aware. The average score for this sample is $\overline{X} = 15.5$.

a. Make a point estimate of the population mean performance score with the mirror present.

b. Make an interval estimate of the population mean so that you are 95% confident that the true mean is in your interval.

4. Researchers have developed a filament that should add to the life expectancy of light bulbs. The standard 60-watt bulb burns for an average of $\mu = 750$ hours with $\sigma = 20$. A sample of $n = 100$ bulbs is prepared using the new filament. The average life for this sample is $\overline{X} = 820$ hours.

a. Use these sample data to make a point estimate of the mean life expectancy for the new filament.

b. Make an interval estimate so that you are 80% confident that the true mean is in your interval.

c. Make an interval estimate so that you are 99% confident that the true mean is in your interval.

5. A poultry farm supplies chickens to a fast-food restaurant chain. The chickens are sold by weight and average $\mu = 65$ ounces. The distribution of weights is normal with $\sigma = 4.9$ ounces. The farmer is interested in changing to a new brand of chicken food. However, the new food is more expensive and will not be economically feasible unless it results in an average weight increase of at least 3 ounces per chicken. A sample of $n = 30$ chicks is selected to be tested on the new food. At maturity, the weights for these chickens are as follows: 74, 72, 65, 79, 75, 73, 68, 75, 78, 69, 72, 75, 79, 81, 73, 63, 69, 73, 77, 73, 64, 73, 63, 78, 72, 71, 62, 72, 71, 74.

a. Construct an 80% confidence interval for the population mean weight for chickens raised on the new feed.

b. Based on your confidence interval, should the farmer switch to the new food? Explain your answer.

6. What factors affect the width of the confidence interval? How is the width affected by each of these factors?

7. A psychologist has developed a new personality questionnaire for measuring self-esteem and would like to estimate the population parameters for the test scores. The questionnaire is administered to a sample of $n = 25$ subjects. This sample has an average score of $\overline{X} = 43$ with $SS = 2400$.

a. Provide an unbiased estimate for the population standard deviation.

b. Make a point estimate for the population mean.

c. Make an interval estimate of μ so that you are 90% confident that the value for μ is in your interval.

8. A toy manufacturer asks a developmental psychologist to test children's responses to a new product. Specifically, the manufacturer wants to know how long, on average, the toy captures children's attention. The psychologist tests a sample of $n = 9$ children and measures how long they play with the toy before they get bored. This sample had a mean of $\overline{X} = 31$ minutes with $SS = 648$.

a. Make a point estimate for μ.

b. Make an interval estimate for μ using a confidence level of 95%.

9. A random sample of $n = 11$ scores is selected from a population with unknown parameters. The scores in the sample are as follows: 12, 5, 9, 9, 10, 14, 7, 10, 14, 13, 8.

a. Provide an unbiased estimate of the population standard deviation.

b. Use the sample data to make a point estimate for μ and to construct the 95% confidence interval for μ.

10. A vocabulary skills test designed for 6-year-old children has been standardized to produce a mean score of $\mu = 50$. A researcher would like to use this test in an experiment with 5-year-old children. Before beginning the experiment, however, the researcher would like some indication of how well 5-year-olds can perform on this test. Therefore, a sample of $n = 21$ 5-year-old children is given the test. The data for this sample are as follows:

VOCABULARY TEST SCORES						
42	56	49	37	43	46	47
48	57	39	40	51	49	50
36	45	52	47	49	40	53

a. Use the data to make a point estimate of the population mean for 5-year-old children.

b. Make an interval estimate of the mean so that you are 95% confident that the true mean is in your interval.

c. On the basis of your confidence interval, can the researcher be 95% confident that the population mean for 5-year-olds is lower than the mean for 6-year-olds?

11. A curious student would like to know the average number of books owned by college professors. A

random sample of 12 professors is selected, and the student counts the number of books owned by each professor. The data obtained by the student are as follows:

346, 134, 208, 640, 276, 318
211, 453, 152, 281, 109, 334

a. Use these sample data to make a point estimate of the population mean.
b. Use the data to make an interval estimate of the population mean so that you are 95% confident that the mean is in your interval.
c. Based on these data, the 80% confidence interval for the population mean extends from 229.87 to 347.13. Does this mean that 80% of all college professors own between 229.87 and 347.13 books? Explain your answer.

12. A psychologist is studying the relation between weight and hormone levels. A random sample of rats is selected, and the sample is divided into two groups of five rats each. The rats in one group are given daily injections of a "growth" hormone, and the rats in the second group are injected with a harmless salt solution. During a 2-week test period, the psychologist records the amount of weight gained by each rat. The data are as follows:

HORMONE	CONTROL
$\bar{X} = 22$	$\bar{X} = 8$
$SS = 140$	$SS = 180$

Use the data to estimate how much extra weight gain the hormone produces. Make a point estimate and an interval estimate so that you are 80% confident that the true mean difference is in your interval.

13. A psychologist would like to know how much difference there is between the problem-solving ability of 8-year-old children versus 10-year-old children. A random sample of 10 children is selected from each age group. The children are given a problem-solving test, and the results are summarized as follows:

8-YEAR-OLDS	10-YEAR-OLDS
$n = 10$	$n = 10$
$\bar{X} = 36$	$\bar{X} = 43$
$SS = 110$	$SS = 250$

a. Use the sample data to make a point estimate of the mean difference between 8-year-olds' and 10-year-olds' problem-solving ability.
b. Make an interval estimate of the mean difference so that you are 90% confident that the real difference is in your interval.

14. A developmental psychologist would like to know how much difference there is in vocabulary development between 6-year-old boys versus 6-year-old girls. Random samples of $n = 5$ boys and $n = 10$ girls are obtained, and each child is given a standardized vocabulary test. The average score for the boys is $\bar{X} = 84$ with $SS = 120$ and the average score for the girls is $\bar{X} = 91$ with $SS = 270$.
a. Use the sample data to make a point estimate of the population mean difference.
b. Make an interval estimate of the mean difference so that you are 90% confident that the true mean difference is in your interval.

15. A researcher is investigating the effectiveness of a new sleeping pill. A random sample of twenty insomniacs is obtained. Half are given the new sleeping pill to try for one week and the other half are given a placebo (sugar pill). Each person is asked to record the amount of time needed to fall asleep each evening. the average time for the $n = 10$ subjects with the real medication is $\bar{X} = 18.7$ minutes with $SS = 160$ and the average time for the placebo group is $\bar{X} = 32.5$ minutes with $SS = 200$.
a. Use the sample data to make a point estimate of the population mean difference.
b. Make an interval estimate of the mean difference so that you are 80% confident that the true mean difference is in your interval.

16. The following data were obtained from an independent-measures experiment comparing two experimental treatments.

TREATMENT 1		TREATMENT 2	
12	18	21	14
16	19	19	23
11	13	24	18
12	15	20	22

a. Use the sample data to make a point estimate of the population mean difference between the two treatments.
b. Make an interval estimate of the population mean difference so that you are 80% confident that the real mean difference is in your interval.

17. For the following studies, state whether estimation or hypothesis testing is required. Also, is an independent- or a repeated-measures *t* statistic appropriate?

    a. An educator wants to determine how much mean difference can be expected for the population in SAT scores following an intensive review course. Two samples are selected. The first group takes the review course and the second receives no treatment. SAT scores are subsequently measured for both groups.

    b. A psychiatrist would lke to test the effectiveness of a new antipsychotic medication. A sample of patients is first assessed for the severity of psychotic symptoms. Then the patients are placed on drug therapy for 2 weeks. The severity of their symptoms is assessed again at the end of the treatment.

18. A researcher is investigating the relation between reaction time and room temperature. A sample of $n = 16$ subjects is obtained and each person's reaction time is measured in a 70° room and again in a room where the temperature is 95°. On average, this sample showed a reaction time that was 45 milliseconds faster in the 70° room with *SS* for the difference scores equal to 6000.

    a. Use the sample data to make a point estimate of the difference in reaction time produced by the change in temperature.

    b. Make an interval estimate of the population mean difference so that you are 95% confident that the real population mean difference is in your interval.

19. A researcher is testing the effectiveness of a blood-pressure medication. A sample of $n = 25$ subjects is obtained, and each person's blood pressure is measured before beginning the medication. After 3 weeks, each person's blood pressure is measured again and the researcher records the amount of change for each individual. For this sample, the average blood pressure decreased by 14.6 points with $SS = 2400$.

    a. Use the sample data to make a point estimate of the mean reduction in blood pressure for the general population.

    b. Make an interval estimate of the population mean change so that you are 80% confident that the true mean is located in your interval.

20. A researcher would like to determine how much reaction time is impaired after drinking only four ounces of alcohol. A random sample is obtained and each person's reaction time is measured before and after drinking the alcohol. The difference scores for this sample are as follows:

    24, 35, 28, 10, −1, 32, 18, 26, 34, 20, 41

    a. Use the sample data to make a point estimate of the change in reaction time for the general population.

    b. Make an interval estimate of the population mean difference so that you are 95% confident that the true mean is located in your interval.

21. A researcher would like to evaluate the improvement in reading speed that results from a 1-hour speed-reading course. A sample of $n = 30$ students is obtained and each person's reading speed is measured before and after the 1-hour course. For this sample, the average subject increased reading speed by 125 words per minute with $SS = 5800$. Make a point estimate and a 90% confidence interval estimate of the average improvement in reading speed for the general population.

CHAPTER 13

INTRODUCTION TO ANALYSIS OF VARIANCE

CONTENTS

PREVIEW

"But I read the chaper four times! How could I possibly have failed the exam!"

Most of you probably have had the experience of reading a textbook and suddenly realizing that you have no idea of what was said on the past few pages. Although you have been reading the words, your mind has wandered off, and the meaning of the words never reaches memory. In an influential paper on human memory, Craik and Lockhart (1972) proposed a *levels of processing* theory of memory that can account for this phenomenon. In general terms, this theory says that all perceptual and mental processing leaves behind a memory trace. However, the quality of the memory trace depends on the level or the depth of the processing. If you superficially skim the words in a book, your memory also will be superficial. On the other hand, when you think about the meaning of the words and try to understand what you are reading, the result will be a good, substantial memory that should serve you well on exams. In general, deeper processing results in better memory.

Rogers, Kuiper, and Kirker (1977) conducted an experiment demonstrating the effect of levels of processing. Subjects in this experiment were shown lists of words and asked to answer questions about each word. The questions were designed to require different levels of processing, from superficial to deep. In one experimental condition, subjects were simply asked to judge the physical characteristics of each printed word ("Is it printed in capital letters or small letters?") A second condition asked about the sound of each word ("Does it rhyme with 'boat'?"). In a third condition, subjects were required to process the meaning of each word ("Does it have the same meaning as 'attractive'?"). The final condition required subjects to understand each word and relate its meaning to themselves. ("Does this word describe you?"). After going through the complete list, all subjects were given a surprise memory test. As you can see in Figure 13.1, deeper processing resulted in better memory. Remember, none of these subjects was trying to memorize the words; they were simply reading through the list answering questions. However, the more they processed and understood the words, the better they recalled the words on the test.

In terms of human memory the Rogers et al. experiment is notable because it demonstrates the importance of "self" in memory. You are most likely to remember material that is directly related to you. In terms of statistics, however, this study is notable because it compares four different treatment conditions in a single experiment. Although it may seem like a small step to go from two treatments (as in the *t* tests in Chapters 10 and 11) to four treatments, there is a tremendous gain in experimental sophistication. Suppose, for example, that Rogers et al. had decided to examine only two levels of processing: one based on physical characteristics and one based on sound. In this simplified experiment, they would have made only *one* comparison: physical versus sound. In the real experiment, however, they used four conditions and were able to make *six* different comparisons:

Figure 13.1

Mean recall as a function of the level of processing. Rogers, T. B., Kuiper, N. A., & Kirker, W. S. (1977). Self-reference and the encoding of personal information. *Journal of Personality and Social Psychology, 35,* 677–688. Copyright (1977) by the American Psychological Association. Adapted by permission of the author.

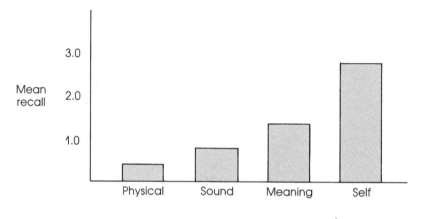

Physical versus sound

Physical versus meaning

Physical versus self

Sound versus meaning

Sound versus self

Meaning versus self

To gain this experimental sophistication, there is some cost. Specifically, you no longer can use the familiar *t* tests we encountered in Chapters 10 and 11. Instead, you now must learn a new statistical technique which is designed for experiments consisting of two or more sets of data. This new, general-purpose procedure is called analysis of variance.

13.1 OVERVIEW

Analysis of variance (ANOVA) is a hypothesis-testing procedure used to determine if mean differences exist for two or more treatments (or populations). As with all inferential procedures, ANOVA uses sample data as the basis for drawing conclusions about populations. A diagram of a situation where analysis of variance would be used is shown in Figure 13.2.

For an independent-measures experiment, a separate sample is taken for each of the treatment conditions. Because it is very unlikely that any two samples will be identical, even if they come from the same population, we have assumed that the samples in Figure 13.2 have different scores and different means. The purpose of ANOVA is to decide whether the differences between the samples are simply due to chance (sampling error) or whether there are systematic treatment effects that have caused the scores in one group to be different from the scores in another. More precisely, the alternatives can be stated as follows:

Remember, we would expect samples to differ because of sampling error (Chapter 7).

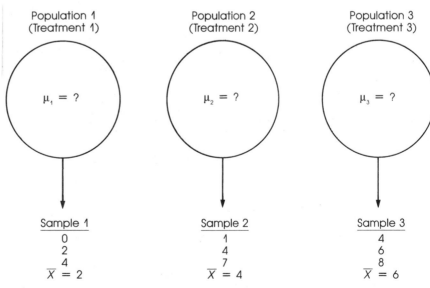

Figure 13.2

A typical situation where ANOVA would be used. Three separate samples are obtained to evaluate the mean differences among three populations (or treatments) with unknown means.

1. The populations for all treatments are really the same (μ's for each population are identical); the mean difference between the samples occurred due to chance; that is, sampling error.

2. The populations for the treatments are different (they have different μ's); the mean difference between the samples is due to the effect of the treatment.

The hypothesis test for ANOVA will attempt to differentiate between these two alternatives by computing a test statistic that is very similar to the t statistics used in the preceeding chapters. For the t statistic, we computed a value for t as follows:

$$t = \frac{\text{mean difference between samples}}{\text{difference expected from sampling error}}$$

$$= \frac{\text{mean difference between samples}}{\text{standard error}}$$

For ANOVA, the test statistic is called an F-ratio and has the following structure:

$$F = \frac{\text{variance (differences) between sample means}}{\text{variance (differences) expected from sampling error}}$$

Notice that the F-ratio is based on *variance* instead of sample mean difference. The reason for this change is that analysis of variance is used in situations where there are more than two sample means. With three sample means, for example, it would be impossible to compute a single value for the sample mean difference. However, by computing variance, you can determine whether the three sample means are clustered close together (small variance) or whether there are big differences among the sample means (large variance). For example, if the three sample means are $\overline{X} = 7$, $\overline{X} = 9$, and $\overline{X} = 10$, the differences between samples are relatively small, and the variance for these three numbers would be small. On the other hand, if the three sample means are $\overline{X} = 2$, $\overline{X} = 12$, and $\overline{X} = 23$, the differences among samples are relative large and the variance would be large.

With either the F-ratio or the t statistic, a large value indicates that the sample mean difference is more than chance. To determine whether the sample difference is *significantly* more than chance, we must compare the obtained test statistic with the criterion value that is established by the alpha level for the hypothesis test.

It may appear that analysis of variance and t tests are simply two different ways of doing exactly the same job: testing for mean differences. In some respects this is true—both tests use sample data to test hypotheses about population means. However, ANOVA has a tremendous advantage over t tests. Specifically, t tests are limited to situations where there are only two treatments to compare. The major advantage of ANOVA is that it can be used to compare two or more treatments.

In addition, ANOVA can be used with either an independent-measures or a repeated-measures experimental design, and ANOVA can be used to evaluate the results of research studies that involve more than one independent variable. In this chapter we focus our attention on research situations that use an independent-measures design (a separate sample for each treatment condition) and have only one independent variable. The next two chapters explore the flexibility of ANOVA by considering repeated-measures experiments (Chapter 14) and experiments with two independent variables (Chapter 15).

STATISTICAL HYPOTHESES FOR ANOVA

The following example will be used to introduce the statistical hypotheses for ANOVA. Suppose a psychologist examined learning performance under three temperature conditions: 50°, 70°, and 90°. Three samples of subjects are selected, one sample for each treatment condition. The purpose of the study is to determine whether room temperature affects learning performance. In statistical terms, we want to decide between two hypotheses: the null hypothesis (H_0), which says temperature has no effect, and the alternative hypothesis (H_1), which states that temperature does affect learning. In symbols, the null hypothesis states

$$H_0: \quad \mu_1 = \mu_2 = \mu_3$$

That is, there are no differences among the means of the populations that receive the three treatments. The population means are all the same. Once again, notice that hypotheses are always stated in terms of population parameters, even though we use sample data to test them.

For the alternative hypothesis we may state that

$$H_1: \quad \text{At least one population mean is different from the others}$$

Notice that we have not given any specific alternative hypothesis. This is because there are many different alternatives possible, and it would be tedious to list them all. One alternative, for example, would be that the first two populations are identical but that the third is different. Another alternative states that the last two means are the same but that the first is different. Other alternatives might be

$$H_1: \quad \mu_1 \neq \mu_2 \neq \mu_3 \qquad \text{all three means are different}$$
$$H_1: \quad \mu_1 = \mu_3 \qquad \qquad \mu_2 \text{ is different}$$

It should be pointed out that a researcher typically entertains only one (or at most a few) of these alternative hypotheses. Usually a theory or the outcomes of previous studies will dictate a specific prediction concerning the treatment effect. For the sake of simplicity, we will state a general alternative hypothesis rather than try to list all the possible specific alternatives.

13.2 THE LOGIC OF ANALYSIS OF VARIANCE

The formulas and calculations required in ANOVA are somewhat complicated, but the logic that underlies the whole procedure is fairly straightforward. Therefore, this section will give a general picture of analysis of variance before we start looking at the details. We will introduce the logic of ANOVA

Table 13.1

Hypothetical data from an experiment examining learning performance under three temperature conditions*

TREATMENT 1 50° (SAMPLE 1)	TREATMENT 2 70° (SAMPLE 2)	TREATMENT 3 90° (SAMPLE 3)
0	4	1
1	3	2
3	6	2
1	3	0
0	4	0
$\overline{X} = 1$	$\overline{X} = 4$	$\overline{X} = 1$

*Note that there are three separate samples, with $n = 5$ in each sample. The dependent variable is the number of problems solved correctly.

with the help of the hypothetical data in Table 13.1. These data represent the results of an independent-measures experiment comparing learning performance under three temperature conditions.

One obvious characteristic of the data in Table 13.1 is that the scores are not all the same. In everyday language, the scores are different: in statistical terms, the scores are variable. Our goal is to measure the amount of variability (the size of the differences) and to explain where it comes from.

The first step is to determine the total variability for the entire set of data. To compute the total variability, we will combine all the scores from all the separate samples to obtain one general measure of variability for the complete experiment. Once we have measured the total variability, we can begin to break it apart into separate components. The word *analysis* means dividing into smaller parts. Because we are going to analyze variability, the process is called *analysis of variance*. This analysis process divides the total variability into two basic components:

1. Between-Treatments Variability. Looking at the data in Table 13.1, we clearly see that much of the variability in the scores is due to general differences between treatment conditions. For example, the scores in the 70° condition tend to be much higher ($\overline{X} = 4$) than the scores in the 50° condition ($\overline{X} = 1$). We will calculate the variability between treatments to provide a measure of the overall differences between treatment conditions— that is, the differences among sample means.

2. Within-Treatments Variability. In addition to the general differences between treatment conditions, there is variability within each sample. Looking again at Table 13.1, the scores in the 70° condition are not all the same; they are variable. The within-treatments variability will provide a measure of the variability inside each treatment condition.

Analyzing the total variability into these two components is the heart of analysis of variance. We will now examine each of the components in more detail.

BETWEEN-TREATMENTS VARIABILITY

Whenever you compare two samples representing two treatment conditions, there are three possible explanations for the differences (variability) between sample means:

1. Treatment Effect. It is possible that the different treatments have caused the samples to be different. In Table 13.1, the scores in sample 1 were obtained in a 50° room, and the scores in sample 2 were obtained in a 70° room. It is possible that the difference between these two samples is due in part to the different temperatures.

2. Individual Differences. Subjects enter an experiment with different backgrounds, abilities, and attitudes; that is, they are unique individuals. Whenever you compare separate samples (different groups of individuals), it is possible that the differences between samples are simply the result of individual differences.

3. Experimental Error. Whenever you make a measurement, there is a chance of error. The error could be caused by poor equipment, lack of attention, or unpredictable changes in the event you are measuring. This kind of uncontrolled and unexplained difference is called *experimental error,* and it can cause two samples to be different.

Thus, when we compute the variability between treatments, we are measuring differences that could be due to any of these three factors or any combination of the three.

WITHIN-TREATMENTS VARIABILITY

There are only two possible explanations for variability within a treatment condition:

1. Individual Differences. The scores are obtained from different individuals, which could explain why the scores are variable.

2. Experimental Error. There always is a chance that the differences are caused by experimental error.

Notice that the variability inside a treatment condition cannot be attributed to any treatment effect because all subjects within a treatment condition are treated exactly the same. Thus, the differences within a treatment are not systematic or predictable but rather are due to chance. The analysis, or partitioning, of variability is diagrammed in Figure 13.3.

Figure 13.3

The independent-measures analysis of variance partitions, or analyzes, the total variability into two components: variability between treatments and variability within treatments.

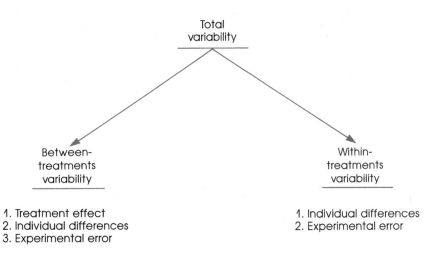

THE F-RATIO: THE TEST STATISTIC FOR ANOVA

Once we have analyzed the total variability into two basic components (between treatments and within treatments), we simply compare them. The comparison is made by computing a statistic called an *F-ratio*. For the independent-measures ANOVA, the *F*-ratio has the following structure:

$$F = \frac{\text{variance between treatments}}{\text{variance within treatments}} \tag{13.1}$$

When we express each component of variability in terms of its sources (see Figure 13.3), the structure of the *F*-ratio is

$$F = \frac{\text{treatment effect} + \text{individual differences} + \text{experimental error}}{\text{individual differences} + \text{experimental error}} \tag{13.2}$$

You should note that the between-treatments variability and the within-treatments variability differ in only one respect: the variability (mean differences) caused by the treatment effect. This single difference between the numerator and denominator of the *F*-ratio is crucial in determining if a treatment effect has occurred. Remember, the whole purpose for doing the experiment and the analysis is to find out whether or not the treatment has any effect. Let's consider the two possibilities:

1. H_0 is true, and there is no treatment effect. In this case, the numerator and denominator of the *F*-ratio are measuring the same variance:

$$F = \frac{0 + \text{individual differences} + \text{experimental error}}{\text{individual differences} + \text{experimental error}}$$

When H_0 is true and the treatment effect is zero, the *F*-ratio is expected to equal 1.

2. If H_0 is false, then a treatment effect does exist, and the *F*-ratio becomes

$$F = \frac{\text{treatment effect} + \text{individual differences} + \text{experimental error}}{\text{individual differences} + \text{experimental error}}$$

The numerator of the ratio should be larger than the denominator, and the *F*-ratio is expected to be larger than 1.00. Ordinarily, the presence of a large treatment effect is reflected in a large value for the *F*-ratio.

In more general terms, the denominator of the *F*-ratio measures only uncontrolled and unexplained (often called *unsystematic*) variability. For this reason, the denominator of the *F*-ratio is called the *error term*. The numerator of the *F*-ratio always includes the same unsystematic variability as in the error term, but it also includes any systematic differences caused by the treatment effect. The goal of ANOVA is to find out whether or not a treatment effect exists.

DEFINITION

For ANOVA, the denominator of the *F*-ratio is called the *error term*. The error term provides a measure of the variance due to chance. When the treatment effect is zero (H_0 is true), the error term measures the same sources of variance as the numerator of the *F*-ratio, so the value of the F-ratio is expected to be nearly equal to 1.00. (Technically, the average value for F-ratios is slightly larger than 1.00 when H_0 is true.)

LEARNING CHECK

1. ANOVA is a statistical procedure that compares two or more treatment conditions for differences in variance. (True or false?)

2. In ANOVA what value is expected on the average for the F-ratio when the null hypothesis is true?

3. What happens to the value of the F-ratio if differences between treatments are increased? What happens to the F-ratio if variability inside the treatments is increased?

4. In ANOVA, the total variability is partitioned into two parts. What are these two variability components called, and how are they used in the F-ratio?

ANSWERS

1. False. Although ANOVA uses variability in the computations, the purpose of the test is to evaluate differences in *means* between treatments.

2. When H_0 is true, the expected value for the F-ratio is 1.00 because the top and bottom of the ratio are both measuring the same variance.

3. As differences between treatments increase, the F-ratio will increase. As variability within treatments increases, the F-ratio will decrease.

4. The two components are between-treatments variability and within-treatments variability. Between treatments is the numerator of the F-ratio and within treatments is the denominator.

13.3 ANOVA VOCABULARY, NOTATION, AND FORMULAS

Before we introduce the notation, let's look at some special terminology that is used for ANOVA. The first term we will need from the ANOVA vocabulary is the word *factor*. This term is used in place of the words *independent variable*. Therefore, for the experiment shown in Table 13.1, the factor is temperature.

DEFINITION

In analysis of variance, a *factor* is an independent variable.

Because this experiment has only one independent variable, it is called a *single-factor experiment*. There are more complex experiments that use more than one factor. For example, in Chapter 15 we examine two-factor experiments—that is, experiments with two independent variables.

The second term you need to know is *levels*. The levels in an experiment consist of the different values used in the factor. For example, in the learning experiment (Table 13.1) we are using three values of temperature. Therefore, the temperature factor has three levels.

DEFINITION   The individual treatment conditions that make up a factor are called *levels* of the factor.

Because ANOVA most often is used to examine data from more than two treatment conditions (and more than two samples), we will need a notation system to help keep track of all the individual scores and totals. To help introduce this notational system, we will use the hypothetical data from Table 13.1 again. The data are reproduced in Table 13.2 along with some of the notation and statistics that will be described.

1. The letter k is used to identify the number of treatment conditions, that is, the number of levels of the factor. For an independent-measures experiment, k also specifies the number of separate samples. For the data in Table 13.2, there are three treatments, so $k = 3$.

2. The number of scores in each treatment is identified by a lowercase letter n. For the example in Table 13.2, $n = 5$ for all the treatments. If the samples are of different sizes, you can identify a specific sample by using a subscript. For example, n_2 is the number of scores in treatment 2.

3. The total number of scores in the entire experiment is specified by a capital letter N. When all the samples are the same size (n is constant), $N = kn$. For the data in Table 13.2, there are $n = 5$ scores in each of the $k = 3$ treatments, so $N = 3(5) = 15$.

4. The total (ΣX) for each treatment condition is identified by the capital letter T. The total for a specific treatment can be identified by adding a numerical subscript to the T. For example, the total for the second treatment in Table 13.2 is $T_2 = 20$.

5. The sum of all the scores in the experiment (the grand total) is identified by G. You can compute G by adding up all N scores or by adding up the treatment totals: $G = \Sigma T$.

6. Although there is no new notation involved, we also have computed SS and $\overline{X}$ for each sample, and we have calculated ΣX^2 for the entire

Because ANOVA formulas require ΣX for each treatment and ΣX for the entire set of scores, we have introduced new notation (T and G) to help identify which ΣX is being used. Remember, T stands for *treatment total* and G stands for *grand total*.

Table 13.2

Hypothetical data from an experiment examining learning performance under three temperature conditions*

	TEMPERATURE CONDITIONS		
1 50°	2 70°	3 90°	
0	4	1	$\Sigma X^2 = 106$
1	3	2	$G = 30$
3	6	2	$N = 15$
1	3	0	$k = 3$
0	4	0	
$T_1 = 5$	$T_2 = 20$	$T_3 = 5$	
$SS_1 = 6$	$SS_2 = 6$	$SS_3 = 4$	
$n_1 = 5$	$n_2 = 5$	$n_3 = 5$	
$\overline{X}_1 = 1$	$\overline{X}_2 = 4$	$\overline{X}_3 = 1$	

*Summary values and notation for an analysis of variance are also presented.

set of $N = 15$ scores in the experiment. These values are given in Table 13.2 and will be important in the formulas and calculations for ANOVA.

ANOVA FORMULAS

Because analysis of variance requires extensive calculations and many formulas, one common problem for students is simply keeping track of the different formulas and numbers. Therefore, we will examine the general structure of the procedure and look at the organization of the calculations before we introduce the individual formulas.

1. The final calculation for ANOVA is the F-ratio, which is composed of two variances:

$$F = \frac{\text{variance between treatments}}{\text{variance within treatments}}$$

2. You should recall that variance for sample data has been defined as

$$\text{sample variance} = s^2 = \frac{SS}{df}$$

Therefore, we will need to compute an SS and a df for the variance between treatments (numerator of F), and we will need another SS and df for the variance within treatments (denominator of F). To obtain these SS and df values, we must go through two separate analyses: First compute SS for the total experiment and analyze it into two components (between and within). Then, compute df for the total experiment and analyze it into two components (between and within).

Thus, the entire process of analysis of variance will require nine calculations: Three values for SS, three values for df, two variances (between and within), and a final F-ratio. However, these nine calculations are all logically related and are all directed toward finding the final F-ratio. Figure 13.4 shows the logical structure of ANOVA calculations.

Figure 13.4

The structure of ANOVA calculations.

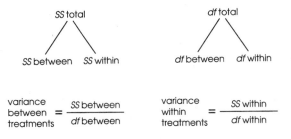

ANALYSIS OF SUM OF SQUARES (SS)

The ANOVA requires that we first compute a total variability and then partition this value into two components: between treatments and within treatments. This analysis is outlined in Figure 13.5. We will examine each of the three components separately.

1. Total Sum of Squares, SS_{total}. As the name implies, SS_{total} is simply the sum of squares for the entire set of N scores. We calculate this value by using the computational formula for SS:

$$SS = \Sigma X^2 - \frac{(\Sigma X)^2}{N}$$

To make this formula consistent with the ANOVA notation, we substitute the letter G in place of ΣX and obtain

$$SS_{total} = \Sigma X^2 - \frac{G^2}{N} \tag{13.3}$$

Applying this formula to the set of data in Table 13.2, we obtain

$$SS_{total} = 106 - \frac{30^2}{15}$$
$$= 106 - 60$$
$$= 46$$

2. Within-Treatments Sum of Squares, SS_{within}. Now we are looking at the variability inside each of the treatment conditions. We already have computed the SS within each of the three treatment conditions (Table 13.2): $SS_1 = 6$, $SS_2 = 6$, and $SS_3 = 4$. To find the overall within-treatment sum of squares, we simply add these values together:

$$SS_{within} = \Sigma SS_{\text{inside each treatment}} \tag{13.4}$$

For the data in Table 13.2, this formula gives

Figure 13.5

Partitioning the sum of squares *(SS)* for the independent-measures analysis of variance.

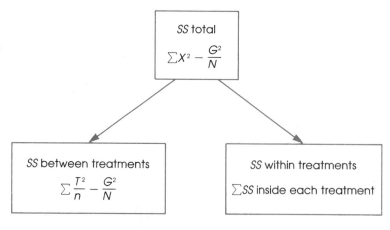

ALTERNATIVE FORMULA FOR SS_{within}

YOU SHOULD know that there is an alternative formula for finding SS_{within}. This formula is developed briefly in the following three steps:

1. First, recall that the two SS components add up to the total SS:

$$SS_{within} + SS_{between} = SS_{total}$$

2. By simple algebra we obtain the relation

$$SS_{within} = SS_{total} - SS_{between}$$

3. Finally, substituting the equations for SS_{total} and $SS_{between}$, we obtain

$$SS_{within} = \Sigma X^2 - \frac{G^2}{N} - \left(\Sigma \frac{T^2}{n} - \frac{G^2}{N} \right)$$

$$= \Sigma X^2 - \frac{G^2}{N} - \Sigma \frac{T^2}{n} + \frac{G^2}{N}$$

$$= \Sigma X^2 - \Sigma \frac{T^2}{n}$$

This alternative formula for SS_{within} can help simplify the calculations for ANOVA. To find all three SS values, you must compute only three numbers: ΣX^2, $\Sigma T^2/n$, and G^2/N. These three values are sufficient to satisfy the three SS formulas.

$$SS_{within} = 6 + 6 + 4$$
$$= 16$$

Box 13.1 provides an alternative formula for SS_{within}.

3. Between-Treatments Sum of Squares, $SS_{between}$. Before we introduce the equation for $SS_{between}$, consider what we have found so far. The total variability for the data in Table 13.2 is $SS_{total} = 46$. We intend to partition this total into two parts (see Figure 13.5). One part, SS_{within}, has been found to be equal to 16. This means that $SS_{between}$ must be equal to 30 in order for the two parts (16 and 30) to add up to the total (46). The equation for the between treatments sum of squares should produce a value of $SS_{between} = 30$. You should recall that the variability between treatments is measuring the differences between treatment means. Conceptually, the most direct way of measuring the amount of variability among the treatment means is to compute the sum of squares for the set of means. To do this, we begin by computing the overall mean for the entire set of N scores in the experiment. This overall mean will be identified by the symbol $\overline{G}$, indicating the grand mean. For the data in Table 13.2, the grand total is $G = 30$ for a set of $N = 15$ scores, so the grand mean is $\overline{X} = {}^{30}\!/_{15} = 2$. Next, we measure the extent to which each individual sample mean deviates from the grand mean:

$$\text{deviation} = (\overline{X} - \overline{G})$$

Then we square these deviations and sum the results to obtain the sum of squared deviations (SS) for the set of sample means

$$SS_{means} = \Sigma(\overline{X} - \overline{G})^2$$

Because each individual treatment mean represents a sample of n scores, each of the squared deviations is multiplied by n to obtain a complete measure of the between-treatments sum of squares:

$$SS_{between} = \Sigma n(\overline{X} - \overline{G})^2 \qquad (13.5)$$

Applying this formula to the data in Table 13.2, we obtain

$$SS_{between} = 5(1 - 2)^2 + 5(4 - 2)^2 + 5(1 - 2)^2$$
$$= 5 + 20 + 5$$
$$= 30$$

Notice that the result $SS_{between} = 30$, is exactly what we predicted. The two parts from the analysis (between and within) add up to the total:

$$SS_{total} = SS_{within} = SS_{between}$$
$$46 = 16 + 30$$

Although formula 13.5 is conceptually the most direct way of computing the amount of variability among the treatment means, this formula can be awkward to use, especially when the means are not whole numbers. For this reason, we generally will use an algebraically equivalent formula that uses the treatment totals (T values) instead of the means:

$$SS_{between} = \Sigma \frac{T^2}{n} - \frac{G^2}{N} \qquad (13.6)$$

Using this new formula with the data in Table 13.2, we obtain

$$SS_{between} = \frac{5^2}{5} + \frac{20^2}{5} + \frac{5^2}{5} - \frac{30^2}{15}$$
$$= 5 + 80 + 5 - 60$$
$$= 90 - 60$$
$$= 30$$

At this point of the analysis, the work may be checked to see if total SS equals between-treatments SS plus within-treatments SS.

Notice that this result is identical to the value we obtained using formula 13.5.

The formula for each SS and the relationships among these three values are shown in Figure 13.5.

THE ANALYSIS OF DEGREES OF FREEDOM (df)

The analysis of degrees of freedom (df) follows the same pattern as the analysis of SS. First, we will find df for the total set of N scores, and then we will partition this value into two components: degrees of freedom between treatments and degrees of freedom within treatments. In computing degrees of freedom, there are two important considerations to keep in mind:

1. Each df value is associated with a specific SS value.

2. Normally, the value of df is obtained by counting the number of items that were used to calculate SS and then subtracting 1. For example, if you compute SS for a set of n scores, then $df = n - 1$.

With this in mind, we will examine the degrees of freedom for each part of the analysis:

1. Total Degrees of Freedom, df_{total}. To find the df associated with SS_{total}, you must first recall that this SS value measures variability for the entire set of N scores. Therefore, the df value will be

$$df_{\text{total}} = N - 1 \tag{13.7}$$

For the data in Table 13.2, the total number of scores is $N = 15$, so the total degrees of freedom would be

$$df_{\text{total}} = 15 - 1$$
$$= 14$$

2. Within-Treatments Degrees of Freedom, df_{within}. To find the df associated with SS_{within}, we must look at how this SS value is computed. Remember, we first find SS inside each of the treatments and then add these values together. Each of the treatment SS values measures variability for the n scores in the treatment, so each SS will have $df = n - 1$. When all these individual treatment values are added together, we obtain

$$df_{\text{within}} = \Sigma(n - 1) \tag{13.8}$$

For the experiment we have been considering, each treatment has $n = 5$ scores. This means there are $n - 1 = 4$ degrees of freedom inside each treatment. Because there are three different treatment conditions, this gives a total of 12 for the within-treatments degrees of freedom. Notice that this formula for df simply adds up the number of scores in each treatment (the n values) and subtracts 1 for each treatment. If these two stages are done separately, you obtain

$$df_{\text{within}} = N - k \tag{13.9}$$

(Adding up all the n values gives N. If you subtract 1 for each treatment, then altogether you have subtracted k because there are k treatments.) For the data in Table 13.2, $N = 15$ and $k = 3$, so

$$df_{\text{within}} = 15 - 3$$
$$= 12$$

3. Between-Treatments Degrees of Freedom, df_{between}. The df associated with SS_{between} can be found by considering the SS formula. This SS formula measures the variability among the treatment means or totals. To find df_{between}, simply count the number of T values (or means) and subtract 1. Because the number of treatments is specified by the letter k, the formula for df is

$$df_{\text{between}} = k - 1 \tag{13.10}$$

For the data in Table 13.2, there are three different treatment conditions (three T values), so the between-treatments degrees of freedom is

Figure 13.6

Partitioning degrees of freedom *(df)* for the independent-measures analysis of variance.

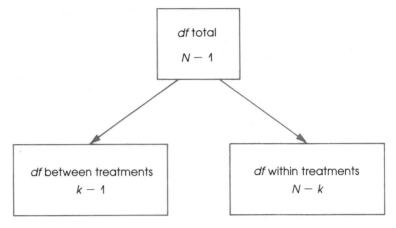

$$df_{\text{between}} = 3 - 1$$
$$= 2$$

Notice that the two parts we obtained from this analysis of degrees of freedom add up to equal the total degrees of freedom:

$$df_{\text{total}} = df_{\text{within}} + df_{\text{between}}$$
$$14 = 12 + 2$$

The complete analysis of degrees of freedom is shown in Figure 13.6.

CALCULATION OF VARIANCES (MS) AND THE F-RATIO

The final step in the analysis of variance procedure is to compute the variance between treatments and the variance within treatments in order to calculate the *F*-ratio (see Figure 13.4). You should recall (from Chapter 4) that variance is defined as the average squared deviation. For a sample, you compute this average by the following formula:

$$\text{variance} = \frac{SS}{n - 1} = \frac{SS}{df}$$

In ANOVA it is customary to use the term *mean square, or simply MS,* in place of the term *variance.* Note that variance is the *mean squared* deviation, so this terminology is quite sensible. For the final *F*-ratio you will need an *MS* between treatments and an *MS* within treatments. In each case,

$$MS = \frac{SS}{df} \tag{13.11}$$

For the data we have been considering,

$$MS_{\text{between}} = \frac{SS_{\text{between}}}{df_{\text{between}}} = \frac{30}{2} = 15$$

and

$$MS_{\text{within}} = \frac{SS_{\text{within}}}{df_{\text{within}}} = \frac{16}{12} = 1.33$$

We now have a measure of the variance (or differences) between the treatments and a measure of the variance within the treatments. The F-ratio simply compares these two variances:

$$F = \frac{MS_{\text{between}}}{MS_{\text{within}}}$$

(13.12)

For the experiment we have been examining, the data give an F-ratio of

$$F = \frac{15}{1.33} = 11.28$$

It is useful to organize the results of the analysis in one table called an *ANOVA summary table*. The table shows the source of variability (between-treatments, within-treatments, and total variability), *SS, df, MS,* and *F.* For the previous computations, the ANOVA summary table is constructed as follows:

SOURCE	SS	df	MS	
Between treatments	30	2	15	$F = 11.28$
Within treatments	16	12	1.33	
Total	46	14		

Although these tables are no longer commonly used in published reports, they do provide a concise method for presenting the results of an analysis. (Note that you can conveniently check your work: Adding the first two entries in the *SS* column (30 + 16) yields the total *SS.* The same applies to the *df* column.) When using analysis of variance, you might start with a blank ANOVA summary table and then fill in the values as they are calculated. With this method you will be less likely to "get lost" in the analysis, wondering what to do next.

For this example, the obtained value of $F = 11.28$ indicates that the numerator of the F-ratio is substantially bigger than the denominator. If you recall the conceptual structure of the F-ratio as presented in formulas 13.1 and 13.2, the F value we obtained indicates that the differences between treatments are substantially greater than would be expected by chance, providing evidence that a treatment effect really exists. Stated in terms of the experimental variables, it appears that temperature does have an effect on learning performance. However, to properly evaluate the F-ratio, we must examine the F distribution.

13.4 THE DISTRIBUTION OF F-RATIOS

In analysis of variance, the F-ratio is constructed so that the numerator and denominator of the ratio are measuring exactly the same variance when the null hypothesis is true (see formula 13.2). In this situation we expect the value of F to be around 1.00. The problem now is to define precisely what we mean by "around 1.00." What values are considered to be close to 1.00, and what values are far away? To answer this question, we need to look at all the possible F values, that is, the *distribution of F-ratios*.

Before we examine this distribution in detail, you should note two obvious characteristics:

1. Because F-ratios are computed from two variances (the numerator and denominator of the ratio), F values always will be positive numbers. Remember, variance is always positive.

2. When H_0 is true, the numerator and denominator of the F-ratio are measuring the same variance. In this case, the two sample variances should be about the same size, so the ratio should be near 1. In other words, the distribution of F-ratios should pile up around 1.00.

With these two factors in mind we can sketch the distribution of F-ratios. The distribution is cut off at zero (all positive values), piles up around 1.00, and then tapers off to the right (see Figure 13.7). The exact shape of the F distribution depends on the degrees of freedom for the two variances in the F-ratio. You should recall that the precision of a sample variance depends on the number of scores or the degrees of freedom. In general, the variance for a large sample (large *df*) provides a more accurate estimate of the population variance. Because the precision of the *MS* values depends on *df*, the shape of

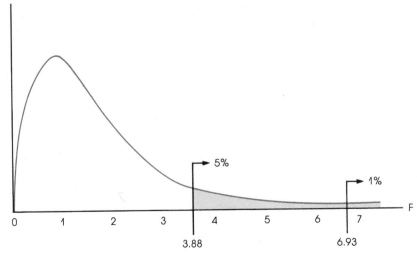

Figure 13.7

The distribution of F-ratios with *df* = 2, 12. Of all the values in the distribution, only 5% are larger than F = 3.88, and only 1% are larger than F = 6.93.

the F distribution also will depend on the df values for the numerator and denominator of the F-ratio. With very large df values, nearly all the F-ratios will be clustered very near to 1.00. With smaller df values, the F distribution is more spread out.

For analysis of variance we expect F near 1.00 if H_0 is true, and we expect a large value for F if H_0 is not true. In the F distribution, we need to separate those values that are reasonably near 1.00 from the values that are significantly greater than 1.00. These critical values are presented in an F distribution table in Appendix B, page A-26. To use the table, you must know the df values for the F-ratio (numerator and denominator), and you must know the alpha level for the hypothesis test. It is customary for an F table to have the df values for the numerator of the F-ratio printed across the top of the table. The df values for the denominator of F are printed in a column on the left-hand side. A portion of the F distribution table is shown in Table 13.3. For the temperature experiment we have been considering, the numerator of the F-ratio (between treatments) has $df = 2$ and the denominator of the F-ratio (within treatments) has $df = 12$. This F-ratio is said to have "degrees of freedom equal to 2 and 12." The degrees of freedom would be written as $df = 2, 12$. To use the table, you would first find $df = 2$ across the top of the table and $df = 12$ in the first column. When you line up these two values, they point to a pair of numbers in the middle of the table. These numbers give the critical cutoffs for $\alpha = .05$ and $\alpha = .01$. With $df = 2, 12$, for example, the numbers in the table are 3.88 and 6.93. These values indicate that the most unlikely 5% of the distribution ($\alpha = .05$) begins at a value of 3.88. The most extreme 1% of the distribution begins at a value of 6.93 (see Figure 13.7).

In the temperature experiment we obtained an F-ratio of 11.28. According to the critical cutoffs in Figure 13.7, this value is extremely unlikely (it is in the most extreme 1%). Therefore, we would reject H_0 with α set at either .05 or .01 and conclude that temperature does have a significant effect on learning performance.

Table 13.3

A portion of the F distribution table. Entries in roman type are critical values for the .05 level of significance and bold type values are for the .01 level of significance.

DEGREES OF FREEDOM DENOMINATOR	DEGREES OF FREEDOM: NUMERATOR					
	1	2	3	4	5	6
10	4.96	4.10	3.71	3.48	3.33	3.22
	10.04	**7.56**	**6.55**	**5.99**	**5.64**	**5.39**
11	4.84	3.98	3.59	3.36	3.20	3.09
	9.65	**7.20**	**6.22**	**5.67**	**5.32**	**5.07**
12	4.75	3.88	3.49	3.26	3.11	3.00
	9.33	**6.93**	**5.95**	**5.41**	**5.06**	**4.82**
13	4.67	3.80	3.41	3.18	3.02	2.92
	9.07	**6.70**	**5.74**	**5.20**	**4.86**	**4.62**
14	4.60	3.74	3.34	3.11	2.96	2.85
	8.86	**6.51**	**5.56**	**5.03**	**4.69**	**4.46**

1. Calculate SS_{total}, $SS_{between}$, and SS_{within} for the following set of data:

TREATMENT 1	TREATMENT 2	TREATMENT 3	
$n = 10$	$n = 10$	$n = 10$	$N = 30$
$T = 10$	$T = 20$	$T = 30$	$G = 60$
$SS = 27$	$SS = 16$	$SS = 23$	$\Sigma X^2 = 206$

2. A researcher uses an ANOVA to compare three treatment conditions with a sample of $n = 8$ in each treatment. For this analysis, find df_{total}, $df_{between}$, and df_{within}.

3. With $\alpha = .05$, what value forms the boundary for the critical region in the distribution of F-ratios with $df = 2, 24$?

ANSWERS   1. $SS_{total} = 86$; $SS_{between} = 20$; $SS_{within} = 66$

2. $df_{total} = 23$, $df_{between} = 2$, and $df_{within} = 21$

3. The critical value is 3.40.

13.5 EXAMPLES OF HYPOTHESIS TESTING WITH ANOVA

Although we have seen all the individual components of ANOVA, the following example demonstrates the complete ANOVA process using the standard four-step procedure for hypothesis testing.

EXAMPLE 13.1   The data depicted in Table 13.4 were obtained from an independent-measures experiment designed to measure the effectiveness of three pain relievers (A, B, and C). A fourth group that received a placebo (sugar pill) also was tested.

Example 13.1 is analyzed with the Minitab commands ONEWAY and AOVONEWAY (see Section 20.7).

The purpose of the analysis is to determine whether these sample data provide evidence of any significant differences among the four drugs. The dependent variable is the amount of time (in seconds) that subjects can withstand a painfully hot stimulus.

Table 13.4

The effect of drug treatment on the amount of time (in seconds) a stimulus is endured

PLACEBO	DRUG A	DRUG B	DRUG C	
0	0	3	8	$N = 12$
0	1	4	5	$G = 36$
3	2	5	5	$\Sigma X^2 = 178$
$T = 3$	$T = 3$	$T = 12$	$T = 18$	
$SS = 6$	$SS = 2$	$SS = 2$	$SS = 6$	

STEP 1 The first step is to state the hypotheses and select an alpha level:

$$H_0: \quad \mu_1 = \mu_2 = \mu_3 = \mu_4 \quad \text{(no treatment effect)}$$

$$H_1: \quad \text{At least one of the treatment means is different}$$

We will use $\alpha = .05$.

STEP 2 To locate the critical region for the F-ratio, we first must determine degrees of freedom for MS_{between} and MS_{within} (the numerator and denominator of F). For these data, the total degrees of freedom would be

$$df_{\text{total}} = N - 1$$
$$= 12 - 1$$
$$= 11$$

Analyzing this total into two components, we obtain

$$df_{\text{between}} = k - 1$$
$$= 4 - 1$$
$$= 3$$
$$df_{\text{within}} = N - k$$
$$= 12 - 4$$
$$= 8$$

The F-ratio for these data will have $df = 3, 8$. The distribution of all the possible F-ratios with $df = 3, 8$ is presented in Figure 13.8. Almost always (95% of the time) we should obtain an F-ratio less than 4.07 if H_0 is true.

STEP 3 To compute the F-ratio for these data, you must go through the series of calculations outlined in Figure 13.4. The calculations can be summarized as follows:

a. Analyze the SS to obtain SS_{between} and SS_{within}.

Figure 13.8

The distribution of F-ratios with $df = 3, 8$. The critical value for $\alpha = .05$ is $F = 4.07$.

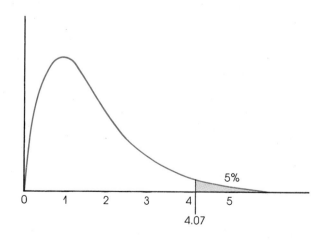

b. Use the *SS* values and the *df* values (from Step 2) to calculate $MS_{between}$ and MS_{within}.

c. Finally, use the two *MS* values (variances) to compute the *F*-ratio.

Analysis of SS. First we will compute the total *SS* and then the two components as indicated in Figure 13.4:

$$SS_{total} = \Sigma X^2 - \frac{G^2}{N}$$

$$= 178 - \frac{36^2}{12}$$

$$= 178 - 108$$

$$= 70$$

$$SS_{within} = \Sigma SS_{inside\ each\ treatment}$$

$$= 6 + 2 + 2 + 6$$

$$= 16$$

$$SS_{between} = \Sigma \frac{T^2}{n} - \frac{G^2}{N}$$

$$= \frac{3^2}{3} + \frac{3^2}{3} + \frac{12^2}{3} + \frac{18^2}{3} - \frac{36^2}{12}$$

$$= 3 + 3 + 48 + 108 - 108$$

$$= 54$$

Calculation of mean squares. Now we must compute the variance or *MS* for each of the two components:

$$MS_{between} = \frac{SS_{between}}{df_{between}} = \frac{54}{3} = 18$$

$$MS_{within} = \frac{SS_{within}}{df_{within}} = \frac{16}{8} = 2$$

Calculation of F. Finally, we compute the *F*-ratio:

$$F = \frac{MS_{between}}{MS_{within}} = \frac{18}{2} = 9.00$$

STEP 4 *Statistical decision.* The *F* value we obtained, $F = 9.00$, is in the critical region (see Figure 13.8). It is very unlikely ($p < .05$) that we will obtain a value this large if H_0 is true. Therefore, we reject H_0 and conclude that there is a significant treatment effect.

 SPSS^x A-80

Example 13.1 demonstrated the complete, step-by-step application of the ANOVA procedure. There are three additional points that can be made using this example.

First, you should look carefully at the statistical decision. We have rejected H_0 and concluded that not all the treatments are the same. But we have not determined which ones are different. Is drug A different from the placebo? Is drug A different from drug B? Unfortunately, these questions remain unanswered. We do know that at least one difference exists (we rejected H_0), but additional analysis is necessary to find out exactly where this difference is. This problem is addressed in Section 13.6.

Second, it is common in experimental reports to present the obtained F-ratio, the degrees of freedom, and the alpha level in one concise phrase. For the data in Example 13.1, this phrase would be

$$F(3, 8) = 9.00, p < .05$$

This phrase indicates that our F-ratio has $df = 3, 8$, we obtained a value of $F = 9.00$ from the data, and the F value was in the critical region with alpha equal to .05.

Third, the results can be presented in an analysis of variance summary table. The summary table for the analysis in Example 13.1 is as follows:

SOURCE	SS	df	MS	
Between treatments	54	3	18	$F = 9.00$
Within treatments	16	8	2	
Total	70	11		

AN ALTERNATIVE VIEW OF THE ANOVA ANALYSIS

The next example is intended to give you a better understanding of exactly what is measured by the between-treatments and the within-treatments variances. By modifying the original set of data, we will create two extreme data sets that will demonstrate how the between-treatments variability and the within-treatments variability are related to the actual scores from an experiment.

EXAMPLE 13.2

We begin with the same set of scores used in Example 13.1. However, for purposes of demonstration, we will adjust the original data to create two new sets of scores so that

1. One set contains *only* variability between treatments.
2. One set contains *only* variability within treatments.

The original data and the two modified sets are shown in Table 13.5.

Between-treatments data. First, consider the data set in the lower left-hand side of Table 13.5. For these data, the *only* variability is *between treatments*. To create these data, we have changed each individual's score to the mean value for that treatment. For example, all the individuals in the placebo group have been assigned the same score, $X = 1$, which is the mean for the placebo treatment. Notice that there is no variability within treatments for these data (each treatment group has $SS = 0$). Also notice that these modified scores have exactly the same differences between treatments as the original scores; that is, the treatment totals (T values) are the same as in the original data.

Table 13.5

The process of analyzing variability by modifying the scores in a set of data.

ORIGINAL DATA

PLACEBO	DRUG A	DRUG B	DRUG C
0	0	3	8
0	1	4	5
3	2	5	5
$T = 3$	$T = 3$	$T = 12$	$T = 18$
$SS = 6$	$SS = 2$	$SS = 2$	$SS = 6$

$$N = 12 \quad \Sigma X^2 = 178 \quad G = 36$$

BETWEEN-TREATMENTS DATA (ALL VARIABILITY WITHIN TREATMENTS HAS BEEN REMOVED.)

PLACEBO	DRUG A	DRUG B	DRUG C
1	1	4	6
1	1	4	6
1	1	4	6
$T = 3$	$T = 3$	$T = 12$	$T = 18$
$SS = 0$	$SS = 0$	$SS = 0$	$SS = 0$

$$N = 12 \quad \Sigma X^2 = 162 \quad G = 36$$

WITHIN-TREATMENTS DATA (ALL VARIABILITY BETWEEN TREATMENTS HAS BEEN REMOVED.)

PLACEBO	DRUG A	DRUG B	DRUG C
2	2	2	5
2	3	3	2
5	4	4	2
$T = 9$	$T = 9$	$T = 9$	$T = 9$
$SS = 6$	$SS = 2$	$SS = 2$	$SS = 6$

$$N = 12 \quad \Sigma X^2 = 124 \quad G = 36$$

Within-treatments data. Now consider the data set in the lower right-hand side of Table 13.5. For these data, the *only* variability is *within treatments.* To create these data, we have adjusted the original scores so that each of the four treatment conditions has exactly the same total. For the placebo group, for example, we added 2 points to each individual's score. For drug A we added 2 points to each scores. For drug B we subtracted 1 point, and for drug C we subtracted 3 points. Notice that there is no variability between treatments for these data (all four treatments have exactly the same mean). Also notice that these modified scores have exactly the same within-treatments variability as the original scores; that is, the *SS* values for the four treatments are the same as in the original data.

The three data sets in Table 13.5 illustrate the process of analyzing variability.

1. The original data (top of Table 13.5) show the total variability for the actual scores. By computing *SS* for this entire set of scores, we obtain SS_{total}.

$$SS_{\text{total}} = \Sigma X^2 - \frac{G^2}{N}$$

$$= 178 - \frac{36^2}{12}$$

$$= 178 - 108$$

$$= 70$$

2. For the *between-treatments data* (lower left of Table 13.5), we have removed all the within-treatment variability. Thus, all the variability in the data set is between treatments. By computing SS_{total} for this set of scores, we will obtain the same value as $SS_{between}$.

$$SS_{total} = \Sigma X^2 - \frac{G^2}{N} \qquad SS_{between} = \Sigma \frac{T^2}{n} - \frac{G^2}{N}$$

$$= 162 - \frac{36^2}{12} \qquad\qquad = \frac{3^2}{3} + \frac{3^2}{3} + \frac{12^2}{3} + \frac{18^2}{3} - \frac{36^2}{12}$$

$$= 162 - 108 \qquad\qquad = 3 + 3 + 48 + 108 - 108$$

$$= 54 \qquad\qquad\qquad = 54$$

Notice that the between-treatments variability accounts for all the variability. Also note that this is exactly the same value we obtained for $SS_{between}$ in the original ANOVA (Example 13.1).

3. For the within-treatments data (lower right of Table 13.5), we have removed all the between-treatments variability (the differences between treatments have been eliminated). For these data, all the variability in the scores is within treatments. By computing SS_{total} for this set of scores, we obtain the same value as SS_{within}.

$$SS_{total} = \Sigma X^2 - \frac{G^2}{N} \qquad SS_{within} = \Sigma\, SS_{each\ treatment}$$

$$\qquad\qquad\qquad\qquad\qquad\quad = 6 + 2 + 2 + 6$$

$$= 124 - \frac{36^2}{12} \qquad\qquad\qquad = 16$$

$$= 124 - 108$$

$$= 16$$

Notice that this is exactly the same value we obtained for SS_{within} in the original ANOVA (Example 13.1).

AN EXAMPLE WITH UNEQUAL SAMPLE SIZES

In the previous example all the samples were exactly the same size (equal n's). However, the formulas for ANOVA can be used when the sample size varies within an experiment. With unequal sample sizes you must take care to be sure that each value of n is matched with the proper T value in the equations. You also should note that the general ANOVA procedure is most accurate when used to examine experimental data with equal sample sizes. Therefore, researchers generally try to plan experiments with equal n's. However, there are circumstances where it is impossible or impractical to have an equal number of subjects in every treatment condition. In these situations, ANOVA still provides a valid test, especially when the samples are relatively large and when the discrepancy between sample sizes is not extreme.

EXAMPLE 13.3

A psychologist conducts an experiment to compare learning performance for three species of monkeys. The animals are tested individually on a delayed-response task. A raisin is hidden in one of three containers while the animal is viewing from its cage window. A shade is then pulled over the window for 1 minute to block the view. After this delay period, the monkey is allowed to respond by tipping over one container. If its response is correct, the monkey is rewarded with the raisin. The number of trials it takes before the animal makes five consecutive correct responses is recorded. The experimenter used all of the available animals from each species, which resulted in unequal sample sizes (n). The data are summarized in Table 13.6.

STEP 1 *State hypothesis and select alpha.*

$$H_0: \quad \mu_1 = \mu_2 = \mu_3$$
$$H_1: \quad \text{At least one population is different from the others}$$
$$\alpha = .05$$

STEP 2 *Locate the critical region.* To find the critical region, we first must determine the *df* values for the *F*-ratio:

$$df_{total} = N - 1 = 20 - 1 = 19$$
$$df_{between} = k - 1 = 3 - 1 = 2$$
$$df_{within} = N - k = 20 - 3 = 17$$

The *F*-ratio for these data will have $df = 2, 17$. With $\alpha = .05$, the critical value for the *F*-ratio is 3.59.

STEP 3 *Compute the F-ratio.* First compute *SS* for all three parts of the analysis:

$$SS_{total} = \Sigma X^2 - \frac{G^2}{N}$$
$$= 3400 - \frac{200^2}{20}$$
$$= 3400 - 2000$$
$$= 1400$$

$$SS_{between} = \Sigma \frac{T^2}{n} - \frac{G^2}{N} = \frac{T_1^2}{n_1} + \frac{T_2^2}{n_2} + \frac{T_3^2}{n_3} - \frac{G^2}{N}$$
$$= \frac{36^2}{4} + \frac{140^2}{10} + \frac{24^2}{6} - \frac{200^2}{20}$$
$$= 324 + 1960 + 96 - 2000$$
$$= 380$$

Table 13.6

The performance of different species of monkeys on a delayed-response task

	VERVET	RHESUS	BABOON	
	$n = 4$	$n = 10$	$n = 6$	$N = 20$
	$\overline{X} = 9$	$\overline{X} = 14$	$\overline{X} = 4$	$G = 200$
	$T = 36$	$T = 140$	$T = 24$	$\Sigma X^2 = 3400$
	$SS = 200$	$SS = 500$	$SS = 320$	

$$SS_{\text{within}} = \Sigma SS_{\text{inside each treatment}}$$
$$= 200 + 500 + 320$$
$$= 1020$$

Finally, compute the MS values and the F-ratio:

$$MS_{\text{between}} = \frac{SS}{df} = \frac{380}{2} = 190$$

$$MS_{\text{within}} = \frac{SS}{df} = \frac{1020}{17} = 60$$

$$F = \frac{MS_{\text{between}}}{MS_{\text{within}}} = \frac{190}{60} = 3.17$$

STEP 4 *Make a decision.* Because the obtained F-ratio is not in the critical region, we fail to reject H_0 and conclude that these data do not provide evidence of significant differences among the three populations of monkeys in terms of average learning performance.

LEARNING CHECK 1. The following data sumarize the results of an experiment using three separate samples to compare three treatment conditions:

TREATMENT 1	TREATMENT 2	TREATMENT 3	
$n = 5$	$n = 5$	$n = 5$	
$T = 5$	$T = 10$	$T = 30$	$\Sigma X^2 = 325$
$SS = 45$	$SS = 25$	$SS = 50$	

Do these data provide evidence of any significant mean differences among the treatments? Test with $\alpha = .05$.

2. A researcher reports an F-ratio with $df = 2, 30$ for an independent-measures analysis of variance. How many treatment conditions were compared in the experiment? How many subjects participated in the experiment?

ANSWERS 1. The following summary table presents the results of the analysis:

SOURCE	SS	df	MS	
Between	70	2	35	$F = 3.5$
Within	120	12	10	
Total	190	14		

The critical value for F is 3.88. The obtained value for F is not in the critical region and we fail to reject H_0.

2. There were 3 treatment conditions ($df_{\text{between}} = k - 1 = 2$). A total of $N = 33$ individuals participated ($df_{\text{within}} = 30 = N - k$).

13.6 POST HOC TESTS

In analysis of variance, the null hypothesis states that there is no treatment effect:

$$H_0: \quad \mu_1 = \mu_2 = \mu_3 = \cdots$$

When you reject the null hypothesis, you conclude that the means are not all the same. Although this appears to be a simple conclusion, in most cases it actually creates more questions than it answers. When there are only two treatments in an experiment, H_0 will state that $\mu_1 = \mu_2$. If you reject this hypothesis, the conclusion is quite straightforward; i.e., the two means are not equal ($\mu_1 \neq \mu_2$). However, when you have more than two treatments, the situation immediately becomes more complex. With $k = 3$, for example, rejecting H_0 indicates that not all the means are the same. Now you must decide which ones are different. Is μ_1 different from μ_2? Is μ_1 different from μ_3? Is μ_2 different from μ_3? Are all three different? The purpose of *post hoc tests* is to answer these questions.

As the name implies, post hoc tests are done after an analysis of variance. More specifically, these tests are done after ANOVA when

1. You reject H_0 and
2. There are three or more treatments ($k \geq 3$).

Rejecting H_0 indicates that at least one difference exists among the treatments. With $k = 3$ or more, the problem is to find where the differences are.

In general, a post hoc test enables you to go back through the data and compare the individual treatments two at a time. In statistical terms, this is called making *pairwise comparisons*. For example, with $k = 3$, we would compare μ_1 versus μ_2, then μ_2 versus μ_3, and then μ_1 versus μ_3. In each case, we are looking for a significant mean difference.

You might wonder why we do not perform t tests for all possible pairs of groups. This approach may cause a problem in avoiding Type I errors. Remember, each time you do a hypothesis test, you select an alpha level. For this reason, researchers often make a distinction between the *testwise* alpha level and the *experimentwise* alpha level. The testwise alpha level is simply the alpha level you select for each individual hypothesis test. The experimentwise alpha level is the total probability of a Type I error that is accumulated from all the separate tests in the experiment. It is the experimentwise alpha level that is most important when doing multiple comparisons between all possible pairs of groups. The more comparisons you make, the greater the experimentwise alpha level and the greater the risk of a Type I error. The problem with simply doing t tests for all possible pairs of treatment groups is that the experimentwise alpha level may be quite large.

Fortunately, many post hoc tests have been developed that attempt to control the experimentwise alpha level. We will examine two of these commonly used procedures: Tukey's HSD test and the Scheffé test.

TUKEY'S HONESTLY SIGNIFICANT DIFFERENCE (HSD) TEST   The first post hoc test we will consider is Tukey's HSD test. We have selected Tukey's HSD test because it is a commonly used test in psychological research.

Tukey's test allows you to compute a single value that determines the minimum difference between treatment means that is necessary for significance. This value, called the *honestly significant difference,* or HSD, is then used to compare any two treatment conditions. If the mean difference exceeds Tukey's HSD, you conclude that there is a significant difference between the treatments. Otherwise you cannot conclude that the treatments are significantly different. The formula for Tukey's HSD is

$$HSD = q \sqrt{\frac{MS_{within}}{n}} \qquad (13.13)$$

The q value used in Tukey's HSD test is called a Studentized range statistic.

where the value of q is found in Table B5 (Appendix B, page A-29), MS_{within} is the within-treatments variance from the ANOVA, and n is the number of scores in each treatment. Tukey's test requires that the sample size n be the same for all treatments. To locate the appropriate value of q, you must know the number of treatments in the overall experiment (k) and the degrees of freedom for MS_{within} (the error term in the F-ratio) and select an alpha level (generally the same α used for the ANOVA).

EXAMPLE 13.4 To outline the procedure for conducting post hoc tests with Tukey's HSD, we will use the data from the pain-reliever study in Example 13.1. The data are reproduced in summary form in Table 13.7. The within-treatments variance for these data is $MS_{within} = 2.00$ with $df = 8$.

With $\alpha = .05$ and $k = 4$, the value of q for these data is $q = 4.53$. Tukey's HSD is

$$HSD = q \sqrt{\frac{MS_{within}}{n}}$$
$$= 4.53 \sqrt{\frac{2.00}{3}}$$
$$= 3.70$$

Therefore, the mean difference between any two samples must be at least 3.70 to be significant. Using this value, we can make the following four conclusions:

1. Drug A is not significantly different from the placebo (both have $\overline{X} = 1$).

Table 13.7

Pain threshold data for four different pain relievers.

	1, PLACEBO	2, DRUG A	3, DRUG B	4, DRUG C
	$n = 3$	$n = 3$	$n = 3$	$n = 3$
	$T = 3$	$T = 3$	$T = 12$	$T = 18$
	$\overline{X} = 1$	$\overline{X} = 1$	$\overline{X} = 4$	$\overline{X} = 6$

2. Drug B is not significantly different from either the placebo or drug A ($\overline{X} = 4$ versus $\overline{X} = 1$).

3. Drug C is significantly different from both the placebo and drug A ($\overline{X} = 6$ versus $\overline{X} = 1$).

4. Drug C is not significantly different from drug B ($\overline{X} = 6$ versus $\overline{X} = 4$).

Thus, drug C is the only one that produced significantly more pain relief than the placebo, and drug C is significantly better than drug A.

You also should notice that posttests can lead to apparently contradictory results. In this case, for example, we have found that there is no significant difference between drug A and drug B, and we have found that there is no significant difference between drug B and drug C. This combination of outcomes might lead you to expect that there is no significant difference between drug A and drug C. However the test did show a significant difference. The answer to this apparent contradiction is in the criterion of statistical significance. The differences between A and B or between B and C were too small to satisfy the criterion of significance. However, when these differences are combined, the total difference between A and C is large enough to meet the criterion of statistical significance.

THE SCHEFFE TEST

Because it uses an extremely cautious method for reducing the risk of a Type I error, the *Scheffé test* has the distinction of being one of the safest of all possible post hoc tests. The Scheffé test uses an *F*-ratio to test for a significant difference between any two treatment conditions. The numerator of the *F*-ratio is an *MS* between treatments that is calculated using *only the two treatments you want to compare*. The denominator is the same *MS* within treatments that was used for the overall ANOVA. The "safety factor" for the Scheffé test comes from the following two considerations:

1. Although you are comparing only two treatments, the Scheffé test uses the value of k from the original experiment to compute *df* between treatments. Thus, *df* for the numerator of the *F*-ratio is $k - 1$.

2. The critical value for the Scheffé *F*-ratio is the same as was used to evaluate the *F*-ratio from the overall ANOVA. Thus, Scheffé requires that every posttest satisfy the same criteria used for the complete analysis of variance. The following example uses the data from Example 13.1 (Table 13.7) to demonstrate the Scheffé posttest procedure.

EXAMPLE 13.5

Rather than test all the possible comparisons of the four treatment conditions shown in Table 13.7, we will begin with the largest mean difference and then test progressively smaller differences until we find one that is not significant. For these data, the largest difference is between the placebo ($T = 3$) and drug C ($T = 18$). The first step is to compute SS_{between} for these two treatments.

The grand total, G, for these two treatments is found by adding the two treatment totals ($G = 3 + 18$), and N is found by adding the number of scores in the two treatments ($N = 3 + 3$).

$$SS_{between} = \Sigma \frac{T^2}{n} - \frac{G^2}{N}$$

$$= \frac{3^2}{3} + \frac{18^2}{3} - \frac{21^2}{6}$$

$$= 37.5$$

Although we are comparing only two treatments, these two were selected from an experiment consisting of $k = 4$ treatments. The Scheffé test uses the overall experiment ($k = 4$) to determine the degrees of freedom between treatments. Therefore, $df_{between} = k - 1 = 3$, and the MS between treatments is

$$MS_{between} = \frac{SS_{between}}{df_{between}} = \frac{37.5}{3} = 12.5$$

Scheffé also uses the within-treatments variance from the complete experiment, $MS_{within} = 2.00$ with $df = 8$, so the Scheffé F-ratio is

$$F = \frac{MS_{between}}{MS_{within}} = \frac{12.5}{2} = 6.25$$

With $df = 3, 8$ and $\alpha = .05$, the critical value for F is 4.07 (see Table B.4). Therefore, our F-ratio is in the critical region and we conclude that there is a significant difference between the placebo and drug C. Because the data for drug A and the placebo are equivalent (both have $T = 3$), we also conclude that drug C is significantly different from drug A.

Next, we consider the second largest mean difference for the data: drug B ($T = 12$) versus the placebo ($T = 3$). Again, we compute $SS_{between}$ using only these two treatment groups.

$$SS_{between} = \Sigma \frac{T^2}{n} - \frac{G^2}{N}$$

$$= \frac{3^2}{3} + \frac{12^2}{3} - \frac{15^2}{6}$$

$$= 13.5$$

As before, the Scheffé test uses the overall experiment ($k = 4$) to determine df between treatments. Thus $df_{between} = k - 1 = 3$, and $MS_{between}$ for this comparison is

$$MS_{between} = \frac{SS_{between}}{df_{between}} = \frac{13.5}{3} = 4.5$$

Using $MS_{within} = 2$ with $df = 8$, we obtain a Scheffé F-ratio of

$$F = \frac{MS_{between}}{MS_{within}} = \frac{4.5}{2} = 2.25$$

With $df = 3, 8$ and $\alpha = .05$, the obtained F-ratio is less than the critical value of 4.07. Because the F-ratio is not in the critical region, our decision is that these data do not provide sufficient evidence to conclude that there is a significant difference between the placebo and drug B. Because the mean difference between the placebo and drug B is larger than any of the remaining pairs of treatments, we can conclude that none of the other pairwise comparisons would be significant with the Scheffé test.

Thus the conclusion from the Scheffé posttest is that drug C is significantly different from both the placebo and drug A. These are the only significant differences for this experiment (using Scheffé), and these differences are the source of the significant F-ratio obtained for the overall ANOVA.

13.7 THE RELATION BETWEEN ANOVA AND t TESTS

When you have data from an independent-measures experiment with only two treatment conditions, you can use either a t test (Chapter 10) or independent-measures ANOVA. In practical terms, it makes no difference which you choose. These two statistical techniques always will result in the same statistical decision. In fact, the two methods use many of the same calculations and are very closely related in several other respects. The basic relation between t statistics and F-ratios can be stated in an equation:

$$F = t^2$$

This relation can be explained by first looking at the structure of the formulas for F and t.

The structure of the t statistic compares the actual difference between the samples (numerator) with the standard difference that would be expected by chance (denominator).

$$t = \frac{\text{mean difference}}{\text{standard error}} = \frac{\text{difference between samples}}{\text{difference expected by chance}}$$

The structure of the F-ratio also compares differences between samples versus the difference due to chance or error.

$$F = \frac{\text{variance between treatments}}{\text{variance within treatments}}$$

However, the numerator and denominator of the F-ratio measure variances, or mean squared differences. Therefore, we can express the F-ratio as follows:

$$F = \frac{(\text{differences between samples})^2}{(\text{differences expected by chance})^2}$$

The fact that the *t* statistic is based on differences and the *F*-ratio is based on *squared* differences leads to the basic relation $F = t^2$.

There are several other points to consider in comparing the *t* statistic to the *F*-ratio.

1. It should be obvious that you will be testing the same hypotheses whether you choose a *t* test or ANOVA. With only two treatments, the hypotheses for either test are

$$H_0: \quad \mu_1 = \mu_2$$
$$H_1: \quad \mu_1 \neq \mu_2$$

2. The degrees of freedom for the *t* statistic and the *df* for the denominator of the *F*-ratio (df_{within}) are identical. For example, if you have two samples, each with six scores, the independent-measures *t* statistic will have $df = 10$, and the *F*-ratio will have $df = 1, 10$. In each case, you are adding the *df* from the first sample ($n - 1$) and the *df* from the second sample.

3. The distribution of *t* and the distribution of *F*-ratios match perfectly if you take into consideration the relation $F = t^2$. Consider the *t* distribution with $df = 18$ and the corresponding *F* distribution with $df = 1$, 18 that are presented in Figure 13.9. Notice the following relations:

   a. If each of the *t* values is squared, then all of the negative values will become positive. As a result, the whole left-hand side of the *t* distribution (below zero) will be flipped over to the positive side. This creates a nonsymmetrical, positively skewed distribution, that is, the *F* distribution.

Figure 13.9

The distribution of *t*-scores with $df = 18$ and the corresponding distribution of *F*-ratios with $df = 1$, 18. Notice that the critical values for $\alpha = .05$ are $t = \pm 2.101$ and that $F = 2.101^2 = 4.41$.

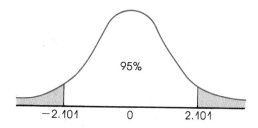

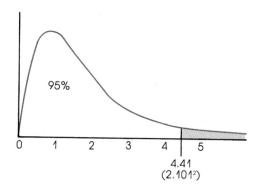

b. For $\alpha = .05$, the critical region for t is determined by values greater than $+2.101$ or less than -2.101. When these boundaries are squared, you get

$$\pm 2.101^2 = 4.41$$

Notice that 4.41 is the critical value for $\alpha = .05$ in the F distribution. Any value that is in the critical region for t will end up in the critical region for F-ratios after it is squared.

ASSUMPTIONS FOR THE INDEPENDENT-MEASURES ANOVA

The independent-measures ANOVA requires the same three assumptions that were necessary for the independent-measures t hypothesis test:

1. The observations within each sample must be independent (see page 255).

2. The populations from which the samples are selected must be normal.

3. The populations from which the samples are selected must have equal variances (homogeneity of variance).

Ordinarily, researchers are not overly concerned with the assumption of normality, especially when large samples are used, unless there are strong reasons to suspect the assumption has not been satisfied. The assumption of homogeneity of variance is an important one. If a researcher suspects it has been violated, it can be tested by Hartley's F-max test for homogeneity of variance (Chapter 10, page 281).

LEARNING CHECK

1. The Scheffé post hoc test uses between-treatments df from the original ANOVA even though $SS_{between}$ is calculated for a pair of treatments. (True or false?)

2. An ANOVA produces an F-ratio with $df = 1, 34$. Could the data have been analyzed with a t test? What would be the degrees of freedom for the t statistic?

3. With $k = 2$ treatments, are post hoc tests necessary when the null hypothesis is rejected? Explain why or why not.

ANSWERS

1. True

2. If the F-ratio has $df = 1, 34$, then the experiment compared only two treatments, and you could use a t statistic to evaluate the data. The t statistic would have $df = 34$.

3. No. Post hoc tests are used to determine which treatments are different. With only two treatment conditions, there is no uncertainty as to which two treatments are different.

SUMMARY

1. Analysis of variance is a statistical technique that is used to test for mean differences among two or more treatment conditions or among two or more populations. The null hypothesis for this test states that there are no differences among the population means. The alternative hypothesis states that at least one mean is different from the others. Although analysis of variance can be used with either an independent- or a repeated-measures experiment, this chapter examined only independent-measures designs, that is, experiments with a separate sample for each treatment condition.

2. The test statistic for analysis of variance is a ratio of two variances called an F-ratio. The F-ratio is structured so that the numerator and denominator measure the same variance when the null hypothesis is true. In this way, the existence of a significant treatment effect is apparent if the data produce an "unbalanced" F-ratio. The variances in the F-ratio are called mean squares, or MS values. Each MS is computed by

$$MS = \frac{SS}{df}$$

3. For the independent-measures analysis of variance, the F-ratio is

$$F = \frac{MS_{between}}{MS_{within}}$$

The $MS_{between}$ measures differences among the treatments by computing the variability of the treatment means or totals. These differences are assumed to be produced by three factors.
   a. Treatment effects (if they exist)
   b. Individual differences
   c. Experimental error

The MS_{within} measures variability inside each of the treatment conditions. This variability is assumed to be produced by two factors:
   a. Individual differences
   b. Experimental error

With these factors in mind, the F-ratio has the following structure

$$F = \frac{\text{treatment effect} + \text{individual diff's.} + \text{experimental error}}{\text{individual diff's.} + \text{experimental error}}$$

Figure 13.10

Formulas for ANOVA.

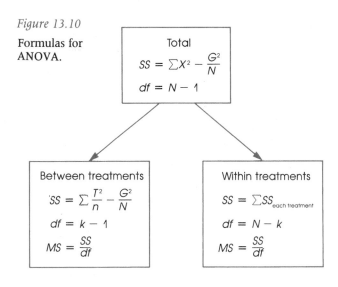

$$F\text{-ratio} = \frac{MS \text{ between treatments}}{MS \text{ within treatments}}$$

When there is no treatment effect (H_0 is true), the numerator and denominator of the F-ratio are measuring the same variance, and the obtained ratio should be near 1.00. If there is a significant treatment effect, the numerator of the ratio should be larger than the denominator, and the obtained F value should be much greater than 1.00.

4. The formulas for computing each SS, df, and MS value are presented in Figure 13.10, which also shows the general structure for the analysis of variance.

5. The F-ratio has two values for degrees of freedom, one associated with the MS in the numerator and one associated with the MS in the denominator. These df values are used to find the critical value for the F-ratio in the F distribution table.

6. When the decision from an analysis of variance is to reject the null hypothesis and when the experiment contained more than two treatment conditions, it is necessary to continue the analysis with a post hoc test such as Tukey's HSD test or the Scheffé test. The purpose of these tests is to determine exactly which treatments are significantly different and which are not.

KEY TERMS

analysis of variance (ANOVA)	individual differences	factor	distribution of F-ratios
between-treatments variability	experimental error	levels	post hoc tests
within-treatments variability	F-ratio	mean square (MS)	Scheffé test
treatment effect	error term	ANOVA summary table	Tukey's HSD test

——— *Focus on Problem Solving* ———

1. The words and labels used to describe the different components of variance can help you remember the ANOVA formulas. For example, *total* refers to the total experiment. Therefore, the SS_{total} and df_{total} values are based on the whole set of N scores. The word *within* refers to the variability inside (within) the treatment groups. Thus, the value for SS_{within} is based on an SS value from each group, computed from the scores *within* each group. Finally, *between* refers to the variability (or differences) between treatments. The $SS_{between}$ component measures the differences between treatments (T_1 versus T_2, and so on), and $df_{between}$ is simply the number of T values (k) minus 1.

2. When you are computing SS and df values, always calculate all three components (total, between, and within) separately, then check your work by making sure that the *between-treatments* and *within-treatments* components add up to the *total*.

3. Because ANOVA requires a fairly lengthy series of calculations, it helps to organize your work. We suggest that you compute all of the SS values first, followed by the df values, then the two MS values, and finally the F-ratio. If you use the same system all the time (practice it!), you will be less likely to get lost in the middle of a problem.

4. The previous two focus points are facilitated by using an ANOVA summary table (for example, see page 361). The first column has the heading *source*. Listed below the heading are the three sources of variability (between, within, and total). The second and third columns have the heading SS and df. These can be filled in as you perform the appropriate computations. The last column is headed MS for the mean square values.

5. Remember that an F-ratio has two separate values for df: A value for the numerator and one for the denominator. Properly reported, the $df_{between}$ value is stated first. You will need both df values when consulting the F distribution table for the critical F value. You should recognize immediately that an error has been made if you see an F-ratio reported with a single value for df.

6. When you encounter an F-ratio and its df values reported in the literature, you should be able to reconstruct much of the original experiment. For example, if you see "$F(2, 36) = 4.80$," you should realize that the experiment compared $k = 3$ treatment groups (because $df_{between} = k - 1 = 2$), with a total of $N = 39$ subjects participating in the experiment (because $df_{within} = N - k = 36$).

7. Keep in mind that a large value for F indicates evidence for a treatment effect. A combination of factors will yield a large F value. One such factor is a large value for $MS_{between}$ in the numerator of the ratio. This will occur when there are large differences between groups, as would be expected when a treatment

effect occurs. Another factor that contributes to a large F value would be a small value for MS_{within} on the bottom of the F ratio. This will occur when there is a little error variability, reflected in low variability within groups.

——— *Demonstration 13.1* ———

ANALYSIS OF VARIANCE

A human factors psychologist studied three computer keyboard designs. Three samples of individuals were given material to type on a particular keyboard and the number of errors committed by each subject was recorded. The data are as follows:

> Keyboard A: 0 4 0 1 0
> Keyboard B: 6 8 5 4 2
> Keyboard C: 6 5 9 4 6

Does typing performance differ significantly among the three types of keyboards?

STEP 1 State the hypotheses and specify alpha.

The null hypothesis states that there is no difference among the keyboards in terms of number of errors committed. In symbols, we would state

H_0: $\mu_1 = \mu_2 = \mu_3$ (there is no effect of type of keyboard used)

As noted previously in this chapter, there are a number of possible statements for the alternative hypothesis. Here, we state the general alternative hypothesis.

H_1: At least one of the treatment means is different.

That is, there is an effect of the type of keyboard on typing performance. We will set alpha at $\alpha = .05$.

STEP 2 Locate the critical region.

To locate the critical regions, we must obtain the values for $df_{between}$ and df_{within}.

$$df_{between} = k - 1 = 3 - 1 = 2$$
$$df_{within} = N - k = 15 - 3 = 12$$

The F-ratio for this problem will have $df = 2, 12$. The F distribution table is consulted for $df = 2$ in the numerator and $df = 12$ in the denominator. The critical F value for $\alpha = .05$ is $F = 3.88$. The obtained F ratio must exceed this value to reject H_0.

STEP 3 Perform the analysis.

The analysis involves the following steps:

1. Compute T and SS for each sample and obtain G and ΣX^2 for all ($N = 15$) scores.

2. Perform the analysis of SS.

3. Perform the analysis of df.

4. Calculate mean squares.

5. Calculate the F-ratio.

Compute T, SS, G, and ΣX^2. We will use the computational formula for the SS of each sample. The calculations are illustrated with the following tables.

KEYBOARD A		KEYBOARD B		KEYBOARD C	
X	X^2	X	X^2	X	X^2
0	0	6	36	6	36
4	16	8	64	5	25
0	0	5	25	9	81
1	1	4	16	4	16
0	0	2	4	6	36
$\Sigma X = 5$	$\Sigma X^2 = 17$	$\Sigma X = 25$	$\Sigma X^2 = 145$	$\Sigma X = 30$	$\Sigma X^2 = 194$

For keyboard A, T and SS are computed using only the $n = 5$ scores of this sample:

$$T_1 = \Sigma X = 0 + 4 + 0 + 1 + 0 = 5$$

$$SS_1 = \Sigma X^2 - \frac{(\Sigma X)^2}{n} = 17 - \frac{(5)^2}{5} = 17 - \frac{25}{5} = 17 - 5$$

$$= 12$$

For keyboard B, T and SS are computed for its $n = 5$ scores

$$T_2 = \Sigma X = 25$$

$$SS_2 = \Sigma X^2 - \frac{(\Sigma X)^2}{n} = 145 - \frac{(25)^2}{5} = 145 - \frac{625}{5} = 145 - 125$$

$$= 20$$

For the last sample, keyboard C, we obtain:

$$T_3 = \Sigma X = 30$$

$$SS_3 = \Sigma X^2 - \frac{(\Sigma X)^2}{n} = 194 - \frac{(30)^2}{5} = 194 - \frac{900}{5} = 194 - 180$$

$$= 14$$

The grand total (G) for $N = 15$ scores is

$$G = \Sigma T = 5 + 25 + 30 = 60$$

The ΣX^2 for all $N = 15$ scores in this study can be obtained by summing the X^2 columns for the three samples. For these data we obtain

$$\Sigma X^2 = 17 + 145 + 194 = 356$$

Perform the analysis of SS. We will compute SS_{total} followed by its two components.

$$SS_{total} = \Sigma X^2 - \frac{G^2}{N} = 356 - \frac{60^2}{15} = 356 - \frac{3600}{15}$$

$$= 356 - 240 = 116$$

$$SS_{within} = \Sigma SS_{inside\ each\ treatment}$$

$$= 12 + 20 + 14$$

$$= 46$$

$$SS_{between} = \Sigma \frac{T^2}{n} - \frac{G^2}{N}$$

$$= \frac{5^2}{5} + \frac{25^2}{5} + \frac{30^2}{5} - \frac{60^2}{15}$$

$$= \frac{25}{5} + \frac{625}{5} + \frac{900}{5} - \frac{3600}{15}$$

$$= 5 + 125 + 180 - 240$$

$$= 70$$

Analyze degrees of freedom. We will compute df_{total}. Its components, $df_{between}$ and df_{within}, were previously calculated (Step 2).

$$df_{total} = N - 1 = 15 - 1 = 14$$

$$df_{between} = 2$$

$$df_{within} = 12$$

Calculate the MS values. The values for $MS_{between}$ and MS_{within} are determined.

$$MS_{between} = \frac{SS_{between}}{df_{between}} = \frac{70}{2} = 35$$

$$MS_{within} = \frac{SS_{within}}{df_{within}} = \frac{46}{12} = 3.83$$

Compute the F-ratio. Finally, we can compute F.

$$F = \frac{MS_{between}}{MS_{within}} = \frac{35}{3.83} = 9.14$$

STEP 4 Make a decision about H_0 and state a conclusion.

The obtained F of 9.14 exceeds the critical value of 3.88. Therefore, we can reject the null hypothesis. The type of keyboard used has a significant effect of the number of errors committed, $F(2, 12) = 9.14$, $p < .05$. The following table summarizes the results of the analysis.

SOURCE	SS	df	MS	
Between treatments	70	2	35	$F = 9.14$
Within treatments	46	12	3.83	
Total	116	14		

PROBLEMS

1. Explain why the expected value for an F-ratio is equal to 1.00 when there is no treatment effect?

2. Describe the similarities between an F-ratio and a t statistic.

3. Explain why you should use ANOVA instead of several t tests to evaluate mean differences when an experiment consists of three or more treatment conditions.

4. Describe *when* and *why* posttests are used. Explain why you would not need to do posttests for an experiment with only $k = 2$ treatment conditions.

5. Use the following set of data.
   a. Without doing any calculations (just look at the data), what value should be obtained for the variance between treatments? ($MS_{between} = ?$)
   b. Based on your answer to part a, what value would be obtained for the F-ratio for these data?
   c. Calculate $SS_{between}$ and $MS_{between}$ to verify your answers.

TREATMENTS		
I	II	
1	2	
4	5	$G = 16$
0	0	$\Sigma X^2 = 56$
3	1	
$T = 8$	$T = 8$	
$SS = 10$	$SS = 14$	

6. For the following set of data, without doing any calculations (just look at the data), what value should be obtained for the variance within treatments? ($MS_{within} = ?$)

TREATMENTS		
I	II	
1	3	
1	3	$G = 16$
1	3	$\Sigma X^2 = 40$
1	3	
$T = 4$	$T = 12$	

7. A psychologist would like to examine the relative effectiveness of three therapy techniques for treating mild phobias. A sample of $N = 15$ individuals who display a moderate fear of spiders is obtained. These individuals are randomly assigned (with $n = 5$) to each of the three therapies. The dependent variable is a measure of reported fear of spiders after therapy. The data are as follows:

THERAPY A	THERAPY B	THERAPY C	
5	3	1	
2	3	0	
2	0	1	$G = 30$
4	2	2	$\Sigma X^2 = 86$
2	2	1	
$T = 15$	$T = 10$	$T = 5$	
$SS = 8$	$SS = 6$	$SS = 2$	

Do these data indicate that there are any significant differences among the three therapies? Test at the .05 level of significance.

8. Use the following sample:

0	4
2	2
1	5
5	1

a. Calculate SS for the entire sample of eight scores.

b. Now treat each column as a separate sample of $n = 4$ scores and calculate SS for each of the two samples.

c. Again treating each column as a separate sample, find the total (T) for each group and compute $SS_{between}$ for these two samples.
[*Note:* You should find that the within-samples SS (from part b) and the between-samples SS (from part c) add up to the total SS from part a.]

9. The following data are from an experiment comparing three treatment conditions with a separate sample of $n = 4$ in each treatment.

	TREATMENTS		
I	II	III	
0	1	8	$G = 48$
4	5	5	
0	4	6	$\Sigma X^2 = 284$
4	2	9	
$T = 8$	$T = 12$	$T = 28$	
$SS = 16$	$SS = 10$	$SS = 10$	

a. Use an ANOVA with $\alpha = .05$ to determine whether there are any significant differences among the three treatments.

b. Use Tukey's HSD test to find exactly which treatments are different from each other. Again, use the .05 level of significance.

10. A psychologist would like to examine how the rate of presentation affects people's ability to memorize a list of words. A list of 20 words is prepared. For one group of subjects the list is presented at the rate of one word every ½ second. The next group gets one word every second. The third group has one word every 2 second, and the fourth group has one word every 3 seconds. After the list is presented, the psychologist asks each person to recall the entire list. The dependent variable is the number of errors in recall. The data from this experiment are as follows:

½ SECOND	1 SECOND	2 SECOND	3 SECOND	
4	0	3	0	
6	2	1	2	$G = 32$
2	2	2	1	
4	0	2	1	$\Sigma X^2 = 104$
$T = 16$	$T = 4$	$T = 8$	$T = 4$	
$SS = 8$	$SS = 4$	$SS = 2$	$SS = 2$	

a. Can the psychologist conclude that the rate of presentation has a significant effect on memory? Test at the .05 level.

b. Use the Tukey HSD test to determine which rates of presentation are statistically different and which are not.

11. The following data represent scores from three different treatment conditions.

TREATMENT 1	TREATMENT 2	TREATMENT 3	
1	3	2	$N = 12$
1	3	2	
1	3	2	$\Sigma X^2 = 56$
1	3	2	$G = 24$
$T = 4$	$T = 12$	$T = 8$	

a. Just looking at the data, describe the relative amount of variability between treatments versus within treatments.

b. Calculate SS_{total}, $SS_{between}$, and SS_{within}. You should find that all of the variability for these data comes from differences between treatments.

12. A psychologist would like to show that background noise can interfere with a student's concentration and therefore cause poorer performance on complex mental tasks. A sample of 12 students is obtained, and the psychologist randomly assigns these students to three separate groups. Each group is given a standard problem-solving task. One group works on this task under quiet conditions, one group works with soft background music, and the third group works with a loud radio tuned to a popular rock station. For each student the psychologist measures the number of errors on the task. The results from this experiment are summarized as follows:

QUIET	SOFT MUSIC	LOUD MUSIC	
$n = 4$	$n = 4$	$n = 4$	$\Sigma X^2 = 71$
$T = 4$	$T = 6$	$T = 14$	
$SS = 2$	$SS = 4$	$SS = 3$	

Can the psychologist conclude that the background noise had an effect on performance? Test at the .05 level of significance.

13. A psychologist using an independent-measures experimental design to compare different teaching methods reports an F-ratio of $F = 3.87$ with $df = 3, 28$.

a. How many teaching methods (treatments) were being compared?

b. How many subjects participated in the total experiment?

c. Were there significant differences among the teaching methods?

14. The following data represent the results of an independent-measures experiment comparing two treatment conditions.

TREATMENT 1	TREATMENT 2
1	5
2	4
2	3
4	2
1	6

a. Use an analysis of variance with $\alpha = .05$ to test for a significant difference between the two treatment means.

b. Use an independent-measures t statistic to test for a significant difference. (Remember, you should find the basic relation, $F = t^2$.)

15. Use an analysis of variance with $\alpha = .05$ to determine whether the following data provide evidence of any significant differences among the three treatments:

TREATMENT 1	TREATMENT 2	TREATMENT 3	
$n = 4$	$n = 5$	$n = 6$	$N = 15$
$T = 2$	$T = 10$	$T = 18$	$G = 30$
$SS = 13$	$SS = 21$	$SS = 26$	$\Sigma X^2 = 135$

16. A pharmaceutical company has developed a drug that is expected to reduce hunger. To test the drug, three samples of rats are selected with $n = 10$ in each sample. The first sample receives the drug every day. The second sample is given the drug once a week, and the third sample receives no drug at all. The dependent variable is the amount of food eaten by each rat over a 1-month period. These data are analyzed by an analysis of variance, and the results are reported in the following summary table. Fill in all missing values in the table. (*Hint:* Start with the *df* column.)

SOURCE	SS	df	MS	
Between treatments	___	___	___	$F = 12$
Within treatments	54	___	___	
Total	___	___		

17. The following summary table presents the results of an ANOVA from an experiment comparing four treatment conditions with a sample of $n = 10$ in each treatment. Complete all missing values in the table.

SOURCE	SS	df	MS	
Between treatments	___	___	15	$F =$ ___
Within treatments	108	___	___	
Total	___	___		

18. A common science-fair project involves testing the effects of music on the growth of plants. For one of these projects, a sample of 24 newly sprouted bean plants is obtained. These plants are randomly assigned to four treatments, with $n = 6$ in each group. The four conditions are: rock music, heavy metal, country, and classical. The dependent variable is the height of each plant after 2 weeks. The data from this experiment were examined using an ANOVA and the results are summarized in the following table. Fill in all missing values.

SOURCE	SS	df	MS	
Between treatments	___	___	10	$F =$ ___
Within treatments	40	___	___	
Total	___	___		

19. A developmental psychologist is examining problem-solving ability for grade school children. Random samples of 5-year-old, 6-year-old, and 7-year-old children are obtained with $n = 3$ in each sample. Each child is given a standardized problem-solving task, and the psychologist records the number of errors. These data are as follows:

5-YEAR-OLDS	6-YEAR-OLDS	7-YEAR-OLDS	
5	6	0	$G = 30$
4	4	1	$\Sigma X^2 = 138$
6	2	2	
$T = 15$	$T = 12$	$T = 3$	
$SS = 2$	$SS = 8$	$SS = 2$	

a. Use these data to test whether there are any significant differences among the three age groups. Use $\alpha = .05$.

b. Use the Scheffé test to determine which groups are different.

20. A psychologist would like to demonstrate that the combination of two drugs can often produce much different effects than either of the drugs taken separately. Four random samples are selected with $n = 5$ in each sample. One group is given a sugar pill (no drug), one group is given drug A, another group is given drug B, and the final group is given drugs A and B together. Each person is then given a logic test measuring basic reasoning ability. The data are summarized as follows:

SUGAR PILL	DRUG A	DRUG B	DRUGS A AND B	
$T = 0$	$T = 5$	$T = 5$	$T = 20$	$\Sigma X^2 = 122$
$SS = 7$	$SS = 8$	$SS = 7$	$SS = 10$	

a. Can the psychologist conclude that there are any significant differences among the treatments? Test at the .05 level.

b. Use the Scheffé test to determine which treatments are different.

21. Several studies indicate that handedness (left-handed/right-handed) is related to differences in brain function. Because different parts of the brain are specialized for specific behaviors, this means that left- and right-handed people should show different skills or talents. To test this hypothesis, a psychologist tested pitch discrimination (a component of musical ability) for three groups of subjects: left-handed, right-handed, and ambidextrous. The data from this study are as follows:

RIGHT-HANDED	LEFT-HANDED	AMBIDEXTROUS	
6	1	2	
4	0	0	
3	1	0	$G = 30$
4	1	2	$\Sigma X^2 = 102$
3	2	1	
$T = 20$	$T = 5$	$T = 5$	
$SS = 6$	$SS = 2$	$SS = 4$	

Each score represents the number of errors during a series of pitch discrimination trials.

a. Do these data indicate any differences among the three groups? Test with $\alpha = .05$.

b. Use the F-max test to determine whether these data satisfy the homogeneity of variance assumption (see Chapter 10).

22. Betz and Thomas (1979) have reported a distinct connection between personality and health. They identified three personality types who differ in their susceptibility to serious, stress-related illness (heart attack, high blood pressure, etc.). The three personality types are alphas, who are cautious and steady; betas, who are carefree and outgoing; and gammas, who tend toward extremes of behavior such as being overly cautious or very careless. Sample data representing general health scores for each of these three groups are as follows. A low score indicates poor health.

ALPHAS		BETAS		GAMMAS	
43	44	41	52	36	29
41	56	40	57	38	36
49	42	36	48	45	42
52	53	51	55	25	40
41	21	52	39	41	36

a. Compute the mean for each personality type. Do these data indicate a significant difference among the three types? Test with $\alpha = .05$.

b. Use the Scheffé test to determine which groups are different. Explain what happened in this study.

23. Do weather conditions affect people's moods? To examine this question, a researcher selected three samples of college students and administered a mood inventory questionnaire to each student. One group was tested on a dreary, overcast, and drizzly day. The second group was tested during a violent thunderstorm, and the third group was tested on a bright sunny day. The data are as follows:

DREARY		STORMY		BRIGHT	
6	9	8	12	13	10
10	12	10	6	6	13
5	7	8	9	10	8
12	8	14	10	9	12
7	10	7	7	15	11

Do these data indicate that weather has an effect on mood? Test at the .05 level of significance.

24. A psychologist is interested in the extent to which physical attractiveness can influence judgment of other personal characteristics such as intelligence or ability. The psychologist selected three groups of subjects who were to play the role of a company personnel manager. Each subject was given a stack of job applications which included a photograph of the applicant. One of these applications was previously selected as the test stimulus. For one group of subjects, this application contained a photograph of a very attractive woman. For the second group, the photograph was of an average-looking woman. For the third group, a photo of a very unattractive woman was attached to the application. The subjects were instructed to rate the quality of each job applicant (0 = "very poor" to 10 = "excellent"). The psychologist recorded the rating of the test stimulus for each subject. These data are as follows:

ATTRACTIVE			AVERAGE			UNATTRACTIVE		
5	4	4	6	5	3	4	3	1
3	5	6	6	6	7	3	1	2
4	3	8	5	4	6	2	4	3
3	5	4	8	7	8	2	1	2

a. Compute the means of the groups and draw a graph showing the results.
b. Use an ANOVA with $\alpha = .05$ to determine whether there are any significant differences among these three groups.

c. Use the Scheffé test to determine which groups are different.
d. Based on the results of the post hoc test, describe the relation between physical attractiveness and the job ratings.

25. A researcher evaluating the effects of a drug designed an experiment using three different drug doses (small, medium, and large). A separate sample of subjects was tested for each drug dose, and the researcher obtained the following scores:

SMALL	MEDIUM	LARGE
14	16	24
19	20	18
13	15	20
17	18	18
18	19	22
21	23	24

a. Use an analysis of variance to determine whether there are any significant differences among these three drug doses. Set $\alpha = .05$.
b. Use the F-max test to determine whether these data satisfy the homogeneity of variance assumption.

CHAPTER 14

REPEATED-MEASURES ANALYSIS OF VARIANCE (ANOVA)

TOOLS YOU WILL NEED

The following items are considered essential background material for this chapter. If you doubt your knowledge of any of these items, you should review the appropriate chapter or section before proceeding.

- Introduction to analysis of variance (Chapter 13)
- The logic of analysis of variance
- ANOVA notation and formulas
- Distribution of *F*-ratios
- Repeated-measures design (Chapter 11)

CONTENTS

PREVIEW

In the early 1970s, it was discovered that the brain manufactures and releases morphinelike substances called endorphins (see Snyder, 1977). Among many possible functions, these substances are thought to act as natural pain killers. For example, acupuncture may relieve pain because the acupuncture needles stimulate a release of endorphins in the brain. It also is thought that endorphins are responsible for reducing pain for long-distance runners and may produce the "runner's high."

Gintzler (1980) studied changes in pain threshold during pregnancy and examined how these changes are related to endorphin activity. Gintzler tested pregnant rats in several sessions spaced at regular intervals throughout their pregnancies (a rat's pregnancy lasts only 3 weeks). In a test session, a rat received a series of foot shocks that increased in intensity. The intensity of shock that elicited a jump response was recorded as the index of pain threshold. In general, the rats showed less sensitivity to shock (increased thresholds) as the pregnancy progressed. The change in threshold from one session to another was gradual, up until just a day or two before birth of the pups. At that point there was an abrupt increase in pain threshold. Gintzler also found evidence that the change in pain sensitivity was due to enhanced activity of endorphins. Perhaps a natural pain-killing mechanism

prepares these animals for the stress of giving birth.

You should recognize Gintzler's experiment as an example of a repeated-measures design: each rat was observed repeatedly at several different times during the course of pregnancy. You also should recognize that it would be inappropriate to use the repeated-measures t statistic to evaluate the data because each subject is measured in *more than* 2 conditions. As noted in Chapter 13, whenever the number of levels of a treatment is greater than 2, analysis of variance (ANOVA) should be performed rather than multiple t tests. Because each t test has a risk of Type I error, doing several t tests would result in an unacceptably large experimentwise alpha level, making the probability of a Type I error for the entire set of tests undesirably high. The ANOVA, on the other hand, provides a single test statistic the (F-ratio) for the experiment.

In this chapter we will examine how the repeated-measures design is analyzed with ANOVA. As you will see, many of the notational symbols and computations are the same as those used for the independent-measures ANOVA. In fact, your best preparation for this chapter is a good understanding of the basic ANOVA procedure presented in Chapter 13.

14.1 OVERVIEW

In the previous chapter we introduced the statistical technique of analysis of variance, and we examined how this hypothesis-testing procedure is used for independent-measures experimental designs. In this chapter we will examine how data from a repeated-measures experiment are evaluated using ANOVA. You should recall that an independent-measures design uses a separate sample for each treatment condition. A repeated-measures experiment, on the other hand, uses a single sample, so that the same individuals are measured in each of the treatment conditions. In both experimental designs, ANOVA is used to determine whether or not the sample data provide evidence of mean differences between two or more treatment conditions. As always, the null hypothesis states that there are no mean differences among the treatments: In symbols,

$$H_0 : \quad \mu_1 = \mu_2 = \mu_3 = \cdots$$

The alternative hypothesis states that the treatments are not all the same. As before, we will not list all the possible alternative hypotheses but rather will simple state

$$H_1 : \quad \text{At least one treatment mean is different from the others}$$

When repeated-measures designs were first introduced in Chapter 11, we noted that this type of experiment is particularly useful when a researcher wants to examine how behavior changes over time or across different treatment conditions in the same individuals. As a result, repeated-measures designs are used commonly to examine development (over time), to chart the course of learning (at different levels of practice), or simply to examine performance under different conditions. We also noted in Chapter 11 that a repeated-measures experiment has the advantage of being more powerful than an independent-measures design because it eliminates individual differences. Because the same individuals are tested in each treatment condition, differences between treatments cannot be attributed to differences between groups of subjects.

As we shall see, many of the notational symbols and computations for repeated-measures ANOVA are identical to those used for the independent-measures design. In fact, the repeated-measures ANOVA can be viewed as a two-stage process where the first stage is exactly the same analysis that was used for the independent-measures analysis (Chapter 13). However, the fact that the repeated-measures analysis eliminates individual differences will produce a fundamental change in the structure of the final F-ratio. To introduce this change, we will begin with the general logic of the repeated-measures ANOVA and then look at the details of notation and formulas.

14.2 THE LOGIC OF REPEATED-MEASURES ANOVA

ANOVA evaluates mean differences between two or more treatments by comparing the actual differences versus the amount of difference that would be expected by chance. This comparison is made in an F-ratio, which is a ratio of two variances.

$$F = \frac{\text{variance between treatments}}{\text{variance due to chance}} \tag{14.1}$$

$$= \frac{\text{variance (differences) between treatments}}{\text{variance (differences) expected by sampling error}}$$

As with the independent-measures ANOVA, a large value for the F-ratio indicates that the sample mean differences are more than would be expected by chance. We will examine in more detail the two variance components that comprise the numerator and denominator of the F-ratio.

VARIANCE BETWEEN TREATMENTS

The variance between treatments provides a measure of the actual mean differences between treatment conditions in an experiment. What might cause the scores in one treatment to be different from scores in another treatment? For a repeated-measures design, there are only two answers to this question.

1. Treatment Effect. It is possible that the different treatment conditions actually do produce different effects and therefore cause the individuals' scores to be higher (or lower) in one condition than in another. Remember, the purpose of the experiment is to determine whether or not a treatment effect exists.

2. Experimental Error. Any time behavior is measured, error may be introduced. The error may be inherent in the accuracy of the measurement tools, or it might be attributed to uncontrolled conditions in the laboratory, such as noises or changes in room temperature. This kind of uncontrolled and unsystematic error may cause the individuals' scores in one condition to be different from their scores in another condition.

Notice that we have not listed "individual differences" as a possible explanation for variance between treatments. Remember, a repeated-measures design uses the same individuals in every treatment condition, so any differences between treatments cannot be attributed to individual differences.

VARIANCE DUE TO CHANCE: THE ERROR TERM

The error term (denominator of the F-ratio) is intended to provide a measure of the amount of variance expected by chance. In addition, the error term is intended to produce a balanced F-ratio when the null hypothesis is true and there is no treatment effect. For the repeated-measures ANOVA, this means that the denominator of the F-ratio should provide a measure of variance due to experimental error, so the final F-ratio has the following structure:

$$F = \frac{\text{treatment effect} + \text{experimental error}}{\text{experimental error}} \tag{14.2}$$

Notice that when the treatment effect is zero, the top and bottom of the F-ratio are measuring the same variance, and the expected value of F is 1.00.

To obtain a measure of variance due to experimental error, we begin with the variance within treatments. You should recall that the differences (or variance) inside each treatment condition come from two sources:

1. Individual Differences. Within each treatment, the scores come from different individuals.

2. Experimental Error. This uncontrolled and unsystematic error always could be the source of differences between scores.

The denominator of the repeated-measures F-ratio requires a measure of variance that is due *only* to experimental error. To obtain this measure, we will analyze the within-treatments variability into two separate components: the variance from individual differences and the variance from experimental error.

Figure 14.1 summarizes the complete analysis of variance for a repeated-measures design. Note that the analysis consists of a two-stage process. In the first stage, the total variance is partitioned into two components: (1) variance

Figure 14.1

The partitioning of variability for a repeated-measures experiment.

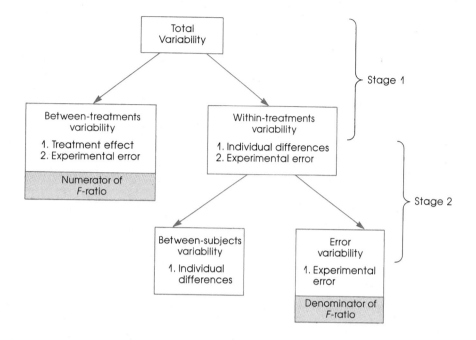

between treatments, and (2) variance within treatments. This stage is identical to the analysis we conducted for an independent-measures design (see Chapter 13). The second stage of the analysis is necessary to separate individual differences and experimental error. This is accomplished by computing the variance between subjects and subtracting it from the variance within treatments. The residual, error variance, provides a measure of experimental error and is used as the error term in the *F*-ratio.

The term *residual* is often used in place of *error*.

LEARNING CHECK

1. What sources contribute to between-treatments variability for the repeated-measures design?

2. What sources of variability contribute to within-treatments variability?

3. **a.** Describe the structure of the *F*-ratio for a repeated-measures ANOVA.

   b. Compare it to the *F*-ratio structure for the independent-measures ANOVA (Chapter 13). How do they differ?

4. In the second stage of analysis, within-treatments variability is partitioned into _____ variability and _____ variability.

ANSWERS

1. treatment effect, experimental error

2. individual differences, experimental error

3. **a.** $F = \dfrac{\text{treatment effect} + \text{experimental error}}{\text{experimental error}}$

b. For the independent-measures ANOVA, individual differences contribute variability to both between-treatments variability and the error term of the F-ratio.

4. between-subjects variability, error variability

14.3 NOTATION AND FORMULAS FOR REPEATED-MEASURES ANOVA

We will use the data in Table 14.1 to help introduce the notation and formulas for the repeated-measures ANOVA. The data represent manual dexterity scores for a sample of $n = 4$ people measured over a series of three practice sessions. The goal of the experiment is to examine changes in manual dexterity performance (dependent variable) as a function of practice (independent variable). Most of the notation for a repeated-measures study is identical to the notation used in an independent-measures experiment. The following list reviews the notation system.

1. The letter k identifies the number of treatment conditions. For Table 14.1, $k = 3$.

2. The number of scores in each treatment is identified by the lowercase letter n. For a repeated-measures study, n is the same for all treatments because the same sample is used in all treatments. In Table 14.1, $n = 4$.

3. The total number of scores in the entire experiment is identified by an uppercase N. For these data, $N = 12$.

Remember, we are using T and G to help differentiate ΣX for treatments and ΣX for the entire set of scores.

4. The sum of all the scores in the experiment is G. The value of G corresponds to ΣX for all N scores and specifies the grand total for the experiment. For Table 14.1, $G = 36$.

5. The sum of the scores in each treatment condition is identified by the letter T, for treatment total.

6. We also identify the sum of squares for each treatment (SS) and the sum of the squared scores (ΣX^2) for the entire experiment.

Table 14.1

Manual dexterity scores as a function of amount of practice (Test session)

	TEST SESSION			
PERSON	SESSION 1	SESSION 2	SESSION 3	P
A	3	3	6	12
B	2	2	2	6
C	1	1	4	6
D	2	4	6	12
	$T_1 = 8$	$T_2 = 10$	$T_3 = 18$	
	$SS_1 = 2$	$SS_2 = 5$	$SS_3 = 11$	
$G = 36$	$\Sigma X^2 = 140$	$k = 3$ $n = 4$	$N = 12$	

7. The repeated-measures design includes one new notational symbol. The total of the scores for each individual is identified by the letter P, for "person total." In Table 14.1, person A has scores of 3, 3, and 6, so the total for this person is $P = 12$. The P values are used to help measure individual differences in the analysis.

FORMULAS FOR REPEATED-MEASURES ANOVA

The F-ratio for ANOVA requires two measures of sample variance: between-treatments variance and error variance. As always, sample variance is computed by

$$\text{sample variance} = s^2 = \frac{SS}{df}$$

To compute each of the variances in the F-ratio we will need an SS value and a df value. These values are obtained by conducting a complete analysis of the sum of squares following the outline shown in Figure 14.1 and a separate analysis of degrees of freedom. These two analyses are described in detail in the following sections.

ANALYSIS OF THE SUM OF SQUARES (SS)

We will continue to use the data in Table 14.1 to demonstrate the ANOVA formulas. As shown in Figure 14.2, the repeated-measures ANOVA can be viewed as a two-stage process. The first stage of the analysis separates the total variability into two components: between treatments and within treatments. This stage of the analysis is exactly the same as the process used for an independent-measures experiment (Chapter 13).

Stage 1 The first step in the analysis of SS is to compute SS_{total}, which measures the total variability for the entire set of N scores.

Figure 14.2

The partitioning of sum of squares (SS) for a repeated-measures analysis of variance.

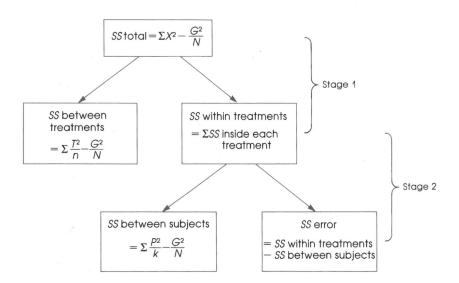

$$SS_{total} = \Sigma X^2 - \frac{G^2}{N} \qquad (14.3)$$

Using this formula for the data in Table 14.1, we obtain

$$SS_{total} = 140 - \frac{(36)^2}{12}$$

$$= 140 - 108 = 32$$

The next step is to partition SS_{total} into two components: between treatments and within treatments (see Figure 14.2). The $SS_{between\ treatments}$ measures the mean differences among the treatment conditions and is computed using the treatment totals (T's). The formula for this SS value is

$$SS_{between\ treatments} = \Sigma \frac{T^2}{n} - \frac{G^2}{N} \qquad (14.4)$$

For the data in Table 14.1, we obtain

$$SS_{between\ treatments} = \frac{8^2}{4} + \frac{10^2}{4} + \frac{18^2}{4} - \frac{36^2}{12}$$

$$= 16 + 25 + 81 - 108$$

$$= 14$$

The $SS_{within\ treatments}$ measures the variability inside the treatment conditions. To compute this value, we simply add the SS values from each of the separate treatment conditions.

$$SS_{within\ treatments} = \Sigma SS_{inside\ each\ treatment} \qquad (14.5)$$

For the experiment in Table 14.1, we obtain

$$SS_{within\ treatments} = 2 + 5 + 11$$

$$= 18$$

To check your calculations, you should always compute all three SS values and verify that the two components add up to the total.

This completes the first stage of the analysis (see Figure 14.2). You should notice that the formulas and computations up to this point are identical to those of the independent-measures ANOVA. You also should note that the two SS components (between and within) add up to the total SS.

Stage 2 The second stage of the analysis involves partitioning the SS_{within} into two components: $SS_{between\ subjects}$ and SS_{error} (see Figure 14.2). As you will see, we actually compute only $SS_{between\ subjects}$ and then subtract this value from SS_{within}. The residual is SS_{error}.

Because the same individuals are used in every treatment in a repeated-measures experiment, it is possible to measure the variability due to individual differences. If you examine the data in Table 14.1, you will notice that some individuals tend to have higher scores than others. These individual differences are reflected in the P values, or person totals. To evaluate the individual differences, we compute an $SS_{between\ subjects}$ that measures the variability among the person totals, the P values. The formula for $SS_{between\ subjects}$ is

14.1

THE RELATION BETWEEN
$SS_{\text{between subjects}}$ AND $SS_{\text{between treatments}}$

THE DATA for a repeated-measures experiment are normally presented in a matrix, with the treatment conditions determining the columns and the subjects defining the rows. The data in Table 14.1 provide an example of this normal presentation. The calculation of $SS_{\text{between treatments}}$ is intended to provide a measure of the variability, or differences between the treatments—that is, a measure of the mean differences between *columns* in the data matrix. For the data in Table 14.1, the column totals are 8, 10, and 18. These values are variable, and $SS_{\text{between treatments}}$ measures the amount of variability.

The following table reproduces the data from Table 14.1, but now we have turned the data matrix sidewise so that the subjects define the columns and the treatment conditions define the rows.

In this new form, the variability, or differences between the columns, represents the between-subject variability. The calculation of $SS_{\text{between subjects}}$ now has exactly the same structure as the original calculation of $SS_{\text{between treatments}}$. The column totals are now P values (instead of T values), and the number of scores in each column is now identified by k (instead of n); except for this change in notation, the formula for $SS_{\text{between subjects}}$ is exactly the same as the formula for $SS_{\text{between treatments}}$. For these data, the person totals (column totals) are 12, 6, 6, and 12. These values are variable, and $SS_{\text{between subjects}}$ measures the amount of variability.

		PERSON			
SESSION	A	B	C	D	
1	3	2	1	2	$T = 8$
2	3	2	1	4	$T = 10$
3	6	2	4	6	$T = 18$
	$P = 12$	$P = 6$	$P = 6$	$P = 12$	

$$SS_{\text{between subjects}} = \Sigma \frac{P^2}{k} - \frac{G^2}{N}$$

(14.6)

Notice that the formula for $SS_{\text{between subjects}}$ is similar in structure to the formula for $SS_{\text{between treatments}}$ (see Box 14.1). The person totals (P values) are used instead of treatment totals (T values). Each P value is divided by the number of scores that were added together to obtain P, or by k. Remember, each person was measured repeatedly, once for each treatment. There are k treatment conditions, and thus k scores are used to get a person total. For the example, $SS_{\text{between subjects}}$ is

$$SS_{\text{between subjects}} = \Sigma \frac{P^2}{k} - \frac{G^2}{N}$$
$$= \frac{12^2}{3} + \frac{6^2}{3} + \frac{6^2}{3} + \frac{12^2}{3} - \frac{36^2}{12}$$
$$= 48 + 12 + 12 + 48 - 108$$
$$= 120 - 108$$
$$= 12$$

The final step in the analysis is to obtain SS_{error} by subtracting $SS_{between\ subjects}$ from SS_{within} (see Figure 14.2).

$$SS_{error} = SS_{within\ treatments} - SS_{between\ subjects} \qquad (14.7)$$

Substituting the values we have already obtained for SS_{within} and $SS_{between\ subjects}$ into the formula, we obtain

$$SS_{error} = 18 - 12$$
$$= 6$$

Subtracting the variability due to individual differences from $SS_{within\ treatments}$ is the easiest way to compute SS_{error}.

ANALYSIS OF DEGREES OF FREEDOM (DF) Each of the SS values in analysis of variance has a corresponding degrees of freedom. In general terms, SS measures the variability for a set of "things," such as scores, treatment totals, people, and so on, and the df value for each SS is determined by the number of items minus one. For a set of n scores, for example, $df = n - 1$. The df formulas for the first stage of the repeated-measures analysis are identical to those in the independent-measures ANOVA. Figure 14.3 presents the complete analysis of degrees of freedom. You may want to refer to this figure as you read the following section on df formulas.

Stage 1 Remember, the total SS measures the variability for the entire set of N scores. The total df is computed by

$$df_{total} = N - 1 \qquad (14.8)$$

For the data in Table 14.1,

$$df_{total} = 12 - 1$$
$$= 11$$

Figure 14.3

The partitioning of degrees of freedom for a repeated-measures experiment.

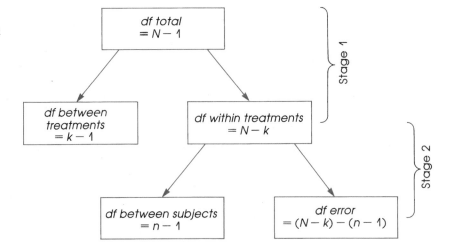

The between-treatments SS is based on the k treatment totals (T's), and the corresponding df is

$$df_{\text{between treatments}} = k - 1 \tag{14.9}$$

For the data in Table 14.1,

$$
\begin{aligned}
df_{\text{between treatments}} &= 3 - 1 \\
&= 2
\end{aligned}
$$

The within-treatments SS was obtained by summing the SS values for each of the treatment conditions. Each of these SS values has $df = n - 1$, and $df_{\text{within treatments}}$ is obtained by summing these df values.

$$df_{\text{within}} = \Sigma (n - 1) = N - k \tag{14.10}$$

For the data in Table 14.1,

$$
\begin{aligned}
df_{\text{within}} &= 12 - 3 \\
&= 9
\end{aligned}
$$

This completes the first stage of the analysis of degrees of freedom (see Figure 14.3). As always, you should check that the two components (between and within) add up to the total.

Stage 2   In the second stage of the analysis, the variability within treatments is partitioned into two components: between subjects and error. The between-subjects SS measures the variability among the person totals, the P values. Because the number of P values is n, the between-subjects df is given by

$$df_{\text{between subjects}} = n - 1 \tag{14.11}$$

Using the data from Table 14.1,

$$
\begin{aligned}
df_{\text{between subjects}} &= 4 - 1 \\
&= 3
\end{aligned}
$$

The final step in the analysis is to find df for the error variance. Remember, the variability due to error is not computed directly but rather is defined as the residual that is left when you subtract between-subject variability (individual differences) from the within-treatments variability. We obtain df_{error} in exactly the same manner.

$$
\begin{aligned}
df_{\text{error}} &= df_{\text{within}} - df_{\text{between subjects}} \\
&= (N - k) - (n - 1)
\end{aligned}
\tag{14.12}
$$

For the data in Table 14.1,

$$
\begin{aligned}
df_{\text{error}} &= 9 - 3 \\
&= 6
\end{aligned}
$$

CALCULATION OF THE VARIANCES (*MS*) AND THE *F*-RATIO

The *F*-ratio is a ratio of two variances. These variances, called mean squares (*MS*), are obtained by dividing a sum of squares by degrees of freedom. The *MS* in the numerator of the *F*-ratio, in part, is influenced by the amount of treatment effect that is present. This is the between treatments *MS*, and it is calculated by dividing the between-treatments *SS* by between-treatments *df*:

$$MS_{\text{between treatments}} = \frac{SS_{\text{between treatments}}}{df_{\text{between treatments}}} \tag{14.13}$$

The error term of the *F*-ratio consists of MS_{error} for a repeated-measures ANOVA. This *MS* is computed by dividing the error *SS* by the error *df*:

$$MS_{\text{error}} = \frac{SS_{\text{error}}}{df_{\text{error}}} \tag{14.14}$$

The *F*-ratio therefore consists of

$$F = \frac{MS_{\text{between treatments}}}{MS_{\text{error}}} \tag{14.15}$$

Once again, notice that the repeated-measures *F*-ratio uses MS_{error} as an error term in place of MS_{within}. The new error term is used because it maintains the expected *F*-ratio of 1.00 if the null hypothesis is true. This is confirmed when the structure of the repeated-measures *F*-ratio is examined:

$$F = \frac{\text{treatment effect} + \text{experimental error}}{\text{experimental error}}$$

When H_0 is true, the treatment effect will be zero, and the expected value of the *F*-ratio is 1.00. Alternatively, when H_0 is false, the presence of a treatment effect in the numerator of the *F*-ratio should give us a large value that falls in the critical region.

For the data in Table 14.1, we obtain the following *MS* values:

$$MS_{\text{between treatments}} = \frac{SS_{\text{between treatments}}}{df_{\text{between treatments}}}$$
$$= \frac{14}{2}$$
$$= 7$$

$$MS_{\text{error}} = \frac{SS_{\text{error}}}{df_{\text{error}}}$$
$$= \frac{6}{6}$$
$$= 1$$

The *F*-ratio for the example is obtained by dividing the between-treatments *MS* by the error *MS*:

$$F = \frac{MS_{\text{between treatments}}}{MS_{\text{error}}}$$

$$= \frac{7}{1}$$

$$= 7$$

The degrees of freedom for the F-ratio are determined by the two variances that form the numerator and denominator. For the repeated-measures ANOVA, the numerator and denominator are between treatments and error, respectively. The df values for the F-ratio are reported as

$$df = df_{\text{between treatments}}, \, df_{\text{error}}$$

Therefore, the df values associated with the repeated-measures F-ratio in our example are

$$df = 2, 6$$

Caution! A very common mistake is to use the value of within-treatments df instead of error df. Remember, the error term for a repeated-measures ANOVA is not the same as that of an independent-measures ANOVA.

The obtained F-ratio is evaluated by the same general procedure used for the independent-measures ANOVA. The experimenter must consult the F distribution table (page A-26) to find the critical value of F. The df values printed across the top of the table are values for the df associated with the numerator of the F-ratio (between-treatments df). The column on the left-hand side of the table contains df values associated with the denominator of the F-ratio. For a repeated-measures ANOVA, this value is the error df.

LEARNING CHECK

1. $SS_{\text{within treatments}} - SS_{\text{between subjects}} =$ _____

2. What two df components are associated with the repeated-measures F-ratio? How are they computed?

3. For the following set of data, compute all of the SS components for a repeated-measures ANOVA:

SUBJECT	TREATMENT				
	1	2	3	4	
A	2	2	2	2	$G = 32$
B	4	0	0	4	$\Sigma X^2 = 96$
C	2	0	2	0	
D	4	2	2	4	

4. Which two MS components are used to form the F-ratio of the repeated-measures ANOVA? How are they computed?

ANSWERS

1. SS_{error}

2. between-treatments df and error df; $df_{\text{between treatments}} = k - 1$; $df_{\text{error}} = (N - k) - (n - 1)$

3. $SS_{\text{total}} = 32$, $SS_{\text{between treatments}} = 10$, $SS_{\text{within treatments}} = 22$, $SS_{\text{between subjects}} = 8$, $SS_{\text{error}} = 14$

4. between treatments MS and error MS;

$$MS_{\text{between treatments}} = \frac{SS_{\text{between treatments}}}{df_{\text{between treatments}}}$$

$$MS_{\text{error}} = \frac{SS_{\text{error}}}{df_{\text{error}}}$$

14.4 TESTING HYPOTHESES WITH THE REPEATED-MEASURES ANOVA

Let us consider a complete example of hypothesis testing with a repeated-measures study. This task will be accomplished in the four steps that should be familiar by now: (1) State hypotheses and set the alpha level, (2) compute *df* and locate the critical region, (3) compute the test statistic, and (4) evaluate the hypotheses.

EXAMPLE 14.1

Example 14.1 is analyzed with the Minitab command ANOVA (see Section 20.7).

A school psychologist would like to test the effectiveness of a behavior-modification technique in controlling classroom outbursts of unruly children. A teacher is instructed to use the response-cost technique. Every time a child disrupts the class, he or she is told that the behavior has cost him or her 10 minutes of free time. That is, the free-time period is shortened for each unruly act. For a sample of $n = 4$ children, the number of outbursts is measured for a day before the treatment is initiated and again 1 week, 1 month, and 6 months after the response-cost technique began. Note that the measurements taken after the response-cost technique is administered serve as a long-term follow-up on the effectiveness of the treatment. This underscores the usefulness of the repeated-measures design in evaluating the effectiveness of clinical treatments. The data are summarized in Table 14.2.

Table 14.2

The effect of response-cost treatment on the number of outbursts in class after different periods of time

SUBJECT	BEFORE TREATMENT	ONE WEEK AFTER	ONE MONTH AFTER	SIX MONTHS AFTER	P
A	8	2	1	1	12
B	4	1	1	0	6
C	6	2	0	2	10
D	8	3	4	1	16
	$T_1 = 26$	$T_2 = 8$	$T_3 = 6$	$T_4 = 4$	
	$SS_1 = 11$	$SS_2 = 2$	$SS_3 = 9$	$SS_4 = 2$	
	$n = 4$ $k = 4$	$N = 16$	$G = 44$	$\Sigma X^2 = 222$	

STEP 1 *State the hypotheses and select an alpha level.* According to the null hypothesis, the response-cost technique will be ineffective in producing a change in the number of classroom disruptions. In symbols the null hypothesis states that

$$H_0: \quad \mu_{\text{before}} = \mu_{1 \text{ week}} = \mu_{1 \text{ month}} = \mu_{6 \text{ months}}$$

The alternative hypothesis may take on many forms. Somewhere among the four levels of the treatment there will be a difference. Because there are a number of possibilities, the alternative hypothesis states that

$$H_1: \quad \text{At least one mean is different from the others}$$

For the level of significance, the experimenter selects $\alpha = .05$. In other words, the researcher is willing to take only a 5% chance of committing a Type I error.

STEP 2 *Find df and locate the critical region.* For a repeated-measures study, the degrees of freedom associated with the F-ratio are between-treatments df and error df. In this example,

We have computed only those df values that are needed to evaluate the F-ratio. However, it is useful to compute all df components of ANOVA in order to check the computations (see Figure 14.3).

$$df_{\text{between treatments}} = k - 1$$
$$= 4 - 1$$
$$= 3$$

$$df_{\text{error}} = (N - k) - (n - 1)$$
$$= (16 - 4) - (4 - 1)$$
$$= 12 - 3$$
$$= 9$$

Therefore, for this F-ratio $df = 3, 9$. Consulting the F distribution table for $\alpha = .05$, we observe that the critical region begins with $F = 3.86$. Figure 14.4 illustrates the distribution. An obtained F-ratio that exceeds this critical value justifies rejecting H_0.

STEP 3 *Compute the test statistic.* To compute the F-ratio, we must first calculate the values for SS, df, and MS. This analysis begins by finding the value for total SS.

$$SS_{\text{total}} = \Sigma X^2 - \frac{G^2}{N}$$
$$= 222 - \frac{44^2}{16}$$
$$= 222 - 121$$
$$= 101$$

Total variability is partitioned into between-treatments SS and within-treatments SS. For between-treatments variability, we get

Figure 14.4

The critical region in the *F* distribution for α = .05 and *df* = 3, 9.

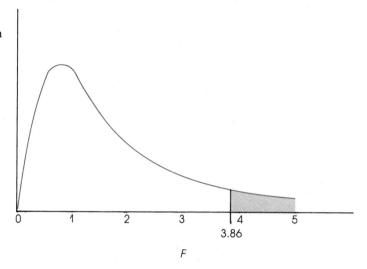

$$SS_{\text{between treatments}} = \Sigma \frac{T^2}{n} - \frac{G^2}{N}$$

$$= \frac{26^2}{4} + \frac{8^2}{4} + \frac{6^2}{4} + \frac{4^2}{4} - \frac{44^2}{16}$$

$$= 169 + 16 + 9 + 4 - 121$$

$$= 77$$

The first stage of the partitioning of variability is completed by computing within-treatments *SS*:

At this point of the analysis, the work may be checked to see if total *SS* equals between-treatments *SS* plus within-treatments *SS*.

$$SS_{\text{within treatments}} = \Sigma SS_{\text{inside each treatment}}$$

$$= 11 + 2 + 9 + 2$$

$$= 24$$

In the second stage of the analysis, within-treatments *SS* is partitioned into between-subjects *SS* and error *SS*. This analysis is accomplished by first calculating between-subjects *SS* and then subtracting it from within-treatments *SS*. The residual will be error *SS*:

$$SS_{\text{between subjects}} = \Sigma \frac{P^2}{k} - \frac{G^2}{N}$$

$$= \frac{12^2}{4} + \frac{6^2}{4} + \frac{10^2}{4} + \frac{16^2}{4} - \frac{44^2}{16}$$

$$= 36 + 9 + 25 + 64 - 121$$

$$= 13$$

$$SS_{\text{error}} = SS_{\text{within treatments}} - SS_{\text{between subjects}}$$

$$= 24 - 13$$

$$= 11$$

Finally, we can compute the *MS* values and then the *F*-ratio. The repeated-measures *F*-ratio uses between-treatments *MS* in the numerator and error *MS* in the denominator. These are readily obtained by dividing *SS* by the appropriate number of degrees of freedom:

$$MS_{\text{between treatments}} = \frac{SS_{\text{between treatments}}}{df_{\text{between treatments}}}$$

$$= \frac{77}{3}$$

$$= 25.67$$

$$MS_{\text{error}} = \frac{SS_{\text{error}}}{df_{\text{error}}}$$

$$= \frac{11}{9}$$

$$= 1.22$$

$$F = \frac{MS_{\text{between treatments}}}{MS_{\text{error}}}$$

$$= \frac{25.67}{1.22}$$

$$= 21.04$$

STEP 4   *Evaluate the hypotheses.* The obtained *F*-ratio is 21.04. This value falls in the critical region that begins at 3.86. The statistical decision is to reject the null hypothesis. The school psychologist may conclude that the response-cost technique had an effect on the number of disruptions. A report might state:

> There was a significant effect of response-cost training on the number of outbursts exhibited by the children, $F(3, 9) = 21.04$, $p < .05$.

The complete results of the analysis are summarized in Table 14.3.

POST HOC TESTS WITH REPEATED MEASURES   Recall that ANOVA provides an overall test of significance for the treatment. When the null hypothesis is rejected, it only indicates that there is a difference between at least two of the treatment means. If $k = 2$, it is obvious where the

Table 14.3

Analysis of variance summary for Example 14.1.

SOURCE	SS	df	MS	F
Between treatments	77	3	25.67	21.04
Within treatments	24	12		
Between subjects	13	3		
Error	11	9	1.22	
Total	101	15		

difference lies in the experiment. However, when k is greater than 2, the situation becomes more complex. To determine exactly where significant differences exist, the researcher must follow the ANOVA with post hoc tests. In Chapter 13 we used Tukey's HSD and the Scheffé test to make these multiple comparisons among treatment means. These two procedures attempt to control the overall alpha level by making adjustments for the number of potential comparisons.

For a repeated-measures ANOVA, Tukey's HSD and the Scheffé test can be used in the exact same manner as was done for the independent-measures ANOVA, *provided* that you substitute MS_{error} in place of MS_{within} in the formulas and use df_{error} in place of df_{within} when locating the critical value in a statistical table. It should be noted that statisticians are not in complete agreement about the appropriate error term in post hoc tests for repeated-measures designs (for an excellent discussion, see Keppel, 1973).

14.5 ADVANTAGES OF THE REPEATED-MEASURES DESIGN

When we first encountered the repeated-measures design (Chapter 11), it was noted that this type of experiment has certain advantages and disadvantages. On the bright side, a repeated-measures study may be desirable if the supply of subjects is limited. A repeated-measures experiment is economical in that the experimenter can get by using fewer subjects. However, the disadvantages may be very great. These take the form of carry-over effects, such as fatigue, that can make the interpretation of the data very difficult.

Now that we have examined the repeated-measures ANOVA, we can introduce another advantage, namely, the elimination of the role of variability due to individual differences. Consider the structure of the F-ratio for both the independent- and repeated-measures designs. For the independent-measures design, the F-ratio takes the following form:

$$F = \frac{\text{treatment effect} + \text{individual differences} + \text{experimental error}}{\text{individual differences} + \text{experimental error}}$$

The structure of the repeated-measures F-ratio reveals that the influence of individual differences has been eliminated altogether:

$$F = \frac{\text{treatment effect} + \text{experimental error}}{\text{experimental error}}$$

The removal of individual differences from the analysis becomes an advantage in situations where very large individual differences exist among the subjects being studied. When individual differences are extraordinarily large, the presence of a treatment effect may be masked if an independent-measures study is performed. In this case, a repeated-measures design would be more sensitive in detecting a treatment effect, because individual differences do not influence the value of the F-ratio.

This point will become evident in the following example. Suppose an experiment is performed in two ways, with an independent-measures design and a repeated-measures experiment. Also, let's suppose that we know how much variability is accounted for by the different sources of variance. For example,

$$\text{treatment effect} = 10 \text{ units of variance}$$

$$\text{individual differences} = 1000 \text{ units of variance}$$

$$\text{experimental error} = 1 \text{ unit of variance}$$

Notice that a very large amount of the variability in the experiment is due to individual differences. By comparing the F-ratios of both types of experiments, we will be able to see a fundamental difference between the two types of experimental designs. For the independent-measures experiment, we obtain

$$F = \frac{\text{treatment effect} + \text{individual differences} + \text{experimental error}}{\text{individual differences} + \text{experimental error}}$$

$$= \frac{10 + 1000 + 1}{1000 + 1}$$

$$= \frac{1011}{1001}$$

$$= 1.01$$

However, the repeated-measures F-ratio provides a different outcome:

$$F = \frac{\text{treatment effect} + \text{experimental error}}{\text{experimental error}}$$

$$= \frac{10 + 1}{1}$$

$$= \frac{11}{1}$$

$$= 11$$

All things (sources of variability) being equal, the repeated-measures F-ratio is larger. In this example, the F-ratio is much larger for the repeated-measures study because the individual differences, which are extremely large, have been removed (see Box 14.2). In the independent-measures ANOVA, the presence of a treatment effect is obscured by the influence of individual differences. This problem is remedied by the repeated-measures design in which variability due to individual differences has been partitioned out of the analysis. When the amount of individual differences is great, a repeated-measures experiment may provide a more sensitive test for a treatment effect. In statistical terms, a repeated-measures test has more *power* than an independent-measures test; that is, it is more likely to reject a false H_0.

TO GET some idea of a situation that results in a large MS_{error}, it is useful to examine hypothetical data in the form of a graph. Suppose an experimenter examines the effect of amount of reward on maze performance in rats. A sample of $n = 4$ rats that have learned to solve a maze is subsequently tested in all four reward conditions: 2, 4, 6, and 8 grams of food reward. The experimenter measures the speed with which they solve the maze after experiencing the new amount of reward. The broken line in Figure 14.5 represents a graph of the means of each treatment. The speed of maze running seems to increase with amount of reward.

Figure 14.5 also shows a set of hypothetical data for each individual (solid lines) that would produce the treatment means (broken line). Notice that there are individual differences in these data. The subject totals (P values) differ, indicating that some subjects generally run faster than others. Also note that the individual differences are consistent from one treatment to the next. For example, in all four treatment conditions subject 1 is fastest, and subject 2 is slowest. This means that much of the variability within treatments is due to consistent, predictable individual differences. When the individual differences are subtracted out of the analysis, the result will be a very small value for MS_{error}. Remember that a small value for MS_{error} will tend to produce a large value for the F-ratio, indicating a significant difference between treatments. The consistency in these data can be described in another way that may help you to understand the F-ratio. For the data in Figure 14.5 the effect of the treatment is consistent for all subjects: Every rat shows an increase in speed when the amount of reward is increased. Because the treatment effect is very consistent, you should expect to find a significant difference between treatments.

Figure 14.6 depicts another possibility for individual subjects. Although these data will produce the same treatment means as the previous example (Figure 14.5), the treatment effect is no longer consistent across subjects. Now when the amount of reward is increased, some subjects run faster, and some run slower. Because the treatment effect is not consistent, you should not expect to find significant differences between treatments. Also note that the data in Figure 14.6 do not show consistent individual differences from one treatment to another. For example,

subject 2 is the slowest rat in the first treatment but is the fastest in the second treatment. Because there are no consistent individual differences, most of the variability within treatments is due to experimental error. As a result, MS_{error} will be large and will tend to produce a relatively small F-ratio.

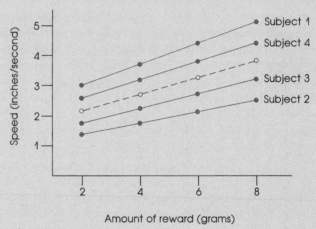

Figure 14.5

The effect of amount of reward on running speed. Treatment means are depicted by the broken line. Individual scores for each subject at each level of reward are shown by solid lines.

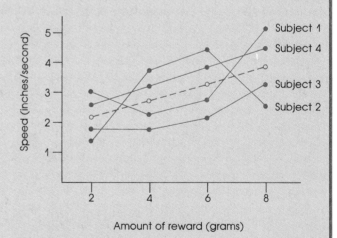

Figure 14.6

The effect of amount of reward on running speed. The treatment means are depicted by the broken line. Individual scores for each subject at each level of reward are shown by solid lines.

14.6 ASSUMPTIONS OF THE REPEATED-MEASURES ANOVA

The basic assumptions for the repeated-measures ANOVA are identical to those required for the independent-measures ANOVA.

1. The observations within each treatment condition must be independent (see page 255).

2. The population distribution within each treatment must be normal. (As before, the assumption of normality is important only with small samples.)

3. The variances of the population distributions for each treatment should be equivalent.

For the repeated-measures ANOVA, there is an additional assumption, called homogeneity of covariance. Basically, it refers to the requirement that the relative standing of each subject is maintained in each treatment condition. This assumption will be violated if the effect of the treatment is not consistent for all of the subjects or if carry-over effects exist for some but not other subjects. This issue is a very complex one and beyond the scope of this book. However, methods do exist for dealing with violations of this assumption (for a discussion, see Keppel, 1973).

LEARNING CHECK

1. It has been suggested that pupil size increases during emotional arousal. A researcher would therefore like to see if the increase in pupil size is a function of the type of arousal (pleasant versus aversive). A random sample of five subjects is selected for the study. Each subject views *all* three stimuli: neutral, pleasant, and aversive photographs. The neutral photograph portrays a plain brick building. The pleasant photograph consists of a young man and woman sharing a large ice cream cone. Finally, the aversive stimulus is a graphic photograph of an automobile accident. Upon viewing each stimulus, the pupil size is measured (in millimeters) with sophisticated equipment. The data are as follows. Perform an ANOVA and make a conclusion about the findings.

| | STIMULUS | | |
SUBJECT	NEUTRAL	PLEASANT	AVERSIVE
A	4	8	3
B	3	6	3
C	2	5	2
D	3	3	6
E	3	8	1

ANSWER

SOURCE	SS	df	MS	F
Between treatments	30	2	15	4.29
Within treatments	34	12		
Between subjects	6	4		
Error	28	8	3.5	
Total	64	14		

$F(2, 8) = 4.29$. For an alpha level of .05, the obtained F-ratio fails to reach statistical significance. The null hypothesis cannot be rejected. There is not sufficient evidence for an effect of stimulus type on pupil size.

SUMMARY

1. ANOVA for a repeated-measures design initially partitions total variability into between-treatments SS and within-treatments SS.

2. Between-treatments SS is influenced by the treatment effect and experimental error. Individual differences do not play a role in this source of variability because the same sample of subjects serves in all treatments.

3. Within-treatments SS is affected by individual differences and experimental error.

4. The structure of the repeated-measures F is

$$F = \frac{\text{treatment effect} + \text{experimental error}}{\text{experimental error}}$$

5. To obtain the error term for the F-ratio, within-treatments SS is partitioned into between-subjects SS and error SS.

6. Degrees of freedom are partitioned in a similar fashion. That is, there is a df value for each SS value in the analysis.

7. The estimated variances, or MS values, are computed by dividing each SS used in the F-ratio by the appropriate df value. For the repeated-measures ANOVA.

$$MS_{\text{between treatments}} = \frac{SS_{\text{between treatments}}}{df_{\text{between treatments}}}$$

$$MS_{\text{error}} = \frac{SS_{\text{error}}}{df_{\text{error}}}$$

8. The F-ratio for the repeated-measures ANOVA is computed by

$$F = \frac{MS_{\text{between treatments}}}{MS_{\text{error}}}$$

9. When the obtained F-ratio is significant (that is, H_0 is rejected), it indicates that a significant difference lies between at least two of the treatment conditions. To determine exactly where the difference lies, post hoc comparisons may be made. Post tests, such as Tukey's HSD, use MS_{error} rather than $MS_{\text{within treatments}}$ and df_{error} instead of $df_{\text{within treatments}}$.

10. A repeated-measures ANOVA eliminates the influence of individual differences from the analysis. If individual differences are extremely large, a treatment effect might be masked in an independent-measures experiment. In this case, a repeated-measures design might be a more sensitive test for a treatment effect.

KEY TERMS

between-treatments variability

within-treatments variability

between-subjects variability

error variability

treatment effect

individual differences

experimental error

mean squares

F-ratio

— *Focus on Problem Solving* ——————————

1. Before you begin a repeated-measures ANOVA, complete all the preliminary calculations needed for the ANOVA formulas. This requires that you find the total for each treatment (T's), the total for each person (P's), the grand total (G), the SS for each treatment condition, and ΣX^2 for the entire set of N scores. As a partial check on these calculations, be sure that the T values add up to G and that the P values have a sum of G.

2. To help remember the structure of repeated-measures ANOVA, keep in mind that a repeated-measures experiment eliminates the contribution of individual differences. There are no individual differences contributing to the numerator of the F-ratio ($MS_{\text{between treatments}}$) because the same individuals are used for all treatments. Therefore, you must also eliminate individual differences in the denominator. This is accomplished by partitioning within-treatments variability into two components: between-subjects variability and error variability. It is the MS value for error variability that is used in the denominator of the F-ratio.

3. As with any ANOVA, it helps to organize your work so you do not get lost. Compute the SS values first, followed by the df values. You can then calculate the MS values and the F-ratio. Filling in the columns on an ANOVA summary table (for example, page 405) as you do the computations will help guide your way through the problem.

4. Be careful when using df values to find the critical F value. Remember, df_{error} (*not* df_{within}) is used for the denominator.

— *Demonstration 14.1* ——————————

REPEATED-MEASURES ANOVA

The following data were obtained from an experiment examining the effect of sleep deprivation on motor-skills performance. A sample of five subjects was tested on a motor-skills task after 24 hours of sleep deprivation, tested again after 36 hours, and once more after 48 hours. The dependent variable is the number of errors made on the motor skills task.

SUBJECT	24 HOURS	36 HOURS	48 HOURS
A	0	0	6
B	1	3	5
C	0	1	5
D	4	5	9
E	0	1	5

Do these data indicate that the number of hours of sleep deprivation has a significant effect on motor skill performance?

STEP 1   *State the hypotheses and specify alpha.* The null hypothesis states that there are no differences among the three deprivation conditions. In symbols,

$$H_0: \quad \mu_1 = \mu_2 = \mu_3$$

The general form of the alternative hypothesis states that there are differences among the conditions.

$$H_1: \quad \text{At least one of the treatment means is different.}$$

We will set alpha at $\alpha = .05$.

STEP 2   *Locate the critical region.* To locate the critical region, we must obtain the df values for the F-ratio, specifically, $df_{\text{between treatments}}$ for the numerator and df_{error} for the denominator. (Often it is easier to postpone this step until the analysis of the df values in Step 3.)

$$df_{\text{between treatments}} = k - 1 = 3 - 1 = 2$$

$$
\begin{aligned}
df_{\text{error}} &= (N - k) - (n - 1) \\
&= (15 - 3) - (5 - 1) \\
&= 12 - 4 \\
&= 8
\end{aligned}
$$

Thus, the final F-ratio will have $df = 2, 8$. With $\alpha = .05$, the critical value for the F-ratio is $F = 4.46$. The obtained F-ratio must exceed this critical value to reject H_0.

STEP 3   *Perform the analysis.* The complete repeated-measures ANOVA can be divided into a series of stages:

1. Compute the summary statistics for the data. This involves calculating T and SS for each treatment condition, obtaining G and ΣX^2 for the entire set of scores, and finding the P totals for each person.
2. Perform the first stage of the analysis: Separate the total variability (SS and df) into the between- and within-treatment components.
3. Perform the second stage of the analysis: Separate the within-treatment variability (SS and df) into the between-subjects and error components.
4. Calculate the mean squares for the F-ratio.
5. Calculate the F-ratio.

Compute summary statistics. We will use the computational formula to obtain SS for each treatment condition. These calculations will also provide numerical values for the treatment totals (T), G, and ΣX^2.

24 HOURS		36 HOURS		48 HOURS	
X	X^2	X	X^2	X	X^2
0	0	0	0	6	36
1	1	3	9	5	25
0	0	1	1	5	25
4	16	5	25	9	81
0	0	1	1	5	25
$\Sigma X = 5$	$\Sigma X^2 = 17$	$\Sigma X = 10$	$\Sigma X^2 = 36$	$\Sigma X = 30$	$\Sigma X^2 = 192$

For the 24-hour condition,

$$T = \Sigma X = 5$$

$$SS = \Sigma X^2 - \frac{(\Sigma X)^2}{n} = 17 - \frac{5^2}{5} = 17 - 5 = 12$$

For the 36-hour condition,

$$T = \Sigma X = 10$$

$$SS = \Sigma X^2 - \frac{(\Sigma X)^2}{n} = 36 - \frac{10^2}{5} = 36 - 20 = 16$$

For the 48-hour condition,

$$T = \Sigma X = 30$$

$$SS = \Sigma X^2 - \frac{(\Sigma X)^2}{n} = 192 - \frac{30^2}{5} = 192 - 180 = 12$$

The grand total is obtained by summing the three treatment totals.

$$G = \Sigma T = 5 + 10 + 30 = 45$$

The value of ΣX^2 for the entire set of scores is obtained by summing the ΣX^2 values from each of the treatment conditions.

$$\Sigma X^2 = 17 + 36 + 192 = 245$$

The person totals, P values, are obtained by summing the three scores for each individual.

$$P_1 = 0 + 0 + 6 = 6$$

$$P_2 = 1 + 3 + 5 = 9$$

$$P_3 = 0 + 1 + 5 = 6$$

$$P_4 = 4 + 5 + 9 = 18$$

$$P_5 = 0 + 1 + 5 = 6$$

Stage 1 of the analysis. We begin by analyzing SS:

$$SS_{total} = \Sigma X^2 - \frac{G^2}{N} = 245 - \frac{45^2}{15} = 245 - 135 = 110$$

$$SS_{between} = \Sigma \frac{T^2}{n} - \frac{G^2}{N} = \frac{5^2}{5} + \frac{10^2}{5} + \frac{30^2}{5} - \frac{45^2}{15}$$
$$= 5 + 20 + 180 - 135$$
$$= 205 - 135$$
$$= 70$$

$$SS_{within} = \Sigma SS_{each\ treatment} = 12 + 16 + 12 = 40$$

For this stage, the *df* values are:

$$df_{total} = N - 1 = 15 - 1 = 14$$
$$df_{between} = k - 1 = 3 - 1 = 2$$
$$df_{within} = N - k = 15 - 3 = 12$$

Stage 2 of the analysis. We begin by analyzing SS_{within}.

$$SS_{between\ subjects} = \Sigma \frac{P^2}{k} - \frac{G^2}{N}$$
$$= \frac{6^2}{3} + \frac{9^2}{3} + \frac{6^2}{3} + \frac{18^2}{3} + \frac{6^2}{3} - \frac{45^2}{15}$$
$$= 171 - 135$$
$$= 36$$

$$SS_{error} = SS_{within} - SS_{between\ subjects}$$
$$= 40 - 36$$
$$= 4$$

For Stage 2, the *df* values are:

$$df_{between\ subjects} = n - 1 = 5 - 1 = 4$$
$$df_{error} = (N - k) - (n - 1)$$
$$= 12 - 4 = 8$$

Calculate the two MS values.

$$MS_{between} = \frac{SS_{between}}{df_{between}} = \frac{70}{2} = 35$$

$$MS_{error} = \frac{SS_{error}}{df_{error}} = \frac{4}{8} = 0.50$$

Calculate the F-ratio.

$$F = \frac{MS_{between}}{MS_{error}} = \frac{35}{0.50} = 70.00$$

STEP 4 *Make a decision about H_0 and state a conclusion.* The obtained F-ratio, $F = 70.00$, exceeds the critical value of 4.26. Therefore, we reject the null hypothesis. We conclude that the number of hours of sleep deprivation has a significant effect on the number of errors committed, $F(2, 8) = 70.00$, $p < .05$. The following table summarizes the results of the analysis.

SOURCE	SS	df	MS	
Between treatments	70	2	35	$F = 70.00$
Within treatments	40	12		
Between subjects	36	4		
Error	4	8	0.50	
Total	110	14		

PROBLEMS

1. What advantages does a repeated-measures design have over an independent-measures design?

2. How does the error term differ for repeated- versus independent-measures ANOVA?

3. It has been demonstrated that when subjects must memorize a list of words serially (in the order of presentation) words at the beginning and end of the list are remembered better than words in the middle. This observation has been called the *serial-position effect*. The following data represent the number of errors made in recall of the first eight, second eight, and last eight words in the list:

	SERIAL POSITION		
PERSON	FIRST	MIDDLE	LAST
A	1	5	0
B	3	7	2
C	5	6	1
D	3	2	1

   a. Compute the mean number of errors for each position and draw a graph of the data.
   b. Is there evidence for a significant effect of serial position? Test at the .05 level of significance. Based on the ANOVA, explain the results of the study.

4. A researcher reports an F-ratio with $df = 3, 36$ for a repeated-measures ANOVA.
   a. How many treatment conditions were evaluated in this experiment?

   b. How many subjects participated in this experiment?

5. A researcher conducts a repeated-measures experiment using a sample of $n = 12$ subjects to evaluate the differences among three treatment conditions. If the results are examined with an ANOVA, what would be the df values for the F-ratio?

6. The following data were obtained to compare three experimental treatments:

TREATMENTS		
1	2	3
2	4	6
5	5	5
1	2	3
0	1	2

   a. If these data were obtained from an *independent-measures design,* then could you conclude that there is a significant difference among the treatment conditions? Test with alpha set at .05.
   b. If these data were obtained from a *repeated-measures design,* so that each row of scores represents data from a single subject, then could you conclude that there is a significant difference among the treatments? Test at the .05 level of significance.
   c. Explain the difference in the results of part a and part b.

7. To determine the long-term effectiveness of relaxation training on anxiety, a researcher uses a repeated-measures study. A random sample of $n = 10$ subjects is first tested for the severity of anxiety with a standardized test. In addition to this pretest, subjects are tested again 1 week, 1 month, 6 months, and 1 year after treatment. The investigator used ANOVA to evaluate these data, and portions of the results are presented in the following summary table. Fill in the missing values. (*Hint:* Start with the *df* values.)

SOURCE	SS	df	MS	
Between treatments	___	___	___	$F = 5$
Within treatments	500	___		
Between subjects	___	___		
Error	___	___	10	
Total		___	___	

8. An educational psychologist is studying student motivation in elementary school. A sample of $n = 5$ students is followed over three years from fourth grade to sixth grade. Each year the students complete a questionnaire measuring their motivation and enthusiasm for school. The psychologist would like to know whether there are significant changes in motivation across the three grade levels. The data from this study are as follows:

STUDENT	FOURTH GRADE	FIFTH GRADE	SIXTH GRADE
A	4	3	1
B	8	6	4
C	5	3	3
D	7	4	2
E	6	4	0

a. Compute the mean motivation score for each grade level.
b. Use an ANOVA to determine whether there are any significant differences in motivation among the three grade levels. Use the .05 level of significance.

9. The following data represent a second sample of $n = 5$ students from the motivation study described in Problem 8.

STUDENT	FOURTH GRADE	FIFTH GRADE	SIXTH GRADE
A	10	0	4
B	0	10	0
C	4	6	0
D	14	0	6
E	2	4	0

a. Compute the mean motivation score for each grade level.
b. Use an ANOVA to determine whether there are any significant differences in motivation among the three grade levels. Use the .05 level of significance.
c. You should find that the means for these data are identical to the means obtained in Problem 8. How do you explain the fact that the two ANOVAs produce different results?

10. The following data represent idealized results from an experiment comparing two treatments. Notice that the mean for treatment II is 4 points higher than the mean for treatment I. Also notice that this 4-point treatment effect is perfectly consistent for all subjects.

PERSON	TREATMENTS	
	I	II
A	1	5
B	4	8
C	7	11
D	4	8
E	6	10
F	2	6
	$T = 24$	$T = 48$
	$\overline{X} = 4$	$\overline{X} = 8$

a. Calculate the within-treatments SS for these data.
b. Calculate the between-subjects SS for these data. You should find that all of the within-treatments variability is accounted for by variability between subjects; that is, $SS_{within} = SS_{between\ subjects}$. For these data, the treatment effect is perfectly consistent across subjects and there is no error variability ($SS_{error} = 0$).

11. A teacher studies the effectiveness of a reading skills course on comprehension. A sample of $n = 15$ students is studied. The instructor assesses their comprehension with a standardized reading test. The test

is administered at the beginning of the course, at midterm, and at the end of the course. The instructor uses analysis of variance to determine whether or not a significant change has occurred in the students' reading performance. The following summary table presents a portion of the ANOVA results. Provide the missing values in the table. (Start with *df* values.)

SOURCE	SS	df	MS	
Between treatments	___	___	24	F = 8
Within treatments	120	___		
Between subjects	___	___		
Error	___	___	___	
Total	___	___		

12. The following summary table presents the results of an ANOVA from a repeated-measures experiment comparing four treatment conditions with a sample of $n = 10$ subjects. Fill in all missing values in the table.

SOURCE	SS	df	MS	
Between treatments	___	___	20	F = ___
Within treatments	___	___		
Between subjects	36	___		
Error	___	___	___	
Total	150	___		

13. A researcher reports an *F*-ratio with $df = 2, 40$ from a repeated-measures experiment.
  a. How many treatment conditions were compared in this experiment?
  b. How many subjects participated in the experiment?

14. A psychologist studies the effect of practice on maze learning in rats. Rats are tested in the maze in one daily session for 4 days. The psychologist records the number of errors made in each daily session. The data are as follows:

	SESSION			
RAT	1	2	3	4
1	3	1	0	0
2	3	2	2	1
3	6	3	1	2

Is there evidence for a practice effect? Use the .05 level of significance.

15. A psychologist is asked by a dog food manufacturer to determine if animals will show a preference among three new food mixes recently developed. The psychologist takes a sample of $n = 6$ dogs. They are deprived of food overnight and presented simultaneously with three bowls of the mixes on the next morning. After 10 minutes, the bowls are removed, and the amount of food (in ounces) consumed is determined for each type of mix. The data are as follows:

	MIX		
SUBJECT	1	2	3
1	3	2	1
2	0	5	1
3	2	7	3
4	1	6	5
5	1	2	3
6	3	0	3

Is there evidence for a significant preference? Test at the .05 level of significance.

16. A repeated-measures experiment comparing only two treatments can be evaluated with either a *t* statistic or an ANOVA. As we found with the independent-measures design, the *t* test and the ANOVA will produce equivalent conclusions, and the two test statistics are related by the equation $F = t^2$.

The following data are from a repeated-measures study.

SUBJECT	TREATMENT 1	TREATMENT 2	DIFFERENCE
1	2	4	+2
2	1	3	+2
3	0	10	+10
4	1	3	+2

  a. Use a repeated-measures *t* statistic with $\alpha = .05$ to determine whether or not the data provide evidence of a significant difference between the two treatments.
  b. Use a repeated-measures ANOVA with $\alpha = .05$ to evaluate the data. (You should find $F = t^2$.) (*Caution:* ANOVA calculations are done with the *X* values, but for *t* you use the difference scores.)

17. The following data are from an experiment comparing three different treatment conditions:

A	B	C
0	1	2
2	5	5
1	2	6
5	4	9
2	8	8

  a. If the experiment uses an *independent-measures design,* then can the researcher conclude that the treatments are significantly different? Test at the .05 level of significance.
  b. If the experiment were done with a *repeated-measures design,* should the researcher conclude that the treatments are significantly different? Set alpha at .05 again.
  c. Explain why the results are different in the analyses of parts a and b.

18. A researcher used an analysis of variance to evaluate the results from a single-factor repeated-measures experiment. The reported *F*-ratio was $F(2, 28) = 6.35$.
  a. How many different treatments were compared in this experiment?
  b. How many subjects participated in the experiment?

19. A manufacturer of business machines would like to compare the four most popular brands of electric typewriters. A sample of eight typists is selected, and each typist spends 15 minutes testing each of the four typewriters and then rates its performance. The manufacturer would like to know if there are any significant differences among the four brands. The data from this study were examined using an analysis of variance. The results are shown in the following summary table. Fill in all missing values.

SOURCE	SS	df	MS	
Between treatments	270	___	___	*F* = 9
Within treatments	___	___		
Between subjects	___	___		
Error	___	___	___	
Total	680	___		

20. When a stimulus is presented continuously and it does not vary in intensity, the individual will eventually perceive the stimulus as less intense or not perceive it at all. This phenomenon is known as sensory adaptation. Years ago Zigler (1932) studied adaptation for skin (cutaneous) sensation by placing a small weight on part of the body and measuring how much time lapsed until subjects reported they felt nothing at all. Suppose a researcher does a similar study, comparing adaptation for four regions of the body for a sample of $n = 7$ subjects. A 500-milligram weight is gently placed on the region, and the latency (in seconds) for a report that it is no longer felt is recorded for each subject. The data are as follows:

	AREA OF STIMULATION			
SUBJECT	BACK OF HAND	LOWER BACK	MIDDLE OF PALM	CHIN BELOW LOWER LIP
1	6.5	4.6	10.2	12.1
2	5.8	3.5	9.7	11.8
3	6.0	4.2	9.9	11.5
4	6.7	4.7	8.1	10.7
5	5.2	3.6	7.9	9.9
6	4.3	3.5	9.0	11.3
7	7.4	4.8	10.8	12.6

Is there a significant effect of area of stimulation on the latency of adaptation? Set the alpha level to .01.

21. A scientist tests two drugs for their effects on insomnia. A sample of $n = 8$ insomniacs is pretested with a placebo before bedtime, and the latency to onset of sleep is measured to serve as a baseline. A week later, the subjects receive the first drug before bedtime, and the time that lapses between drug administration and sleep onset is measured again. Finally, a week later the second drug is tested in the same fashion. The latency to sleep onset (in minutes) is presented for each subject on every test. The data are as follows:

SUBJECT	PRETEST	DRUG 1	DRUG 2
E.B.	136	24	33
K.F.	92	107	21
T.Z.	117	98	111
J.R.	65	51	49
R.E.	129	29	37
A.G.	172	112	70
P.S.	89	122	145
D.W.	84	22	16

Is there a significant effect on latency? Test at the .05 level of significance.

22. A sample of 14-week-old infants is studied in a perception experiment. The infants are presented with three line drawings successively for 5 minutes each. The designs vary in their complexity. The researcher records how much time (in seconds) is spent viewing each of the stimuli. The data are as follows:

| | AMOUNT OF COMPLEXITY | | |
INFANT	LOW	MODERATE	HIGH
A	63	112	39
B	210	73	80
C	94	314	83
D	219	232	115
E	54	396	76
F	120	352	100

Is there a significant preference among the three stimuli? Test at the .01 level of significance.

23. An industrial psychologist examines the effect of hourly wages and piecework pay on productivity. A random sample of $n = 10$ workers is studied. These workers are assembling small circuit boards for appliances and are getting paid at an hourly rate. The psychologist records the number of circuit boards assembled in 1 day for this pay schedule. The workers are later switched to a piecework rate, in which they get paid according to the number of circuit boards assembled, not the number of hours worked. Again, the number of boards assembled is recorded for 1 day. The results are as follows:

SUBJECT	HOURLY RATE	PIECEWORK
1	74	82
2	59	70
3	70	63
4	67	91
5	79	87
6	61	75
7	80	96
8	72	68
9	69	60
10	57	67

a. Perform an ANOVA to determine if a significant effect occurred. Use the .05 level of significance.
b. Use a repeated-measures t test to analyze the data. Again, set alpha to .05. Compare the results of parts a and b. Remember, $F = t^2$ (Chapter 13).

24. A researcher is examining the effect of sleep deprivation on basic mental processes. A sample of eight subjects is obtained. These subjects agree to stay awake for a total of 48 hours. Every 12 hours the researcher gives each subject a series of arithmetic problems as a test of mental alertness. The number of problems worked correctly in 10 minutes is recorded for each subject. The data are as follows:

| | HOURS AWAKE | | | |
SUBJECT	12	24	36	48
1	8	7	8	6
2	10	12	9	11
3	9	9	8	10
4	7	8	6	6
5	12	10	10	8
6	10	9	12	8
7	7	7	6	8
8	9	10	11	11

On the basis of these data can the researcher conclude that sleep deprivation has a significant effect on basic mental processing? Test with $\alpha = .05$.

25. The researcher in Problem 24 also wanted to examine the subjects' own perceptions of their mental functioning. Immediately before the subjects started each set of arithmetic problems, they were asked to rate their own abilities using a scale from 10 (normal) to 1 (severely impaired). The data from this part of the experiment are as follows:

| | HOURS AWAKE | | | |
SUBJECT	12	24	36	48
1	10	9	6	2
2	9	8	5	5
3	10	8	7	3
4	10	9	6	4
5	9	7	6	2
6	8	9	4	1
7	9	8	7	2
8	9	7	6	4

a. Do these data indicate that subjects perceive a change in performance as they become more tired? Test with $\alpha = .05$.
b. Write a brief description of the results of the entire experiment, combining the data from Problem 24 and Problem 25.

CHAPTER 15

TWO-FACTOR ANALYSIS OF VARIANCE (INDEPENDENT MEASURES)

TOOLS YOU WILL NEED

The following items are considered essential background material for this chapter. If you doubt your knowledge of any of these items, you should review the appropriate chapter or section before proceeding.

- Introduction to analysis of variance (Chapter 13)
- The logic of analysis of variance
- ANOVA notation and formulas
- Distribution of *F*-ratios

CONTENTS

Imagine that you are seated at your desk, ready to take the final exam in statistics. Just before the exams are handed out, a television crew appears and sets up a camera and lights aimed directly at you. They explain that they are filming students during exams for a television special. You are told to ignore the camera and go ahead with your exam.

Would the presence of a TV camera affect your performance on an exam? For some of you, the answer to this question is "definitely yes" and for others, "probably not." In fact, both answers are right; whether or not the TV camera affects performance depends on your personality. Some of you would become terribly distressed and self-conscious, while others really could ignore the camera and go on as if everything were normal.

In an experiment that duplicates the situation we have described, Shrauger (1972) tested subjects on a concept formation task. Half the subjects worked alone (no audience), and half the subjects worked with an audience of people who claimed to be interested in observing the experiment. Shrauger also divided the subjects into two groups on the basis of personality: those high in self-esteem and those low in self-esteem. The dependent variable for this experiment was the number of errors on the concept formation task. Data similar to those obtained by Shrauger are shown in Figure 15.1. Notice that the audience had no effect on the high-self-esteem subjects. However, the low-self-esteem subjects made nearly twice as many errors with an audience as when working alone.

We have presented Shrauger's study as an introduction to experiments that have two independent variables. In this study, the independent variables are

1. Audience (present or absent)
2. Self-esteem (high or low)

The results of this study indicate that the effect of one variable (audience) depends on another variable (self-esteem).

You should realize that it is quite common to have experimental variables that interact in this way. For example, a particular drug may have a profound effect on some patients and have no effect whatsoever on others. Some children develop normally in a single-parent home, while others show serious difficulties. In general, the effects of a particular treatment often depend on other factors. To determine whether two variables are interdependent, it is necessary to examine both variables together in a single experiment. In this chapter we will introduce the experimental techniques that are used for experiments with two independent variables.

Figure 15.1

Results of an experiment examining the effect of an audience on the number of errors made in a concept formation task for subjects who are rated either high or low in self-esteem. Notice that the effect of the audience depends on the self-esteem of the subjects.

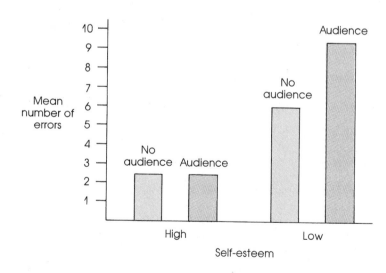

Shrauger, J.S. (1972). Self-esteem and reactions to being observed by others. *Journal of Personality and Social Psychology, 23,* 192–200. Copyright (1972) by the American Psychological Association. Adapted by permission of the author.

15.1 OVERVIEW

In the preceeding two chapters, we examined analysis of variance for research designs using a single independent variable. In this chapter, we consider research situations involving two independent variables—that is, two-factor experiments.

An example of a two-factor experiment is shown in Figure 15.2. This experiment compares two different programs for teaching third-grade mathematics and three different class sizes. Thus, the independent variables are teaching program and class size. The dependent variable is the mathematics achievement test score obtained for each child at the end of the school year. You should recall that the different values for each factor are called the *levels* of the factor. For this example, the program factor has two levels (program I and program II), and the class-size factor has three levels (18 students, 24 students, and 30 students).

Notice that the structure of a two-factor experiment can be represented by a matrix listing the values of one factor across the top and the values for the second factor down the left-hand side. Each box, or *cell*, in the matrix represents a specific treatment condition. For example, the lower left-hand cell in Figure 15.2 contains scores for those students who were taught by program II in a class containing 18 students.

The two-factor analysis of variance will allow the researcher to test for mean differences in this experiment. Specifically, the ANOVA will test for

1. Mean difference between the two teaching programs
2. Mean differences between the three class sizes
3. Any other mean differences that may result from unique combinations of a specific teaching program and a specific class size (For example, program I may be especially effective with a small class of only 18 students.)

Figure 15.2

The structure of a two-factor experiment presented as a matrix. The factors are teaching program and class size. There are two levels for the program factor (program I and program II), and there are three levels for the class-size factor (18 students, 24 students, and 30 students).

| | Factor B (class size) | | |
	18-student class	24-student class	30-student class
Program I	Scores for $n = 15$ subjects taught by program I in a class of 18	Scores for $n = 15$ subjects taught by program I in a class of 24	Scores for $n = 15$ subjects taught by program I in a class of 30
Program II	Scores for $n = 15$ subjects taught by program II in a class of 18	Scores for $n = 15$ subjects taught by program II in a class of 24	Scores for $n = 15$ subjects taught by program II in a class of 30

Factor B (program)

Thus, the two-factor ANOVA combines three separate hypothesis tests in one analysis. Each of these three tests will be based on its own F-ratio computed from the data. The three F-ratios will all have the same basic structure.

$$F = \frac{\text{variance (differences) between sample means}}{\text{variance (differences) expected from sampling error}}$$

As always in ANOVA, a large value for the F-ratio indicates that the sample mean differences are greater than chance. To determine whether the obtained F-ratios are *significantly* greater than chance, we will need to compare each F-ratio with the critical values found in the F-distribution table in Appendix B.

15.2 MAIN EFFECTS AND INTERACTIONS

As noted in the previous section, a two-factor ANOVA actually involves three distinct hypothesis tests. In this section, we will examine these three tests in more detail.

Traditionally, the two independent variables in a two-factor experiment are identified as *factor A* and *factor B*. For the experiment presented in Figure 15.2, teaching program would be factor A and class size would be factor B. The goal of the experiment is to evaluate the mean differences that may be produced by either of these factors independently or by the two factors acting together.

MAIN EFFECTS One purpose of the experiment is to determine whether differences in teaching program (factor A) result in differences in student performance. To answer this question, we will compare the mean score for all students taught in program I versus the mean score for students taught in program II. Notice that this process evaluates mean differences between the rows in Figure 15.2.

To make this process more concrete, we have presented a set of hypothetical data in Table 15.1. This table shows the mean score for each of the treatment conditions (cells) as well as the mean for each column (each class size) and for each row (teaching program). These data indicate that students in program I obtained an average test score of $\overline{X} = 79$. In contrast, program II resulted in a mean score of $\overline{X} = 69$. The differences between these

Table 15.1

Hypothetical data from an experiment examining two different teaching programs (factor A) and three different class sizes (factor B)

	18-STUDENT CLASS SIZE	24-STUDENT CLASS SIZE	30-STUDENT CLASS SIZE	
PROGRAM I	$\overline{X} = 85$	$\overline{X} = 77$	$\overline{X} = 75$	$\overline{X} = 79$
PROGRAM II	$\overline{X} = 75$	$\overline{X} = 67$	$\overline{X} = 65$	$\overline{X} = 69$
	$\overline{X} = 80$	$\overline{X} = 72$	$\overline{X} = 70$	

means constitutes what is called the *main effect* for programs, or the *main effect for factor A.*

Similarly, the main effect for factor B (class size) is defined by the mean differences between columns of the matrix. For the data in Table 15.1, students taught in a class of 18 obtained an average test score of $\overline{X} = 80$. Students in a class of 24 averaged only $\overline{X} = 72$, and students in a class of 30 achieved a mean score of $\overline{X} = 70$. The differences among these means constitute the *main effect* for class size, or the *main effect for factor B.*

DEFINITION   The mean differences among the levels of one factor are referred to as the *main effect* of that factor. If the design of the experiment is represented as a matrix with one factor determining the rows and the second factor determining the columns, then the main effect for the first factor would evaluate the mean differences among the rows, and the main effect for the second factor would evaluate the mean differences among the columns.

The evaluation of main effects will make up two of the three hypothesis tests contained in a two-factor ANOVA. We will state hypotheses concerning the main effect of factor A and the main effect of factor B and then calculate two separate F-ratios to evaluate the hypotheses.

For the example we are considering, factor A involves the comparison of two different teaching programs. The null hypothesis would state that there is no difference between the two programs—that is, teaching program has no effect on test performance. In symbols,

$$H_0: \quad \mu_{A1} = \mu_{A2}$$

The alternative hypothesis is that the two programs do produce different test scores:

$$H_1: \quad \mu_{A1} \neq \mu_{A2}$$

To evaluate these hypotheses, we will compute an F-ratio that compares the actual mean difference between the two programs versus the amount of difference that would be expected by chance (sampling error).

$$F = \frac{\text{variance (differences) between the means for factor } A}{\text{variance (differences) expected from sampling error}}$$

$$= \frac{\text{variance (differences) between row means}}{\text{variance (differences) expected by sampling error}}$$

Similarly, factor B involves the comparison of three different class sizes. The null hypothesis states that, overall, there are no differences among the three class sizes. In symbols,

$$H_0: \quad \mu_{B1} = \mu_{B2} = \mu_{B3}$$

As always, the alternative hypothesis states that there are differences:

$$H_1: \quad \text{At least one mean is different from the others.}$$

Again, the *F*-ratio will compare the obtained mean differences among the three class sizes versus the difference that would be expected by chance.

$$F = \frac{\text{variance (differences) between the means for factor } B}{\text{variance (differences) expected from sampling error}}$$

$$= \frac{\text{variance (differences) between column means}}{\text{variance (differences) expected by sampling error}}$$

INTERACTIONS In addition to evaluating the main effects for each of the two independent variables, the two-factor ANOVA allows you to evaluate other mean differences that may result from unique combinations of the two factors. For example, it is possible for the effects of a treatment depend on the specific circumstances under which it is administered. Or, it is possible that a treatment affects one group differently than it does another. When the effects of one treatment (factor) depend on a second treatment (factor), you have an *interaction*.

DEFINITION There is an *interaction* between two factors if the effect of one factor depends on the levels of the second factor. When the two factors are identified as *A* and *B*, the interaction is identified as the *A* × *B* interaction.

To make the concept of an interaction more concrete, we will reexamine the data shown in Table 15.1. For these data, there is no interaction. Specifically, the effect of the program variable (factor *A*) does not depend on class size (factor *B*). Overall, these data show a 10-point difference between the two programs, $\overline{X} = 79$ versus $\overline{X} = 69$. This 10-point difference is the main effect for program. Notice that this 10-point effect is *constant* for each of the three class sizes. That is, within each column of the matrix, you find exactly the same 10-point difference between the two programs. Thus, the program effect does not depend on class size and there is no interaction.

Now consider the data shown in Table 15.2. These new data show exactly the same main effects that existed in Table 15.1 (the column means and the row means have not been changed). But now there is an interaction between the two factors. Specifically, the 10-point main effect for the program ($\overline{X} = 79$ versus $\overline{X} = 69$) is *not constant* across the three class sizes: For classes of 18 students, there is zero difference between programs; with 24 students, there

Table 15.2

Hypothetical data from an experiment examining two different teaching programs (factor *A*) and three different class sizes (factor *B*). These data show the same main effects as the data in Table 15.1, but the individual treatment means have been modified to produce an interaction.

	18-STUDENT CLASS SIZE	24-STUDENT CLASS SIZE	30-STUDENT CLASS SIZE	
PROGRAM I	$\overline{X} = 80$	$\overline{X} = 77$	$\overline{X} = 80$	$\overline{X} = 79$
PROGRAM II	$\overline{X} = 80$	$\overline{X} = 67$	$\overline{X} = 60$	$\overline{X} = 69$
	$\overline{X} = 80$	$\overline{X} = 72$	$\overline{X} = 70$	

is a 10-point difference; and for classes of 30 students, the program difference is 20 points. For these data, the effect of factor A (program difference) does depend on class size (the levels of factor B), so there is an interaction.

Finally, consider the two graphs shown in Figure 15.3. The graph on the left-hand size of the figure shows the data from Table 15.1 (no interaction) and the graph on the right-hand side shows the data from Table 15.2 (interaction). Notice that when there is no interaction in a set of data, the lines in the graph are parallel. In the left-hand graph, the effect of programs (10-point difference) is constant across the three class sizes which results in a constant distance between the two lines. On the other hand, when there is an interaction, the lines in the graph will not be parallel. In the right-hand figure, the program effect (distance between the lines) varies from one class size to the next and the resulting lines are not parallel. In general, an easy way to spot an interaction is to look for lines that are not parallel—that is, look for lines that converge or cross.

To evaluate the interaction, the two-factor ANOVA first identifies mean differences between the treatment conditions that cannot be explained by the main effects. For the data in Table 15.1 [or Figure 15.3(a)], for example, the mean difference between the two cells in each column can be explained by the 10-point main effect for program. In this case, the overall 10-point difference between the two programs completely explains the difference between treatments for all of the three class sizes considered. By contrast, the data in Table 15.2 [or Figure 15.3(b)] show mean differences between treatment conditions that cannot be explained by the main effects. For example, the data show a 20-point difference between program I and

Figure 15.3

(a) Graph showing the data from Table 15.1 where there is no interaction. (b) Graph of the data from Table 15.2 showing an interaction between program and class size.

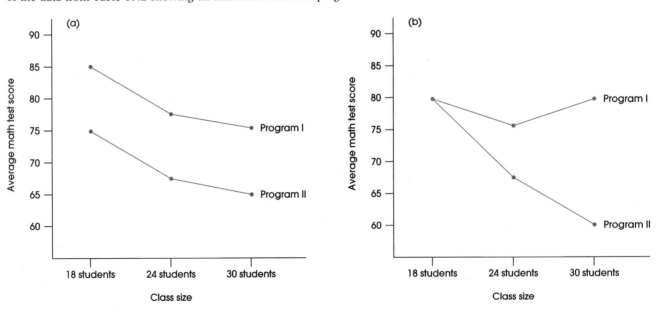

program II when classes contain 30 students. This 20-point difference cannot be explained by the 10-point main effect for programs. After these "extra" mean differences are identified, they are evaluated by an F-ratio with the following structure:

$$F = \frac{\text{variance (mean differences) not explained by main effects}}{\text{variance (differences) expected from sampling error}}$$

The null hypothesis for this F-ratio simply states that there is no interaction:

H_0: There is no interaction between factors A and B. The effect of factor A does not depend on the levels of factor B (and B does not depend on A).

The alternative hypothesis is that there is an interaction between the two factors:

H_1: The effect of one factor does depend on the levels of the other factor.

Thus, the two-factor ANOVA is composed of three distinct hypothesis tests:

1. The main effect of factor A (often called the A-effect)
2. The main effect of factor B (called the B-effect)
3. The interaction (called the $A \times B$ interaction)

In each case we are looking for mean differences between treatments that are larger than would be expected by chance and in each case the magnitude of the treatment effect will be evaluated by an F-ratio. Each of the three F-ratios will have the same basic structure:

$$F = \frac{\text{variance between treatments}}{\text{variance within treatments}}$$

The between-treatments variance is assumed to be caused by three things:

1. Treatment effect (either factor A, or factor B, or $A \times B$ interaction)
2. Individual differences (there are different subjects for each treatment condition)
3. Experimental error (there always is a margin of error in measurements)

The variability within treatments will provide a measure of the variability expected by chance. Differences within treatments are assumed to be caused by

1. Individual differences
2. Experimental error

With these components of variability in mind, the three F-ratios will all have the basic form:

$$F = \frac{\text{treatment effect} + \text{individual differences} + \text{experimental error}}{\text{individual differences} + \text{experimental error}}$$

The level of significance helps us decide if the value for the F-ratio is sufficiently larger than 1.00.

As always, a value of F near 1.00 indicates that there is no treatment effect (the numerator and denominator of F are nearly the same). A value of F much greater than 1.00 indicates that the treatment effect is real.

LEARNING CHECK

1. A researcher assesses verbal ability in children, both male and female, at 5 or 9 years of age. The mean test scores for the groups are as follows:

5-year-old males, $\bar{X} = 20$
5-year-old females, $\bar{X} = 22$
9-year-old males, $\bar{X} = 30$
9-year-old females, $\bar{X} = 45$

   a. Draw a graph of the data. (*Hint:* Put age on the X-axis and test score on the Y-axis. Use separate lines for males and females.)

   b. Judging from the graph, does there appear to be an interaction between age and sex? Explain your answer.

2. A two-factor ANOVA makes *three* hypothesis tests. What are they?

3. It is impossible to have an interaction unless there are also main effects present (True or false?)

ANSWERS **1. a.**

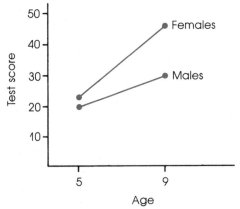

   b. The graph indicates an interaction because the lines are not parallel. The difference between males and females depends on age.

2. The three separate hypothesis tests in the two-factor ANOVA are the main effect for the first factor, main effect for the second factor, and the interaction between the two factors.

3. false

15.3 NOTATION AND FORMULAS

The general format for any two-factor experiment is shown in Figure 15.4. Notice that we have identified the factors by using the letters A and B. By convention, the number of levels of factor A is specified by the symbol a and the number of levels of factor B is specified by b. The $A \times B$ matrix gives a picture of the total experiment, with each cell corresponding to a specific treatment condition. In the example shown in Figure 15.4, $a = 2$ and $b = 3$, so we have a total of $ab = 2 \times 3 = 6$ different treatment conditions.

It is possible to use either an independent or a repeated-measures experimental design with a two-factor experiment. In this chapter, we will only look at independent-measures designs. By definition, independent measures means that there is a separate group of subjects for each treatment condition, that is, a separate sample for each cell in the experimental design. For the experiment shown in Figure 15.4, there are six treatment conditions, so we would need six different groups of subjects.

To develop the formulas for the two-factor analysis of variance, we must be able to specify all the totals, numbers, and SS values in the data. The notation system for the two-factor design is as follows:

1. G = the grand total of all the scores in the experiment
2. N = the total number of scores in the entire experiment
3. a = the number of levels of factor A
4. b = the number of levels of factor B
5. n = the number of scores in each treatment condition (in each cell of the $A \times B$ matrix)
6. The totals for each treatment condition will be specified by using the capital letters (A and B) that represent that condition. For example, A_1B_2 would represent the total of the scores in the cell where the level of A is 1 and the level of B is 2. When we want to talk in general about the cell totals, we will refer to the AB totals (without specifying a particular cell). Notice that there are n scores in each AB total.

In addition, A_1 will refer to the total of all the scores for subjects in the first level of factor A (all the scores in the first row of the $A \times B$ matrix). A_2 refers

---

Figure 15.4

Matrix showing the general design of a two-factor experiment. The factors are identified by the letters A and B. The levels of each factor are identified by adding numerals to the factor letters; for example, the third level of factor B is identified by B_3.

Factor B

		Level B_1	Level B_2	Level B_3
Factor A	Level A_1	Treatment (cell) A_1B_1	Treatment (cell) A_1B_2	Treatment (cell) A_1B_3
	Level A_2	Treatment (cell) A_2B_1	Treatment (cell) A_2B_2	Treatment (cell) A_2B_3

to the total for the second row, and so on. When speaking in general about the row totals, we will refer to the *A* totals. Notice that there are *bn* scores in each *A* total. In a similar way, B_1 will refer to the total of all the scores in the first column. In general, the column totals will be called *B* totals. Note that you add *an* scores to obtain each *B* total.

FORMULAS   The general structure for the analysis of a two-factor experiment is shown in Figure 15.5. At the first level of the analysis, the total variability is separated into two components: between-treatments variability and within-treatments variability. You should notice that this first stage is identical to the structure used for the single-factor analysis of variance in Chapters 13 and 14 (see Figures 13.4 and 14.1). The second level of the analysis partitions the between-treatments variability into separate components. With a two-factor experiment, the differences between treatment conditions (cells) could be caused by either of the two factors (*A* or *B*) or by the interaction. These three components are examined individually in the second stage of the analysis.

The goal of this analysis is to compute the variance values needed for the three *F*-ratios. We will need three between-treatments variances (one for factor *A*, one for factor *B*, and one for the interaction), and we will need a within-treatments variance. Each of these variances (or means squares) will be determined by a sum of squares value (*SS*) and a degrees of freedom value (*df*):

Remember, in ANOVA a variance is called a mean square, or MS.

$$\text{mean square} = MS = \frac{SS}{df}$$

The actual formulas for the two-factor analysis of variance are almost identical to the formulas for the single-factor analysis (Chapters 13 and 14). You may find it useful to refer to these chapters for a more detailed

Figure 15.5

Structure of the analysis for a two-factor analysis of variance.

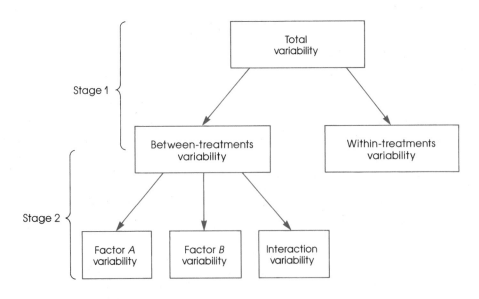

Table 15.3

Hypothetical data for a two-factor experiment with two levels of factor *A* and three levels of factor *B.*[a]

		FACTOR B			
		B_1	B_2	B_3	
		1	7	3	
		6	7	1	
		1	11	1	
	A_1	1	4	6	$A_1 = 60$
		1	6	4	
		$AB = 10$	$AB = 35$	$AB = 15$	
		$SS = 20$	$SS = 26$	$SS = 18$	
FACTOR A		0	0	0	
		3	0	2	
		7	0	0	
	A_2	5	5	0	$A_2 = 30$
		5	0	3	
		$AB = 20$	$AB = 5$	$AB = 5$	
		$SS = 28$	$SS = 20$	$SS = 8$	
		$B_1 = 30$	$B_2 = 40$	$B_3 = 20$	$N = 30$
					$G = 90$
					$\Sigma X^2 = 520$

[a]The individual scores are given for each treatment cell (n = 5), along with the cell totals (AB values) and the SS for each cell.

explanation of the formulas. To help demonstrate the use of the formulas, we will use the data in Table 15.3. You should notice that the analysis consists of two parts; we must analyze the *SS* values as well as the *df* values. We will begin with the analysis of the sum of squares (*SS*).

ANALYSIS OF SUM OF SQUARES

Total sum of squares, SS_{total} SS_{total} computes the sum of squares for the total set of *N* scores:

$$SS_{total} = \Sigma X^2 - \frac{G^2}{N} \tag{15.1}$$

You should notice that this formula is identical to the *SS* formula that was used for single-factor ANOVA in Chapters 13 and 14 [see formulas (13.3) and (14.3)].

For the data in Table 15.3, this total sum of squares would be

$$SS_{total} = 520 - \frac{90^2}{30}$$
$$= 520 - 270$$
$$= 250$$

Within-treatments sum of squares, SS_{within} The variability within, or "inside," the treatments is found by simply calculating *SS* for each individual cell and then adding up these *SS* values. The formula is

$$SS_{\text{within}} = \Sigma \, SS_{\text{inside each treatment cell}} \qquad\qquad (15.2)$$

For the data in Table 15.3, SS_{within} is

$$SS_{\text{within}} = 20 + 26 + 18 + 28 + 20 + 8$$
$$= 120$$

Between-treatments sum of squares, SS_{between}   In the single-factor analysis of variance the formula for computing sum of squares between treatments focused on the treatment totals (T values) and computed SS for these totals:

$$SS_{\text{between}} = \Sigma\frac{T^2}{n} - \frac{G^2}{N}$$

In the two-factor design, each treatment corresponds to a particular cell, and the cell totals are identified by AB rather than T, so the between-treatments formula becomes

$$SS_{\text{between}} = \Sigma\frac{AB^2}{n} - \frac{G^2}{N} \qquad\qquad (15.3)$$

This SS is also called $SS_{\text{between cells}}$. It measures between-cell variability.

Applying this formula to the data in Table 15.1 gives

$$SS_{\text{between}} = \frac{10^2}{5} + \frac{35^2}{5} + \frac{15^2}{5} + \frac{20^2}{5} + \frac{5^2}{5} + \frac{5^2}{5} - \frac{90^2}{30}$$
$$= 20 + 245 + 45 + 80 + 5 + 5 - 270$$
$$= 400 - 270$$
$$= 130$$

This completes the first level of the analysis. When you are performing the calculations for a two-factor analysis of variance, you should stop at this stage and be sure that the two components add up to the total:

$$SS_{\text{total}} = SS_{\text{between}} + SS_{\text{within}}$$
$$250 = 120 + 130$$

We now move to the second level of the analysis. Remember, we are still measuring treatment effects or differences between treatments. But now we want to determine how much of the overall treatment effect can be attributed to factor A, how much is due to factor B, and how much is due to the interaction between these two factors. To compute the SS for each of the two separate factors, we will continue to use the same basic formula for sum of squares between treatments. The first part of this formula uses the total for each treatment condition and the number of scores in each condition (see formula 15.3). For factor A, the totals are identified by A's and the number of scores in each level of A is given by bn. Thus, the formula for SS between the levels of factor A would be

$$SS_A = \Sigma\frac{A^2}{bn} - \frac{G^2}{N} \qquad\qquad (15.4)$$

To get an A total, we must sum scores across the levels of factor B. Therefore, bn (or 15) scores are added to obtain an A total.

The A totals for the data in Table 15.3 are $A_1 = 60$ and $A_2 = 30$. Each of these totals is obtained by adding up a set of $3(5) = 15$ scores. Therefore, the sum of squares for factor A would be

$$SS_A = \frac{60^2}{15} + \frac{30^2}{15} - \frac{90^2}{30}$$
$$= 240 + 60 - 270$$
$$= 30$$

For factor B, the totals are identified by B's, and the number of scores in each total is determined by an. The formula for sum of squares for factor B is

$$SS_B = \Sigma \frac{B^2}{an} - \frac{G^2}{N} \tag{15.5}$$

To get a B total, we must sum across levels of factor A. Therefore, an (or 10) scores are added to find the B total.

For the data in Table 15.3, this SS would be

$$SS_B = \frac{30^2}{10} + \frac{40^2}{10} + \frac{20^2}{10} - \frac{90^2}{30}$$
$$= 90 + 160 + 40 - 270$$
$$= 20$$

Finally, the SS for the interaction is found by subtraction. According to Figure 15.5, the between-treatments variability is partitioned into three parts: factor A, factor B, and the interaction. Therefore, if you start with $SS_{between}$ and subtract out SS_A and SS_B, the amount that is left will be the SS for the interaction. Thus, the "formula" for the interaction is

$$SS_{A \times B} = SS_{between} - SS_A - SS_B \tag{15.6}$$

Using this formula on the data from Table 15.3 gives

$$SS_{A \times B} = 130 - 30 - 20$$
$$= 80$$

The complete analysis of SS for the data in Table 15.3 is presented in Figure 15.6. Notice that the separate parts at each level of the analysis add up to the total amount of variability at the level above. For example, the SS for factor A, factor B, and the $A \times B$ interaction add up to the $SS_{between}$.

ANALYSIS OF DEGREES OF FREEDOM

Each SS value in the analysis of variance has a corresponding degrees of freedom. Normally, SS measures the amount of variability (or differences) among a number of things. The corresponding df value is found by counting the number of things and subtracting 1. For a set of n scores, for example, $df = n - 1$. Using this general principle, we will define the df value associated with each of the SSs in the analysis.

Figure 15.6

Analysis of the sum of squares (SS) for a two-factor experiment. The values are those obtained from the data in Table 15.3.

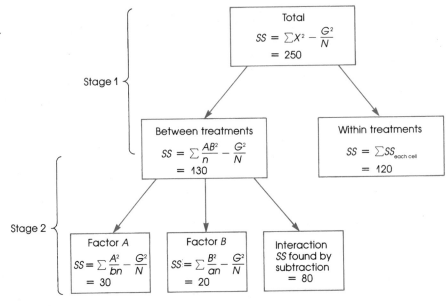

Total degrees of freedom, df_{total}   The df_{total} is simply the degrees of freedom associated with the SS_{total}. When we computed this SS, we used all N scores. Therefore,

$$df_{total} = N - 1 \qquad\qquad (15.7)$$

For the data in Table 15.3, there are a total of $N = 30$ scores, so $df_{total} = 29$.

Degrees of freedom within treatments, df_{within}   To compute SS_{within}, we added up the SS values inside each of the treatment conditions. Because there are n scores inside each treatment, each SS value has $df = n - 1$. When these are added up, you get

$$df_{within} = \Sigma(n - 1) \qquad\qquad (15.8)$$
$$= N - ab$$

For the data in Table 15.3, there are $n = 5$ scores in each treatment condition. Therefore, $df = 4$ inside each treatment. Summing over the six treatments gives an overall within-treatments df of 24. This same value is obtained if we start with $N = 30$ scores and subtract $ab = 6$ treatments.

Degrees of freedom between treatments, $df_{between}$ $SS_{between}$ was computed using the AB totals from each of the treatment cells. Because there are ab separate cells,

$$df_{between} = ab - 1 \qquad\qquad (15.9)$$

The example we are considering has a total of six treatment conditions (two levels of factor A and three levels of factor B). Therefore, the between-treatments $df = 3 \times 2 - 1 = 6 - 1 = 5$.

Notice that the analysis of the *df* values follows the same pattern shown in Figure 15.5. Specifically, the $df_{between}$ and the df_{within} will combine to equal the df_{total}:

$$df_{total} = df_{between} + df_{within}$$
$$29 = 5 + 24$$

Degrees of freedom for factor A, df_A   The *SS* for factor *A* measures the variability among the *A* totals. Because the number of levels of factor *A* is identified by *a*,

$$df_A = a - 1 \tag{15.10}$$

Because there are two levels of factor $A(a = 2)$ in Table 15.3, this factor would have $df = 1$.

Degrees of freedom for factor B, df_B   There are *b* different levels for factor *B*, and the *SS* for factor *B* is computed by using these totals. Therefore,

$$df_B = b - 1 \tag{15.11}$$

For the data we are considering, factor *B* has three levels ($b = 3$), so factor *B* would have $df = 2$.

Degrees of freedom for the interaction, $df_{A \times B}$ The *df* for the $A \times B$ interaction can be computed two different ways. First, you can use the structure of the analysis shown in Figure 15.5 to find $df_{A \times B}$ by subtraction. If you start with $df_{between}$ and subtract the *df* values for factors *A* and *B*, the value that is left will be *df* for the interaction:

$$df_{A \times B} = df_{between} - df_A - df_B \tag{15.12}$$

The data in Table 15.3 have $df_{between}$ equal to 5, df_A equal to 1, and df_B equal to 2. Therefore, the *df* for the interaction would be

$$df_{A \times B} = 5 - 1 - 2$$
$$= 2$$

An easy shortcut for finding *df* for the interaction is to notice that

$$df_{A \times B} = df_A df_B \tag{15.13}$$

Using this shortcut formula for the data in Table 15.3, the $A \times B$ interaction would have $df = 1 \times 2 = 2$. An intuitive explanation of this formula for *df* is presented in Box 15.1.

The complete analysis of *df* values is shown in Figure 15.9. Again, notice that the separate components always add up to the total. For example, the $df_{between}$ (5) and the df_{within} (24) add up to the df_{total} (29).

15.1 ADDITIVE AND MULTIPLICATIVE RELATION BETWEEN FACTORS

ONE WAY to think about interactions is to consider the difference between factors that multiply together and factors that add together.

When there is no interaction, the effect of one factor simply adds to the effect of the other factor. This situation is shown in Figure 15.7. Notice that the effect of factor A is to add three points to each mean (the means in A_2 are each three points greater than the corresponding means in A_1). When these means are placed in a graph, the lines for A_1 and A_2 are parallel. There is no interaction. When an additive relation exists between the two factors, there is no interaction.

An interaction means that there is a nonadditive relation. A multiplicative relation is one example of a nonadditive relation. Consider the data shown in Figure 15.8. In this case, the effect of factor A is to multiply each mean by three points (each mean in A_2 is three times greater than the corresponding mean in A_1). When these means are placed in a

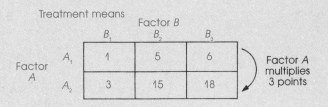

Treatment means

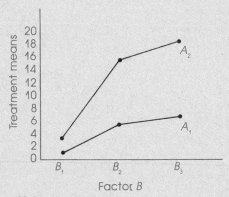

Figure 15.8

Treatment means for a two-factor experiment showing a multiplicative relation between the two factors. Notice that there is a large $A \times B$ interaction.

graph, the lines for A_1 and A_2 are not parallel. This time there is an interaction.

The notation used to represent an interaction is consistent with this idea of a multiplicative relation between two factors. For example, an interaction is identified as $A \times B$. Also, you can find the degrees of freedom for an interaction by multiplication:

$$df \text{ for } A \times B = df \text{ for } A \times df \text{ for } B$$

The notion that a multiplicative relation can be described as an interaction is common in areas other than statistics. For example, pharmacists often speak of "drug interactions." This term is used when the effects of one drug multiply the effects of another. You should note that in some cases the multiplication produces a much greater effect than would be expected by simply "adding" the two drugs together. In other cases, two drugs can cancel each other so that the combination is less effective than would be expected by simple addition.

Treatment means

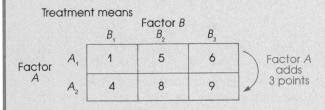

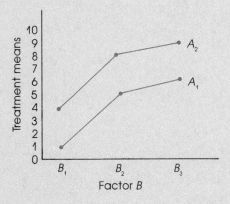

Figure 15.7

Treatment means for a two-factor experiment showing an additive relation between the two factors. Notice that there is no $A \times B$ interaction.

Figure 15.9

Analysis of the degrees of freedom for a two-factor analysis of variance. The values are those obtained from the data in Table 15.3.

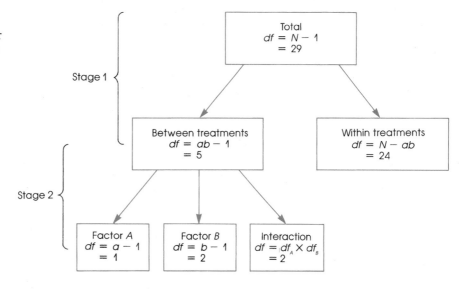

MEAN SQUARES (*MSs*) AND *F*-RATIOS   The final step in the analysis is to compute the mean square values and the *F*-ratios. Recall that each mean square (*MS*) is actually a sample variance and is computed from the *SS* and *df* values:

$$MS = \frac{SS}{df}$$

For the example we are considering,

$$MS \text{ for } A = MS_A = \frac{SS_A}{df_A} = \frac{30}{1} = 30$$

$$MS \text{ for } B = MS_B = \frac{SS_B}{df_B} = \frac{20}{2} = 10$$

$$MS \text{ for } A \times B = MS_{A \times B} = \frac{SS_{A \times B}}{df_{A \times B}} = \frac{80}{2} = 40$$

The denominator of each *F*-ratio will have MS_{within}:

$$MS_{\text{within}} = \frac{SS_{\text{within}}}{df_{\text{within}}} = \frac{120}{24} = 5.$$

For factor *A*, the *F*-ratio is

$$F = \frac{MS_A}{MS_{\text{within}}} = \frac{30}{5} = 6.00$$

This *F*-ratio has $df = 1, 24$ ($df = 1$ for the numerator of the ratio and $df = 24$ for the denominator). Commonly, this would be written as

$$F(1, 24) = 6.00$$

For factor B,

$$F(2,24) = \frac{MS_B}{MS_{\text{within}}}$$

$$= \frac{10}{5}$$

$$= 2.00$$

And for the $A \times B$ interaction,

This analysis may be done with the Minitab command TWOWAY (see Section 20.7).

$$F(2, 24) = \frac{MS_{A \times B}}{MS_{\text{within}}}$$

$$= \frac{40}{5}$$

$$= 8.00$$

To determine whether or not these values fall in the critical region and thereby indicate a significant treatment effect, it is necessary to look at the distribution of F-ratios. The F distributions for $df = 1, 24$ and for $df = 2, 24$ are shown in Figure 15.10. The critical values are shown for the .05 level of significance (check the table on page A-26).

Caution: Be sure to check the appropriate critical region. Factors A and B have different critical values because these factors have different values for degrees of freedom in this example.

Note that for factor A our obtained F-ratio of $F(1, 24) = 6.00$ is in the critical region. This indicates that the obtained difference between treatments (the numerator of the ratio) is significantly greater than what would be expected by chance (the denominator of the ratio). We conclude that factor A does have a significant effect.

On the other hand, the obtained F-ratio for factor B, $F(2, 24) = 2.00$, is not in the critical region. According to these data, factor B does not have a significant effect; that is, the difference we obtained is not larger than would be expected by chance.

Finally, the F-ratio for the $A \times B$ interaction, $F(2, 24) = 8.00$, is in the critical region. This indicates that there is a significant interaction. There are several equivalent ways of expressing this result. You could say that the

Figure 15.10

Distribution of F for $df = 1, 24$ for evaluating the F-ratio for factor A and the distribution with $df = 2, 24$ for evaluating factor B and the $A \times B$ interaction. In each case, the critical value for $\alpha = .05$ is shown.

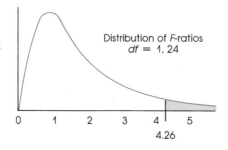

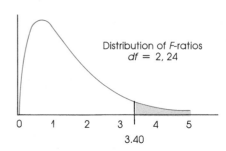

specific combinations of factors A and B produce significant differences. Or you could say that the effect of factor A depends on the different levels of factor B. Or you could say that the effect of factor B depends on the different levels of factor A.

 SPSS^x A-81

To make these conclusions more concrete, the data from the experiment are graphed in Figure 15.11. The significant main effect for factor A is seen in the fact that the line for A_1 is generally higher than the line for A_2. The average difference between these lines is the A-effect.

To visualize the B-effect, image a point midway between the two dots above B_1 on the graph. Do the same thing for the two dots above B_2 and for the dots above B_3. Now draw a line connecting these three imaginary points. You should find that this line is nearly horizontal; as you move across the line from B_1 to B_2 to B_3, there is not much change in the mean score. This indicates that factor B does not have much effect and supports our conclusion that the main effect for B is not significant.

The interaction is easy to see because the two lines in the graph are not parallel. You can describe this interaction by focusing on the distance between the lines at each level of factor B. At B_1, for example, the A_1 line is lower. But at B_2, the A_1 line goes considerably higher than A_2, etc. This description is equivalent to saying that the A-effect (the distance between the lines) depends on the levels of B.

A concise summary of the formulas and structure for the two-factor analysis of variance is presented in Figure 15.12. This figure contains nearly all of the information you need to conduct the analysis and should help you to understand the relationships among all the parts.

Figure 15.11

Graph of the data from Table 15.3, showing the means for each of the six different treatment combinations (cells) in the experiment.

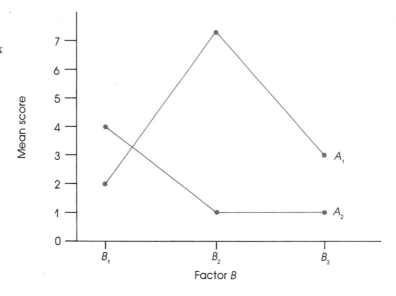

Figure 15.12

The complete analysis of variance for an independent measures two-factor design.

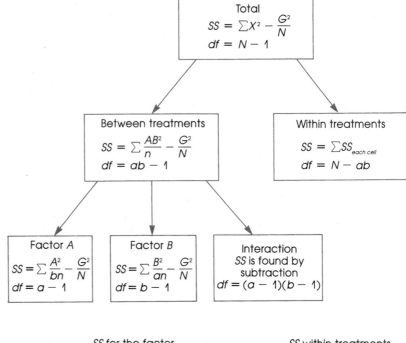

$$MS_{factor} = \frac{SS \text{ for the factor}}{df \text{ for the factor}}$$

This MS is computed for A, B, and the interaction.

$$MS_{error\ term} = \frac{SS \text{ within treatments}}{df \text{ within treatments}}$$

The same MS is used as the error term for all three F-ratios.

LEARNING CHECK   1. The following data summarize the results from a two-factor, independent-measures experiment.

	FACTOR B		
	B_1	B_2	B_3
A_1	$n = 10$ $AB = 0$ $\overline{X} = 0$ $SS = 30$	$n = 10$ $AB = 10$ $\overline{X} = 1$ $SS = 40$	$n = 10$ $AB = 20$ $\overline{X} = 2$ $SS = 50$
A_2	$n = 10$ $AB = 40$ $\overline{X} = 4$ $SS = 60$	$n = 10$ $AB = 30$ $\overline{X} = 3$ $SS = 50$	$n = 10$ $AB = 20$ $\overline{X} = 2$ $SS = 40$

FACTOR A (label at left of table, rows A_1 and A_2)

$\Sigma X^2 = 610$

a. Sketch a graph similar to those in Figure 15.3 to show the results of this experiment.

b. Looking at your graph, does there appear to be a main effect for factor A? Does factor B have an effect? Is there an interaction?

c. Use an analysis of variance with $\alpha = .05$ to evaluate the effects of factor A, factor B, and the $A \times B$ interaction for these data.

ANSWERS **1. a.** Your graph should show two converging lines.

b. In a graph, the points for level 1 of factor A are much lower than the means for level 2. This mean difference indicates a main effect for factor A. There is no main effect for factor B. The fact that the lines are not parallel indicates an interaction.

c. The results of the ANOVA are summarized in the following table:

SOURCE	SS	df	MS	
Between treatments	100	5		
Factor A	60	1	60	$F = 12.00$
Factor B	0	2	0	$F = 0$
$A \times B$ interaction	40	2	20	$F = 4.00$
Within treatments	270	54	5	
Total	370	59		

(*Note:* The fact that $SS_B = 0$ should be clear from looking at the data. The B totals are all the same; they are not variable.)

15.4 EXAMPLES OF THE TWO-FACTOR ANOVA

Example 15.1 presents the complete hypothesis testing procedure for a two-factor independent-measures experiment.

EXAMPLE 15.1 In 1968 Stanley Schachter published an article in *Science* reporting a series of experiments on obesity and eating behavior. One of these studies examined the hypothesis that obese individuals do not respond to internal, biological signals of hunger. In simple terms, this hypothesis says that obese individuals tend to eat whether or not their bodies are actually hungry.

In Schachter's experiment subjects were led to believe that they were taking part in a "taste test." All subjects were told to come to the experiment without eating for several hours beforehand. The experiment used two independent variables or factors:

1. Weight (obese versus normal subjects)

2. Full stomach versus empty stomach (half the subjects were given a full meal, as much as they wanted, after arriving at the experiment, and half were left hungry)

All subjects were then invited to taste and rate five different types of crackers. The dependent variable was the number of crackers eaten by each subject.

The prediction for this study was that the obese subjects would eat the same amount of crackers whether or not they were full. The normal subjects were expected to eat more with empty stomachs and less with full stomachs. Notice that the primary prediction of this study is that there will be an interaction between weight and fullness.

Hypothetical data similar to those obtained by Schachter are presented in Table 15.4.

For this analysis, we will identify weight as factor A and fullness as factor B.

STEP 1   *State hypotheses and select* α. For factor A the null hypothesis states that there is no difference in the amount eaten for normal versus obese subjects. In symbols,

$$H_0: \quad \mu_{A_1} = \mu_{A_2}$$

$$H_1: \quad \mu_{A_1} \neq \mu_{A_2}$$

For factor B the null hypothesis states that the amount eaten will be the same for full-stomach subjects as for empty-stomach subjects. In symbols,

$$H_0: \quad \mu_{B_1} = \mu_{B_2}$$

$$H_1: \quad \mu_{B_1} \neq \mu_{B_2}$$

For the $A \times B$ interaction the null hypothesis can be stated two different ways. First, if there is a difference in eating between the full-stomach and empty-stomach conditions, it will be the same for normal and obese subjects. Second, if there is a difference in eating between the normal and obese subjects, it will be the same for the full-stomach and empty-stomach conditions. In more general terms,

Table 15.4

Results from an experiment examining the eating behavior of normal and obese individuals who have either a full or an empty stomach[a]

FACTOR A (WEIGHT)		FACTOR B (FULLNESS)		
		EMPTY STOMACH	FULL STOMACH	
	NORMAL	$n = 20$ $\bar{X} = 22$ $AB = 440$ $SS = 1540$	$n = 20$ $\bar{X} = 15$ $AB = 300$ $SS = 1270$	$A_1 = 740$
	OBESE	$n = 20$ $\bar{X} = 17$ $AB = 340$ $SS = 1320$	$n = 20$ $\bar{X} = 18$ $AB = 360$ $SS = 1266$	$A_1 = 700$
		$B_1 = 780$	$B_2 = 660$	$G = 1440$ $\Sigma X^2 = 31{,}836$ $N = 80$

[a]The dependent variable is the number of crackers eaten in a taste test (hypothetical data).

H_0:   The effect of factor A does not depend on the levels of factor B (and B does not depend on A)

H_1:   The effect of one factor does depend on the levels of the other factor

We will use $\alpha = .05$ for all tests.

STEP 2   *Locate the critical region.* To locate the critical values for each of the three F-ratios, we first must determine the df values. For these data (Table 15.4),

$$df_{\text{total}} = N - 1 = 79$$

$$df_{\text{between}} = ab - 1 = 3$$

$$df_{\text{within}} = N - ab = 76$$

$$df_A = a - 1 = 1$$

$$df_B = b - 1 = 1$$

$$df_{A \times B} = df_A df_B = 1$$

Notice that the F distribution table has no entry for $df = 1, 76$. A close and conservative estimate of this critical value may be obtained by using $df = 1, 70$ (critical $F = 3.98$). Whenever there is no entry for the df value of the error term, use the nearest smaller value in the table.

Thus, all three F-ratios will have $df = 1, 76$. With $\alpha = .05$, the critical F value is 3.98 for all three tests.

STEP 3   *Use the data to compute the F-ratios.* First, we will analyze the SS values:

$$SS_{\text{total}} = \Sigma X^2 - \frac{G^2}{N} = 31{,}836 - \frac{1440^2}{80}$$

$$= 31{,}836 - 25{,}920$$

$$= 5916$$

$$SS_{\text{between}} = \Sigma \frac{AB^2}{n} - \frac{G^2}{N}$$

$$= \frac{440^2}{20} + \frac{300^2}{20} + \frac{340^2}{20} + \frac{360^2}{20} - \frac{1440^2}{80}$$

$$= 26{,}440 - 25{,}920$$

$$= 520$$

$$SS_{\text{within}} = \Sigma SS_{\text{inside each cell}}$$

$$= 1540 + 1270 + 1320 + 1266$$

$$= 5396$$

$$SS_A = \Sigma \frac{A^2}{bn} - \frac{G^2}{N}$$

$$= \frac{740^2}{40} + \frac{700^2}{40} - \frac{1440^2}{80}$$

$$= 25{,}940 - 25{,}920$$

$$= 20$$

$$SS_B = \Sigma \frac{B^2}{an} - \frac{G^2}{N}$$

$$= \frac{780^2}{40} + \frac{660^2}{40} - \frac{1440^2}{80}$$

$$= 26,100 - 25,920$$

$$= 180$$

$$SS_{A \times B} = SS_{\text{between}} - SS_A - SS_B$$

$$= 520 - 20 - 180$$

$$= 320$$

The MS values needed for the F-ratios are

$$MS_A = \frac{SS_A}{df_A} = \frac{20}{1} = 20$$

$$MS_B = \frac{SS_B}{df_B} = \frac{180}{1} = 180$$

$$MS_{A \times B} = \frac{SS_{A \times B}}{df_{A \times B}} = \frac{320}{1} = 320$$

$$MS_{\text{within}} = \frac{SS_{\text{within}}}{df_{\text{within}}} = \frac{5396}{76} = 71$$

Finally, the F-ratios are

$$F_A = \frac{MS_A}{MS_{\text{within}}} = \frac{20}{71} = 0.28$$

$$F_B = \frac{MS_B}{MS_{\text{within}}} = \frac{180}{71} = 2.54$$

$$F_{A \times B} = \frac{MS_{A \times B}}{MS_{\text{within}}} = \frac{320}{71} = 4.51$$

STEP 4 *Make decisions.* For these data, factor *A* (weight) has no significant effect; $F(1, 76) = 0.28$. Statistically, there is no difference in the number of crackers eaten by normal versus obese subjects.

Similarly, factor *B* (fullness) has no significant effect; $F(1, 76) = 2.54$. Statistically, the number of crackers eaten by full subjects is no different from the number eaten by hungry subjects. (*Note:* This conclusion concerns the combined group of normal and obese subjects. The interaction concerns these two groups separately. See Box 15.2 for information concerning the interpretation of results when there is a significant interaction.)

These data produce a significant interaction; $F(1, 76) = 4.51$, $p < .05$. This means that the effect of fullness does depend on weight. Specifically, the degree of fullness did affect the normal subjects, but it has no effect on the obese subjects.

As we saw in Chapters 13 and 14, the results from an ANOVA can be organized in a summary table, which shows all the components of

15.2 INTERPRETING INTERACTIONS AND MAIN EFFECTS

WHEN A two-factor ANOVA produces a significant interaction, you should use the interaction (not the main effects) as the basis for interpreting the results of the experiment. This point is demonstrated by the data in Figure 15.13. The figure shows the results (means) for a two-factor experiment comparing the weight loss achieved from two different diet programs (factor *A*) for men versus women (factor *B*).

Notice that the data show no main effect for type of diet—overall, there is no difference between the mean score for diet 1 versus diet 2. Also, the data show no main effect for sex—the overall mean for the men is exactly the same as the mean for the women. However, these results should not be interpreted as showing that there is no difference between the two diets, nor should you conclude that there is no difference in weight loss for men versus women.

In this example, the data show a clear difference between the two diets; however, this difference depends on whether you are looking at the data for men or the data for women. For men, diet 1 produces substantially higher scores than diet 2. For women, the reverse is true. This is the basic concept of an interaction: The effects of one factor (diet) depend on the levels of the other factor (gender).

Whenever a two-factor ANOVA produces a significant interaction, the results from the main effects can be misleading. A significant interaction requires that you look beyond the main effects and examine the individual means to interpret the results.

Mean weight loss

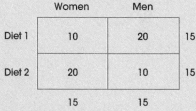

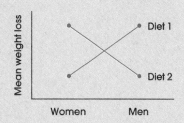

Figure 15.13

Hypothetical data from a two-factor experiment comparing two diets for men versus women. The numbers in the matrix and the points in the graph represent the mean weight loss for each treatment condition.

the analysis (*SS, df,* etc.) as well as the final *F*-ratios. For this example, the summary table would be as follows:

SOURCE	SS	df	MS	F
Between treatments	520	3		
Factor *A* (weight)	20	1	20	0.28
Factor *B* (fullness)	180	1	180	2.54
A × *B* Interaction	320	1	320	4.51
Within treatments	5396	76	71	
Total	5916	79		

REDUCTION OF UNCONTROLLED VARIANCE BY A TWO-FACTOR DESIGN

One advantage of a two-factor experiment is that it allows you to "control" some of the variability within an experiment. The following example demonstrates how you can "add" a second factor to a single-factor experiment in order to reduce the error variability and thereby increase the chances of obtaining a significant treatment effect. The rationale for this technique comes from the fact that the independent-measures analysis of variance uses the variability within treatments (MS_{within}) as the denominator of the F-ratio. This variance inside the treatments provides a measure of how much variability is expected just by chance, that is, how much variability is due to individual differences and experimental error.

Often the variability within treatments is not all unexplained and uncontrolled variance. For example, a researcher may notice that a particular treatment seems to have a large effect on the young animals in the sample but not much effect on the older animals. In this case, much of the variability within the treatment condition is caused by the age of the animals. Whenever variability can be explained or predicted in this way, it is possible to measure it and remove it from the F-ratio. The following example demonstrates this process.

EXAMPLE 15.2

The data in Table 15.5 represent the outcome of a single-factor experiment comparing two treatment conditions. Each treatment condition contains $n = 10$ subjects, 5 males and 5 females.

Using a single-factor ANOVA on these data, the researcher obtains

$$SS_{between} = \Sigma \frac{T^2}{n} - \frac{G^2}{N}$$

$$= \frac{40^2}{10} + \frac{60^2}{10} - \frac{100^2}{20}$$

$$= 520 - 500$$

$$= 20$$

Table 15.5

Hypothetical data from a single-factor experiment comparing two treatment conditions[a]

TREATMENT 1		TREATMENT 2
3		5
3		4
1		3
2		5
1	Males	3
7	Females	7
7		7
5		8
6		9
5		9
$T_1 = 40$		$T_2 = 60$
$SS_1 = 48$		$SS_2 = 48$

[a]Each treatment contains a sample of $n = 10$ subjects, 5 males and 5 females.

The within-treatments SS for these data is

$$SS_{\text{within}} = \Sigma SS_{\text{inside each treatment}}$$
$$= 48 + 48$$
$$= 96$$

The MS values are

$$MS_{\text{between}} = \frac{SS}{df} = \frac{20}{1}$$
$$= 20$$

$$MS_{\text{within}} = \frac{SS}{df} = \frac{96}{18}$$
$$= 5.33$$

The resulting F-ratio is $F(1, 18) = 3.75$, which is not in the critical region. Therefore, the researcher must conclude that these data do not demonstrate a significant treatment effect.

The researcher noticed, however, that much of the variability inside the treatments appears to come from the fact that the females tend to have higher scores than the males. If this is true, then much of the within-treatments variability (the denominator of the F-ratio) can be explained. Table 15.6 reproduces the data, but this time the scores for males and females are separated by using sex as a second factor. If we call the original treatments factor A and use sex as factor B, the two-factor ANOVA gives the following results:

Table 15.6

The same hypothetical data shown in Table 15.6 with a second factor (sex) added to create a two-factor experiment

$$SS_A = \Sigma\frac{A^2}{bn} - \frac{G^2}{N}$$

$$= \frac{40^2}{10} + \frac{60^2}{10} - \frac{100^2}{20}$$

$$= 20$$

(Notice that the treatment effect is the same whether you use a one- or a two-factor analysis.)

$$SS_B = \Sigma\frac{B^2}{an} - \frac{G^2}{N}$$

$$= \frac{30^2}{10} + \frac{70^2}{10} + \frac{100^2}{20}$$

$$= 80$$

(This is the variability due to sex differences.) The SS for the $A \times B$ interaction is zero for these data. (Check it for yourself.)

With the data arranged in a two-factor design, SS_{within} is

$$SS_{within} = SS_{inside\ each\ cell}$$

$$= 4 + 4 + 4 + 4$$

$$= 16$$

Finally, the mean square values are

$$MS_A = \frac{SS_A}{df_A} = \frac{20}{1}$$

$$= 20$$

$$MS_B = \frac{SS_B}{df_B} = \frac{80}{1}$$

$$= 80$$

$$MS_{within} = \frac{SS_{within}}{df_{within}} = \frac{16}{16}$$

$$= 1$$

The F-ratios are as follows:

For factor A: $F(1, 16) = \frac{20}{1} = 20$

For factor B: $F(1, 16) = \frac{80}{1} = 80$

Now the treatment effect (factor A) gives an F-ratio of 20, which is in the critical region. The researcher can conclude that there is a significant treatment effect.

The difference between the two analyses is entirely in the denominator of the F-ratios. In the two-factor analysis, much of the "error" variability is accounted for and removed from the denominator of the F-ratio. This makes it much more likely to obtain a significant result. You also should notice that the two-factor analysis provides additional information about the second factor and the interaction between the two factors.

15.5 ASSUMPTIONS FOR THE TWO-FACTOR ANOVA

The validity of the analysis of variance presented in this chapter depends on the same three assumptions we have encountered with other hypothesis tests for independent-measures experiments (the t test in Chapter 10 and the single-factor ANOVA in Chapter 13):

1. The observations within each sample must be independent (see page 255).

2. The populations from which the samples are selected must be normal.

3. The populations from which the samples are selected must have equal variances (homogeneity of variance).

As before, the assumption of normality generally is not a cause for concern, especially when the sample size is relatively large. The homogeneity of variance assumption is more important, and if it appears that your data fail to satisfy this requirement, you should conduct a test for homogeneity before you attempt the ANOVA. Hartley's F-max test (see page 281) allows you to use the sample variances from your data to determine whether there is evidence for any differences among the population variances.

HIGHER-ORDER FACTORIAL DESIGNS

The basic concepts of the two-factor ANOVA can be extended to more complex designs involving three or more factors. A three-factor design, for example, might look at academic performance scores for two different teaching methods (factor A), for boys versus girls (factor B), and for first-grade versus second-grade classes (factor C). The logic of the analysis and many of the formulas from the two-factor ANOVA are simply extended to the three- (or more) factor situation. In a three-factor experiment, for example, you would evaluate the main effects for each of the three factors and you would evaluate a set of two-way interactions: $A \times B$, $B \times C$, and $A \times C$. In addition, however, the extra factor introduces the potential for a three-way interaction: $A \times B \times C$.

The general logic for defining and interpreting higher-order interactions follows the pattern set by two-way interactions. For example, a two-way interaction, $A \times B$, means that the effect of factor A depends on the levels of factor B. Extending this definition, a three-way interaction, $A \times B \times C$, indicates that the two-way interaction between A and B depends on the levels of factor C. Although you may have a good understanding of two-way interactions and you may grasp the general idea of a three-way interaction, most people have great difficulty comprehending or interpreting a four- (or more) way interaction. For this reason, factorial experiments involving three or more factors can produce very complex results that are difficult to understand and, thus, often have limited practical value.

SUMMARY

1. An experiment with two independent variables is called a two-factor experiment. Such an experiment can be diagrammed as a matrix by listing the levels of one factor across the top and the levels of the other factor down the side. Each *cell* in the matrix corresponds to a specific combination of the two factors.

2. Traditionally, the two factors are identified as factor *A* and factor *B*. The purpose of the analysis of variance is to determine whether there are any significant mean differences among the treatment conditions or cells in the experimental matrix. These treatment effects are classified as follows:
   a. The *A*-effect: Differential effects produced by the different levels of factor *A*.
   b. The *B*-effect: Differential effects produced by the different levels of factor *B*.

c. The *A* × *B* interaction: Differences that are produced by unique combinations of *A* and *B*. An interaction exists when the effect of one factor depends on the levels of the other factor.

3. The two-factor analysis of variance produces three *F*-ratios: one for factor *A*, one for factor *B*, and one for the *A* × *B* interaction. Each *F*-ratio has the same basic structure:

$$F = \frac{MS_{\text{treatment effect}}(\text{either } A \text{ or } B \text{ or } A \times B)}{MS_{\text{within}}}$$

The formulas for *SS*, *df*, and *MS* values for the two-factor ANOVA are presented in Figure 15.12.

KEY TERMS

two-factor experiment   matrix   cells   main effect   interaction

Focus on Problem Solving

1. Before you begin a two-factor ANOVA, you should take time to organize and summarize the data. It is best if you summarize the data in a matrix with rows corresponding to the levels of one factor and columns corresponding to the levels of the other factor. In each cell of the matrix, show the number of scores (*n*), the total and mean for the cell, and the *SS* within the cell. Also, compute the row totals and column totals that will be needed to calculate main effects.

2. To draw a graph of the results from a two-factor experiment, first prepare a matrix with each cell containing the mean for that treatment condition.

Next, list the levels of factor B on the X-axis (B_1, B_2, etc.) and put the scores (dependent variable) on the Y-axis. Starting with the first row of the matrix, place a dot above each B level so that the height of the dot corresponds to the cell mean. Connect the dots with a line, and label the line A_1. In the same way, construct a separate line for each level of factor A (that is, a separate line for each row of the matrix). In general, your graph will be easier to draw and easier to understand if the factor with the larger number of levels is placed on the X-axis (factor B in this example).

3. The concept of an interaction is easier to grasp if you sketch a graph showing the means for each treatment. Remember, parallel lines indicate no interaction. Crossing or converging lines indicate that the effect of one treatment depends on the levels of the other treatment you are examining. This indicates that an interaction exists between the two treatments.

4. For a two-factor ANOVA, there are three separate F-ratios. These three F-ratios use the same error term in the denominator (MS_{within}). On the other hand, these F-ratios will have different numerators and may have different df values associated with each of these numerators. Therefore, you must be careful when you look up the critical F values in the table. The two factors and the interaction may have different critical F values.

5. As we have mentioned in previous ANOVA chapters, it helps tremendously to organize your computations; start with SS and df values and then compute MS values and F-ratios. Once again, using an ANOVA summary table (see page 000) can be of great assistance.

Demonstration 15.1

TWO-FACTOR ANOVA

The following data are from an experiment examining the phenomenon of encoding specificity. According to this psychological principle, recall of information will be best if the testing conditions are the same as the conditions that existed at the time of learning.

The experiment involves presenting a group of students with a lecture on an unfamiliar topic. One week later, the students are given a test on the lecture material. To manipulate the conditions at the time of learning, some students receive the lecture in a large classroom, and some hear the lecture in a small classroom. For those students who were lectured in the large room, one-half are tested in the same large room, and the others are changed to the small room for testing. Similarly, one-half of the students who were lectured in the small room are tested in the same small room, and the other half are tested in the large room. Thus, the experiment involves four groups of subjects in a two-factor design, as shown in the following table. The score for each subject is the number of correct answers on the test.

		TESTING CONDITION	
		LARGE TESTING ROOM	SMALL TESTING ROOM
LECTURE CONDITION	LARGE LECTURE ROOM	15 20 11 18 16	5 8 1 1 5
	SMALL LECTURE ROOM	1 4 2 5 8	22 15 20 17 16

Do these data indicate that the size of the lecture room and/or testing room has a significant effect on test performance?

STEP 1   *State the hypotheses and specify* α. The two-factor ANOVA evaluates three separate sets of hypotheses:

1. The main effect of lecture room size: Is there a significant difference in test performance for students who received the lecture in a large room versus students who received the lecture in a small room? With lecture room size identified as factor A, the null hypothesis states that there is no difference between the two room sizes. In symbols,

$$H_0: \quad \mu_{A_1} = \mu_{A_2}$$

The alternative hypothesis states that there is a difference between the two lecture room sizes.

$$H_1: \quad \mu_{A_1} \neq \mu_{A_2}$$

2. The main effect of testing room size: Is there a significant difference in test performance for students who were tested in a large room versus students who were tested in a small room? With testing room size identified as factor B, the null hypothesis states that there is no difference between the two room sizes. In symbols,

$$H_0: \quad \mu_{B_1} = \mu_{B_2}$$

The alternative hypothesis states that there is a difference between the two testing room sizes.

$$H_1: \quad \mu_{B_1} \neq \mu_{B_2}$$

3. The interaction between lecture room size and testing room size. The null hypothesis states that there is no interaction:

H_0: The effect of testing room size does not depend on the size of the lecture room.

The alternative hypothesis states that there is an interaction:

H_1: The effect of testing room size does depend on the size of the lecture room.

Notice that the researcher is not predicting any main effects for this study: There is no prediction that one room size is better than another for either learning or for testing. However, the researcher is predicting that there will be an interaction. Specifically, the small testing room should be better for students who learned in the small room, and the large testing room should be better for students who learned in the large room. Remember, the principle of encoding specificity states that the better the match between testing and learning conditions, the better the recall.

We will set alpha at $\alpha = .05$.

STEP 2 *Locate the critical region.* To locate the critical region, we must obtain the *df* values for each of the three *F*-ratios. Specifically, we will need df_A, df_B, and $df_{A \times B}$ for the numerators and df_{within} for the denominator. (Often it is easier to postpone this step until the analysis of the *df* values in Step 3.)

$$df_A = a - 1 = 2 - 1 = 1$$

$$df_B = b - 1 = 2 - 1 = 1$$

$$df_{A \times B} = (a - 1)(b - 1) = (1)(1) = 1$$

$$df_{within} = N - ab = 20 - (2)(2) = 20 - 4 = 16$$

Thus, all three *F*-ratios will have $df = 1, 16$. With $\alpha = .05$, the critical value for each *F*-ratio is $F = 4.49$. For each test, the obtained *F*-ratio must exceed this critical value to reject H_0.

STEP 3 *Perform the analysis.* The complete two-factor ANOVA can be divided into a series of stages:

1. Compute the summary statistics for the data. This involves calculating the *AB* total and *SS* for each treatment condition, finding the *A* totals and *B* totals for the rows and columns, respectively, and obtaining *G* and ΣX^2 for the entire set of scores.

2. Perform the first stage of the analysis: Separate the total variability (*SS* and *df*) into the between- and within-treatment components.

3. Perform the second stage of the analysis: Separate the between-treatment variability (*SS* and *df*) into the *A*-effect, *B*-effect, and interaction components.

4. Calculate the mean squares for the *F*-ratios.

5. Calculate the *F*-ratios.

Compute summary statistics. We will use the computational formula to obtain *SS* for each treatment condition. These calculations will also provide numerical values for the row and column totals (*A* and *B*) as well as *G* and ΣX^2.

LARGE TESTING LARGE LECTURE		SMALL TESTING LARGE LECTURE	
X	X^2	X	X^2
15	225	5	25
20	400	8	64
11	121	1	1
18	324	1	1
16	256	5	25
$\Sigma X = 80$	$\Sigma X^2 = 1326$	$\Sigma X = 20$	$\Sigma X^2 = 116$

$$SS = \Sigma X^2 - \frac{(\Sigma X)^2}{n}$$

$$= 1326 - \frac{80^2}{5}$$

$$= 1326 - 1280$$

$$= 46$$

$$AB = \Sigma X = 80$$

$$SS = \Sigma X^2 - \frac{(\Sigma X)^2}{n}$$

$$= 116 - \frac{20^2}{5}$$

$$= 116 - 80$$

$$= 36$$

$$AB = \Sigma X = 20$$

LARGE TESTING SMALL LECTURE		SMALL TESTING SMALL LECTURE	
X	X^2	X	X^2
1	1	22	484
4	16	15	225
2	4	20	400
5	25	17	289
8	64	16	256
$\Sigma X = 20$	$\Sigma X^2 = 110$	$\Sigma X = 90$	$\Sigma X^2 = 1654$

$$SS = \Sigma X^2 - \frac{(\Sigma X)^2}{n}$$

$$= 110 - \frac{20^2}{5}$$

$$= 110 - 80$$

$$= 30$$

$$AB = \Sigma X = 20$$

$$SS = \Sigma X^2 - \frac{(\Sigma X)^2}{n}$$

$$= 1654 - \frac{90^2}{5}$$

$$= 1654 - 1620$$

$$= 34$$

$$AB = \Sigma X = 90$$

The column totals (factor *B*) are $B_1 = 100$ and $B_2 = 110$. The row totals (factor *A*) are $A_1 = 100$ and $A_2 = 110$. The grand total for these data is $G = 210$, and ΣX^2 for the entire set can be obtained by summing the ΣX^2 values for the four treatment conditions.

$$\Sigma X^2 = 1326 + 116 + 110 + 1654 = 3206$$

For this study there are two levels for factor A and for factor B, so $a = b = 2$, and there are $n = 5$ scores in each of the four conditions, so $N = 20$.

Stage 1 of the analysis. We begin by analyzing SS into two basic components:

$$SS_{total} = \Sigma X^2 - \frac{G^2}{N} = 3206 - \frac{210^2}{20} = 3206 - 2205 = 1001$$

$$SS_{between\ cells} = \Sigma\frac{AB^2}{n} - \frac{G^2}{N} = \frac{80^2}{5} + \frac{20^2}{5} + \frac{20^2}{5} + \frac{90^2}{5} - \frac{210^2}{20}$$
$$= 1280 + 80 + 80 + 1620 - 2205$$
$$= 3060 - 2205$$
$$= 855$$

$$SS_{within} = \Sigma SS_{each\ cell} = 46 + 36 + 30 + 34 = 146$$

For this stage, the *df* values are:

$$df_{total} = N - 1 = 20 - 1 = 19$$

$$df_{between\ cells} = ab - 1 = 4 - 1 = 3$$

$$df_{within} = N - ab = 20 - 4 = 16$$

Stage 2 of the analysis. We begin by analyzing $SS_{between}$.

$$SS_A = \Sigma\frac{A^2}{bn} - \frac{G^2}{N}$$
$$= \frac{100^2}{10} + \frac{110^2}{10} - \frac{210^2}{20}$$
$$= 1000 + 1210 - 2205$$
$$= 5$$

$$SS_B = \Sigma\frac{B^2}{an} - \frac{G^2}{N}$$
$$= \frac{100^2}{10} + \frac{110^2}{10} - \frac{210^2}{20}$$
$$= 1000 + 1210 - 2205$$
$$= 5$$

$$SS_{A\times B} = SS_{between\ cells} - SS_A - SS_B$$
$$= 855 - 5 - 5$$
$$= 845$$

For stage 2, the *df* values are

$$df_A = a - 1 = 2 - 1 = 1$$

$$df_B = b - 1 = 2 - 1 = 1$$

$$df_{A\times B} = (a - 1)(b - 1) = (1)(1) = 1$$

Calculate the MS values.

$$MS_A = \frac{SS_A}{df_A} = \frac{5}{1} = 5$$

$$MS_B = \frac{SS_B}{df_B} = \frac{5}{1} = 5$$

$$MS_{A \times B} = \frac{SS_{A \times B}}{df_{A \times B}} = \frac{845}{1} = 845$$

$$MS_{\text{within}} = \frac{SS_{\text{within}}}{df_{\text{within}}} = \frac{146}{16} = 9.125$$

Calculate the F-ratios.
For factor A (lecture-room size),

$$F = \frac{MS_A}{MS_{\text{within}}} = \frac{5}{9.125} = 0.55$$

For factor B (testing-room size),

$$F = \frac{MS_B}{MS_{\text{within}}} = \frac{5}{9.125} = 0.55$$

For the $A \times B$ interaction,

$$F = \frac{MS_{A \times B}}{MS_{\text{within}}} = \frac{845}{9.125} = 92.60$$

STEP 4   *Make a decision about each H_0 and state conclusions.* For factor A, lecture-room size, the obtained F-ratio, $F = 0.55$, is not in the critical region. Therefore, we fail to reject the null hypothesis. We conclude that the size of the lecture room does not have a significant effect on test performance, $F(1, 16) = 0.55$, $p > .05$.

For factor B, testing-room size, the obtained F-ratio, $F = 0.55$, is not in the critical region. Therefore, we fail to reject the null hypothesis. We conclude that the size of the testing room does not have a significant effect on test performance, $F(1, 16) = 0.55$, $p > .05$.

For the $A \times B$ interaction the obtained F-ratio, $F = 92.60$, exceeds the critical value of $F = 4.46$. Therefore, we reject the null hypothesis. We conclude that there is a significant interaction between lecture-room size and testing-room size, $F(1, 16) = 92.60$, $p < .05$.

Notice that the significant interaction means that you must be cautious interpreting the main effects (see Box 15.2). In this experiment, for example, the size of the testing room (factor B) does have an effect on performance, depending on which room was used for the lecture. Specifically, performance is higher when the testing room and lecture room match, and performance is lower when the lecture and testing occur in different rooms.

The following table summarizes the results of the analysis.

SOURCE	SS	df	MS	
Between cells	855	3		
A (lecture room)	5	1	5	F = 0.55
B (testing room)	5	1	5	F = 0.55
A × B interaction	845	1	845	F = 92.60
Within cells	146	16	9.125	
Total	1001	19		

PROBLEMS

1. Sketch a graph for each of the following sets of data. (*Hint:* Place the levels of B on the X-axis and mean score on the y-axis. Use two separate graph lines for the levels of A.) State whether or not the graph indicates the presence on an interaction between factors A and B.

a.

	FACTOR B	
	B_1	B_2
FACTOR A A_1	$\bar{X} = 40$	$\bar{X} = 10$
A_2	$\bar{X} = 60$	$\bar{X} = 30$

b.

	FACTOR B	
	B_1	B_2
FACTOR A A_1	$\bar{X} = 20$	$\bar{X} = 20$
A_2	$\bar{X} = 10$	$\bar{X} = 50$

c.

	FACTOR B	
	B_1	B_2
FACTOR A A_1	$\bar{X} = 20$	$\bar{X} = 20$
A_2	$\bar{X} = 10$	$\bar{X} = 10$

2. Sketch a graph showing the results of a 2 × 2 factorial experiment for each of the following descriptions:
   a. There is an A-effect and no B-effect and no interaction.
   b. There is an A-effect and a B-effect but no interaction.

c. There is an interaction but no A-effect and no B-effect.

3. A researcher studies the effects of need for achievement and task difficulty on problem solving. A two-factor design is used, in which there are two levels of amount of achievement motivation (high versus low need for achievement) and four levels of task difficulty, yielding eight treatment cells. Each cell consists of n = 6 subjects. The number of errors each subject made was recorded and the data were analyzed. The following table summarizes the results of the ANOVA, but it is not complete. Fill in the missing values. (Start with df values.)

SOURCE	SS	df	MS	
Between treatments	280	—		
Main effect for achievement motivation	—	—	—	F = —
Main effect for task difficulty	—	—	48	F = —
Interaction	120	—	—	F = —
Within treatments	—	—	—	
Total	600	—		

4. The results of a two-factor experiment are examined using an ANOVA, and the researcher reports an F-ratio for factor A with df = 1, 54 and an F-ratio for factor B with df = 2, 108. Explain why this report cannot be correct.

5. The following sets of data represent three potential results from an experiment evaluating computer monitors. The two factors in the experiment are: (A) color of the monitor screen (amber versus green), and (B) the size of the monitor screen (9

inches, 12 inches, and 15 inches). The dependent variable is the ease of use for each monitor as judged by a sample of computer users. The value reported in each cell is the mean rating for the monitor.

Data set 1

	9 INCHES	12 INCHES	15 INCHES
AMBER	5	7	9
GREEN	3	5	7

Data set 2

	9 INCHES	12 INCHES	15 INCHES
AMBER	3	7	3
GREEN	1	5	1

Data set 3

	9 INCHES	12 INCHES	15 INCHES
AMBER	9	5	1
GREEN	1	5	9

For each set of data:

a. Sketch a graph showing the results of the two-factor experiment.

b. In general, is one color monitor generally rated higher than the other? (Describe the A-effect.)

c. In general, how does the size of the monitor screen affect ratings of ease of use? (Describe the B-effect.)

d. Does there appear to be an interaction between color and size? Explain your answer.

6. The following data are from a two-factor experiment with $n = 10$ subjects in each treatment condition (each cell):

		FACTOR B	
		B_1	B_2
FACTOR A	A_1	$AB = 40$ $SS = 70$	$AB = 10$ $SS = 80$
	A_2	$AB = 30$ $SS = 73$	$AB = 20$ $SS = 65$

$$\Sigma X^2 = 588$$

Test for a significant A-effect, B-effect, and $A \times B$ interaction using $\alpha = .05$ for all tests.

7. The following data are from an experiment examining the extent to which different personality types are affected by distraction. Individuals were selected to represent two different personality types: introverts and extroverts. Half the individuals in each group were tested on a monotonous task in a relatively quiet, calm room. The individuals in the other half of each group were tested in a noisy room filled with distractions. The dependent variable was the number of errors committed by each individual. The results of this experiment are as follows:

		FACTOR B (PERSONALITY)	
		INTROVERT	EXTROVERT
FACTOR A (DISTRACTION)	QUIET	$n = 5$ $AB = 10$ $SS = 15$	$n = 5$ $AB = 10$ $SS = 25$
	NOISY	$n = 5$ $AB = 20$ $SS = 10$	$n = 5$ $AB = 40$ $SS = 30$

$$\Sigma X^2 = 520$$

Use an ANOVA with $\alpha = .05$ to evaluate these results. Describe how distraction and personality affect performance.

8. The following data were obtained from an independent-measures experiment using $n = 5$ subjects in each treatment condition:

		FACTOR B	
		B_1	B_2
FACTOR A	A_1	$AB = 15$ $SS = 80$	$AB = 25$ $SS = 90$
	A_2	$AB = 5$ $SS = 70$	$AB = 55$ $SS = 80$

$$\Sigma X^2 = 1100$$

a. Compute the means for each cell and draw a graph showing the results of this experiment. Your graph should be similar to those shown in Figure 15.3.

b. Just from looking at your graph, does there appear to be a main effect for factor A? What about factor B? Does there appear to be an interaction?

c. Use an analysis of variance with $\alpha = .05$ to evaluate these data.

9. Many species of animals communicate using odors. A researcher suspects that specific chemicals contained in the urine of male rats can influence the behavior of other males in the colony. The researcher predicts that male rats will become anxious and more active if they think they are in territory that has been marked by another male. Also, it is predicted that these chemicals will have no effect on female rats. To test this theory, the researcher obtains samples of 15 male and 15 female rats. One-third of each group is tested in a sterile cage. Another one-third of each group is tested in a cage that has been painted with a small amount of the chemicals. The rest of the rats are tested in a cage that has been painted with a large amount of the chemicals. The dependent variable is the activity level of each rat. The data from this experiment are as follows:

	FACTOR B (AMOUNT OF CHEMICAL)		
	NONE	SMALL	LARGE
FACTOR A (SEX) MALE	$n = 5$ $AB = 10$ $SS = 15$	$n = 5$ $AB = 20$ $SS = 19$	$n = 5$ $AB = 30$ $SS = 31$
FEMALE	$n = 5$ $AB = 10$ $SS = 19$	$n = 5$ $AB = 10$ $SS = 21$	$n = 5$ $AB = 10$ $SS = 15$

$$\Sigma X^2 = 460$$

Use an ANOVA with $\alpha = .05$ to test the researcher's predictions. Explain the results.

10. It has been demonstrated in a variety of experiments that memory is best when the conditions at the time of testing are identical to the conditions at the time of learning. This phenomenon is called *encoding specificity* because the specific cues that you use to learn (or encode) new information are the best possible cues to help you recall the information at a later time. In an experimental demonstration of encoding specificity, Tulving and Osler (1968) prepared a list of words to be memorized. For each word on the list, they selected an associated word to serve as a cue. For example, if the word *queen* were on the list, the word *lady* would be a cue. Four groups of subjects participated in the experiment. One group was given the cues during learning and during the recall test. Another group received the cues only during recall. A third group received the cues only during learning, and the final group was not given any cues at all. The dependent variable was the number of words correctly recalled. Data similar to Tulving and Osler's results are as follows:

		CUES AT LEARNING	
		YES	NO
CUES AT RECALL	YES	$n = 10$ $\overline{X} = 3$ $SS = 22$	$n = 10$ $\overline{X} = 1$ $SS = 15$
	NO	$n = 10$ $\overline{X} = 1$ $SS = 16$	$n = 10$ $\overline{X} = 1$ $SS = 19$

$$\Sigma x^2 = 192$$

Use an ANOVA with $\alpha = .05$ to evaluate these data. Describe the results.

11. The following data summarize the results of a two-factor experiment with $n = 5$ in each treatment condition (each cell):

		FACTOR B			
		B_1	B_2	B_3	B_4
FACTOR A	A_1	$AB = 5$ $SS = 40$	$AB = 5$ $SS = 50$	$AB = 5$ $SS = 30$	$AB = 5$ $SS = 40$
	A_2	$AB = 5$ $SS = 30$	$AB = 15$ $SS = 30$	$AB = 15$ $SS = 50$	$AB = 25$ $SS = 50$

$$\Sigma X^2 = 560$$

Use an ANOVA with $\alpha = .05$ to evaluate the results of this experiment.

12. The following data show the results of a two-factor experiment with $n = 10$ in each treatment condition (cell):

		FACTOR B	
		B_1	B_2
FACTOR A	A_1	$\bar{X} = 4$ $SS = 40$	$\bar{X} = 2$ $SS = 50$
	A_2	$\bar{X} = 3$ $SS = 50$	$\bar{X} = 1$ $SS = 40$

$$\Sigma X^2 = 480$$

a. Sketch a graph showing the results of this experiment. (See Figure 15.3 for examples.)
b. Looking at your graph, does there appear to be an $A \times B$ interaction? Does factor A appear to have any effect? Does factor B appear to have any effect?
c. Evaluate these data using an ANOVA with $\alpha = .05$.

13. The following data are from an experiment examining the influence of a specific hormone on eating behavior. Three different drug doses were used, including a control condition (no drug), and the experiment measured eating behavior for males and females. The dependent variable was the amount of food consumed over a 48-hour period.

	NO DRUG	SMALL DOSE	LARGE DOSE
MALES	1 6 1 1 1	7 7 11 4 6	3 1 1 6 4
FEMALES	0 3 7 5 5	0 0 0 5 0	0 2 0 0 3

Use an ANOVA with $\alpha = .05$ to evaluate these data and describe the results (i.e., the drug effect, the sex difference, and the interaction).

14. Hyperactivity in children usually is treated by counseling, or by drugs, or by both. The following data are from an experiment designed to evaluate the effectiveness of these different treatments. The dependent variable is a measure of attention span (how long each child was able to concentrate on a specific task).

	DRUG	NO DRUG
COUNSELING	$n = 10$ $AB = 140$ $SS = 40$	$n = 10$ $AB = 80$ $SS = 36$
NO COUNSELING	$n = 10$ $AB = 120$ $SS = 45$	$n = 10$ $AB = 100$ $SS = 59$

$$\Sigma X^2 = 5220$$

a. Use an ANOVA with $\alpha = .05$ to evaluate these data.
b. Do the data indicate that the drug has a significant effect? Does the counseling have an effect? Describe these results in terms of the effectiveness of the drug and counseling and their interaction.

15. In the preview section of this chapter we presented an experiment that examined the effect of an audience on the performance of two different personality types. Data from this experiment are as follows. The dependent variable is the number of errors made by each subject.

		ALONE	AUDIENCE
SELF-ESTEEM	HIGH	3 6 2 2 4 7	9 4 5 8 4 6
	LOW	7 7 2 6 8 6	10 14 11 15 11 11

Use an ANOVA with $\alpha = .05$ to evaluate these data. Describe the effect of the audience and the effect of personality on performance.

16. The general relation between performance and arousal level is described by the Yerkes-Dodson law. This law states that performance is best at a moderate level of arousal. When arousal is too low, people don't care about what they are doing, and performance is poor. At the other extreme, when arousal is too high, people become overly anxious, and performance suffers. In addition, the exact form of the relation between arousal and performance depends on the difficulty of the task. The following data demonstrate the Yerkes-Dodson law. The dependent variable is a measure of performance.

		AROUSAL LEVEL		
		LOW	MEDIUM	HIGH
TASK DIFFICULTY	EASY	$n = 10$ $AB = 80$ $SS = 30$	$n = 10$ $AB = 100$ $SS = 36$	$n = 10$ $AB = 120$ $SS = 45$
	HARD	$n = 10$ $AB = 60$ $SS = 42$	$n = 10$ $AB = 100$ $SS = 27$	$n = 10$ $AB = 80$ $SS = 36$

$$\Sigma X^2 = 5296$$

a. Sketch a graph showing the mean level of performance for each treatment condition.
b. Use a two-factor ANOVA to evaluate these data.
c. Describe and explain the main effect for task difficulty.
d. Describe and explain the interaction between difficulty and arousal.

17. The following matrix presents the results of a two-factor experiment with two levels of factor A, two levels of factor B, and $n = 10$ subjects in each treatment condition. Each value in the matrix is the mean score for the subjects in that treatment condition. Notice that one of the mean values is missing.

		FACTOR B	
		B_1	B_2
FACTOR A	A_1	10	40
	A_2	30	?

a. What value should be assigned to the missing mean so that the resulting data would show no main effect for factor A?
b. What value should be assigned to the missing mean so that the data would show no main effect for factor B?
c. What value should be assigned to the missing mean so that the data would show no interaction?

18. Individuals who are identified as having an antisocial personality disorder also tend to have reduced physiological responses to painful or anxiety-producing stimuli. In everyday terms, these individuals show a limited physical response to fear, guilt, or anxiety. One way of measuring this response is with the galvanic skin response (GSR). Normally, when a person is aroused, there is an increase in perspiration which causes a measurable reduction in the electrical resistance on the skin. The following data represent the results of an experiment measuring GSR for normal and antisocial individuals in regular and stress-provoking situations:

		AROUSAL LEVEL			
		BASELINE		STRESS	
PERSONALITY	NORMAL	27	25	15	21
		26	23	20	18
		19	24	14	21
		27	26	19	24
		21	19	13	17
	ANTISOCIAL	24	26	29	22
		28	29	27	25
		23	27	22	20
		25	22	20	29
		21	25	28	21

a. Compute the cell means and sketch a graph of the results.
b. Use an ANOVA with $\alpha = .05$ to evaluate these data.
c. Explain the findings of this study.

19. A psychologist would like to evaluate the effectiveness of a special counseling program for students with math anxiety. Students from a freshman math class are assessed as being either high or low in math anxiety. Half of each group participates in the counseling program, while the other students continue without any special counseling. Each student's performance in the course is measured by the grade on the final exam. These data are as follows:

		COUNSELING		NO COUNSELING	
MATH ANXIETY	HIGH	72	61	75	64
		61	63	72	87
		85	82	85	76
		52	68	78	79
	LOW	64	87	75	93
		89	94	78	71
		92	75	90	84
		61	73	84	86

a. Use an analysis of variance to evaluate these data. Use the .05 level of significance for all tests.
b. Based on the results of your analysis, can the psychologist conclude that the counseling program has any effect? Is the effectiveness of the program different for students high in math anxiety versus students low in math anxiety?

20. A school psychologist is examining students' responses to a trial program in self-paced instruction. In this program, students are left on their own to determine how quickly (or slowly) they work through a set of required material. The psychologist suspects that self-motivated students will do well in this program but that other students may find it difficult. The psychologist identifies samples of students with "internal" personality types (self-motivated) and "external" personality types. Half of each group is placed in the self-paced program, and half remains in a normal, well-structured classroom. The final grades for these students are as follows:

	INTERNAL		EXTERNAL	
SELF-PACED	84	64	71	86
	83	85	68	64
	91	93	75	72
	75	90	73	65
STRUCTURED CLASS	86	85	76	90
	83	91	81	85
	92	76	78	83
	72	84	71	72

a. Use an analysis of variance to evaluate these data. Make all tests at the .05 level of significance.
b. Describe the results of the ANOVA in terms of the two independent variables.

21. In addition to measuring classroom performance, the psychologist in Problem 20 also measured each student's attitude toward his or her course. Attitudes were measured on a 10-point scale with 10 being best ("I completely enjoyed the course"). These attitude scores are as follows:

	INTERNAL		EXTERNAL	
SELF-PACED	8	8	3	4
	10	10	5	3
	10	7	3	5
	9	8	7	6
	7	9	5	5
STRUCTURED CLASS	8	7	8	8
	6	6	9	7
	5	7	10	6
	10	5	7	9
	7	8	9	8

a. Use an ANOVA with $\alpha = .05$ to evaluate these data.

b. Describe the results. (Is one type of instruction preferred over the other? Is one personality type generally more positive or negative than the other? Does preference for the type of instruction depend on personality?

22. The process of interference is assumed to be responsible for much of forgetting in human memory. New information going into memory interferes with the information that already is there. One demonstration of interference examines the process of forgetting while people are asleep versus while they are awake. Because there should be less interference during sleep, there also should be less forgetting. The following data are the results from an experiment examining four groups of subjects. All subjects were given a list of words to remember. Then half of the subjects went to sleep, and the others stayed awake. Within both the asleep and the awake groups, half of the subjects were tested after 2 hours, and the rest were tested after 8 hours. The dependent variable is the number of words correctly recalled.

	DELAY OF MEMORY TEST			
	2 HOURS		8 HOURS	
ASLEEP	5	7	6	4
	6	10	8	4
	4	5	5	7
	3	8	10	8
	6	5	7	6
AWAKE	3	2	1	2
	4	3	0	1
	5	4	0	2
	3	2	1	0
	2	4	1	1

a. Use a two-factor ANOVA to examine these data.

b. Describe and explain the interaction.

23. Most adolescents experience a growth spurt when they are between 12 and 15 years old. This period of dramatic growth generally occurs earlier for girls than for boys. A psychologist studying the physical development of adolescents recorded the gain in height (in centimeters) over a 1-year period for boys and girls ranging in age from 11 to 15. Separate samples were used for each age group. The data are as follows:

	AGE				
	11 YEARS	12 YEARS	13 YEARS	14 YEARS	15 YEARS
MALES	4	4	6	8	9
	5	5	7	7	8
	6	4	5	10	6
	5	6	4	9	7
	4	4	7	10	6
	5	6	6	7	7
FEMALES	5	8	7	4	1
	7	7	6	3	2
	6	9	6	3	2
	5	10	7	5	1
	6	9	5	3	1
	6	8	6	4	2

a. Compute the mean gain in height for each of these 10 groups and draw a graph showing the results of this study.

b. By just looking at your graph, how would you describe the difference between the growth spurt for boys and the growth spurt for girls?

c. Use an analysis of variance to evaluate these data. Perform all tests with $\alpha = .05$.

d. Do the results of the ANOVA support your description of these data?

24. It has been demonstrated that children who watch violent television shows tend to be more aggressive than children who are not exposed to television violence. However, there is some question as to whether this effect exists only for shows with human characters or whether it also occurs for violent cartoons. A hypothetical experiment to address this question is presented here. A large sample of pre-school children is obtained. One group from this sample watches a violent TV show with human characters for half an hour. A second group watches violent cartoons. Two other groups serve as control groups: One watches nonviolent human shows, and the other watches nonviolent cartoons. After watching these television shows, all four groups are placed together in a large playroom, and a psychologist records the number of aggressive actions for each child.

a. Identify the two independent variables (factors) and the dependent variable for this experiment.

b. Suppose that the psychologist is predicting that exposure to human violence will affect behavior but that cartoon violence will not. If the psychol-

ogist is correct, what outcomes are expected for the ANOVA? Predict both main effects and the interaction. (*Note:* It may help to sketch a graph of the predicted results.)

c. Suppose that the psychologist predicts that cartoon violence and human violence will affect behavior equally. In this case, what outcomes are expected for the ANOVA? Predict both main effects and the interaction.

25. The following hypothetical data represent one possible outcome of the experiment described in Problem 24:

	VIOLENT		NONVIOLENT	
HUMAN CHARACTERS	6	2	3	5
	3	4	2	3
	2	5	1	2
	5	4	4	4
	3	6	2	3
CARTOON CHARACTERS	5	2	1	3
	4	5	3	2
	3	3	2	2
	4	3	3	3
	3	4	4	4

a. Use an ANOVA to evaluate these data. Set $\alpha = .05$ for all tests.

b. Describe the results of this experiment.

TOOLS YOU WILL NEED

The following items are considered essential background material for this chapter. If you doubt your knowledge of any of these items, you should review the appropriate chapter or section before proceeding.

- Sum of squares (*SS*) (Chapter 4)
  - Computational formula
  - Definitional formula
- *z*-scores (Chapter 4)
- Hypothesis testing (Chapter 8)

CONTENTS

PREVIEW

Having been a student and taken exams for much of your life, you probably have noticed a curious phenomenon. In every class there are some students who zip through exams and turn in their papers while everyone else is still on page 1. Other students cling to their exams and are still working frantically when the instructor announces that time is up and demands that all papers be turned in. Have you wondered what grades these students receive? Are the students who finish first the best in the class, or are they completely ignorant and simply accepting their failure? Are the A students the last to finish because they are compulsively checking and rechecking their answers? To help answer these questions, we carefully observed a recent exam and recorded the amount of time each student spent and the grade each student received. These data are shown in Figure 16.1. Note that we have listed time along the X-axis and grade on the Y-axis. Each student is identified by a point in the graph with the point located directly above the student's time and directly across from the student's grade. Also note that we have drawn a line through the middle of the data points in Figure 16.1. The line helps make the relationship between time and grade more obvious. The graph shows that the highest grades tend to go to the students who finished their exams early. Students who held their papers to the bitter end tended to have low grades.

In statistical terms, these data show a correlation between time and grade. In this chapter we will see how correlations are used to measure and describe relations. Just as a sample mean provides a concise description of

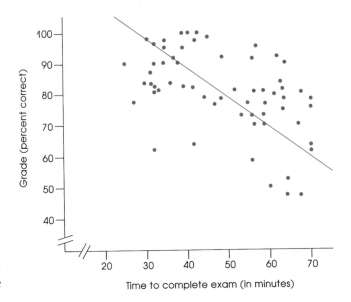

Figure 16.1

The relationship between exam grade and time needed to complete the exam. Notice the general trend in these data: Students who finish the exam early tend to have better grades.

an entire sample, a correlation will provide a description of a relationship. We also will look at how correlations are used and interpreted. For example, now that you have seen the relation between time and grades, don't you think it might be a good idea to start turning in your exam papers a little sooner? Wait and see.

16.1 OVERVIEW

Correlation is a statistical technique that is used to measure and describe a relationship between two variables. Usually, the two variables are simply observed as they exist naturally in the environment—there is no attempt to control or manipulate the variables. For example, a researcher interested in the relation between nutrition and IQ could observe (and record) the dietary patterns for a group of preschool children and then measure IQ scores for the same group. Notice that the researcher is not trying to manipulate the children's diet or IQ but is simply observing what occurs naturally. You also should notice that a correlation requires two scores for each individual (one

Figure 16.2

The same set of $n = 6$ pairs of scores (X and Y values) is shown in a table and in a scatterplot. Notice that the scatterplot allows you to see the relationship between X and Y.

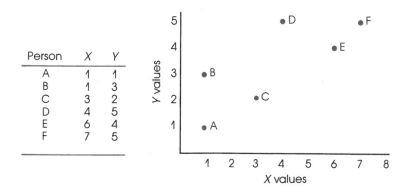

Person	X	Y
A	1	1
B	1	3
C	3	2
D	4	5
E	6	4
F	7	5

score from each of the two variables). These scores normally are identified as X and Y. The pairs of scores can be listed in a table, or they can be presented graphically in a scatterplot (see Figure 16.2). In the scatterplot, the X values are placed on the horizontal axis of a graph, and the Y values are placed on the vertical axis. Each individual is then identified by a single point on the graph so that the coordinates of the point (the X and Y values) match the individual's X score and Y score. The value of the scatterplot is that it allows you to see the nature of the relationship (see Figure 16.2).

THE CHARACTERISTICS OF A RELATIONSHIP

A correlation measures three characteristics of the relation between X and Y. These three characteristics are as follows:

1. The Direction of the Relationship. Correlations can be classified into two basic categories: positive and negative.

DEFINITIONS

In a *positive correlation*, the two variables tend to move in the same direction: When the X variable increases, the Y variable also increases; if the X variable decreases, the Y variable also decreases.

In a *negative correlation*, the two variables tend to go in opposite directions. As the X variable increases, the Y variable decreases. That is, it is an inverse relationship.

The direction of a relationship is identified by the sign of the correlation. A positive value ($+$) indicates a positive relationship; a negative value ($-$) indicates a negative relation. The following example provides a description of positive and negative relations.

EXAMPLE 16.1

Remember that the actual data appear as *points* in the figures. The dashed lines have been added as visual aids to help make the direction of the relationship easier to see.

Suppose you run the drink concession at the football stadium. After several seasons you begin to notice a relationship between the temperature at game time and the beverages you sell. Specifically, you have noted that when the temperature is high, you tend to sell a lot of beer. When the temperature is low, you sell relatively little beer [see Figure 16.3(a)]. This is an example of a positive correlation. At the same time, you have noted a relation between temperature and coffee sales: On cold days

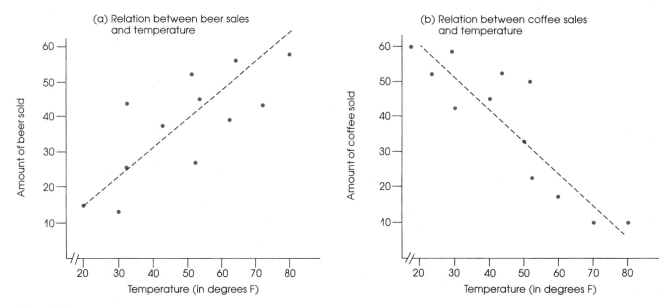

Figure 16.3

Examples of positive and negative relationships. Beer sales are positively related
to temperature, and coffee sales are negatively related to temperature.

you sell much more coffee than on hot days [see Figure 16.2(b)]. This is
an example of a negative relation.

2. The Form of the Relation. In the preceding coffee and beer examples, the relationships tend to have a linear form; that is, the points in the
scatterplot tend to form a straight line. Notice that we have drawn a line
through the middle of the data points in each figure to help show the relation. The most common use of correlation is to measure straight-line relations. However, you should note that other forms of relationship do exist
and that there are special correlations used to measure them. Figure
16.4(a) shows the typical relation between practice and performance. This
is not a straight-line relationship. In the early stages of practice, performance increases rapidly. But with a great deal of practice, the improvement in performance becomes less noticeable. (Ask anyone who has taken
piano lessons for 10 years.) Figure 16.4(b) shows the relation between vocabulary scores and gender for 5-year-old children. Again, this is not a
straight-line relation. These data show a tendency for females to have
higher scores than males. Many different types of correlations exist. In
general, each type is designed to evaluate a specific form of relationship.
In this text we will concentrate on the correlation that measures linear
relations.

3. The Degree of the Relationship. Finally, a correlation measures
how well the data fit the specific form being considered. For example, a
linear correlation measures how well the data points fit on a straight line.

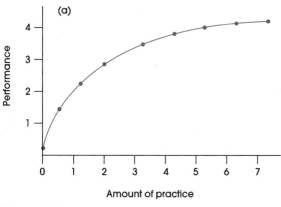
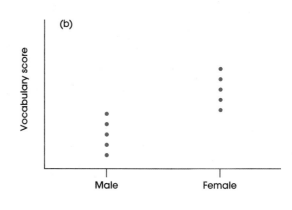

Figure 16.4

Examples of relationships that are not linear. (a) Relationship between performance and amount of practice. (b) Relationship between vocabulary score and gender.

A correlation of −1.00 also indicates a perfect fit. The direction of the relation (positive or negative) should be considered separately from the degree of the relationship.

A *perfect correlation* always is identified by a correlation of 1.00, and indicates a perfect fit whereas a correlation of 0 indicates no fit at all. Intermediate values represent the degree to which the data points approximate the perfect fit. The numerical value of the correlation also reflects the degree to which there is a consistent, predictable relation between the two variables. Again, a correlation of 1.00 (or −1.00) indicates a perfectly consistent relation.

Examples of different values for linear correlations are shown in Figure 16.5. Notice that in each example we have sketched a line around the data points. This line, called an *envelope* because it encloses the data, often helps you to see the overall trend in the data.

Figure 16.5

Examples of different values for linear correlations: (a) shows a good positive relation, approximately +0.90; (b) shows a relatively poor negative correlation, approximately −0.40; (c) shows a perfect negative correlation, −1.00; (d) shows no linear trend, 0.00.

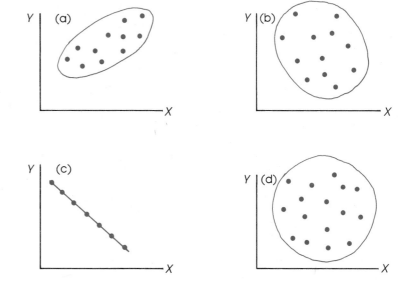

WHERE AND WHY CORRELATIONS ARE USED

Although correlations have a number of different applications, a few specific examples are presented next to give an indication of the value of this statistical measure.

1. Prediction. If two variables are known to be related in some systematic way, it is possible to use one of the variables to make accurate predictions about the other. For example, when you applied for admission to college, you were required to submit a great deal of personal information, including your scores on the Scholastic Aptitude Test (SAT). College officials want this information so they can predict your chances of success in college. It has been demonstrated over several years that SAT scores and college grade point averages are correlated. Students who do well on the SAT tend to do well in college; students who have difficulty with the SAT tend to have difficulty in college. Based on this relationship, the college admissions office can make a prediction about the potential success of each applicant. You should note that this prediction is not perfectly accurate. Not everyone who does poorly on the SAT will have trouble in college. That is why you also submit letters of recommendation, high school grades, and other information with your application.

2. Validity. Suppose a psychologist develops a new test for measuring intelligence. How could you show that this test truly is measuring what it claims; that is, how could you demonstrate the validity of the test? One common technique for demonstrating validity is to use a correlation. If the test actually is measuring intelligence, then the scores on the test should be related to other measures of intelligence, for example, standardized IQ tests, performance on learning tasks, problem-solving ability, etc. The psychologist could measure the correlation between the new test and each of these other measures of intelligence in order to demonstrate that the new test is valid.

3. Reliability. In addition to evaluating the validity of a measurement procedure, correlations are also used to determine reliability. A measurement procedure is considered reliable to the extent that it produces stable, consistent measurements. That is, a reliable measurement procedure will produce the same (or nearly the same) scores when the same individuals are measured under the same conditions. For example, if your IQ were measured as 113 last week, you would expect to obtain nearly the same score if your IQ were measured again this week. One way to evaluate reliability is to use correlations to determine the relationship between two sets of measurements. When reliability is high, the correlation between two measurements should be strong and positive.

4. Theory Verification. Many psychological theories make specific predictions about the relationship between two variables. For example, a theory may predict a relation between brain size and learning ability; a developmental theory may predict a relationship between the parents' IQs and the child's IQ; a social psychologist may have a theory predicting a relation between personality type and behavior in a social situation. In each case, the prediction of the theory could be tested by determining the correlation between the two variables.

LEARNING CHECK 1. If the world were fair, would you expect a positive or negative relationship between grade point average *(X)* and weekly studying hours *(Y)* for college students?

2. Data suggest that on average children from large families have lower IQs than children from small families. Do these data indicate a positive or negative relation between family size and average IQ?

3. If you are measuring linear relationship, correlations of +0.50 and −0.50 are equally good in terms of how well the data fit on a straight line. (True or false?)

4. It is impossible to have a correlation greater than +1.00 or less than −1.00. (True or false?)

ANSWERS 1. Positive. More hours studying should be associated with higher grade point averages.

2. negative

3. True. The degree of fit is measured by the magnitude of the correlation independent of sign.

4. True. Correlations are always from +1.00 to −1.00.

16.2 THE PEARSON CORRELATION

By far the most common correlation is the Pearson correlation (or the Pearson product-moment correlation).

DEFINITION   The *Pearson correlation* measures the degree and direction of linear relation between two variables.

The Pearson correlation is identified by the letter *r*. Conceptually, this correlation is computed by

$$r = \frac{\text{degree to which } X \text{ and } Y \text{ vary together}}{\text{degree to which } X \text{ and } Y \text{ vary separately}}$$

$$= \frac{\text{covariability of } X \text{ and } Y}{\text{variability of } X \text{ and } Y \text{ separately}}$$

When there is a perfect linear relation, every change in the *X* variable is accompanied by a corresponding change in the *Y* variable. In Figure 16.5(c), for example, every time the value of *X* increases, there is a perfectly predictable decrease in *Y*. The result is a perfect linear relation, with *X* and *Y* always varying together. In this case, the covariability (*X* and *Y* together) is identical to the variability of *X* and *Y* separately, and the formula produces a correlation of −1.00. At the other extreme, when there is no linear relation, a change in the X variable does not correspond to any predictable change in Y. In this case there is no covariability, and the resulting correlation is zero.

THE SUM OF PRODUCTS OF DEVIATIONS

To calculate the Pearson correlation, it is necessary to introduce one new concept: the sum of products of deviations. In the past we have used a similar concept, SS (the sum of squared deviations), to measure the amount of variability for a single variable. The *sum of products*, or SP, provides a parallel procedure for measuring the amount of covariability between two variables. The value for SP can be calculated with either a definitional formula or a computational formula.

The *definitional formula* for the sum of products is

$$SP = \Sigma(X - \overline{X})(Y - \overline{Y}) \tag{16.1}$$

This formula instructs you to first find the product of each X deviation and Y deviation and then add up these products. Notice that the terms in the formula define the value being calculated: the sum of the products of the deviations.

The *computational formula* for the sum of products is

Caution: The n in this formula refers to the number of pairs of scores.

$$SP = \Sigma XY - \frac{\Sigma X \Sigma Y}{n} \tag{16.2}$$

Because the computational formula uses the original scores (X and Y values), it usually results in easier calculations than those required with the definitional formula. However, both formulas will always produce the same value for SP.

You may have noted that the formulas for SP are similar to the formulas you have learned for SS (sum of squares). The relation between the two sets of formulas is described in Box 16.1. The following example demonstrates the calculation of SP with both formulas.

EXAMPLE 16.2

The same set of $n = 4$ pairs of scores will be used to calculate SP, first using the definitional formula and then the computational formula.

For the definitional formula, you need deviation scores for each of the X values and each of the Y values. Note that the mean for the X's is $\overline{X} = 3$ and that the mean for the Y's is $\overline{Y} = 5$. The deviations and the products of deviations are shown in the following table:

Caution: The signs (+ and −) are critical in determining the sum of products, SP.

| SCORES | | DEVIATIONS | | PRODUCTS |
X	Y	$X - \overline{X}$	$Y - \overline{Y}$	$(X - \overline{X})(Y - \overline{Y})$
1	3	−2	−2	+4
2	6	−1	+1	−1
4	4	+1	−1	−1
5	7	+2	+2	+4
				+6 = SP

16.1   COMPARING THE *SP*
       AND *SS* FORMULAS

IT WILL help you to learn the formulas for *SP* if you note the similarity between the two *SP* formulas and the corresponding formulas for *SS* that were presented in Chapter 4. The definitional formula for *SS* is

$$SS = \Sigma(X - \bar{X})^2$$

In this formula, you must square each deviation, which is equivalent to multiplying it by itself. With this in mind, the formula can be rewritten as

$$SS = \Sigma(X - \bar{X})(X - \bar{X})$$

The similarity between the *SS* formula and the *SP* formula should be obvious—the *SS* formula uses squares and the *SP* formula uses products. This same relationship exists for the computational formulas. For *SS*, the computational formula is

$$SS = \Sigma X^2 - \frac{(\Sigma X)^2}{n}$$

As before, each squared value can be rewritten so that the formula becomes

$$SS = \Sigma XX - \frac{\Sigma X \Sigma X}{n}$$

Again, you should note the similarity in structure between the *SS* formula and the *SP* formula. If you remember that *SS* uses squares and *SP* uses products, the two new formulas for the sum of products should be easy to learn.

For these scores, the sum of the products of the deviations is $SP = +6$.

For the computational formula, you need the sum of the X values, the sum of the Y values, and the sum of the XY product for each pair. These values are as follows:

X	Y	XY	
1	3	3	
2	6	12	
4	4	16	
5	7	35	
12	20	66	Totals

Substituting the sums in the formula gives

$$SP = \Sigma XY - \frac{\Sigma X \Sigma Y}{n}$$

$$= 66 - \frac{12(20)}{4}$$

$$= 66 - 60$$

$$= 6$$

Note that both formulas produce the same result, $SP = 6$.

CALCULATION OF THE PEARSON CORRELATION

By using the sum of products to measure the covariability between X and Y, the formula for the Pearson correlation becomes

$$r = \frac{SP}{\sqrt{SS_X SS_Y}}$$

(16.3)

Note that you *multiply SS* for X and *SS* for Y in the denominator of the Pearson formula.

Notice that the variability for X is measured by the SS for the X-scores and the variability for Y is measured by SS for the Y-scores. The following example demonstrates the use of this formula with a simple set of scores.

EXAMPLE 16.3

The Pearson correlation is computed for the following set of $n = 5$ pairs of scores:

X	Y
0	1
10	3
4	1
8	2
8	3

Before starting any calculations, it is useful to put the data in a scatterplot and make a preliminary estimate of the correlation. These data have been graphed in Figure 16.6. Looking at the scatterplot, it appears that there is a very good (but not perfect) positive correlation. You should expect an approximate value of $r = +0.8$ or $+0.9$. To find the Pearson correlation, we will need SP, SS for X, and SS for Y. Each of these values is calculated using the definitional formula.

Figure 16.6

Scatterplot of the data from Example 16.3.

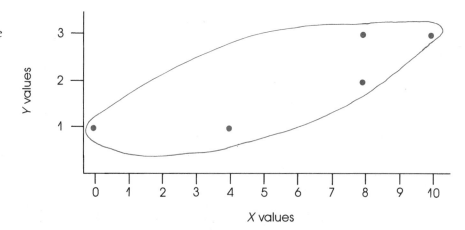

For the sum of products,

SCORES		DEVIATIONS		PRODUCTS
X	Y	$X - \bar{X}$	$Y - \bar{Y}$	$(X - \bar{X})(Y - \bar{Y})$
0	1	−6	−1	+6
10	3	+4	+1	+4
4	1	−2	−1	+2
8	2	+2	0	0
8	3	+2	+1	+2
				$+14 = SP$

For the X values,

X	$X - \bar{X}$	$(X - \bar{X})^2$
0	−6	36
10	+4	16
4	−2	4
8	+2	4
8	+2	4
		$64 = SS$ for X

For the Y values,

Y	$Y - \bar{Y}$	$(Y - \bar{Y})^2$
1	−1	1
3	+1	1
1	−1	1
2	0	0
3	+1	1
		$4 = SS$ for Y

Correlations are computed with Minitab using CORRELATION (see Section 20.8)

By using these values, the Pearson correlation is

$$r = \frac{SP}{\sqrt{SS_X SS_Y}} = \frac{14}{\sqrt{64(4)}}$$

$$= \frac{14}{16} = +0.875$$

Note that the value we obtained is in agreement with the prediction based on the scatterplot.

THE PEARSON CORRELATION AND z-SCORES

The Pearson correlation measures the relation between an individual's location in the X distribution and his or her location in the Y distribution. For example, a positive correlation means that individuals who score high on X also tend to score high on Y. Similarly, a negative correlation indicates that individuals with high X scores tend to have low Y scores.

You should recall from Chapter 5 that z-scores provide a precise way to identify the location of an individual score within a distribution. Because the Pearson correlation measures the relation between locations and because z-scores are used to specify locations, the formula for the Pearson correlation can be expressed entirely in terms of z-scores:

$$r = \frac{\sum z_X z_Y}{n} \qquad\qquad (16.4)$$

In this formula, z_X identifies each individual's position within the X distribution, and z_Y identifies the position within the Y distribution. The product of the z-scores (like the product of the deviation scores) determines the strength and direction of the correlation.

Because z-scores are considered to be the best way to describe a location within a distribution, formula 16.4 often is considered to be the best way to define the Pearson correlation. However, you should realize that this formula requires a lot of tedious calculations (changing each score to a z-score), so it rarely is used to calculate a correlation.

LEARNING CHECK

1. Describe what is measured by a Pearson correlation.

2. Can SP ever have a value less than zero?

3. Calculate the sum of products of deviations *(SP)* for the following set of scores. Use the definitional formula and then the computational formula. Verify that you get the same answer with both formulas.

X	Y
1	0
3	1
7	6
5	2
4	1

Remember, it is useful to sketch a scatterplot and make an estimate of the correlation before you begin calculations.

4. Compute the Pearson correlation for the following data:

X	Y
2	9
1	10
3	6
0	8
4	2

ANSWERS

1. The Pearson correlation measures the degree and direction of linear relationship between two variables.

2. Yes. SP can be positive, negative, or zero depending on the relation between X and Y.

3. $SP = 19$ 4. $r = -\dfrac{16}{20} = -0.80$

16.3 UNDERSTANDING AND INTERPRETING THE PEARSON CORRELATION

When you encounter correlations, there are four additional considerations that you should bear in mind:

1. Correlation simply describes a relationship between two variables. It does not explain why the two variables are related. Specifically, a correlation should not and cannot be interpreted as proof of a cause-and-effect relation between the two variables.

2. The value of a correlation can be affected greatly by the range of scores represented in the data.

3. One or two extreme data points, often called *outriders,* can have a dramatic effect on the value of a correlation.

4. When judging "how good" a relationship is, it is tempting to focus on the numerical value of the correlation. For example, a correlation of +0.5 is halfway between 0 and 1.00 and therefore appears to represent a moderate degree of relation. However, a correlation should not be interpreted as a proportion. Although a correlation of 1.00 does mean that there is a 100% perfectly predictable relation between X and Y, a correlation of 0.5 does not mean that you can make predictions with 50% accuracy. To describe how accurately one variable predicts the other, you must square the correlation. Thus, a correlation of $r = 0.5$ provides only $r^2 = 0.5^2 = 0.25$, or 25% accuracy.

Each of these four points will now be discussed in detail.

CORRELATION AND CAUSATION

One of the most common errors in interpreting correlations is to assume that a correlation necessarily implies a cause-and-effect relation between the two variables. We constantly are bombarded with reports of relationships: Cigarette smoking is related to heart disease; alcohol consumption is related to birth defects; carrot consumption is related to good eyesight. Do these relationships mean that cigarettes cause heart disease or carrots cause good eyesight? The answer is *no.* Although there may be a causal relation, the simple existence of a correlation does not prove it. This point should become clear in the following hypothetical example.

EXAMPLE 16.4

Suppose we select a variety of different cities and towns throughout the United States and measure the number of serious crimes (Y variable) and the number of churches (X variable) for each. A scatterplot showing hypothetical data for this study is presented in Figure 16.7. Notice that this scatterplot shows a strong, positive correlation between churches and crime. You also should note that these are realistic data. It is reasonable that the smaller towns would have less crime and fewer churches and that the large cities would have large values for both variables. Does this relation mean that churches cause crime? Does it mean

Figure 16.7

Hypothetical data showing the logical relation between the number of churches and the number of serious crimes for a sample of U.S. cities.

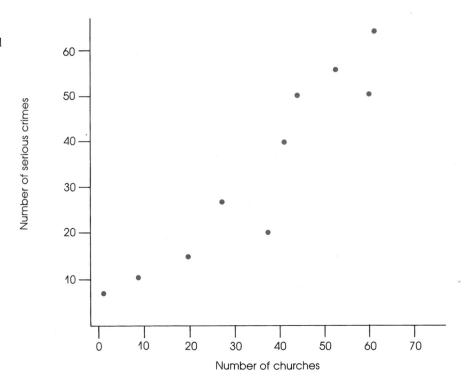

that crime causes churches? It should be clear that the answer is no. Although a strong correlation exists between churches and crime, the real cause of the relationship is the size of the population.

CORRELATION AND RESTRICTED RANGE

Whenever a correlation is computed from scores that do not represent the full range of possible values, you should be cautious in interpreting the correlation. Suppose, for example, you are interested in the relationship between IQ and creativity. If you select a sample of your fellow college students, your data probably would represent only a limited range of IQ scores (most likely from 110 to 130). The correlation within this restricted range could be completely different from the correlation that would be obtained from a full range of IQ scores. Two extreme examples are shown in Figure 16.8.

Figure 16.8(a) shows an example where there is strong positive relation between *X* and *Y* when the entire range of scores is considered. However, this relation is obscured when the data are limited to a *restricted range*. In Figure 16.8(b) there is no consistent relation between *X* and *Y* for the full range of scores. However, when the range of *X* values is restricted, the data show a strong positive relation.

To be safe, you should not generalize any correlation beyond the range of data represented in the sample. For a correlation to provide an accurate description for the general population, there should be a wide range of *X* and *Y* values in the data.

(a)

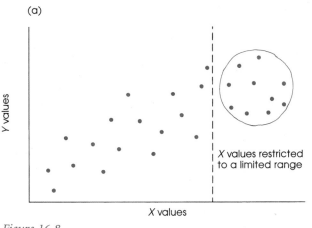

(b)

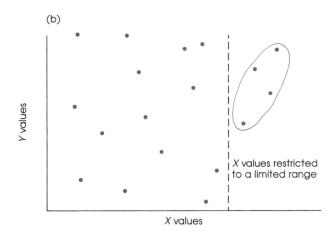

Figure 16.8

(a) An example where the full range of X and Y values show a strong, positive correlation but the restricted range of scores produces a correlation near zero. (b) An example where the full range of X and Y values show a correlation near zero but the scores in the restricted range produce a strong, positive correlation.

OUTRIDERS

An outrider is an individual with X and/or Y values that are substantially greater (or smaller) than the values obtained for the other individuals in a data set. A single outrider can have a dramatic effect on the value obtained for a correlation. This phenomenon is shown in Figure 16.9. Figure 16.9(a) shows a set of $n = 5$ data points where the correlation between X and Y is near zero (the actual value is $r = -0.08$). In Figure 16.9(b) one extreme data point has been added to the original set. When this outrider is included, a strong, positive correlation emerges (the correlation is now $r = 0.85$). Notice that the single outrider drastically alters the correlation and, thereby, can change the interpretation of the relationship between X and Y.

CORRELATION AND THE STRENGTH OF THE RELATION

A correlation measures the degree of relation between two variables on a scale from 0 to 1.00. Although this number provides a measure of the degree of relationship, many researchers prefer to square the correlation and use the resulting value to measure the strength of the relationship.

One of the common uses of correlation is for prediction. If two variables are correlated, you can use the value of one variable to predict the other. For example, college admissions officers do not just guess which applicants are likely to do well; they use other variables (SAT scores, high school grades, etc.) to predict which students are most likely to be successful. These predictions are based on correlations. By using correlations, the admissions officers expect to make more-accurate predictions than would be obtained by just guessing. In general, the squared correlation (r^2) measures the gain in accuracy that is obtained from using the correlation for prediction instead of just guessing.

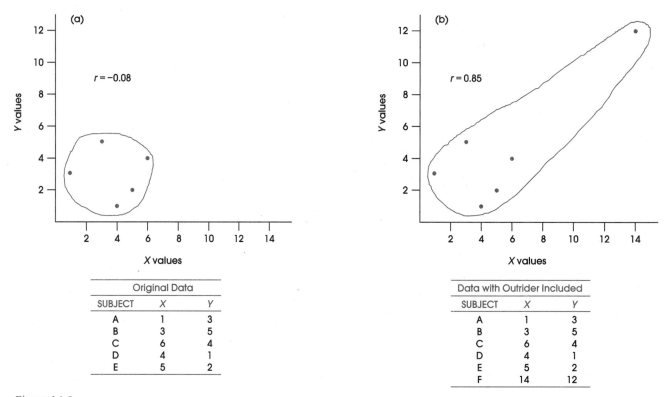

Figure 16.9

A demonstration of how one extreme data point (an outrider) can influence the value of a correlation.

DEFINITION   The value r^2 is called the *coefficient of determination* because it measures the proportion of variability in one variable that can be determined from the relationship with the other variable. A correlation of $r = 0.80$ (or -0.80), for example, means that $r^2 = 0.64$ (or 64%) of the variability in the Y scores can be predicted from the relation with X.

A more detailed discussion of the coefficient of determination is presented in Section 16.6. For now, you simply should realize that whenever two variables are consistently related, it is possible to use one variable to predict the values of the second variable. The amount of variability that can be predicted is determined by r^2 (see Figure 16.10).

One final consideration concerning the interpretation of correlations is presented in Box 16.2.

(a) With $r = 0$, X and Y are independent. None of the Y variability can be predicted from X; $r^2 = 0$.

(b) With $r = 0.8$, the Y variability is partially predicted from the relation with X; $r^2 = 0.64$ or 64%.

(c) With $r = 1$, all the Y variability is predicted from the relation with X; $r^2 = 1.00$ or 100%.

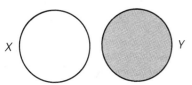
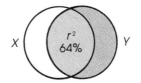
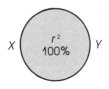

Figure 16.10

A graphic representation of the coefficient of determination, r^2. See text for further explanation.

16.4 HYPOTHESIS TESTS WITH THE PEARSON CORRELATION

The Pearson correlation is generally computed for sample data. Quite often, however, the sample correlation is used to provide information about the entire population. For example, a psychologist would like to know whether there is a relation between IQ and creativity. This is a general question concerning a population. To answer the question, a sample would be selected and the sample data would be used to compute the correlation value. You should recognize this process as an example of inferential statistics: using samples to draw inferences about populations. In the past, we have been concerned primarily with using sample means as the basis for answering questions about population means. In this section we will examine the procedures for using a sample correlation as the basis for testing hypotheses about the corresponding population correlation.

The basic question for this hypothesis test is whether or not a correlation exists in the population. The null hypothesis says "No, there is no correlation in the population," or "The population correlation is zero." The alternative hypothesis is "Yes, there is a real, nonzero, correlation in the population." Because the population correlation is traditionally represented by ρ (the Greek letter rho), these hypotheses would be stated in symbols as

Directional hypotheses for a "one-tailed" test would specify either a positive correlation ($\rho > 0$) or a negative correlation ($\rho < 0$).

$$H_0: \quad \rho = 0 \quad \text{(no population correlation)}$$
$$H_1: \quad \rho \neq 0 \quad \text{(there is a real correlation)}$$

The correlation from the sample data *(r)* will be used to evaluate these hypotheses. As always, samples are not expected to be identical to the populations from which they come. Specifically, you should note that it is possible to obtain a nonzero sample correlation even when the population value is zero. This is particularly true when you have a small sample (see Figure 16.12). The question for this hypothesis test is whether the obtained

CONSIDER THE following problem:

Explain why the rookie of the year in major-league baseball usually does not perform as well in his second season.

Notice that this question does not appear to be statistical or mathematical in nature. However, the answer to the question is directly related to the statistical concepts of correlation and regression. Specifically, there is a simple observation about correlations known as *regression toward the mean*.

DEFINITION   When there is a less-than-perfect correlation between two variables, extreme scores (high or low) on one variable tend to be paired with less extreme scores (more toward the mean) on the second variable. This fact is called *regression toward the mean*.

Figure 16.11 shows a scatterplot with a less-than-perfect correlation between two variables. The data points in this figure might represent batting averages for baseball rookies in 1990 (variable 1) and batting averages for the same players in 1991 (variable 2). Because the correlation is less than perfect, the highest scores on variable 1 are generally *not* the highest scores on variable 2. In baseball terms, the rookies with the highest averages in 1990 do not have the highest averages in 1991.

Remember that a correlation does not explain *why* one variable is related to the other; it simply says that there is a relation. The correlation cannot explain why the best rookie does not perform as well in his second year. But, because the correlation is not perfect, it is a statistical fact that extremely high scores in one year generally will *not* be paired with extremely high scores in the next year.

Regression toward the mean often poses a problem for interpreting experimental results. Suppose, for example, that you want to evaluate the effects of a special preschool program for disadvantaged children. You select a sample of children who score extremely low on an academic performance test. After participating in your preschool program, these children score significantly higher on the test. Why did their scores improve? One answer is that the special program helped. But, an alternative answer is regression toward the mean. If there is a less-than-perfect correlation between scores on the first test and scores on the second test (which is usually the case), individuals with extremely low scores on test 1 will tend to have higher scores on test 2. It is a statistical fact of life, not necessarily the result of any special program.

Now try using the concept of regression toward the mean to explain the following phenomena:

1. You have a truly outstanding meal at a restaurant. However, when you go back with a group of friends, you find that the food is disappointing.

2. You have the highest score on exam I in your statistics class but score only a little above average on exam II.

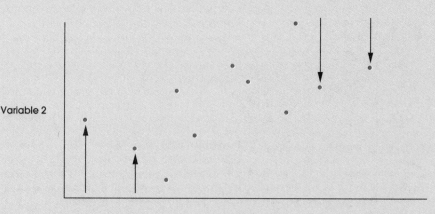

Figure 16.11

A demonstration of regression toward the mean. The figure shows a scatterplot for a set of data with a less-than-perfect correlation. Notice that the highest scores on variable 1 (extreme right-hand points) are not the highest scores on variable 2 but are displaced downward toward the mean. Also, the lowest scores on variable 1 (extreme left-hand points) are not the lowest scores on variable 2 but are displaced upward toward the mean.

Variable 2

Variable 1

Figure 16.12

Scatterplot of a population of *X* and *Y* values with a near zero correlation. However, a small sample of *n* = 3 data points from this population shows a relatively strong, positive correlation. Data points in the sample are circled.

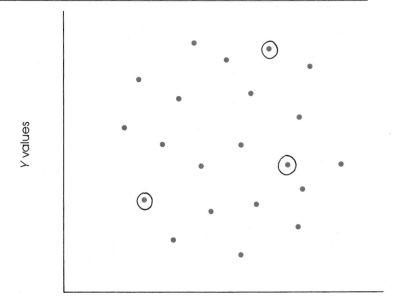

Y values

X values

sample correlation provides sufficient evidence to conclude that a real, nonzero correlation exists in the population. Although it is possible to conduct this hypothesis test by calculating either a *t* statistic or an *F*-ratio, the detailed computations have been completed and are summarized in Appendix B, Table B.6. To use the table, you must know the sample size (*n*), the magnitude of the sample correlation (independent of sign), and the alpha level. If the magnitude of the sample correlation (*r*) equals or exceeds the value given in the table, then we reject H_0 conclude that there is significant evidence for a correlation in the population. To demonstrate the use of the table, suppose you have a sample of *n* = 30 and want to test a nondirectional hypothesis about the population with α = .05. In this case, the table indicates that your sample correlation must be greater than or equal to 0.361 to be significant.

The table lists critical values in terms of degrees of freedom: *df* = *n* − 2. Remember to subtract 2 when using this table.

LEARNING CHECK

1. A researcher obtains a correlation of *r* = −.41 for a sample of *n* = 30 individuals. Does this sample provide sufficient evidence to conclude that there is a significant, nonzero correlation in the population? Assume a nondirectional test with α = .05.

2. For a sample of *n* = 20, how large a correlation is needed to conclude at the .05 level that there is a nonzero correlation in the population? Assume a nondirectional test.

3. As sample size gets smaller, what happens to the magnitude of the correlation necessary for significance? Explain why this occurs.

ANSWERS   1. Yes. For $n = 30$, the critical value is $r = 0.361$. The sample value is in the critical region.

2. For $n = 20$ the critical value is $r = 0.444$.

3. As the sample size gets smaller, the magnitude of the correlation needed for significance gets larger. With a small sample, it is easy to get a relatively good correlation just by chance (see Figure 16.12). Therefore, a small sample requires a very large correlation before you can be confident that there is a real (nonzero) relation in the population.

16.5 OTHER MEASURES OF RELATIONSHIP

Although the Pearson correlation is the most commonly used method for evaluating the relationship between two variables, there are many other measures of relationship that exist. Many of these alternative correlations are simply special applications of the Pearson formula. In this section we examine three alternative correlations. Notice that each alternative simply applies the Pearson formula to data with special characteristics.

THE SPEARMAN CORRELATION   The Spearman correlation is intended to measure the degree and direction of relationshp between two variables where both variables are measured on ordinal scales; that is, both X and Y consist of ranks. The Spearman correlation is identified by the symbol r_s and is computed using the regular Pearson equation (formula 16.3) with the ranked data.

The Spearman correlation generally is used in one of the following two situations.

1. The original data for both X and Y are ranks. For example, a first-grade teacher may rank-order the students in a class in terms of leadership ability (X variable) and then rank-order the same students in terms of social development (Y variable). Thus, each student would have a rank for X (first, second, third, and so on for leadership) and a rank for Y. The Spearman correlation would measure the relationship between leadership ability and social development.

2. The original data consist of interval-scale or ratio-scale scores, but the researcher chooses to rank-order the scores before computing the correlation. For example, a set of data may have one or two extreme scores that would distort the Pearson correlation (see page 479). The process of ranking will eliminate a huge difference between one extreme score and the rest of the data points. This process is demonstrated in the following example.

EXAMPLE 16.5   A researcher obtains two measurements (X and Y values for each individual in a sample of $n = 5$. One of these individuals has extremely high scores relative to the rest of the sample. However, when the scores are ranked, the extreme individual no longer appears as an extreme outrider in the group.

ORIGINAL SCORES			RANKED SCORES		
SUBJECT	X	Y	SUBJECT	X RANK	Y RANK
A	3	8	A	1 (1ST)	2 (2ND)
B	7	6	B	3 (3RD)	1 (1ST)
C	4	9	C	2 (2ND)	3 (3RD)
D	8	10	D	4 (4TH)	4 (4TH)
E	19	24	E	5 (5TH)	5 (5TH)

The Spearman correlation is examined in greater detail in Chapter 19.

THE POINT-BISERIAL CORRELATION

The point-biserial correlation is used to measure the relationship between two variables in situations where one variable is measured on an interval or ratio scale ("regular" scores) but the *second variable has only two different values.* Variables with only two values are called *dichotomous variables.* Some examples of dichotomous variables are

1. Male versus female
2. College graduate versus not a college graduate
3. Firstborn child versus later-born child
4. Success versus failure on a particular task
5. Over 30 years old versus under 30 years old

It is customary to use the numerical values 0 and 1, but any two different numbers would work equally well and would not affect the value of the correlation.

To compute the point-biserial correlation, the dichotomous variable is first converted to numerical values by assigning a value of zero (0) to one category and a value of one (1) to the other category. Then, the regular Pearson correlation formula is used with the converted data. This process is demonstrated in the following example.

EXAMPLE 16.6

The following data represent measurements of attitude (X) and gender (Y) for each individual in a sample of $n = 8$. In the original data, one variable consists of two categories: male and female. In the converted data the categories are assigned numerical values: male = 0 and female = 1. The point-biserial correlation is obtained by using the Pearson formula for the converted data.

Because the assignment of numerical values 0 and 1 to male and female is arbitrary, the sign (+ or −) of the point-biserial correlation is unimportant.

ORIGINAL DATA		CONVERTED DATA	
ATTITUDE SCORE X	GENDER Y	ATTITUDE SCORE X	GENDER Y
8	MALE	8	0
7	FEMALE	7	1
4	MALE	4	0
6	MALE	6	0
1	FEMALE	1	1
9	MALE	9	0
3	FEMALE	3	1
4	FEMALE	4	1

THE RELATION BETWEEN THE POINT-BISERIAL CORRELATION AND THE INDEPENDENT-MEASURES *t* HYPOTHESIS TEST

You may have noticed that the data for a point-biserial correlation are identical to the data that are used for an independent-measures *t* hypothesis test (Chapter 10). The dichotomous variable can be used to separate the sample into two independent groups. For example, the data from Example 16.6 could be reorganized and presented as follows:

MALES	FEMALES
8	7
4	1
6	3
9	4

With the data in this form, the independent-measures *t* would be used to evaluate the mean difference between the two groups.

In many respects the point-biserial correlation and the hypothesis tests (*t* or ANOVA) are evaluating the same thing. Both statistical techniques are examining the relation between two variables—for this example, the relation between sex and attitude. Specifically,

1. The correlation is measuring the degree of relationship between the two variables. A large correlation (near 1.00) would indicate that there is a consistent, predictable relation between sex and attitude. The correlation measures the *strength* of the relationship. The value of r^2, the coefficient of determination, describes how much of the variability in the attitude scores can be predicted on the basis of sex.

2. On the other hand, the independent-measures hypothesis test is evaluating the mean difference between groups. A large value for *t* would indicate that there is a consistent, predictable tendency for one sex to have attitudes different from the other. The hypothesis test determines whether the mean difference in attitude between males and females is more than can be explained by chance.

In fact, the point-biserial correlation and the independent-measures t are directly related by the following equation:

$$t^2 = \frac{r^2}{(1 - r^2)/(N - 2)}$$

In general, a large value for t (indicating a significant difference) will be accompanied by a large value for r (indicating a strong relationship).

THE PHI-COEFFICIENT   When both variables (X and Y) measured for each individual are dichotomous, the correlation between the two variables is called the phi-coefficient. To compute phi (ϕ), you follow a two-step procedure:

1. Convert each of the dichotomous variables to numerical values by assigning a 0 to category 1 and a 1 to category 2 for each of the variables.

2. Use the regular Pearson formula with the converted scores.

This process is demonstrated in the following example.

EXAMPLE 16.7   A researcher is interested in examining the relation between birth-order position and personality. A random sample of $n = 8$ individuals is obtained and each individual is classified in terms of birth-order position as firstborn or only child versus later-born. Then each individual's personality is classified as either introvert or extrovert.

The original measurements are then converted to numerical values by the following assignments:

BIRTH ORDER	PERSONALITY
1st or only child = 0	Introvert = 0
Later-born child = 1	Extrovert = 1

The original data and the converted scores are as follows:

ORIGINAL DATA		CONVERTED SCORES	
BIRTH ORDER X	PERSONALITY Y	BIRTH ORDER X	PERSONALITY Y
1st	Introvert	0	0
3rd	Extrovert	1	1
Only	Extrovert	0	1
2nd	Extrovert	1	1
4th	Extrovert	1	1
2nd	Introvert	1	0
Only	Introvert	0	0
3rd	Extrovert	1	1

The Pearson correlation formula would then be used with the converted data to compute the phi-coefficient.

Because the assignment of numerical values is arbitrary (either category could be designated 0 or 1), the sign of the resulting correlation is meaningless. As with most correlations, the *strength* of the relationship is best described by the value of r^2, the coefficient of determination, which measures how much of the variability in one variable is predicted or determined by the association with the second variable.

We also should note that although the phi-coefficient can be used to assess the relationship between two dichotomous variables, the more common statistical procedure is a chi-square statistic, which is examined in Chapter 17.

LEARNING CHECK

1. Define a *dichotomous* variable.

2. The following data represent job-related stress scores for a sample of $n = 8$ individuals. These people also are classified by salary level.

   a. Convert the data into a form suitable for the point-biserial correlation.

   b. Compute the point-biserial correlation for these data.

SALARY OVER $40,000	SALARY UNDER $40,000
8	4
7	2
5	1
3	3

ANSWERS

1. A dichotomous variable has only two possible values.

2. Salary level is a dichotomous variable and can be coded as 0 = over $40,000, 1 = under $40,000 for each subject. The resulting point-biserial correlation is -0.719.

16.6 INTRODUCTION TO REGRESSION

Earlier in this chapter we introduced the Pearson correlation as a technique for describing and measuring the linear relation between two variables. Figure 16.13 presents hypothetical data showing the relation between SAT scores and college grade-point average (GPA). Note that the figure shows a good, but not perfect, positive relation. Also note that we have drawn a line through the middle of the data points. This line serves several purposes:

a. The line makes the relation between SAT and GPA easier to see.

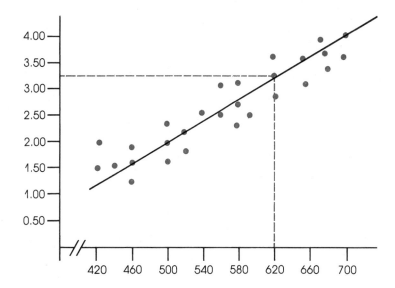

Figure 16.13

Hypothetical data showing the relation between SAT scores and GPA with a regression line drawn through the data points. The regression line defines a precise, one-to-one relation between each *X* value (SAT score) and its corresponding *Y* value (GPA).

b. The line identifies the center, or "central tendency," of the relation, just as the mean describes central tendency for a set of scores. Thus the line provides a simplified description of the relation. For example, if the data points were removed, the straight line would still give a general picture of the relation between SAT and GPA.

c. Finally, the line can be used for prediction. The line establishes a precise relation between each X value (SAT score) and a corresponding Y value (GPA). For example, an SAT score of 620 corresponds to a GPA of 3.40 (see Figure 16.13). Thus, the college admissions office could use the straight line relation to predict that a student entering college with an SAT score of 620 should achieve a college GPA of approximately 3.40.

Our goal in this section is to develop a procedure that identifies and defines the straight line that provides the best fit for any specific set of data. You should realize that this straight line does not have to be drawn on a graph; it can be presented in a simple equation. Thus, our goal is to find the equation for the line that best describes the relationship for a set of *X* and *Y* data.

LINEAR EQUATIONS In general, a *linear relation* between two variables *X* and *Y* can be expressed by the equation $Y = bX + a$, where *b* and *a* are fixed constants.

For example, a local tennis club charges a fee of $5 per hour plus an annual membership fee of $25. With this information, the total cost of playing tennis can be computed using a *linear equation* that describes the relation between the total cost (*Y*) and the number of hours (*X*).

$$Y = 5X + 25$$

In the general linear equation, the value of *b* is called the *slope*. The slope determines how much the *Y* variable will change when *X* is increased by one

Note that a positive slope means that Y increases when X increases, and a negative slope indicates that Y decreases when X increases.

point. For the tennis club example, the slope is $b = \$5$ and indicates that your total cost will increase by $5 for each hour you play. The value of a in the general equation is called the *Y-intercept* because it determines the value of Y when $X = 0$. (On a graph, the a value identifies the point where the line intercepts the Y-axis.) For the tennis club example, $a = \$25$; there is a \$25 charge even if you never play tennis.

Figure 16.14 shows the general relation between cost and number of hours for the tennis club example. Notice that the relation results in a straight line. To obtain this graph, we picked any two values of X and then used the equation to compute the corresponding values for Y. For example,

when $X = 10$:	when $X = 30$:
$Y = bX + a$	$Y = bX + a$
$= \$5(10) + \$25$	$= \$5(30) + \$25$
$= \$50 + \$25$	$= \$150 + \$25$
$= \$75$	$= \$175$

When drawing a graph of a linear equation, it is wise to compute and plot a least three points to be certain you have not made a mistake.

Next, these two points are plotted on the graph: one point at $X = 10$ and $Y = 75$, the other point at $X = 30$ and $Y = 175$. Because two points completely determine a straight line, we simply drew the line so that it passed through these two points.

Because a straight line can be extremely useful for describing a relation between two variables, a statistical technique has been developed that provides a standardized method for determining the best fitting straight line for any set of data. The statistical procedure is regression and the resulting straight line is called the regression line.

DEFINITION

The statistical technique for finding the best-fitting straight line for a set of data is called *regression*, and the resulting straight line is called the *regression line*.

Figure 16.14

Relationship between total cost and number of hours playing tennis. The tennis club charges a $25 membership fee plus $5 per hour. The relation is described by a linear equation:

total cost = $5(number of hours) + $25
$Y = bX + a$

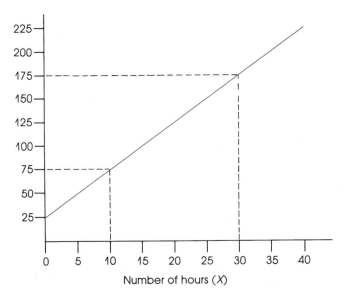

Number of hours (X)

The goal for regression is to find the best-fitting straight line for a set of data. To accomplish this goal, however, it is first necessary to define precisely what is meant by "best fit." For any particular set of data it is possible to draw lots of different straight lines that all appear to pass through the center of the data points. Each of these lines can be defined by a linear equation of the form

$$Y = bX + a$$

where b and a are constants that determine the slope and Y-intercept of the line, respectively. Each individual line has its own unique values for b and a. The problem is to find the specific line that provides the best fit to the actual data points.

LEARNING CHECK

1. Identify the slope and Y-intercept for the following linear equation:

$$Y = -3X + 7$$

2. Use the linear equation $Y = 2X - 7$ to determine the value of Y for each of the following values of X.

   X values: 1, 3, 5, 10

3. If the slope constant (b) in a linear equation is positive, then a graph of the equation will be a line tilted from lower left to upper right. (True or false?)

ANSWERS

1. Slope $= -3$ and Y-intercept $= +7$.

2.

X	Y
1	−5
3	−1
5	3
10	13

3. True. A positive slope indicates that Y increases (goes up in the graph) when X increases (goes to the right in the graph).

THE LEAST-SQUARES SOLUTION

To determine how well a line fits the data points, the first step is to define mathematically the distance between the line and each data point. For every X value in the data, the linear equation will determine a Y value on the line. This value is the predicted Y and is called $\hat{Y}$("Y hat"). The distance between this predicted value and the actual Y value in the data is determined by

$$\text{distance} = Y - \hat{Y}$$

Notice that we simply are measuring the vertical distance between the actual data point (Y) and the predicted point on the line. This distance measures the error between the line and the actual data (see Figure 16.15).

Figure 16.15.

The distance between the actual data point (*Y*) and the predicted point on the line ($\hat{Y}$) is defined as $Y - \hat{Y}$. The goal of regression is to find the equation for the line that minimizes these distances.

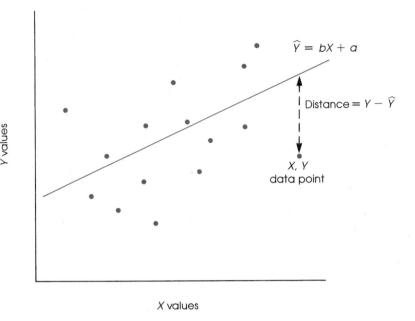

Because some of these distances will be positive and some will be negative, the next step is to square each distance in order to obtain a uniformly positive measure of error. Finally, to determine the total error between the line and the data, we sum the squared errors for all of the data points. The result is a measure of overall squared error between the line and the data:

$$\text{total squared error} = \Sigma\,(Y - \hat{Y})^2$$

Now we can define the *best-fitting* line as the one that has the smallest total squared error. For obvious reasons, the resulting line is commonly called the *least-squared-error* solution.

In symbols, we are looking for a linear equation of the form.

$$\hat{Y} = bX + a$$

For each value of *X* in the data, this equation will determine the point on the line ($\hat{Y}$) *that gives the best prediction of Y.* The problem is to find the specific values for *a* and *b* that will make this the best fitting line.

The calculations that are needed to find this equation require calculus and some sophisticated algebra, so we will not present the details of the solution. The results, however, are relatively straightforward, and the solutions for *b* and *a* are as follows:

A commonly used alternative formula for the slope is

$$b = r\,\frac{s_Y}{s_X}$$

where s_X and s_Y are the standard deviations for *X* and *Y*, respectively.

$$b = \frac{SP}{SS_X} \qquad\qquad (16.5)$$

where *SP* is the sum of products and SS_X is the sum of squares for the *X*-scores.

$$a = \overline{Y} - b\overline{X} \qquad\qquad (16.6)$$

Note that these two formulas determine the linear equation that provides the best prediction of Y values. This equation is called the regression equation for Y.

DEFINITION The *regression equation for Y* is the linear equation

$$\hat{Y} = bX + a$$

where the constants b and a are determined by formulas (16.5) and (16.6), respectively. This equation results in the least squared error between the data points and the line.

You should notice that the values of SS and SP are needed in the formulas for b and a just as they are needed to compute the Pearson correlation. An example demonstrating the calculation and use of this best fitting line is presented now.

EXAMPLE 16.8 The following table presents X and Y scores for a sample of $n = 5$ individuals. These data will be used to demonstrate the procedure for determining the linear regression equation for predicting Y values.

X	Y	$X - \bar{X}$	$Y - \bar{Y}$	$(X - \bar{X})(Y - \bar{Y})$	$(X - \bar{X})^2$
7	11	2	5	10	4
4	3	−1	−3	3	1
6	5	1	−1	−1	1
3	4	−2	−2	4	4
5	7	0	1	0	0
				16 = SP	10 = SS_X

For these data $\Sigma X = 25$, so $\bar{X} = 5$. Also, $\Sigma Y = 30$, so $\bar{Y} = 6$. These means have been used to compute the deviation scores for each X and Y value. The final two columns show the products of the deviation scores and the squared deviations for X. Based on these values,

$$SP = \Sigma (X - \bar{X})(Y - \bar{Y}) = 16$$

$$SS_X = \Sigma (X - \bar{X})^2 = 10$$

Our goal is to find the values for b and a in the linear equation so that we obtain the best fitting straight line for these data.

By using formulas 16.5 and 16.6, the solutions for b and a are

Regression may be done with Minitab using the command REGRESS (see Section 20.8).

$$b = \frac{SP}{SS_X} = \frac{16}{10} = 1.6$$

$$a = \bar{Y} - b\bar{X}$$
$$= 6 - 1.6(5)$$
$$= 6 - 8$$
$$= -2$$

The resulting regression equation is

$$\hat{Y} = 1.6X - 2$$

The original data and the regression line are shown in Figure 16.16.

 SPSS^x A-82

As we noted at the beginning of this section, one common use of regression equations is for prediction. For any given value of X, we can use the equation to compute a predicted value for Y. For the equation from Example 16.8, an individual with an X score of $X = 5$ would be predicted to have a Y score of

$$\hat{Y} = 1.6X - 2$$
$$= 1.6(5) - 2$$
$$= 8 - 2$$
$$= 6$$

Although regression equations can be used for prediction, there are a few cautions that should be considered whenever you are interpreting the predicted values:

1. The predicted value is not perfect (unless $r = +1.00$ or -1.00). If you examine Figure 16.16, it should be clear that the data points do not fit perfectly on the line. In general, there will be some error between the predicted Y values (on the line) and the actual data. Although the amount

Figure 16.16

The scatterplot for the data in Example 16.8 is shown with the best-fitting straight line. The predicted Y values ($\hat{Y}$) are on the regression line. Unless the correlation is perfect ($+1.00$ or -1.00), there will be some error between the actual Y values and the predicted Y values. The larger the correlation, the less the error will be.

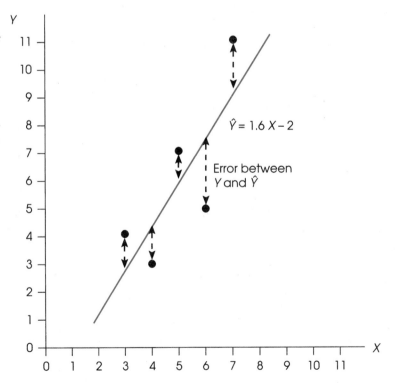

of error will vary from point to point, on average the errors will be directly related to the magnitude of the correlation. With a correlation near 1.00 (or −1.00) the data points will generally be close to the line (small error), but as the correlation gets nearer to zero, the magnitude of the error will increase. The statistical procedure for measuring this error is described in the following section.

2. The regression equation should not be used to make predictions for X values that fall outside the range of values covered by the original data. For Example 16.8, the X values ranged from $X = 3$ to $X = 7$ and the regression equation was calculated as the best-fitting line within this range. Because you have no information about the X-Y relation outside this range, the equation should not be used to predict Y for any X value lower than 3 or greater than 7.

LEARNING CHECK   **1.** Sketch a scatterplot for the following data, that is, a graph showing the X, Y data points:

X	Y
1	4
3	9
5	8

a. Find the regression equation for predicting Y and X. Draw this line on your graph. Does it look like the best fitting line?

b. Use the regression equation to find the predicted Y value corresponding to each X in the data.

ANSWERS   **1. a.** $SS_X = 8$, $SP = 8$, $b = 1$, $a = 4$.
The equation is

$$\hat{Y} = X + 4$$

b. The predicted Y values are 5, 7, and 9.

THE STANDARD ERROR OF ESTIMATE   It is possible to determine a best-fitting regression equation for any set of data by simply using the formulas already presented. The linear equation you obtain is then used to generate predicted Y values for any known value of X. However, it should be clear that the accuracy of this prediction depends on how well the points on the line correspond to the actual data points, that is, the amount of error between the predicted values $\hat{Y}$ and the actual scores, Y values. Figure 16.17 shows two different sets of data that have exactly the same regression equation. In one case there is a perfect correlation ($r = +1$) between X and Y, so the linear equation fits the data perfectly. For the second set of data, the predicted Y values on the line only approximate the real data points.

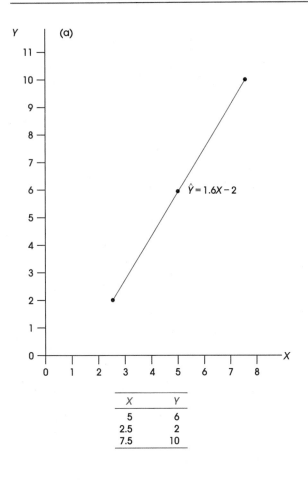

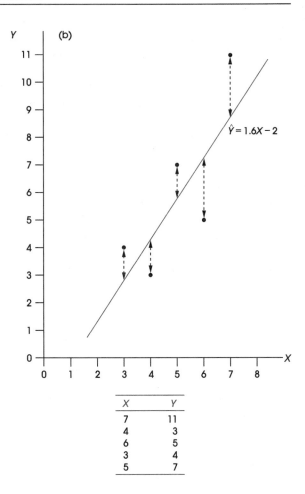

X	Y
5	6
2.5	2
7.5	10

X	Y
7	11
4	3
6	5
3	4
5	7

Figure 16.17

(a) Scatterplot showing data points that perfectly fit the regression equation $\hat{Y} = 1.6X - 2$. Note that the correlation is $r = 1.00$. (b) Scatterplot for the data from Example 16.8.

Notice there is error between the actual data points and the predicted Y values of the regression line.

A regression equation, by itself, allows you to make predictions, but it does not provide any information about the accuracy of the predictions. To measure the precision of the regression, it is customary to compute a standard error of estimate.

DEFINITION   The *standard error of estimate* gives a measure of the standard distance between a regression line and the actual data points.

Conceptually, the standard error of estimate is very much like a standard deviation: Both provide a measure of standard distance. You also should note that the calculation of the standard error of estimate is very similar to the calculation of standard deviation.

To calculate the standard error of estimate, we first will find a sum of squared deviations (*SS*). Each deviation will measure the distance between the actual Y value (from the data) and the predicted Y value (from the regression line). This sum of squares is commonly called SS_{error} because it measures the sum of squared distances, or errors, between the actual data and the predicted values:

$$SS_{error} = \Sigma (Y - \hat{Y})^2 \tag{16.7}$$

The obtained SS value is then divided by its degrees of freedom to obtain a measure of variance. This procedure should be very familiar:

$$\text{variance} = \frac{SS}{df}$$

The degrees of freedom for the standard error of estimate are $df = n - 2$. The reason for having $n - 2$ degrees of freedom, rather than the customary $n - 1$, is that we now are measuring deviations from a line rather than deviations from a mean. You should recall that it is necessary to know SP to find the slope of the regression line (the value of b in the equation). To calculate SP, you must know the means for both the X- and the Y-scores. Specifying these two means places two restrictions on the variability of the data with the result that the scores have only $n - 2$ degrees of freedom. (A more intuitive explanation for the fact that the SS_{error} has $df = n - 2$ comes from the simple observation that it takes exactly two points to determine a straight line. If there are only two data points, they must fit perfectly on a straight line so there will be no error. It is only when you have more than two points that there is some freedom in determining the best-fitting line.)

The final step in the calculation of the standard error of estimate is to take the square root of the variance in order to obtain a measure of standard distance. The final equation is

$$\text{standard error of estimate} = \sqrt{\frac{SS_{error}}{df}} = \sqrt{\frac{\Sigma(Y - \hat{Y})^2}{n - 2}}$$

The following example demonstrates the calculation of this standard error.

EXAMPLE 16.9 The data in Example 16.8 will be used to demonstrate the calculation of the standard error of estimate. These data have the regression equation:

$$\hat{Y} = 1.6X - 2$$

Using this regression equation, we have computed the predicted Y value, the error, and the squared error for each individual in the data.

DATA		PREDICTED Y VALUE $\hat{Y} = 1.6X - 2$	ERROR $Y - \hat{Y}$	SQUARED ERROR $(Y - \hat{Y})^2$
X	Y			
7	11	9.2	1.8	3.24
4	3	4.4	−1.4	1.96
6	5	7.6	−2.6	6.76
3	4	2.8	1.2	1.44
5	7	6.0	1.0	1.00
				$14.40 = SS_{error}$

For these data, the sum of the squared errors is $SS_{error} = 14.40$. With $n = 5$, the data have $df = n - 2 = 3$, so the standard error of estimate is

$$\text{standard error of estimate} = \sqrt{\frac{SS_{error}}{df}} = \sqrt{\frac{14.40}{3}} = 2.19$$

Remember, the standard error of estimate provides a measure of how accurately the regression equation predicts the Y values. In this case, the standard distance between the actual data points and the regression line is measured by standard error of estimate = 2.19.

RELATION BETWEEN STANDARD ERROR AND THE CORRELATION

It should be clear from Example 16.9 that the standard error of estimate is directly related to the magnitude of the correlation between X and Y. If the correlation is near 1.00 or (-1.00), the data points will be clustered close to the line, and the standard error of estimate will be small. As the correlation gets nearer to zero, the line will provide less accurate predictions, and the standard error of estimate will grow larger. Earlier (page 479) we observed that squaring the correlation provides a measure of the accuracy of prediction: r^2 is called the coefficient of determination because it determines what proportion of the variability in Y is predicted by the relationship with X. Figure 16.18 should help make this concept more concrete. In the figure we show three sets of data: one with a correlation of $r = 0$, one with $r = 0.8$, and one with a perfect correlation of $r = 1.00$. In each figure, the variability in the Y-scores is represented by the black vertical lines showing the deviation from the mean for each value of Y. In addition, we have drawn colored vertical lines to show the unpredicted (error) variability in Y by measuring the deviation from the regression line for each value of Y.

In Figure 16.8(a), there is no correlation between X and Y, so all the variability in Y is unpredicted, error variability. In this case, the coefficient of determination is zero, which means that none of the Y variability can be predicted from the association with X.

Figure 16.18(b), however, shows that the error variability (colored lines) is substantially less than the original variability in the Y-scores (black lines). In this case, the coefficient of determination is $r^2 = 0.64$, which means that 64% of the Y variability can be predicted from the association with X.

Finally, Figure 16.8(c) shows that the unpredicted variability is completely eliminated with a correlation of 1.00. Now the coefficient of determination is $r^2 = 1.00$, which means that 100% of the Y variability is predictable from the association with X.

Because r^2 measures the predicted portion of the variability in Y, we can use the expression $1 - r^2$ to measure the unpredicted, or error, portion. With a correlation of $r = 0.80$, for example, the predicted portion of the Y variability is

$$r^2 = 0.64 \qquad (\text{or } 64\%)$$

The remaining, unpredicted portion is

—·— Variability of Y scores (deviation from mean)
------ Error variability (deviation from regression line)

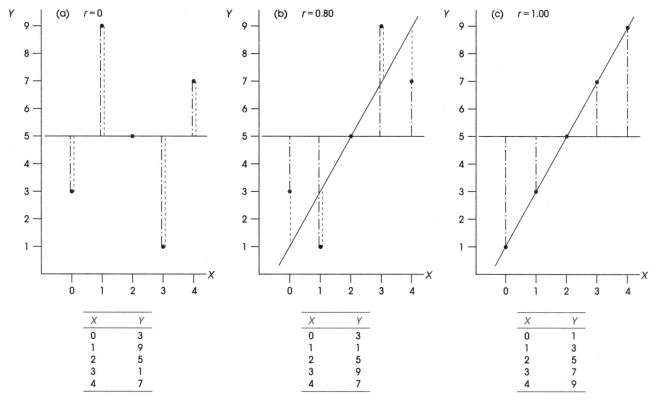

Figure 16.18

Error variability as a function of the magnitude of the correlation. (a) Data where the correlation is zero and all the
variability in the Y scores is unpredicted error variability.

(b) The correlation is $r = 0.80$ and the error variability is
reduced. (c) A perfect correlation, where there is no unpredicted error variability.

$$1 - r^2 = 1 - 0.64 = 0.36 \quad \text{(or 36\%)}$$

The unpredicted variability is exactly what we have defined as error
variability in the standard error of estimate. Because the total variability in Y
is measured by SS_Y, the error portion can be calculated as

$$SS_{\text{error}} = (1 - r^2)SS_Y \tag{16.9}$$

Notice that when $r = 1.00$ there is no error (perfect prediction), and that as
the correlation approaches zero the error will grow larger. By using this
formula for SS_{error}, the standard error of estimate can be computed as

$$\text{standard error of estimate} = \sqrt{\frac{SS_{\text{error}}}{df}} = \sqrt{\frac{(1 - r^2)SS_Y}{n - 2}}$$

The following example demonstrates this new formula.

EXAMPLE 16.10 The same data used in Examples 16.8 and 16.9 are reproduced in the following table.

X	Y	$X - \bar{X}$	$Y - \bar{Y}$	$(X - \bar{X})^2$	$(Y - \bar{Y})^2$	$(X - \bar{X})(Y - \bar{Y})$
7	11	2	5	4	25	10
4	3	−1	−3	1	9	3
6	5	1	−1	1	1	−1
3	4	−2	−2	4	4	4
5	7	0	1	0	1	0
				$SS_X = 10$	$SS_Y = 40$	$SP = 16$

For these data, the Pearson correlation is

$$r = \frac{SP}{\sqrt{SS_X SS_Y}} = \frac{16}{\sqrt{10(40)}} = \frac{16}{20} = 0.80$$

With $SS_Y = 40$ and a correlation of 0.80, the error portion of the Y variability is

$$SS_{error} = (1 - r^2)SS_Y = (1 - 0.64)(40)$$
$$= 0.36(40)$$
$$= 14.40$$

Notice that the new formula for SS_{error} produces exactly the same value that we obtained by summing the squared errors in Example 16.9. Also note that this new formula is generally much easier to use because it requires only the correlation value (r) and the SS for Y. The primary point of this example, however, is that the standard error of estimate is closely related to the value of the correlation. With a large correlation (near +1.00 or −1.00) the data points will be close to the regression line, and the standard error of estimate will be small. As a correlation gets smaller (near zero), the data points move away from the regression line and the standard error of estimate gets larger.

LEARNING CHECK **1.** Use the following set of data:

X	Y	
1	4	$SS_X = 10$
2	1	
3	7	$SS_Y = 90$
4	13	
5	10	$SP = 24$

a. Find the regression equation for predicting Y from X.

b. Use the regression equation to find the predicted Y value for each X in the data.

c. Find the error $(Y - \hat{Y})$ for each data point. Square each error value and sum the results to find SS_{error}.

d. Calculate the Pearson correlation for these data.

e. Use the correlation and SS_Y to compute S_{error}.

2. Assuming all other factors are held constant, what happens to the standard error of estimate as the correlation between X and Y moves toward zero?

ANSWERS **1. a.** $\hat{Y} = 2.4X - 0.2$

b–c.

Y	$\hat{Y}$	ERROR	ERROR^2
4	2.2	1.8	3.24
1	4.6	−3.6	12.96
7	7.0	0	0
13	9.4	3.6	12.96
10	11.8	−1.8	3.24
			$32.40 = SS_{error}$

d. $r = 0.80$

e. $(1 - r^2)SS_Y = 0.36(90) = 32.40 = SS_{error}$

2. The standard error of estimate would get larger.

SUMMARY

1. A correlation measures the relationship between two variables X and Y. The relationship is described by three characteristics:

a. *Direction.* A relation can be either positive or negative. A positive relation means that X and Y vary in the same direction. A negative relation means that X and Y vary in opposite directions. The sign of the correlation (+ or −) specifies the direction.

b. *Form.* The most common form for a relation is a straight line. However, special correlations exist for measuring other forms. The form is specified by the type of correlation used. For example, the Pearson correlation measures linear form.

c. *Degree.* The magnitude of the correlation measures the degree to which the data points fit the specified form. A correlation of 1.00 indicates a perfect fit, and a correlation of 0 indicates no degree of fit.

2. The most commonly used correlation is the Pearson correlation, which measures the degree of linear rela-

tionship. The Pearson correlation is identified by the letter r and is computed by

$$r = \frac{SP}{\sqrt{SS_X SS_Y}}$$

In this formula, SP is the sum of products of deviations and can be calculated either with a definitional formula or a computational formula:

definitional formula: $SP = \Sigma(X - \bar{X})(Y - \bar{Y})$

computational formula: $SP = \Sigma XY - \dfrac{\Sigma X \Sigma Y}{n}$

3. The Pearson correlation and z-scores are closely related because both are concerned with the location of individuals within a distribution. When X and Y

scores are transformed into z-scores, the Pearson correlation can be computed by

$$r = \frac{\Sigma z_X z_Y}{n}$$

4. A correlation between two variables should not be interpreted as implying a causal relation. Simply because X and Y are related does not mean that X causes Y or that Y causes X.

5. When the X or Y values used to compute a correlation are limited to a relatively small portion of the potential range, you should exercise caution in generalizing the value of the correlation. Specifically, a limited range of values can either obscure a strong relation or exaggerate a poor relation.

6. To evaluate the strength of a relation, you should square the value of the correlation. The resulting value, r^2, is called the *coefficient of determination* because it measures the portion of the variability in one variable that can be predicted using the relationship with the second variable.

7. Special correlations exist to measure relationships between variables with specific characteristics. The Spearman correlation is used when both variables are measured on ordinal scales. The point-biserial correlation is used when one of the two variables is dichotomous, and the phi-coefficient is used when both variables are dichotomous.

8. When there is a general linear relation between two variables X and Y, it is possible to construct a linear equation that allows you to predict the Y value corresponding to any known value of X:

$$\text{predicted } Y \text{ value} = \hat{Y} = bX + a$$

The technique for determining this equation is called regression. By using a *least-squares* method to minimize the error between the predicted Y values and the actual Y values, the best fitting line is achieved when the linear equation has

$$b = \frac{SP}{SS_X} \quad \text{and} \quad a = \bar{Y} - b\bar{X}$$

9. The linear equation generated by regression (called the *regression equation*) can be used to compute a predicted Y value for any value of X. The accuracy of the prediction is measured by the standard error of estimate, which provides a measure of the standard distance (or error) between the predicted Y value on the line and the actual data point. The standard error of estimate is computed by

$$\text{standard error of estimate} = \sqrt{\frac{SS_{\text{error}}}{n-2}}$$

where SS_{error} may be computed directly from the error scores,

$$SS_{\text{error}} = \Sigma(Y - \hat{Y})^2$$

or as a proportion of the original Y variability,

$$SS_{\text{error}} = (1 - r^2)SS_Y$$

KEY TERMS

correlation	sum of products (SP)	point-biserial correlation	Y-intercept
positive correlation	restricted range	phi-coefficient	regression equation for Y
negative correlation	coefficient of determination	linear relationship	regression
perfect correlation		linear equation	regression line
Pearson correlation	Spearman correlation	slope	standard error of estimate

—— *Focus on Problem Solving* ——

1. A correlation always has a value from $+1.00$ to -1.00. If you obtain a correlation outside this range, then you have made a computational error.

2. When interpreting a correlation, do not confuse the sign ($+$ or $-$) with its numerical value. The sign and numerical value must be considered separately.

Remember, the sign indicates the direction of the relationship between X and Y. On the other hand, the numerical value reflects the strength of the relationship, or how well the points approximate a linear (straight-line) relationship. Therefore, a correlation of -0.90 is just as strong as a correlation of $+0.90$. The signs tell us that the first correlation is an inverse relationship.

3. Before you begin to calculate a correlation, you should sketch a scatterplot of the data and make an estimate of the correlation. (Is it positive or negative? Is it near 1 or near 0?). After computing the correlation, compare your final answer with your original estimate.

4. The definitional formula for the sum of products (SP) should be used only when you have a small set (n) of scores and the means for X and Y are both whole numbers. Otherwise, the computational formula will produce quicker, easier, and more accurate results.

5. For computing a correlation, n is number of individuals (and, therefore, the number of *pairs* of X and Y values).

6. To draw a graph from a linear equation, choose any three values for X, put each value in the equation, and calculate the corresponding values for Y. Then plot the three (X, Y) points on the graph. Its a good idea to use $X = 0$ for one of the three values because this will give you the Y-intercept. You can get a quick idea of what the graph should look like if you know the Y-intercept and the slope. Remember, the Y-intercept is the point where the line crosses the Y-axis, and the slope identifies the tilt of the line. For example, suppose the Y-intercept is 5 and the slope is -3. The line would pass through the point $(0, 5)$, and its slope indicates that the Y value goes down 3 points each time X increases by 1.

7. Rather than memorizing the formula for the Y-intercept in the regression equation, simply remember that the graphed line of the regression equation always goes through the point $(\overline{X}, \overline{Y})$. Therefore, if you plug the mean value for X ($\overline{X}$) into the regression equation, the result equals the mean value for Y ($\overline{Y}$).

$$\overline{Y} = b\overline{X} + a$$

If you simply solve this equation for a, you get the formula for the Y-intercept.

$$a = \overline{Y} - b\overline{X}$$

Demonstration 16.1

CORRELATION AND REGRESSION

For the following data, calculate the Pearson correlation and find the regression equation.

PERSON	X	Y
A	0	4
B	2	1
C	8	10
D	6	9
E	4	6

STEP 1 *Sketch a scatterplot.* We have constructed a scatterplot for the data (Figure 16.19) and placed an envelope around the data points to make a preliminary estimate of the correlation. Note that the envelope is narrow and elongated. This indicates that the correlation is large—perhaps 0.80 to 0.90. Also, the correlation is positive because increases in *X* are generally accompanied by increases in *Y*.

We can sketch a straight line through the middle of the envelope and data points. Now, we can roughly approximate the slope and *Y*-intercept of the best-fit line. This is only an educated guess, but it will tell us what values are reasonable when we actually compute the regression line. The line has a positive slope (as *X* increases, *Y* increases) and it intersects the *Y* axis in the vicinity of +2.

STEP 2 *Obtain the values for SS and SP.* To compute the Pearson correlation, we must find the values for SS_X, SS_Y, and *SP*. These values are needed for the regression equation as well. The following table illustrates these calculations with the computational formulas for *SS* and *SP*.

X	Y	X^2	Y^2	XY
0	4	0	16	0
2	1	4	1	2
8	10	64	100	80
6	9	36	81	54
4	6	16	36	24

$\Sigma X = 20$ $\Sigma Y = 30$ $\Sigma X^2 = 120$ $\Sigma Y^2 = 234$ $\Sigma XY = 160$

For SS_X, we obtain

$$SS_X = \Sigma X^2 - \frac{(\Sigma X)^2}{n} = 120 - \frac{20^2}{5} = 120 - \frac{400}{5} = 120 - 80$$
$$= 40$$

For *Y*, sum of squares is

$$SS_Y = \Sigma Y^2 - \frac{(\Sigma Y)^2}{n} = 234 - \frac{30^2}{5} = 234 - \frac{900}{5} = 234 - 180$$
$$= 54$$

The sum of products equals

$$SP = \Sigma XY - \frac{\Sigma X \Sigma Y}{n} = 160 - \frac{20(30)}{5} = 160 - \frac{600}{5} = 160 - 120$$
$$= 40$$

STEP 3 *Compute the Pearson correlation.* For these data, the Pearson correlation is

$$r = \frac{SP}{\sqrt{SS_X SS_Y}} = \frac{40}{\sqrt{40(54)}} = \frac{40}{\sqrt{2160}} = \frac{40}{46.48}$$
$$= 0.861$$

Figure 16.19

The scatterplot for the data of Demonstration 16.1. An envelope is drawn around the points to estimate the magnitude of the correlation. A line is drawn through the middle of the envelope to roughly estimate the *Y*-intercept for the regression equation.

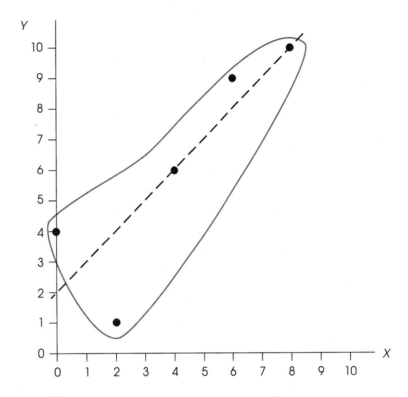

In Step 1, our preliminary estimate for the correlation was between $+0.80$ and $+0.90$. The calculated correlation is consistent with this estimate.

STEP 4   *Compute the values for the regression equation.* The general form of the regression equation is

$$\hat{Y} = bX + a$$

We will need to compute the values for the slope (b) of the line and the *Y*-intercept (a). For slope, we obtain

$$b = \frac{SP}{SS_X} = \frac{40}{40} = +1$$

The formula for the *Y*-intercept is

$$a = \overline{Y} - b\overline{X}$$

Thus, we will need the values for the sample means. For these data, the sample means are

$$\overline{X} = \frac{\Sigma X}{n} = \frac{20}{5} = 4$$

$$\overline{Y} = \frac{\Sigma Y}{n} = \frac{30}{5} = 6$$

Now we can compute the Y-intercept.

$$a = 6 - 1(4) = 6 - 4 = 2$$

Finally, the regression equation is

$$\hat{Y} = bX + a$$
$$= 1X + 2$$

or $\hat{Y} = X + 2$

PROBLEMS

1. What information is provided by the sign ($+$ or $-$) of a correlation?

2. For each of the following sets of scores, calculate SP using the definitional formula and then using the computational formula:

SET 1		SET 2		SET 3	
X	Y	X	Y	X	Y
1	3	0	7	1	5
2	6	4	3	2	0
4	4	0	5	3	1
5	7	4	1	2	6

3. Use the following set of data.

DATA	
X	Y
8	2
9	2
2	4
1	5
5	2

a. Sketch a graph showing the location of the five (X, Y) points.
b. Just looking at your graph, estimate the value of the Pearson correlation.
c. Compute the Pearson correlation for this data set.

4. For this problem we have used the same X and Y values that appeared in Problem 3, but we have changed the X, Y pairings:

DATA	
X	Y
8	4
9	5
2	2
1	2
5	2

a. Sketch a graph showing these reorganized data.
b. Estimate the Pearson correlation just by looking at your graph.
c. Compute the Pearson correlation. (*Note:* Much of the calculation for this problem was done already in Problem 3.)
If you compare the results of Problem 3 and Problem 4, you will see that the correlation measures the relation between X and Y. These two problems use the same X and Y values, but they differ in the way X and Y are related.

5. With a very small sample, a single point can have a large influence on the magnitude of a correlation. Use the following data set.

X	Y
0	1
10	3
4	1
8	2
8	3

a. Sketch a graph showing the X, Y points.
b. Estimate the value of the Pearson correlation.
c. Compute the Pearson correlation.

d. Now we will change the value of one of the points. For the first individual in the sample ($X = 0$ and $Y = 1$), change the Y value to $Y = 6$. What happens to the graph of the X, Y points? What happens to the Pearson correlation? Compute the new correlation.

6. In the following data there are three scores (X, Y, and Z) for each of the $n = 5$ individuals:

X	Y	Z
3	5	5
4	3	2
2	4	6
1	1	3
0	2	4

a. Sketch a graph showing the relation between X and Y. Compute the Pearson correlation between X and Y.

b. Sketch a graph showing the relation between Y and Z. Compute the Pearson correlation between Y and Z.

c. Given the results of parts a and b, what would you predict for the correlation between X and Z?

d. Sketch a graph showing the relation between X and Z. Compute the Pearson correlation for these data.

e. What general conclusion can you make concerning relations among correlations? If X is related to Y and Y is related to Z, does this necessarily mean that X is related to Z?

7. Use the following set of data.

X	Y
1	2
2	4
3	1
4	5
5	3
6	9
7	10
8	7
9	8
10	6

a. Sketch a graph showing the X, Y points.

b. Compute the Pearson correlation for the full set of data.

c. Compute the Pearson correlation using only the first five individuals in the sample (the five smallest X values).

d. Compute the Pearson correlation for the final five individuals in the sample (the five largest X values).

e. Explain why the results from parts c and d are so different from the overall correlation obtained in part b.

8. Use the following set of data.

X	Y
5	2
6	4
0	2
8	4
6	3

a. Sketch a scatterplot showing the X and Y values. Just by looking at your graph, estimate the Pearson correlation for these data.

b. Compute the Pearson correlation.

c. Add 3 points to each Y value and sketch a new scatterplot showing the new X and Y values. Just by looking at your graph, estimate what happens to the Pearson correlation when a constant is added to each score.

d. Compute the Pearson correlation for the data from part c.

9. Use the following set of data.

X	Y
1	2
2	8
3	0
1	3
3	2

a. Sketch a scatterplot showing the X and Y values. Just by looking at your graph, estimate the Pearson correlation for these data.

b. Compute the Pearson correlation.

c. Multiply each Y value by 3 and sketch a new scatterplot showing the new X and Y values. Just by looking at your graph, estimate what happens to the Pearson correlation when each score is multiplied by a constant.

d. Compute the Pearson correlation for the data from part c.

10. If you obtain a random sample of $n = 2$ people and measure each person's annual salary and shoe size, what would you expect to obtain for the Pearson correlation? (Be careful. Try making up some data points to see what happens.) How would you interpret a correlation of $r = +1.00$ obtained for a sample of $n = 2$? Should you generalize this sample correlation and conclude that a strong relationship between X and Y exists in the population?

11. A psychologist would like to determine whether there is any consistent relationship between intelligence and creativity. A random sample of $n = 18$ people is obtained, and the psychologist administers a standardized IQ test and a creativity test to each individual. Using these data, the psychologist obtained a Pearson correlation of $r = +0.20$ between IQ and creativity. Do these sample data provide sufficient evidence to conclude that a correlation exists in the population? Test at the .05 level of significance, one tail.

12. A high school counselor would like to know if there is a relation between mathematical skill and verbal skill. A sample of $n = 25$ students is selected, and the counselor records achievement test scores in mathematics and English for each student. The Pearson correlation for this sample is $r = +0.50$. Do these data provide sufficient evidence for a real relationship in the population? Test at the .05 level, two tails.

13. A psychology instructor asked each student to report the number of hours he or she had spent preparing for the final exam. In addition, the instructor recorded the number of incorrect answers on each student's exam. These data are as follows:

HOURS	NUMBER WRONG
4	5
0	12
2	3
3	1
6	4

a. Compute the Pearson correlation between study hours and number wrong.
b. Convert the original scores to ranks and compute the Spearman correlation for these data.
c. Sketch a scatterplot for the original X and Y values and a scatterplot for the ranks. Notice that the

extreme data point (0 hours and 12 wrong) has less influence after the data are ranked.

14. To test the effectiveness of a new studying strategy, a psychologist randomly divides a sample of 8 students into two groups with $n = 4$ in each group. The students in one group receive training in the new studying strategy. Then all students are given 30 minutes to study a chapter from a history textbook before they take a quiz on the chapter. The quiz scores for the two groups are as follows:

TRAINING	NO TRAINING
9	4
7	7
6	3
10	6

a. Convert these data into a form suitable for the point-biserial correlation. (Use $X = 1$ for training, $X = 0$ for no training, and the quiz score for Y.)
b. Calculate the point-biserial correlation for these data.

15. The data in Problem 14 showed a mean difference of 3 points between the training group and the no training group ($\overline{X} = 8$ versus $\overline{X} = 5$). Because there is a 3-point difference, you would expect to find that quiz scores are related to training (there is a nonzero correlation). Now consider the following data, where there is no mean difference between the two groups:

TRAINING	NO TRAINING
2	4
5	7
6	3
7	6

a. Without doing any calculations, estimate the point-biserial correlation for these data.
b. Convert the data to a form suitable for the point-biserial, and compute the correlation.

16. A researcher would like to evaluate the relationship between a person's age and his or her preference between two leading brands of cola. In a sample of 12 people, the researcher found that 5 out of 8 people over 30 years old preferred brand A, and only 1 out of 4 people under 30 years old preferred brand A.

a. Convert the data to a form suitable for computing the phi-coefficient. (Code the two age categories as 0 and 1 for the X variable and code the preferred brand of soft drink as 0 and 1 for the Y variable.)

b. Compute the phi-coefficient for the data.

17. Sketch a graph showing the linear equation $Y = 3X - 2$.

18. Two major companies supply laboratory animals for psychologists. Company A sells laboratory rats for $6 each and charges a $10 fee for delivery. Company B sells rats for only $5 each but has a $20 delivery charge. In each case the delivery fee is a one-time charge and does not depend on the number of rats in the order.

a. For each company, what is the linear equation that defines the total cost (Y) as a function of the number of rats (X)? Each equation should be of the form

$$Y = bX + a$$

b. What would the total cost be for an order of 10 rats from company A? From company B?

c. If you were buying 20 rats, which company gives you the better deal?

19. For the following set of data, find the linear regression equation for predicting Y from X:

X	Y
0	9
2	9
4	7
6	3

20. a. Find the regression equation for the following data:

X	Y
1	2
4	7
3	5
2	1
5	14
3	7

b. Compute the predicted Y value for each X in the data.

c. Compute the error ($Y - \hat{Y}$) for each individual and find SS_{error} for these data.

21. A set of $n = 6$ pairs of X and Y values has a Pearson correlation of $r = +0.60$ and $SS_Y = 100$. If you are using these data as the basis for a regression equation,

a. On average, how much error would you expect if the regression equation were used to predict the Y-score for a specific individual? That is, find the standard error of estimate.

b. How much error would you expect if the sample size were $n = 102$ instead of $n = 6$?

c. How much error would you expect if the sample correlation were r $= +0.80$ instead of 0.60?

22. For the following data:

X	Y
3	12
0	8
4	18
2	12
1	8

a. Compute the Pearson correlation.

b. Find the regression equation for predicting Y from X.

c. Compute the standard error of estimate.

23. A college professor claims that the scores on the first exam provide an excellent indication of how students will perform throughout the term. To test this claim, first-exam score and final scores were recorded for a sample of $n = 12$ students in an introductory psychology class. The data are as follows:

FIRST EXAM	FINAL GRADE
62	74
73	93
88	68
82	79
85	91
77	72
94	96
65	61
91	92
74	82
85	93
98	95

a. Is the professor right? Is there a significant correlation between scores on the first exam and final grades? Test with $\alpha = .01$.

b. How accurately do the exam scores predict final grades? Compute the standard error of estimate.

24. The correlation between IQ measured at age 2 and IQ at age 18 is only $r = 0.31$. Assume that this correlation is based on a sample of 22 people.

a. Do these data provide evidence for a significant relation between IQ at age 2 and IQ at 18? Test at the .05 level of significance.

b. If the IQ scores for the 18-year-olds had $SS = 5220$, how accurately can you predict adult IQ based on the 2-year-old's score? (Find the standard error of estimate.)

25. A photographer has noticed that a freshly mixed batch of chemicals will develop photographs faster than an old batch of chemicals. The photographer keeps records of the time needed to develop a print and the age of the chemicals:

AGE OF CHEMICALS (DAYS)	TIME TO DEVELOP (SECONDS)
1	35
4	38
6	40
9	44
12	49
14	52

a. Use these data to find the regression equation for predicting time as a function of age of the chemicals.

b. Using your regression equation, predict how long it should take to develop a print if the chemicals are 10 days old.

c. Calculate the standard error of estimate to determine a degree of accuracy for your prediction in part b.

CHAPTER 17

THE CHI-SQUARE STATISTIC: TESTS FOR GOODNESS OF FIT AND INDEPENDENCE

TOOLS YOU WILL NEED

The following items are considered essential background material for this chapter. If you doubt your knowledge of any of these items, you should review the appropriate chapter or section before proceeding.

- Proportions (math review, Appendix A)
- Frequency distributions (Chapter 2)

CONTENTS

PREVIEW

Once in a while we hear a horrifying report in which passersby observe a person in trouble and yet do not go to the victim's aid. Some people have attributed bystander apathy to the alienating and dehumanizing aspect of modern life, but Darley and Latané (1968) suggested that the number of witnesses is a key variable in determining if aid will be given. Specifically, if one person observes someone in trouble, the observer tends to feel personally responsible and is likely to assist. However, if there is a group of observers, the responsibility for the victim is spread thin among the witnesses, and it is less likely that anyone will help. This interpretation has been called *diffusion of responsibility*.

In an experimental test of this phenomenon, Darley and Latané (1968) asked subjects to participate in group discussions concerning problems adjusting to college life. To ensure anonymity, each participant sat in a separate room, and the discussion was held over an intercom. The discussion groups consisted of either 2 people, 3 people, or 6 people. Actually, there was only one real subject in each group; the rest of the people were "confederates," or research assistants posing as subjects.

At some point during the discussion, the researchers played a tape recording over the intercom, giving the appearance that one of the participants was having an epileptic seizure. Darley and Latané recorded how many subjects tried to help the "victim" and how many did not. The findings are summarized in Table 17.1. Notice that the data for this study consist of frequencies, not scores. For example, when there were only 2 people in the group (subject and victim), the data show 11 subjects helping and only 2 who did not help (85% helped). When there were 3 people in the group, the helping rate

Table 17.1
The relationship between the size of group and the type of response to the victim.

	GROUP SIZE		
	2	3	6
ASSISTANCE	11	16	4
NO ASSISTANCE	2	10	9

J. M. Darley and B. Latané (1968). Bystander intervention in emergencies: Diffusion of responsibility. *Journal of Personality and Social Psychology, 8,* 377–383. Copyright (1968) by the American Psychological Association. Adapted with permission of the publisher and author.

dropped to 16 out of 26 (62%). Finally, when the group size was 6, only 4 out of 13 subjects (31%) tried to help the victim. Clearly the data show a trend—the larger the group, the less likely that someone will help. However, these data represent a relatively small sample. Can we be sure that the results generalize to the entire population? This is a question of statistical inference, and what we need is a hypothesis test that works with frequency data.

In this chapter we will examine a statistic called *chi-square*, which is used to test hypotheses about the form and shape of frequency distributions. Unlike earlier hypothesis tests that used scores (X values), the data for chi-square are simply frequencies. Incidently, we will return to the bystander apathy study later in the chapter.

17.1 OVERVIEW: PARAMETRIC AND NONPARAMETRIC STATISTICAL TESTS

All the statistical tests we have examined thus far are designed to test hypotheses about specific population parameters. For example, we used *t* tests to assess hypotheses about μ and later about $\mu_1 - \mu_2$. In addition, these tests typically make assumptions about the shape of the population distribution and about other population parameters. Recall that for analysis of variance the population distributions are assumed to be normal and homogeneity of variance is required. Because these tests all concern parameters and require assumptions about parameters, they are called *parametric tests*.

Another general characteristic of parametric tests is that they require a numerical score for each individual in the sample. The scores then are added, squared, averaged, and otherwise manipulated using basic arithmetic. In terms of measurement scales, parametric tests require data from an interval or a ratio scale (see Chapter 1).

Often, researchers are confronted with experimental situations that do not conform to the requirements of parametric tests. In these situations it may not be appropriate to use a parametric test. Remember, when the assumptions of a test are violated, the test may lead to an erroneous interpretation of the data. Fortunately, there are several hypothesis testing techniques that provide alternatives to parametric tests. These alternatives are called *nonparametric tests*.

In this chapter, we introduce some commonly used nonparametric tests. You should notice that these nonparametric tests usually do not state hypotheses in terms of a specific parameter, and they make few (if any) assumptions about the population distribution. For the latter reason, nonparametric tests sometimes are called *distribution-free tests*. Another distinction is that nonparametric tests are well suited for data that are measured on nominal or ordinal scales. Finally, you should be warned that nonparametric tests generally are not as sensitive as parametric tests; nonparametric tests are more likely to fail in detecting a real difference between two treatments. Therefore, whenever the experimental data give you a choice between a parametric and a nonparametric test, you always should choose the parametric alternative.

17.2 THE CHI-SQUARE TEST FOR GOODNESS OF FIT

Parameters such as the mean and standard deviation are the most common way to describe a population, but there are situations where a researcher has questions about the shape of a frequency distribution. For example,

How does the number of women lawyers compare with the number of men in the profession?

Of the three leading brands of soft drinks, which is preferred by most Americans? Which brands are second and third, and how big are the differences in popularity among the three?

To what extent are different ethnic groups represented in the population of your city?

Notice that each of the preceding examples asks a question about *how many*—in other words, these are all questions about frequencies. The chi-square test for goodness of fit is specifically designed to answer this type of question. In general terms, this chi-square test is a hypothesis-testing procedure that uses the frequency distribution for a sample to test hypotheses about the corresponding frequency distribution for a population.

The name of the test comes from the Greek letter χ (chi, pronounced "kye") that is used to identify the test statistic.

DEFINITION   The chi-square test for *goodness of fit* determines how well the frequency distribution for a sample fits the population distribution that is specified by the null hypothesis.

You should recall from Chapter 2 that a frequency distribution is defined as a record of the number of individuals located in each category of the scale of measurement. In a frequency distribution graph, the categories that make up the scale of measurement are listed on the X-axis. In a frequency distribution table, the categories are listed in the first column. With chi-square tests, however, it is customary to present the scale of measurement as a series of boxes with each box corresponding to a separate category on the scale. The frequency corresponding to each category is simply presented as a number written inside the box. Figure 17.1 shows how a distribution of eye colors for a set of $n = 40$ students can be presented either as a graph, a table, or a series of boxes. Notice that the scale of measurement for this example consists of four categories of eye color (brown, blue, green, other).

THE NULL HYPOTHESIS FOR THE GOODNESS-OF-FIT TEST

For the chi-square test of goodness of fit, the null hypothesis specifies the proportion (or percentage) of the population in each category. For example a hypothesis might state that 90% of all lawyers are men and only 10% are women. The simplest way of presenting this hypothesis, is to put the hypothesized proportions in the series of boxes representing the scale of measurement:

	MEN	WOMEN
H_0:	90%	10%

Although it is conceivable that a researcher could choose any proportions for the null hypothesis, there usually is some well-defined rationale for stating a null hypothesis. Generally H_0 will fall into one of the following categories.

Figure 17.1

Distribution of eye colors for a sample of $n = 40$ individuals. The same frequency distribution is shown as a bar graph, as a table, and with the frequencies written in a series of boxes.

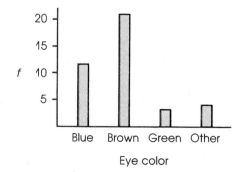

Eye color (X)	f
Blue	12
Brown	21
Green	3
Other	4

Blue	Brown	Green	Other
12	21	3	4

1. No Preference. The null hypothesis often states that there is no preference among the different categories. In this case, H_0 states that the population is divided equally among the categories. For example, a hypothesis stating that there is no preference among the three leading brands of soft drinks would specify a population distribution as follows:

	BRAND X	BRAND Y	BRAND Z
H_0:	$\frac{1}{3}$	$\frac{1}{3}$	$\frac{1}{3}$

2. No Difference from a Comparison Population. The null hypothesis can state that the frequency distribution for one population is not different from the distribution that is known to exist for another population. For example, suppose it is known that 60% of U.S. residents favor the president's foreign policy and 40% are in opposition. A researcher might wonder if this same pattern of attitudes exists among Europeans. The null hypothesis would state that there is no difference between the two populations and specify the Europeans would be distributed as follows:

	FAVOR	OPPOSE
H_0:	60%	40%

Because the null hypothesis for the goodness-of-fit test specifies an exact distribution for the population, the alternative hypothesis (H_1) simply states that the population distribution has a different shape from that specified in H_0. If the null hypothesis stated that the population is equally divided among three categories, the alternative hypothesis would say that the population is not divided equally.

THE DATA FOR THE GOODNESS-OF-FIT TEST

The data for a chi-square test are remarkably simple. There is no need to calculate a sample mean or *SS*, you just select a sample of *n* individuals and count how many are in each category. The resulting values are called *observed frequencies*. The symbol for observed frequency is f_o. For example, the following data represent observed frequencies for a sample of $n = 40$ subjects. Each person was given a personality questionnaire and classified into one of three personality categories: A, B, or C.

CATEGORY A	CATEGORY B	CATEGORY C	
15	19	6	$n = 40$

Notice that each individual in the sample is classified into one and only one of the categories. Thus, the frequencies in this example represent three completely separate groups of individuals: 15 who were classified as category A, 19 classified as B, and 6 classified as C. Also note that the observed frequencies add up to the total sample size: $\Sigma f_o = n$.

DEFINITION

The *observed frequency* is the number of individuals from the sample who are classified in a particular category. Each individual is counted in one and only one category.

EXPECTED FREQUENCIES   The general goal of the chi-square test for goodness of fit is to compare the data (the observed frequencies) with the null hypothesis. The problem is to determine how well the data fit the distribution specified in H_0—hence the name *goodness of fit*.

The first step in the chi-square test is to determine how the sample distribution should look if the null hypothesis were exactly right. Suppose the null hypothesis states that the population is distributed in three categories with the following proportions:

CATEGORY A	CATEGORY B	CATEGORY C
25%	50%	25%

If this hypothesis is correct, how would you expect a random sample of $n = 40$ individuals to be distributed among the three categories? It should be clear that your best strategy is to predict 25% of the sample would be in category A, 50% would be in category B, and 25% would be in category C. To find the exact frequency expected for each category, multiply the sample size *(n)* by the proportion (or percentage) from the null hypothesis. For this example you would expect

25% of 40 = 0.25(40) = 10 individuals in category A

50% of 40 = 0.50(40) = 20 individuals in category B

25% of 40 = 0.25(40) = 10 individuals in category C

The frequency values predicted from the null hypothesis are called *expected frequencies*. The symbol for expected frequency is f_e, and the expected frequency for each category is computed by

$$\text{expected frequency} = f_e = pn \tag{17.1}$$

where p is the proportion stated in the null hypothesis and n is the sample size.

DEFINITION   The *expected frequency* for each category is the frequency value that is predicted from the null hypothesis and the sample size *(n)*.

THE CHI-SQUARE STATISTIC   The general purpose of any hypothesis test is to determine whether the sample data support or refute a hypothesis about the population. In the chi-square test for goodness of fit, the sample is expressed as a set of observed frequencies (f_o values), and the null hypothesis has been used to generate a set of expected frequencies (f_e values). The *chi-square statistic* simply measures how well the data (f_o) fit the hypothesis (f_e). The symbol for the chi-square statistic is χ^2. The formula for the chi-square statistic is

$$\text{chi-square} = \chi^2 = \Sigma \frac{(f_o - f_e)^2}{f_e} \tag{17.2}$$

17.1 THE CHI-SQUARE FORMULA

WE HAVE seen that the chi-square formula compares observed frequencies to expected frequencies in order to assess how well the sample data match the hypothesized data. This function of the chi-square statistic is easy to spot in the numerator of the equation, $(f_o - f_e)^2$. The difference between the observed and expected frequencies is found first. The greater this difference, the more discrepancy there is between what is observed and what is expected. The difference is then squared to remove the negative signs (large discrepancies may have negative signs as well as positive signs). The summation sign in front of the equation indicates that we must examine the amount of discrepancy for every category. Why, then, must we divide the squared differences by f_e for each category before we sum the category values? Basically, we would view the $f_o - f_e$ discrepancies in a different light if f_e were very small or very large.

Suppose you were going to throw a party and you *expected* 1000 people to show up. However, at the party you counted the number of guests and *observed* that 1040 actually showed up. Forty more guests than expected are no major problem when all along you were planning for 1000. There will still probably be enough beer and potato chips for everyone. On the other hand, suppose you had a party and you expected 10 people to attend but instead 50 actually showed up. Forty more guests in this case spell big trouble. How "significant" the discrepancy is depends in part on what you were originally expecting. With very large expected frequencies, allowances are made for more error between f_o and f_e. This is accomplished in the chi-square formula by dividing the squared discrepancy for each category, $(f_o - f_e)^2$, by its expected frequency.

As the formula indicates, the value of chi-square is computed by the following steps:

1. Find the difference between f_o (the data) and f_e (the hypothesis) for each category.

2. Square the difference. This ensures that all values are positive.

3. Next, divide the squared difference by f_e. A justification for this step is given in Box 17.1.

4. Finally, sum the values from all the categories.

THE CHI-SQUARE DISTRIBUTION AND DEGREES OF FREEDOM

It should be clear from the chi-square formula that the value of chi-square is measuring the discrepancy between the observed frequencies (data) and the expected frequencies (H_0). When there are large differences between f_o and f_e the value of chi-square will be large, and we will conclude that the data do not fit the hypothesis. Thus, a large value for chi-square will lead us to reject H_0. On the other hand, when the observed frequencies are very close to the expected frequencies, chi-square will be small and we will conclude that there is a very good fit between the data and the hypothesis. Thus, a small chi-square value indicates that we should fail to reject H_0. To decide whether a particular chi-square value is "large" or "small," we must refer to a *chi-square distribution*. This distribution is the set of chi-square values for all the possible random samples when H_0 is true. Much like other distributions we have examined (t distribution, F distribution), the chi-square distribution is a theoretical distribution with well-defined characteristics. Some of these characteristics are easy to infer from the chi-square formula.

1. The formula for chi-square involves adding squared values, so you can never obtain a negative value. Thus, all chi-square values are zero or larger.

2. When H_0 is true, you expect the data (f_o values) to be close to the hypothesis (f_e values). Thus, we expect chi-square values to be small when H_0 is true.

These two factors suggest that the typical chi-square distribution will be positively skewed (see Figure 17.2). Note that small values, near zero, are expected when H_0 is true, and large values (in the right-hand tail) are very unlikely. Thus, unusually large values of chi-square will form the critical region for the hypothesis test.

Although the typical chi-square distribution is positively skewed, there is one other factor that plays a role in the exact shape of the chi-square distribution—the number of categories. You should recall that the chi-square formula requires that you sum values from every category. The more categories you have, the more likely it is that you will obtain a large sum for the chi-square value. On the average, chi-square will be larger when you are summing over 10 categories than when you are summing over only 3 categories. As a result, there is a whole family of chi-square distributions, with the exact shape of each distribution determined by the number of categories used in the study. Technically, each specific chi-square distribution is identified by degrees of freedom (df) rather than the number of categories. For the goodness-of-fit test, the degrees of freedom are determined by

$$df = C - 1 \qquad \text{(17.3)}$$

where C is the number of categories. A brief discussion of this df formula is presented in Box 17.2. Figure 17.3 shows the general relation between df and the shape of the chi-square distribution. Note that the typical chi-square value (the mode) gets larger as the number of categories is increased.

Figure 17.2

Chi-square distributions are positively skewed. The critical region is placed in the extreme tail, which reflects large chi-square values.

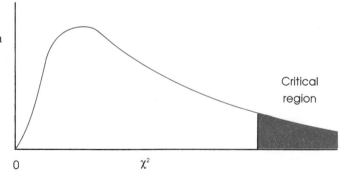

0   χ^2

Critical region

Figure 17.3

The shape of the chi-square distribution for different values of *df*. As the number of categories increase, the peak (mode) of the distribution has a larger chi-square value.

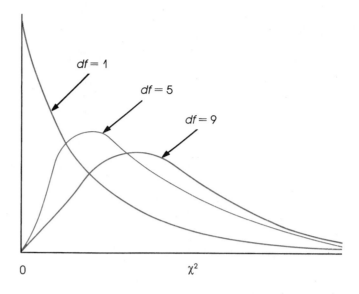

LOCATING THE CRITICAL REGION FOR A CHI-SQUARE TEST

To evaluate the results of a chi-square test, we must determine whether the chi-square statistic is large or small. Remember, an unusually large value indicates a big discrepancy between the data and the hypothesis and suggests that we reject H_0. To determine whether or not a particular chi-square value is significantly large, you first select an alpha level, typically .05 or .01. Then, you consult the table entitled The Chi-Square Distribution (Appendix B). A portion of the chi-square distribution table is shown in Table 17.2. The first column in the table lists *df* values for chi-square. The top row of the table lists proportions of area in the extreme right-hand tail of the distribution. The numbers in the body of the table are the critical values of chi-square. The table shows, for example, in a chi-square distribution with *df* = 3, only 5% (0.05) of the values are larger than 7.81, and only 1% (0.01) are larger than 11.34.

Table 17.2

A portion of the table of critical values for the chi-square distribution

		PROPORTION IN CRITICAL REGION			
df	0.10	0.05	0.025	0.01	0.005
1	2.71	3.84	5.02	6.63	7.88
2	4.61	5.99	7.38	9.21	10.60
3	6.25	7.81	9.35	11.34	12.84
4	7.78	9.49	11.14	13.28	14.86
5	9.24	11.07	12.83	17.09	16.75
6	10.64	12.59	14.45	16.81	18.55
7	12.02	14.07	16.01	18.48	20.28
8	13.36	17.51	17.53	20.09	21.96
9	14.68	16.92	19.02	21.67	23.59

A CLOSER LOOK
AT DEGREES OF FREEDOM

17.2

DEGREES OF freedom for the chi-square test literally measure the number of free choices that exist when you are determining the null hypothesis or the expected frequencies. For example, when you are classifying individuals into three categories, you have exactly two free choices in stating the null hypothesis. You may select any two proportions for the first two categories, but then the third proportion is determined. If you hypothesize 25% in the first category and 50% in the second category, then the third category must be 25% in order to account for 100% of the population. In general, you are free to select proportions for all but one of the categories, but then the final proportion is determined by the fact that the entire set must total 100%. Thus, you have $C - 1$ free choices, where C is the number of categories: degrees of freedom, df, equals $C - 1$.

The same restriction holds when you are determining the expected frequencies. Again suppose that you have three categories and a sample of $n = 40$ individuals. If you specify expected frequencies of $f_e = 10$ for the first category and $f_e = 20$ for the second category, then you must use $f_e = 10$ for the final category.

CATEGORY A	CATEGORY B	CATEGORY C	
10	20	???	$n = 40$

As before, you may distribute the sample freely among the first $C - 1$ categories, but then the final category is determined by the total number of individuals in the sample.

EXAMPLE OF THE CHI-SQUARE TEST FOR GOODNESS OF FIT

We will use the same step-by-step process for testing hypotheses with chi-square as we used for other hypothesis tests. In general, the steps consists of stating the hypotheses, locating the critical region, computing the test statistic, and making a decision about H_0. The following example demonstrates the complete process of hypothesis testing with the goodness-of-fit test.

EXAMPLE 17.1   A researcher is interested in the factors that are involved in course selection. A sample of 50 students is asked, "Which of the following factors is most important to you when selecting a course?" Students must choose one and only one of the following alternatives:

1. Interest in course topic
2. Ease of passing the course
3. Instructor for the course
4. Time of day course is offered

The frequency distribution of responses for this sample is summarized in Table 17.3. Do any of these factors play a greater role than others for course selection?

STEP 1   We must state the hypotheses and select a level of significance. The hypotheses may be stated as follows:

H_0:   The population of students shows no preference in selecting any one of the four factors over the others. Thus, the

Table 17.3

Part A: The most important factor in course selection (observed frequencies).

	INTEREST IN TOPIC	EASE OF PASSING	COURSE INSTRUCTOR	TIME OF DAY
f_o	18	17	7	8

It is acceptable for expected frequencies to have fractional or decimal values.

Part B: The expected frequencies for Example 17.1

	INTEREST IN TOPIC	EASE OF PASSING	COURSE INSTRUCTOR	TIME OF DAY
f_e	12.5	12.5	12.5	12.5

four factors are named equally often, and the population distribution has the following proportions:

INTEREST IN TOPIC	EASE OF PASSING	COURSE INSTRUCTOR	TIME OF DAY
$\frac{1}{4}$	$\frac{1}{4}$	$\frac{1}{4}$	$\frac{1}{4}$

H_1:   In the population of students, one or more of these factors plays a greater role in course selection (the factor is named more frequently by students).

The level of significance is set at a standard value, $\alpha = .05$.

STEP 2   The value for degrees of freedom is determined, and then the critical region is located. For this example, the value for degrees of freedom is

$$df = C - 1 = 4 - 1 = 3$$

For $df = 3$ and $\alpha = .05$, the table for critical values of chi-square indicates that the critical χ^2 has a value of 7.81. The critical region is sketched in Figure 17.4.

STEP 3   The expected frequencies for all categories must be determined, and then the chi-square statistic can be calculated. If H_0 were true and the

Figure 17.4

For Example 17.1, the critical region begins at a chi-square value of 7.81.

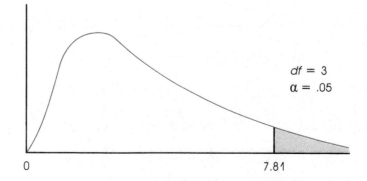

$df = 3$
$\alpha = .05$

0   7.81

students display no response preference for the four alternatives, then the proportion of the population responding to each category would be $\frac{1}{4}$. Because the sample size (n) is 50, the null hypothesis predicts expected frequencies of 12.5 for all categories (Table 17.3):

$$f_e = pn = \tfrac{1}{4}(50) = 12.5$$

Using the observed and the expected frequencies from Table 17.3, the chi-square statistic may now be calculated:

$$
\begin{aligned}
\chi^2 = \Sigma \frac{(f_o - f_e)^2}{f_e} \\
= \frac{(18 - 12.5)^2}{12.5} + \frac{(17 - 12.5)^2}{12.5} + \frac{(7 - 12.5)^2}{12.5} + \frac{(8 - 12.5)^2}{12.5} \\
= \frac{30.25}{12.5} + \frac{20.25}{12.5} + \frac{30.25}{12.5} + \frac{20.25}{12.5} \\
= 2.42 + 1.62 + 2.42 + 1.62 \\
= 8.08
\end{aligned}
$$

STEP 4   The obtained chi-square value is in the critical region. Therefore, H_0 is rejected, and the researcher may conclude that the subjects mentioned some of the factors more than others in response to the question about course selection. In a research report, the investigator might state:

> The students showed a significant response preference to the question concerning factors involved in course selection, $\chi^2(3, n = 50) = 8.08, p < .05$.

Note that the form of reporting the chi-square value is similar to that of other statistical tests we have encountered. Degrees of freedom and the sample size are indicated in the parentheses after the χ^2 symbol. This information is followed by the obtained chi-square value and then by the probability that a Type I error has been committed.

LEARNING CHECK   1. A researcher for an insurance company would like to know if high-performance, overpowered automobiles are more likely to be involved in accidents than other types of cars. For a sample of 50 insurance claims, the investigator classifies the automobiles as high-performance, subcompact, midsize, or full-size. The observed frequencies are as follows:

Observed Frequencies of Insurance Claims

HIGH-PERFORMANCE	SUBCOMPACT	MIDSIZE	FULL-SIZE	TOTAL
20	14	7	9	50

In determining the f_e values, assume that only 10% of the cars in the population are the high-performance variety. However, subcompacts, midsize cars, and full-size cars make up 40%, 30%, and 20%, respectively. Can the researcher conclude that the observed pattern of accidents does not fit the predicted (f_e) values? Test with $\alpha = .05$.

a. In a few sentences, state the hypotheses.

b. Determine the value for df and locate the critical region.

c. Determine f_e values and compute chi-square.

d. Make a decision regarding H_0.

ANSWERS   **1. a.** H_0: In the population, no particular type of car shows a disproportionate number of accidents. H_1: In the population, a disproportionate number of the accidents occur with certain types of cars.

b. $df = 3$; the critical χ^2 value is 7.81.

c. The f_e values for high-performance, subcompact, midsize, and full-size cars are 5, 20, 15, and 10, respectively. The obtained chi-square is 51.17.

d. Reject H_0.

17.3 THE CHI-SQUARE TEST FOR INDEPENDENCE

The chi-square statistic may also be used to test whether or not there is a relationship between two variables. In this situation, each individual in the sample is measured or classified on two separate variables. For example, a group of students could be classified in terms of personality (introvert, extrovert) and in terms of color preference (red, yellow, green, or blue). Usually the data from this classification are presented in the form of a matrix, where the rows correspond to the categories of one variable and the columns correspond to the categories of the second variable. Table 17.4 presents some hypothetical data for a sample of $n = 400$ students who have been classified by personality and color preference. The number in each box, or cell, of the matrix depicts the frequency of that particular group. In Table 17.4, for example, there are 20 introverted students who selected red as their preferred color and 180 extroverted students who preferred red. To obtain these data the researcher first selects a random sample of $n = 400$ students. Each student is then given a personality test, and each student is asked to select a preferred color from among the four choices. Notice that the classification is based on the measurements for each student, the researcher does not assign students to categories. Also notice that the data consist of frequencies, not scores, from a sample. These sample data will be used to test a hypothesis about the corresponding population frequency distribution. Once again we will be using the chi-square statistic for the test, but in this case the test is called the chi-square *test for independence*.

THE NULL HYPOTHESIS   The null hypothesis for the chi-square test for independence states that there is no relationship between the two variables being measured; that is, the two variables are independent. For the example we have been considering, H_0 could be stated as

H_0:   For the general population of students, color preference is independent of personality.

The alternative hypothesis, H_1, says that there is a relation between the two variables. For this example, H_1 states that color preference does depend on personality.

OBSERVED AND EXPECTED FREQUENCIES   The chi-square test for independence uses the same basic logic that was used for the goodness-of-fit test. First, a sample is selected and each individual is classified or categorized. Because the test for independence considers two variables, every individual is classified on both variables, and the resulting frequency distribution is presented as a two-dimensional matrix (see Table 17.4). As before, the frequencies in the sample distribution are called observed frequencies and are identified by the symbol f_o.

The next step is to find the frequency distribution that would be predicted from the null hypothesis. As before, the frequencies generated from H_0 are called expected frequencies and are identified by the symbol f_e. Once the expected frequencies are obtained, we will compute a chi-square statistic to determine how well the data (observed values) fit the hypothesis (expected values). Before we get to the chi-square formula, however, we must face the relatively complex task of finding expected frequencies for the chi-square test of independence. The data in Table 17.4 will be used to help introduce the calculation of expected frequencies.

The data in Table 17.4 provide a set of observed frequencies. Our problem is to find the set of expected frequencies for this example. Remember, expected frequencies specify how the sample would be distributed if the null hypothesis were correct. Therefore, the f_e values are based on the null hypothesis and the sample size. We will begin by examining H_0. For this example, the null hypothesis states

We could state H_0 as "personality is independent of color preference."

H_0:   Color preference is independent of personality

If this hypothesis is correct we would expect no consistent, predictable differences between the color preferences for introverts versus the color preferences for extroverts. For example, if we found that 60% of the introverts preferred red, we would expect that approximately 60% of the extroverts also would prefer red. On the other hand, a big difference in the color preference

Table 17.4

Color preferences according to personality types

	RED	YELLOW	GREEN	BLUE	
INTROVERT	20	6	30	44	100
EXTROVERT	180	34	50	36	300
	200	40	80	80	$n = 400$

distributions for introverts versus extroverts would indicate that there is a relation between the two variables. For example, if the data showed that 60% of the extroverts chose red but only 10% of the introverts preferred red, we would probably conclude that color preference is related to personality.

In general, when two variables are independent, the distribution for one variable will not depend on the categories of the second variable. In other words, the frequency distribution for one variable will have the *same shape* (same proportions) for all categories of the second variable.

DEFINITION   Two variables are *independent* when the frequency distribution for one variable is not related to (or dependent on) the categories of the second variable. As a result, the frequency distribution for one variable will have the same shape for all categories of the second variable.

Thus, we can restate the null hypothesis for this example as follows:

H_0:   The frequency distribution for color preference has the same shape for all categories of personality.

Now, we are ready to look at the size of the sample.

The data in Table 17.4 represent a sample of $n = 400$ individuals. However, this total sample is already divided into a set of predetermined subgroups. For example, the sample contains 100 introverts and a separate group of 300 extroverts. Similarly, the total sample consists of 200 people who selected red as their favorite color, 40 people who picked yellow, 80 who choose green, and 80 who preferred blue. These subgroup sizes are crucial to the calculation of expected frequencies. Fortunately, the subgroup numbers are easily obtained by reading the row totals and the column totals from the data (the observed frequencies).

Part A of Table 17.5 presents an empty frequency distribution table, listing only row totals and column totals. This empty table identifies the general characteristics of the sample ($n = 400$, with 100 introverts, etc.). To find the

---

Table 17.5

Expected frequencies for color preferences and personality types

Part A: An empty frequency distribution matrix showing only the row totals and column totals. These numbers describe the basic characteristics of the sample from Table 17.4

	RED	YELLOW	GREEN	BLUE	
INTROVERT					100
EXTROVERT					300
	200	40	80	80	

Part B: Expected frequencies. This is the distribution that is predicted by the null hypothesis.

	RED	YELLOW	GREEN	BLUE	
INTROVERT	50	10	20	20	100
EXTROVERT	150	30	60	60	300
	200	40	80	80	

expected frequencies, we must determine how the sample should be distributed according to the null hypothesis. In other words, our problem is to fill in the empty spaces in the table.

Once again, the null hypothesis states that the distribution of color preferences should have the same shape for introverts as for extroverts. But what is the "distribution of color preferences"? The best information we have about this distribution comes from the sample data. The column totals from the sample show the following distribution (see part A of Table 17.5):

$$200 \text{ out of } 400 \text{ choose red:} \quad \frac{200}{400} = 50\% \text{ red}$$

$$40 \text{ out of } 400 \text{ choose yellow:} \quad \frac{40}{400} = 10\% \text{ yellow}$$

$$80 \text{ out of } 400 \text{ choose green:} \quad \frac{80}{400} = 20\% \text{ green}$$

$$80 \text{ out of } 400 \text{ choose blue:} \quad \frac{80}{400} = 20\% \text{ blue}$$

If H_0 is true, we would expect to obtain this same distribution of color preferences for both introverts and extroverts. Therefore, expected frequencies can be obtained by applying the color-preference distribution equally to the set of 100 introverts and to the set of 300 extroverts. The resulting f_e values are as follows.

For the 100 introverts, we expect

$$50\% \text{ choose red:} \quad f_e = 0.50(100) = 50$$
$$10\% \text{ choose yellow:} \quad f_e = 0.10(100) = 10$$
$$20\% \text{ choose green:} \quad f_e = 0.20(100) = 20$$
$$20\% \text{ choose blue:} \quad f_e = 0.20(100) = 20$$

For the 300 extroverts, we expect

$$50\% \text{ choose red:} \quad f_e = 0.50(300) = 150$$
$$10\% \text{ choose yellow:} \quad f_e = 0.10(300) = 30$$
$$20\% \text{ choose green:} \quad f_e = 0.20(300) = 60$$
$$20\% \text{ choose blue:} \quad f_e = 0.20(300) = 60$$

These expected frequencies are shown in part B of Table 17.5. Notice that the row totals and column totals for the expected frequencies are the same as those for the original data in Table 17.4.

A SIMPLE FORMULA FOR DETERMINING EXPECTED FREQUENCIES

Although you should understand that expected frequencies are derived directly from the null hypothesis and the sample characteristics, it is not necessary to go through extensive calculations in order to find f_e values. In fact, there is a simple formula that determines f_e for any cell in the frequency distribution table.

$$f_e = \frac{f_c f_r}{n} \qquad (17.4)$$

where f_c is the frequency total for the column (column total), f_r is the frequency total for the row (row total), and n is the number of individuals in the entire sample. To demonstrate this formula, we will compute the expected frequency for introverts selecting red in Table 17.5(A). First note that this cell is located in the top row and first column in the table. The column total is $f_c = 200$, the row total is $f_r = 100$, and the sample size is $n = 400$. Using these values in formula 17.4, we obtain

$$f_e = \frac{f_c f_r}{n} = \frac{200(100)}{400} = 50$$

Notice that this is identical to the expected frequency we obtained using percentages from the overall distribution.

THE CHI-SQUARE STATISTIC AND DEGREES OF FREEDOM

The chi-square test of independence uses exactly the same chi-square formula as the test for goodness of fit:

$$\chi^2 = \Sigma \frac{(f_o - f_e)^2}{f_e}$$

As before, the formula measures the discrepancy between the data (f_o values) and the hypothesis (f_e values). A large discrepancy will produce a large value for chi-square and will indicate that H_0 should be rejected. To determine whether a particular chi-square statistic is significantly large, you must first determine degrees of freedom (df) for the statistic and then consult the chi-square distribution in the appendix. For the chi-square test of independence, degrees of freedom are based on the number of cells for which you can freely choose expected frequencies. You should recall that the f_e values are partially determined by the sample size (n) and by the row totals and column totals from the original data. These various totals restrict your freedom in selecting expected frequencies. This point is illustrated in Table 17.6. Once three of the f_e values have been selected, all the other f_e values in the table are also determined. In general, the row totals and column totals restrict the final

Table 17.6

Degrees of freedom and expected frequencies. Once three values have been selected, all the remaining expected frequencies are determined by the row totals and the column totals. This example has only three free choices, so $df = 3$.

	RED	YELLOW	GREEN	BLUE	
	50	10	20	?	100
	?	?	?	?	300
	200	40	80	80	

choices in each row and column. Thus, we may freely choose all but one expected frequency in each row and all but one f_e in each column. The total number of f_e values that you can freely choose is $(R - 1)(C - 1)$, where R is the number of rows and C is the number of columns. The degrees of freedom for the chi-square test of independence are given by the formula

$$df = (R - 1)(C - 1) \tag{17.5}$$

AN EXAMPLE OF THE CHI-SQUARE TEST FOR INDEPENDENCE

The steps for the chi-square test of independence should be familiar by now. First, the hypotheses are stated, and an alpha level is selected. Second, the value for degrees of freedom is computed, and the critical region is located. Third, expected frequencies are determined, and the chi-square statistic is computed. Finally, a decision is made regarding the null hypothesis. The following example demonstrates the complete hypothesis-testing procedure.

E X A M P L E   1 7 . 2

This example is analyzed with Minitab using the command CHISQUARE (see Section 20.9).

Darley and Latané(1968) did a study that examined the relationship between the number of observers and aid-giving behaviors (see the Preview). The group sizes consisted of two people (subject and victim), three people, or six people. The investigators categorized the response of a subject in terms of whether or not the observer exhibited any helping behaviors when the victim (actually another laboratory worker) staged an epileptic seizure. The data are presented in Table 17.7. Do aid-giving behaviors depend on group size?

STEP 1 *State the hypotheses and select a level of significance.* According to the null hypothesis, group size and helping behavior are independent of each

Table 17.7

The relationship between size of group and the type of response to the victim.

Part A: Observed frequencies.

	Group Size			
	2	3	6	TOTALS
ASSISTANCE	11	16	4	31
NO ASSISTANCE	2	10	9	21
TOTALS	13	26	13	

Part B: Expected frequencies.

	Group Size			
	2	3	6	TOTALS
ASSISTANCE	7.75	15.5	7.75	31
NO ASSISTANCE	5.25	10.5	5.25	21
TOTALS	13	26	13	

J. M. Darley and B. Latané(1968). Bystander intervention in emergencies: Diffusion of responsibility. *Journal of Personality and Social Psychology, 8,* 377–383. Copyright (1968) by the American Psychological Association. Adapted with permission of the publisher and first author.

other in the population. That is, the absence or presence of aid-giving behavior should not be related to the number of observers. The alternative hypothesis would state that the absence or presence of helping behavior is dependent on group size. The level of significance is set at $\alpha = .05$.

STEP 2 *Calculate the degrees of freedom and locate the critical region.* For the chi-square test of independence,

$$df = (R - 1)(C - 1)$$

Therefore, for this study.

$$df = (2 - 1)(3 - 1) = 1(2) = 2$$

With two degrees of freedom and a level of significance of .05, the critical value for χ^2 is 5.99 (see table for critical values of chi-square).

STEP 3 *Determine the expected frequencies and calculate the chi-square statistic.* As noted before, it is quicker to use the computational formula to determine the f_e values, rather than the percentage method. The expected frequency for each cell is as follows:

1. Group size 2—showed aid-giving behavior:

$$f_e = \frac{f_c f_r}{n} = \frac{13(31)}{52} = 7.75$$

2. Group size 3—showed aid-giving behavior:

$$f_e = \frac{26(31)}{52} = 15.5$$

3. Group size 6—showed aid-giving behavior:

$$f_e = \frac{13(31)}{52} = 7.75$$

4. Group size 2—no aid-giving behavior:

$$f_e = \frac{13(21)}{52} = 5.25$$

5. Group size 3—no aid-giving behavior:

$$f_e = \frac{26(21)}{52} = 10.5$$

6. Group size 6—no aid-giving behavior:

$$f_e = \frac{13(21)}{52} = 5.25$$

Note that the row totals and column totals for the expected frequencies are the same as the totals for the observed frequencies.

The expected frequencies are summarized in Table 17.7. Using these expected frequencies along with the observed frequencies (part A of Table 17.7), we can now calculate the value for the chi-square statistic:

$$\chi^2 = \Sigma \frac{(f_o - f_e)^2}{f_e}$$

$$= \frac{(11 - 7.75)^2}{7.75} + \frac{(16 - 15.5)^2}{15.5} + \frac{(4 - 7.75)^2}{7.75}$$

$$+ \frac{(2 - 5.25)^2}{5.25} + \frac{(10 - 10.5)^2}{10.5} + \frac{(9 - 5.25)^2}{5.25}$$

$$= 1.363 + 0.016 + 1.815 + 2.012 + 0.024 + 2.679$$

$$= 7.91$$

STEP 4 *Make a decision regarding the null hypothesis.* The obtained chi-square value exceeds the critical value (5.99). Therefore, the decision is to reject H_0 and conclude that there is a relationship between group size and the likelihood that someone will aid another person in trouble. For purposes of reporting the data, the researchers could state that there is a significant relationship between size of group and helping behavior, $\chi^2(2, n = 52) = 7.91$, $p < .05$. By examining the observed frequencies in part A of Table 17.7, we see that the likelihood of aid-giving behavior decreases as group size increases.

SPSS^x A-83

LEARNING CHECK 1. A researcher suspects that color blindness is inherited by a sex-linked gene. This possibility is examined by looking for a relationship between gender and color vision. A sample of 1000 people is tested for color blindness, and then they are classified according to their sex and color vision status (normal, red-green blind, other color blindness). Is color blindness related to gender? The data are as follows:

Observed Frequencies of Color Vision Status According to Sex

	NORMAL COLOR VISION	RED-GREEN COLOR BLINDNESS	OTHER COLOR BLINDNESS	TOTALS
MALE	320	70	10	400
FEMALE	580	10	10	600
TOTALS	900	80	20	

a. State the hypotheses.
b. Determine the value for *df* and locate the critical region.
c. Compute the f_e values and then chi-square.
d. Make a decision regarding H_0.

ANSWERS 1. a. H_0: In the population, there is no relationship between gender and color vision. H_1: In the population, gender and color vision are related.

b. $df = 2$; critical $\chi^2 = 5.99$ for $\alpha = .05$.

c. f_e values are as follows:

Expected Frequencies

	NORMAL	RED-GREEN	OTHER
MALE	360	32	8
FEMALE	540	48	12

Obtained $\chi^2 = 83.44$

d. Reject H_0.

17.4 ASSUMPTIONS AND RESTRICTIONS FOR CHI-SQUARE TESTS

To use a chi-square test for goodness of fit or a test of independence, several conditions must be satisfied. For any statistical test, violation of assumptions and restrictions will cast doubt on the results. For example, the probability of committing a Type I error may be distorted when assumptions of statistical tests are not satisfied. Some important assumptions and restrictions for using chi-square tests are the following:

1. Independence of Observations. This is *not* to be confused with the concept of independence between *variables* as seen in the test of independence (Section 17.3). One consequence of independent observations is that each observed frequency is generated by a different subject. A chi-square test would be inappropriate if a person could produce responses that can be classified in more than one category or contribute more than one frequency count to a single category. (See page 255 for more information on independence.)

2. Size of Expected Frequencies. A chi-square test should not be performed when the expected frequency of any cell is less than 5. The chi-square statistic can be distorted when f_e is very small. Consider the chi-square computations for a single cell. Suppose the cell has values of $f_e = 1$ and $f_o = 5$. The contribution of this cell to the total chi-square value is

$$\text{cell} = \frac{(f_o - f_e)^2}{f_e} = \frac{(5 - 1)^2}{1} = \frac{4^2}{1} = 16$$

Now consider another instance, where $f_e = 10$ and $f_o = 14$. The difference between the observed and expected frequency is still 4, but the contribution of this cell to the total chi-square value differs from that of the first case:

$$\text{cell} = \frac{(f_o - f_e)^2}{f_e} = \frac{(14 - 10)^2}{10} = \frac{4^2}{10} = 1.6$$

It should be clear that a small f_e value can have a great influence on the chi-square value. This problem becomes serious when f_e values are less than 5. When f_e is very small, what would otherwise be a minor discrepancy between f_o and f_e will now result in large chi-square values. The test is too sensitive when f_e values are extremely small. One way to avoid small expected frequencies is to use large samples.

17.5 SPECIAL APPLICATIONS OF THE CHI-SQUARE TESTS

At the beginning of this chapter we introduced the chi-square tests as examples of nonparametric tests. Although nonparametric tests serve a function that is uniquely their own, they also can be viewed as alternatives to the common parametric techniques that were examined in earlier chapters. In general, nonparametric tests are used as substitutes for parametric techniques in situations where one of the following occurs:

1. The data do not meet the assumptions needed for a standard parametric test.
2. The data consist of nominal or ordinal measurements, so that it is impossible to compute standard descriptive statistics such as the mean and standard deviation.

In this section we will examine some of the relationships between chi-square tests and the parametric procedures for which they may substitute.

CHI-SQUARE AND THE PEARSON CORRELATION

The chi-square test of independence and the Pearson correlation are both statistical techniques intended to evaluate the relationship between two variables. The type of data obtained in a research study determines which of these two statistical procedures is appropriate.

The Pearson correlation is used to evaluate a relationship in situations where both variables consist of numerical values; that is, X and Y are numbers obtained from measurement on interval or ratio scales. The chi-square test for independence, on the other hand, is used in situations where the data are obtained by classifying individuals into categories, usually determined by a nominal or ordinal scale of measurement. Although both statistical techniques are used to measure the relationship between two variables, the distinction between them is determined by the type of data that a researcher has obtained. For the chi-square test, the numbers in the data are frequencies, not scores. For the Pearson correlation, the scores are numerical values.

THE PHI-COEFFICIENT

In Chapter 16 (page 487) we introduced the phi-coefficient as a correlational statistic for measuring the degree of association between two dichotomous variables. A dichotomous variable is one for which there are exactly two categories of measurement; for example, gender can be classified as male or female; people's opinions concerning a new law can be classified as ''for'' or

Figure 17.5

Hypothetical data showing the first four individuals in a sample where each person is classified on two dichotomous variables. The original data (top of figure) can be reorganized into a form suitable for computing the phi-coefficient (lower left) or into a form suitable for computing a chi-square test for independence (lower right).

Original Data

SUBJECT	SEX	OPINION
A	Male	For
B	Female	For
C	Female	Against
D	Male	For

Data Coded as Numerical Values (0 and 1) for Computing the Phi-coefficient

SUBJECT	SEX	OPINION
A	0	0
B	1	0
C	1	1
D	0	0

Data Organized in a Frequency Distribution for Computing Chi-square

	OPINION FOR	AGAINST
MALE	2	0
FEMALE	1	1

"against." The phi-coefficient allows you to compute a correlation measuring the degree of relation between two such variables.

The same data that are used to compute the phi-coefficient can be reorganized into a matrix of frequencies that is suitable for the chi-square test for independence. This process is shown in Figure 17.5. In the figure, the original data show that each individual is classified according to gender (male, female) and according to opinion concerning a proposal to ban smoking in all college buildings (for, against). To compute the phi-coefficient, the original data are transformed into numerical values by substituting values of 0 and 1 for the two categories of each variable, and the Pearson formula is used. The transformed data are shown in the lower left-hand side of Figure 17.5. On the other hand, the original two variables can be used to create a 2 × 2 matrix with the categories of one variable determining the two columns and the categories of the second variable determining the two rows of the matrix. This process is demonstrated in the lower right-hand side of Figure 17.5. The number in each cell of the matrix is the frequency, or number of individuals classified in that cell. The chi-square statistic is computed from the frequency data using the procedures described in Section 17.3. The value for the phi-coefficient (ϕ) may be computed directly from chi-square by the following formula:

$$\phi = \sqrt{\frac{\chi^2}{n}}$$

(17.6)

A strong relationship between the two variables will produce a large value (near 1.00) for the phi-coefficient.

INDEPENDENT-MEASURES t AND ANOVA

The independent-measures t test and ANOVA are statistical procedures used to examine the relationship between an independent variable and a dependent variable. Both tests require that the scores for the dependent variable consist of numerical values measured on an interval or a ratio scale. The chi-square test for independence often can be used as a substitute for t or ANOVA, particularly in the following situations:

1. The independent variable is actually a quasi-independent variable (Chapter 1) consisting of distinct subject groups (men versus women; 8-year-olds versus 10-year-olds)

2. The dependent variable involves classifying individuals into nominal or ordinal categories.

For example, suppose a researcher is interested in examining the difference in vocabulary skills between 4-year-old boys and girls. The data for this study would require two independent samples (boys versus girls). If each child's vocabulary skill were measured by a numerical score, the mean difference between boys and girls could be evaluated using either an independent-measures t test or ANOVA. On the other hand, if each child were simply classified as being either high, medium, or low with respect to vocabulary skill, the data would be suitable for a chi-square test. Examples of both types of data are shown in Table 17.8.

THE MEDIAN TEST FOR INDEPENDENT SAMPLES

The median test provides a nonparametric alternative to the independent-measures t hypothesis test (or ANOVA) in situations where the data do not meet the assumptions for the t statistic (or F-ratio). The median test is used to determine whether there is a significant difference in the distribution of scores from two or more independent samples.

The null hypothesis for the median test states that the populations from which the samples were obtained are all distributed evenly around a common median. The alternative hypothesis is that the population distributions are significantly different and do not share a common median.

Table 17.8

Two possible sets of data from a study comparing vocabulary skills for 5-year-old boys versus girls. In Data Set A, vocabulary skill is measured by numerical scores suitable for an independent-measures t (or ANOVA) hypothesis test. In Data Set B, each child's vocabulary skill is classified into one of three categories (high, medium, low) and the numbers represent the frequency, or number of children in each category.

DATA SET A VOCABULARY SCORES	
BOYS	GIRLS
18	20
4	9
21	24
17	18
10	5
3	11
.	.
.	.
.	.

DATA SET B
FREQUENCY DISTRIBUTION
OF VOCABULARY SKILL

	BOYS	GIRLS
HIGH	6	11
MEDIUM	12	14
LOW	8	7

The first step in conducting the median test is to combine all the scores from the separate samples into one group and then find the median for the combined group (see Chapter 3, page 79, for instructions for finding the median). Next, a matrix is constructed with a column for each of the separate samples and two rows: one row for individuals scoring above the combined median and one row for individuals scoring below the combined median. Finally, frequencies are entered in the cells of the matrix with each frequency corresponding to the number of individuals in the specific sample (column) who scored above the combined median (top row) and who scored below the combined median (bottom row).

The frequency distribution matrix is evaluated using a chi-square test for independence. The expected frequencies and a value for chi-square are computed exactly as described in Section 17.3. A significant value for chi-square indicates that the discrepancy between the individual sample distributions is greater than would be expected by chance.

The median test is demonstrated in the following example.

EXAMPLE 17.3   The following data represent self-esteem scores obtained from a sample of $n = 40$ children. The children are then separated into three groups based on their level of academic performance (high, medium, low). The median test will evaluate whether there is a significant relation between self-esteem and level of academic performance.

SELF-ESTEEM SCORES FOR CHILDREN AT THREE LEVELS OF ACADEMIC PERFORMANCE							
HIGH		MEDIUM				LOW	
22	14	22	13	24	20	11	19
19	18	18	22	25	16	13	15
12	21	19	15	14	19	20	16
20	18	11	18	24	10	10	18
23	20	12	19	15	12	15	11

The median for the combined group of $n = 40$ scores is $X = 17$ (exactly 20 scores are above this value and 20 are below). For the first sample, 8 out of 10 scores are above the combined median. For the second sample, 9 out of 20 are above the median, and for the third sample, only 3 out of 10 are above the median. These observed frequencies are shown in the following matrix.

ACADEMIC PERFORMANCE

	HIGH	MEDIUM	LOW
ABOVE MEDIAN	8	9	3
BELOW MEDIAN	2	11	7

The expected frequencies for this test are as follows:

ACADEMIC PERFORMANCE

	HIGH	MEDIUM	LOW
ABOVE MEDIAN	5	10	5
BELOW MEDIAN	5	10	5

The chi-square statistic is,

$$\chi^2 = \frac{9}{5} + \frac{9}{5} + \frac{1}{10} + \frac{1}{10} + \frac{4}{5} + \frac{4}{5} = 5.40$$

With $df = 2$ and $\alpha = .05$, the critical value for chi-square is 5.99. The obtained chi-square of 5.40 does not fall in the critical region, so we would fail to reject the null hypothesis. These data do not provide sufficient evidence to conclude that there are significant differences among the self-esteem distributions for these three groups of students.

A few words of caution are in order concerning the interpretation of the median test. First, the median test is *not* a test for mean differences. Remember, the mean for a distribution can be strongly affected by a few extreme scores. Therefore, the mean and median for a distribution are not necessarily the same, and they may not even be related. The results from a median test *cannot* be interpreted as indicating that there is (or is not) a difference between means.

Second, you may have noted that the median test does not directly compare the median from one sample with the median from another. Thus, the median test is not a test for significant differences between medians. Instead, this test compares the distribution of scores for one sample versus the distribution for another sample. If the samples are distributed evenly around a common point (the group median), the test will conclude that there is no significant difference. On the other hand, finding a significant difference simply indicates that the samples are not distributed evenly around the common median. Thus, the best interpretation of a significant result is that there is a *difference in the distributions* of the samples.

TESTING DIFFERENCES IN PROPORTIONS FOR INDEPENDENT SAMPLES

Although the chi-square test of independence is typically viewed as a method for testing the relationship between two variables, it also serves the purpose of testing for differences in proportions between two (or more) independent samples. When the individuals in each sample are classified into categories, the chi-square test can be used to determine whether the proportions (shape of the distribution) for one sample are significantly different from the proportions obtained for another sample. Consider the following example.

EXAMPLE 17.4 Suppose the city is considering a budget proposal that would allocate extra funding toward the renovation of city parks. A survey is conducted to measure public opinion concerning this proposal. A total of 300 individuals respond to the survey; 100 who live within the city limits, and 200 from the surrounding suburbs. Of the city respondents, 68% (68 out of 100) favor the proposal. But only 43% (86 out of 200) of the suburban respondents favor using tax money for city parks. Is there a significant difference in opinion between these two groups?

This question can be answered using the chi-square test for independence. The data from the survey are the observed frequencies and can be summarized in a matrix as follows:

	FAVOR	OPPOSE	
CITY	68	32	100
SUBURB	86	114	200
	154	146	

The expected frequencies and the value for chi-square would be computed exactly as described in Section 17.3. A significant value for chi-square would indicate a significant difference in the distribution of preference for city dwellers versus the distribution for suburbanites.

SUMMARY

1. Chi-square tests are a type of nonparametric technique that tests hypotheses about the form of the entire frequency distribution. Two types of chi-square tests are the test for goodness of fit and the test for independence. The data for these tests consist of the frequency of observations that fall into various categories of a variable.

2. The test for goodness of fit compares the frequency distribution for a sample to the frequency distribution that is predicted by H_0. The test determines how well the observed frequencies (sample data) fit the expected frequencies (data predicted by H_0).

3. The expected frequencies for the goodness-of-fit test are determined by

    expected frequency $= f_e = pn$

    where p is the hypothesized proportion (according to H_0) of observations falling into a category and n is the size of the sample.

4. The chi-square statistic is computed by

    chi-square $= \chi^2 = \Sigma \dfrac{(f_o - f_e)^2}{f_e}$

    where f_o is the observed frequency for a particular category and f_e is the expected frequency for that category. Large values for χ^2 indicate that there is a large discrepancy between the observed (f_o) and expected (f_e) frequencies and may warrant rejection of the null hypothesis.

5. Degrees of freedom for the test for goodness of fit are

    $df = C - 1$

    where C is the number of categories in the variable. Degrees of freedom measure the number of categories for which f_e values can be freely chosen. As can be seen from the formula, all but the last f_e value to be determined are free to vary.

6. The chi-square distribution is positively skewed and begins at the value of zero. Its exact shape is determined by degrees of freedom.

7. The test for independence is used to assess the relationship between two variables. The null hypothesis states that the two variables in question are independent of each other. That is, the frequency distribution for one variable does not depend on the categories of

the second variable. On the other hand, if a relationship does exist, then the form of the distribution for one variable will depend on the categories of the other variable.

8. For the test for independence, the expected frequencies for H_0 can be directly calculated from the marginal frequency totals,

$$f_e = \frac{f_c f_r}{n}$$

where f_c is the total column frequency and f_r is the total row frequency for the cell in question.

9. Degrees of freedom for the test for independence are computed by

$$df = (R - 1)(C - 1)$$

where R is the number of row categories and C is the number of column categories.

10. For the test of independence, a large chi-square value means there is a large discrepancy between the f_o and f_e values. Rejecting H_0 in this test provides support for a relationship between the two variables.

11. Both chi-square tests (for goodness of fit and independence) are based on the assumption that each observation is independent of the others. That is, each observed frequency reflects a different individual, and no individual can produce a response that would be classified in more than one category or more than one frequency in a single category.

12. The chi-square statistic is distorted when f_e values are small. Chi-square tests, therefore, are restricted to situations where f_e values are 5 or greater. The test should not be performed when the expected frequency of any cell is less than 5.

13. The test for independence also can be used to test whether two sample distributions share a common median. Observed frequencies are obtained by classifying each individual as above or below the median value for the combined samples. A significant value for chi-square indicates a difference between the two sample distributions.

KEY TERMS

goodness-of-fit test	expected frequencies	distribution of chi-square	test for independence
observed frequencies	chi-square statistic	median test	

———— *Focus on Problem Solving* ————

1. The expected frequencies that you calculate must satisfy the constraints of the sample. For the goodness-of-fit test, $\Sigma f_e = \Sigma f_o = n$. For the test of independence, the row totals and column totals for the expected frequencies should be identical to the corresponding totals for the observed frequencies.

2. It is entirely possible to have fractional (decimal) values for expected frequencies. Observed frequencies, however, are always whole numbers.

3. Whenever $df = 1$, the difference between observed and expected frequencies $(f_o - f_e)$ will be identical (the same value) for all cells. This makes the calculation of chi-square easier.

4. Although you are advised to compute expected frequencies for all categories (or cells), you should realize that it is not essential to calculate all f_e values separately. Remember, df for chi-square identifies the number of f_e values that are free to vary. Once you have calculated that number of f_e values, the remaining f_e values are determined. You can get these remaining values by subtracting the calculated f_e values from their corresponding row or column totals.

5. Remember, unlike previous statistical tests, the degrees of freedom (df) for a chi-square test are *not* determined by the sample size (n). Be careful!

Demonstration 17.1

TEST FOR INDEPENDENCE

A manufacturer of watches would like to examine preferences for digital versus analog watches. A sample of $n = 200$ people is selected and these individuals are classified by age and preference. The manufacturer would like to know if there is a relationship between age and watch preference. The observed frequencies (f_0) are as follows:

		PREFERENCE		
		DIGITAL	ANALOG	UNDECIDED
Age	UNDER 30	90	40	10
	OVER 30	10	40	10

STEP 1 *State the hypotheses and select an alpha level.* The null hypothesis states that there is no relationship between the two variables.

> H_0: Preference is independent of age. That is, the frequency distribution of preference has the same form for people under 30 as for people over 30.

The alternative hypothesis states that there is a relationship between the two variables.

> H_1: Preference is related to age. That is, the type of watch preferred depends on a person's age.

We will set alpha to $\alpha = .05$.

STEP 2 *Locate the critical region.* Degrees of freedom for the chi-square test for independence are determined by

$$df = (C - 1)(R - 1)$$

For these data,

$$df = (3 - 1)(2 - 1) = 2(1) = 2$$

For $df = 2$ with $\alpha = .05$, the critical chi-square value is 5.99. Thus, our obtained chi-square must exceed 5.99 to be in the critical region and to reject H_0.

STEP 3 *Compute the test statistic.* Computing the chi-square statistic requires the following preliminary calculations:

1. Obtain the row and column totals
2. Calculate expected frequencies

Row and column totals. We start by determining the row and column totals from the original observed frequencies, f_o.

	DIGITAL	ANALOG	UNDECIDED	TOTALS
UNDER 30	90	40	10	140
OVER 30	10	40	10	60
COLUMN TOTALS	100	80	20	$n = 200$

Expected frequencies, f_e. For the test for independence, the following formula is used to obtain expected frequencies:

$$f_e = \frac{f_c f_r}{n}$$

For people under 30, we obtain the following expected frequencies.

$$f_e = \frac{100(140)}{200} = \frac{14000}{200} = 70 \text{ for digital}$$

$$f_e = \frac{80(140)}{200} = \frac{11200}{200} = 56 \text{ for analog}$$

$$f_e = \frac{20(140)}{200} = \frac{2800}{200} = 14 \text{ for undecided}$$

For individuals over 30, the expected frequencies are as follows:

$$f_e = \frac{100(60)}{200} = \frac{6000}{200} = 30 \text{ for digital}$$

$$f_e = \frac{80(60)}{200} = \frac{4800}{200} = 24 \text{ for analog}$$

$$f_e = \frac{20(60)}{200} = \frac{1200}{200} = 6 \text{ for undecided}$$

The following table summarizes the expected frequencies.

	DIGITAL	ANALOG	UNDECIDED
UNDER 30	70	56	14
OVER 30	30	24	6

The chi-square statistic. The chi-square statistic is computed from the formula,

$$\chi^2 = \Sigma \frac{(f_o - f_e)^2}{f_e}$$

That is, we must

1. Find the $f_o - f_e$ difference for each cell.
2. Square these differences.

3. Divide the squared differences by f_e.

4. Sum the results of 3.

The following table summarizes these calculations.

CELL	f_o	f_e	$(f_o - f_e)$	$(f_o - f_e)^2$	$(f_o - f_e)^2/f_e$
Under 30—digital	90	70	20	400	5.71
Under 30—analog	40	56	−16	256	4.57
Under 30—undecided	10	14	−4	16	1.14
Over 30—digital	10	30	−20	400	13.33
Over 30—analog	40	24	16	256	10.67
Over 30—undecided	10	6	4	16	2.67

Finally, we can sum the last column to get the chi-square value.

$$\chi^2 = 5.71 + 4.57 + 1.14 + 13.33 + 10.67 + 2.67$$
$$= 38.09$$

STEP 4 *Make a decision about H_0 and state the conclusion.* The chi-square value is in the critical region. Therefore, we can reject the null hypothesis. There is a relationship between watch preference and age, $\chi^2(2, n = 200) = 38.09$, $p < .05$.

PROBLEMS

1. A large discount store has prepared a customer survey to determine which factors influence people to shop in the store. A sample of $n = 100$ people is obtained and each person as asked to identify from a list of alternatives the most important factor influencing their choice to shop in the store. The data are as follows:

CONVENIENT LOCATION	LOW PRICES	GOOD SELECTION	OTHER
30	40	20	10

On the basis of these data can you conclude that there is any specific factor (or factors) that is most often cited as being important? Test at the .05 level of significance.

2. A psychology professor noted that a large number of the student representatives on the student government appear to come from the departments of history and political science. In the total college, history majors account for only 6% of the student body and political science accounts for only 8% of the stu-

dents. The numbers in student government are as follows:

HISTORY	POLITICAL SCIENCE	OTHER
12	17	71

Based on these data, can the professor conclude that departmental representation on student government is significantly different from what would be expected by chance? Test at the .05 level of significance.

3. A researcher noticed that one of the laboratory rats seemed to have a strong preference for taking the right-hand branch in a *T*-maze. During a series of 20 trials, this rat took the right-hand branch 17 times and went left only 3 times. Explain why you should not use a chi-square goodness-of-fit test to evaluate these data.

4. A researcher is investigating the physical characteristics that influence whether or not a person's face is

judged as beautiful. The researcher selects a photograph of a woman and then creates two modifications of the photo by (1) moving the eyes slightly farther apart and (2) moving the eyes slightly closer together. The original photograph and the two modifications are then shown to a sample of $n = 150$ college students, and each student is asked to select the "most beautiful" of the three faces. The distribution of responses was as follows:

ORIGINAL PHOTO	EYES MOVED APART	EYES MOVED TOGETHER
51	72	27

Do these data indicate any significant preferences among the three versions of the photograph? Test at the .05 level of significance.

5. A marketing researcher would like to determine if a preference exists among adult readers for one of the three leading weekly news magazines. In a telephone survey, a sample of $n = 1000$ people are asked to select the magazine they like the most: *Newsweek*, *Time*, or *U.S. News and World Report*. The observed frequencies are as follows:

SELECTION

	NEWSWEEK	TIME	U.S. NEWS
f_o	342	355	303

Is there a significant preference? Test at the .05 level of significance.

6. It is known that blood type varies among different populations of people. In the United States, for example, types O, A, B, and AB blood make up 45%, 41%, 10%, and 4% of the population, respectively. Suppose blood type is determined for a sample of $n = 136$ individuals from a foreign country. The resulting frequency distribution is as follows:

BLOOD TYPE

	O	A	B	AB
f_o	43	38	41	14

Is there a significant difference between this distribution and what we would expect for the United States? Set alpha at .05.

7. Suppose an opinion poll taken in 1970 revealed the following data regarding the legalization of marijuana: 15% in favor of, 79% against, and 6% no opinion regarding legalization. Suppose you took a random sample of $n = 220$ people today and obtained the following data:

ATTITUDE TOWARD LEGALIZATION OF MARIJUANA

	FOR	AGAINST	NO OPINION
f_o	38	165	17

Is there a significant difference between the current data and what were obtained in 1970? Use the .05 level of significance.

8. A consumer research organization recently conducted a taste-test comparing three major brands of diet cola. A random sample of $n = 200$ people was obtained. Each person tasted all three brands and then selected his or her favorite. The frequency distribution from this study is as follows:

BRAND X	BRAND Y	BRAND Z
78	51	71

Do these data indicate any significant preferences among the three brands? Test at the .05 level of significance.

9. A questionnaire given to last year's freshman class indicated that 30% intended to be science majors, 50% intended to major in social science or humanities, and 20% were interested in professional programs. A random sample of 100 students from the current freshman class yielded the following frequency distribution:

INTENDED MAJOR

SCIENCES	SOCIAL SCIENCE OR HUMANITIES	PROFESSIONAL
35	40	25

a. On the basis of these data, should the university officials conclude that there has been a significant change in student interests? Test at the .05 level of significance.

b. If twice as many students had been sampled with the result that the observed frequencies were doubled in each of the three categories, would there be evidence for a significant change? Again, test with $\alpha = .05$.

c. How do you explain the different conclusions for parts a and b?

10. A psychologist would like to determine if there is a relationship between extroversion and cigarette smoking. A random sample of 150 people is selected. Each person is given a standard personality inventory to classify him or her as an introvert or extrovert. Each must also provide information about how much he or she smokes (never, less than a pack per day, more than a pack per day). The observed frequencies are as follows:

NUMBER OF CIGARETTES PER DAY

	NONE	LESS THAN A PACK	MORE THAN A PACK
Extrovert	50	12	28
Introvert	50	8	2

Can the psychologist conclude there is a relationship between these personality types and smoking behavior? Set alpha at .05.

11. A scientist would like to see if there is a relationship between handedness and eye preference. A random sample of $n = 150$ subjects is selected. For each subject the researcher determines two things: (1) whether the person is left-handed or right-handed and (2) which eye the person prefers to use when looking through a camera viewfinder. The observed frequencies are as follow:

HAND PREFERENCE

		LEFT	RIGHT
Eye Preference	LEFT	20	40
	RIGHT	10	80

Is there a relationship between the two variables? Test at the .01 level of significance.

12. A researcher is interested in the relation between IQ and vocabulary for 5-year-old children.
  a. Explain how the relationship might be examined using a Pearson correlation. Specifically, describe the data that the researcher would need to collect.
  b. Explain how the relationship might be examined using a chi-square test for independence. Again, describe the data that the researcher would need to collect.

13. The U.S. Senate recently considered a controversial amendment for school prayer. The amendment did not get the required two-thirds majority, but the results of the vote are interesting when viewed in terms of the party affiliation of the senators. The data are as follows:

PRAYER AMENDMENT VOTE (MARCH 1984)

		YES	NO
Party	DEMOCRAT	19	26
	REPUBLICAN	37	18

Is there a relationship between political party affiliation and prayer amendment vote? Test with $\alpha = .05$.

14. A school board would like to study a proposal to eliminate the cost-of-living raises for next year and replace them with merit raises (raises based on evaluation of performance). The board decides to assess the attitudes toward the proposal among those individuals who are working in the school system. Specifically, the school board would like to know if attitude is related to the type of position the person holds. The observed frequencies are as follows:

TYPE OF POSITION

	TEACHERS	ADMINISTRATION	COUNSELORS
APPROVE MERIT RAISES	265	14	33
AGAINST MERIT RAISES	124	37	21

Is there a relationship between the two variables? Test at the .01 level of significance.

15. McClelland (1961) suggested that the strength of a person's need for achievement can predict behavior in a number of situations, including risk-taking situations. This experiment is patterned after his work. A random sample of college students is given a standardized test that measures the need for achievement. On the basis of their test scores, they are classified into high achievers and low achievers. They are then confronted with a task for which they can select the level of difficulty. Their selections are classified as "cautious" (low risk of failure), "moderate" risk, or "high" risk of failure. The observed frequencies for this study are as follows:

RISK TAKEN BY SUBJECT

	CAUTIOUS	MODERATE	HIGH
HIGH ACHIEVER	8	24	6
LOW ACHIEVER	17	7	16

Can you conclude there is a relationship between the need for achievement and risk-taking behavior? Set alpha to .05. Describe the outcome of the study.

16. A researcher believes that people with low self-esteem will avoid situations that will focus attention on themselves. A random sample of $n = 72$ people is selected. Each person is given a standardized test that measures self-esteem and is classified as high, medium, or low in self-esteem. The subjects are then placed in a situation in which they must choose between performing a task in front of other people or by themselves. The researcher notes which task is chosen. The observed frequencies are as follows:

TASK CHOSEN

	AUDIENCE	NO AUDIENCE
LOW SELF-ESTEEM	4	16
MEDIUM SELF-STEEM	14	14
HIGH SELF-ESTEEM	18	6

Is there a relationship between self-esteem and the task chosen? Use $\alpha = .05$.

17. A social psychology experiment examined the effect of success or failure on people's willingness to help others. In this experiment, individual subjects were given a task that was either very easy or impossible to perform. Thus, some subjects were guaranteed to succeed, and some were doomed to fail. As subjects left the testing room, they encountered a student who was trying to reach a telephone from a wheel chair. The psychologist recorded how many subjects stopped to help. The data from this experiment are presented in the following table:

	SUCCESS	FAILURE
HELP	16	11
NO HELP	9	14

On the basis of these data, can the psychologist conclude that there is a significant relation between people's willingness to help and their personal experience of success or failure. Test at the .05 level of significance.

18. Professors at the local college claim that the older, nontraditional students are better scholars than the typical college-age students. To test this hypothesis a professor records the age and final exam score for each individual in a class of 20. The data are as follows:

older students:	89	73	96	92	80	65
	77	76	79			

younger students:	81	67	59	75	71	80
	94	73	70	62	73	

a. Find the median for the entire class of $n = 20$ students.
b. Use the median test to determine whether there is a significant difference between the distribution of scores for older students versus younger students. Use $\alpha = .05$.

19. A survey of 200 students from the Springfield school district found a median family income of $36,593. Of the 60 students from single-parent households, only 21 were above the median. The remaining 140 students were from two-parent households, and 79 of them had incomes above the median. Do these data indicate a significant difference between the two groups of students? Test at the .05 level of significance.

20. A recent student survey at the state university included a question concerning increasing institutional support for intercollegiate athletics. When the responses were categorized according to opinion and gender, the following distribution was obtained:

	YES	NO	NO OPINION
MALES	110	60	10
FEMALES	65	35	20

Do these data indicate that the distribution of opinions differs for males versus females? Test with $\alpha = .05$.

21. At freshman orientation last fall, individual faculty members presented small groups of students with information concerning the different academic majors at the college. At the end of the presentation, each student was asked to identify a preference for academic major. Although the faculty members were trained to be objective, there is some concern that the faculty may have presented biased information to

make their own academic areas appear more interesting. To determine whether there is a relation between student choices and faculty affiliation, the following distribution was constructed:

STUDENT CHOICE

		SCI.	HUM.	ARTS
	SCI.	24	12	3
Faculty Affiliation	HUM.	20	30	10
	ARTS	15	12	21

Based on these data, can you conclude that the distribution of student choices is related to the academic area of the faculty member making the presentation? Test at the .05 level of significance.

CHAPTER 18   THE BINOMIAL TEST

TOOLS YOU WILL NEED

The following items are considered essential background material for this chapter. If you doubt your knowledge of any of these items, you should review the appropriate chapter or section before proceeding.

- Binomial distribution (Chapter 6)

- z-Score hypothesis tests (Chapter 8)

- Chi-square test for goodness of fit (Chapter 17)

CONTENTS

In 1960 Eleanor Gibson and Richard Walk designed a classic piece of apparatus to test depth perception (Gibson and Walk, 1960). Their device, called a *visual cliff*, consisted of a wide board with a deep drop (the cliff) to one side and a shallow drop on the other side. An infant was placed on the board and then observed to see whether he or she crawled off the shallow side or crawled off the cliff. (*Note:* Infants who moved to the deep side actually crawled onto a sheet of heavy glass, which prevented them from falling. Thus, the deep side only appeared to be a cliff—hence the name *visual cliff*.)

Gibson and Walk reasoned that if infants are born with the ability to perceive depth, they would recognize the deep side and not crawl off the cliff. On the other hand, if depth perception is a skill that develops over time through learning and experience, then infants should not be able to perceive any difference between the shallow and the deep sides.

Out of 27 infants who moved off the board, only 3 ventured onto the deep side at any time during the experiment. Gibson and Walk interpreted these data as convincing evidence that depth perception is innate.

The infants showed a systematic preference for the shallow side.

You should notice immediately that the data from this experiment are different from any we have encountered before. There aren't any scores. Gibson and Walk simply counted the number of infants who went off the deep end and the number who went to the shallow side. Still, we would like to use these data to make statistical decisions. Do these sample data provide sufficient evidence to make a confident conclusion about depth perception in the population? Suppose 8 of the 27 infants had crawled to the deep side. Would you still be convinced that there is a significant preference for the shallow side? What about 12 out of 27?

Notice that we are asking questions about probability and statistical significance. In this chapter we will examine the statistical techniques designed for use with data similar to those obtained in the visual cliff experiments. Each individual in the sample is classified into one of two possible categories (for example, deep or shallow), and we simply count the number in each category. These frequency data are then used to draw inferences about the general population.

18.1 OVERVIEW

In Chapter 6 we introduced the concept of binomial data. You should recall that binomial data exist whenever a measurement procedure classifies individuals into exactly two distinct categories. For example, the outcomes from tossing a coin can be classified as heads and tails; people can be classified as male or female; plastic products can be classified as recyclable or nonrecyclable. In general, binomial data exist when

1. The measurement scale consists of exactly two categories.
2. Each individual observation in a sample is classified in only one of the two categories.
3. The sample data consist of the frequency or number of individuals in each category.

The traditional notation system for binomial data identifies the two categories as A and B and identifies the probability (or proportion) associated with each category as p and q, respectively. For example, a coin toss results in either heads (A) or tails (B), with probabilities $p = \frac{1}{2}$ and $q = \frac{1}{2}$.

In this chapter we will examine the statistical process of using binomial data for testing hypotheses about the values of p and q for the population. This type of hypothesis test is called a *binomial test*.

DEFINITION   A *binomial test* uses sample data to evaluate hypotheses about the values of p and q for a population consisting of binomial data.

Consider the following two situations:

1. In a sample of $n = 34$ color-blind students, 30 are male and only 4 are female. Does this sample indicate that color-blindness is significantly more common for males in the general population?

2. In 1980 only 10% of American families had incomes below the poverty level. This year, in a sample of 100 families, 19 were below the poverty level. Does this sample indicate that there has been a significant change in the population proportions?

Notice that both of these examples have binomial data (exactly two categories). Although the data are relatively simple, we are asking the same statistical question about significance that is appropriate for a hypothesis test: Do the sample data provide sufficient evidence to make a conclusion about the population?

18.2   LOGIC AND FORMULAS FOR THE BINOMIAL TEST

As noted earlier, the data for a binomial situation consist of frequencies: the number of individuals classified in category A and the number classified in category B. We focus attention on the number of individuals classified in category A and identify this variable with the symbol X. For a sample of $n = 20$ coin tosses, for example, the variable X would be the number of heads.

You should recall from Chapter 6 that X can have any value from 0 to n and that each value of X has an associated probability. In a sample of $n = 20$ coin tosses, you could obtain any value from 0 heads up to 20 heads, and each of the possible outcomes has a specific probability. The distribution of probabilities for each value of X is called the binomial distribution.

As we noted in Chapter 6, when the values pn and qn are both equal to or greater than 10, the binomial distribution approximates a normal distribution. This fact is important because it allows us to compute z-scores and use the unit normal table to answer probability questions about binomial events. In particular, when pn and qn are both at least 10, the binomial distribution will have the following properties:

1. The shape of the distribution is approximately normal.

2. The mean of the distribution is $\mu = pn$.

3. The standard deviation of the distribution is

$$\sigma = \sqrt{npq}$$

With these parameters in mind, it is possible to compute a z-score corresponding to each value of X in the binomial distribution

$$z = \frac{X - \mu}{\sigma} = \frac{X - pn}{\sqrt{npq}} \qquad \text{[See formula (6.4).]} \qquad \text{(18.1)}$$

This is the basic z-score formula that will be used for the binomial test. However, we will modify the formula slightly to make it more compatable with the logic of the binomial hypothesis test. The modification consists of dividing both the numerator and the denominator of the z-score by n. (You should realize that dividing both the numerator and denominator by the same value does not change the value of the z-score.) The resulting equation is

$$z = \frac{X/n - p}{\sqrt{pq/n}}$$ (18.2)

For the binomial test, the values in this formula are defined as follows:

1. X/n is the proportion of individuals in the sample data who are classified in category A.
2. p is the hypothesized value (from H_0) for the proportion of individuals in the population who are classified in category A.
3. $\sqrt{pq/n}$ is the standard error for the sampling distribution of X/n and provides a measure of the standard distance between the sample statistic (X/n) and the population parameter (p).

Thus, the structure of the binomial z-score [formula (18.2)] can be expressed as

$$z = \frac{X/n - p}{\sqrt{pq/n}} = \frac{\begin{array}{c}\text{sample} \quad \text{hypothesized} \\ \text{proportion} - \text{population} \\ \text{(data)} \quad \text{proportion}\end{array}}{\text{standard error}}$$

The logic underlying the binomial test is exactly the same as we encountered with the original z-score hypothesis test in Chapter 8. The hypothesis test involves comparing the sample data with the hypothesis. If the data are consistent with the hypothesis, we will conclude that the hypothesis is reasonable. But if there is a big discrepancy between the data and the hypothesis, we will reject the hypothesis. The value of the standard error will provide a benchmark for determining whether the discrepancy between the data and the hypothesis is more than would be expected by chance. The alpha level for the test will provide a criterion for deciding whether or not the discrepancy is significant. The hypothesis-testing procedure is demonstrated in the following section.

18.3 THE BINOMIAL TEST

The binomial test will follow the same four-step procedure presented earlier with other examples for hypothesis testing. The four steps are summarized as follows.

STEP 1 *State the hypotheses.* In the binomial test the null hypothesis specifies values for the population proportions p and q. For example, a null hypothesis might state that for particular coin, $P(\text{heads}) = \frac{1}{2}$ and $P(\text{tails}) = \frac{1}{2}$. Note that the null hypothesis often states that there is "nothing wrong or unusual" about the population probabilities or proportions. For example, this hypothesis states that the coin is balanced, so that heads and tails are equally likely. Also notice that the null hypothesis requires that you specify a value only for p, the proportion associated with category A. The value of q is directly determined from p by the relation $q = 1 - p$. Finally, you should realize that the hypothesis, as always, addresses the probabilities or proportions for the *population*. Although we will use a sample to test the hypotheses, the hypothesis itself always concerns a population.

STEP 2   *Locate the critical region.* When both values for pn and qn are greater than or equal to 10, the z-scores defined by equation (18.1) or (18.2) will form an approximately normal distribution. Thus, the unit normal table can be used to find the boundaries for the critical region. With $\alpha = .05$, for example, you may recall that the critical region is defined as z-score values greater than $+1.96$ or less than -1.96.

STEP 3   *Compute the test statistic (z-score).* At this time you obtain a sample of n individuals (or events) and count the number of times category A occurs in the sample. The number of occurences of A in the sample is the X value for equation (18.1) or (18.2). Because the two z-score equations are equivalent, you may use either one for the hypothesis test. Usually, equation (18.1) is easier to use because it involves larger numbers (fewer decimals) and it is less likely to be affected by rounding error.

STEP 4   *Make a decision.* If the z-score for the sample data is in the critical region, you reject H_0 and conclude that the discrepancy between the sample proportions and the hypothesized population proportions is significantly greater than chance. That is, the data are not consistent with the null hypothesis, so H_0 must be wrong. On the other hand, if the z-score is not in the critical region, you fail to reject H_0.

The following example demonstrates a complete binomial test.

EXAMPLE 18.1   In the preview section we described the *visual cliff* experiment designed to examine depth perception in infants. To summarize briefly, an infant is placed on a wide board that has an apparently deep drop on one side and a relatively shallow drop on the other. An infant who is able to perceive depth should avoid the deep side and move toward the shallow side. Without depth perception, the infant should show no preference between the two sides. In the experiment, only 3 out of 27 infants moved onto the deep side. The purpose of the hypothesis test is to determine whether these data demonstrate that infants have a significant preference for the shallow side.

This is a binomial hypothesis testing situation. The two categories are

A = move off the deep side

B = move off the shallow side

STEP 1   The null hypothesis states that for the general population of infants, there is no preference between the deep and shallow sides; the direction of movement is determined by chance. In symbols,

$$H_0: \quad p = P(\text{deep side}) = \tfrac{1}{2} \quad (\text{and } q = \tfrac{1}{2})$$

$$H_1: \quad p \neq \tfrac{1}{2} \qquad\qquad (\text{There is a preference.})$$

We will use $\alpha = .05$.

STEP 2   With a sample of $n = 27$, $pn = 13.5$ and $qn = 13.5$. Both values are greater than 10, so the distribution of z-scores will be approximately normal. With $\alpha = .05$, the critical region is determined by boundaries of $z = \pm 1.96$.

STEP 3   For this experiment the data consist of $X = 3$ out of $n = 27$. Using equation 18.1, these data produce a z-score value of

$$z = \frac{X - pn}{\sqrt{npq}} = \frac{3 - 13.5}{\sqrt{27(\frac{1}{2})(\frac{1}{2})}} = \frac{-10.5}{2.60} = -4.04$$

To use equation 18.2, you first compute the sample proportion, $X/n = 3/27 = 0.111$. The z-score is then

$$z = \frac{X/n - p}{\sqrt{pq/n}} = \frac{0.111 - 0.5}{\sqrt{\frac{1}{2}(\frac{1}{2})/27}} = \frac{-0.389}{0.096} = -4.05$$

Within rounding error, the two equations produce the same result.

STEP 4   Because the data are in the critical region, our decision is to reject H_0. These data do provide sufficient evidence to conclude that there is a significant preference for the shallow side. Gibson and Walk interpreted these data as convincing evidence that depth perception is innate.

ASSUMPTIONS FOR THE BINOMIAL TEST

The binomial test requires two very simple assumptions:

1. The sample must consist of *independent* observations (see Chapter 9, page 255).
2. The values for pn and qn must both be greater than or equal to 10 to justify using the unit normal table for determining the critical region.

LEARNING CHECK

1. The makers of Brand X beer claim that people like their beer more than the leading brand. The basis for this claim is an experiment in which 64 beer drinkers compared the two brands in a side-by-side taste test. In this sample, 38 preferred Brand X and 26 preferred the leading brand. Do these data support the claim that there is a significant preference? Test at the .05 level.

ANSWER   **1.** H_0: $p = \frac{1}{2} = q$, $X = 38$, $\mu = 32$, $\sigma = 4$, $z = +1.50$, fail to reject H_0. Conclude that there is no evidence for a significant preference.

18.4 THE RELATION BETWEEN CHI-SQUARE AND THE BINOMIAL TEST

You may have noticed that the binomial test evaluates the same basic hypotheses as the chi-square test for goodness of fit; that is, both tests evaluate how well the sample proportions fit a hypothesis about the population proportions. When an experiment produces binomial data, these two tests are equivalent, and either one may be used. The relation between the two tests can be expressed by the equation

$$\chi^2 = z^2$$

where χ^2 is the statistic from the chi-square test for goodness of fit and z is the z-score from the binomial test.

To demonstrate the relation between the goodness-of-fit test and the binomial test, we will reexamine the data from Example 18.1.

STEP 1   *Hypotheses.* In the visual cliff experiment from Example 18.1, the null hypothesis states that there is no preference between the shallow side and the deep side. For the binomial test, the null hypothesis states

$$H_0: \quad p = P(\text{deep side}) = q = P(\text{shallow side}) = \frac{1}{2}$$

The chi-square test for goodness of fit would state the same hypothesis, specifying the population proportions as

	SHALLOW SIDE	DEEP SIDE
H_0:	$\frac{1}{2}$	$\frac{1}{2}$

STEP 2   *Critical region.* For the binomial test, the critical region is located by using the unit normal table. With $\alpha = .05$, the critical region consists of any z-score value beyond ± 1.96. The chi-square test would have $df = 1$, and with $\alpha = .05$, the critical region consists of chi-square values greater than 3.84. Notice that the basic relation, $\chi^2 = z^2$, holds:

$$3.84 = (1.96)^2$$

STEP 3   *Test statistic.* For the binomial test (Example 18.1), we obtained a z-score of $z = -4.04$. For the chi-square test, the expected frequencies would be

	SHALLOW SIDE	DEEP SIDE
f_e	13.5	13.5

With observed frequencies of 24 and 3, respectively, the chi-square statistic is

$$\chi^2 = \frac{(24 - 13.5)^2}{13.5} + \frac{(3 - 13.5)^2}{13.5}$$

$$= \frac{(10.5)^2}{13.5} + \frac{(10.5)^2}{13.5}$$

$$= 8.167 + 8.167$$

$$= 16.33$$

With a little rounding error, the values obtained for the z-score and chi-square are related by the equation

$$\chi^2 = z^2$$

$$16.33 = (4.04)^2$$

STEP 4   *Decision.* Because the critical values for both tests are related by the equation $\chi^2 = z^2$ and the test statistics are related in the same way, these two tests *always* will result in the same statistical conclusion.

18.5 THE SIGN TEST

Although hypothesis tests with the binomial distribution are used in many situations, there is one specific case that merits special attention. Throughout this book we have observed that one of the basic experimental designs is repeated measures. You should recall that in a repeated-measures experiment each subject is measured in several different experimental conditions; that is, you "repeat measurements" on the same subjects. The binomial test can use the data from a repeated-measures experiment to test hypotheses about the difference between two treatment conditions. In this situation, the binomial test commonly is called a *sign test.*

The data for the sign test require that each individual be measured in two experimental conditions. The researcher then records the *direction of the difference* between the treatments. An example is as follows:

SUBJECT	TREATMENT		DIRECTION OF DIFFERENCE
	1	2	
1	18	14	− (decrease)
2	23	10	− (decrease)
3	17	12	− (decrease)
4	31	33	+ (increase)
5	27	24	− (decrease)

Notice that the magnitude of the treatment effect is not important; the researcher records only the direction of the effect. Traditionally, increases and decreases in scores are noted by plus and minus signs in the data; hence the name *sign test.*

The null hypothesis for the sign test states that there is no difference between the two treatments. Therefore, any change in a subject's score is due to chance. In terms of probabilities, this means that increases and decreases are equally likely, so

$$p = P(\text{increase}) = \frac{1}{2}$$

$$q = P(\text{decrease}) = \frac{1}{2}$$

Because the data from the repeated measures experiment have been transformed into two categories (increases and decreases), we now have dichotomous data appropriate for a binomial test. The null hypothesis specifies probabilities for these two categories ($p = \frac{1}{2} = q$). A complete example of a sign test follows.

EXAMPLE 18.2   A researcher would like to test the effectiveness of a new antidepressant drug. A sample of 36 severely depressed patients is selected. These patients are clinically evaluated by a committee of psychiatrists before and after receiving the drug. In the judgment of the psychiatrists, 23 patients improved after being given the drug, and the remaining 13 patients worsened.

STEP 1   *State the hypothesis.* The null hypothesis states that the drug has no effect. Any change in the patients is due to chance, so increases and decreases are equally likely. Expressed as probabilities, the hypotheses are

$$H_0: \quad p = P(\text{improve}) = \frac{1}{2}$$

$$q = P(\text{worsen}) = \frac{1}{2}$$

$$H_1: \quad p \neq q \quad \text{(Changes are consistently in one direction or the other.)}$$

Set $\alpha = .05$.

STEP 2   *Locate the critical region.* With $p = q = \frac{1}{2}$ and $n = 36$, the normal approximation to the binomial distribution is appropriate:

$$pn = qn = 18 \quad \text{(both greater than 10)}$$

With $\alpha = .05$, the critical region is defined as the most extreme 5% of the distribution. This portion is bounded by z-scores of $z = +1.96$ at one extreme and $z = -1.96$ at the other.

STEP 3   *Compute the test statistic.* For this sample we have $X = 23$ patients who improved. This score corresponds to a z-score of

$$z = \frac{X - pn}{\sqrt{npq}} = \frac{23 - 18}{\sqrt{36(\frac{1}{2})(\frac{1}{2})}} = \frac{5}{3} = 1.67$$

STEP 4   *Make a decision.* Because the data are not in the critical region, we fail to reject H_0. These data do not provide sufficient evidence (with $\alpha = .05$) to conclude that the drug has any consistent effect on the patients.

ZERO DIFFERENCES IN THE SIGN TEST

You should notice that the null hypothesis in the sign test refers only to those individuals who show some difference between treatment 1 versus treatment 2. The null hypothesis states that if there is any change in an individual's score, then the probability of an increase is equal to the probability of a decrease. Stated in this form, the null hypothesis does not consider individuals who show zero difference between the two treatments. As a result, the usual recommendation is that these individuals be discarded from the data and the value of n be reduced accordingly. However, if the null hypothesis is interpreted more generally, it states that there is no difference between the two treatments. Phrased this way, it should be clear that individuals who show no difference actually are supporting the null hypothesis and should not be discarded. Therefore, an alternative approach to the sign test is to divide individuals who show zero differences equally between the positive and negative categories. (With an odd number of zero differences, discard one and divide the rest evenly.) This alternative results in a more conservative test; that is, the test is more likely to fail to reject the null hypothesis.

EXAMPLE 18.3

It has been demonstrated that stress or exercise causes an increase in the concentration of certain chemicals called endorphins in the brain. Endorphins are similar to morphine and produce a generally relaxed feeling and a sense of well-being. The endorphins may explain the "high" experienced by long-distance runners. To demonstrate this phenomenon, a researcher tested pain tolerance for 40 athletes before and after they completed a mile run. Immediately after running, the ability to tolerate pain increased for 21 of the athletes, decreased for 12, and showed no change for the remaining 7.

Following the standard recommendation for handling zero differences, you would use $n = 33$ for the sign test because only 33 subjects showed any difference between the two treatments. The other 7 athletes are eliminated from the sample. With the more conservative approach, only 1 of the 7 athletes who showed no difference would be discarded, and the other 6 would be divided equally between the two categories. This would result in a total of $n = 39$ in the sample data with 24 (21 + 3) in one category and 15 (12 + 3) in the other.

WHEN TO USE THE SIGN TEST

In many cases, data from a repeated-measures experiment can be evaluated using either a sign test or a repeated- measures t test. In general, you should use the t test whenever possible. Because the t test uses the actual difference scores (not just the signs), it makes maximum use of the available information and results in a more powerful test. However, there are some cases where a t test cannot or should not be used, and in these situations the sign test can be valuable. Three specific cases where a t test is inappropriate or inconvenient will now be described.

1. When you have infinite or undetermined scores, a t test is impossible, and the sign test is appropriate. Suppose, for example, you are evaluating the effects of a sedative drug on problem-solving ability. A sam-

BEFORE	AFTER	DIFFERENCE
20	23	+3
14	39	+25
27	Failed	+??
.	.	.
.	.	.
.	.	.

ple of rats is obtained, and each animal's performance is measured before and after receiving the drug. Hypothetical data are shown in the left margin. Note that the third rat in this sample failed to solve the problem after receiving the drug. Because there is no score for this animal, it is impossible to compute a sample mean, an *SS*, or a *t* statistic. But you could do a sign test because you know that the animal made more errors (an increase) after receiving the drug.

2. Often it is possible to describe the difference between two treatment conditions without precisely measuring a score in either condition. In a clinical setting, for example, a doctor can say whether a patient is improving, growing worse, or showing no change even though the patient's condition is not precisely measured by a score. In this situation, the data are sufficient for a sign test, but you could not compute a *t* statistic without individual scores.

3. Often a sign test is done as a preliminary check on an experiment before serious statistical analysis begins. For example, a researcher may predict that scores in treatment 2 should be consistently greater than scores in treatment 1. However, examination of the data after 1 week indicates that only 8 of 15 subjects showed the predicted increase. On the basis of these preliminary results, the researcher may choose to reevaluate the experiment before investing additional time.

LEARNING CHECK 1. A developmental psychologist is using a behavior-modification program to help control the disruptive behavior of 40 children in a local school. After 1 month, 26 of these children have improved, 10 are worse, and 4 show no change in behavior. On the basis of these data, can the psychologist conclude that the program is working? Test at the .05 level.

ANSWER 1. Discarding the 4 subjects who showed zero difference, $X = 26$ increases out of $n = 36$; $z = 2.67$; reject H_0; the program is working.

SUMMARY

1. The binomial test is used with dichotomous data, that is, when each individual in the sample is classified in one of two categories. The two categories are identified as *A* and *B*, with probabilities of

$$P(A) = p \quad \text{and} \quad P(B) = q$$

2. The binomial distribution gives the probability for each value of *X*, where *X* equals the number of occurences of category *A* in a sample of *n* events. For example, *X* equals the number of heads in $n = 10$ tosses of a coin.

3. When *pn* and *qn* are both at least 10, the binomial distribution is closely approximated by a normal distribution with

$$\mu = pn$$
$$\sigma = \sqrt{npq}$$

By using this normal approximation, each value of *X* has a corresponding *z*-score:

$$z = \frac{X - \mu}{\sigma} = \frac{X - pn}{\sqrt{npq}} \quad \text{or} \quad z = \frac{X/n - p}{\sqrt{pq/n}}$$

4. The binomial test uses sample data to test hypotheses about the binomial proportions, p and q, for a population. The null hypothesis specifies p and q, and the binomial distribution (or the normal approximation) is used to determine the critical region.

5. One common use of the binomial distribution is for the sign test. This test evaluates the difference between two treatments using the data from a repeated measures design. The difference scores are coded as being either increases $(+)$ or decreases $(-)$. Without a consistent treatment effect, the increases and decreases should be mixed randomly so the null hypothesis states that

$$P(\text{increase}) = \tfrac{1}{2} = P(\text{decrease})$$

With dichotomous data and hypothesized values for p and q, this is a binomial test.

KEY TERMS

dichotomous data	binomial distribution	binomial test	sign test

Focus on Problem Solving

1. For all binomial tests, the values of p and q must sum to 1.00 (or 100%).

2. Remember that both pn and qn must be at least 10 before you can use the normal distribution to determine critical values for a binomial test.

3. Although the binomial test usually specifies the critical region in terms of z-scores, it is possible to identify the X values that determine the critical region. With $\alpha = .05$, the critical region is determined by z-scores greater than 1.96 or less than -1.96. That is, to be significantly different from chance, the individual score must be above (or below) the mean by at least 1.96 standard deviations. For example, in an ESP experiment where an individual is trying to predict the suit of a playing card for a sequence of $n = 64$ trials, chance probabilities would be

$$p = P(\text{right}) = \tfrac{1}{4} \qquad q = P(\text{wrong}) = \tfrac{3}{4}$$

For this example, the binomial distribution would have a mean of $pn = (\tfrac{1}{4})(64) = 16$ right and a standard deviation of $\sqrt{npq} = \sqrt{64(\tfrac{1}{4})(\tfrac{3}{4})} = \sqrt{12} = 3.46$. To be significantly different from chance, a score must be above (or below) the mean by at least $1.96(3.46) = 6.78$. Thus, with a mean of 16, an individual would need to score above 22.78 $(16 + 6.78)$ or below 9.22 $(16 - 6.78)$ to be significantly different from chance.

Demonstration 18.1

THE BINOMIAL TEST

The population of students in the psychology department at the State College consists of 60% females and 40% males. Last semester, the psychology of gender course had a total of 36 students, of which 26 were female and only 10 were male. Can you conclude from these data that the gender course attracts more females than would be expected by chance? Test at the .05 level of significance.

STEP 1 *State the hypotheses and specify alpha.* The null hypothesis states that the male/female proportions for the gender class are not different from the population proportions. In symbols,

$$H_0: \quad p = P(\text{female}) = 0.60 \quad \text{and} \quad q = P(\text{male}) = 0.40$$

The alternative hypothesis is that the proportions for this class are different from the population proportions.

$$H_1: \quad p \neq 0.60 \quad (\text{and } q \neq 0.40)$$

We will set alpha at $\alpha = .05$.

STEP 2 *Locate the critical region.* Because pn and qn are both greater than 10, we can use the normal approximation to the binomial distribution. With $\alpha = .05$, the critical region is defined as any z-score value greater than $+1.96$ or less than -1.96.

STEP 3 *Calculate the test statistic.* The sample has 26 females out of 36 students, so the sample proportion is

$$\frac{X}{n} = \frac{26}{36} = 0.72$$

The corresponding z-score [using formula (18.2)] is

$$z = \frac{X/n - p}{\sqrt{pq/n}} = \frac{0.72 - 0.60}{\sqrt{\dfrac{0.60(0.40)}{36}}} = \frac{0.12}{0.0816} = 1.47$$

STEP 4 *Make a decision about H_0 and state a conclusion.* The obtained z-score is not in the critical region Therefore, we fail to reject the null hypothesis. On the basis of these data, you cannot conclude that the male/female proportions in the gender class are significantly different from the proportions in the psychology department as a whole.

PROBLEMS

1. An extensive survey 2 years ago indicated that 80% of the population of New York State favored income tax over sales tax as a means of increasing state revenue. In a recent sample of 100 people, 72 preferred income tax, and 28 preferred sales tax. Do these data indicate a significant change in opinion? Test at the .05 level of significance. (*Caution:* Be careful in setting the values of p and q for H_0. They are not equal.)

2. In a recent study examining color preferences in infants, 30 babies were offered a choice between a red rattle and a green rattle. Twenty-five of the 30 selected the red rattle. Do these data provide evidence for a significant color preference? Test at the .01 level of significance.

3. A college dormitory recently sponsored a taste comparison between two major soft drinks. Of the 64 students who participated, 39 selected brand A, and only 25 selected brand B. Do these data indicate a significant preference? Test at the .05 level of significance.

4. An automobile manufacturer is developing a computer for its cars. Among other things, the computer will "talk" to the driver to warn of open doors, unfastened seat belts, low fuel levels, and so on. The company would like to know whether the computer should have a masculine or feminine voice. When two voices were tested with a sample of 36 people, 30 preferred the masculine voice and only 6 preferred the feminine voice. Do these data represent a significant preference? Use an alpha of .05.

5. Nationwide, only 4% of the population develops ulcers each year. In a sample of 200 executive vice presidents, 40 had developed ulcers during the previous 12 months. Do these data indicate that vice presidents have an incidence of ulcers different from the general population? Test at the .05 level of significance.

6. Use $\alpha = .05$ to answer each of the following questions. Use the normal approximation to the binomial distribution.
   a. For a true-false test with 20 questions, how many would you have to get right to do significantly better than chance?
   b. How many would you need to get right on a 40-question test?
   c. How many would you need to get right on a 100-question test?

7. A multiple-choice exam has 48 questions, each with four possible answers. What score (X = number correct) is needed on this exam to do significantly better than chance? Assume a one-tailed test with $\alpha = .05$.

8. Children with attention-deficit-disorder (ADD) often lack the ability to sustain attention on a single task for any extended period. Often this disorder is treated with a medication called Ritalin. To demonstrate the effectiveness of this medication, a researcher obtains a sample of $n = 40$ ADD children from a special-education program. Each child is asked to draw a picture of the school building before drug treatment begins. One week after beginning the Ritalin treatment, each child is again asked to draw a picture of the building. The pair of drawings from each student is then given to an art teacher to be evaluated. For 32 of the 40 students, the second picture is judged to be a more detailed and more sophisticated drawing. Do these data indicate that the students' pictures were significantly different after

they began treatment with Ritalin? Test at the .05 level of significance.

9. The habituation technique is one method that is used to examine memory for infants. The procedure involves presenting a stimulus to an infant (usually projected on the ceiling above the crib) for a fixed time period and recording how long the infant spends looking at the stimulus. After a brief delay, the stimulus is presented again. If the infant spends less time looking at the stimulus during the second presentation, it is interpreted as indicating that the stimulus is remembered and therefore is less novel and less interesting than it was on the first presentation. This procedure is used with a sample of $n = 30$ two-week-old infants. For this sample, 22 infants spent less time looking at the stimulus during the second presentation than during the first. Do these data indicate a significant difference? Test at the .01 level of significance.

10. Thirty percent of the students in the local elementary school are classified as only children (no siblings). However, in the special program for talented and gifted children, 43 out of 90 students are only children. Is the proportion of only children in the special program significantly different from the proportion for the school? Test at the .05 level of significance.

11. Last year the college counseling center offered a workshop for students who claimed to suffer from extreme exam anxiety. Of the 45 students who attended the workshop, 31 had higher grade point averages this semester than they did last year. Do these data indicate a significant difference from what would be expected by chance? Test at the .01 level of significance.

12. A social psychologist is examining the transition from elementary school to a middle school. One aspect of this transition is that elementary students spend all day with a single teacher and the same group of classmates. In the middle school, the students move from teacher to teacher with a different set of classmates each class period. The psychologist believes that the lack of social stability in the middle school will cause the students to place more importance on belonging to a well-defined peer group. To test this hypothesis, the psychologist gave a questionnaire to the elementary students and found that only 35% rated peer-group membership as being important or very important. When the same questionnaire was given to a sample of $n = 50$ middle school students, 38 rated peer-group membership as important or very important. Do these data indicate

a significant difference between the two school groups? Test at the .05 level of significance.

13. In the general population, 8 out of 10 people can be hypnotized. A researcher suspects that the ability to be hypothesized is partially determined by an individual's personality. A sample of $n = 80$ subjects is obtained. All these subjects are known to be *field independent*, which means that they tend to rely on internal cues rather than external cues for making judgements. The researcher finds that 51 of these 80 subjects can be hypnotized. Do these data indicate that field-independent people are different from the general population in terms of their ability to be hypnotized? Use an alpha of .05.

14. In a study of human memory, Sachs (1967) demonstrated that people recall the meaning of verbal material but tend to forget the exact word-for-word details. In this study, people read a passage of text. Then the people were shown a test sentence and asked whether or not the identical sentence had appeared in the text. In one condition the test sentence was phrased differently but has the same meaning as a sentence that was in the text. For example, the sentence in the test might be "The boy hit the ball," and the test sentence might be "The ball was hit by the boy." If only 27 out of 45 people correctly notice that change in the sentence, can you conclude that their performance is significantly better than chance? Test at the .05 level of significance.

15. A psychologist examining the psychology of art appreciation selected an abstract painting that had no obvious top or bottom. Hangers were placed on the painting so that it could be hung with any one of the four sides at the top. This painting was shown to a sample of $n = 50$ undergraduates, and each was asked to hang the painting in whatever orientation "looked best." Twenty-five of the subjects in this sample placed the painting so that the correct side was up. Is this significantly better than would be expected by chance? Test with $\alpha = .05$.

16. The National Weather Service reports that for the first 70 days of this year, 42 days have had temperatures lower than last year, 22 days had higher temperatures, and 6 days show no difference. Do these data indicate that this year's temperatures are significantly different from last year's? Test at the .05 level.

17. A sample of 40 children is selected for an experiment to evaluate the effect of teacher's sex on classroom performance. Each child is given a task while being observed by a male teacher and then a similar task while being observed by a female teacher. Of these 40 children, 20 were judged to work better for the female teacher, 8 worked better for the male teacher, and 12 worked equally well in the two situations. Do these results indicate that the teacher's sex has a significant influence on performance? Test with $\alpha = .05$.

18. An English professor conducts a special 1-week course in writing skills for freshmen who are poorly prepared for college-level writing. To test the effectiveness of this course, each student in a recent class of $n = 36$ was required to write a short paragraph describing a painting before the course started. At the end of the course, the students were once again required to write a paragraph describing the same painting. The students' paragraphs were then given to another instructor to be evaluated. For 25 students the writing was judged to be better after the course. For the rest of the class, the first paragraph was judged to be better. Do these results indicate a significant change in performance? Test at the .05 level of significance.

19. A television commercial claims that four out of five people prefer Brand X potato chips over Brand Y. If this claim is based on a sample of $n = 50$ (40 out of 50 preferred Brand X), is there evidence for a significant preference? Use the normal approximation to the binomial distribution and test with $\alpha = .05$.

20. Biofeedback training is often used to help people who suffer migraine headaches. A recent study found that 29 out of 50 subjects reported a decrease in the frequency and severity of their headaches after receiving biofeedback training. Of the remaining subjects in this study, 10 reported that their headaches were worse, and 11 reported no change.
    a. Discard the zero difference subjects and use a sign test with $\alpha = .05$ to determine whether or not the biofeedback produced a significant difference.
    b. Divide the zero difference subjects between the two groups and use a sign test to evaluate the effect of biofeedback training.

21. The sense of smell plays an important role in the taste of food. A favorite demonstration of this fact involves having people hold their noses while tasting slices of apple and onion. Without smell, these two taste much the same. In a sample of 25 people who tried this demonstration, only 15 were able to identify the onion correctly. Is this significantly better than chance? Test at the .05 level of significance.

CHAPTER 19

STATISTICAL TECHNIQUES FOR ORDINAL DATA: MANN-WHITNEY AND WILCOXON TESTS AND SPEARMAN CORRELATION

CONTENTS

PREVIEW

Americans have a passion for ranking things. Everyone wants to know who is number 1. Just turn on the television for an hour and you are likely to learn answers to such interesting questions as

What is the best-selling car in the United States?
What pain reliever is most preferred by doctors?
What college football team is ranked first in the polls?

You might even learn what television show is currently number 1 in the Neilson ratings.

Part of the fascination with ranks is that they are easy to obtain and they are easy to understand. For example, what is your favorite ice-cream flavor? Notice that you do not need to conduct any sophisticated measurement to arrive at an answer. There is no need to rate 31 different flavors on a 100-point scale, and you don't need to worry about how much difference there is between your first and second choices.

You may recall from Chapter 1 that ranking is an example of measurement on an ordinal scale. In general, ordinal scales are less demanding and less sophisticated than the interval or ratio scales that are most commonly used to measure variables. Because ordinal scales are less demanding, they are easier to use. On the other hand, because they are less sophisticated, they can cause some problems for statistical analysis. Consider the data presented in Table 19.1. The table shows the top 20 American cities according to overall quality of life as they are listed in the *Places Rated Almanac* (1989). The almanac evaluates each city on a variety of factors, such as climate, cost of living, crime rate, and cultural attractions. These evaluations are combined into a composite score for each city, and the cities are rank-ordered according to their total scores (*Note:* A low score is better.) Table 19.1 shows the final rank for each city and its composite score.

Because the ranks in Table 19.1 are numbers, it is tempting to try to perform some routine calculations with them. However, one simple example should demonstrate the problems that can arise when doing arithmetic with ranks. According to the table, Washington, D.C. is ranked number 4 and San Diego, California, is ranked number 5. With only a 1-point difference between these two cities, it would appear that they are rated about the same. Now consider Nassau-Suffolk, New York, ranked number 10 and Miami-Hialeah, Florida, ranked number 20. There is a 10-point difference between the two cities, which would suggest a substan-

Table 19.1

The top 20 American cities rated for overall quality of life.

RANK	CITY	SCORE
1.	Seattle, WA	666
2.	San Francisco, CA	676
3.	Pittsburgh, PA	679
4.	Washington, DC	702
5.	San Diego, CA	760
6.	Boston, MA	761
7.	New York, NY	786
8.	(Tie) Louisville, KY	801
	(Tie) Anaheim−Santa Ana, CA	801
10.	Nassau-Suffolk, NY	802
11.	Atlanta, GA	812
12.	Cleveland, OH	815
13.	Philadelphia, PA	817
14.	Cincinnati, OH	820
15.	Los Angeles−Long Beach, CA	833
16.	Salt Lake City−Ogden, UT	834
17.	Baltimore, MD	839
18.	Chicago, IL	851
19.	Oakland, CA	856
20.	Miami-Hialeah FL	860

tial difference in their ratings. However, if you look at the rating scores, a strange thing can be observed: the difference between Washington and San Diego is exactly the same as the difference between Nassau-Suffolk and Miami-Hialeah.

	PAIR 1	
CITY	RANK	SCORE
Washington	4	702
San Diego	5	760

	PAIR 2	
CITY	RANK	SCORE
Nassau-Suffolk	10	802
Miami-Hialeah	20	860

How can there be such an apparent contradiction between the ranks and the scores? The source of the contradictions comes from a limitation of ordinal scales—they do not tell you *how much difference* exists between two individuals. The actual distance between fourth and fifth may be no different from the actual distance between tenth and twentieth.

Because ordinal measurements provide limited information, they must be used and interpreted carefully. Attempts to compute average ranks, for example, can produce misleading results. Therefore, you should not use standard statistical procedures such as *t* tests or analysis of variance when data are measured on an ordinal scale. Fortunately, special statistical techniques have been developed for ranked data. It is possible, for example, to determine whether there are significant differences in ranked data or to compute correlations for ranked data. In this chapter, we examine some of the statistical procedures that are designed for ordinal data.

Table 19-1 adapted from *Places Rated Almanac* by Richard Boyer and David Savageau, copyright 1989. Used by permission of the publisher, Prentice Hall Travel, a division of Simon and Schuster, Inc., New York.

19.1 OVERVIEW

The statistical procedures discussed in this chapter are designed for use with data measured on an ordinal scale. This type of measurement simply requires that the individuals be arranged in order from greatest to smallest with respect to the variable being measured. For example, a sample of $n = 10$ people could be ordered in terms of height from tallest to shortest, or they could be ordered in terms of singing ability from best singer to worst singer. The outcome of this ordering process is generally reported as a set of ranks: first (1), second (2), and so on. Thus, measurement on an ordinal scale is essentially equivalent to ranking.

The process of ranking can be based directly on observations of individuals. For example, you could arrange a group of people in order of height by simply comparing them side by side to see who is tallest, who is next tallest, and so on. This kind of direct ordinal measurement is fairly common because it is easy to do. Notice that you do not need any absolute measurement to complete the ranking; that is, you never need to know anyone's exact height. It is necessary only to make relative judgments—given any two individuals, you must decide who is taller. Because ordinal scales do not require any absolute measurements, they can be used with variables that are not routinely measured. Variables such as beauty or talent can be observed, judged, and ranked, although they may be difficult to define and measure with more-sophisticated scales.

In addition to obtaining ranks by direct observation, a researcher may begin with a set of numerical measurements and convert these scores into ranks. For example, if you had a listing of the actual heights for a group of individuals, you could arrange the numbers in order from greatest to least. This process converts data from an interval or ratio scale into ordinal measurements. There are a number of reasons for converting scores into ranks, but the following list should give you some indication of why this might be done.

1. Ranks are simpler. If someone asks you how tall your sister is, you could reply with a specific numerical value, such as 5 feet 7¾ inches

tall. Or, you could answer, "She is a little taller than I am." For many situations, the relative answer would be better.

2. The original scores may violate some of the basic assumptions that underly certain statistical procedures. For example, the t tests and analysis of variance assume that the data come from normal distributions. Also, the independent-measures tests assume that the different populations all have the same variance (the homogeneity of variance assumption). If a researcher suspects that the data do not satisfy these assumptions, it may be safer to convert the scores to ranks and use a statistical technique designed for ranks.

3. Occasionally, an experiment will produce an undetermined, or infinite, score. For example, a rat may show no sign of solving a particular maze after hundreds of trials. This animal has an infinite, or undetermined, score. Although there is no absolute score that can be assigned, you can say that this rat has the highest score for the sample and then rank the rest of the scores by their numerical values.

RANKING TIED SCORES

When you are converting scores into ranks, you may encounter two (or more) identical scores. Whenever, two scores have exactly the same value, their ranks should also be the same. This is accomplished by the following procedure.

1. List the scores in order from smallest to largest. Include tied values in this list.

2. Assign a rank (first, second, etc.) to each position in the ordered list.

3. When two (or more) scores are tied, compute the average of their ranked positions and assign this average value as the final rank for each score.

The process of finding ranks for tied scores is demonstrated here. These scores have been listed in order from smallest to largest.

SCORES	RANK POSITION	FINAL RANK	
3	1	1.5	Average of 1 and 2
3	2	1.5	
5	3	3	
6	4	5	
6	5	5	Average of 4, 5, and 6
6	6	5	
12	7	7	

Note that this example has seven scores and uses all seven ranks. For $X = 12$, the largest score, the appropriate rank is 7. It cannot be given a rank of 6 because that rank has been used for the tied scores.

HYPOTHESIS TESTS AND CORRELATION WITH ORDINAL DATA

The remainder of this chapter examines three statistical procedures that are used with ordinal data. The first two procedures we consider are hypothesis tests. Both tests use sample data to evaluate the difference between two treatments or populations. The Mann-Whitney *U*-test works with data from an independent-measures experiment (two separate samples), and the Wilcoxon test is intended for data from a repeated-measures experiment. The third procedure we consider is a correlation measuring the degree and direction of relationship between two variables measured on ordinal scales.

19.2 THE MANN-WHITNEY *U*-TEST

The Mann-Whitney test is designed to evaluate the difference between two treatments (or two populations) using data from an independent-measures experiment. The calculations for this test require that the individual scores in the two samples be rank-ordered. The mathematics of the Mann-Whitney test is based on the following simple observation:

> A real difference between the two treatments should cause the scores in one sample to be generally larger than the scores in the other sample. If the two samples are combined and all the scores placed in rank order on a line, then the scores from one sample should be concentrated at one end of the line, and the scores from the other sample should concentrate at the other end.
>
> On the other hand, if there is no treatment difference, then large and small scores will be mixed evenly in the two samples because there is no reason for one set of scores to be systematically larger or smaller than the other.

This observation is demonstrated in Figure 19.1.

CALCULATION OF THE MANN-WHITNEY *U* The first steps in the calculations for the Mann-Whitney test have already been discussed. To summarize,

1. A separate sample is obtained from each of the two treatments. We will use n_A to refer to the number of subjects in sample A and n_B to refer to the number in sample B.

2. These two samples are combined, and the total group of $n_A + n_B$ subjects is rank-ordered.

Figure 19.1

In part (a) the scores from the two samples are clustered at opposite ends of the rank ordering. In this case, the data suggest a systematic difference between the two treatments.

Part (b) shows the two samples intermixed evenly along the scale, indicating no consistent difference between treatments.

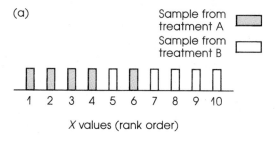

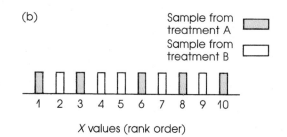

The remaining problem is to decide whether the scores from the two samples are mixed randomly in the rank ordering or whether they are systematically clustered at opposite ends of the scale. This is the familiar question of statistical significance: Are the data simply the result of chance, or has some systematic effect produced these results? We will answer this question exactly as we always have answered it. First, look at all the possible results that could have been obtained. Next, separate these outcomes into two groups:

1. Those results that are reasonably likely to occur by chance
2. Those results that are very unlikely to occur by chance (this is the critical region)

For the Mann-Whitney test, the first step is to identify each of the possible outcomes. This is done by assigning a numerical value to every possible set of sample data. This number is called the Mann-Whitney U. The value of U is computed as if the two samples were two teams of athletes competing in a sports event. Each individual in sample A (the A team) gets one point whenever he or she is ranked ahead of an individual from sample B. The total number of points accumulated for sample A is called U_A. In the same way, a U value, or team total, is computed for sample B. The final Mann-Whitney U is the smaller of these two values. This process is demonstrated in the following example.

EXAMPLE 19.1   We begin with two separate samples with $n = 6$ scores in each.

Sample A (treatment 1):   27,   2,   9,   48,   6,   15

Sample B (treatment 2):   71,   63,   18,   68,   94,   8

Next, the two samples are combined and all 12 scores are placed in rank order. Each individual in sample A is assigned 1 point for every score in sample B that has a higher rank.

| | ORDERED SCORES | | POINTS FOR |
RANK	SCORE	SAMPLE	SAMPLE A
1	2	(A)	6 points
2	6	(A)	6 points
3	8	(B)	
4	9	(A)	5 points
5	15	(A)	5 points
6	18	(B)	
7	27	(A)	4 points
8	48	(A)	4 points
9	63	(B)	
10	68	(B)	
11	71	(B)	
12	94	(B)	

Finally, the points from all the individuals in sample A are combined, and the total number of points is computed for the sample. In this example the total points or the U value for sample A is $U_A = 30$. In the same way you can compute the U value for sample B. You should obtain $U_B = 6$. As a simple check on your arithmetic, note that

$$U_A + U_B = n_A n_B \qquad (19.1)$$

To avoid errors, it is wise to compute both U values and verify that the sum is equal to $n_A n_B$.

For these data,

$$30 + 6 = 6(6)$$

FORMULAS FOR THE MANN-WHITNEY U

Because the process of counting points to determine the Mann-Whitney U can be tedious, especially with large samples, there is a formula that will generate the U value for each sample. To use this formula, you combine the samples and rank-order all the scores as before. Then you must find ΣR_A, which is the sum of the ranks for individuals in sample A and the corresponding ΣR_B for sample B. The U value for each sample is then computed as follows: For sample A,

$$U_A = n_A n_B + \frac{n_A(n_A + 1)}{2} - \Sigma R_A \qquad (19.2)$$

and for sample B,

$$U_B = n_A n_B + \frac{n_B(n_B + 1)}{2} - \Sigma R_B \qquad (19.3)$$

These formulas are demonstrated using the data from Example 19.1. For sample A the sum of the ranks is

$$\Sigma R_A = 1 + 2 + 4 + 5 + 7 + 8$$
$$= 27$$

For sample B the sum of the ranks is

$$\Sigma R_B = 3 + 6 + 9 + 10 + 11 + 12$$
$$= 51$$

By using the special formula, for sample A,

$$U_A = n_A n_B + \frac{n_A(n_A + 1)}{2} - \Sigma R_A$$
$$= 6(6) + \frac{6(7)}{2} - 27$$
$$= 36 + 21 - 27$$
$$= 30$$

For sample B,

$$U_B = n_A n_B + \frac{n_B(n_B + 1)}{2} - \Sigma R_B$$

$$= 6(6) + \frac{6(7)}{2} - 51$$

$$= 36 + 21 - 51$$

$$= 6$$

Notice that these are the same U values we obtained in Example 19.1 using the counting method. The Mann-Whitney U value is the smaller of these two,

$$U = 6$$

HYPOTHESIS TESTS WITH THE MANN-WHITNEY U

Now that we have developed a method for identifying each rank order with a numerical value, the remaining problem is to decide whether the U value provides evidence for a real difference between the two treatment conditions. We will look at each possibility separately.

A large difference between the two treatments will cause all the ranks from sample A to cluster at one end of the scale and all the ranks from sample B to cluster at the other (see Figure 19.1). At the extreme, there will be no overlap between the two samples. In this case, the Mann-Whitney U will be zero because one of the samples will get no points at all. In general, a Mann-Whitney U of zero indicates the greatest possible difference between the two samples. As the two samples become more alike, their ranks begin to intermix, and the U becomes larger. If there is no consistent tendency for one treatment to produce larger scores than the other, then the ranks from the two samples should be intermixed evenly. In terms of a competition between the two samples (the A team versus the B team), a final score of 49 to 51 indicates that the two teams were nearly equal; a final score of 100 to 0 indicates a real difference between the two teams.

Notice that the null hypothesis does not specify any population parameter.

The null hypothesis for the Mann-Whitney test states that there is no systematic difference between the two treatments being compared; that is, there is no real difference between the two populations from which the samples are selected. In this case, the most likely outcome is that the two samples would be similar and that the U value would be relatively large. On the other hand, a very small value of U, near zero, is evidence that the two samples are very different. Therefore, a U value near zero would tend to refute the null hypothesis. The distribution of all the possible U values has been constructed, and the critical values for $\alpha = .05$ and $\alpha = .01$ are presented in Table B.8 of Appendix B. When sample data produce a U that is *less than or equal to* the table value, we reject H_0.

A complete example of a hypothesis test using the Mann-Whitney U follows.

EXAMPLE 19.2   A psychologist interested in the development of manual dexterity prepared a block-manipulation task for 3-year-old children. A sample of 13

This example is analyzed with the Minitab command MANN-WHITNEY (see Section 20.9).

children was obtained, 5 boys and 8 girls. The psychologist recorded the amount of time (in seconds) required by each child to arrange the blocks in a specified pattern. The data are as follows:

Boys: 23, 18, 29, 42, 21

Girls: 37, 56, 39, 34, 26, 104, 48, 25

STEP 1 The null hypothesis states that there is no consistent difference between the two populations. For this example,

H_0: There is no systematic difference between the solution times for boys versus the times for girls

H_1: There is a systematic difference

STEP 2 For a nondirectional test with $\alpha = .05$ and with $n_A = 5$ and $n_B = 8$, the Mann-Whitney table gives a critical value of $U = 6$. If the data produce a U less than or equal to 6, we will reject the null hypothesis.

STEP 3 We will designate the boys as sample A and the girls as sample B. Combining the two samples and arranging the scores in order produces the following result.

Rank	1	2	3	4	5	6	7	8	9	10	11	12	13
Score	18	21	23	25	26	29	34	37	39	42	48	56	104
Sample	A	A	A	B	B	A	B	B	B	A	B	B	B
Points for the girls (B)				2	2		1	1	1		0	0	0

Because the girls (sample B) tend to cluster at the bottom of the rankings, they should have the smaller U. Therefore, we have identified the points for this sample. The girls' point total is $U_B = 7$.

It is not necessary to compute U for the sample boys, but we will continue with this calculation to demonstrate the formula for U. The boys (sample A) have ranks of 1, 2, 3, 6, and 10. The sum is $\Sigma R_A = 22$, so the U_A value is

Notice that the larger sample does not always have the larger point total.

$$U_A = n_A n_B + \frac{n_A(n_A + 1)}{2} - \Sigma R_A$$

$$= 5(8) + \frac{5(6)}{2} - 22$$

$$= 40 + 15 - 22$$

$$= 33$$

To check our calculations,

$$U_A + U_B = n_A n_B$$

$$33 + 7 = 5(8)$$

$$40 = 40$$

The final U is the smaller of the two values, so the Mann-Whitney U statistic is $U = 7$.

STEP 4   Because $U = 7$ is greater than the critical value of $U = 6$, we fail to reject the null hypothesis. At the .05 level of significance, these data do not provide sufficient evidence to conclude that there is a significant difference in manual dexterity between boys and girls at 3 years of age.

SPSS^X A-84

NORMAL APPROXIMATION FOR THE MANN-WHITNEY U

When samples are large (about $n = 20$), the distribution of the Mann-Whitney U statistic tends to approximate a normal shape. In this case the Mann-Whitney hypotheses can be evaluated using a z-score statistic and the unit normal distribution. You may have noticed that the table of critical values for the Mann-Whitney test does not list values for samples larger than $n = 20$. This is because the normal approximation typically is used with larger samples. The procedure for this normal approximation is as follows:

1. Find the U values for sample A and sample B as before. The Mann-Whitney U is the smaller of these two values.

2. When both samples are relatively large (around $n = 20$ or more), the distribution of the Mann-Whitney U statistic tends to form a normal distribution with

$$\mu = \frac{n_A n_B}{2}$$

and

$$\sigma = \sqrt{\frac{n_A n_B (n_A + n_B + 1)}{12}}$$

The Mann-Whitney U obtained from the sample data can be located in this distribution using a z-score:

This approximation is intended for data without tied scores or with very few ties. A special formula has been developed for data with many ties and can be found in most advanced statistics texts such as Hays (1981).

$$z = \frac{X - \mu}{\sigma} = \frac{U - \dfrac{n_A n_B}{2}}{\sqrt{\dfrac{n_A n_B (n_A + n_B + 1)}{12}}} \tag{19.4}$$

3. Use the unit normal table to establish the critical region for this z-score. For example, with $\alpha = .05$ the critical values would be ± 1.96.

An example of this normal approximation to the Mann-Whitney U follows.

EXAMPLE 19.3   To demonstrate the normal approximation, we will use the same data that were used in Example 19.2. This experiment tested manual dexterity for 3-year-olds using a sample of $n = 5$ boys and a sample of $n = 8$ girls. The data produced a value of $U = 7$. (You should realize that when samples are this small, you would normally use the Mann-Whitney table rather than the normal approximation. However, we will use the normal approximation so that we can compare the outcome to the result from the regular Mann-Whitney test.)

STEP 1 The normal approximation does not affect the statement of the hypotheses.

H_0: There is no systematic difference between the manual dexterity scores for boys versus the scores for girls.

H_1: There is a systematic difference.

We will set $\alpha = .05$.

STEP 2 The critical region for this test is defined in terms of z-scores and the normal distribution. The unit normal table states that the extreme 5% of this distribution is located beyond z-scores of ± 1.96 (see Figure 19.2).

STEP 3 The sample value of $U = 7$ is used to compute a z-score from the normal approximation formula.

$$z = \frac{U - \dfrac{n_A n_B}{2}}{\sqrt{\dfrac{n_A n_B (n_A + n_B + 1)}{12}}}$$

$$= \frac{7 - \dfrac{5(8)}{2}}{\sqrt{\dfrac{5(8)(5 + 8 + 1)}{12}}}$$

$$= \frac{-13}{\sqrt{\dfrac{560}{12}}}$$

$$= -1.90$$

Figure 19.2

The normal distribution of z-scores used with the normal approximation to the Mann-Whitney U test. The critical region for $\alpha = .05$ has been shaded.

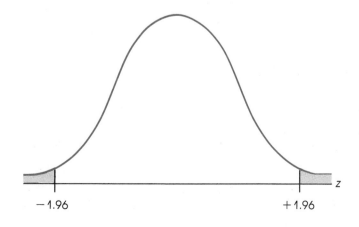

STEP 4

Notice that we reached the same conclusion with the original Mann-Whitney test in Example 19.2.

Because this z-score is not in the critical region, our decision is to fail to reject the null hypothesis. These data do not provide sufficient evidence to conclude that there is a significant difference in manual dexterity between boys and girls at age 3.

ASSUMPTIONS AND CAUTIONS FOR THE MANN-WHITNEY U

The Mann-Whitney U test is a very useful alternative to the independent-measures t test. Because the Mann-Whitney test does not require homogeneity of variance or normal distributions, it can be used in situations where the t test would be inappropriate. However, the U test does require independent observations, and it assumes that the dependent variable is continuous. You should recall from Chapter 1 that a continuous scale has an infinite number of distinct points. One consequence of this fact is that it is very unlikely for two individuals to have exactly the same score. This means that there should be few, if any, tied scores in the data. When sample data do have several tied scores, you should suspect that a basic assumption underlying the Mann-Whitney U test has been violated. In this situation, you should be cautious about using the Mann-Whitney U.

When there are relatively few tied scores in the data the Mann-Whitney test may be used, but you must follow the standard procedure for ranking tied scores.

LEARNING CHECK

1. Rank the following scores, using tied ranks where necessary: 14, 3, 4, 0, 3, 5, 14, 3.

2. An experiment using $n = 25$ in one sample and $n = 10$ in the other produced a Mann-Whitney U of $U = 50$. Assuming that this is the smaller of the two U values, what was the value of U for the other sample?

3. A developmental psychologist is examining social assertiveness for preschool children. Three- and 4-year-old children are observed for 10 hours in a day-care center. The psychologist records the number of times each child initiates a social interaction with another child. The scores for the sample of four boys and nine girls are as follows:

    Boys' scores: 8,   17,   14,   21

    Girls' scores: 18,   25,   23,   21,   34,   28,   32,   30,   13

    Use a Mann-Whitney test to determine whether these data provide evidence for a significant difference in social assertiveness between preschool boys and girls. Test at the .05 level.

4. According to the Mann-Whitney table, a value of $U = 30$ is significant (in the critical region) with $\alpha = .05$ when both samples have $n = 11$. If this value is used in the normal approximation, does it produce a z-score in the critical region?

ANSWERS **1.** Scores: 0 3 3 3 4 5 14 14

Ranks: 1 3 3 3 5 6 7.5 7.5

2. With $n_A = 25$ and $n_B = 10$, the two U values must total $n_A n_B = 25(10) = 250$. If the smaller value is 50, then the larger value must be 200.

3. For the boys, $U = 31.5$. For the girls, $U = 4.5$. The critical value in the table is 4, so fail to reject H_0.

4. $U = 30$ produces a z-scores of $z = -2.00$. This is in the critical region.

19.3 THE WILCOXON SIGNED-RANKS TEST

The Wilcoxon test is designed to evaluate the difference between two treatments using the data from a repeated-measures experiment. The data for the Wilcoxon test consist of the difference scores from the repeated-measures design. The test requires that these differences be ranked from smallest to largest in terms of their *absolute values* (without regard to the sign). This process is demonstrated in the following example.

EXAMPLE 19.4   The following data are from a repeated-measures experiment using a sample of $n = 6$ subjects to compare two treatments conditions:

| | TREATMENTS | | | | |
SUBJECT	1	2	DIFFERENCE	RANK	
1	18	43	+25	6	(Largest)
2	9	14	+5	2	
3	21	20	−1	1	(Smallest)
4	30	48	+18	5	
5	14	21	+7	3	
6	12	4	−8	4	

The null hypothesis for this test states that there is no difference between the two treatments. If this hypothesis is true, any differences that exist in the sample data must be due to chance. Therefore, we would expect positive and negative differences to be intermixed evenly. On the other hand, a consistent difference between the two treatments should cause the scores in one treatment to be consistently larger than scores in the other. This should produce difference scores that tend to be consistently positive or consistently negative. The Wilcoxon test uses the signs and the ranks of the difference scores to decide whether or not there is a significant difference between the two treatments.

CALCULATION AND INTERPRETATION OF THE WILCOXON T

As with most nonparametric tests, the calculations for the Wilcoxon are quite simple. After ranking the absolute values of the difference scores as in Example 19.4, you separate the ranks into two groups: those associated with positive differences and those associated with negative differences. Next, find the sum of the ranks for each group. The smaller of these two sums is the test statistic for the Wilcoxon test and is identified by the letter T. For the data in Example 19.4, the ranks for positive differences are 6, 2, 3, and 5. These ranks sum to $\Sigma R = 16$. The ranks for negative differences are 1 and 4, which sum to $\Sigma R = 5$. The smaller of these two sums is 5, so the Wilcoxon T for these data is $T = 5$.

We noted earlier that a strong treatment effect should cause the difference scores to be consistently positive or consistently negative. In the extreme case, all of the differences will be in the same direction. This will produce a Wilcoxon T of zero. For example, when all of the differences are positive, the sum of the negative ranks will be zero. On the other hand, when there is no treatment effect, the signs of the difference scores should be intermixed evenly. In this case, the Wilcoxon T will be relatively large. In general, a small value T (near zero) provides evidence for a real difference between the two treatment conditions. The distribution of all the possible T values has been constructed, and the critical values for $\alpha = .05$ and $\alpha = .01$ are given in Table B.9 of Appendix B. Whenever sample data produce a T that is *less than or equal to* this critical value, we will reject H_0.

See Box 19.1 for information concerning how the distribution of Wilcoxon T values is constructed.

TIED SCORES AND ZERO SCORES

Although the Wilcoxon test does not require normal distributions, it does assume that the dependent variable is continuous. As noted with the Mann-Whitney test, this assumption implies that tied scores should be very unlikely. When ties do appear in sample data, you should be concerned that the basic assumption of continuity has been violated, and the Wilcoxon test may not be appropriate. If there are relatively few ties in the data, most researchers assume that the data actually are continuous but have been crudely measured. In this case, the Wilcoxon test may be used, but the tied values must receive special attention in the calculations.

With the Wilcoxon test, there are two different types of tied scores:

1. When a subject has the same score in treatment 1 and treatment 2, resulting in a zero difference.
2. When two or more subjects have identical different scores.

Remember, the null hypothesis says there is no difference between the two treatments. Subjects with zero difference scores tend to support this hypothesis.

When the data include individuals with zero different scores, some texts recommend that these subjects should be discarded from the analysis and the sample size (n) reduced. However, this procedure ignores the fact that a zero difference is evidence for retaining the null hypothesis. A better procedure is to divide the zero differences evenly between the positives and negatives. (If you have an odd number of zero differences, one should be discarded, and the rest divided evenly.) This second procedure will tend to increase ΣR for both the positive and the negative ranks, which increases the final value of T and makes it more likely that H_0 will be retained.

When you have ties among the difference scores, each of the tied scores should be assigned the average of the tied ranks. This procedure was presented in detail in an earlier section of this chapter (see page 564).

19.1 A CLOSER LOOK AT THE WILCOXON T DISTRIBUTION

YOU MAY have wondered how statisticians develop all the tables you find in the back of statistics books. The Wilcoxon test provides a good opportunity to demonstrate how one of these tables is constructed.

To determine the critical values for a statistical test, you must first look at the distribution of all the possible results that could be obtained. Next, you determine the probability values for each portion of the distribution and identify the results that are very unlikely; that is, results with probability less than .01 or less than .05 (for $\alpha = .01$ or .05, respectively). Usually the calculation of these probabilities requires sophisticated mathematics, but for the Wilcoxon test the computations are relatively simple. For example, suppose you are using a sample of $n = 6$ in a repeated-measures experiment. The results of the experiment would consist of a set of $n = 6$ difference scores that are classified as either positive or negative and then rank-ordered from smallest to largest. For each position in the rank order there are only two possibilities, positive or negative. With two possibilities for the first position, two for the second, two for the third, and so on, there is total of

$$2 \times 2 \times 2 \times 2 \times 2 \times 2 = 64$$

different outcomes. When H_0 is true and there is no systematic treatment effect, all 64 possible outcomes are equally likely and have a probability of $P = \frac{1}{64}$.

Rather than list all 64 possible outcomes, we will focus on results that produce small values for T. For example, there are only two outcomes that result in $T = 0$: Either all 6 difference scores are negative, so

that the positive ranks sum to zero, or all six are positive and the negative ranks sum to zero. Thus, only 2 out of 64 possible results will give $T = 0$. In terms of probabilities.

$$P(T = 0) = \frac{2}{64} = 0.031$$

Because an outcome with $T = 0$ has a probability less than .05, we can conclude that data producing this outcome are significant at the $\alpha = .05$ level of significance.

Similarly, there are only two outcomes that produce $T = 1$: Either there is exactly one positive difference with a rank of 1, or there is one negative difference with a rank of 1. Thus,

$$P(T = 1) = \frac{2}{64} = 0.031$$

By combining the two probabilities obtained so far, we can find the probability of obtaining a T value less than or equal to 1.

$$P(T \leq 1) = P(T = 0 \text{ or } 1) = \frac{4}{64} = 0.062$$

Notice that the probability of T being less than or equal to 1 is greater than .05. Thus, experimental results that produce $T = 1$ would not be significant at the .05 level of significance. These probabilities are reflected in the critical values listed in the Wilcoxon table. Checking the table, you will find that the critical value for $n = 6$ and $\alpha = .05$ is $T = 0$. Thus, an outcome of $T = 0$ is significant ($p < .05$), but an outcome of $T = 1$ is not significant ($p > .05$).

HYPOTHESIS TESTS WITH THE WILCOXON T

A complete example of the Wilcoxon test showing some tied scores will now be presented.

EXAMPLE 19.5

This example is analyzed with the Minitab command WTEST (see Section 20.9).

The local Red Cross has conducted an intensive campaign to increase blood donations. This campaign has been concentrated in 10 local businesses. In each company, the goal was to increase the percentage of employees who participate in the blood donation program. Figures showing the percent participation from last year (before the campaign) and from this year are as follows. We will use the Wilcoxon test to decide whether these data provide evidence that the campaign had a significant impact on blood donations. Note that the 10 companies are listed in rank order according to the absolute value of the difference scores.

COMPANY	PERCENT PARTICIPATION			RANK DISCARDING ZEROS	RANK INCLUDING ZEROS
	BEFORE	AFTER	DIFFERENCE		
A	18	18	0	—	1.5
B	24	24	0	—	1.5
C	31	30	−1	1	3
D	28	24	−4	2	4
E	17	24	+7	3	5
F	16	24	+8	4	6
G	15	26	+11	5.5	7.5
H	18	29	+11	5.5	7.5
I	20	36	+16	7	9
J	9	28	+19	8	10

Note: We will conduct the Wilcoxon test using the recommendation that zero differences be discarded. Following this test, we will examine what would happen if the zero differences were included.

STEP 1 The null hypothesis states that the campaign had no effect. Therefore, any differences are due to chance, and there should be no consistent pattern.

STEP 2 The two companies with zero differences are discarded, and n is reduced to 8. With $n = 8$ and $\alpha = .05$, the critical value for the Wilcoxon test is $T = 3$. A sample value that is less than or equal to 3 will lead us to reject H_0.

STEP 3 For these data, the positive differences have ranks of 3, 4, 5.5, 5.5, 7, and 8:

$$\Sigma R_+ = 33$$

The negative differences have ranks of 1 and 2:

$$\Sigma R_- = 3$$

The Wilcoxon T is the smaller of these sums, so $T = 3$.

STEP 4 The T value from the data is in the critical region. This value is very unlikely to occur by chance ($p < .05$); therefore, we reject H_0 and conclude that there is a significant change in participation after the Red Cross campaign.

Note: If we include the zero differences in this test, then $n = 10$, and with $\alpha = .05$ the critical value for the Wilcoxon T is 8. Because the zero differences are tied for first and second in the ordering, each is given a rank of 1.5. One of these ranks is assigned to the positive group and one to the negative group. As a result, the sums are

$$\Sigma R_+ = 1.5 + 5 + 6 + 7.5 + 7.5 + 9 + 10$$
$$= 46.5$$

and

$$\Sigma R_- = 1.5 + 3 + 4$$
$$= 8.5$$

The Wilcoxon T is the smaller of these two sums, $T = 8.5$. Because this T value is larger than the critical value, we fail to reject H_0 and conclude that these data do not indicate a significant change in blood donor participation.

By including the zero differences in the test, we have changed the statistical conclusion. Remember, the zero differences are an indication that the null hypothesis is correct. When zero differences are considered, the test is more likely to retain H_0.

LEARNING CHECK

1. A physician is testing the effectiveness of a new arthritis drug by measuring patients' grip strength before and after they receive the drug. The difference scores for 10 patients are as follows: +3, +46, +16, −2, +38, +14, 0 (no change), −8, +25, and +41. Each score is the difference in strength, with a positive value indicating a stronger grip after receiving the drug. Use a Wilcoxon test to determine whether these data provide sufficient evidence to conclude that the drug has a significant effect. Test at the .05 level.

ANSWER

1. The Wilcoxon $T = 4$. Because one patient showed no change, n is reduced to 9, and the critical value is $T = 6$. Therefore, we reject H_0 and conclude that there is a significant effect.

19.4 THE SPEARMAN CORRELATION

In Chapter 16 we introduced the concept of correlation as a statistical method for measuring and describing the relation between two variables. As we noted in Chapter 16, the Pearson correlation, which measures linear relationship, is by far the most commonly used measure of relationship. However, there are other correlations that have been developed for special purposes or for special types of data. One of these other correlations is called the *Spearman correlation*.

The Spearman correlation measures the relation between two variables that are both measured on ordinal scales. As we have noted, ordinal data are fairly common because they often are easier to obtain than interval or ratio data. If only one of the variables is measured on an ordinal scale, it usually is easy to convert the other variable to ranks so that a Spearman correlation can be computed.

Figure 19.3

Hypothetical data showing the relationship between practice and performance. Although this relation is not linear, there is a consistent positive relationship. An increase in performance tends to accompany an increase in practice.

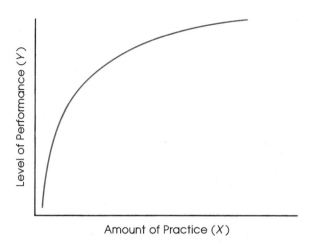

In addition to measuring relationships for ordinal data, the Spearman correlation can be used as a valuable alternative to the Pearson correlation with data from interval or ratio scales. As we have noted, the Pearson correlation measures the degree of linear relation between the two variables—that is, how well the data points fit on a straight line. However, a researcher often expects the data to show a *consistent* relationship but not necessarily a *linear* relation. For example, a researcher may be investigating the relation between amount of practice (X) and level of performance (Y). For these data the researcher expects a good positive relation; more practice leads to better performance. However, the relation probably does not fit a linear form, so a Pearson correlation would not be appropriate (see Figure 19.3). In this situation, the Spearman correlation can be used to obtain a measure of the consistency of relationship, independent of its specific form.

The reason that the Spearman correlation measures consistency, rather than form, comes from a simple observation: When two variables are consistently related, their ranks will be linearly related. For example, a perfectly consistent positive relation means that every time the X variable increases, the Y variable also increases. Thus, the smallest value of X is paired with the smallest value of Y, the second-smallest value of X is paired with the second-smallest value of Y, and so on. This phenomenon is demonstrated in the following example.

EXAMPLE 19.6

PERSON	X	Y
A	4	9
B	2	2
C	10	10
D	3	8

The data in the margin represent X and Y scores for a sample of $n = 4$ people. Note that person B has the lowest X score and the lowest Y score. Similarly, person D has the second-lowest score for both X and Y, person A has the third-lowest scores, and person C has the highest scores. These data show a perfectly consistent relation: Each increase in X is accompanied by an increase in Y. However, the relation is not linear, as can be seen in the graph of the data in Figure 19.4.

Now observe what happens when the X and Y scores are converted to ranks. Again, person B has the lowest X and Y scores, so this individual is ranked first on both variables. Similarly, person D is ranked sec-

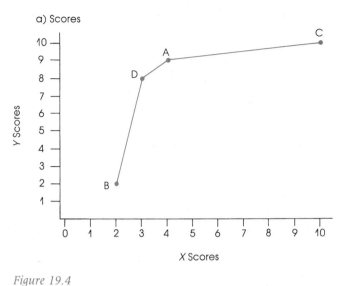

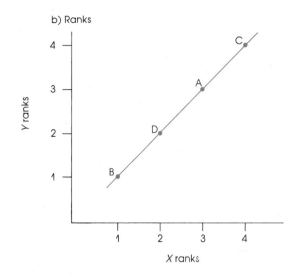

Figure 19.4

Scatterplots showing the scores and the ranks for the data in Example 19.6. Notice that there is a consistent, positive relation between the X and Y scores, although it is not a linear relation. Also notice that the scatterplot of the ranks shows a perfect linear relationship.

PERSON	X RANK	Y RANK
A	3	3
B	1	1
C	4	4
D	2	2

ond on both variables, person A is ranked third, and person C is ranked fourth (table at left). When the ranks are placed in a graph (see Figure 19.4), the result is a perfect linear relation.

The preceeding example has demonstrated that a consistent relationship among scores produces a linear relation when the scores are converted to ranks. Thus, if you want to measure the consistency of a relationship for a set of scores, you can simply convert the scores to ranks and then use the Spearman correlation to measure the correlation for the ranked data. The degree of relationship for the ranks (the Spearman correlation) provides a measure of the degree of consistency for the original scores.

Once again, the Spearman correlation measures the relation between two variables when both are measured on ordinal scales (ranks). There are two general situations where the Spearman correlation is used:

1. Spearman is used when the original data are ordinal; that is, when the X and Y values are ranks.

2. Spearman is used when a researcher wants to measure the consistency of a relation between X and Y, independent of the specific form of the relation. In this case the original scores are first converted to ranks; then the Spearman correlation is used to measure the relationship for the ranks. Incidently, when there is a consistently one-directional relation between two variables, the relation is said to be *monotonic*. Thus, the Spearman correlation can be used to measure the degree of monotonic relation between two variables.

The word *monotonic* describes a sequence that is consistently increasing (or decreasing). Like the word *monotonous*, it means constant and unchanging.

CALCULATION OF THE SPEARMAN CORRELATION

The calculation of the Spearman correlation is remarkably simple, provided you know how to compute a Pearson correlation. First, be sure that you have ordinal data (ranks) for the X scores and the Y scores. (If necessary, convert the original data into ranks. The smallest X value is called 1, the next smallest is 2, and so on. Note that the X and Y scores are ranked separately.) Then, compute a Pearson correlation using the ranks.

That's all there is to it. When you use the Pearson correlation formula for ordinal data, the result is called a Spearman correlation. The Spearman correlation is identified by the symbol r_s to differentiate it from the Pearson correlation. The complete process of computing the Spearman correlation, including ranking scores, is demonstrated in Example 19.7.

EXAMPLE 19.7

The following data show a nearly perfect monotonic relation between X and Y. When X increases, Y tends to decrease, and there is only one reversal in this general trend. To compute the Spearman correlation, we first rank the X and Y values, and we then compute the Pearson correlation for the ranks.

We have listed the X values in order so that the trend is easier to recognize.

ORIGINAL DATA			RANKS		
X	Y		X	Y	XY
3	12		1	5	5
4	5		2	3	6
5	6		3	4	12
10	4		4	2	8
13	3		5	1	5
					$36 = \Sigma XY$

The scatterplots for the original data and the ranks are shown in Figure 19.5. To compute the correlation, we will need SS for X, SS for Y,

Figure 19.5

Scatterplots showing the scores and the ranks for the data in Example 19.7.

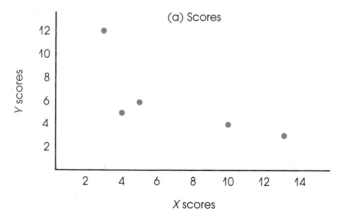

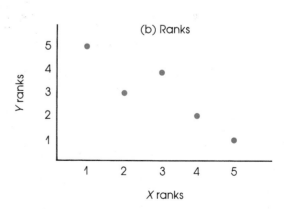

and *SP*. Remember, all these values are computed with the ranks, not the original scores.

The X ranks are simply the integers 1, 2, 3, 4, 5. These values have $\Sigma X = 15$ and $\Sigma X^2 = 55$. The *SS* for the X ranks is

$$SS_X = \Sigma X^2 - \frac{(\Sigma X)^2}{n},$$

$$= 55 - \frac{(15)^2}{5}$$

$$= 55 - 45$$

$$= 10$$

You should note that the ranks for Y are identical to the ranks for X; that is, they are the integers 1, 2, 3, 4, and 5. Therefore, *SS* for Y will be identical to *SS* for X:

$$SS_Y = 10$$

To compute the *SP* value, we need ΣX, ΣY, and ΣXY for the ranks. The XY values are listed in the table with the ranks, and we already have found that both the X's and the Y's have a sum of 15. Using these values, we obtain

$$SP = \Sigma XY - \frac{(\Sigma X)(\Sigma Y)}{n}$$

$$= 36 - \frac{(15)(15)}{5}$$

$$= 36 - 45$$

$$= -9$$

The final Spearman correlation is

$$r_s = \frac{SP}{\sqrt{(SS_X)(SS_Y)}}$$

$$= \frac{-9}{\sqrt{10(10)}}$$

$$= -0.9$$

The Spearman correlation indicates that the data show a strong (nearly perfect) negative trend.

SPECIAL FORMULA FOR THE SPEARMAN CORRELATION

After the original X values and Y values have been ranked, the calculations necessary for *SS* and *SP* can be greatly simplified. First, you should note that the X ranks and the Y ranks are really just a set of integers 1, 2, 3, 4, . . . , n. To compute the mean for these integers, you can locate the midpoint of the series by $\bar{X} = (n + 1)/2$. Similarly, the SS for this series of integers can be computed by

$$SS = \frac{n(n^2 - 1)}{12} \qquad \text{(Try it out.)}$$

Also, because the X ranks and the Y ranks are the same values, SS for X will be identical to SS for Y.

Because calculations with ranks can be simplified and because the Spearman correlation uses ranked data, these simplifications can be incorporated into the final calculations for the Spearman correlation. Instead of using the Pearson formula after ranking the data, you can put the ranks directly into a simplified formula:

$$r_s = 1 - \frac{6\Sigma D^2}{n(n^2 - 1)} \tag{19.5}$$

Caution: In this formula, you compute value of the fraction and then subtract from 1. The 1 is not part of the fraction.

where D is the difference between the X rank and the Y rank for each individual. This special formula will produce the same result that would be obtained from the Pearson formula. However, you should note that this special formula can be used only after the scores have been converted to ranks and only when there are no ties among the ranks. If there are relatively few tied ranks, the formula still may be used, but it loses accuracy as the number of ties increases. The application of this formula is demonstrated in the following example.

EXAMPLE 19.8   To demonstrate the special formula for the Spearman correlation, we will use the same data that were presented in Example 19.7. The ranks for these data are shown again here:

RANKS		DIFFERENCE	
X	Y	D	D^2
1	5	4	16
2	3	1	1
3	4	1	1
4	2	−2	4
5	1	−4	16
			38 = ΣD^2

Using the special formula for the Spearman correlation, we obtain

$$r_s = 1 - \frac{6\Sigma D^2}{n(n^2 - 1)}$$

$$= 1 - \frac{6(38)}{5(25 - 1)}$$

$$= 1 - \frac{19}{10}$$

$$= -0.90$$

Notice that this is exactly the same answer that we obtained in Example 19.7 using the Pearson formula on the ranks.

1. Describe what is measured by a Spearman correlation, and explain how this correlation is different from the Pearson correlation.

2. Identify the two procedures that can be used to compute the Spearman correlation.

3. Compute the Spearman correlation for the following set of scores.

X	Y
2	7
12	38
9	6
10	19

1. The Spearman correlation measures the consistency of the direction of the relation between two variables. The Spearman correlation does not depend on the form of the relation, whereas the Pearson correlation measures how well the data fit a linear form.

2. After the X and Y values have been ranked, you can compute the Spearman correlation by using either the special formula or the Pearson formula.

3. $r_s = 0.80$

SUMMARY

1. The Mann-Whitney and Wilcoxon tests are nonparametric alternatives to the independent-measures t and repeated-measures t tests, respectively. These tests do not require normal distributions or homogeneity of variance. Both tests require that the data be rank-ordered, and they assume that the dependent variable is continuously distributed. For both tests the null hypothesis states that there is no difference between the two treatments being compared.

2. The Mann-Whitney U can be computed either by a counting process or by a formula. A small value of U (near zero) is evidence of a difference between the two treatments. With the counting procedure, U is determined by the following:
   a. The scores from the two samples are combined and ranked from smallest to largest.
   b. Each individual in sample A is awarded one point for every member of sample B with a larger rank.

c. U_A equals the total points for sample A. U_B is the total for sample B. The Mann-Whitney U is the smaller of these two values.

In formula form,

$$U_A = n_A n_B + \frac{n_A(n_A + 1)}{2} - \Sigma R_A$$

$$U_B = n_A n_B + \frac{n_B(n_B + 1)}{2} - \Sigma R_B$$

3. For large samples, larger than those normally presented in the Mann-Whitney table, the normal distribution can be used to evaluate the difference between the two treatments. This normal approximation to the Mann-Whitney is used as follows:
   a. Find the value of U as before.

b. The Mann-Whitney U is converted to a z-score by the formula

$$z = \frac{U - \dfrac{n_A n_B}{2}}{\sqrt{\dfrac{n_A n_B (n_A + n_B + 1)}{12}}}$$

c. If this z-score is in the critical region of the unit normal distribution, the null hypothesis is rejected.

4. The test statistic for the Wilcoxon test is called a T score. A small value of T (near zero) provides evidence of a difference between the two treatments. T is computed as follows:
a. Compute a difference score (treatment 1 versus treatment 2) for each individual in the sample.
b. Rank these difference scores from smallest to largest without regard to the signs.

c. Sum the ranks for the positive differences, and sum the ranks for the negative differences. T is the smaller of these two sums.

5. The Spearman correlation (r_s) measures the consistency of direction in the relation between X and Y, that is, the degree to which the relation is one-directional, or monotonic. The Spearman correlation is computed by a two-stage process:
a. Rank the X scores and the Y scores.
b. Compute the Pearson correlation using the ranks.

Note: After the X and Y values are ranked, you may use a special formula to determine the Spearman correlation:

$$r_s = 1 - \frac{6\Sigma D^2}{n(n^2 - 1)}$$

where D is the difference between the X rank and the Y rank for each individual. This formula is accurate only when there are no tied scores in the data.

KEY TERMS

Mann-Whitney U

Wilcoxon T

Spearman correlation

normal approximation to the Mann-Whitney U

monotonic relation

—— *Focus on Problem Solving* ——

1. In computing the Mann-Whitney U, it will sometimes be obvious from the data which sample has the smaller U value. Even if this is the case, you should still compute both U values so that your computations can be checked using the formula

$$U_A + U_B = n_A n_B$$

2. Contrary to the previous statistical tests, the Mann-Whitney U and the Wilcoxon T are significant when the obtained value is equal to or *less than* the critical value in the table.

3. For the Wilcoxon T, remember to ignore the signs of the differences scores when assigning ranks to them.

4. When using the special formula for the Spearman correlation, remember that the fraction is computed separately and then subtracted from 1. Students often include the 1 as a part of the numerator, or they get so absorbed in computing the fractional part of the equation that they forget to subtract it from 1. Be careful using this formula.

5. When computing a Spearman correlation, be sure that both X and Y values have been ranked. Sometimes the data will consist of one variable already ranked with the other variable on an interval or ratio scale. If one variable is ranked, do not forget to rank the other.

Demonstration 19.1

THE MANN-WHITNEY *U*-TEST

A local police expert claims to be able to judge an individual's personality on the basis of his or her handwriting. To test this claim, 10 samples of handwriting are obtained: 5 come from prisoners convicted of violent crimes, and 5 come from psychology majors at the college. The expert ranks the handwriting samples from first to tenth, with 1 representing the most antisocial personality. The rankings are as follows:

RANKING	SOURCE
1	Prisoner
2	Prisoner
3	Student . . . 3 points
4	Prisoner
5	Prisoner
6	Student . . . 1 point
7	Prisoner
8	Student . . . 0 points
9	Student . . . 0 points
10	Student . . . 0 points

STEP 1 The null hypothesis states that there is no difference between the two populations. For this example, H_0 states that the police expert cannot differentiate the handwriting for prisoners from the handwriting for students.

The alternative hypothesis says there is a discernible difference.

STEP 2 For $\alpha = .05$ and with $n_A = n_B = 5$, the Mann-Whitney table gives a critical value of $U = 2$. If our data produce a U less than or equal to 2, we will reject the null hypothesis.

STEP 3 We designate the students as sample A and the prisoners as sample B. Because the students tended to cluster at the bottom of the rankings, they should have the smaller U. Therefore, we have identified the points for this sample. The students' point total is $U_A = 4$.

Because we have found the smaller of the two U values, it is not necessary to compute U for the sample of prisoners. However, we will continue with this calculation to demonstrate the formula for U. The sample of prisoners has ranks 1, 2, 4, 5, and 7. The sum is $\Sigma R_B = 19$, so the U_B value is

$$U_B = n_A n_B + \frac{n_B(n_B + 1)}{2} - \Sigma R_B$$

$$= 5(5) + \frac{5(6)}{2} - 19$$

$$= 25 + 15 - 19$$

$$= 21$$

To check our calculations,

$$U_A + U_B = n_A n_B$$

$$4 + 21 = 5(5)$$

$$25 = 25$$

The final U is the smaller of the two values, so the Mann-Whitney U statistic is $U = 4$.

STEP 4   Because $U = 4$ is not in the critical region, we fail to reject the null hypothesis. With $\alpha = .05$, these data do not provide sufficient evidence to conclude that there is a discernible difference in handwriting between the two populations.

———— *Demonstration 19.2* ————

THE WILCOXON SIGNED-RANKS TEST

A researcher obtains a random sample of $n = 7$ individuals and tests each person in two different treatment conditions. The data for this sample are as follows.

SUBJECT	TREATMENT 1	TREATMENT 2	DIFFERENCE
1	8	24	+16
2	12	10	− 2
3	15	19	+ 4
4	31	52	+21
5	26	20	− 6
6	32	40	+ 8
7	19	29	+10

STEP 1   *State the hypotheses and select alpha.* The hypotheses for the Wilcoxon test do not refer to any specific population parameter.

H_0:   There is no systematic difference between the two treatments.

H_1:   There is a consistent difference between the treatments that causes the scores in one treatment to be generally higher than the scores in the other treatment.

We will use $\alpha = .05$.

STEP 2   *Locate the critical region.* A small value for the Wilcoxon T indicates that the difference scores were consistently positive or consistently negative, which indicates a systematic treatment difference. Thus, small values will tend to refute H_0. With $n = 7$ and $\alpha = .05$, the Wilcoxon table shows that a T value of 2 or smaller is needed to reject H_0.

STEP 3   *Compute the test statistic.* The calculation of the Wilcoxon T is very simple but requires several stages:

   a. Ignoring the signs (+ or −), rank the difference scores from smallest to largest.

b. Compute the sum of the ranks for the positive differences and the sum for the negative differences.

c. The Wilcoxon T is the smaller of the two sums.

For these data, we have the following.

DIFFERENCE	RANK	
(+) 16	6	$\Sigma R_+ = 6 + 2 + 7 + 4 + 5 = 24$
(−) 2	1	
(+) 4	2	
(+) 21	7	$\Sigma R_- = 1 + 3 = 4$
(−) 6	3	
(+) 8	4	
(+) 10	5	

The Wilcoxon T is $T = 4$.

STEP 4   *Make a decision.* The obtained T value is not in the critical region. These data are not significantly different from chance. Therefore, we fail to reject H_0 and conclude that there is not sufficient evidence to suggest a systematic difference between the two treatment conditions.

Demonstration 19.3

THE SPEARMAN CORRELATION

The following data will be used to demonstrate the calculation of the Spearman correlation. Both X and Y values are measurements on interval scales.

X	Y
5	12
7	18
2	9
15	14
10	13

STEP 1   *Rank the X and Y values.* Remember, the X values and Y values are ranked separately.

X SCORE	Y SCORE	X RANK	Y RANK
5	12	2	2
7	18	3	5
2	9	1	1
15	14	5	4
10	13	4	3

STEP 2   *Use the special Spearman formula to compute the correlation.* The special Spearman formula requires that you first find the difference (D) between the X rank and the Y rank for each individual and then square the differences and find the sum of the squared differences.

X RANK	Y RANK	D	D²
2	2	0	0
3	5	2	4
1	1	0	0
5	4	1	1
4	3	1	1
			$6 = \Sigma D^2$

Using this value in the Spearman formula, we obtain

$$r_s = 1 - \frac{6\Sigma D^2}{n(n^2 - 1)}$$

$$= 1 - \frac{6(6)}{5(24)}$$

$$= 1 - \frac{3}{10}$$

$$= 0.70$$

There is a positive relation between X and Y for these data. The Spearman correlation is fairly high, which indicates a very consistent positive relation.

PROBLEMS

1. The following data are scores from two separate samples, each representing a different treatment condition:

SAMPLE 1, TREATMENT 1	SAMPLE 2, TREATMENT 2
8	22
10	16
15	20
12	24
17	14
9	23
13	19

a. Sketch a frequency distribution histogram for these data. Put both samples in the same histogram (use different colors or shading to differentiate the two treatments).

b. Just by looking at your frequency distribution sketch, does it appear that the two samples came from the same population or from two different populations?

c. Compute the Mann-Whitney U for these data. By using the .05 level of significance, do these data provide evidence of a significant difference between the two treatments?

2. An instructor teaches two sections of the same statistics course. All students take a common final exam, and the instructor receives a printout of the grades in rank order (lowest to highest). For the morning section with $n = 14$ students, the sum of the ranks is $\Sigma R = 192$. The afternoon section with $n = 10$ students has $\Sigma R = 108$. Do these data indicate a significant difference between the two sections? Test at the .05 level.

3. A researcher is trying to determine which of two species of laboratory rats should be housed in the psychology department. A sample of $n = 10$ rats is obtained for each species, and the researcher records the amount of food each rat consumes during a 1-week period. The data are as follows:

species A: 7, 9, 14, 20, 16, 18, 10, 22, 25, 13

species B: 24, 19, 21, 26, 21, 29, 13, 28, 32, 17

Do these data indicate that one species eats significantly more than the other? Use a Mann-Whitney test with $\alpha = .05$.

4. A doctor has been collecting data on the birth weight of newborn children for smoking and nonsmoking mothers:

smoking mothers: 92 oz,   111 oz,   108 oz, 120 oz,   101 oz

nonsmoking mothers: 127 oz,   118 oz,   134 oz, 136 oz,   109 oz,   122 oz, 115 oz,   129 oz,   113 oz

Do these data indicate a significant difference in birth weight between these two groups? Use a Mann-Whitney U-Test at the .05 level of significance.

5. A psychologist studying problem-solving ability presents subjects with a set of five anagrams to unscramble. (An anagram is a word with the letters rearranged into a random order.) In one condition, the anagrams are all pronounceable sequences (e.g., CAWTH), and in a second condition the anagrams are unpronounceable (e.g., HTWCA). In each condition, the psychologist records the amount of time needed to solve all five anagrams:

SUBJECT	PRONOUNCEABLE	UNPRONOUNCEABLE
1	189	130
2	167	94
3	208	185
4	143	82
5	156	148
6	119	124
7	129	91
8	175	107

Do these data indicate a significant difference between the two conditions? Use a Wilcoxon test with $\alpha = .05$.

6. In a hidden-figures task, subjects are required to find a specific shape that is contained within a more complex drawing. In an experiment using this task, the same figure was presented twice to each subject. On one presentation the figure was oriented so that all the lines were vertical and horizontal. On the other presentation, the figure was rotated so that all the lines were oblique. The dependent variable was the amount of time needed to locate and identify the hidden figure. Use a Wilcoxon test to determine whether the following data indicate a significant difference between the two orientations:

SUBJECT	HORIZONTAL-VERTICAL	OBLIQUE
1	8 seconds	13 seconds
2	10 seconds	35 seconds
3	7 seconds	12 seconds
4	3 seconds	11 seconds
5	12 seconds	10 seconds
6	17 seconds	29 seconds
7	8 seconds	9 seconds
8	14 seconds	38 seconds
9	5 seconds	21 seconds
10	13 seconds	9 seconds

7. Hyperactive children often are treated with a stimulant such as Ritalin to improve their attention spans. In one test of this drug treatment, hyperactive children were given a boring task to work on. A psychologist recorded the amount of time (in seconds) each child spent on the task before becoming distracted. Each child's performance was measured before he or she received the drug and again after the drug was administered. Because the scores on this task are extremely variable, the psychologist decided to convert the data to ranks. Use a Wilcoxon test with $\alpha = .05$ to determine whether the following data provide evidence that the drug has a significant effect:

CHILD	TREATMENT 1 (WITHOUT THE DRUG)	TREATMENT 2 (WITH THE DRUG)
1	28	135
2	15	309
3	183	150
4	48	224
5	30	25
6	233	345
7	21	43
8	110	188
9	12	15

8. Rank the following scores and compute the Spearman correlation between X and Y:

X	Y
7	19
2	4
11	34
15	28
32	104

9. A professor in the art department would like to demonstrate that art classes make a real contribution to artistic ability. A random sample of $n = 6$ seniors is selected from a drawing class. The professor obtains a sample drawing from each student and the drawings are ranked (best to worst). In addition, the professor records the number of art courses that each student has completed. These data are as follows:

RANK OF STUDENT'S DRAWING	NUMBER OF ART COURSES
3	2
4	1
6	0
1	7
5	1
2	4

Compute the correlation between drawing ability and education. (*Note:* First you must determine which correlation to use for these data.)

10. There are several tied scores in the following data:

X	Y
9	6
9	14
12	14
12	14
26	14
26	18

a. Compute the Spearman correlation by first ranking and then using the Pearson formula.
b. Compute the Spearman correlation using the special Spearman formula on the ranks.
c. Compare the results from the two different formulas. In general, how do tied scores affect the results with the special formula?

11. Monkeys raised in isolation tend to have difficulty adjusting to a social situation as adults. In an experimental demonstration of this phenomenon, a sample of 16 newborn monkeys was obtained. Eight of these monkeys were raised in isolation, and the other 8 were left to be reared in the colony. After 10 months, the 8 isolated monkeys were returned to the colony. Two months later, all 16 monkeys were ranked in terms of their position in the colony dominance hierarchy (number 1 being most dominant). These rankings are as follows:

ISOLATED MONKEYS		NOT ISOLATED	
SUBJECT	RANKING	SUBJECT	RANKING
1	13	9	3
2	7	10	12
3	10	11	5
4	16	12	1
5	6	13	4
6	14	14	2
7	11	15	8
8	15	16	9

Do these data provide evidence that isolation affects social dominance? Test at the .05 level of significance.

12. As part of a product testing program, a paint manufacturer painted 12 houses in a suburban community. Six of the houses were painted with the company's own product, and the other 6 were painted with a competitor's paint. After 5 years a panel of home owners inspected the 12 houses and ranked them according to how well the paint was holding up. The rankings are as follows:

ranks for company's paint: 1, 3, 4, 5, 7, 8

ranks for competitor's paint: 2, 6, 9, 10, 11, 12

Do these data indicate a significant difference between the two brands of paint? Test with $\alpha = .05$.

13. One assumption for parametric tests with independence-measures data is that the different treatment conditions have the same variance (homogeneity of variance assumption). However, a treatment effect that increases the mean often will also increase the variability. In this situation, the parametric t test or ANOVA is not justified and a Mann-Whitney test should be used. The following data represent an example of this situation:

TREATMENT 1 (SAMPLE A)	TREATMENT 2 (SAMPLE B)
1	8
5	20
0	14
2	27
4	6
2	10
3	19

a. Compute the mean and variance for each sample. Note the difference between the two sample variances.

b. Use a Mann-Whitney test, with $\alpha = .05$, to test for a significant difference between the two treatments.

14. Quite often you have a choice between a parametric and a nonparametric statistical test; for example, you could use either a t test or a Wilcoxon test for the same set of data. In general, the parametric test is the better choice because it uses more of the information available in the data and is more likely to produce a correct interpretation of the experimental outcome. The following data are difference scores from a repeated-measures design: 11, 3, −1, 10, 17, 15, −6, −4, 5, 13. Using $\alpha = .05$, test for a significant difference using both a t test and the Wilcoxon test. Explain why the two tests lead to different conclusions.

15. The American Automobile Club has classified states according to how strictly they enforce drinking-while-intoxicated (DWI) laws. The 20 states representing the 10 most strict and 10 most lax enforcers have been ranked by per capita traffic fatalities (1 = lowest). These data are as follows:

STATE	TRAFFIC FATALITIES RANK POSITION	DWI ENFORCEMENT
A	1	Strict
B	2	Strict
C	3	Strict
D	4	Lax
E	5	Strict
F	6	Strict
G	7	Lax
H	8	Strict
I	9	Lax
J	10	Lax
K	11	Strict
L	12	Strict
M	13	Lax
N	14	Strict
O	15	Lax
P	16	Strict
Q	17	Lax
R	18	Lax
S	19	Lax
T	20	Lax

Do these data indicate that DWI enforcement has a significant effect on traffic fatalities? Test at the .05 level of significance.

16. A new cold remedy contains a chemical that causes drowsiness and disorientation. Part of the testing for this drug involved measuring maze-learning performance for rats. Individual rats were tested with and without the drug. The dependent variable is the number of errors before the rat solves the maze. In the drug condition, two rats failed to solve the maze after 200 errors and were simply marked as "failed."

SUBJECT	NO DRUG	DRUG
1	28	125
2	43	90
3	37	(Failed)
4	16	108
5	47	40
6	51	75
7	23	91
8	31	23
9	26	115
10	53	55
11	26	(Failed)
12	32	87

Do these data indicate that the drug has a significant effect on maze-learning performance? Test at the .05 level of significance.

17. A researcher has developed a simple test that is intended to measure general intelligence. To evaluate the validity of this test, the researcher administers it to a class of 12 seventh-grade students. In addition, the teacher for this class is asked to rank-order the students in terms of intelligence with 1 being the smartest child in the class. The teacher's ranking and the test score for each child are as follows:

TEACHER'S RANKING	TEST SCORE
1	41
2	47
3	36
4	42
5	41
6	39
7	40
8	36
9	32
10	39
11	35
12	33

a. Compute the Spearman correlation for these data. (*Note:* You must change the test scores to ranks before you begin.)
b. On the basis of this correlation, does it appear that the researcher's test is a good measure of intelligence?

18. A common concern for students (and teachers) is the assignment of grades for essays or term papers. Because there are no absolute right or wrong answers, these grades must be based on a judgment of quality. To demonstrate that these judgments actually are reliable, an English instructor asked a colleague to rank-order a set of term papers. The ranks and the instructor's grades for these papers are as follows:

RANK	GRADE
1	A
2	B
3	A
4	B
5	B
6	C
7	D
8	C
9	C
10	D
11	E

a. Calculate the Spearman correlation for these data. *Note:* You must convert the letter grades to ranks.
b. Based on this correlation, does it appear that there is reasonable agreement between these two instructors in their judgment of the papers?

19. In the following data, X and Y are related by the equation $Y = X^2$:

X	Y
0	0
1	1
2	4
3	9
4	16
5	25

a. Sketch a graph showing the relation between X and Y. Describe the relationship shown in your graph.
b. Compute the Spearman correlation for these data.

20. A physiological psychologist is interested in the relationship between brain weight and learning ability. It is expected that there should be a consistent relationship, but the psychologist has no prediction concerning the form (linear or nonlinear) of the rela-

tion. The data for a sample of $n = 10$ animals are as follows:

BRAIN WEIGHT	LEARNING SCORE
1.04	1.5
2.75	1.8
4.14	1.9
7.81	1.6
8.11	2.1
8.35	4.5
8.50	4.2
8.73	6.2
8.81	10.3
8.97	14.7

a. Explain why the Spearman correlation is appropriate for these data.
b. Calculate the Spearman correlation.

21. For the vast majority of right-handed people, language is controlled in the left hemisphere of the brain. The left hemisphere also manages motor control for the right side of the body. Because language and fine motor control with the right hand are dependent on the same general area of the brain, these two activities can interfere with each other if an individual tries both at the same time. To demonstrate this fact, a psychologist asked subjects to balance a ruler on the index finger of their right hand. The psychologist recorded the amount of time the ruler was balanced under two conditions. In one condition the subject was allowed to concentrate on balancing the ruler. In the second condition, the subject was required to recite a nursery rhyme while balancing the ruler. The data for this experiment are as follows:

SUBJECT	JUST BALANCING	BALANCING AND RECITING
1	43 seconds	15 seconds
2	127 seconds	21 seconds
3	18 seconds	25 seconds
4	28 seconds	6 seconds
5	21 seconds	10 seconds
6	47 seconds	9 seconds
7	12 seconds	14 seconds
8	25 seconds	6 seconds
9	53 seconds	24 seconds
10	17 seconds	11 seconds

On the basis of these data, can the psychologist conclude that the language task (nursery rhyme) significantly interferes with right-hand motor skill? Use a Wilcoxon test with $\alpha = .05$.

22. Psychosis such as schizophrenia often is expressed in the artistic work produced by patients. To test the reliability of this phenomenon, a psychologist collected 10 paintings done by schizophrenic patients and another 10 paintings done by normal college students. A professor in the art department was asked to rank-order all 20 paintings in terms of bizarreness. These ranks are as follows:

ranks for schizophrenics: 1, 3, 4, 5, 6, 8, 9 11, 12, 14

ranks for students: 2, 7, 10, 13, 15, 16, 17, 18, 19, 20

On the basis of these data, can the psychologist conclude that there is a significant difference between the paintings for these two populations? Test at the .05 level of significance.

23. Individuals who are rated high in need for achievement (nAch) tend to work harder and longer than individuals rated low in nAch. In a laboratory test, 12 individuals rated high in nAch and 8 individuals rated low in nAch were given a mechanical puzzle to solve. Unknown to the subjects, there was no solution to the puzzle. The psychologist observing these subjects recorded the amount of time each person persisted on the task before giving up. There was a 20-minute time limit for each subject. The scores (in minutes) for the 8 subjects rated low in nAch were 6, 3, 7, 3, 2, 10, 12, 8. Of the 12 subjects rated high in nAch, 3 worked for the full 20 minutes and had to be stopped by the psychologist. The scores for the other 9 subjects were 9, 17, 13, 8, 5, 15, 16, 18, 11. Do these data indicate a significant difference between two personality types in terms of their persistence? Test at the .05 level of significance.

24. Several studies suggest that prejudice between groups can be reduced if people are given an opportunity for interaction on an equal status basis. One of these studies involved a specially structured summer camp for children. In this camp, all of the administrative and counseling positions were divided equally between blacks and whites. Thus, the campers experienced a situation where blacks and whites were equal in number and in status. Each child's attitude toward opposite-race children was tested before and after the camp. These data are as follows:

CHILD	BEFORE	AFTER
1	6	13
2	10	10
3	8	9
4	11	10
5	7	15
6	12	15
7	4	6
8	10	17
9	12	10
10	9	12
11	14	18
12	7	12

Because the attitude scale used in this study was an ordinal scale, use a Wilcoxon test to determine whether or not these data indicate a significant change in attitude. Test at the .05 level.

CHAPTER 20 | # INTRODUCTION TO MINITAB*

TOOLS YOU WILL NEED

The following items are considered essential background material for this chapter. If you doubt your knowledge of any of these items, you should review the appropriate chapter or section before proceeding.

- Frequency distributions (Chapter 2)
- Stem and leaf displays (Chapter 2)
- Central tendency (Chapter 3)
- Variability (Chapter 4)
- Hypothesis tests (Chapters 8–11)
- Estimation (Chapter 12)
- Analysis of variance (Chapters 13–15)
- Correlation and regression (Chapter 16)
- Chi-square (Chapter 17)
- Mann-Whitney test and Wilcoxon test (Chapter 19)

CONTENTS

* Portions of this chapter were adapted with permission from the *Minitab Primer* © copyright by Minitab, Inc. 1986, 1987. No portion of this chapter may be reproduced, stored or transmitted in any form or by any means without permission of Minitab, Inc.

PREVIEW

Many of the problems and exercises in this book have relatively simple data sets and can be readily analyzed with a basic calculator. However, as the size of the data set increases, the calculator becomes less useful in reducing the tedium of repetitive or complex computations. Imagine, for example, that you have collected data from hundreds or thousands of subjects. The analyses for that much data would be unwieldy for a calculator, even more so if the individual scores are large values or have decimals. The computer, on the other hand, can make very short work of large amounts of data and complex analyses. There are a great many statistical software packages available to perform these analyses. In this chapter, we will highlight Minitab, an easy-to-use statistical software package applied at many colleges as well as in industry and business.

Although many people initially learn to use computers with great trepidation, they later wonder how they ever got along without computers for data analysis, word processing, maintaining business records and the like. Their fears are overcome by the reward of getting tedious work done quickly, efficiently, and correctly. Although the lure of computing can be strong, a word of caution is in order. Despite the marvel of desktop computing, the computer will not (at least not yet) do the thinking for you. There is a well-known quip among computer people: Garbage in, garbage out. That is, if you expect to get meaningful output, you will need to know what information and which instructions to give to the computer. In a similar vein, a statistics professor of mine once told me, "The computer doesn't know where the numbers are coming from." Thus, it is still necessary that you understand the statistical procedures that are being performed by the computer. You will still have to select the appropriate analysis for your specific application. You will have to instruct the computer what to do, and you will still have to interpret the printout.

20.1 GETTING STARTED

Minitab is a statistical analysis program that is available for many types of computers, including PC-compatible machines. This chapter describes the fundamentals of using Minitab, including analyses from previous chapters in this book. Because there are Minitab versions for many types of computers, starting the program may vary from computer to computer. Your instructor can help you start the program. The purpose of this chapter is to familiarize you with the basic operation of the Minitab worksheet and commands. To help acquaint you with this program, we begin by introducing an example and by showing you a simple Minitab session.

EXAMPLE 20.1   A statistics instructor gives a quiz to a section of $n = 25$ students. On the quiz the students note how many hours they studied during the past week. The instructor records the hours studied and the quiz score for each student. These data are entered into the computer and saved in a file, or *worksheet,* called SECTION2. Once the data are in the computer, the instructor can use Minitab commands to review the data, transform the quiz scores into percentages, create a histogram showing the distribution of scores, and calculate statistics such as the mean or a correlation. Table 20.1 shows a Minitab session after the data were entered and stored. We have underlined the commands typed by the user to make them stand out. The remaining text is typed by the computer.

```
MTB > RETRIEVE 'SECTION2'

  WORKSHEET SAVED  5/2/1991

Worksheet retrieved from file: SECTION2.MTW
MTB > INFO

COLUMN    NAME      COUNT
C1        HOURS        25
C2        SCORE        25

CONSTANTS USED: NONE

MTB > DESCRIBE C1 C2

                N      MEAN    MEDIAN    TRMEAN     STDEV    SEMEAN
HOURS          25     5.680     6.000     5.739     2.704     0.541
SCORE          25    14.040    15.000    14.174     4.541     0.908

              MIN       MAX        Q1        Q3
HOURS       0.000    10.000     3.500     7.500
SCORE       5.000    20.000    10.500    17.000

MTB > CORRELATION OF 'HOURS' VS 'SCORE'

Correlation of HOURS and SCORE = 0.812

MTB > LET C3 = 'SCORE'/20*100
MTB > NAME C3 'PERCENT'
MTB > HISTOGRAM C3

Histogram of PERCENT   N = 25

Midpoint   Count
      30       2   **
      40       3   ***
      50       1   *
      60       1   *
      70       3   ***
      80       5   *****
      90       7   *******
     100       3   ***
```

Table 20.1

An illustration of a Minitab session. The user entered the commands that are underlined. Text produced by the computer is not underlined.

Although you may not understand all the computer printout shown in Table 20.1, it should give you some appreciation of the power of Minitab. With just seven simple commands, we have instructed Minitab to perform a variety of statistical manipulations. The remainder of this chapter provides a more detailed explanation of how Minitab operates, including a complete description of the commands used in Table 20.1 as well as many other Minitab functions.

AN OVERVIEW: THE WORKSHEET AND COMMANDS

Minitab consists of a worksheet plus commands. The worksheet is where you keep your data while you are running Minitab. The commands are used to analyze and manage (store, retrieve, edit) the data while they are in the worksheet.

The worksheet consists of rows and columns as well as constants (Table 20.2). A column is designed to hold a series of numbers for a variable, such as the quiz scores for 25 students. Columns are identified by C1, C2, C3, and so on. On the other hand, a constant holds just one number, such as the mean of the quiz scores. Constants are designated K1, K2, K3, and so on.

Table 20.2

The Minitab Worksheet. Columns are numbered C1, C2, and so on. The symbol for constants is K, and they are similarly numbered K1, K2, etc.

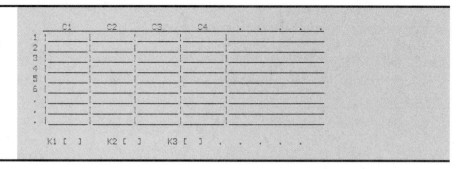

DEFINITIONS

The *columns* of the worksheet are used for holding data, with each variable studied assigned to a particular column. The number of *rows* in any column will correspond to the number (*n*) of observations made for that variable.

A *constant* on the worksheet holds a single value assigned by the user.

The Minitab worksheet is a temporary storage area for your data. Think of it as a scratch pad on which you can perform computations and analyses. Whenever you begin a Minitab session, a new worksheet is created. Until you enter numbers into the worksheet, it is empty and looks like the chart in Table 20.2. We must emphasize the temporary nature of the worksheet. Whenever you end a Minitab session, the worksheet and any data in it disappear. Therefore, if you have important data in the worksheet, it must be saved in a file before exiting Minitab. The command for saving data is explained in Section 20.2.

On most computers, Minitab is started by typing MINITAB and pressing the Return (or Enter) key. Minitab will follow with a few introductory remarks followed by the MTB> prompt. You instruct Minitab to do things by typing command names after each MTB> prompt and pressing the Enter key. Most Minitab commands consist of a command name followed by one or more arguments. Minitab will recognize approximately 180 command names, most of which are simple English words, such as READ, PLOT, and DESCRIBE. Arguments can be numerical values, columns (C1, C2, C3, and so on), constants (K1, K2, and the like), file names, or column names. For Example 20.1, the first line of the Minitab session (Table 20.1) shows the command RETRIEVE, followed by a single argument, a file named SECTION2.

DEFINITIONS

Commands consist of a command name and, usually, an argument list. The *command name* is a simple word instructing the computer to perform a particular task. The *argument* specifies the columns, constants, or file name on which the command will operate.

There are several shortcuts for entering commands. You can abbreviate command names by typing only their first four letters. You can add or delete text between command names and arguments as you see fit. Also, you can refer to columns by number or name (see Section 20.3 for naming columns). In Example 20.1, the third and fourth commands (Table 20.1) can be

```
MTB > HISTOGRAM C3;
SUBC> INCREMENT = 5.

Histogram of PERCENT    N = 25

Midpoint     Count
    25.00        1  *
    30.00        1  *
    35.00        2  **
    40.00        1  *
    45.00        1  *
    50.00        0
    55.00        0
    60.00        1  *
    65.00        2  **
    70.00        1  *
    75.00        3  ***
    80.00        2  **
    85.00        5  *****
    90.00        2  **
    95.00        1  *
   100.00        2  **
```

Table 20.3

The use of the INCREMENT subcommand with HISTOGRAM. The underlined commands are entered by the user. The computer provides remaining text.

shortened as follows (again, we have underlined the material that you enter):

MTB > <u>DESC C1 C2</u>

MTB > <u>CORR C1 C2</u>

In situations where several consecutive column numbers are specified in the argument, we can abbreviate the argument by inserting a hyphen. For example, if we wanted descriptive statistics for data in columns C1, C2, C3, and C4, the command could be written as follows:

MTB > <u>DESCRIBE C1−C4</u>

USING SUBCOMMANDS

Some Minitab commands can be followed by one or more subcommands. To tell Minitab that subcommands are to follow, end a command line with a semicolon (;). Minitab will respond with a new prompt, SUBC>, rather than MTB>. Each subcommand must be placed on a separate line, and all but the final subcommand must end with a semicolon. The final subcommand must end with a period. Then the command and subcommands will carry out their tasks and the MTB> prompt will return. In Example 20.1, the last command is HISTOGRAM C3, which creates a frequency distribution histogram for the percents in column C3 (Table 20.1). Notice that the distance between each midpoint in the histogram is 10 points. This distance was automatically selected by Minitab, but you can specify some other distance with the INCREMENT subcommand. Table 20.3 illustrates the use of this subcommand to set up histogram midpoints that are 5 points apart. Compare the results to those of Table 20.1.

ENDING YOUR SESSION

To end a Minitab session, you type STOP. This will return you to the operating system of your computer. It will also clear the worksheet for your next session. If the data in your current worksheet are important, the worksheet should be saved before the Minitab session is ended; *otherwise the data will be lost when the session is ended.* Section 20.2 examines entering and saving data in the worksheet.

HELP   Minitab has a useful and very complete HELP facility that you can access at any time. To learn how to use HELP, type HELP HELP after the MTB> prompt. You can see what commands Minitab has by typing HELP COMMANDS. Finally, you can get help on a specific command by typing HELP followed by the command name. For example, to get assistance in using the command HISTOGRAM, you can type

MTB > HELP HISTOGRAM

LEARNING CHECK

1. In the Minitab worksheet, the data for each variable are assigned to a column. (True or false?)

2. What is the distinction between a command name and a command argument?

3. Once data are entered into the Minitab worksheet, they are permanently stored. (True or false?)

4. You can end a Minitab session by typing the command _____.

5. Assistance can be obtained during a Minitab session by using the _____command.

ANSWERS

1. True. Each column contains the data for one variable.

2. A command name specifies the task for Minitab to perform (e.g., to make a histogram, to compute a correlation). The argument indicates the columns, variable names, or files to be used in the task.

3. False. The worksheet is temporary. Data in it are deleted when you end the Minitab session unless the worksheet is saved with a special command.

4. STOP   5. HELP

20.2 ENTERING AND SAVING DATA

The first task in any Minitab session is entering data into the Minitab worksheet. This can be accomplished in three ways: directly from the keyboard, from a saved Minitab worksheet, or from a data file on your computer.

ENTERING DATA FROM THE KEYBOARD   There are two commands you can use to enter data directly from the keyboard, SET and READ. The SET command puts all the numbers you type into one column. For example, to enter numbers into C1, you type

MTB > <u>SET C1</u>

Minitab will respond with a new prompt, DATA>, and then wait for you to type in a number. For example, you might type the following:

DATA> <u>2 4 6.5 0.2</u>

Caution: If C1 already contains data, using SET C1 again will write over the original data.

Minitab will place these four numbers into the first four rows of C1 and once again respond with the DATA> prompt. You may continue to place numbers in this column, for example, by typing

DATA> <u>10 −0.1 14</u>

Do not use commas on the data lines. Minitab will read 1,312 as 1   312.

These numbers are placed into the next three rows of C1. Notice that there is no special format, other than leaving at least one space between each number. You include any decimal points and negative signs that are necessary. When you have finished entering numbers in column C1, type END on a data line by itself:

DATA> <u>END</u>

Minitab returns to the MTB> prompt.

The READ command enters data into several columns at once. For example, you can enter data into columns C2, C3, and C4 as follows:

MTB > <u>READ C2−C4</u>
DATA > <u>1 2 3</u>
DATA > <u>4 5 6</u>
DATA > <u>7 8 9</u>
DATA > <u>10 11 12</u>
DATA > <u>END</u>

Caution: If columns C2, C3, and C4 already contain data, then using READ C2−C4 will write over the original data.

With this example using READ, the first number entered on each DATA line goes into C2, the second number on each line is placed into C3, and the last number on each line is put in C4. Again, a space is placed between each number during entry.

Now we can look at all the data we have just entered. This is done using the PRINT command, followed by specification of the columns we want to view.

MTB > <u>PRINT C1−C4</u>

Minitab then displays your worksheet.

```
ROW      C1       C2      C3      C4
  1       2        1       2       3
  2       4        4       5       6
  3      6.5       7       8       9
  4      0.2      10      11      12
  5      10
  6     -0.1
  7      14
```

SAVING AND RETRIEVING A WORKSHEET

It is important to distinguish between the Minitab worksheet and a *saved* worksheet. As noted earlier, the Minitab worksheet provides temporary storage for your data. Data entered when you begin your Minitab session is deleted when you end the session. However, during the session you can permanently store your Minitab worksheet using the SAVE command followed by a worksheet name. In Example 20.1, the data were originally stored as follows:

MTB > <u>SAVE 'SECTION2'</u>

You choose the name of the worksheet. It may contain both letters and numbers and should be placed in single quotation marks. The SAVE command takes a "snapshot" of the Minitab worksheet at a particular moment in time. Any changes made to the data later in the session will not be stored unless you use the SAVE command again. Thus, it is a good idea to save your worksheet near the end of the session, even if you used the SAVE command earlier.

Saved worksheets are special (binary) files that only Minitab can access. They are very fast to store and retrieve and contain both numbers (the data) and column names. You gain access to a saved worksheet by the RETRIEVE command. For example, at the start of a Minitab session, the data from the saved worksheet SECTION2 are retrieved as follows:

MTB > <u>RETRIEVE 'SECTION2'</u>

It should be noted that if the SECTION2 worksheet is not located in your current directory, Minitab will respond with an error message to tell you that the requested worksheet does not exist. In that case, you will have to supply a pathname that tells Minitab where to find the saved worksheet. On microcomputers running MS-DOS (PC compatibles) you might have to type a path that resembles the following, for instance:

MTB > <u>RETRIEVE 'C:\MINITAB\GRADES\SECTION2'</u>

Here the computer is instructed to search drive C through the specified path for a file named SECTION2. Minitab fetches SECTION2, places its content into the Minitab worksheet, and responds with the MTB> prompt. Note that anytime you enter a RETRIEVE command, the new data you are retrieving will replace whatever was previously in the worksheet.

ENTERING DATA FROM AN ASCII FILE

Often your data already reside in a file on your computer. Most computers use a standardized code called ASCII. If your data file is a standard text (or ASCII) file, you can input its contents directly into the Minitab worksheet. It is important to distinguish between these data files and the saved worksheets, which were discussed in the previous section. Data files are stored in the standard ASCII format that other software programs, such as data editors, can readily access and read. They can also easily be transferred from computer to computer. The commands READ and SET are used with these data files (note that SAVE and RETRIEVE are used with saved Minitab worksheets). Unlike saved worksheets, ASCII files do not store column numbers and names. These must be entered each time you use the file.

If all the data in your file are observations of a single variable, then you will want to put them into a single column on the worksheet. To illustrate how this is done, we will assume that the following data are stored in a standard text file named EXAMPLE:

$$11 \quad 22 \quad 33$$
$$44 \quad 55 \quad 66$$
$$77 \quad 88 \quad 99$$

To place all nine numbers from this file into C5 of your worksheet, you would use the SET command, as follows:

MTB > SET 'EXAMPLE' C5

Column C5 now contains 11, 22, 33, 44, 55, 66, 77, 88, 99. As you can see, Minitab reads the data file one row at a time from left to right.

If your data file contains observations from several variables (one observation from each variable in each row), then the data are entered with the READ command. For example, to enter the data from the EXAMPLE file into C6, C7, and C8 of the worksheet, you type

MTB > READ 'EXAMPLE' C6–C8

The Minitab worksheet now contains the following data:

ROW	C6	C7	C8
1	11	22	33
2	44	55	66
3	77	88	99

STORING DATA IN AN ASCII FILE

You can store some or all of the worksheet data in an ASCII file that other software packages can read. The WRITE command is used for this purpose. For example, consider the following command statement:

MTB > WRITE 'DATFIL' C1–C2

Minitab creates a standard ASCII file called DATFIL and places the contents of C1 and C2 in it. The contents of any data file created with WRITE can be entered into the Minitab worksheet using READ (or SET if there is only one column of data).

LEARNING CHECK

1. Data can be entered into the worksheet with SET or READ. What is the difference between these commands?

2. You can store your entire worksheet using the command _____ and gain access to it with _____.

3. Once your worksheet is saved during a session, any changes made to the worksheet later in the session will be automatically included in the saved file. (True or false?)

4. The advantage of storing data in ASCII files is that other computer software can often read these files. (True or false?)

ANSWERS   **1.** With SET, the data are entered into one column. READ enters the data into two or more columns that are specified in the argument.

2. SAVE; RETRIEVE (the argument for each command must specify a file name)

3. False. The modified worksheet must be saved.

4. True

20.3 SOME USEFUL COMMANDS

There are a number of commands that allow you to view, manipulate, and edit your worksheet. A summary of a few of the most useful commands are summarized next.

CHECKING THE WORKSHEET STATUS

Once you have retrieved a worksheet, you may wonder what variables and constant it contains. The easiest way to check the status of your worksheet is to use the INFO command. For Example 20.1, the status check proceeds as follows:

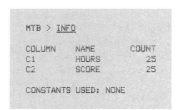

```
MTB > INFO

COLUMN      NAME        COUNT
C1          HOURS         25
C2          SCORE         25

CONSTANTS USED: NONE
```

As you can see, INFO lists all the columns and constants that contain data, column names (when applicable), and the number of values in each column.

NAMING VARIABLES

Preceding sections have shown named columns. Naming columns makes your variables much easier to identify and reference and your output easier to read. In Example 20.1, the following command was used to name the columns.

MTB > NAME C1 'HOURS' C2 'SCORE'

The names you choose may be from one to eight characters in length. Once you have named a variable, you may refer to it by its name or column number. Thus, the second command in Example 20.1 may be stated as

MTB > DESCRIBE C1 C2

```
MTB > PRINT C1 C2

ROW        HOURS        SCORE
 1            8           17
 2            7           19
 3            5           15
 4            6           14
 5            5           16
 6            1            9
 7            3            7
 8            9           20
 9            3            8
10            6           16
11            7           17
12            7           18
13            4           13
14            3           17
15            6           13
16            9           17
17            6           15
18           10           17
19            2            7
20            6           15

CONTINUE?
```

Table 20.4

Using the PRINT command to view the data for Example 20.1.

or

MTB > <u>DESCRIBE 'HOURS' 'SCORE'</u>

Whenever you refer to a variable name, you must enclose the name in single quotation marks. You may change the name of a variable by issuing another NAME command for that column.

VIEWING DATA

You can view data in your worksheet anytime using the PRINT command. For Example 20.1, the PRINT command can view the contents of C1 and C2, as illustrated in Table 20.4. When the columns you are printing contain more data than will fit on a single screen, Minitab will display one screen at a time. After each screen it will ask you if you want to continue. To conserve space, type the letter N after the CONTINUE prompt. You may, of course, respond with Y to view additional data.

CORRECTING ERRORS IN DATA

There are several ways you can edit the worksheet. You can use the LET command to substitute a new value for an incorrect one. Suppose the fifteenth value in C1 (Table 20.4) should have been 8 instead of 6. You can change that value by using the LET command and the following arguments.

MTB > <u>LET C1 (15) = 8</u>

A new value, 8, is now assigned to the fifteenth observation (row) of C1. Because you can always substitute a column name for a column number, you could have stated the command as follows:

MTB > <u>LET 'HOURS' (15) = 8</u>

Table 20.5

The screen display for the data editor, which is activated by pressing the Esc key. Note that the highlighted cursor appears at the first score in C1. The data are from Example 20.1.

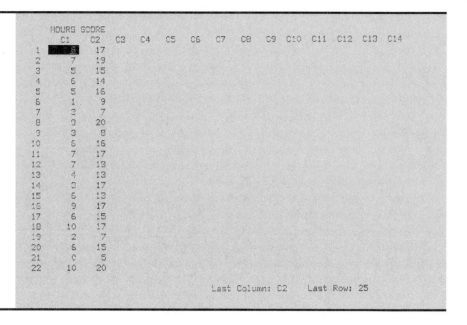

Note that the row number must always be enclosed in parentheses. Also, two other commands, INSERT and DELETE, can be used to correct the worksheet. You can learn about these commands by typing HELP INSERT and HELP DELETE.

THE ON-SCREEN DATA EDITOR

Release 7 of Minitab has a new feature for the PC version. It is an on-screen data editor that allows you to view and edit the worksheet, much like most spreadsheet software. To activate the data editor, press the Escape (Esc) key. Minitab will then display your worksheet. Table 20.5 shows the screen display for Example 20.1 after Esc is pressed. The screen displays the columns and rows of the worksheet and any data that are in them. The first score in C1 will be highlighted by the computer (Table 20.5) and a small flashing bar, called a cursor, will be present. To change a score in the worksheet, you press the cursor arrows (↑   ↓   →   ←) to move the highlighted cursor to the score you want to change. You then simply enter the new value.

DEFINITION

The *cursor* is a small flashing bar or square on the screen that indicates where a character will appear when you press a key. On some computer displays the cursor is highlighted.

Notice that the entire worksheet cannot fit on the screen. The lower left corner of the screen indicates the last column and row that contain data. In this example, the screen can fit only 22 rows, but there are actually 25 scores per column. You can display the last rows by toggling (repeatedly pressing) the down arrow (↓).

There are other useful keys that allow you to move the cursor highlight quickly. The Page Down (PgDn) key lets you view the next screen of data, and avoids the trouble of toggling the down arrow. The page up (PgUp) key moves the screen display in the opposite direction. The Home key moves the cursor highlight to the top of the screen and the End key moves it to the bottom of the screen. Pressing the Control key (Ctrl) with Home or End will move the highlight to the top (C1, row 1) or bottom (last column, last row) of the entire set of data. When you have finished editing the worksheet, press the Esc key, and the MTB> prompt will return to the screen. You may now enter Minitab commands to analyze the data. It is important to note that when you have edited a worksheet, the changes you have made are not permanent. You must now save the edited worksheet. This warning also applies to corrections made by the LET command.

ARITHMETIC TRANSFORMATIONS

The LET command in Example 20.1 created a new variable by computing the percent for each quiz score. The results were placed in C3 (Table 20.1). This example illustrates an arithmetic transformation. Algebraic expressions used in the LET command (for example, C3 = 'SCORE'/20*100) may contain the following operators:

+   addition
−   subtraction
*   multiplication
/   division
** raising to a power (exponents)

In addition, LET commands may contain functions for square root (SQRT), for computing the mean and standard deviation (MEAN, STDEV), and many others. For example, to take the square root of the data in column C2 and place the results in C4, the command would state

MTB > LET C4 = SQRT(C2)

Notice that the argument that follows SQRT, in this case C2, must be enclosed in parentheses. When using statistical functions that yield a single value, you may assign the result of the LET command to a constant. A few examples using the data from Example 20.1 follow:

```
MTB > LET K1 = MEAN(C1)
MTB > LET K2 = STDEV(C1)
MTB > LET K3 = MEDIAN(C1)
MTB > PRINT K1-K3
K1      5.68000
K2      2.70370
K3      6.00000
```

SENDING OUTPUT TO THE PRINTER

When you work through a Minitab session, your results are displayed on the screen in front of you. You can also produce a permanent record of the results of an analysis by sending the output to the printer. This is accomplished by entering the following command:

MTB > PAPER

All the commands you enter after the PAPER command, as well as the results or analyses of those commands, will be sent to the printer and to your screen simultaneously. Although simultaneous printing will occur on the PC version, on some computers the output is sent to a temporary print file instead of directly to a printer. When you exit Minitab, this file is automatically printed and then deleted.

If you want a complete record of your entire Minitab session—its commands and results—then PAPER should be used at the beginning of your session. Also, you can produce a page advance (form feed) on your printer anytime by entering the following command:

MTB > NEWPAGE

When you want to stop sending output to a printer, enter

MTB > NOPAPER

During a single Minitab session, you can start and stop sending output to a printer as many times as you wish by alternating between PAPER and NOPAPER.

When using a mainframe computer terminal, the OUTFILE command can be used to obtain printed output. This command will place the output of any subsequent commands into the file specified. For example, the commands

MTB > OUTFILE 'RESULTS'
DATA > HISTOGRAM C1

create a histogram for the data in column 1 and places the output in a file named RESULTS. Later, you may use the system commands for your particular mainframe computer to print the contents of the RESULTS file.

LEARNING CHECK

1. What information will the command INFO provide?

2. Given the following commands:

NAME C1 'AGE' C2 'GPA' C3 'SCORE'
DESCRIBE C1 C2 C3

a. What is the purpose of the first command?
b. What are other ways to state the DESCRIBE command?
c. What command could you enter to view the data on this worksheet?

3. For the previous example, suppose we enter

LET C2 (11) = 3.2
LET K1 = MEAN (C2)

What will these commands do?

4. Which of the following commands allows you to send output to the printer?

a. PRINT
b. NEWPAGE

c. PAPER

d. WRITE

ANSWERS
1. A list of the columns with data, variable names, number of scores in each column, and the constants used

2. **a.** The worksheet columns C1, C2, and C3 are named AGE, GPA, and SCORE, respectively.

   b. DESC C1 C2 C3 or DESC 'AGE' 'GPA' 'SCORE'

   c. PRINT C1 C2 C3

3. The first command changes the eleventh score in C2 to 3.2. The second command calculates the mean for C2 and stores it as constant K1.

4. c

20.4 DESCRIPTIVE STATISTICS

Minitab will perform a variety of basic descriptive procedures. For example, it permits you to depict your data graphically in various histograms and scatterplots. Some plots summarize your data, others depict patterns in your data over time, and still others illustrate the relationship between two variables. Additionally, Minitab can provide measures of central tendency and variability. We illustrate these procedures in this section. Remember, commands consist of command names and arguments. The command name specifies the analysis or operation to done, and the arguments indicate which columns or constants are to be used. Once again, we underline the material that the user is supposed to type. Text provided by the computer is not underlined.

TABLES AND GRAPHS
There are several ways to summarize a frequency distribution. We already demonstrated the use of HISTOGRAM in Tables 20.1 and 20.3. The command HISTOGRAM is followed by one or more column numbers or names. A frequency distribution histogram is constructed for the data in each column listed in the argument. The subcommand INCREMENT may be used with HISTOGRAM to assign a desired interval between the midpoints in the histogram (see Table 20.3). Remember, to use a subcommand, the command must end in a semicolon. A SUBC> prompt will appear on the screen. Then you may type in the subcommand, ending with a period.

Minitab can produce a display similar to a histogram, called a dotplot. For Example 20.1, the following command is entered:

MTB > DOTPLOT C1

A dotplot is constructed by Minitab for the data in column C1 (Figure 20.1). Of course, we could have used the variable name in the argument, in which case we would enter DOTPLOT 'HOURS'. Each dot on the dotplot represents

Figure 20.1

Minitab results for the command DOTPLOT. The data from Example 20.1 were used.

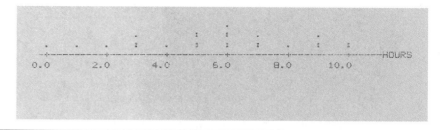

one score from C1. Minitab automatically selects the scales for all plots unless you specify your own with subcommands such as INCREMENT. Typing HELP DOTPLOT will provide assistance.

You can also depict the relationship between two variables by using a scatterplot. A scatterplot (Chapter 16) is created with the PLOT command. Its argument specifies the two columns or variable names that you would like plotted. For the data in Example 20.1, the scatterplot is constructed as follows:

MTB > <u>PLOT 'SCORE' 'HOURS'</u>

The results are shown in Figure 20.2.

In the scatterplot, an asterisk is displayed for each pair of observations. If several data points are repeated, such as (6, 16) in this example, then a number appears instead of an asterisk. The number 2 on the scatterplot indicates that the coordinates (6, 16) appear twice in the data. Notice that the variable listed first in the argument of the command is plotted on the Y-axis (vertical axis) and the second variable is plotted on the X-axis (horizontal axis). Finally, Minitab has a number of subcommands for PLOT that allow you to specify the scales and labels on the axes. Type HELP PLOT to learn more about these options.

Numbers also replace asterisks when data points are so close on the graph that asterisks would be overlapping.

STEM AND LEAF DISPLAYS

Stem and leaf displays (Chapter 2) are created by the command STEM-AND-LEAF. Its argument lists the column numbers or names for the data to be used in the display. Consider the data from Table 2.3 (page 58), which we will enter into the worksheet with SET:

Figure 20.2

A scatterplot generated by the command PLOT for the data in Example 20.1.

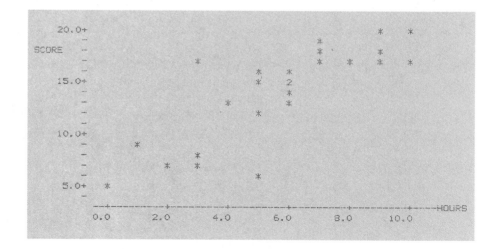

```
 2        3  23
 2        3
 3        4  2
 4        4  6
 5        5  2
 8        5  679
10        6  23
11        6  8
(4)       7  1344
 9        7  668
 6        8  123
 3        8  5
 2        9  3
 1        9  7
```

Table 20.6

A stem and leaf display for the data from Table 2.2. The Minitab command STEM-AND-LEAF was used. The abbreviated command STEM will produce the same printout.

```
MTB  > SET C1
DATA > 83 82 63 62 93 78 71 68 33 76 52 97
DATA > 85 42 46 32 57 59 56 73 74 74 81 76
DATA > END
```

Next we enter the command to create the display.

```
MTB > STEM-AND-LEAF C1
```

The resulting display is shown in Table 20.6. The second column in the printout shows the stems. The leaves are displayed to the right of the stems. A unique feature of the Minitab stem and leaf display is the addition of cumulative frequencies (the first column in the display). Moving down this column from the top, cumulative frequencies are shown until you reach the stem that contains the 50th percentile. The frequency for that particular stem is entered in parentheses: (4). That is, the stem and leaves of 7 1344 contain the 50th percentile of the distribution, and this stem has 4 scores in it (71 73 74 74). Starting from the bottom of the column and moving up, cumulative frequencies are again shown. These, too, stop when the stem with the 50th percentile is reached. This additional column helps you find the middle of the distribution at a glance.

CENTRAL TENDENCY AND VARIABILITY

We demonstrated (Table 20.1) the use of the DESCRIBE command to provide basic descriptive measures of central tendency and variability. When the argument of this command has more than one column designated, descriptive measures will be provided for each column (Table 20.1). Notice that DESCRIBE provides many measures we covered in early chapters: the mean, median, standard deviation (STDEV), standard error (SEMEAN), and the first (Q1) and third (Q3) quartiles (Table 20.1). The TRMEAN is a trimmed mean. For this measure, the lowest 5% and the highest 5% of the distribution are trimmed and the mean is computed for the remaining (middle) 90% of the scores. Thus, the trimmed mean is less influenced by extreme scores in the distribution.

Also, we noted previously how the LET command (Section 20.3) can be used to obtain descriptive measures. LET allows you to assign the values for the MEAN, MEDIAN, and STDEV to constants (K1, K2, and so on). Finally, in Section 20.7, we demonstrate how to obtain cell means for a two-factor experiment with the TABLE command.

1. Describe the tasks are being performed by the following command and subcommand:

   DOTPLOT 'AGE';
   INCREMENT = 5.

2. Given the following command:

   PLOT 'GPA' 'SCORE'

   a. What type of graph will Minitab produce?
   b. How will the axes be labeled?

3. Consider the following Minitab printout.

	N	MEAN	MEDIAN	TRMEAN	STDEV	SEMEAN
AGE	43	20.279	20.000	20.128	3.050	0.465

	MIN	MAX	Q1	Q3
AGE	15.000	29.000	18.000	21.000

   a. What command produced this printout?
   b. Explain the content of the printout.

1. The data for the variable named AGE are presented in a dotplot. The subcommand sets up increments of 5 points on the scale of the dotplot.

2. a. A scatterplot is constructed.
   b. The Y (vertical) axis is labeled GPA. The X (horizontal) axis is labeled SCORE.

3. a. DESCRIBE 'AGE'
   b. For a variable named AGE, the mean for 43 individuals is 20.279. The median is 20 and the trimmed mean (the mean excluding the smallest 5% and largest 5% of the distribution) is 20.128. The standard deviation and standard error of the mean are 3.05 and 0.465, respectively. The smallest score is $X = 15$ and the largest is $X = 29$. Finally, the first and third quartiles are 18 and 21, respectively.

20.5 HYPOTHESIS TESTS WITH THE t STATISTIC

Minitab will perform hypothesis tests with the t statistic for a single-sample study (Chapter 9), an independent-measures experiment (Chapter 10), or a related-samples (repeated-measures) study (Chapter 11). This section summarizes each of these analyses.

```
TEST OF MU = 4.000 VS MU N.E. 4.000

          N      MEAN    STDEV    SE MEAN        T     P VALUE
HOURS    25      5.680   2.704    0.541       3.11     0.0048
```

Table 20.7

The results of a single-sample *t* test using the command TTEST. The professor wanted to determine if the hours spent studying by students differ significantly from the national average, $\mu = 4$.

THE SINGLE-SAMPLE *t* STATISTIC

The single-sample *t* test (Chapter 9) is performed by the TTEST command. Let's look at Example 20.1 again. A sample of $n = 25$ students indicated how many hours they studied statistics in a week. Suppose that the professor knows that the national average is $\mu = 4.0$ hours per course for college students. A single-sample *t* test can be used to determine if the sample mean differs significantly from the population mean (note that the value for σ is not known). The command is stated as follows:

MTB > TTEST 4.0 'HOURS'

The first part of the argument is the value for the population mean, according to H_0 ($\mu = 4.0$). The second part specifies the column or variable name for the data. The results are shown in Table 20.7. The printout displays the sample size, mean, standard deviation (STDEV), and standard error (SE MEAN). Finally, the obtained *t* value is provided as well as its probability when H_0 is true.

THE INDEPENDENT-MEASURES *t* TEST

The TWOSAMPLE command is used for the independent-measures *t* test (Chapter 10). Consider the following data, which were used for Example 10.2, a study of the effects of imagery on memory.

DATA FROM EXAMPLE 10.2 (NUMBERS OF WORDS RECALLED)				
Group 1	24	23	16	17	19
(no images)	13	17	20	15	26
Group 2	18	19	23	29	30
(images)	31	29	26	21	24

The first step is entering the data onto the worksheet. This is easily accomplished using SET.

MTB > SET C1
DATA > 24 23 16 17 19 13 17 20 15 26
DATA > END
MTB > SET C2
DATA > 18 19 23 29 30 31 29 26 21 24
DATA > END

Table 20.8

An independent-measures *t* test using the data from Example 10.2. The command TWOSAMPLE was used with the subcommand POOLED.

```
TWOSAMPLE T FOR GROUP1 VS GROUP2
              N       MEAN      STDEV    SE MEAN
GROUP1       10      19.00       4.22       1.3
GROUP2       10      25.00       4.71       1.5

95 PCT CI FOR MU GROUP1 - MU GROUP2: (-10.2, -1.8)

TTEST MU GROUP1 = MU GROUP2 (VS NE): T= -3.00  P=0.0077  DF=  18

POOLED STDEV =        4.47
```

Next, we use TWOSAMPLE to begin the analysis. Its argument indicates the two columns that contain the data for the two treatment groups. We also use the POOLED subcommand so that the estimated standard error is computed using pooled variance (Chapter 10).

> MTB > <u>TWOSAMPLE C1 C2;</u>
> SUBC > <u>POOLED.</u>

Remember, a semicolon is used at the end to the command statement when using subcommands. The results of the analysis are presented in Table 20.8. Notice that TWOSAMPLE provides descriptive statistics for each group, the 95% confidence interval for $\mu_1-\mu_2$, the *t* statistic for the hypothesis test, and the probability (*P*) of committing a Type I error if H_0 is rejected. Of course, you would not reject H_0 unless *P* is less than your alpha level (for example, $p < .05$).

THE REPEATED-MEASURES *t* TEST

For the repeated-measures *t* test (Chapter 11), the TTEST command is used again, only the data that are analyzed consist of difference scores (where $D = X_2 - X_1$). To demonstrate this analysis, let's take another look at Example 11.1. A researcher studies the effect of relaxation training on asthma attacks. The numbers of doses of medication needed before and after training are recorded for each subject. The data from Table 11.3 are displayed again here.

PATIENT	DATA FROM EXAMPLE 11.1 WEEK BEFORE TRAINING	WEEK AFTER TRAINING
A	9	4
B	4	1
C	5	5
D	4	0
E	5	1

First, the before-and-after scores for each subject should be entered in C1 and C2, respectively, using the READ command.

> MTB > <u>READ C1 C2</u>
> DATA > <u>9   4</u>
> DATA > <u>4   1</u>

```
TEST OF MU = 0.000 VS MU N.E. 0.000

           N     MEAN    STDEV   SE MEAN        T    P VALUE
C3         5   -3.200    1.924    0.860    -3.72      0.020

MTB > NOPAPER
```

Table 20.9

A repeated-measures *t* test for the data in Example 11.1 was performed. The command TTEST was used for a column containing difference scores.

DATA > <u>5   5</u>

DATA > <u>4   0</u>

DATA > <u>5   1</u>

DATA > <u>END</u>

Next, the difference scores are computed and placed in C3 using the LET command.

MTB > <u>LET C3 = C2 − C1</u>

Finally, the TTEST command is used to perform the analysis. Because H_0 states that there is no change, $\mu_D = 0$. Thus, zero is the first argument. The second argument is C3 because this column contains the *D*-scores.

MTB > <u>TTEST 0 C3</u>

Table 20.9 shows the results of the analysis. Descriptive statistics are provided for the sample of *D*-scores as well as the obtained *t* value and its probability when H_0 is true.

ONE-TAILED TESTS

One-tailed (directional) tests may be performed on any of the preceding *t* tests by using the ALTERNATIVE subcommand. If the critical region is placed in the right-hand tail, then the subcommand should state ALTERNATIVE = +1. To place the critical region on the left side of the distribution, use ALTERNATIVE = −1.

LEARNING CHECK

1. Why is the POOLED subcommand used with TWOSAMPLE?

2. To do a repeated-measures *t* test, you must first calculate difference scores and store them in a column on the worksheet. (True or false?)

3. A subcommand ALTERNATIVE = −1 is used with a *t* test command. What does this subcommand do?

ANSWERS

1. TWOSAMPLE performs an independent-measures *t* test. The POOLED subcommand computes the standard error with pooled variance, the method recommended in this textbook.

2. True

3. A one-tailed test is used for the *t* test. Because −1 is used, the critical region is set in the left-hand tail of the *t* distribution.

20.6 ESTIMATION

Minitab can be used to construct confidence interval estimates for the population mean (μ) or population mean difference ($\mu_1 - \mu_2$, or μ_D). These methods were described in Chapter 12.

ESTIMATION WITH z-SCORES

When the value for the population standard deviation is known, estimation is performed with a z-score. The Minitab command for this purpose is ZINTERVAL. For example, suppose we know that a population of scores is normally distributed and has a standard deviation of $\sigma = 6$. A sample of $n = 9$ individuals is selected from this population; their scores are as follows:

sample data: 17   14   18   17   10   14   19   12   14

We are going to construct the 90% confidence interval. The data are entered into the Minitab worksheet using SET.

MTB > SET C1
DATA > 17 14 18 17 10 14 19 12 14
DATA > END

The confidence interval is constructed using ZINTERVAL. The first argument in the command is the percent confidence for the interval. If you do not specify a confidence level, Minitab will automatically use 95% and select the appropriate z-score values. The next argument for this command is the value for the population standard deviation (SIGMA=). Finally, the column number or name that contains the data is specified. For this example, the entire command is entered as follows:

MTB > ZINTERVAL 90 SIGMA=6 C1

This command could be written as follows: ZINTERVAL 90 6 C1. The SIGMA= is not necessary and is used just for clarity.

The results are shown in Table 20.10. The printout specifies the assumed population standard deviation ($\sigma = 6$) and the sample size, mean, and standard deviation (STDEV). It also shows the standard error (SE MEAN), which was obtained by dividing σ by $\sqrt{n}$. Finally, it indicates that the 90% confidence interval for μ is between 11.71 and 18.29.

ESTIMATION WITH THE SINGLE-SAMPLE t STATISTIC

When the population standard deviation is not known, the sample standard deviation is used in its place, and estimated standard error is computed. Then the t statistic is used to construct a confidence interval. The Minitab command

---

Table 20.10

A 90% confidence interval for μ was determined by ZINTERVAL. The population standard deviation is $\sigma = 6$.

```
THE ASSUMED SIGMA =6.00

           N      MEAN    STDEV   SE MEAN    90.0 PERCENT C.I.
C1         9     15.00    2.96     2.00    (  11.71,    18.29)
```

	N	MEAN	STDEV	SE MEAN	95.0 PERCENT C.I.
C1	9	70.00	3.24	1.08	(67.51, 72.49)

Table 20.11

The 95% confidence interval for μ was constructed using the command TINTERVAL. The value for the population standard deviation is not known.

TINTERVAL will perform these tasks. Consider the following sample data collected from an unknown population:

sample data: 75 70 73 68 64 72 69 71 68

Let's construct the 95% confidence interval for μ. The argument for TINTERVAL must specify the confidence level and the column number or name for the data. The following commands illustrate the data entry and use of TINTERVAL.

> MTB > <u>SET C1</u>
> DATA > <u>75 70 73 68 64 72 69 71 68</u>
> DATA > <u>END</u>
> MTB > <u>TINTERVAL 95 C1</u>

Note: The 95 is not necessary in TINTERVAL. When percent confidence is omitted from the command, it automatically uses 95%.

The printout is displayed in Table 20.11. It looks the same at the printout for ZINTERVAL (Table 20.10); however, in this case SE MEAN is the *estimated* standard error, which is computed by dividing the sample standard deviation, s, by $\sqrt{n}$.

ESTIMATION WITH THE INDEPENDENT-MEASURES *t* STATISTIC

A confidence interval for the mean difference between two populations, $\mu_1 - \mu_2$, is provided by the command TWOSAMPLE. This command was previously used to perform an independent-measures t test (Section 20.5). Along with the t test, this command also provides the 95% confidence interval for $\mu_1 - \mu_2$ (see Table 20.8). You may specify a different level of confidence in the command. For the independent-measures study on page 613, we could have specified

> MTB > <u>TWOSAMPLE 90 C1 C2;</u>
> SUBC > <u>POOLED.</u>

An independent-measures t test will be performed exactly as before (page 614); however, now the 90% confidence interval will be displayed in the printout. Note once again that we use the POOLED subcommand with TWOSAMPLE so that pooled variance is used in computing the standard error.

ESTIMATION WITH THE REPEATED-MEASURES *t* STATISTIC

For the repeated-measures study, we will construct an confidence interval for μ_D. This task is accomplished by the TINTERVAL command, only now we use data that consist of difference scores. In Section 20.5, we performed a t test for

Table 20.12

TINTERVAL was used to create the 80% confidence interval for μ_D.

	N	MEAN	STDEV	SE MEAN	80.0 PERCENT C.I.
C3	5	-3.200	1.924	0.860	(-4.519, -1.881)

a repeated-measures study (page 614). Now let's construct the 80% confidence interval for μ_D. First the data were entered using READ. Next, difference scores were computed for each subject using LET and stored in C3. These steps are shown on pages 614–615. Finally, TINTERVAL is used to construct the confidence interval.

> MTB > <u>TINTERVAL 80 C3</u>

Table 20.12 shows the printout. Remember, this printout depicts an analysis of D-scores. Thus, MEAN is $\overline{D}$, STDEV is the standard deviation of D-scores, and SE MEAN is the standard error of $\overline{D}$, $s_{\overline{D}}$. Finally, the 80% confidence interval for μ_D is provided.

LEARNING CHECK   **1.** Describe what the following commands do.

> MTB > <u>ZINTERVAL 80 15 'IQ'</u>
> MTB > <u>TINTERVAL 'WEIGHT'</u>

2. What command will provide a confidence interval estimate for $\mu_1 - \mu_2$?

3. List the steps and commands, including data entry, for constructing a confidence interval for μ_D.

ANSWERS   **1.** The first command constructs the 80% confidence interval for a variable named IQ. The population standard deviation is $\sigma = 15$ and z-scores are used for the estimate. The second command constructs the 95% confidence interval for a variable named WEIGHT. The t statistic is used for the estimate because the population standard deviation is not known.

2. TWOSAMPLE is used for this estimate. The POOLED subcommand should be used.

3. The scores for each subject are entered into two columns using READ. Difference scores are computed and placed into a third column with LET. Finally, TINTERVAL is used to construct the confidence interval for the D-scores.

20.7 ANALYSIS OF VARIANCE (ANOVA)

Minitab can perform an analysis of variance (ANOVA) for an independent-measures study (Chapter 13), a repeated-measures study (Chapter 14), and a two-factor experiment (Chapter 15). Each type of analysis uses a different

Minitab command with its own command structure, as illustrated in the following examples.

INDEPENDENT-MEASURES (SINGLE-FACTOR) ANOVA

A single-factor ANOVA (Chapter 13) can be performed with either AOVONE-WAY or ONEWAY. The difference between these two commands is in how the data must be organized in the worksheet. For AOVONEWAY, each treatment group has its own column of data. If, for example, there are k = 4 treatments, enter the data from each treatment into columns C1 through C4. On the other hand, ONEWAY places all the data in one column, say C1. A second column would contain the corresponding group number for each score. We demonstrate the use of both commands with the data from Example 13.1:

| | DATA FROM EXAMPLE 13.1 | | |
PLACEBO	DRUG A	DRUG B	DRUG C
0	0	3	8
0	1	4	5
3	2	5	5

For AOVONEWAY, the data from Example 13.1 are entered into four separate columns, each column containing the data of one treatment group. We demonstrate this with the SET command.

```
MTB  > SET C1
DATA > 0 0 3
DATA > END
MTB  > SET C2
DATA > 0 1 2
DATA > END
MTB  > SET C3
DATA > 3 4 5
DATA > END
MTB  > SET C4
DATA > 8 5 5
DATA > END
```

The ANOVA is performed by using the AOVONEWAY command and specifying the column numbers that contain the data.

```
MTB > AOVONEWAY C1–C4
```

The results of the analysis are summarized in Table 20.13. It provides the ANOVA summary table, descriptive statistics, and 95% confidence interval for each treatment group.

For ONEWAY, all the data are entered into one column. A second column contains the group identification number (for example, 1, 2, 3, . . . , k) for

Table 20.13

The results for the AOVONEWAY command using the data from Example 13.1. ONEWAY will produce the same output.

```
ANALYSIS OF VARIANCE
SOURCE     DF       SS        MS        F        p
FACTOR      3     54.00     18.00     9.00     0.006
ERROR       8     16.00      2.00
TOTAL      11     70.00
                                      INDIVIDUAL 95 PCT CI'S FOR MEAN
                                      BASED ON POOLED STDEV
  LEVEL      N      MEAN     STDEV   ----+---------+---------+---------+---
C1           3     1.000     1.732  (---------*---------)
C2           3     1.000     1.000  (---------*---------)
C3           3     4.000     1.000                 (---------*---------)
C4           3     6.000     1.732                        (---------*---------)
                                      ----+---------+---------+---------+---
POOLED STDEV =     1.414             0.0       2.5       5.0       7.5
```

each score in the first column. First, we enter the data with the READ command. The scores are placed in C1 and the group numbers, in C2.

> MTB > READ C1 C2
> DATA > 0 1
> DATA > 0 1
> DATA > 3 1
> DATA > 0 2
> DATA > 1 2
> DATA > 2 2
> DATA > 3 3
> DATA > 4 3
> DATA > 5 3
> DATA > 8 4
> DATA > 5 4
> DATA > 5 4
> DATA > END

Now the ONEWAY command can be used for these data. Its argument first specifies the column that contains the data and then the column with the group identifiers.

> MTB > ONEWAY C1 C2

The results obtained with ONEWAY are identical to those of AOVONEWAY (Table 20.13).

REPEATED-MEASURES ANOVA

ANOVA for a repeated-measures study (Chapter 14) can be accomplished using the Minitab command ANOVA. This command is versatile. It can perform analyses on very complex experimental designs, often called *mixed designs* because they contain both repeated-measures and independent-measures factors in the same experiment. Although these experimental designs are beyond the scope of this text, the ANOVA command is also useful for performing a single-factor, repeated-measures analysis. We will use the data from Example 14.1 (Table 14.2, page 402) to demonstrate the use of this command:

SUBJECT	DATA FROM EXAMPLE 14.1			
	BEFORE TREATMENT	ONE WEEK AFTER	ONE MONTH AFTER	SIX MONTHS AFTER
A	8	2	1	1
B	4	1	1	0
C	6	2	0	2
D	8	3	4	1

For the repeated-measures analysis, we use one column to identify the subjects (1, 2, 3, . . . , n) and a second column to identify the level of the repeated-measures factor (1, 2, 3, . . . , k). The third column contains the scores for the dependent variable. For example, the data for the first subject would be entered into the first three columns as follows:

```
MTB  > READ C1—C3
DATA > 1 1 8
DATA > 1 2 2
DATA > 1 3 1
DATA > 1 4 1
```

Notice that subject A is identified by 1 in C1, the levels of the factor are coded in C2 (before treatment level is 1, one week after is 2, and so on), and the scores (dependent variable) are placed in C3. Thus, each subject will have four DATA lines because four measurements were taken ($k = 4$). The remaining data are entered as follows:

```
DATA > 2 1 4
DATA > 2 2 1
DATA > 2 3 1
DATA > 2 4 0
DATA > 3 1 6
DATA > 3 2 2
DATA > 3 3 0
DATA > 3 4 2
DATA > 4 1 8
DATA > 4 2 3
DATA > 4 3 4
DATA > 4 4 1
DATA > END
```

For convenience, we will name these columns S for subject, T for time tested, and Y for the dependent variable.

Table 20.14

The printout for a repeated-measures analysis of variance. The command ANOVA was used for the data from Example 14.1.

```
Factor      Type Levels Values
T           fixed     4    1      2      3      4
S           fixed     4    1      2      3      4

Analysis of Variance for Y

Source    DF         SS        MS       F      P
T          3     77.000    25.667   21.00  0.000
S          3     13.000     4.333    3.55  0.061
Error      9     11.000     1.222
Total     15    101.000
```

MTB > NAME C1='S' C2='T' C3='Y'

The argument for the ANOVA command provides a specification of the experimental design. For a repeated-measures ANOVA, it has the following form:

$$\text{dependent variable} \atop \text{column or name} = {\text{factor column} \atop \text{or name}} \quad {\text{subject column} \atop \text{or name}}$$

Thus, the analysis for Example 14.1 is initiated as follows:

MTB > ANOVA Y = T S

Note the variable names in the argument of this command do not need to be placed in single quotes. The printout of the analysis for Example 14.1 is shown in Table 20.14. The ANOVA summary table is similar to Table 14.3 (page 405). Under "Source" it lists the effect of factor T (time of testing), S (variability between subjects), error variability, and total variability. The table also provides an F ratio for between-subjects (S), something that we ordinarily do not report. It measures whether or not there are significant differences among the subjects.

TWO-FACTOR ANALYSIS OF VARIANCE

The command TWOWAY is used to perform a two-factor analysis of variance. The argument for this command specifies three columns (or column names). One column contains codes to indicate the levels of factor A (1, 2, 3, . . . , a). A second column specifies levels for factor B (1, 2, 3, . . . , b). Finally, a third column contains the data (scores) for the dependent variable. We will demonstrate this analysis with the data in Table 15.3 (page 431), which are reproduced here.

DATA FROM TABLE 15.3

FACTOR B

		B_1					B_2					B_3			
FACTOR A	A_1	1	6	1	1	1	7	7	11	4	6	3	1	1	6	4
	A_2	0	3	7	5	5	0	0	0	5	0	0	2	0	0	3

We enter the data using READ. C1 will contain codes for levels of factor A (1 or 2), C2 will have codes for factor B (1, 2, or 3), and C3 will contain the scores.

```
MTB  > READ C1–C3
DATA > 1 1 1
DATA > 1 1 6
DATA > 1 1 1
DATA > 1 1 1
DATA > 1 1 1
DATA > 1 2 7
DATA > 1 2 7
DATA > 1 2 11
DATA > 1 2 4
DATA > 1 2 6
DATA > 1 3 3
DATA > 1 3 1
DATA > 1 3 1
DATA > 1 3 6
DATA > 1 3 4
DATA > 2 1 0
DATA > 2 1 3
DATA > 2 1 7
DATA > 2 1 5
DATA > 2 1 5
DATA > 2 2 0
DATA > 2 2 0
DATA > 2 2 0
DATA > 2 2 5
DATA > 2 2 0
DATA > 2 3 0
DATA > 2 3 2
DATA > 2 3 0
DATA > 2 3 0
DATA > 2 3 3
DATA > END
```

The analysis is done with TWOWAY. The argument first specifies the column that contains the data and then the columns for factors A and B, respectively. We illustrate its use, along with naming the columns.

```
MTB > NAME C1='A' C2='B'
MTB > TWOWAY C3 'A' 'B'
```

Table 20.15 shows the printout for TWOWAY. Note that the ANOVA summary table does not provide the F-ratios. These you will have to compute from the MS values in the table. See Chapter 15 if you need a review of computing F-ratios (pages 437–438).

Table 20.15

TWOWAY was used to perform a two-factor analysis of variance for the data from Table 15.3.

```
ANALYSIS OF VARIANCE  C3

SOURCE          DF        SS        MS
A                1     30.00     30.00
B                2     20.00     10.00
INTERACTION      2     80.00     40.00
ERROR           24    120.00      5.00
TOTAL           29    250.00
```

You can obtain means for each *AB* cell by using TABLE followed by the subcommand MEAN. The argument for the TABLE command specifies the columns that contain the codes for factor levels. The MEAN subcommand indicates the column that stores the scores for the dependent variable. For this example, we would enter the following:

> MTB > <u>TABLE 'A' 'B';</u>
> SUBC > <u>MEAN C3.</u>

The printout of cell means is shown in Table 20.16.

LEARNING CHECK

1. What is the fundamental difference between AOVONEWAY and ONE-WAY in conducting analysis of variance?

2. Which of the following commands is used to perform analysis of variance for a repeated-measures study?
   a. AOVONEWAY
   b. ANOVA
   c. TWOWAY
   d. REPEAT

3. How are data entered into the worksheet for a two-factor analysis of variance?

4. How are cell means obtained for a two-factor experiment?

ANSWERS

1. For AOVONEWAY, the data from each treatment group are entered in their own columns. For ONEWAY, one column contains all the data from the study and a second column contains the group identification numbers.

2. b

Table 20.16

Cell means for the two-factor analysis of variance were obtained with the command TABLE and subcommand MEAN. Row and column means are labeled ALL.

```
ROWS: A      COLUMNS: B

           1        2        3       ALL

  1     2.0000   7.0000   3.0000   4.0000
  2     4.0000   1.0000   1.0000   2.0000
ALL     3.0000   4.0000   2.0000   3.0000

   CELL CONTENTS --
            C3:MEAN
```

3. Using READ, each subject's score is entered into one column, level of factor *A* (1, 2, 3, . . . a) into a second column, and level of factor *B* (1, 2, 3, . . . b) into a third column.

4. The command TABLE is used with the subcommand MEAN.

20.8 CORRELATION AND REGRESSION

The CORRELATION command is demonstrated in Table 20.1 at the beginning of the chapter. In the argument for this command, you specify the columns (C1, C2 for example) or variable names for which the correlation is to be calculated. In Example 20.1, the command was stated as follows:

MTB > <u>CORRELATION OF 'HOURS' VS 'SCORE'</u>

It could have been stated more simply as

MTB > <u>CORRELATION 'HOURS' 'SCORE'</u>

or

MTB > <u>CORR C1 C2</u>

If you specify more than two variables in the CORRELATION command, Minitab will provide correlations for all possible variable pairings.

Regression is accomplished with the REGRESS command. For the data in Example 20.1, the command could be stated as

MTB > <u>REGRESS C2 1 C1</u>

or

MTB > <u>REGRESS 'SCORE' 1 'HOURS'</u>

In this command, the column number or name for the *Y* variable is specified first in the argument (SCORE in this case). Next the number of predictor variables is specified. For simple linear regression, this value always will be 1. Finally, the *X* variable (or predictor) is specified. The results of the regression analysis are shown in Table 20.17. Notice that the results provide the regression equation. It also shows the standard error of estimate ($s = 2.707$) and r^2 (expressed as a percent). The ANOVA summary allows one to determine how much variability is explained by the regression line and how much variability is due to error. The *F*-ratio tests the significance of the regression line.

LEARNING CHECK **1.** For the command

REGRESS 'GPA' 1 'SCORE'

which is the predictor and which is the *Y* variable?

Table 20.17

Minitab results for regression using REGRESS. The data are from Example 20.1.

```
The regression equation is
SCORE = 6.29 + 1.36 HOURS

Predictor       Coef       Stdev      t-ratio         p
Constant       6.292       1.281         4.91      0.000
HOURS         1.3641      0.2043         6.68      0.000

s = 2.707      R-sq = 66.0%       R-sq(adj) = 64.5%

Analysis of Variance

SOURCE         DF            SS           MS          F         p
Regression      1         326.46       326.46      44.56     0.000
Error          23         168.50         7.33
Total          24         494.96

Unusual Observations
Obs.    HOURS     SCORE        Fit  Stdev.Fit   Residual    St.Resid
 14       3.0    17.000     10.384      0.770      6.616       2.55R
 25       5.0     6.000     13.112      0.559     -7.112      -2.69R

R denotes an obs. with a large st. resid.
```

2. What will the following commands do?

> CORR C1 C2 C3 C4
> CORRELATION 'AGE' 'WEIGHT'

ANSWERS   **1.** SCORE is the predictor variable and GPA is the *Y* variable.

2. The first command will find the correlation between every pair of variables in columns C1, C2, C3, and C4. The second command finds the correlation between variables named AGE and WEIGHT.

20.9   NONPARAMETRIC STATISTICAL TESTS

Minitab will perform a variety of nonparametric tests. Remember, these are often used when assumptions for parametric tests have been violated or the scale of measurement necessitates the use of a nonparametric test. We describe Minitab commands for several useful nonparametric tests.

CHI-SQUARE TEST FOR INDEPENDENCE   The chi-square test for independence (Chapter 17) is performed by using CHISQUARE. The observed frequencies from a classification matrix are first entered in the worksheet with READ. Then CHISQUARE specifies the columns in which the observed frequencies are found. Minitab calculates the expected frequencies and the chi-square statistic. The following commands demonstrate this analysis using the data from Example 17.2 (Table 17.7, page 528).

> MTB > READ C1–C3
> DATA > 11 16 4

Table 20.18

The results of a chi-square test of independence for the data in Example 17.2. The CHISQUARE command was used to perform the analysis.

```
Expected counts are printed below observed counts
              C1        C2        C3     Total
    1         11        16         4        31
            7.75     15.50      7.75

    2          2        10         9        21
            5.25     10.50      5.25

Total         13        26        13        52

ChiSq =   1.363 +   0.016 +   1.815 +
          2.012 +   0.024 +   2.679 = 7.908
df = 2
```

DATA > 2 10 9

DATA > END

MTB > CHISQUARE C1–C3

Table 20.18 shows the results provided by Minitab. It displays the observed and expected frequencies for each cell, the computation of chi-square, and the value for *df*.

THE MANN-WHITNEY TEST

The Mann-Whitney U (Chapter 19) is used to evaluate the difference between two treatments (or populations) using two independent samples. Recall that the test requires the data from both samples to be rank-ordered. The Minitab command MANN-WHITNEY will perform the entire analysis (including ranking). We demonstrate this analysis with the data from Example 19.2 (page 568). The manual dexterity scores for boys and girls in that example are as follows:

DATA FROM EXAMPLE 19.2

Boys: 23   18   29   42   21

Girls: 37   56   39   34   26   104   48   25

First, the two samples of data are entered into separate columns. We use SET rather than READ because the sample sizes (n) are unequal.

MTB > SET C1

DATA > 23 18 29 42 21

DATA > END

MTB > SET C2

DATA > 37 56 39 34 26 104 48 25

DATA > END

Next, we use the MANN-WHITNEY command. Its argument specifies the column numbers or names for the data.

MTB > MANN-WHITNEY C1 C2

Table 20.19

The printout for a Mann-Whitney test. The MANN-WHITNEY command was used for the data from Example 19.2.

```
Mann-Whitney Confidence Interval and Test

C1           N =   5     Median =        23.00
C2           N =   8     Median =        38.00
Point estimate for ETA1-ETA2 is         -14.00
95.2 pct c.i. for ETA1-ETA2 is (-35.00,3.01)
W = 22.0
Test of ETA1 = ETA2  vs.  ETA1 n.e. ETA2 is significant at 0.0673

Cannot reject at alpha = 0.05
```

The printout for this analysis is shown in Table 20.19. It shows the sample size and median for both groups, a point estimate and confidence interval for the population median difference, and the test statistic. The test statistic for this analysis is not the U statistic that was used in Chapter 20. This Mann-Whitney analysis provides a test statistic known as W. In this instance, $W = 22$. Note that this actually is the sum of the ranks for group A, ΣR_A, which was used in Example 19.2 to obtain the value for U. The printout also notes the difference between groups "is significant at 0.0673." This value is the probability of committing a Type I error if the null hypothesis is rejected. However, with the alpha level appropriately set at .05, the difference between groups is not significant.

THE WILCOXON SIGNED-RANKS TEST

The Wilcoxon signed-ranks test (Chapter 19) is used to evaluate the difference between two treatments for a repeated-measures study. This test is based on ranks of the difference scores. The WTEST command will rank difference scores (discarding zero differences) and perform the Wilcoxon test. The Wilcoxon test is demonstrated with the data from Example 19.5 (page 575).

DATA FROM EXAMPLE 19.5
Differences scores: 0   0   −1   −4   +7   +8   +11   +11   +16   +19

The first step is entering the difference scores into the Minitab worksheet.

> MTB > <u>SET C1</u>
> DATA > <u>0 0 −1 −4 7 8 11 11 16 19</u>
> DATA > <u>END</u>

If you enter the raw scores for each subject using READ, then you could have Minitab calculate the difference scores by using LET. This was demonstrated for the repeated-measures *t* test (Section 20.5, page 614).

Then, we initiate the Wilcoxon test with WTEST, specifying the column that contains the difference scores.

> MTB > <u>WTEST C1</u>

The results are displayed in the Minitab printout (Table 20.20). Notice that the printout indicates a sample of $n = 10$ individuals, with $n = 8$ used for the test. The lower n for the test occurred because the two zero difference scores

```
TEST OF MEDIAN = 0.000000 VERSUS MEDIAN N.E. 0.000000

              N FOR    WILCOXON              ESTIMATED
         N    TEST     STATISTIC   P-VALUE    MEDIAN
C1       10    8        33.0        0.042      7.000
```

Table 20.20

The results of a Wilcoxon test for the data from Example 19.5. The Minitab command WTEST was used.

were discarded. The Wilcoxon statistic reported in the printout is not the Wilcoxon T but the sum of the ranks for positive differences, ΣR_+. The probability (P-VALUE) for this statistic is less than the alpha level of .05. Thus, the null hypothesis is rejected, and we can conclude that there is a significant effect.

LEARNING CHECK

1. For the chi-square test for independence, all observed frequencies are first entered into a single column using SET. (True or false?)

2. The command MANN-WHITNEY will not rank your data. You must first enter ranks into a column and specify that column in the argument for the command. (True or false?)

3. For the Wilcoxon test, you must first compute difference scores for the raw data and enter them into the worksheet. Then you use the command WTEST on the difference scores. (True or false?)

ANSWERS

1. False. Observed frequencies are entered into more than one column using READ.

2. False. MANN-WHITNEY performs the ranking of raw scores.

3. True

SOME FINAL NOTES

This chapter has summarized the fundamentals of Minitab, focusing on basic procedures that are relevant to the topics covered in this textbook. However, Minitab is capable of much more, and there are many other commands and subcommands in this software. For those that wish to delve into Minitab's full capabilities, we refer you to the *Minitab Reference Manual*, Release 7 (1989), published by Minitab, Inc.

As of this writing, Release 8 of Minitab is in its final stages of preparation. The Release 7 commands and procedures will work for the new version as well. However, the PC version (DOS compatible) of the new release will also have features that facilitate its use. These features include pull-down menus for command selection and windows that display command options and the variables in your worksheet. Thus, you will not have to remember command syntax, subcommand names, variable names, or column numbers. You will be able to select your commands, options, and variables from the keyboard or with a mouse. Experienced Release 7 users will still be able to enter commands following MTB prompts, bypassing the menus entirely.

KEY TERMS

worksheet	command	SUBC> prompt	ASCII file
column	argument	DATA> prompt	on-screen editor
row	MTB> prompt	saved worksheet	cursor
constant	subcommand		

LIST OF COMMANDS

DATA MANAGEMENT
SET
END
READ
PRINT
SAVE
RETRIEVE
WRITE
NAME
LET

GRAPHS AND DESCRIPTIVE STATISTICS
HISTOGRAM
DOTPLOT
PLOT
HISTOGRAM
DESCRIBE
STEM-AND-LEAF
TABLE

MEASURES OF RELATIONSHIP
CORRELATION
REGRESS

HYPOTHESIS TESTS
TTEST
TWOSAMPLE
AOVONEWAY
ONEWAY
ANOVA
TWOWAY

PRINTER AND OUTPUT COMMANDS
PAPER
NEWPAGE
NOPAPER
OUTFILE

MISCELLANEOUS
HELP
STOP
INFO

ESTIMATION
ZINTERVAL
TINTERVAL

NONPARAMETRIC TESTS
CHISQUARE
MANN-WHITNEY
WTEST

PROBLEMS

Data Set 1

The following data set consists of attitude scores for an opinion survey given to college students. Problems 1–5 pertain to these data.

Attitude Scores

9	73	62	52	14	46
31	26	74	61	13	5
79	58	16	62	7	55
77	43	30	18	23	11
42	78	10	66	72	25

1. For Data Set 1, construct a histogram and a dotplot.

2. Obtain descriptive statistics (such as the mean, median, trimmed mean, standard deviation, and so on) for the distribution of attitude scores.

3. Construct a stem-and-leaf display.

4. The general population has an average attitude score of $\mu = 52$. Use a t test to determine whether or not the college students differ significantly from the general population.

5. Construct the 90% confidence interval for the population mean for college students.

Data Set 2

For each subject in this study, blood alcohol concentration (BAC) and reaction time (RT) were measured. Problems 6–9 refer to these data.

BAC	RT
.07	235
.00	205
.10	250
.15	244
.05	230
.14	263
.12	250
.00	190
.06	228
.05	233
.03	211
.08	233
.10	250
.04	214

6. Obtain descriptive statistics for BAC and RT.

7. Construct a scatterplot for these data. Place BAC on the X-axis.

8. Compute the correlation for these variables.

9. Use regression to obtain the equation for the best fit line, with blood alcohol concentration (BAC) as the predictor for reaction time (RT).

Data Set 3

The following data are from an independent measures study. These data are used in problems 10–13.

TREATMENT 1			TREATMENT 2		
62	45	52	42	12	37
63	63	59	28	21	33
58	68	38	51	14	26
66	67	61	15	47	18
59	60	68	33	22	28
53	51	67	39	56	19
30	48		20	16	

10. Provide descriptive statistics for both treatments in Data Set 3.

11. Construct dotplots for both groups.

12. Perform a t test to determine if there is a difference between the two treatments. Use pooled variance in the analysis.

13. Conduct a Mann-Whitney test on these data.

Data Set 4

These data are from a repeated-measures study in which subjects were tested before and after receiving a treatment. Problems 14–18 use these data.

BEFORE	AFTER
46	74
52	58
56	90
35	64
53	39
71	65
50	75
72	85
53	79
39	82
88	90
61	77

14. Construct separate histograms for the BEFORE and AFTER data.

15. Obtain descriptive statistics for data taken before and after treatment.

16. Use a repeated-measures t test to determine if there is a significant change.

17. Construct the 80% confidence interval for μ_D.

18. Perform the Wilcoxon test on data set 4.

Data Set 5

In this study, four independent samples of subjects were used to test the effect of several treatments. These data are used for problems 19–21.

CONTROL	TREATMENT A	TREATMENT B	TREATMENT C
12	15	15	34
20	19	6	21
15	24	9	17
17	28	19	15
15	26	5	32
9	14	11	38
10	30	4	33
19	26	6	20
15	10	20	34
18	22	7	24

19. Provide descriptive statistics for each group.

20. Construct a dotplot for each group.

21. Perform an analysis of variance to see if there is a significant effect.

Data Set 6

These are data from a two-factor experiment. These data are used in problems 22 and 23.

FACTOR B

		B_1	B_2
FACTOR A	A_1	3, 5, 6 3, 4, 8	9, 8, 11 12, 14, 10
	A_2	4, 9, 7 9, 6, 8	8, 8, 6 9, 8, 11
	A_3	10, 11, 8 14, 7, 9	5, 4, 3 4, 3, 1
	A_4	15, 13, 12 10, 16, 15	1, 2, 2 4, 1, 3

22. Perform a two-factor analysis of variance for data set 6.

23. Create a table of cell means.

Data Set 7

In a repeated-measures study, subjects are tested once before treatment to establish a baseline, then tested one week and six months following treatment. Problem 24 refers to data set 7.

SUBJECT	BEFORE TREATMENT	ONE WEEK AFTER	SIX MONTHS AFTER
A	16	10	9
B	10	12	6
C	11	9	8
D	17	9	5
E	14	10	3
F	11	7	3

24. Perform a repeated-measures analysis of variance for data set 7 to determine if there was an effect of the treatment.

Data Set 8

Children are given a test to determine if they are introverted or extraverted. For this sample, birth order (first born, middle born, last born) is also noted. This results in the following observed frequencies of these classifications.

BIRTH ORDER

	First Born	Middle Born	Last Born
Introvert	11	4	2
Extravert	4	5	10

25. Is there a relationship between birth order and whether a person is introverted or extraverted? Perform a chi-square test of independence.

APPENDIX A   BASIC MATHEMATICS REVIEW

PREVIEW

This appendix reviews some of the basic math skills that are necessary for the statistical calculations presented in this book. Many students already will know some or all of this material. Others will need to do extensive work and review. To help you assess your own skills, we are including a skills assessment exam here. You should allow approximately 30 minutes to complete the test. When you finish, grade your test using the answer key on page A-19.

Notice that the test is divided into four sections. If you miss more than three questions in any section of the test, you probably need help in that area. Turn to the section of this appendix that corresponds to your problem area. In each section, you will find a general review, some examples, and some additional practice problems. After reviewing the appropriate section and doing the practice problems, turn to the end of the appendix. You will find another version of the skills assessment exam. If you still miss more than three questions in any section of the exam, continue studying. Get assistance from an instructor or tutor if necessary. At the end of this appendix is a list of recommended books for individuals who need a more extensive review than can be provided here. We must stress that mastering this material now will make the rest of the course much easier.

SKILLS ASSESSMENT EXAM

SECTION 1

(corresponding to Sections A.1 and A.2 of this appendix)

1. The fraction $\frac{3}{4}$ corresponds to a percentage of _____.
2. Express 30% as a fraction.
3. Convert $\frac{12}{40}$ to a decimal.
4. $\frac{2}{13} + \frac{8}{13} = ?$
5. $1.375 + 0.25 = ?$
6. $\frac{2}{5} \times \frac{1}{4} = ?$
7. $\frac{1}{8} + \frac{2}{3} = ?$
8. $3.5 \times 0.4 = ?$
9. $\frac{1}{5} \div \frac{3}{4} = ?$
10. $3.75/0.5 = ?$

11. In a group of 80 students, 20% are psychology majors. How many psychology majors are in this group?
12. A company reports that two-fifths of its employees are women. If there are 90 employees, how many are women?

SECTION 2

(corresponding to Section A.3 of this appendix)

1. $3 + (-2) + (-1) + 4 = ?$
2. $6 - (-2) = ?$
3. $-2 - (-4) = ?$
4. $6 + (-1) - 3 - (-2) - (-5) = ?$
5. $4 \times (-3) = ?$
6. $-2 \times (-6) = ?$

7. $-3 \times 5 = ?$

8. $-2 \times (-4) \times (-3) = ?$

9. $12 \div (-3) = ?$

10. $-18 \div (-6) = ?$

11. $-16 \div 8 = ?$

12. $-100 \div (-4) = ?$

SECTION 3

(corresponding to Section A.4 of this appendix)

For each equation, find the value of X.

1. $X + 6 = 13$

2. $X - 14 = 15$

3. $5 = X - 4$

4. $3X = 12$

5. $72 = 3X$

6. $X/5 = 3$

7. $10 = X/8$

8. $3X + 5 = -4$

9. $24 = 2X + 2$

10. $(X + 3)/2 = 14$

11. $(X - 5)/3 = 2$

12. $17 = 4X - 11$

SECTION 4

(corresponding to Section A.5 of this appendix)

1. $4^3 = ?$

2. $\sqrt{25 - 9} = ?$

3. If $X = 2$ and $Y = 3$, then $XY^3 = ?$

4. If $X = 2$ and $Y = 3$, then $(X + Y)^2 = ?$

5. If $a = 3$ and $b = 2$, then $a^2 + b^2 = ?$

6. $-3^3 = ?$

7. $-4^4 = ?$

8. $\sqrt{4} \times 4 = ?$

9. $36/\sqrt{9} = ?$

10. $(9 + 2)^2 = ?$

11. $5^2 + 2^3 = ?$

12. If $a = 3$ and $b = -1$, then $a^2b^3 = ?$

The answers to the skills assessment exam are at the end of the appendix (page A-19).

A.1 SYMBOLS AND NOTATION

Table A.1 presents the basic mathematical symbols that you should know, and it provides examples of their use. Statistical symbols and notation will be introduced and explained throughout this book as they are needed. Notation for exponents and square roots is covered separately at the end of this appendix.

Parentheses are a useful notation because they specify and control the order of computations. Everything inside the parentheses is calculated first. For example,

$$(5 + 3) \times 2 = 8 \times 2 = 16$$

Changing the placement of the parentheses also changes the order of calculations. For example,

$$5 + (3 \times 2) = 5 + 6 = 11$$

Table A.1

SYMBOL	MEANING	EXAMPLE
$+$	Addition	$5 + 7 = 12$
$-$	Subtraction	$8 - 3 = 5$
$\times$, ( )	Multiplication	$3 \times 9 = 27$, $3(9) = 27$
$\div$, /	Division	$15 \div 3 = 5$, $15/3 = 5$, $\frac{15}{3} = 5$
$>$	Greater than	$20 > 10$
$<$	Less than	$7 < 11$
$\neq$	Not equal to	$5 \neq 6$

A.2 PROPORTIONS: FRACTIONS, DECIMALS, AND PERCENTAGES

A proportion is a part of a whole and can be expressed as a fraction, or a decimal or a percentage. For example, in a class of 40 students, only 3 failed the final exam.

The proportion of the class that failed can be expressed as a fraction,

$$\text{fraction} = \tfrac{3}{40}$$

or as a decimal value,

$$\text{decimal} = 0.075$$

or a percentage,

$$\text{percentage} = 7.5\%$$

In a fraction, the bottom value (the denominator) indicates the number of equal pieces into which the whole is split. Here the "pie" is split into four equal pieces:

If the denominator has a larger value, say 8, then each piece of the whole pie is smaller:

A larger denominator indicates a smaller fraction of the whole.

The value on top of the fraction (the numerator) indicates how many pieces of the whole are being considered. Thus, the fraction $\tfrac{3}{4}$ indicates that the whole is split evenly into four pieces and that three of them are being used:

A fraction is simply a concise way of stating a proportion: "Three out of four" is equivalent to $\tfrac{3}{4}$. To convert the fraction to a decimal, you divide the numerator by the denominator:

$$\tfrac{3}{4} = 3 \div 4 = 0.75$$

To convert the decimal to a percentage, simply multiply by 100 and place a percent sign (%) after the answer:

$$0.75 \times 100 = 75\%$$

The U.S. money system is a convenient way of illustrating the relationship between fractions and decimals. "One quarter," for example, is one-fourth $\left(\frac{1}{4}\right)$ of a dollar, and its decimal equivalent is 0.25. Other familiar equivalencies are as follows:

	DIME	QUARTER	50-CENT PIECE	75 CENTS
Fraction	$\frac{1}{10}$	$\frac{1}{4}$	$\frac{1}{2}$	$\frac{3}{4}$
Decimal	0.10	0.25	0.50	0.75
Percentage	10%	25%	50%	75%

FRACTIONS

1. Finding Equivalent Fractions The same proportional value can be expressed by many equivalent fractions. For example,

$$\frac{1}{2} = \frac{2}{4} = \frac{10}{20} = \frac{50}{100}$$

To create equivalent fractions, you can multiply the numerator and denominator by the same value. As long as both the numerator and denominator of the fraction are multiplied by the same value, the new fraction will be equivalent to the original. For example,

$$\frac{3}{10} = \frac{9}{30}$$

because both the numerator and denominator of the original fraction have been multiplied by 3. Dividing the numerator and denominator of a fraction by the same value will also result in an equivalent fraction. By using division, you can reduce a fraction to a simpler form. For example,

$$\frac{40}{100} = \frac{2}{5}$$

because both the numerator and denominator of the original fraction have been divided by 20.

You can use these rules to find specific equivalent fractions. For example, find the fraction that has a denominator of 100 and is equivalent to $\frac{3}{4}$. That is,

$$\frac{3}{4} = \frac{?}{100}$$

Notice that the denominator of the original fraction must be multiplied by 25 to produce the denominator of the desired fraction. For the two fractions to be equal, both the numerator and the denominator must be multiplied by the same number. Therefore, we also multiply the top of the original fraction by 25 and obtain

$$\frac{3 \times 25}{4 \times 25} = \frac{75}{100}$$

2. Multiplying Fractions To multiply two fractions, you first multiply the numerators and then multiply the denominators. For example,

$$\frac{3}{4} \times \frac{5}{7} = \frac{3 \times 5}{4 \times 7} = \frac{15}{28}$$

3. Dividing Fractions To divide one fraction by another, you invert the second fraction and then multiply. For example,

$$\frac{1}{2} \div \frac{1}{4} = \frac{1}{2} \times \frac{4}{1} = \frac{1 \times 4}{2 \times 1} = \frac{4}{2}$$

4. Adding and Subtracting Fractions Fractions must have the same denominator before you can add or subtract them. If the two fractions already have a common denominator, you simply add (or subtract as the case may be) *only* the values in the numerators. For example,

$$\frac{2}{5} + \frac{1}{5} = \frac{3}{5}$$

Suppose you divided a pie into five equal pieces (fifths). If you first ate two-fifths of the pie and then another one-fifth, the total amount eaten would be three-fifths of the pie:

If the two fractions do not have the same denominator, you must first find equivalent fractions with a common denominator before you can add or subtract. The product of the two denominators will always work as a common denominator for equivalent fractions (although it may not be the lowest common denominator). For example,

$$\frac{2}{3} + \frac{1}{10} = ?$$

Because these two fractions have different denominators, it is necessary to convert each into an equivalent fraction and find a common denominator. We will use $3 \times 10 = 30$ as the common denominator. Thus the equivalent fraction of each is

$$\frac{2}{3} = \frac{20}{30} \quad \text{and} \quad \frac{1}{10} = \frac{3}{30}$$

Now the two fractions can be added:

$$\frac{20}{30} + \frac{3}{30} = \frac{23}{30}$$

5. Comparing the Size of Fractions When comparing the size of two fractions with the same denominator, the larger fraction will have the larger numerator. For example,

$$\frac{5}{8} > \frac{3}{8}$$

The denominators are the same, so the whole is partitioned into pieces of the same size. Five of these pieces is more than three of them:

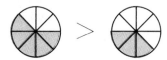

When two fractions have different denominators, you must first convert them to fractions with a common denominator to determine which is larger. Consider the following fractions:

$$\frac{3}{8} \quad \text{and} \quad \frac{7}{16}$$

If the numerator and denominator of $\frac{3}{8}$ are multiplied by 2, the resulting equivalent fraction will have a denominator of 16:

$$\frac{3}{8} = \frac{3 \times 2}{8 \times 2} = \frac{6}{16}$$

Now a comparison can be made between the two fractions:

$$\frac{6}{16} < \frac{7}{16}$$

Therefore,

$$\frac{3}{8} < \frac{7}{16}$$

DECIMALS

1. Converting Decimals to Fractions   Like a fraction, a decimal represents part of the whole. The first decimal place to the right of the decimal point indicates how many tenths are used. For example,

$$0.1 = \frac{1}{10} \qquad 0.7 = \frac{7}{10}$$

The next decimal place represents $\frac{1}{100}$, the next $\frac{1}{1000}$, the next $\frac{1}{10,000}$, and so on. To change a decimal to a fraction, just use the number without the decimal point for the numerator. Use the denominator that the last (on the right) decimal place represents. For example,

$$0.32 = \frac{32}{100}$$
$$0.5333 = \frac{5333}{10,000}$$
$$0.05 = \frac{5}{100}$$
$$0.001 = \frac{1}{1000}$$

2. Addition and Subtraction   To add and subtract decimals, the only rule is that you must keep the decimal points in a straight vertical line. For example,

$$
\begin{array}{r}
0.27 \\
+\ 1.326 \\
\hline
1.596
\end{array}
\qquad
\begin{array}{r}
3.595 \\
-\ 0.67 \\
\hline
2.925
\end{array}
$$

3. Multiplying Decimals To multiply two decimal values, you first multiply the two numbers ignoring the decimal points. Then you position the decimal point in the answer so that the number of digits to the right of the decimal point is equal to the total number of decimal places in the two numbers being multiplied. For example,

$$
\begin{array}{r}
1.73 \\
\times\ 0.251 \\
\hline
173 \\
865 \\
346 \\
\hline
0.43423
\end{array}
$$

(two decimal places)
(three decimal places)

(five decimal places)

$$
\begin{array}{r}
0.25 \\
\times\ 0.005 \\
\hline
125 \\
00 \\
00 \\
\hline
0.00125
\end{array}
$$

(two decimal places)
(three decimal places)

(five decimal places)

4. Dividing Decimals The simplest procedure for dividing decimals is based on the fact that dividing two numbers is identical to expressing them as a fraction:

$0.25 \div 1.6$ is identical to $\frac{0.25}{1.6}$

You now can multiply both the numerator and denominator of the fraction by 10, 100, 1000, or whatever number is necessary to remove the decimal places. Remember, multiplying both the numerator and denominator of a fraction by the *same* value will create an equivalent fraction. Therefore,

$$
\frac{0.25}{1.6} = \frac{0.25 \times 100}{1.6 \times 100} = \frac{25}{160}
$$

The result is a division problem without any decimal places in the two numbers.

PERCENTAGES

1. Converting a Percentage to a Fraction or Decimal To convert a percentage to a fraction, remove the percent sign, place the number in the numerator, and use 100 for the denominator. For example,

$52\% = \frac{52}{100}$ $\qquad$ $5\% = \frac{5}{100}$

To convert a percentage to a decimal, remove the percent sign and divide by 100, or simply move the decimal point two places to the left. For example,

$83\% = 83. = 0.83$

$14.5\% = 14.5 = 0.145$

$5\% = 5. = 0.05$

2. Arithmetic Operations with Percentages   There are situations when it is best to express percent values as decimals in order to perform certain arithmetic operations. For example, what is 45% of 60? This question may be stated as

$$45\% \times 60 = ?$$

The 45% should be converted to decimal form to find the solution to this question. Therefore,

$$0.45 \times 60 = 27$$

LEARNING CHECK

1. Convert $\frac{3}{25}$ to a decimal.

2. Convert $\frac{3}{8}$ to a percentage.

3. Next to each set of fractions, write "true" if they are equivalent and "false" if they are not:
   a. $\frac{3}{8} = \frac{9}{24}$ _____
   b. $\frac{7}{9} = \frac{17}{19}$ _____
   c. $\frac{2}{7} = \frac{4}{14}$ _____

4. Compute the following:
   a. $\frac{1}{6} \times \frac{7}{10}$ **b.** $\frac{7}{8} - \frac{1}{2}$ **c.** $\frac{9}{10} \div \frac{2}{3}$ **d.** $\frac{7}{22} + \frac{2}{3}$

5. Identify the larger fraction of each pair:
   a. $\frac{7}{10}, \frac{21}{100}$ **b.** $\frac{3}{4}, \frac{7}{12}$ **c.** $\frac{22}{3}, \frac{19}{3}$

6. Convert the following decimals into fractions:
   a. 0.012   **b.** 0.77   **c.** 0.005

7. $2.59 \times 0.015 = ?$

8. $1.8 \div 0.02 = ?$

9. What is 28% of 45?

ANSWERS   **1.** 0.12   **2.** 37.5%   **3. a.** True   **b.** False   **c.** True
4. a. $\frac{7}{60}$ **b.** $\frac{3}{8}$ **c.** $\frac{27}{20}$ **d.** $\frac{65}{66}$ **5. a.** $\frac{7}{10}$ **b.** $\frac{3}{4}$ **c.** $\frac{22}{3}$
6. a. $\frac{12}{1000}$ **b.** $\frac{77}{100}$ **c.** $\frac{5}{1000}$ **7.** 0.03885   **8.** 90   **9.** 12.6

A.3   NEGATIVE NUMBERS

Negative numbers are used to represent values less than zero. Negative numbers may occur when you are measuring the difference between two scores. For example, a researcher may want to evaluate the effectiveness of a propaganda film by measuring people's attitude with a test both before and after viewing the film:

	BEFORE	AFTER	AMOUNT OF CHANGE
Person A	23	27	+4
Person B	18	15	−3
Person C	21	16	−5

Notice that the negative sign provides information about the direction of the difference: a plus sign indicates an increase in value, and a minus sign indicates a decrease.

Because negative numbers are frequently encountered, you should be comfortable working with these values. This section reviews basic arithmetic operations using negative numbers. You should also note that any number without a sign (+ or −) is assumed to be positive.

1. Addition with Negative Numbers   When adding numbers that include negative values, simply interpret the negative sign as subtraction. For example,

$$3 + (-2) + 5 = 3 - 2 + 5 = 6$$

When adding a long string of numbers, it often is easier to add all the positive values to obtain the positive sum and then add all of the negative values to obtain the negative sum. Finally, you subtract the negative sum from the positive sum. For example,

$$-1 + 3 + (-4) + 3 + (-6) + (-2)$$

positive sum = 6   negative sum = 13

Answer: $6 - 13 = -7$

2. Subtraction with Negative Numbers   To subtract a negative number, change it to positive and add. For example,

$$4 - (-3) = 4 + 3 = 7$$

This rule is easier to understand if you think of subtraction as "taking away." In the preceding example, if you substitute $7 - 3$ in place of the original 4 (note that $7 - 3 = 4$), you obtain

$$4 - (-3)$$

$7 - 3 - (-3)$ (substitution of $7 - 3$ for 4)

$7 - 3$ "take away" -3 (-3 "take away" -3 is zero)

7 (7 is the remainder)

3. Multiplying and Dividing Negative Numbers   When the two numbers being multiplied (or divided) have the same sign, the result is a positive number. When the two numbers have different signs, the result is negative. For example,

$$3 \times (-2) = -6$$

$$-4 \times (-2) = +8$$

The first example is easy to explain by thinking of multiplication as repeated addition. In this case,

$$3 \times (-2) = (-2) + (-2) + (-2) = -6$$

You take three negative 2s, which result in a total of negative 6. In the second example, we are multiplying by a negative number. This amounts to repeated subtraction. That is,

$$-4 \times (-2) = -(-2) - (-2) - (-2) - (-2)$$
$$= 2 + 2 + 2 + 2 = 8$$

By using the same rule for both multiplication and division, we ensure that these two operations are compatible. For example,

$$-6 \div 3 = -2$$

which is compatible with

$$3 \times (-2) = -6$$

Also,

$$8 \div (-4) = -2$$

which is compatible with

$$-4 \times (-2) = +8$$

LEARNING CHECK

1. Complete the following calculations:
   a. $3 + (-8) + 5 + 7 + (-1) + (-3)$
   b. $5 - (-9) + 2 - (-3) - (-1)$
   c. $3 - 7 - (-21) + (-5) - (-9)$
   d. $4 - (-6) - 3 + 11 - 14$
   e. $9 + 8 - 2 - 1 - (-6)$
   f. $9 \times (-3)$
   g. $-7 \times (-4)$
   h. $-6 \times (-2) \times (-3)$
   i. $-12 \div (-3)$
   j. $18 \div (-6)$

ANSWERS

1. **a.** 3   **b.** 20   **c.** 21   **d.** 4   **e.** 20
   f. -27 **g.** 28   **h.** -36 **i.** 4   **j.** -3

A.4 BASIC ALGEBRA: SOLVING EQUATIONS

An equation is a mathematical statement that indicates two quantities are identical. For example,

$$12 = 8 + 4$$

Often an equation will contain an unknown (or variable) quantity that is identified with a letter or symbol rather than a number. For example,

$$12 = 8 + X$$

In this event, your task is to find the value of X that makes the equation "true," or balanced. For this example, an X value of 4 will make a true equation. Finding the value of X is usually called *solving the equation*.

To solve an equation, there are two points to be kept in mind:

1. Your goal is to have the unknown value *(X)* isolated on one side of the equation. This means that you need to remove all of the other numbers and symbols that appear on the same side of the equation as the X.

2. The equation will remain balanced provided you treat both sides exactly the same. For example, you could add 10 points to *both* sides, and the solution (the X value) for the equation would be unchanged.

FINDING THE SOLUTION FOR AN EQUATION   We will consider four basic types of equations and the operations needed to solve them.

1. When X Has a Value Added to It   An example of this type of equation is

$$X + 3 = 7$$

Your goal is to isolate X on one side of the equation. Thus, you must remove the $+3$ on the left-hand side. The solution is obtained by subtracting 3 from *both* sides of the equation:

$$X + 3 - 3 = 7 - 3$$
$$X = 4$$

The solution is $X = 4$. You should always check your solution by returning to the original equation and replacing X with the value you obtained for the solution. For this example,

$$X + 3 = 7$$
$$4 + 3 = 7$$
$$7 = 7$$

2. When X Has a Value Subtracted from It   An example of this type of equation is

$$X - 8 = 12$$

In this example, you must remove the -8 from the left-hand side. Thus, the solution is obtained by adding 8 to *both* sides of the equation:

$$X - 8 + 8 = 12 + 8$$
$$X = 20$$

Check the solution

$$X - 8 = 12$$

$$20 - 8 = 12$$

$$12 = 12$$

3. When X is Multiplied by a Value   An example of this type of equation is

$$4X = 24$$

In this instance, it is necessary to remove the 4 that is multiplied by X. This may be accomplished by dividing both sides of the equation by 4:

$$\frac{4X}{4} = \frac{24}{4}$$

$$X = 6$$

Check the solution:

$$4X = 24$$

$$4(6) = 24$$

$$24 = 24$$

4. When X is Divided by a Value   An example of this type of equation is

$$\frac{X}{3} = 9$$

Now the X is divided by 3, so the solution is obtained by multiplying by 3. Multiplying both sides yields

$$3\left(\frac{X}{3}\right) = 9(3)$$

$$X = 27$$

For the check,

$$\frac{X}{3} = 9$$

$$\frac{27}{3} = 9$$

$$9 = 9$$

SOLUTIONS FOR MORE-COMPLEX EQUATIONS

More-complex equations can be solved by using a combination of the preceding simple operations. Remember, at each stage you are trying to isolate X on one side of the equation. For example,

$$3X + 7 = 22$$

$$3X + 7 - 7 = 22 - 7 \qquad \text{(remove } +7 \text{ by subtracting 7 from both sides)}$$

$$3X = 15$$

$$\frac{3X}{3} = \frac{15}{3} \qquad \text{(remove 3 by dividing both side by 3)}$$

$$X = 5$$

To check this solution, return to the original equation and substitute 5 in place of X:

$$3X + 7 = 22$$

$$3(5) + 7 = 22$$

$$15 + 7 = 22$$

$$22 = 22$$

Following is another type of complex equation that is frequently encountered in statistics:

$$\frac{X + 3}{4} = 2$$

First, remove the 4 by multiplying both sides by 4:

$$4\left(\frac{X + 3}{4}\right) = 2(4)$$

$$X + 3 = 8$$

Now remove the $+3$ by subtracting 3 from both sides:

$$X + 3 - 3 = 8 - 3$$

$$X = 5$$

To check this solution, return to the original equation and substitute 5 in place of X:

$$\frac{X + 3}{4} = 2$$

$$\frac{5 + 3}{4} = 2$$

$$\frac{8}{4} = 2$$

$$2 = 2$$

LEARNING CHECK **1.** Solve for X and check the solutions:

a. $3X = 18$ **b.** $X + 7 = 9$ **c.** $X - 4 = 18$ **d.** $5X - 8 = 12$

e. $\dfrac{X}{9} = 5$ **f.** $\dfrac{X + 1}{6} = 4$ **g.** $X + 2 = -5$ **h.** $\dfrac{X}{5} = -5$

i. $\dfrac{2X}{3} = 12$ **j.** $\dfrac{X}{3} + 1 = 3$

A.5 EXPONENTS AND SQUARE ROOTS

EXPONENTIAL NOTATION   A simplified notation is used whenever a number is being multiplied by itself. The notation consists of placing a value, called an exponent, on the right-hand side of and raised above another number called a base. For example,

$7^3 \leftarrow$ exponent

$\uparrow$
base

The exponent indicates how many times the base is multiplied by itself. Some examples are the following:

$7^3 = 7(7)(7)$ (read "7 cubed," or "7 raised to the third power")

$5^2 = 5(5)$ (read "5 squared")

$2^5 = 2(2)(2)(2)(2)$ (read "2 raised to the fifth power")

There are a few basic rules about exponents that you will need to know for this course. They are outlined here.

1. Numbers Raised to One or Zero   Any number raised to the first power equals itself. For example,

$6^1 = 6$

Any number (except zero) raised to the zero power equals 1. For example,

$9^0 = 1$

2. Exponents for Multiple Terms   The exponent applies only to the base that is just in front of it. For example,

$XY^2 = XYY$

$a^2b^3 = aabbb$

3. Negative Bases Raised to an Exponent   If a negative number is raised to a power, then the result will be positive for exponents that are even and negative for exponents that are odd. For example,

$$-4^3 = -4(-4)(-4)$$

$$= 16(-4)$$

$$= -64$$

and

$$-3^4 = -3(-3)(-3)(-3)$$
$$= 9(-3)(-3)$$
$$= 9(9)$$
$$= 81$$

4. Exponents and Parentheses If an exponent is present outside of parentheses, then the computations within the parentheses are done first, and the exponential computation is done last:

$$(3 + 5)^2 = 8^2 = 64$$

Notice that the meaning of the expression is changed when each term in the parentheses is raised to the exponent individually:

$$3^2 + 5^2 = 9 + 25 = 34$$

Therefore,

$$X^2 + Y^2 \neq (X + Y)^2$$

5. Fractions Raised to a Power If the numerator and denominator of a fraction are each raised to the same exponent, then the entire fraction can be raised to that exponent. That is,

$$\frac{a^2}{b^2} = \left(\frac{a}{b}\right)^2$$

For example,

$$\frac{3^2}{4^2} = \left(\frac{3}{4}\right)^2$$

$$\frac{9}{16} = \frac{3}{4}\left(\frac{3}{4}\right)$$

$$\frac{9}{16} = \frac{9}{16}$$

SQUARE ROOTS The square root of a value equals a number which when multiplied by itself yields the original value. For example, the square root of 16 equals 4, because 4 times 4 equals 16. The symbol for the square root is called a radical, $\sqrt{\ }$. The square root is taken for a number under the radical. For example,

$$\sqrt{16} = 4$$

The square root is the inverse of raising a number to the second power (squaring). Thus,

$$\sqrt{a^2} = a$$

For example,

$$\sqrt{3^2} = \sqrt{9} = 3$$

Also,

$$(\sqrt{b})^2 = b$$

For example,

$$(\sqrt{64})^2 = 8^2 = 64$$

Computations under the same radical are performed *before* the square root is taken. For example,

$$\sqrt{9 + 16} = \sqrt{25} = 5$$

Note that with addition (or subtraction) separate radicals yield a different result:

$$\sqrt{9} + \sqrt{16} = 3 + 4 = 7$$

Therefore,

$$\sqrt{X} + \sqrt{Y} \neq \sqrt{X + Y}$$
$$\sqrt{X} - \sqrt{Y} \neq \sqrt{X - Y}$$

If the numerator and denominator of a fraction each have a radical, then the entire fraction can be placed under a single radical:

$$\frac{\sqrt{16}}{\sqrt{4}} = \sqrt{\frac{16}{4}}$$

$$\frac{4}{2} = \sqrt{4}$$

$$2 = 2$$

Therefore,

$$\frac{\sqrt{X}}{\sqrt{Y}} = \sqrt{\frac{X}{Y}}$$

Also, if the square root of one number is multiplied by the square root of another number, then the same result would be obtained by taking the square root of the product of both numbers. For example,

$$\sqrt{9} \times \sqrt{16} = \sqrt{9 \times 16}$$

$$3 \times 4 = \sqrt{144}$$

$$12 = 12$$

Therefore,

$$\sqrt{a} \times \sqrt{b} = \sqrt{ab}$$

LEARNING CHECK

1. Perform the following computations:
   a. $(-6)^3$
   b. $(3 + 7)^2$
   c. a^3b^2 when $a = 2$ and $b = -5$
   d. a^4b^3 when $a = 2$ and $b = 3$
   e. $(XY)^2$ when $X = 3$ and $Y = 5$
   f. $X^2 + Y^2$ when $X = 3$ and $Y = 5$
   g. $(X + Y)^2$ when $X = 3$ and $Y = 5$
   h. $\sqrt{5 + 4}$
   i. $(\sqrt{9})^2$
   j. $\dfrac{\sqrt{16}}{\sqrt{4}}$

ANSWERS **1. a.** -216 **b.** 100 **c.** 200 **d.** 432 **e.** 225
          f. 34 **g.** 64 **h.** 3 **i.** 9 **j.** 2

PROBLEMS FOR APPENDIX A   Basic Mathematics Review

1. Convert $\frac{7}{20}$ to a decimal.

2. Express $\frac{9}{25}$ as a percentage.

3. Convert 0.91 to a fraction.

4. Express 0.0031 as a fraction.

5. Next to each set of fractions, write "true" if they are equivalent and "false" if they are not:
   a. $\dfrac{4}{1000} = \dfrac{2}{100}$ _____
   b. $\dfrac{5}{6} = \dfrac{52}{62}$ _____
   c. $\dfrac{1}{8} = \dfrac{7}{56}$ _____

6. Perform the following calculations:
   a. $\dfrac{4}{5} \times \dfrac{2}{3} = ?$
   b. $\dfrac{7}{9} \div \dfrac{2}{3} = ?$
   c. $\dfrac{3}{8} + \dfrac{1}{5} = ?$
   d. $\dfrac{5}{18} - \dfrac{1}{6} = ?$

7. $2.51 \times 0.017 = ?$

8. $3.88 \times 0.0002 = ?$

9. $3.17 + 17.0132 = ?$

10. $5.55 + 10.7 + 0.711 + 3.33 + 0.031 = ?$

11. $2.04 \div 0.2 = ?$

12. $0.36 \div 0.4 = ?$

13. $5 + 3 - 6 - 4 + 3 = ?$

14. $9 - (-1) - 17 + 3 - (-4) + 5 = ?$

15. $5 + 3 - (-8) - (-1) + (-3) - 4 + 10 = ?$

16. $8 \times (-3) = ?$

17. $-22 \div (-2) = ?$

18. $-2(-4) \times (-3) = ?$

19. $84 \div (-4) = ?$

Solve the equations in Problems 20–27 for X.

20. $X - 7 = -2$

21. $9 = X + 3$

22. $\dfrac{X}{4} = 11$

23. $-3 = \dfrac{X}{3}$

24. $\dfrac{X + 3}{5} = 2$

25. $\dfrac{X + 1}{3} = -8$

26. $6X - 1 = 11$

27. $2X + 3 = -11$

28. $-5^2 = ?$

29. $-5^3 = ?$

30. If $a = 4$ and $b = 3$, then $a^2 + b^4 = ?$

31. If $a = -1$ and $b = 4$, then $(a + b)^2 = ?$

32. If $a = -1$ and $b = 5$, then $ab^2 = ?$

33. $\dfrac{18}{\sqrt{4}} = ?$

34. $\sqrt{\dfrac{20}{5}} = ?$

SKILLS ASSESSMENT EXAM A   Follow-up Test

SECTION 1

1. Express $\frac{14}{80}$ as a decimal.

2. Convert $\frac{6}{25}$ to a percentage.

3. Convert 18% to a fraction.

4. $\frac{3}{5} \times \frac{2}{3} = ?$

5. $\frac{5}{24} + \frac{5}{6} = ?$

6. $\frac{7}{12} \div \frac{5}{6} = ?$

7. $\frac{5}{9} - \frac{1}{3} = ?$

8. $6.11 \times 0.22 = ?$

9. $0.18 \div 0.9 = ?$

10. $8.742 + 0.76 = ?$

11. In a statistics class of 72 students, three-eighths of the students received a B on the first test. How many Bs were earned?

12. What is 15% of 64?

SECTION 2

1. $3 - 1 - 3 + 5 - 2 + 6 = ?$

2. $-8 - (-6) = ?$

3. $2 - (-7) - 3 + (-11) - 20 = ?$

4. $-8 - 3 - (-1) - 2 - 1 = ?$

5. $8(-2) = ?$

6. $-7(-7) = ?$

7. $-3(-2)(-5) = ?$

8. $-3(5)(-3) = ?$

9. $-24 \div (-4) = ?$

10. $36 \div (-6) = ?$

11. $-56/7 = ?$

12. $-7/(-1) = ?$

SECTION 3

Solve for X.

1. $X + 5 = 12$

2. $X - 11 = 3$

3. $10 = X + 4$

4. $4X = 20$

5. $\dfrac{X}{2} = 15$

6. $18 = 9X$

7. $\dfrac{X}{5} = 35$

8. $2X + 8 = 4$

9. $\dfrac{X + 1}{3} = 6$

10. $4X + 3 = -13$

11. $\dfrac{X + 3}{3} = -7$

12. $23 = 2X - 5$

SECTION 4

1. $5^3 = ?$

2. $-4^3 = ?$

3. $-2^5 = ?$

4. $-2^6 = ?$

5. If $a = 4$ and $b = 2$, then $ab^2 = ?$

6. If $a = 4$ and $b = 2$, then $(a + b)^3 = ?$

7. If $a = 4$ and $b = 2$, then $a^2 + b^2 = ?$

8. $(11 + 4)^2 = ?$

9. $\sqrt{7^2} = ?$

10. If $a = 36$ and $b = 64$, the $\sqrt{a + b} = ?$

11. $\dfrac{25}{\sqrt{25}} = ?$

12. If $a = -1$ and $b = 2$, then $a^3 b^4 = ?$

ANSWER KEY Skills Assessment Exams

PREVIEW EXAM (P. A-1)

SECTION 1

1. 75%

2. $\dfrac{30}{100}$, or $\dfrac{3}{10}$

3. 0.3

4. $\dfrac{10}{13}$

5. 1.625

6. $\dfrac{2}{20}$

7. $\dfrac{19}{24}$

8. 1.4

9. $\dfrac{4}{15}$

10. 7.5

11. 16

12. 36

SECTION 2

1. 4
2. 8
3. 2
4. 9
5. −12
6. 12

7. −15
8. −24
9. −4
10. 3
11. −2
12. 25

SECTION 3

1. $X = 7$
2. $X = 29$
3. $X = 9$
4. $X = 4$
5. $X = 24$
6. $X = 15$

7. $X = 80$
8. $X = -3$
9. $X = 11$
10. $X = 25$
11. $X = 11$
12. $X = 7$

SECTION 4

1. 64
2. 4
3. 54
4. 25
5. 13
6. −27

7. 256
8. 8
9. 12
10. 121
11. 33
12. −9

FOLLOW-UP EXAM

SECTION 1

1. 0.175

2. 24%

3. $\dfrac{18}{100}$, or $\dfrac{9}{50}$

4. $\dfrac{6}{15}$

5. $\dfrac{25}{24}$

6. $\dfrac{42}{60}$, or $\dfrac{7}{10}$

7. $\dfrac{2}{9}$

8. 1.3442

9. 0.2

10. 9.502

11. 27

12. 9.6

SECTION 2

1. 8
2. −2
3. −25
4. −13
5. −16
6. 49

7. −30
8. 45
9. 6
10. −6
11. −8
12. 7

SECTION 3

1. $X = 7$
2. $X = 14$
3. $X = 6$
4. $X = 5$
5. $X = 30$
6. $X = 2$

7. $X = 175$
8. $X = -2$
9. $X = 17$
10. $X = -4$
11. $X = -24$
12. $X = 14$

SECTION 4

1. 125
2. −64
3. −32
4. 64
5. 16
6. 216

7. 20
8. 225
9. 7
10. 10
11. 5
12. −16

SOLUTIONS TO SELECTED PROBLEMS IN APPENDIX A   Basic Mathematics Review

1. 0.35

2. 36%

4. $\dfrac{31}{10,000}$

5. b. False

6. a. $\dfrac{8}{15}$ **b.** $\dfrac{21}{18}$ **c.** $\dfrac{23}{40}$

7. 0.04267

9. 20.1832

12. 0.9

14. 5

16. -24

17. 11

20. $X = 5$

23. $X = -9$

25. $X = -25$

26. $X = 2$

29. -125

31. 9

32. -25

34. 2

SUGGESTED REVIEW BOOKS

There are many basic mathematics review books available if you need a more extensive review than this appendix can provide. The following books are but a few of the many that you may find helpful:

Barker, V. C., and Aufmann, R. N. (1982). *Essential Mathematics*. Boston: Houghton Mifflin.

Falstein, L. D. (1986). *Basic Mathematics* 2d ed. Reading, Mass.: Addison-Wesley.

Washington, A. J. (1984). *Arithmetic and Beginning Algebra*. Menlo Park, Calif.: Benjamin/Cummings.

APPENDIX B STATISTICAL TABLES

TABLE B.1   THE UNIT NORMAL TABLE*

*Column A lists the *z*-score values.
 Column B provides the proportion of area between the mean and the *z*-score value.
 Column C provides the proportion of area beyond the *z*-score.

Note: Because the normal distribution is symmetrical, areas for negative *z*-scores are the same as those for positive *z*-scores.

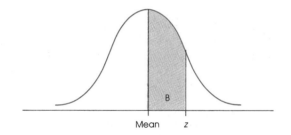

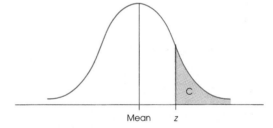

(A)	(B)	(C)	(A)	(B)	(C)	(A)	(B)	(C)
	AREA BETWEEN	AREA BEYOND		AREA BETWEEN	AREA BEYOND		AREA BETWEEN	AREA BEYOND
z	MEAN AND *z*	*z*	*z*	MEAN AND *z*	*z*	*z*	MEAN AND *z*	*z*
0.00	.0000	.5000	0.20	.0793	.4207	0.40	.1554	.3446
0.01	.0040	.4960	0.21	.0832	.4168	0.41	.1591	.3409
0.02	.0080	.4920	0.22	.0871	.4129	0.42	.1628	.3372
0.03	.0120	.4880	0.23	.0910	.4090	0.43	.1664	.3336
0.04	.0160	.4840	0.24	.0948	.4052	0.44	.1700	.3300
0.05	.0199	.4801	0.25	.0987	.4013	0.45	.1736	.3264
0.06	.0239	.4761	0.26	.1026	.3974	0.46	.1772	.3228
0.07	.0279	.4721	0.27	.1064	.3936	0.47	.1808	.3192
0.08	,0319	.4681	0.28	.1103	.3897	0.48	.1844	.3156
0.09	.0359	.4641	0.29	.1141	.3859	0.49	.1879	.3121
0.10	.0398	.4602	0.30	.1179	.3821	0.50	.1915	.3085
0.11	.0438	.4562	0.31	.1217	.3783	0.51	.1950	.3050
0.12	.0478	.4522	0.32	.1255	.3745	0.52	.1985	.3015
0.13	.0517	.4483	0.33	.1293	.3707	0.53	.2019	.2981
0.14	.0557	.4443	0.34	.1331	.3669	0.54	.2054	.2946
0.15	.0596	.4404	0.35	.1368	.3632	0.55	.2088	.2912
0.16	.0636	.4364	0.36	.1406	.3594	0.56	.2123	.2877
0.17	.0675	.4325	0.37	.1443	.3557	0.57	.2157	.2843
0.18	.0714	.4286	0.38	.1480	.3520	0.58	.2190	.2810
0.19	.0753	.4247	0.39	.1517	.3483	0.59	.2224	.2776

TABLE B.1   continued

(A)	(B) AREA BETWEEN	(C) AREA BEYOND	(A)	(B) AREA BETWEEN	(C) AREA BEYOND	(A)	(B) AREA BETWEEN	(C) AREA BEYOND
z	MEAN AND z	z	z	MEAN AND z	z	z	MEAN AND z	z
0.60	.2257	.2743	1.05	.3531	.1469	1.50	.4332	.0668
0.61	.2291	.2709	1.06	.3554	.1446	1.51	.4345	.0655
0.62	.2324	.2676	1.07	.3577	.1423	1.52	.4357	.0643
0.63	.2357	.2643	1.08	.3599	.1401	1.53	.4370	.0630
0.64	.2389	.2611	1.09	.3621	.1379	1.54	.4382	.0618
0.65	.2422	.2578	1.10	.3643	.1357	1.55	.4394	.0606
0.66	.2454	.2546	1.11	.3665	.1335	1.56	.4406	.0594
0.67	.2486	.2514	1.12	.3686	.1314	1.57	.4418	.0582
0.68	.2517	.2483	1.13	.3708	.1292	1.58	.4429	.0571
0.69	.2549	.2451	1.14	.3729	.1271	1.59	.4441	.0559
0.70	.2580	.2420	1.15	.3749	.1251	1.60	.4452	.0548
0.71	.2611	.2389	1.16	.3770	.1230	1.61	.4463	.0537
0.72	.2642	.2358	1.17	.3790	.1210	1.62	.4474	.0526
0.73	.2673	.2327	1.18	.3810	.1190	1.63	.4484	.0516
0.74	.2704	.2296	1.19	.3830	.1170	1.64	.4495	.0505
0.75	.2734	.2266	1.20	.3849	.1151	1.65	.4505	.0495
0.76	.2764	.2236	1.21	.3869	.1131	1.66	.4515	.0485
0.77	.2794	.2206	1.22	.3888	.1112	1.67	.4525	.0475
0.78	.2823	.2177	1.23	.3907	.1093	1.68	.4535	.0465
0.79	.2852	.2148	1.24	.3925	.1075	1.69	.4545	.0455
0.80	.2881	.2119	1.25	.3944	.1056	1.70	.4554	.0446
0.81	.2910	.2090	1.26	.3962	.1038	1.71	.4564	.0436
0.82	.2939	.2061	1.27	.3980	.1020	1.72	.4573	.0427
0.83	.2967	.2033	1.28	.3997	.1003	1.73	.4582	.0418
0.84	.2995	.2005	1.29	.4015	.0985	1.74	.4591	.0409
0.85	.3023	.1977	1.30	.4032	.0968	1.75	.4599	.0401
0.86	.3051	.1949	1.31	.4049	.0951	1.76	.4608	.0392
0.87	.3078	.1922	1.32	.4066	.0934	1.77	.4616	.0384
0.88	.3106	.1894	1.33	.4082	.0918	1.78	.4625	.0375
0.89	.3133	.1867	1.34	.4099	.0901	1.79	.4633	.0367
0.90	.3159	.1841	1.35	.4115	.0885	1.80	.4641	.0359
0.91	.3186	.1814	1.36	.4131	.0869	1.81	.4649	.0351
0.92	.3212	.1788	1.37	.4147	.0853	1.82	.4656	.0344
0.93	.3238	.1762	1.38	.4162	.0838	1.83	.4664	.0336
0.94	.3264	.1736	1.39	.4177	.0823	1.84	.4671	.0329
0.95	.3289	.1711	1.40	.4192	.0808	1.85	.4678	.0322
0.96	.3315	.1685	1.41	.4207	.0793	1.86	.4686	.0314
0.97	.3340	.1660	1.42	.4222	.0778	1.87	.4693	.0307
0.98	.3365	.1635	1.43	.4236	.0764	1.88	.4699	.0301
0.99	.3389	.1611	1.44	.4251	.0749	1.89	.4706	.0294
1.00	.3413	.1587	1.45	.4265	.0735	1.90	.4713	.0287
1.01	.3438	.1562	1.46	.4279	.0721	1.91	.4719	.0281
1.02	.3461	.1539	1.47	.4292	.0708	1.92	.4726	.0274
1.03	.3485	.1515	1.48	.4306	.0694	1.93	.4732	.0268
1.04	.3508	.1492	1.49	.4319	.0681	1.94	.4738	.0262

TABLE B.1 continued

(A) z	(B) AREA BETWEEN MEAN AND z	(C) AREA BEYOND z	(A) z	(B) AREA BETWEEN MEAN AND z	(C) AREA BEYOND z	(A) z	(B) AREA BETWEEN MEAN AND z	(C) AREA BEYOND z
1.95	.4744	.0256	2.42	.4922	.0078	2.88	.4980	.0020
1.96	.4750	.0250	2.43	.4925	.0075	2.89	.4981	.0019
1.97	.4756	.0244	2.44	.4927	.0073	2.90	.4981	.0019
1.98	.4761	.0239	2.45	.4929	.0071	2.91	.4982	.0018
1.99	.4767	.0233	2.46	.4931	.0069	2.92	.4982	.0018
2.00	.4772	.0228	2.47	.4932	.0068	2.93	.4983	.0017
2.01	.4778	.0222	2.48	.4934	.0066	2.94	.4984	.0016
2.02	.4783	.0217	2.49	.4936	.0064	2.95	.4984	.0016
2.03	.4788	.0212	2.50	.4938	.0062	2.96	.4985	.0015
2.04	.4793	.0207	2.51	.4940	.0060	2.97	.4985	.0015
2.05	.4798	.0202	2.52	.4941	.0059	2.98	.4986	.0014
2.06	.4803	.0197	2.53	.4943	.0057	2.99	.4986	.0014
2.07	.4808	.0192	2.54	.4945	.0055	3.00	.4987	.0013
2.08	.4812	.0188	2.55	.4946	.0054	3.01	.4987	.0013
2.09	.4817	.0183	2.56	.4948	.0052	3.02	.4987	.0013
2.10	.4821	.0179	2.57	.4949	.0051	3.03	.4988	.0012
2.11	.4826	.0174	2.58	.4951	.0049	3.04	.4988	.0012
2.12	.4830	.0170	2.59	.4952	.0048	3.05	.4989	.0011
2.13	.4834	.0166	2.60	.4953	.0047	3.06	.4989	.0011
2.14	.4838	.0162	2.61	.4955	.0045	3.07	.4989	.0011
2.15	.4842	.0158	2.62	.4956	.0044	3.08	.4990	.0010
2.16	.4846	.0154	2.63	.4957	.0043	3.09	.4990	.0010
2.17	.4850	.0150	2.64	.4959	.0041	3.10	.4990	.0010
2.18	.4854	.0146	2.65	.4960	.0040	3.11	.4991	.0009
2.19	.4857	.0143	2.66	.4961	.0039	3.12	.4991	.0009
2.20	.4861	.0139	2.67	.4962	.0038	3.13	.4991	.0009
2.21	.4864	.0136	2.68	.4963	.0037	3.14	.4992	.0008
2.22	.4868	.0132	2.69	.4964	.0036	3.15	.4992	.0008
2.23	.4871	.0129	2.70	.4965	.0035	3.16	.4992	.0008
2.24	.4875	.0125	2.71	.4966	.0034	3.17	.4992	.0008
2.25	.4878	.0122	2.72	.4967	.0033	3.18	.4993	.0007
2.26	.4881	.0119	2.73	.4968	.0032	3.19	.4993	.0007
2.27	.4884	.0116	2.74	.4969	.0031	3.20	.4993	.0007
2.28	.4887	.0113	2.75	.4970	.0030	3.21	.4993	.0007
2.29	.4890	.0110	2.76	.4971	.0029	3.22	.4994	.0006
2.30	.4893	.0107	2.77	.4972	.0028	3.23	.4994	.0006
2.31	.4896	.0104	2.78	.4973	.0027	3.24	.4994	.0006
2.32	.4898	.0102	2.79	.4974	.0026	3.30	.4995	.0005
2.33	.4901	.0099	2.80	.4974	.0026	3.40	.4997	.0003
2.34	.4904	.0096	2.81	.4975	.0025	3.50	.4998	.0002
2.35	.4906	.0094	2.82	.4976	.0024	3.60	.4998	.0002
2.36	.4909	.0091	2.83	.4977	.0023	3.70	.4999	.0001
2.37	.4911	.0089	2.84	.4977	.0023	3.80	.49993	.00007
2.38	.4913	.0087	2.85	.4978	.0022	3.90	.49995	.00005
2.39	.4916	.0084	2.86	.4979	.0021	4.00	.49997	.00003
2.40	.4918	.0082	2.87	.4979	.0021			
2.41	.4920	.0080						

TABLE B.2 THE *t* DISTRIBUTION

df	PROPORTION IN ONE TAIL					
	0.25	0.10	0.05	0.025	0.01	0.005
	PROPORTION IN TWO TAILS					
	0.50	0.20	0.10	0.05	0.02	0.01
1	1.000	3.078	6.314	12.706	31.821	63.657
2	0.816	1.886	2.920	4.303	6.965	9.925
3	0.765	1.638	2.353	3.182	4.541	5.841
4	0.741	1.533	2.132	2.776	3.747	4.604
5	0.727	1.476	2.015	2.571	3.365	4.032
6	0.718	1.440	1.943	2.447	3.143	3.707
7	0.711	1.415	1.895	2.365	2.998	3.499
8	0.706	1.397	1.860	2.306	2.896	3.355
9	0.703	1.383	1.833	2.262	2.821	3.250
10	0.700	1.372	1.812	2.228	2.764	3.169
11	0.697	1.363	1.796	2.201	2.718	3.106
12	0.695	1.356	1.782	2.179	2.681	3.055
13	0.694	1.350	1.771	2.160	2.650	3.012
14	0.692	1.345	1.761	2.145	2.624	2.977
15	0.691	1.341	1.753	2.131	2.602	2.947
16	0.690	1.337	1.746	2.120	2.583	2.921
17	0.689	1.333	1.740	2.110	2.567	2.898
18	0.688	1.330	1.734	2.101	2.552	2.878
19	0.688	1.328	1.729	2.093	2.539	2.861
20	0.687	1.325	1.725	2.086	2.528	2.845
21	0.686	1.323	1.721	2.080	2.518	2.831
22	0.686	1.321	1.717	2.074	2.508	2.819
23	0.685	1.319	1.714	2.069	2.500	2.807
24	0.685	1.318	1.711	2.064	2.492	2.797
25	0.684	1.316	1.708	2.060	2.485	2.787
26	0.684	1.315	1.706	2.056	2.479	2.779
27	0.684	1.314	1.703	2.052	2.473	2.771
28	0.683	1.313	1.701	2.048	2.467	2.763
29	0.683	1.311	1.699	2.045	2.462	2.756
30	0.683	1.310	1.697	2.042	2.457	2.750
40	0.681	1.303	1.684	2.021	2.423	2.704
60	0.679	1.296	1.671	2.000	2.390	2.660
120	0.677	1.289	1.658	1.980	2.358	2.617
∞	0.674	1.282	1.645	1.960	2.326	2.576

TABLE B.3   CRITICAL VALUES FOR THE *F*-MAX STATISTIC*

*The critical values for α = .05 are in lightface type, and for α = .01 they are in boldface type.

$n - 1$	2	3	4	5	6	7	8	9	10	11	12
k = NUMBER OF SAMPLES											
4	9.60	15.5	20.6	25.2	29.5	33.6	37.5	41.4	44.6	48.0	51.4
	23.2	**37.**	**49.**	**59.**	**69.**	**79.**	**89.**	**97.**	**106.**	**113.**	**120.**
5	7.15	10.8	13.7	16.3	18.7	20.8	22.9	24.7	26.5	28.2	29.9
	14.9	**22.**	**28.**	**33.**	**38.**	**42.**	**46.**	**50.**	**54.**	**57.**	**60.**
6	5.82	8.38	10.4	12.1	13.7	15.0	16.3	17.5	18.6	19.7	20.7
	11.1	**15.5**	**19.1**	**22.**	**25.**	**27.**	**30.**	**32.**	**34.**	**36.**	**37.**
7	4.99	6.94	8.44	9.70	10.8	11.8	12.7	13.5	14.3	15.1	15.8
	8.89	**12.1**	**14.5**	**16.5**	**18.4**	**20.**	**22.**	**23.**	**24.**	**26.**	**27.**
8	4.43	6.00	7.18	8.12	9.03	9.78	10.5	11.1	11.7	12.2	12.7
	7.50	**9.9**	**11.7**	**13.2**	**14.5**	**15.8**	**16.9**	**17.9**	**18.9**	**19.8**	**21.**
9	4.03	5.34	6.31	7.11	7.80	8.41	8.95	9.45	9.91	10.3	10.7
	6.54	**8.5**	**9.9**	**11.1**	**12.1**	**13.1**	**13.9**	**14.7**	**15.3**	**16.0**	**16.6**
10	3.72	4.85	5.67	6.34	6.92	7.42	7.87	8.28	8.66	9.01	9.34
	5.85	**7.4**	**8.6**	**9.6**	**10.4**	**11.1**	**11.8**	**12.4**	**12.9**	**13.4**	**13.9**
12	3.28	4.16	4.79	5.30	5.72	6.09	6.42	6.72	7.00	7.25	7.48
	4.91	**6.1**	**6.9**	**7.6**	**8.2**	**8.7**	**9.1**	**9.5**	**9.9**	**10.2**	**10.6**
15	2.86	3.54	4.01	4.37	4.68	4.95	5.19	5.40	5.59	5.77	5.93
	4.07	**4.9**	**5.5**	**6.0**	**6.4**	**6.7**	**7.1**	**7.3**	**7.5**	**7.8**	**8.0**
20	2.46	2.95	3.29	3.54	3.76	3.94	4.10	4.24	4.37	4.49	4.59
	3.32	**3.8**	**4.3**	**4.6**	**4.9**	**5.1**	**5.3**	**5.5**	**5.6**	**5.8**	**5.9**
30	2.07	2.40	2.61	2.78	2.91	3.02	3.12	3.21	3.29	3.36	3.39
	2.63	**3.0**	**3.3**	**3.5**	**3.6**	**3.7**	**3.8**	**3.9**	**4.0**	**4.1**	**4.2**
60	1.67	1.85	1.96	2.04	2.11	2.17	2.22	2.26	2.30	2.33	2.36
	1.96	**2.2**	**2.3**	**2.4**	**2.4**	**2.5**	**2.5**	**2.6**	**2.6**	**2.7**	**2.7**

TABLE B.4   THE F DISTRIBUTION*

*Table entries in lightface type are critical values for the .05 level of significance.
Boldface type values are for the .01 level of significance.

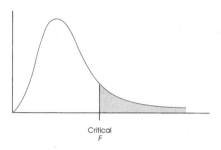

Critical
F

DEGREES OF FREEDOM: DENOMINATOR	DEGREES OF FREEDOM: NUMERATOR															
	1	2	3	4	5	6	7	8	9	10	11	12	14	16	20
1	161	200	216	225	230	234	237	239	241	242	243	244	245	246	248
	4052	**4999**	**5403**	**5625**	**5764**	**5859**	**5928**	**5981**	**6022**	**6056**	**6082**	**6106**	**6142**	**6169**	**6208**
2	18.51	19.00	19.16	19.25	19.30	19.33	19.36	19.37	19.38	19.39	19.40	19.41	19.42	19.43	19.44
	98.49	**99.00**	**99.17**	**99.25**	**99.30**	**99.33**	**99.34**	**99.36**	**99.38**	**99.40**	**99.41**	**99.42**	**99.43**	**99.44**	**99.45**
3	10.13	9.55	9.28	9.12	9.01	8.94	8.88	8.84	8.81	8.78	8.76	8.74	8.71	8.69	8.66
	34.12	**30.82**	**29.46**	**28.71**	**28.24**	**27.91**	**27.67**	**27.49**	**27.34**	**27.23**	**27.13**	**27.05**	**26.92**	**26.83**	**26.69**
4	7.71	6.94	6.59	6.39	6.26	6.16	6.09	6.04	6.00	5.96	5.93	5.91	5.87	5.84	5.80
	21.20	**18.00**	**16.69**	**15.98**	**15.52**	**15.21**	**14.98**	**14.80**	**14.66**	**14.54**	**14.45**	**14.37**	**14.24**	**14.15**	**14.02**
5	6.61	5.79	5.41	5.19	5.05	4.95	4.88	4.82	4.78	4.74	4.70	4.68	4.64	4.60	4.56
	16.26	**13.27**	**12.06**	**11.39**	**10.97**	**10.67**	**10.45**	**10.27**	**10.15**	**10.05**	**9.96**	**9.89**	**9.77**	**9.68**	**9.55**
6	5.99	5.14	4.76	4.53	4.39	4.28	4.21	4.15	4.10	4.06	4.03	4.00	3.96	3.92	3.87
	13.74	**10.92**	**9.78**	**9.15**	**8.75**	**8.47**	**8.26**	**8.10**	**7.98**	**7.87**	**7.79**	**7.72**	**7.60**	**7.52**	**7.39**
7	5.59	4.47	4.35	4.12	3.97	3.87	3.79	3.73	3.68	3.63	3.60	3.57	3.52	3.49	3.44
	12.25	**9.55**	**8.45**	**7.85**	**7.46**	**7.19**	**7.00**	**6.84**	**6.71**	**6.62**	**6.54**	**6.47**	**6.35**	**6.27**	**6.15**
8	5.32	4.46	4.07	3.84	3.69	3.58	3.50	3.44	3.39	3.34	3.31	3.28	3.23	3.20	3.15
	11.26	**8.65**	**7.59**	**7.01**	**6.63**	**6.37**	**6.19**	**6.03**	**5.91**	**5.82**	**5.74**	**5.67**	**5.56**	**5.48**	**5.36**
9	5.12	4.26	3.86	3.63	3.48	3.37	3.29	3.23	3.18	3.13	3.10	3.07	3.02	2.98	2.93
	10.56	**8.02**	**6.99**	**6.42**	**6.06**	**5.80**	**5.62**	**5.47**	**5.35**	**5.26**	**5.18**	**5.11**	**5.00**	**4.92**	**4.80**
10	4.96	4.10	3.71	3.48	3.33	3.22	3.14	3.07	3.02	2.97	2.94	2.91	2.86	2.82	2.77
	10.04	**7.56**	**6.55**	**5.99**	**5.64**	**5.39**	**5.21**	**5.06**	**4.95**	**4.85**	**4.78**	**4.71**	**4.60**	**4.52**	**4.41**
11	4.84	3.98	3.59	3.36	3.20	3.09	3.01	2.95	2.90	2.86	2.82	2.79	2.74	2.70	2.65
	9.65	**7.20**	**6.22**	**5.67**	**5.32**	**5.07**	**4.88**	**4.74**	**4.63**	**4.54**	**4.46**	**4.40**	**4.29**	**4.21**	**4.10**
12	4.75	3.88	3.49	3.26	3.11	3.00	2.92	2.85	2.80	2.76	2.72	2.69	2.64	2.60	2.54
	9.33	**6.93**	**5.95**	**5.41**	**5.06**	**4.82**	**4.65**	**4.50**	**4.39**	**4.30**	**4.22**	**4.16**	**4.05**	**3.98**	**3.86**
13	4.67	3.80	3.41	3.18	3.02	2.92	2.84	2.77	2.72	2.67	2.63	2.60	2.55	2.51	2.46
	9.07	**6.70**	**5.74**	**5.20**	**4.86**	**4.62**	**4.44**	**4.30**	**4.19**	**4.10**	**4.02**	**3.96**	**3.85**	**3.78**	**3.67**
14	4.60	3.74	3.34	3.11	2.96	2.85	2.77	2.70	2.65	2.60	2.56	2.53	2.48	2.44	2.39
	8.86	**6.51**	**5.56**	**5.03**	**4.69**	**4.46**	**4.28**	**4.14**	**4.03**	**3.94**	**3.86**	**3.80**	**3.70**	**3.62**	**3.51**
15	4.54	3.68	3.29	3.06	2.90	2.79	2.70	2.64	2.59	2.55	2.51	2.48	2.43	2.39	2.33
	8.68	**6.36**	**5.42**	**4.89**	**4.56**	**4.32**	**4.14**	**4.00**	**3.89**	**3.80**	**3.73**	**3.67**	**3.56**	**3.48**	**3.36**
16	4.49	3.63	3.24	3.01	2.85	2.74	2.66	2.59	2.54	2.49	2.45	2.42	2.37	2.33	2.28
	8.53	**6.23**	**5.29**	**4.77**	**4.44**	**4.20**	**4.03**	**3.89**	**3.78**	**3.69**	**3.61**	**3.55**	**3.45**	**3.37**	**3.25**

TABLE B.4 continued

DEGREES OF FREEDOM: DENOMINATOR	DEGREES OF FREEDOM: NUMERATOR														
	1	2	3	4	5	6	7	8	9	10	11	12	14	16	20
17	4.45	3.59	3.20	2.96	2.81	2.70	2.62	2.55	2.50	2.45	2.41	2.38	2.33	2.29	2.23
	8.40	**6.11**	**5.18**	**4.67**	**4.34**	**4.10**	**3.93**	**3.79**	**3.68**	**3.59**	**3.52**	**3.45**	**3.35**	**3.27**	**3.16**
18	4.41	3.55	3.16	2.93	2.77	2.66	2.58	2.51	2.46	2.41	2.37	2.34	2.29	2.25	2.19
	8.28	**6.01**	**5.09**	**4.58**	**4.25**	**4.01**	**3.85**	**3.71**	**3.60**	**3.51**	**3.44**	**3.37**	**3.27**	**3.19**	**3.07**
19	4.38	3.52	3.13	2.90	2.74	2.63	2.55	2.48	2.43	2.38	2.34	2.31	2.26	2.21	2.15
	8.18	**5.93**	**5.01**	**4.50**	**4.17**	**3.94**	**3.77**	**3.63**	**3.52**	**3.43**	**3.36**	**3.30**	**3.19**	**3.12**	**3.00**
20	4.35	3.49	3.10	2.87	2.71	2.60	2.52	2.45	2.40	2.35	2.31	2.28	2.23	2.18	2.12
	8.10	**5.85**	**4.94**	**4.43**	**4.10**	**3.87**	**3.71**	**3.56**	**3.45**	**3.37**	**3.30**	**3.23**	**3.13**	**3.05**	**2.94**
21	4.32	3.47	3.07	2.84	2.68	2.57	2.49	2.42	2.37	2.32	2.28	2.25	2.20	2.15	2.09
	8.02	**5.78**	**4.87**	**4.37**	**4.04**	**3.81**	**3.65**	**3.51**	**3.40**	**3.31**	**3.24**	**3.17**	**3.07**	**2.99**	**2.88**
22	4.30	3.44	3.05	2.82	2.66	2.55	2.47	2.40	2.35	2.30	2.26	2.23	2.18	2.13	2.07
	7.94	**5.72**	**4.82**	**4.31**	**3.99**	**3.76**	**3.59**	**3.45**	**3.35**	**3.26**	**3.18**	**3.12**	**3.02**	**2.94**	**2.83**
23	4.28	3.42	3.03	2.80	2.64	2.53	2.45	2.38	2.32	2.28	2.24	2.20	2.14	2.10	2.04
	7.88	**5.66**	**4.76**	**4.26**	**3.94**	**3.71**	**3.54**	**3.41**	**3.30**	**3.21**	**3.14**	**3.07**	**2.97**	**2.89**	**2.78**
24	4.26	3.40	3.01	2.78	2.62	2.51	2.43	2.36	2.30	2.26	2.22	2.18	2.13	2.09	2.02
	7.82	**5.61**	**4.72**	**4.22**	**3.90**	**3.67**	**3.50**	**3.36**	**3.25**	**3.17**	**3.09**	**3.03**	**2.93**	**2.85**	**2.74**
25	4.24	3.38	2.99	2.76	2.60	2.49	2.41	2.34	2.28	2.24	2.20	2.16	2.11	2.06	2.00
	7.77	**5.57**	**4.68**	**4.18**	**3.86**	**3.63**	**3.46**	**3.32**	**3.21**	**3.13**	**3.05**	**2.99**	**2.89**	**2.81**	**2.70**
26	4.22	3.37	2.98	2.74	2.59	2.47	2.39	2.32	2.27	2.22	2.18	2.15	2.10	2.05	1.99
	7.72	**5.53**	**4.64**	**4.14**	**3.82**	**3.59**	**3.42**	**3.29**	**3.17**	**3.09**	**3.02**	**2.96**	**2.86**	**2.77**	**2.66**
27	4.21	3.35	2.96	2.73	2.57	2.46	2.37	2.30	2.25	2.20	2.16	2.13	2.08	2.03	1.97
	7.68	**5.49**	**4.60**	**4.11**	**3.79**	**3.56**	**3.39**	**3.26**	**3.14**	**3.06**	**2.98**	**2.93**	**2.83**	**2.74**	**2.63**
28	4.20	3.34	2.95	2.71	2.56	2.44	2.36	2.29	2.24	2.19	2.15	2.12	2.06	2.02	1.96
	7.64	**5.45**	**4.57**	**4.07**	**3.76**	**3.53**	**3.36**	**3.23**	**3.11**	**3.03**	**2.95**	**2.90**	**2.80**	**2.71**	**2.60**
29	4.18	3.33	2.93	2.70	2.54	2.43	2.35	2.28	2.22	2.18	2.14	2.10	2.05	2.00	1.94
	7.60	**5.42**	**4.54**	**4.04**	**3.73**	**3.50**	**3.33**	**3.20**	**3.08**	**3.00**	**2.92**	**2.87**	**2.77**	**2.68**	**2.57**
30	4.17	3.32	2.92	2.69	2.53	2.42	2.34	2.27	2.21	2.16	2.12	2.09	2.04	1.99	1.93
	7.56	**5.39**	**4.51**	**4.02**	**3.70**	**3.47**	**3.30**	**3.17**	**3.06**	**2.98**	**2.90**	**2.84**	**2.74**	**2.66**	**2.55**
32	4.15	3.30	2.90	2.67	2.51	2.40	2.32	2.25	2.19	2.14	2.10	2.07	2.02	1.97	1.91
	7.50	**5.34**	**4.46**	**3.97**	**3.66**	**3.42**	**3.25**	**3.12**	**3.01**	**2.94**	**2.86**	**2.80**	**2.70**	**2.62**	**2.51**
34	4.13	3.28	2.88	2.65	2.49	2.38	2.30	2.23	2.17	2.12	2.08	2.05	2.00	1.95	1.89
	7.44	**5.29**	**4.42**	**3.93**	**3.61**	**3.38**	**3.21**	**3.08**	**2.97**	**2.89**	**2.82**	**2.76**	**2.66**	**2.58**	**2.47**
36	4.11	3.26	2.86	2.63	2.48	2.36	2.28	2.21	2.15	2.10	2.06	2.03	1.98	1.93	1.87
	7.39	**5.25**	**4.38**	**3.89**	**3.58**	**3.35**	**3.18**	**3.04**	**2.94**	**2.86**	**2.78**	**2.72**	**2.62**	**2.54**	**2.43**
38	4.10	3.25	2.85	2.62	2.46	2.35	2.26	2.19	2.14	2.09	2.05	2.02	1.96	1.92	1.85
	7.35	**5.21**	**4.34**	**3.86**	**3.54**	**3.32**	**3.15**	**3.02**	**2.91**	**2.82**	**2.75**	**2.69**	**2.59**	**2.51**	**2.40**
40	4.08	3.23	2.84	2.61	2.45	2.34	2.25	2.18	2.12	2.07	2.04	2.00	1.95	1.90	1.84
	7.31	**5.18**	**4.31**	**3.83**	**3.51**	**3.29**	**3.12**	**2.99**	**2.88**	**2.80**	**2.73**	**2.66**	**2.56**	**2.49**	**2.37**
42	4.07	3.22	2.83	2.59	2.44	2.32	2.24	2.17	2.11	2.06	2.02	1.99	1.94	1.89	1.82
	7.27	**5.15**	**4.29**	**3.80**	**3.49**	**3.26**	**3.10**	**2.96**	**2.86**	**2.77**	**2.70**	**2.64**	**2.54**	**2.46**	**2.35**
44	4.06	3.21	2.82	2.58	2.43	2.31	2.23	2.16	2.10	2.05	2.01	1.98	1.92	1.88	1.81
	7.24	**5.12**	**4.26**	**3.78**	**3.46**	**3.24**	**3.07**	**2.94**	**2.84**	**2.75**	**2.68**	**2.62**	**2.52**	**2.44**	**2.32**
46	4.05	3.20	2.81	2.57	2.42	2.30	2.22	2.14	2.09	2.04	2.00	1.97	1.91	1.87	1.80
	7.21	**5.10**	**4.24**	**3.76**	**3.44**	**3.22**	**3.05**	**2.92**	**2.82**	**2.73**	**2.66**	**2.60**	**2.50**	**2.42**	**2.30**
48	4.04	3.19	2.80	2.56	2.41	2.30	2.21	2.14	2.08	2.03	1.99	1.96	1.90	1.86	1.79
	7.19	**5.08**	**4.22**	**3.74**	**3.42**	**3.20**	**3.04**	**2.90**	**2.80**	**2.71**	**2.64**	**2.58**	**2.48**	**2.40**	**2.28**

TABLE B.4   continued

DEGREES OF FREEDOM: DENOMINATOR	DEGREES OF FREEDOM: NUMERATOR														
	1	2	3	4	5	6	7	8	9	10	11	12	14	16	20
50	4.03	3.18	2.79	2.56	2.40	2.29	2.20	2.13	2.07	2.02	1.98	1.95	1.90	1.85	1.78
	7.17	**5.06**	**4.20**	**3.72**	**3.41**	**3.18**	**3.02**	**2.88**	**2.78**	**2.70**	**2.62**	**2.56**	**2.46**	**2.39**	**2.26**
55	4.02	3.17	2.78	2.54	2.38	2.27	2.18	2.11	2.05	2.00	1.97	1.93	1.88	1.83	1.76
	7.12	**5.01**	**4.16**	**3.68**	**3.37**	**3.15**	**2.98**	**2.85**	**2.75**	**2.66**	**2.59**	**2.53**	**2.43**	**2.35**	**2.23**
60	4.00	3.15	2.76	2.52	2.37	2.25	2.17	2.10	2.04	1.99	1.95	1.92	1.86	1.81	1.75
	7.08	**4.98**	**4.13**	**3.65**	**3.34**	**3.12**	**2.95**	**2.82**	**2.72**	**2.63**	**2.56**	**2.50**	**2.40**	**2.32**	**2.20**
65	3.99	3.14	2.75	2.51	2.36	2.24	2.15	2.08	2.02	1.98	1.94	1.90	1.85	1.80	1.73
	7.04	**4.95**	**4.10**	**3.62**	**3.31**	**3.09**	**2.93**	**2.79**	**2.70**	**2.61**	**2.54**	**2.47**	**2.37**	**2.30**	**2.18**
70	3.98	3.13	2.74	2.50	2.35	2.23	2.14	2.07	2.01	1.97	1.93	1.89	1.84	1.79	1.72
	7.01	**4.92**	**4.08**	**3.60**	**3.29**	**3.07**	**2.91**	**2.77**	**2.67**	**2.59**	**2.51**	**2.45**	**2.35**	**2.28**	**2.15**
80	3.96	3.11	2.72	2.48	2.33	2.21	2.12	2.05	1.99	1.95	1.91	1.88	1.82	1.77	1.70
	6.96	**4.88**	**4.04**	**3.56**	**3.25**	**3.04**	**2.87**	**2.74**	**2.64**	**2.55**	**2.48**	**2.41**	**2.32**	**2.24**	**2.11**
100	3.94	3.09	2.70	2.46	2.30	2.19	2.10	2.03	1.97	1.92	1.88	1.85	1.79	1.75	1.68
	6.90	**4.82**	**3.98**	**3.51**	**3.20**	**2.99**	**2.82**	**2.69**	**2.59**	**2.51**	**2.43**	**2.36**	**2.26**	**2.19**	**2.06**
125	3.92	3.07	2.68	2.44	2.29	2.17	2.08	2.01	1.95	1.90	1.86	1.83	1.77	1.72	1.65
	6.84	**4.78**	**3.94**	**3.47**	**3.17**	**2.95**	**2.79**	**2.65**	**2.56**	**2.47**	**2.40**	**2.33**	**2.23**	**2.15**	**2.03**
150	3.91	3.06	2.67	2.43	2.27	2.16	2.07	2.00	1.94	1.89	1.85	1.82	1.76	1.71	1.64
	6.81	**4.75**	**3.91**	**3.44**	**3.14**	**2.92**	**2.76**	**2.62**	**2.53**	**2.44**	**2.37**	**2.30**	**2.20**	**2.12**	**2.00**
200	3.89	3.04	2.65	2.41	2.26	2.14	2.05	1.98	1.92	1.87	1.83	1.80	1.74	1.69	1.62
	6.76	**4.71**	**3.88**	**3.41**	**3.11**	**2.90**	**2.73**	**2.60**	**2.50**	**2.41**	**2.34**	**2.28**	**2.17**	**2.09**	**1.97**
400	3.86	3.02	2.62	2.39	2.23	2.12	2.03	1.96	1.90	1.85	1.81	1.78	1.72	1.67	1.60
	6.70	**4.66**	**3.83**	**3.36**	**3.06**	**2.85**	**2.69**	**2.55**	**2.46**	**2.37**	**2.29**	**2.23**	**2.12**	**2.04**	**1.92**
1000	3.85	3.00	2.61	2.38	2.22	2.10	2.02	1.95	1.89	1.84	1.80	1.76	1.70	1.65	1.58
	6.66	**4.62**	**3.80**	**3.34**	**3.04**	**2.82**	**2.66**	**2.53**	**2.43**	**2.34**	**2.26**	**2.20**	**2.09**	**2.01**	**1.89**
∞	3.84	2.99	2.60	2.37	2.21	2.09	2.01	1.94	1.88	1.83	1.79	1.75	1.69	1.64	1.57
	6.64	**4.60**	**3.78**	**3.32**	**3.02**	**2.80**	**2.64**	**2.51**	**2.41**	**2.32**	**2.24**	**2.18**	**2.07**	**1.99**	**1.87**

TABLE B.5 THE STUDENTIZED RANGE STATISTIC (q)*

*The critical values for q corresponding to $\alpha = .05$ (lightface type) and $\alpha = .01$ (boldface type).

df FOR ERROR TERM	k = NUMBER OF TREATMENTS										
	2	3	4	5	6	7	8	9	10	11	12
5	3.64	4.60	5.22	5.67	6.03	6.33	6.58	6.80	6.99	7.17	7.32
	5.70	**6.98**	**7.80**	**8.42**	**8.91**	**9.32**	**9.67**	**9.97**	**10.24**	**10.48**	**10.70**
6	3.46	4.34	4.90	5.30	5.63	5.90	6.12	6.32	6.49	6.65	6.79
	5.24	**6.33**	**7.03**	**7.56**	**7.97**	**8.32**	**8.61**	**8.87**	**9.10**	**9.30**	**9.48**
7	3.34	4.16	4.68	5.06	5.36	5.61	5.82	6.00	6.16	6.30	6.43
	4.95	**5.92**	**6.54**	**7.01**	**7.37**	**7.68**	**7.94**	**8.17**	**8.37**	**8.55**	**8.71**
8	3.26	4.04	4.53	4.89	5.17	5.40	5.60	5.77	5.92	6.05	6.18
	4.75	**5.64**	**6.20**	**6.62**	**6.96**	**7.24**	**7.47**	**7.68**	**7.86**	**8.03**	**8.18**
9	3.20	3.95	4.41	4.76	5.02	5.24	5.43	5.59	5.74	5.87	5.98
	4.60	**5.43**	**5.96**	**6.35**	**6.66**	**6.91**	**7.13**	**7.33**	**7.49**	**7.65**	**7.78**
10	3.15	3.88	4.33	4.65	4.91	5.12	5.30	5.46	5.60	5.72	5.83
	4.48	**5.27**	**5.77**	**6.14**	**6.43**	**6.67**	**6.87**	**7.05**	**7.21**	**7.36**	**7.49**
11	3.11	3.82	4.26	4.57	4.82	5.03	5.20	5.35	5.49	5.61	5.71
	4.39	**5.15**	**5.62**	**5.97**	**6.25**	**6.48**	**6.67**	**6.84**	**6.99**	**7.13**	**7.25**
12	3.08	3.77	4.20	4.51	4.75	4.95	5.12	5.27	5.39	5.51	5.61
	4.32	**5.05**	**5.50**	**5.84**	**6.10**	**6.32**	**6.51**	**6.67**	**6.81**	**6.94**	**7.06**
13	3.06	3.73	4.15	4.45	4.69	4.88	5.05	5.19	5.32	5.43	5.53
	4.26	**4.96**	**5.40**	**5.73**	**5.98**	**6.19**	**6.37**	**6.53**	**6.67**	**6.79**	**6.90**
14	3.03	3.70	4.11	4.41	4.64	4.83	4.99	5.13	5.25	5.36	5.46
	4.21	**4.89**	**5.32**	**5.63**	**5.88**	**6.08**	**6.26**	**6.41**	**6.54**	**6.66**	**6.77**
15	3.01	3.67	4.08	4.37	4.59	4.78	4.94	5.08	5.20	5.31	5.40
	4.17	**4.84**	**5.25**	**5.56**	**5.80**	**5.99**	**6.16**	**6.31**	**6.44**	**6.55**	**6.66**
16	3.00	3.65	4.05	4.33	4.56	4.74	4.90	5.03	5.15	5.26	5.35
	4.13	**4.79**	**5.19**	**5.49**	**5.72**	**5.92**	**6.08**	**6.22**	**6.35**	**6.46**	**6.56**
17	2.98	3.63	4.02	4.30	4.52	4.70	4.86	4.99	5.11	5.21	5.31
	4.10	**4.74**	**5.14**	**5.43**	**5.66**	**5.85**	**6.01**	**6.15**	**6.27**	**6.38**	**6.48**
18	2.97	3.61	4.00	4.28	4.49	4.67	4.82	4.96	5.07	5.17	5.27
	4.07	**4.70**	**5.09**	**5.38**	**5.60**	**5.79**	**5.94**	**6.08**	**6.20**	**6.31**	**6.41**
19	2.96	3.59	3.98	4.25	4.47	4.65	4.79	4.92	5.04	5.14	5.23
	4.05	**4.67**	**5.05**	**5.33**	**5.55**	**5.73**	**5.89**	**6.02**	**6.14**	**6.25**	**6.34**
20	2.95	3.58	3.96	4.23	4.45	4.62	4.77	4.90	5.01	5.11	5.20
	4.02	**4.64**	**5.02**	**5.29**	**5.51**	**5.69**	**5.84**	**5.97**	**6.09**	**6.19**	**6.28**
24	2.92	3.53	3.90	4.17	4.37	4.54	4.68	4.81	4.92	5.01	5.10
	3.96	**4.55**	**4.91**	**5.17**	**5.37**	**5.54**	**5.69**	**5.81**	**5.92**	**6.02**	**6.11**
30	2.89	3.49	3.85	4.10	4.30	4.46	4.60	4.72	4.82	4.92	5.00
	3.89	**4.45**	**4.80**	**5.05**	**5.24**	**5.40**	**5.54**	**5.65**	**5.76**	**5.85**	**5.93**
40	2.86	3.44	3.79	4.04	4.23	4.39	4.52	4.63	4.73	4.82	4.90
	3.82	**4.37**	**4.70**	**4.93**	**5.11**	**5.26**	**5.39**	**5.50**	**5.60**	**5.69**	**5.76**
60	2.83	3.40	3.74	3.98	4.16	4.31	4.44	4.55	4.65	4.73	4.81
	3.76	**4.28**	**4.59**	**4.82**	**4.99**	**5.13**	**5.25**	**5.36**	**5.45**	**5.53**	**5.60**
120	2.80	3.36	3.68	3.92	4.10	4.24	4.36	4.47	4.56	4.64	4.71
	3.70	**4.20**	**4.50**	**4.71**	**4.87**	**5.01**	**5.12**	**5.21**	**5.30**	**5.37**	**5.44**
∞	2.77	3.31	3.63	3.86	4.03	4.17	4.29	4.39	4.47	4.55	4.62
	3.64	**4.12**	**4.40**	**4.60**	**4.76**	**4.88**	**4.99**	**5.08**	**5.16**	**5.23**	**5.29**

T A B L E B . 6   CRITICAL VALUES FOR THE PEARSON CORRELATION*

*To be significant, the sample correlation, r, must be greater than or equal to the critical value in the table.

df = n − 2	LEVEL OF SIGNIFICANCE FOR ONE-TAILED TEST			
	.05	.025	.01	.005
	LEVEL OF SIGNIFICANCE FOR TWO-TAILED TEST			
	.10	.05	.02	.01
1	.988	.997	.9995	.9999
2	.900	.950	.980	.990
3	.805	.878	.934	.959
4	.729	.811	.882	.917
5	.669	.754	.833	.874
6	.622	.707	.789	.834
7	.582	.666	.750	.798
8	.549	.632	.716	.765
9	.521	.602	.685	.735
10	.497	.576	.658	.708
11	.476	.553	.634	.684
12	.458	.532	.612	.661
13	.441	.514	.592	.641
14	.426	.497	.574	.623
15	.412	.482	.558	.606
16	.400	.468	.542	.590
17	.389	.456	.528	.575
18	.378	.444	.516	.561
19	.369	.433	.503	.549
20	.360	.423	.492	.537
21	.352	.413	.482	.526
22	.344	.404	.472	.515
23	.337	.396	.462	.505
24	.330	.388	.453	.496
25	.323	.381	.445	.487
26	.317	.374	.437	.479
27	.311	.367	.430	.471
28	.306	.361	.423	.463
29	.301	.355	.416	.456
30	.296	.349	.409	.449
35	.275	.325	.381	.418
40	.257	.304	.358	.393
45	.243	.288	.338	.372
50	.231	.273	.322	.354
60	.211	.250	.295	.325
70	.195	.232	.274	.302
80	.183	.217	.256	.283
90	.173	.205	.242	.267
100	.164	.195	.230	.254

TABLE B.7 THE CHI-SQUARE DISTRIBUTION*

*The table entries are critical values of χ^2.

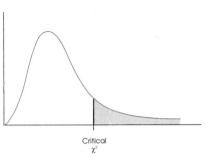

Critical
χ^2

df	PROPORTION IN CRITICAL REGION				
	0.10	0.05	0.025	0.01	0.005
1	2.71	3.84	5.02	6.63	7.88
2	4.61	5.99	7.38	9.21	10.60
3	6.25	7.81	9.35	11.34	12.84
4	7.78	9.49	11.14	13.28	14.86
5	9.24	11.07	12.83	15.09	16.75
6	10.64	12.59	14.45	16.81	18.55
7	12.02	14.07	16.01	18.48	20.28
8	13.36	15.51	17.53	20.09	21.96
9	14.68	16.92	19.02	21.67	23.59
10	15.99	18.31	20.48	23.21	25.19
11	17.28	19.68	21.92	24.72	26.76
12	18.55	21.03	23.34	26.22	28.30
13	19.81	22.36	24.74	27.69	29.82
14	21.06	23.68	26.12	29.14	31.32
15	22.31	25.00	27.49	30.58	32.80
16	23.54	26.30	28.85	32.00	34.27
17	24.77	27.59	30.19	33.41	35.72
18	25.99	28.87	31.53	34.81	37.16
19	27.20	30.14	32.85	36.19	38.58
20	28.41	31.41	34.17	37.57	40.00
21	29.62	32.67	35.48	38.93	41.40
22	30.81	33.92	36.78	40.29	42.80
23	32.01	35.17	38.08	41.64	44.18
24	33.20	36.42	39.36	42.98	45.56
25	34.38	37.65	40.65	44.31	46.93
26	35.56	38.89	41.92	45.64	48.29
27	36.74	40.11	43.19	46.96	49.64
28	37.92	41.34	44.46	48.28	50.99
29	39.09	42.56	45.72	49.59	52.34
30	40.26	43.77	46.98	50.89	53.67
40	51.81	55.76	59.34	63.69	66.77
50	63.17	67.50	71.42	76.15	79.49
60	74.40	79.08	83.30	88.38	91.95
70	85.53	90.53	95.02	100.42	104.22
80	96.58	101.88	106.63	112.33	116.32
90	107.56	113.14	118.14	124.12	128.30
100	118.50	124.34	129.56	135.81	140.17

TABLE B.8A   CRITICAL VALUES OF THE MANN-WHITNEY U FOR $\alpha = .05$*

*Critical values are provided for a *one-tailed* test at $\alpha = .05$ (lightface type) and for a *two-tailed* test at $\alpha = .05$ (boldface type). To be significant for any given n_A and n_B, the obtained U must be *equal to* or *less than* the critical value in the table. Dashes (—) in the body of the table indicate that no decision is possible at the stated level of significance and values of n_A and n_B.

n_B \ n_A	1	2	3	4	5	6	7	8	9	10	11	12	13	14	15	16	17	18	19	20
1	—	—	—	—	—	—	—	—	—	—	—	—	—	—	—	—	—	—	0	0
																			—	—
2	—	—	—	—	0	0	0	1	1	1	1	2	2	2	3	3	3	4	4	4
					—	—	—	**0**	**0**	**0**	**0**	**1**	**1**	**1**	**1**	**1**	**2**	**2**	**2**	**2**
3	—	—	0	0	1	2	2	3	3	4	5	5	6	7	7	8	9	9	10	11
	—	—	—	—	**0**	**1**	**1**	**2**	**2**	**3**	**3**	**4**	**4**	**5**	**5**	**6**	**6**	**7**	**7**	**8**
4	—	—	0	1	2	3	4	5	6	7	8	9	10	11	12	14	15	16	17	18
	—	—	—	**0**	**1**	**2**	**3**	**4**	**4**	**5**	**6**	**7**	**8**	**9**	**10**	**11**	**11**	**12**	**13**	**13**
5	—	0	1	2	4	5	6	8	9	11	12	13	15	16	18	19	20	22	23	25
	—	—	**0**	**1**	**2**	**3**	**5**	**6**	**7**	**8**	**9**	**11**	**12**	**13**	**14**	**15**	**17**	**18**	**19**	**20**
6	—	0	2	3	5	7	8	10	12	14	16	17	19	21	23	25	26	28	30	32
	—	—	**1**	**2**	**3**	**5**	**6**	**8**	**10**	**11**	**13**	**14**	**16**	**17**	**19**	**21**	**22**	**24**	**25**	**27**
7	—	0	2	4	6	8	11	13	15	17	19	21	24	26	28	30	33	35	37	39
	—	—	**1**	**3**	**5**	**6**	**8**	**10**	**12**	**14**	**16**	**18**	**20**	**22**	**24**	**26**	**28**	**30**	**32**	**34**
8	—	1	3	5	8	10	13	15	18	20	23	26	28	31	33	36	39	41	44	47
	—	**0**	**2**	**4**	**6**	**8**	**10**	**13**	**15**	**17**	**19**	**22**	**24**	**26**	**29**	**31**	**34**	**36**	**38**	**41**
9	—	1	3	6	9	12	15	18	21	24	27	30	33	36	39	42	45	48	51	54
	—	**0**	**2**	**4**	**7**	**10**	**12**	**15**	**17**	**20**	**23**	**26**	**28**	**31**	**34**	**37**	**39**	**42**	**45**	**48**
10	—	1	4	7	11	14	17	20	24	27	31	34	37	41	44	48	51	55	58	62
	—	**0**	**3**	**5**	**8**	**11**	**14**	**17**	**20**	**23**	**26**	**29**	**33**	**36**	**39**	**42**	**45**	**48**	**52**	**55**
11	—	1	5	8	12	16	19	23	27	31	34	38	42	46	50	54	57	61	65	69
	—	**0**	**3**	**6**	**9**	**13**	**16**	**19**	**23**	**26**	**30**	**33**	**37**	**40**	**44**	**47**	**51**	**55**	**58**	**62**
12	—	2	5	9	13	17	21	26	30	34	38	42	47	51	55	60	64	68	72	77
	—	**1**	**4**	**7**	**11**	**14**	**18**	**22**	**26**	**29**	**33**	**37**	**41**	**45**	**49**	**53**	**57**	**61**	**65**	**69**
13	—	2	6	10	15	19	24	28	33	37	42	47	51	56	61	65	70	75	80	84
	—	**1**	**4**	**8**	**12**	**16**	**20**	**24**	**28**	**33**	**37**	**41**	**45**	**50**	**54**	**59**	**63**	**67**	**72**	**76**
14	—	2	7	11	16	21	26	31	36	41	46	51	56	61	66	71	77	82	87	92
	—	**1**	**5**	**9**	**13**	**17**	**22**	**26**	**31**	**36**	**40**	**45**	**50**	**55**	**59**	**64**	**67**	**74**	**78**	**83**
15	—	3	7	12	18	23	28	33	39	44	50	55	61	66	72	77	83	88	94	100
	—	**1**	**5**	**10**	**14**	**19**	**24**	**29**	**34**	**39**	**44**	**49**	**54**	**59**	**64**	**70**	**75**	**80**	**85**	**90**
16	—	3	8	14	19	25	30	36	42	48	54	60	65	71	77	83	89	95	101	107
	—	**1**	**6**	**11**	**15**	**21**	**26**	**31**	**37**	**42**	**47**	**53**	**59**	**64**	**70**	**75**	**81**	**86**	**92**	**98**
17	—	3	9	15	20	26	33	39	45	51	57	64	70	77	83	89	96	102	109	115
	—	**2**	**6**	**11**	**17**	**22**	**28**	**34**	**39**	**45**	**51**	**57**	**63**	**67**	**75**	**81**	**87**	**93**	**99**	**105**
18	—	4	9	16	22	28	35	41	48	55	61	68	75	82	88	95	102	109	116	123
	—	**2**	**7**	**12**	**18**	**24**	**30**	**36**	**42**	**48**	**55**	**61**	**67**	**74**	**80**	**86**	**93**	**99**	**106**	**112**
19	0	4	10	17	23	30	37	44	51	58	65	72	80	87	94	101	109	116	123	130
	—	**2**	**7**	**13**	**19**	**25**	**32**	**38**	**45**	**52**	**58**	**65**	**72**	**78**	**85**	**92**	**99**	**106**	**113**	**119**
20	0	4	11	18	25	32	39	47	54	62	69	77	84	92	100	107	115	123	130	138
	—	**2**	**8**	**13**	**20**	**27**	**34**	**41**	**48**	**55**	**62**	**69**	**76**	**83**	**90**	**98**	**105**	**112**	**119**	**127**

TABLE B.8B — CRITICAL VALUES OF THE MANN-WHITNEY U FOR $\alpha = .01$*

*Critical values are provided for a *one-tailed* test at $\alpha = .01$ (lightface type) and for a *two-tailed* test at $\alpha = .01$ (boldface type). To be significant for any given n_A and n_B, the obtained U must be *equal to* or *less than* the critical value in the table. Dashes (—) in the body of the table indicate that no decision is possible at the stated level of significance and values of n_A and n_B.

n_B \ n_A	1	2	3	4	5	6	7	8	9	10	11	12	13	14	15	16	17	18	19	20
1	—	—	—	—	—	—	—	—	—	—	—	—	—	—	—	—	—	—	—	—
2	—	—	—	—	—	—	—	—	—	—	—	—	0	0	0	0	0	0	1	1
													—	—	—	—	—	—	**0**	**0**
3	—	—	—	—	—	—	0	0	1	1	1	2	2	2	3	3	4	4	4	5
							—	—	**0**	**0**	**0**	**1**	**1**	**1**	**2**	**2**	**2**	**2**	**3**	**3**
4	—	—	—	—	0	1	1	2	3	3	4	5	5	6	7	7	8	9	9	10
					—	**0**	**0**	**1**	**1**	**2**	**2**	**3**	**3**	**4**	**5**	**5**	**6**	**6**	**7**	**8**
5	—	—	—	0	1	2	3	4	5	6	7	8	9	10	11	12	13	14	15	16
				—	**0**	**1**	**1**	**2**	**3**	**4**	**5**	**6**	**7**	**7**	**8**	**9**	**10**	**11**	**12**	**13**
6	—	—	—	1	2	3	4	6	7	8	9	11	12	13	15	16	18	19	20	22
				0	**1**	**2**	**3**	**4**	**5**	**6**	**7**	**9**	**10**	**11**	**12**	**13**	**15**	**16**	**17**	**18**
7	—	—	0	1	3	4	6	7	9	11	12	14	16	17	19	21	23	24	26	28
			—	**0**	**1**	**3**	**4**	**6**	**7**	**9**	**10**	**12**	**13**	**15**	**16**	**18**	**19**	**21**	**22**	**24**
8	—	—	0	2	4	6	7	9	11	13	15	17	20	22	24	26	28	30	32	34
			—	**1**	**2**	**4**	**6**	**7**	**9**	**11**	**13**	**15**	**17**	**18**	**20**	**22**	**24**	**26**	**28**	**30**
9	—	—	1	3	5	7	9	11	14	16	18	21	23	26	28	31	33	36	38	40
			0	**1**	**3**	**5**	**7**	**9**	**11**	**13**	**16**	**18**	**20**	**22**	**24**	**27**	**29**	**31**	**33**	**36**
10	—	—	1	3	6	8	11	13	16	19	22	24	27	30	33	36	38	41	44	47
			0	**2**	**4**	**6**	**9**	**11**	**13**	**16**	**18**	**21**	**24**	**26**	**29**	**31**	**34**	**37**	**39**	**42**
11	—	—	1	4	7	9	12	15	18	22	25	28	31	34	37	41	44	47	50	53
			0	**2**	**5**	**7**	**10**	**13**	**16**	**18**	**21**	**24**	**27**	**30**	**33**	**36**	**39**	**42**	**45**	**48**
12	—	—	2	5	8	11	14	17	21	24	28	31	35	38	42	46	49	53	56	60
			1	**3**	**6**	**9**	**12**	**15**	**18**	**21**	**24**	**27**	**31**	**34**	**37**	**41**	**44**	**47**	**51**	**54**
13	—	0	2	5	9	12	16	20	23	27	31	35	39	43	47	51	55	59	63	67
	—	**1**	**3**	**7**	**10**	**13**	**17**	**20**	**24**	**27**	**31**	**34**	**38**	**42**	**45**	**49**	**53**	**56**	**60**	
14	—	0	2	6	10	13	17	22	26	30	34	38	43	47	51	56	60	65	69	73
	—	**1**	**4**	**7**	**11**	**15**	**18**	**22**	**26**	**30**	**34**	**38**	**42**	**46**	**50**	**54**	**58**	**63**	**67**	
15	—	0	3	7	11	15	19	24	28	33	37	42	47	51	56	61	66	70	75	80
	—	**2**	**5**	**8**	**12**	**16**	**20**	**24**	**29**	**33**	**37**	**42**	**46**	**51**	**55**	**60**	**64**	**69**	**73**	
16	—	0	3	7	12	16	21	26	31	36	41	46	51	56	61	66	71	76	82	87
	—	**2**	**5**	**9**	**13**	**18**	**22**	**27**	**31**	**36**	**41**	**45**	**50**	**55**	**60**	**65**	**70**	**74**	**79**	
17	—	0	4	8	13	18	23	28	33	38	44	49	55	60	66	71	77	82	88	93
	—	**2**	**6**	**10**	**15**	**19**	**24**	**29**	**34**	**39**	**44**	**49**	**54**	**60**	**65**	**70**	**75**	**81**	**86**	
18	—	0	4	9	14	19	24	30	36	41	47	53	59	65	70	76	82	88	94	100
	—	**2**	**6**	**11**	**16**	**21**	**26**	**31**	**37**	**42**	**47**	**53**	**58**	**64**	**70**	**75**	**81**	**87**	**92**	
19	—	1	4	9	15	20	26	32	38	44	50	56	63	69	75	82	88	94	101	107
	0	**3**	**7**	**12**	**17**	**22**	**28**	**33**	**39**	**45**	**51**	**56**	**63**	**69**	**74**	**81**	**87**	**93**	**99**	
20	—	1	5	10	16	22	28	34	40	47	53	60	67	73	80	87	93	100	107	114
	0	**3**	**8**	**13**	**18**	**24**	**30**	**36**	**42**	**48**	**54**	**60**	**67**	**73**	**79**	**86**	**92**	**99**	**105**	

TABLE B.9   CRITICAL VALUES OF *T* FOR THE WILCOXON SIGNED-RANKS TEST*

*To be significant, the obtained *T* must be *equal to* or *less than* the critical value. Dashes (—) in the columns indicate that no decision is possible for the stated α and *n*.

	LEVEL OF SIGNIFICANCE FOR ONE-TAILED TEST					LEVEL OF SIGNIFICANCE FOR ONE-TAILED TEST			
	.05	.025	.01	.005		.05	.025	.01	.005
	LEVEL OF SIGNIFICANCE FOR TWO-TAILED TEST					LEVEL OF SIGNIFICANCE FOR TWO-TAILED TEST			
n	.10	.05	.02	.01	*n*	.10	.05	.02	.01
5	0	—	—	—	28	130	116	101	91
6	2	0	—	—	29	140	126	110	100
7	3	2	0	—	30	151	137	120	109
8	5	3	1	0	31	163	147	130	118
9	8	5	3	1	32	175	159	140	128
10	10	8	5	3	33	187	170	151	138
11	13	10	7	5	34	200	182	162	148
12	17	13	9	7	35	213	195	173	159
13	21	17	12	9	36	227	208	185	171
14	25	21	15	12	37	241	221	198	182
15	30	25	19	15	38	256	235	211	194
16	35	29	23	19	39	271	249	224	207
17	41	34	27	23	40	286	264	238	220
18	47	40	32	27	41	302	279	252	233
19	53	46	37	32	42	319	294	266	247
20	60	52	43	37	43	336	310	281	261
21	67	58	49	42	44	353	327	296	276
22	75	65	55	48	45	371	343	312	291
23	83	73	62	54	46	389	361	328	307
24	91	81	69	61	47	407	378	345	322
25	100	89	76	68	48	426	396	362	339
26	110	98	84	75	49	446	415	379	355
27	119	107	92	83	50	466	434	397	373

ACKNOWLEDGMENTS

The statistical tables in Appendix B have been adapted or reprinted, with permission, from the following sources:

TABLE B.1 Appendix 2 of R. Clarke, A. Coladarci, and J. Caffrey, *Statistical Reasoning and Procedures.* Columbus, Ohio: Charles E. Merrill Publishing, 1965.

TABLE B.2 Table III of R. A. Fisher and F. Yates, *Statistical Tables for Biological, Agricultural and Medical Research,* 6th ed. London: Longman Group Ltd., 1974 (previously published by Oliver and Boyd Ltd., Edinburgh).

TABLE B.3 Table 31 of E. Pearson and H. O. Hartley, *Biometrika Tables for Statisticians,* 2nd ed. New York: Cambridge University Press, 1958. Adapted and reprinted with permission of the Biometrika trustees.

TABLE B.4 Table A14 of *Statistical Methods,* 7th ed. by George W. Snedecor and William G. Cochran, Copyright © 1980 by the Iowa State University Press, 2121 South State Avenue, Ames, Iowa 50010.

TABLE B.5 Table 29 of E. Pearson and H. Hartley, *Biometrika Tables for Statisticians,* 3rd ed. New York: Cambridge University Press, 1966. Adapted and reprinted with permission of the Biometrika trustees.

TABLE B.6 Table VI of R. A. Fisher and F. Yates, *Statistical Tables for Biological, Agricultural and Medical Research,* 6th ed. London: Longman Group Ltd., 1974 (previously published by Oliver and Boyd Ltd., Edinburgh).

TABLE B.7 Table 8 of E. Pearson and H. Hartley, *Biometrika Tables for Statisticians,* 3d ed. New York: Cambridge University Press, 1966. Adapted and reprinted with permission of the Biometrika trustees.

TABLE B.8 Table D.10 of *Introductory Statistics* by R. E. Kirk. Copyright © 1978 by Wadsworth, Inc. Reprinted by permission of Brooks/Cole Publishing Company, Monterey, California 93940.

TABLE B.9 Adapted from F. Wilcoxon, S. K. Katti, and R. A. Wilcox, *Critical Values and Probability Levels of the Wilcoxon Rank-Sum Test and the Wilcoxon Signed-Ranks Test.* Wayne, N.J.: American Cyanamid Company, 1963. Also adapted from R. P. Runyon and A. Haber, *Fundamentals of Behavioral Statistics,* 5th ed. Copyright © 1984 by McGraw-Hill (originally by Addison-Wesley), p. 435, Table J. Adapted and reprinted with permission of the American Cyanamid Company and McGraw-Hill, Inc.

Many of the problems in the text require several stages of computation. At each stage there is an opportunity for rounding answers. Depending on the exact sequence of operations used to solve a problem, different individuals will round their answers at different times and in different ways. Also, problems worked on a computer will not be rounded at each stage. As a result, you may obtain answers that are slightly different from those presented here. As long as those differences are small, they probably can be attributed to rounding error and should not be a matter for concern.

CHAPTER 1 INTRODUCTION TO STATISTICS

1. In an experiment the researcher randomly assigns subjects to conditions and manipulates the independent variable. In correlational or quasi-experimental research, preexisting groups of subjects are used and the researcher usually does not manipulate the independent variable.

3. In the experimental method the experimenter manipulates and controls the independent variable to determine whether or not it has any effect on the dependent variable.

5. **a.** quasi-experimental
   b. the dependent variable is vocabulary skill

7. **a.** The researcher could simply find two different offices, one with music and one without, and measure productivity.
   b. The researcher could select one office and measure productivity for one month with music, then for one month without music.
   c. The independent variable is the presence/absence of music. The dependent variable is office productivity.

9. **a.** discrete
   b. ratio scale (zero means no absences)

11. A discrete variable consists of separate, indivisible categories. A continuous variable is divisible into an infinite number of fractional parts.

13. A construct is a hypothetical concept. An operational definition defines a construct in terms of a measurement procedure.

15. **a.** Add 1 to each score then sum the resulting values.
    b. Square each score then sum the squared values.
    c. Subtract 1 from each score and square the resulting values. Then sum the squared values.

17. **a.** $\Sigma X = 8$
    b. $\Sigma Y = 11$
    c. $\Sigma XY = 34$

19. **a.** ΣX^2
    b. $(\Sigma X)^2$

21. **a.** $\Sigma X = -4$
    b. $\Sigma X^2 = 30$
    c. $\Sigma(X + 3) = 11$

23. **a.** $\Sigma X = -3$
    b. $\Sigma Y = 14$
    c. $\Sigma XY = -14$
    d. $\Sigma(Y - 1)^2 = 30$

25. **a.** $\Sigma X = 25$
    b. $\Sigma X^2 = 165$
    c. $(\Sigma X)^2 = 625$
    d. $\Sigma(X - 5)^2 = 41$

CHAPTER 2 **FREQUENCY DISTRIBUTIONS**

1.

X	f	p	%
5	3	.15	15%
4	4	.20	20%
3	8	.40	40%
2	3	.15	15%
1	2	.10	10%

3. $N = \Sigma f = 13$, $\Sigma X = 38$, $\Sigma X^2 = 128$

5. A grouped frequency distribution is used when the original scale of measurement consists of more categories than can be listed simply in a regular table. Around 20 or more categories is generally considered too many for a regular table.

7. The simplest and most complete way to present a set of $N = 7$ scores is to list each individual score. You would need a grouped table to cover a range of 61 to 96, and the grouped table would not tell you the exact value of each score. Also, a grouped table is more complicated than a simple listing of the scores.

9. a. $N = 14$
b. $\Sigma X = 33$

11.

X	f		X	f
30–31	1			
28–29	2		30–34	1
26–27	2		25–29	5
24–25	3		20–24	12
22–23	5		15–19	8
20–21	5		10–14	2
18–19	5			
16–17	3			
14–15	1			
12–13	1			

13.

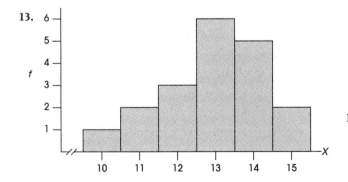

15. a.

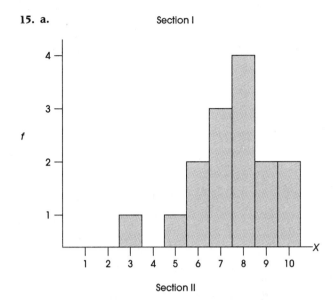

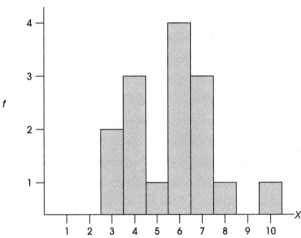

b. The scores in Section I are centered around $X = 8$ and form a negatively skewed distribution. In Section II, the scores are lower (centered around $X = 6$) and there is a tendency toward a positively skewed distribution.

17. a. Independent variable is the number of training sessions and the dependent variable is the time to fall asleep.
b. ratio scale
c. line graph or histogram

d.

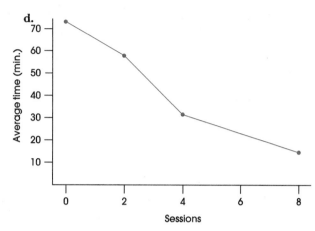

25. a.

X	f
80–89	3
70–79	4
60–69	3
50–59	4
40–49	1
30–39	2
20–29	1

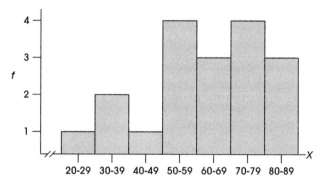

19.

X	f	cf	c%
10	3	20	100%
9	1	17	85%
8	0	16	80%
7	4	16	80%
6	6	12	60%
5	4	6	30%
4	2	2	10%

c. You cannot construct a stem-and-leaf display from a grouped frequency distribution table or graph because the frequency distribution does not identify the individual scores.

21.

X	f	cf	c%
5	7	25	100%
4	8	18	72%
3	5	10	40%
2	3	5	20%
1	2	2	8%

23. a. $X = 3.5$
b. 90%
c. $X = 2.0$
d. 85%
e. $X = 4.25$

27. a.

8	2
7	97384
6	2126
5	82
4	2
3	10
2	63
1	60843
0	997

b.

X	f
80–89	1
70–79	5
60–69	4
50–59	2
40–49	1
30–39	2
20–29	2
10–19	5
0–9	3

c. The group is split with attitudes at both extremes.

CHAPTER 3 CENTRAL TENDENCY

1. Mean = 32/10 = 3.2
Median = 3.5
Mode = 4

3. Mean = 25/8 = 3.125
Median = 3.5
Mode = 4

5. The original $\Sigma X = 90$. With the additional score, $n = 10$ and $\Sigma X = 120$. The new mean is 120/10 = 12.

7. The median is used instead of the mean when there is a skewed distribution (few extreme scores), an open-ended distribution, undetermined scores, or an ordinal scale.

9. If the new value remains on the same side of the median (above or below) as the original value, then the median will not change. However, if a score is changed so that its new value is located on the opposite side of the median as the original value, then the median must be changed.

11. Use the median. The mean cannot be computed with undetermined scores.

13. The original samples have $\Sigma X = 12$ and $\Sigma X = 70$. The combined sample has $\Sigma X = 82$ and $n = 10$. The mean for the combined sample is $82/10 = 8.2$.

15. Mean = 3
Median = 2.5
Mode = 1

17. Although the mean and median would be located in the center of the distribution, they would not be representative of most of the scores. The individual scores would be clustered around the two modes with relatively few scores located in the center.

19. $\Sigma X = 1300$

21. Mean = $33/12 = 2.75$
Median = 2.5
Mode = 2

23. negatively skewed (the mean is displaced toward the tail of the distribution)

25. a.

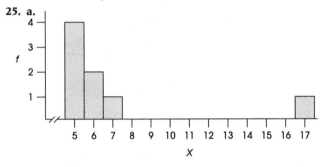

b.

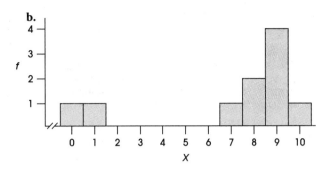

c. In general, the scores in section II are higher. The exceptions are the single high score in section I and the two very low scores in section II.

d. Section I: Mean = 7 and median = 5.5
Section II: Mean = 7 and median = 8.5
The mean does not differentiate these two sections. The median provides a better measure of central tendency.

27. a. Mean = $115/16 = 7.1875$ Median = 6.5
b. Using the mean, the class is above the national norm.
c. Using the median, the class is below the norm.

CHAPTER 4 **VARIABILITY**

1. a. SS is the sum of squared deviation scores.
b. Variance is the mean squared deviation.
c. Standard deviation is the square root of the variance. It provides a measure of the standard distance from the mean.

3. $SS = 20$, $s^2 = 5$, $s = 2.24$

5. a. $\Sigma X = 300$
b. $\Sigma(X - \mu) = 0$ (always)
c. $\Sigma(X - \mu)^2 = SS = 200$

7. SS cannot be less than zero because it is computed by adding squared deviations. Squared deviations are always greater than or equal to zero.

9. The standard deviation, $\sigma = 20$, provides a measure of the standard distance from the mean.

11. A standard deviation of zero means that there is no variability. All the scores have exactly the same value.

13. $SS = 32$

15. a. $\overline{X} = 3$ definitional formula
b. $\overline{X} = 3.2$ computational formula

17. a. $SS = 36$, variance = 9, standard deviation = 3
b. $SS = 36$, variance = 9, standard deviation = 3
c. $SS = 144$, variance = 36, standard deviation = 6
d. Adding a constant to each score does not change any of the deviations and does not change the standard deviation.
e. When each score is multiplied by a constant, the deviations and the standard deviation are also multiplied by the constant.

19. a. standard deviation is 10
b. $SS = 2400$

21. Range = 12 points. $Q1 = 3.5$ and $Q3 = 8.5$. Semi-interquartile range = 2.5. $SS = 120$, $s = 3.30$.

23. $\overline{X} = 0.09$; $s^2 = 0.00015$; $s = 0.0122$

25. a. College students $\overline{X} = 40.6$ and Business Men $\overline{X} = 40.1$. On average, both groups are very accurate.
b. College students $s = 9.22$ and Business Men $s = 2.56$. Age estimates for the business men are generally close to the correct value. The estimates for the college students are much more scattered.

CHAPTER 5 z-SCORES

1. A z-score describes a precise location within a distribution. The sign of the z-score tells whether the location is above (+) or below (−) the mean, and the magnitude tells the distance from the mean in terms of the number of standard deviations.

3. Tom's z-score indicates that he scored far above average for this class. This means that he knows a lot relative to the rest of the students, but it does not mean that he knows a lot about developmental psychology in absolute terms.

5. Because the score, $X = 55$, is above the mean, $\mu = 45$, it must have a positive z-score. Therefore, $z = -2.00$ cannot be correct.

7. a.

X	z	X	z
27	+0.40	28	+0.60
31	+1.20	34	+1.80
29	+0.80	33	+1.60
17	−1.60	19	−1.20
15	−2.00	22	−0.60

b.

X	z	X	z
27	+0.40	32	+1.40
30	+1.00	23	−0.40
10	−3.00	18	−1.40
39	+2.80	35	+2.00

9. a. For the original population $\mu = 10$ and $\sigma = 3$.

b.

X	z	X	z
13	+1.00	10	0
7	−1.00	11	+0.33
12	+0.67	11	+0.33
15	+1.67	10	0
5	−1.67	6	−1.33

11.

X	z	X	z
85	+0.25	130	+2.50
90	+0.50	82	+0.10
110	+1.50	68	−0.60
75	−0.25	80	0
60	−1.00	95	+0.75
45	−1.75	30	−2.50

13. $\sigma = 7$

15. $\mu = 55$ and $\sigma = 5$

17. $\sigma = 20$

19. With $\sigma = 2$, $z = -.50$. This is the higher value.

21. Your z-score is +1.50 which is better than your friend's z-score of +1.10.

23. The numerator of the z-score formula is a deviation score, $X - \mu$. Deviation scores always sum to zero.

25. a. $\mu = 4.4$ and $\sigma = 2.15$

b.

X	z
1	−1.58
3	−0.65
5	+0.28
6	+0.74
7	+1.21

c. For the z-scores the mean is zero and the standard deviation is 1.

d. With a mean of zero the sign indicates direction above or below the mean. With a standard deviation of one, the magnitude of a z-score indicates the number of standard deviations away from the mean.

CHAPTER 6 PROBABILITY

1. a. $p = 45/60 = 0.75$
  b. $p = 25/60 = 0.42$
  c. $p = 5/60 = 0.08$

3. Sampling with replacement means that each individual selected for a sample is returned to the population before the next individual is selected. This sampling method is used to ensure that the probability of selecting any specific individual remains constant.

5. a. 0.1747
  b. 0.6826

  c. 0.4332
  d. 0.7506

7. The portion of the distribution consisting of scores greater than 50 is more than one-half of the whole distribution. The answer must be greater than 0.50.

9. $P(X > 25 \text{ minutes}) = P(z > = -0.50) = 0.6915$

11. a. $p = 0.6915$
  b. $p = 0.0668$
  c. $p = 0.9772$
  d. $p = 0.8664$
  e. $p = 0.2295$

13. **a.** $z = 2.05$, $X = 705$
    b. $z = 0.52$, $X = 552$
    c. $z = 1.30$, Rank = 90.32%
    d. z boundaries $+1.96$ and -1.96; score boundaries 304 and 696
    e. Semi-interquartile range is 67 points (z boundaries for the interquartile range are $+0.67$ and -0.67).

15. **a.** The semi-interquartile range is bounded by $z = 0.67$ and $z = -0.67$. With $\sigma = 10$, the semi-interquartile range is $(0.67)(10) = 6.7$.
    b. With $\sigma = 20$, the semi-interquartile range is $(0.67)(20) = 13.4$.
    c. In general, the semi-interquartile range is equal to 0.67σ.

17. The bottom 25% have z-scores less than -0.67 or scores less than 63. The top 25% have z-scores greater than $+0.67$ or scores greater than 73. The middle 50% have scores between 63 and 73.

19. The Meek: $z < -1.65$; $X < 45.15$
    The Mild: $-1.65 < z < -0.67$; $45.15 < X < 53.97$
    The Average: $-0.67 < z < +0.67$; $53.97 < X < 66.03$
    The Aggressive: $+0.67 < z < +1.65$; $66.03 < X < 74.85$
    The Dangerous: $z > +1.65$; $X > 74.85$

21. **a.** $z = 1.04$, $X = 68.32$

    b. $z = 0.25$, $X = 62$
    c. $z = -0.84$, $X = 53.28$

23. **a.** $z = -1.04$, $X = 104.4$
    b. $z = 1.18$, $X = 137.7$
    c. $z = 1.47$, rank = 92.92%
    d. $z = -1.20$, rank = 11.51%
    e. $z = 0$, rank = 50%
    f. semi-interquartile range = 10.05 points

25. **a.** With four suits possible, the probability of guessing correctly is $p = 1/4$.
    b. With $n = 48$, $p = 1/4$ and $q = 3/4$, it is possible to use the normal approximation to the binomial distribution with $\mu = 12$ and $\sigma = 3$. Using the real limit of 18.5, $P(X > 18.5) = P(z > 2.17) = 0.0150$.

27. **a.** $\mu = pn = 80$
    b. Using the real limit of 95.5, $P(X > 95.5) = P(z > 3.88) = 0.00005$.
    c. Using the real limit of 94.5, $P(X < 94.5) = P(z > 3.63) = 0.9998$
    d. Using the answers from parts b and c, $P(X = 95) = 1.00 - (0.00005 + 0.9998) = 0.00015$

29. If you are just guessing then $p = q = 1/2$, and with $n = 36$ the normal approximation has $\mu = 18$ and $\sigma = 3$. Using the lower real limit of 23.5, $P(X > 23.5) = P(z > 1.83) = 0.0336$.

CHAPTER 7 PROBABILITY AND SAMPLES: THE DISTRIBUTION OF SAMPLE MEANS

1. **a.** The distribution of sample means is the set of all possible sample means for random samples of a specific size (n) from a specific population.
   b. The expected value of $\overline{X}$ is the mean of the distribution of sample means (μ).
   c. The standard error of $\overline{X}$ is the standard deviation of the distribution of sample means ($\sigma_{\overline{x}} = \sigma/\sqrt{n}$).

3. The larger sample ($n = 30$) will have the smaller standard error. On average, $\overline{X}$ from the larger sample will be closer to μ.

5. **a.** Standard error = $100/\sqrt{4} = 50$
   b. Standard error = $100/\sqrt{25} = 20$
   c. Standard error = $100/\sqrt{100} = 10$

7. **a.** $z = -0.50$, $p = 0.3085$
   b. Standard error = 1; $z = -1.00$; $p = 0.1587$

9. **a.** $z = +1.00$, $p = 0.1587$
   b. $z = -2.00$, $p = 0.0228$

11. **a.** Standard error = 6, $z = 1.00$, $p = 0.1587$ (more likely)
    b. Standard error = 2, $z = 1.50$, $p = 0.0668$

13. **a.** $n > 4$
    b. $n > 16$
    c. $n > 400$

15. With a standard error of 0.052 this sample mean corre-

sponds to a z-score of $+5.00$. The probability of obtaining a z-score this extreme is less than 0.00003. It is very unlikely that a random sample of freshmen would score this high. They must be special.

17. **a.** With a standard error of 3.41 this sample mean corresponds to a z-score of $z = 3.14$. A z-score this extreme has a probability of only $p = 0.0008$.
    b. It would be almost impossible to obtain a sample mean this large by random sampling.

19. With $n = 30$ the standard error is 0.55. If the manufacturer's claim is true, this sample mean has a z-score of $z = -2.73$. The probability of obtaining such a sample is $P = 0.0032$. It is extremely unlikely to obtain this sample if the manufacturer's claim is true.

21. With $n = 16$ the standard error is 0.5 and $P(\overline{X} < 31) = P(z < -2) = 0.0228$. This is a very unlikely outcome. The machinery probably needs repair.

23. **a.** With $n = 4$ the standard error is 1. If the shipper's claim is true, the sample mean corresponds to a z-score of $z = -2.00$. The probability of obtaining a value this extreme is $p = 0.0228$.
    b. The manager should suspect that he has been cheated. It is extremely unlikely to obtain this sample if the shipper's claim is true.

CHAPTER 8 INTRODUCTION TO HYPOTHESIS TESTING

1. a. A Type I error is rejecting a true H_0. This can occur if you obtain a very unusual sample with scores that are much different from the general population.
   b. A Type II error is failing to reject a false H_0. This can happen when the treatment effect is very small. In this case the treated sample is not noticeably different from the original population.

3. a. Dependent variable is reaction time and independent variable is the position of the indicator light.
   b. The position of the indicator light has no effect on reaction time.
   c. H_0: $\mu = 200$
      H_1: $\mu \neq 200$
      Where μ refers to the mean reaction time with the light at eye level.
   d. The distribution of sample means is normal with $\mu = 200$ and $\sigma_{\bar{x}} = 4$. The critical region corresponds to z-score values greater than $+1.96$ or less than -1.96.
   e. $\bar{X} = 195$ corresponds to $z = -1.25$. Fail to reject H_0.
   f. With $n = 100$, $\sigma_{\bar{x}} = 2$ and $\bar{X} = 195$ corresponds to $z = -2.50$. Reject H_0. With the larger sample there is less error so the 5 point difference is sufficient to reject the null hypothesis.

5. a. $\bar{X} - \mu$ measures the difference between the sample data and the null hypothesis.
   b. A sample mean is not expected to be identical to the population mean. The standard error indicates how much difference between $\bar{X}$ and μ is expected by chance.

7. The null hypothesis states that the price change has no effect on weekly sales. For these data, $\bar{X} = 161.75$, the standard error is 8.13, and the z-score statistic is -2.86. Reject the null hypothesis and conclude that there has been a significant change in weekly sales.

9. a. If there is no change and the population mean is still $\mu = 8.4$, the standard error is 0.23 and this sample mean corresponds to $z = -5.65$. This is a very unlikely value so reject the null hypothesis and conclude that there has been a change in homework time.
   b. With $n = 20$ the standard error would be 0.74 and the z-score for this sample would be $z = -1.76$. In this case you would fail to reject the null hypothesis.

11. H_0: $\mu = 98.6$ (no change during withdrawal)
    H_1: $\mu \neq 98.6$ (there is a change)

The critical region consists of z-score values greater than $+2.58$ or less than $z = -2.58$. For these data, the sample mean is 99.57, the standard error is 0.16, and $z = 6.06$ which is in the critical region so we reject the null hypothesis and conclude that there is a significant change in temperature during withdrawal.

13. a. H_0: $\mu = 55$ (patients' scores are not different from the normal population). The critical region consists of z-scores greater than $+2.58$ or less than -2.58. For these data, $\bar{X} = 76.62$, the standard error is 2.62, and $z = 8.25$. Reject the null hypothesis. Scores for depressed patients are significantly different from scores for normal individuals on this test.

15. The null hypothesis states that birth weights for infants of smoking mothers are not different from birth weights in the general population. For these data, $X = 2.38$, the standard error is 0.17, and the z-score statistic is $z = -3.06$. Reject H_0, and conclude that infants of smoking mothers are significantly different from infants in the general population.

17. The analyses are contradictory. The critical region for the two-tailed tests consists of the extreme 2.5% in each tail of the distribution. The two-tailed conclusion indicates that the data were not in this critical region. However, the one-tailed test indicates that the data were in the extreme 1% of one tail. Data cannot be in the extreme 1% and at the same time fail to be in the extreme 2.5%.

19. Increasing the alpha level results in increased power and an increased risk of a Type I error.

21. a. Increasing alpha would make the test more powerful but it has the undesirable effect of increasing the risk of a Type I error.
    b. Increasing sample size with a small alpha would increase power and keep the risk of a Type I error small.
    c. Using a one-tailed test would increase power but many researchers would argue that it also produces an indirect increase in the risk of a Type I error.

23. H_0: $\mu \geq 20$ (not reduced), and H_1: $\mu < 20$ (reduced). For these data the standard error is 1 and the z-score is $z = -4.50$. Reject H_0.

25. H_0: $\mu \leq 80$ (not more depressed), and H_1: $\mu > 80$ (more depressed). $\bar{X} = 87.7$. $z = 2.03$. Reject H_0 and conclude that children from divorced families have higher scores on the depression questionnaire.

CHAPTER 9 INTRODUCTION TO THE *t* STATISTIC

1. The *t* statistic is used when the population standard deviation is unknown. You use the sample data to estimate the standard deviation and the standard error.

3. The *t* statistic assumes random sampling from a normal distribution.

5. As *df* increase the *t* distribution becomes less variable (less spread out) and more like a normal distribution. For $\alpha = .05$, the critical *t* values move toward ± 1.96 as *df* increases.

7. a. H_0: $\mu \geq 20$ (not better)
      H_1: $\mu < 20$ (better—fewer trials)

The null hypothesis states that watching other animals will not result in fewer trials needed to solve the problem. H_1 states that performance will improve with watching.

b. In the distribution of t scores with $df = 3$, the critical region consists of values less than -4.541.

c. $t(3) = -5/5 = -1.00$

d. Fail to reject H_0. These data do not provide sufficient evidence to conclude that animals perform significantly better after viewing others.

9. H_0: $\mu = 62$. For these data, $\overline{X} = 48.86$, $s = 16.79$, the standard error is 3.17, and the t statistic is $t = -4.15$. Reject H_0.

11. H_0: $\mu = 7.80$. $\overline{X} = 6.98$ and $s = 0.61$. With a standard error of 0.22, $t(7) = -3.73$. Reject H_0 and conclude that pay for the nonunion workers is significantly different from the union standard.

13. a. H_0: $\mu = 17.5$. For these data, $\overline{X} = 19.73$, $s = 3.28$, the standard error is 0.85, and $t(14) = 2.62$. Reject H_0 and conclude that presentation rate does affect recall.

b. With $\alpha = .01$, $t = 2.62$ is not in the critical region. Fail to reject H_0.

15. H_0: $\mu = 27$. For these data $\overline{X} = 24.58$, $s = 3.48$, and the standard error is 1.01. $t(11) = -2.40$. Reject H_0 and conclude that the data are significantly different from (less time) than the therapist's claim.

17. H_0: $\mu = 10$. $\overline{X} = 9.16$ and $s = 1.43$. With a standard error of 0.37, $t(14) = -2.27$. Reject H_0 and conclude that the rats eat significantly less with high humidity.

19. H_0: $\mu = 5.0$. $\overline{X} = 6.3$ and $s = 2.03$. With a standard error of 0.11, $t(326) = 11.82$. Reject H_0.

CHAPTER 10 HYPOTHESIS TESTS WITH TWO INDEPENDENT SAMPLES

1. a. A single-sample t would be used.

b. An independent-measures hypothesis test to examine the difference between two populations.

c. An independent-measures t would be used to evaluate the difference between the two treatments.

3. The homogeneity of variance assumption specifies that $\sigma_1^2 = \sigma_2^2$ for the two populations from which the samples are obtained. If this assumption is violated, the t statistic can cause misleading conclusions for a hypothesis test.

5. Pooled variance $= 500$, $t(18) = -1.30$. Fail to reject H_0. There is no evidence of a significant difference between the two age groups.

7. a. H_0: $\mu = 60$ (no effect). The data from sample 1 produce a t statistic of $t(8) = -2.00$. Fail to reject H_0. The mean for Treatment A is not significantly different from 60.

b. H_0: $\mu = 60$ (no effect). The data from sample 2 produce a t statistic of $t(8) = 2.00$. Fail to reject H_0. The mean for Treatment B is not significantly different from 60.

c. H_0: $\mu_1 - \mu_2 = 0$ (no difference between treatments A and B). The pooled variance is 9 and the test statistic is $t(16) = -2.84$. Reject H_0 and conclude that there is a significant difference between the two treatments.

d. The results are not contradictory. Treatment A produces a mean that is less than 60, but not enough to be significantly less. Treatment B produces a mean greater than 60, but not enough to be significantly greater. Each treatment appears to have a small (nonsignificant) effect, and the effects are in opposite directions. When the two small effects are combined in the independent-measures test, the result is a significant difference.

9. a. For experiment I, pooled variance $= 10$ and $t(8) = 2.50$. Reject H_0. For experiment II, pooled variance $= 40$ and $t(8) = 1.25$. Fail to reject H_0. For experiment III, pooled variance $= 10$ and $t(8) = 1.00$. Fail to reject H_0.

b. Experiment II has greater variability which produces a larger standard error. In this experiment the 5 point mean difference is not sufficient to reject H_0.

c. In experiment III there is only a 2 point difference between the sample means. This difference is not sufficient to reject H_0.

11. H_0: $(\mu_1 - \mu_2) \leq 0$ (no increase). H_1: $(\mu_1 - \mu_2) > 0$ (increase). Pooled variance $= 30$ and $t(13) = 3.67$. Reject H_0 and conclude that fatigue has a significant effect.

13. For the control group, $\overline{X} = 11.14$ and $SS = 56.86$. For the dog owners, $\overline{X} = 6.4$ and $SS = 17.2$. The pooled variance is 7.41 and $t(10) = 2.98$. Reject H_0. The data show a significant difference between the dog owners and the control group.

15. For the students paid \$1, $\overline{X} = 5.1$ with $SS = 49.80$. For the students paid \$20, $\overline{X} = 2.95$ with $SS = 38.95$. $t(38) = 4.48$. Reject H_0 and conclude that there is a significant difference in opinion concerning the experiment.

17. a.

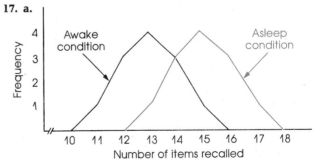

b. For the asleep group $\overline{X} = 15$ and $SS = 14$. For the awake group $\overline{X} = 13$ and $SS = 14$. $t(22) = 4.35$. Reject H_0.

19. For the regular course $\overline{X} = 78.73$ and $SS = 1622.93$. For the programmed course, $\overline{X} = 76.33$ and $SS = 1465.33$. $t(28) = 0.63$. Fail to reject H_0.

21. H_0: $(\mu_1 - \mu_2) \geq 0$ (seniors not higher). H_1: $(\mu_1 - \mu_2) < 0$ (seniors are higher). For the sophomores, $\overline{X} = 21.2$ and $SS = 261.20$. For the seniors, $\overline{X} = 22.15$ and $SS = 246.55$. $t(38) = -0.82$. Fail to reject H_0. There is no evidence of a significant difference.

23. a.

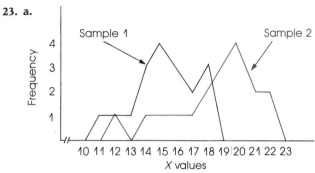

b. The two sets of data appear to come from different populations.

c. For sample #1 $\overline{X} = 15.22$ and $SS = 69.11$. For sample #2 $\overline{X} = 18.5$ and $SS = 130.50$. $t(34) = -4.05$. Reject H_0.

CHAPTER 11 STATISTICAL INFERENCE WITH RELATED SAMPLES

1. a. This is an independent-measures experiment with two separate samples.
  b. This is repeated measures. The same sample is measured twice.
  c. This is a matched-subjects design. The repeated-measures t statistic is appropriate.

3. a. For these data, $s = 10$ and $t(24) = -2.50$. Reject H_0 and conclude that imprisonment changes personality.
  b. With $\alpha = .01$ the decision would be to fail to reject H_0.

5. The researcher expects the beer to increase the time required to respond. Thus, X_2 should be larger than X_1. The hypotheses would be: H_0: $\mu_D \leq 0$ (no increase), H_1: $\mu_D > 0$ (increase).

7. $s = 18$, standard error is 4.65, and $t(14) = -2.75$. Reject H_0 and conclude that the drug significantly reduced blood pressure.

9. H_0: $\mu_D \leq 0$ (no improvement), and H_1: $\mu_D > 0$ (improved scores). For these data, $\overline{D} = 37.19$, $s = 42.25$, the standard error is 10.56, and $t(15) = 3.52$. Reject H_0 and conclude that there was a significant improvement in SAT scores.

11. For these data $\overline{D} = 0.90$, $s = 0.74$, the standard error is 0.22, and $t(10) = 4.09$. Reject H_0 and conclude that the drug has a significant effect.

13. H_0: $\mu_D \geq 0$ (no decrease) For these data, $\overline{D} = -4.20$, $s = 2.95$, the standard error is 1.32, and $t(4) = -3.18$. Reject H_0 and conclude that the treatment significantly reduces nightmares.

15. For these data $\overline{D} = 7.33$, $s = 5.87$, and $t(11) = 4.33$. Reject H_0 and conclude that Ritalin significantly improves performance for hyperkinetic children.

17. For these data, $\overline{D} = 0.50$, $s = 2.02$, and $t(11) = 0.86$. Fail to reject H_0. There is no evidence for a significant difference between the two books.

19. For these data, $\overline{D} = 1.13$, $s = 2.36$, and $t(14) = 1.86$. Fail to reject H_0. The evidence is not sufficient to conclude that the drug has a significant effect.

CHAPTER 12 ESTIMATION

1. a. Use $\overline{X} = 5.8$ for the point estimate of μ.
  b. The amount of change is the difference between 6.3 hours and 5.8 hours. Children are watching TV 0.5 hours less now than in 1970.
  c. With a standard error of 0.20 and $z = \pm 1.28$, estimate μ between 5.544 and 6.056 hours per day.

3. a. Use $\overline{X} = 15.5$ as the point of estimate of μ.
  b. With increased self-awareness the population mean is estimated to be between 13.54 and 17.46 using $z = \pm 1.96$ and a standard error of 1.

5. a. The sample mean is 72.1 with a standard error of 0.91. Using $t = \pm 1.311$, the 80% confidence interval extends from 70.91 ounces to 73.29 ounces.
  b. Yes. A 3 ounce increase would produce a mean weight of 68 ounces. The confidence interval indicates that the new mean should be even larger than this.

7. a. $s = 10$

  b. Use $\overline{X} = 43$ to estimate μ.

  c. Using $t = \pm 1.711$, estimate μ between 39.578 and 46.422.

9. a. $s = 2.91$

  b. Use $\overline{X} = 10.09$ for the point estimate. Using $t = \pm 2.228$ and a standard error of 0.88, the 95% confidence interval extends from 8.13 to 12.05.

11. a. Use $\overline{X} = 288.5$ as the point estimate.

  b. With $df = 11$, $t = \pm 2.201$, and an estimated standard error of 43.02, the 95% confidence interval extends from 193.81 to 383.19.

  c. No. The confidence interval estimates the value of the population mean. It does not estimate what values would be obtained for other samples.

13. a. Use the sample mean difference, $43 - 36 = 7$ to estimate the population mean difference.

  b. With 90% confidence $t = \pm 1.734$, estimate the mean difference between 3.532 and 10.468.

15. a. The sample mean difference, 13.8 minutes, is used to estimate the population difference.

  b. Pooled variance = 20 and standard error = 2. With 80% confidence, $t = \pm 1.330$ and the population mean difference is estimated to be between 11.14 and 16.46.

17. a. With two separate samples, use an independent-measures t statistic to estimate how much difference there is between the review course and control conditions.

  b. This is a repeated-measures hypothesis testing situation. The researcher wants to determine whether or not the medication is effective.

19. a. For the point estimate, use the sample mean difference, 14.6.

  b. For these data, $s = 10$ and the standard error = 2. With 80% confidence, $t = \pm 1.318$ and the population mean difference is estimated to be between 11.964 and 17.236.

21. The sample mean, $\overline{D} = 125$, is used for the point estimate. The sample standard deviation is 14.14 and the standard error is 2.58. With 90% confidence, $t = \pm 1.699$ and the population mean difference is estimated to be between 120.62 and 129.38.

CHAPTER 13 INTRODUCTION TO ANALYSIS OF VARIANCE

1. When there is no treatment effect, the numerator and the denominator of the F-ratio are both measuring the same sources of variability (individual differences and experimental error). In this case, the F-ratio is balanced and should have a value near 1.00.

3. With 3 or more treatment conditions you need 2 or more t tests to evaluate all the mean differences. Each test involves a risk of a Type I error. The more tests you do the more risk there is of a Type I error. The ANOVA performs all of the tests simultaneously with a single, fixed alpha level.

5. a. There is no difference between treatments: Both have $T = 8$ and $\overline{X} = 2$. $MS_{between}$ should be zero.

  b. $F = 0$

  c. $SS_{between} = 0$ and $MS_{between} = 0$

7.

SOURCE	SS	df	MS
Between Treatments	10	2	5.00
Within Treatments	16	12	1.33
Total	26	14	

$F(2,12) = 3.75$

Fail to reject H_0. These data do not provide evidence of any differences among the three therapies.

9. a.

SOURCE	SS	df	MS
Between Treatments	56	2	28
Within Treatments	36	9	4
Total	92	11	

$F(2,9) = 7.00$

Reject H_0 and conclude that there are significant differences among the three treatments.

  b. Tukey's $HSD = 3.95$. Treatments I and II are both significantly different from treatment III, but there is no significant difference between I and II.

11. a. You should recognize that there is no variability within treatments for these data. However, the treatment means are different so there is some variability between treatments.

  b. $SS_{total} = 8$, $SS_{between} = 8$, $SS_{within} = 0$

13. a. $k = 4$

  b. $N = 32$

  c. Yes, $F = 3.87$ is in the critical region at the .05 level of significance.

15.

SOURCE	SS	df	MS
Between Treatments	15	2	7.5
Within Treatments	60	12	5
Total	75	14	

$F(2,12) = 1.50$

Fail to reject H_0. No evidence of any significant differences.

17.

SOURCE	SS	df	MS
Between Treatments	45	3	15
Within Treatments	108	36	3
Total	153	39	

$F(3,36) = 5.00$

19. a.

SOURCE	SS	df	MS
Between Treatments	26	2	13
Within Treatments	12	6	2
Total	38	8	

$F(2,6) = 6.50$

Reject H_0 and conclude that there are significant differences among the three age groups.

b. Beginning with the largest difference between samples, the Scheffé comparisons and F-ratios are as follows:
5 versus 7-year-olds: $F(2, 6) = 6.00$ (significant)
6 versus 7-year-olds: $F(2, 6) = 3.38$ (not significant)
No other differences are significant.

21. a.

SOURCE	SS	df	MS
Between Treatments	30	2	15
Within Treatments	12	12	1
Total	42	14	

$F(2,12) = 15.00$

Reject H_0 and conclude that there are significant differences among the three groups.

b. Of the three samples the largest variance is for the right-handed subjects ($s^2 = 1.50$) and the smallest is for the left-handed subjects ($s^2 = 0.50$). F-max = 3.00 which is not significant. The homogeneity assumption is satisfied.

23. The means and SS values for these data are:

DREARY	STORMY	BRIGHT
$\overline{X} = 8.6$	$\overline{X} = 9.1$	$\overline{X} = 10.7$
$SS = 52.4$	$SS = 54.9$	$SS = 64.1$

SOURCE	SS	df	MS
Between Treatments	24.07	2	12.03
Within Treatments	171.40	27	6.35
Total	195.47	29	

$F(2,27) = 1.90$

Fail to reject H_0. These data do not provide sufficient evidence to conclude that weather affects mood.

25. a.

SOURCE	SS	df	MS
Between Treatments	49.0	2	24.50
Within Treatments	125.5	15	8.37
Total	174.5	17	

$F(2, 15) = 2.93$

Fail to reject H_0. No significant differences.

b. The three sample variances are 9.20, 8.30, and 7.60. F-max = 1.21, not significant. The data support the homogeneity of variance assumption.

CHAPTER 14 REPEATED-MEASURES ANOVA

1. A repeated-measures design generally uses fewer subjects and is more likely to detect a treatment effect because it eliminates variability due to individual differences.

3. a. First $\overline{X} = 3$, second $\overline{X} = 5$, and third $\overline{X} = 1$.

b.

SOURCE	SS	df	MS
Between Treatments	32	2	16
Within Treatments	24	9	
Between Subjects	12	3	
Error	12	6	2
Total	56	11	

$F(2,6) = 8.00$

Reject H_0 and conclude that the number of errors differs significantly with the position in the list. Most errors are made in the middle of the list, with fewer errors at the beginning, and fewest errors on the last items in the list.

5. $df = 2, 22$

7.

SOURCE	SS	df	MS
Between Treatments	200	4	50
Within Treatments	500	45	
Between Subjects	140	9	
Error	360	36	10
Total	700	49	

$F(4,36) = 5.00$

9. a. The means are 6, 4, and 2.

b.

SOURCE	SS	df	MS
Between Treatments	40.00	2	20
Within Treatments	240.00	12	
Between Subjects	37.33	4	
Error	202.67	8	25.33
Total	280.00	14	

$F(2,8) = 0.79$

Fail to reject H_0 There are no significant differences among the three grade levels.

c. The data in problem 9 have substantially more variability within treatments which increases the error variability. As a result, the sample mean differences are not significant.

11.

SOURCE	SS	df	MS
Between Treatments	48	2	24
Within Treatments	120	42	
Between Subjects	36	14	
Error	84	28	3
Total	168	44	

$F = 8.00$

13. a. $k = 3$
b. $n = 21$

15.

SOURCE	SS	df	MS
Between Treatments	12	2	6
Within Treatments	56	15	
Between Subjects	16	5	
Error	40	10	4
Total	68	17	

$F(2,10) = 1.50$

Fail to reject H_0. There are no significant differences among the three mixes.

17. a. For an independent-measures design the ANOVA produces

SOURCE	SS	df	MS
Between Treatments	40	2	20.00
Within Treatments	74	12	6.17
Total	114	14	

$F(2,12) = 3.24$

b. For a repeated-measures design the ANOVA produces

SOURCE	SS	df	MS
Between Treatments	40	2	20.0
Within Treatments	74	12	
Between Subjects	54	4	
Error	20	8	2.5
Total	114	14	

$F(2,8) = 8.00$

c. The independent-measures design includes all the individual differences in the error term (MS_{Within}). As a result the F-ratio, $F(2,12) = 3.24$ is not significant. With a repeated-measures design, the individual differences are removed and the result is a significant F-ratio, $F(2, 8) = 8.00$, $p < .05$.

19.

SOURCE	SS	df	MS
Between Treatments	270	3	90
Within Treatments	410	28	
Between Subjects	200	7	
Error	210	21	10
Total	680	31	

$F = 9$

21.

SOURCE	SS	df	MS
Between Treatments	11260.58	2	5630.29
Within Treatments	36235.38	21	
Between Subjects	19338.63	7	
Error	16896.75	14	1206.91
Total	47495.96	23	

$F(2,14) = 4.67$

Reject H_0 and conclude that there are significant differences among the drugs (and placebo).

23. a.

SOURCE	SS	df	MS
Between Treatments	252.05	1	252.05
Within Treatments	1956.50	18	
Between Subjects	1447.05	9	
Error	509.45	9	56.61
Total	2208.55	19	

$F(1,9) = 4.45$

b. For the difference scores, $\bar{D} = 7.1$ and $SS = 1018.9$. $t(9) = 2.11$.

25. a.

SOURCE	SS	df	MS
Between Treatments	189.84	3	63.28
Within Treatments	28.13	28	
Between Subjects	8.72	7	
Error	19.41	21	0.92
Total	217.97	31	

$F(3,21) = 68.78$

Reject H_0 and conclude that the subjects' self ratings were significantly affected by sleep deprivation.
b. The data show that there was no significant deterioration in performance (problem 24) however, the subjects felt that their abilities were impaired by lack of sleep (problem 25).

SOLUTIONS

CHAPTER 15 **TWO FACTOR ANALYSIS OF VARIANCE (INDEPENDENT MEASURES)**

1. a. no interaction, parallel lines
   b. interaction
   c. no interaction

3.

SOURCE	SS	df	MS
Between Treatments	280	7	
Achievement Need	16	1	16
Task Difficulty	144	3	48
Interaction	120	3	40
Within Treatments	320	40	8
Total	600	47	

$F(1,40) = 2.00$
$F(3,40) = 6.00$
$F(3,40) = 5.00$

5. a.

Data Set 1

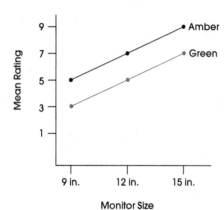

Data Set 2

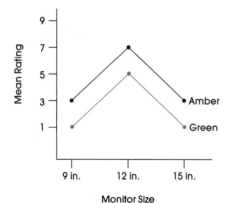

Monitor Size

Data Set 3

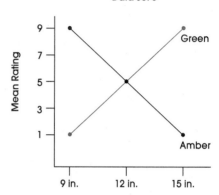

b. The amber monitor is rated slightly higher in data sets #1 and #2. In data set #3 there is no significant main effect for color.

c. In data set #1, the larger the monitor the higher the rating. In set #2 the 12″ size is rated highest, with the other two sizes rated equally. In data set #3 there is no significant main effect for size.

d. No interaction in sets #1 and #2. Data set #3 shows an interaction between size and color.

7.

SOURCE	SS	df	MS
Between Treatments	120	3	
A	80	1	80
B	20	1	20
A × B	20	1	20
Within Treatments	80	16	5
Total	200	19	

$F(1,16) = 16$
$F(1,16) = 4$
$F(1,16) = 4$

Distraction has a significant effect on performance. These results do not provide sufficient evidence to conclude that personality affects performance or that personality interacts with distraction.

9.

SOURCE	SS	df	MS
Between Treatments	70	5	
A	30	1	30
B	20	2	10
A × B	20	2	10
Within Treatments	120	24	5
Total	190	29	

$F(1,24) = 6$
$F(2,24) = 2$
$F(2,24) = 2$

The results indicate that the males are significantly more active than the females. However, the data do not provide sufficient evidence to conclude that the chemical has a significant effect on activity or that the chemical has a different effect on males than on females.

11.

SOURCE	SS	df	MS
Between Treatments	80	7	
A	40	1	40
B	20	3	6.67
A × B	20	3	6.67
Within Treatments	320	32	10
Total	400	39	

$F(1,32) = 4.00$
$F(3,32) = 0.67$
$F(3,32) = 0.67$

Neither of the main effects, nor the interaction is significant at the 0.5 level.

13.

SOURCE	SS	df	MS
Between Treatments	130	5	
A	30	1	30
B	20	2	10
A × B	80	2	40
Within Treatments	120	24	5
Total	250	29	

$F(1,24) = 6$
$F(2,24) = 2$
$F(2,24) = 8$

The significant interaction indicates that the hormone affects the eating behavior of males differently than females. For males, small doses appear to increase eating relative to no drug or a large dose. For females, the drug (in any dose) inhibits eating.

15. a.

SOURCE	SS	df	MS
Between Treatments	216	3	
A (self-esteem)	96	1	96
B (audience)	96	1	96
A × B	24	1	24
Within Treatments	86	20	4.3
Total	302	23	

$F(1,20) = 22.33$
$F(1,20) = 22.33$
$F(1,20) = 5.58$

The significant interaction indicates that the effect of the audience was different for high self-esteem subjects than for low self-esteem subjects. Specifically, the audience produced an increase in errors for the low self-esteem and had little effect on high self-esteem.

17. a. 20
   b. 0
   c. 60

19. a.

SOURCE	SS	df	MS
Between Treatments	944.25	3	
A (anxiety)	578.00	1	578.00
B (counseling)	300.13	1	300.13
A × B	66.13	1	66.13
Within Treatments	2797.75	28	99.92
Total	3742.00	31	

$F(1,28) = 5.78$
$F(1,28) = 3.00$
$F(1,28) = 0.66$

b. The data show no significant main effect for counseling. In addition, there is no interaction which might indicate that the counseling effect depends on the students' level of math anxiety.

21. a.

SOURCE	SS	df	MS
Between Treatments	95.3	3	
A (class type)	8.1	1	8.1
B (personality)	19.6	1	19.6
A × B	67.6	1	67.6
Within Treatments	62.6	36	1.74
Total	157.9	39	

$F(1,36) = 4.66$
$F(1,36) = 11.26$
$F(1,36) = 38.85$

b. Overall there is a significant preference for the structured class (A effect). Overall the internal students are more positive (B effect). However, the interaction indicates that course preference depends on personality type. The internal students prefer the self-paced class and the externals prefer the structured class.

23. a.

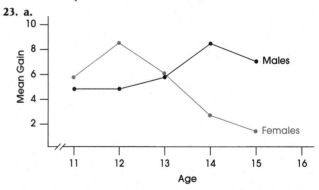

b. The growth spurt for boys occurs around age 14 while the growth spurt for girls occurs around age 12.

c.

SOURCE	SS	df	MS
Between Treatments	248.15	9	
A (sex)	18.15	1	18.15
B (age)	38.07	4	9.52
A × B	191.93	4	47.98
Within Treatments	46.83	50	0.94
Total	294.98	59	

$F(1,50) = 19.31$
$F(4,50) = 10.13$
$F(4,50) = 51.04$

d. The results are consistent with the description in part b.

25. a.

SOURCE	SS	df	MS
Between Treatments	11.0	3	
A (character type)	0.9	1	0.9
B (violence)	10.0	1	10.0
A × B	0.1	1	0.1
Within Treatments	49.4	36	1.37
Total	60.4	39	

$F(1,36) = 0.66$
$F(1,36) = 7.30$
$F(1,36) = 0.07$

b. The results indicate that violence on television affects behavior (B effect) and that this effect does not depend on whether the television characters are human or cartoon figures.

CHAPTER 16 CORRELATION AND REGRESSION

1. A positive correlation indicates that X and Y change in the same direction: As X increases, Y also increases. A negative correlation indicates that X and Y tend to change in opposite directions: As X increases, Y decreases.

3. a.

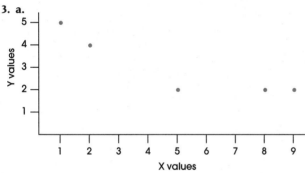

b. Estimate a strong negative correlation, probably $r = -.8$ or $-.9$.

c. $SS_x = 50$, $SS_y = 8$, $SP = -18$, and $r = -.90$.

5. a.

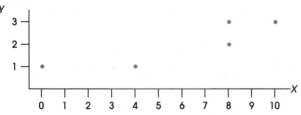

b. It appears to be a strong positive correlation about $r = +.8$ or $+.9$.

c. $SS_x = 64$, $SS_y = 4$, $SP = 14$, and $r = +.875$

d. $SS_x = 64$, $SS_y = 14$, $SP = -16$, and $r = -.535$

7. a.

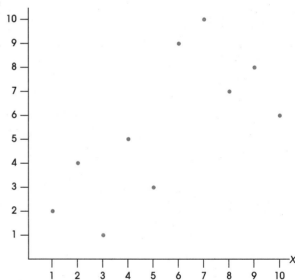

b. $r = 0.697$

c. $r = 0.30$

d. $r = -0.80$

e. The correlations for parts c and d were computed for a restricted range of scores and do not accurately represent the full range of X and Y values.

9. a. The graph shows a very poor, slightly negative correlation.

b. $r = -0.25$

c. The new graph is simply a magnified or enlarged version of the original data. The relation between X and Y is unchanged. Multiplying each score by a constant does not change the Pearson correlation.

d. $r = -0.25$

11. With $n = 18$ and a one-tailed test, the correlation must be greater than 0.400 to be significant at the .05 level. Fail to reject H_0. These data do not provide evidence for a significant correlation.

13. a. $r = -0.588$
b. $r = -0.200$
c.

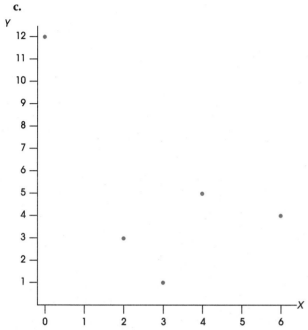

15. a. With no mean difference between the two groups you would expect no relation between training and performance, $r = 0$.

b.

X	Y	$r = 0$
1	2	
1	5	
1	6	
1	7	
0	4	
0	7	
0	3	
0	6	

17.

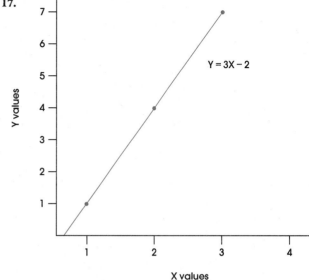

19. $SS_x = 20$, $SS_y = 24$, $SP = -20$. The regression equation is $\hat{Y} = (-1)X + 10$.

21. a. The standard error of estimate is 4.00.
b. The standard error of estimate is 0.80.
c. The standard error of estimate is 3.00.

23. a. $SS_x = 1385.67$, $SS_y = 1586$, $SP = 920$, and $r = +0.621$ which is smaller than the critical value of 0.658.
b. The standard error of estimate is 9.87.

25. a. $\hat{Y} = 1.33X + 32.83$
b. For $X = 10$, $\hat{Y} = 46.13$ seconds
c. The standard error of estimate is 0.73 seconds.

CHAPTER 17 CHI-SQUARE TESTS

1. H_0: The four factors are equally important, $p = .25$ for each factor. The expected frequency is 25 for all four categories. Chi-square $= 20$. Reject H_0 and conclude that the four factors are not equally important.

3. The chi-square test requires that each observed frequency represent a separate and independent observation. In this problem the same rat is observed over and over again, and

it is not reasonable to assume that the different observations are independent.

5. The null hypothesis states that there is no preference among the three magazines ($p = 1/3$ for each). Chi-square $= 4.39$. Fail to reject H_0 and conclude that there is no significant preference.

7. The null hypothesis states that opinions have not changed since 1970 so the distribution should still be 15% for, 79% against, and 6% no opinion. Chi-square = 2.30. Fail to reject H_0. These data do not provide evidence for a change in opinion.

9. a. H_0: The population proportions have not changed and are still 30% science, 50% social science or humanities, and 20% professional. The expected frequencies for these three categories are 30, 50, and 20 respectively. Chi-square = 4.08. Fail to reject H_0 and conclude that there has been no significant change in freshman majors.
   b. With $n = 200$, Chi-square = 8.16. Reject H_0.
   c. A larger sample should be more representative of the population. If the sample continues to be different from the hypothesis as n increases, the difference eventually will be significant.

11. The null hypothesis states that there is no relation between handedness and eye preference. The expected frequencies for left handed subjects are 12 left eye and 18 right eye. For right handed subjects the expected frequencies are 48 for left eye and 72 for right eye. Chi-square = 11.11. There is a significant relation between hand and eye preference.

13. The null hypothesis states that the distribution of votes is independent of political party. The expected frequencies for Democrats are 25.2 Yes and 19.8 No. For Republicans, the expected frequencies are 30.8 Yes and 24.2 No. Chi-square = 6.30. Reject H_0 and conclude that there is a significant relation between vote and party affiliation.

15. The null hypothesis states that there is no relation between need for achievement and risk. The expected frequencies are:

	CAUTIOUS	MODERATE	HIGH
HIGH	12.18	15.10	10.72
LOW	12.82	15.90	11.28

Chi-square = 17.08. Reject H_0.

17. The null hypothesis states that helping behavior is independent of success and failure. The expected frequencies are:

	SUCCESS	FAILURE
HELP	13.5	13.5
NO HELP	11.5	11.5

For these data, chi-square = 2.01. Fail to reject H_0. There is no significant relationship.

19. The expected frequencies are

	SINGLE PARENT	TWO PARENT
ABOVE	30	70
BELOW	30	70

For these data, chi-square = 7.72. Reject the null hypothesis and conclude that there is a significant difference between the two distributions.

21. The expected frequencies are

		SCIENCE	HUMANITIES	ART
	SCI.	15.64	14.31	9.01
FACULTY	HUM.	24.07	22.03	13.87
	ART	19.29	17.66	11.12

(STUDENT CHOICE)

For these data, chi-square = 25.04. Reject the null hypothesis and conclude that there is a significant relation between the faculty members' affiliations and the students' choices.

CHAPTER 18 THE BINOMIAL TEST

1. H_0: $p = .80$ and $q = .20$ (no change). The critical boundaries are $z = \pm 1.96$. With $X = 72$, $\mu = 80$, and $\sigma = 4$, we obtain $z = -2.00$. Reject H_0 and conclude that there has been a significant change in opinion.

3. H_0: $p = q = 1/2$ (no preference). The critical boundaries are $z = \pm 1.96$. With $X = 39$, $\mu = 32$, and $\sigma = 4$, we obtain $z = 1.75$. Fail to reject H_0. There is no evidence of a significant preference between the two drinks.

5. H_0: $p = .04$ and $q = .96$ (no difference between populations). The critical boundaries are $z = \pm 1.96$. With $X = 40$, $\mu = 8$, and $\sigma = 2.77$, we obtain $z = 11.55$. Reject H_0 and conclude that the executives are different from the general population.

7. With $n = 48$, $p = 1/4$, and $q = 3/4$ the binomial distribution would have a mean of 12 and a standard deviation of 3. You would need at least $X = 16.95$ (17 right) to have a z-score above the critical boundary of $z = 1.65$

9. H_0: $p = q = 1/2$ (no difference between the two stimulus presentations). The critical boundaries are $z = \pm 2.58$. The binomial distribution has $\mu = 15$ and $\sigma = 2.74$. With $X = 22$ we obtain $z = 2.55$. Fail to reject H_0 and conclude that there is no significant difference between the first and second presentations.

11. H_0: $p = q = 1/2$ (any change in grade point average is due to chance). The critical boundaries are $z = \pm 2.58$. The binomial distribution has $\mu = 22.5$ and $\sigma = 3.35$. With $X =$

31 we obtain $z = 2.54$. Fail to reject H_0 and conclude that there is no significant change in grade point average after the workshop.

13. H_0: $p = .8$ and $q = .2$ (field dependent subjects are not different from the general population). The critical boundaries are $z = \pm 1.96$. With $X = 51$, $\mu = 64$, and $\sigma = 3.58$, we obtain $z = -3.63$. Reject H_0 and conclude that the field dependent population is significantly different from the general population.

15. H_0: $p = 1/4$ and $q = 3/4$ (people are just guessing). The critical boundaries are $z = \pm 1.96$. With $X = 25$, $\mu = 12.5$, and $\sigma = 3.06$, we obtain $z = 4.08$. Reject H_0 and conclude that the subjects were correct significantly more often than would be expected by chance.

17. H_0: $p = q = 1/2$ (no difference between the two teachers).

The critical boundaries are $z = \pm 1.96$. Discarding the 12 children who showed no difference, the binomial distribution has $\mu = 14$ and $\sigma = 2.65$. With $X = 20$ we obtain $z = 2.26$. Reject H_0 and conclude that the teacher's sex has a significant effect.

19. H_0: $p = q = 1/2$ (no preference between the two brands) The Critical boundaries are $z = \pm 1.96$. The binomial distribution has $\mu = 25$ and $\sigma = 3.54$. With $X = 40$ we obtain $z = 4.24$. Reject H_0 and conclude that there is a significant preference.

21. H_0: $p = q = 1/2$ (no discrimination). The critical boundaries are $z = \pm 1.96$. The binomial distribution has $\mu = 12.5$ and $\sigma = 2.50$. With $X = 15$ we obtain $z = 1.00$. Fail to reject H_0 and conclude that there is no significant evidence of discrimination based on taste.

CHAPTER 19 STATISTICAL TECHNIQUES FOR ORDINAL DATA: MANN-WHITNEY AND WILCOXON TESTS, AND SPEARMAN CORRELATION

1. **a.**

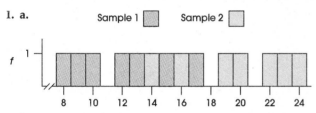

b. The two samples appear to come from different populations.

c. For sample 1 $\Sigma R = 31$ and for sample 2 $\Sigma R = 74$. $U = 3$. Reject H_0 and conclude that the two treatments are different.

3. The null hypothesis states that there is no difference between the two species. For species A $\Sigma R = 73.5$ and for species B $\Sigma R = 136.5$. $U = 18.5$. Reject H_0 and conclude there is a significant difference in eating behavior.

5. The null hypothesis states that there is no difference in the time required to unscramble pronounceable versus unpronounceable anagrams. For increases $\Sigma R = 1$ and for decreases $\Sigma R = 35$. Wilcoxon $T = 1$. Reject H_0.

7. The null hypothesis states that the drug has no effect. For the increases $\Sigma R = 39$ and for the decreases $\Sigma R = 6$. Wilcoxon $T = 6$. Fail to reject H_0. These data do not provide sufficient evidence to conclude that the drug works.

9. First rank the number of art courses then compute the Spearman correlation. $r_s = -0.986$.

11. For the isolated monkeys $\Sigma R = 92$ and $U = 8$. For the not-isolated monkeys $\Sigma R = 44$ and $U = 56$. Reject H_0. Isolation has a significant effect on social dominance.

13. **a.** For sample A $\overline{X} = 2.43$ and $s^2 = 2.95$. For sample B $\overline{X} = 14.86$ and $s^2 = 56.81$.

b. The null hypothesis states that there is no difference between the two treatments. For sample A $\Sigma R = 28$ and for sample B $\Sigma R = 77$. $U = 0$. Reject H_0.

15. For the strict states $\Sigma R = 78$ and $U = 77$. For the lax states $\Sigma R = 132$ and $U = 23$. Reject H_0 and conclude that DWI enforcement has a significant effect on traffic fatalities.

17. **a.** Using The Pearson formula on the ranks, the Spearman correlation is $r_s = -.749$ (using the special formula, $r_s = -.740$).

b. The relatively strong negative correlation indicates that students who score high on the test tend to be ranked low (1st, 2nd, etc.) by the teacher. It appears that the test scores are in general agreement with the teacher's ranking.

19. **a.** The graph shows an accelerating increase in Y as X increases.

b. The Spearman correlation is $r_s = +1.00$. The relation is perfectly monotonic.

21. The null hypothesis states that speaking will have no effect on balancing. For the increases $\Sigma R = 4$ and for the decreases $\Sigma R = 51$. Wilcoxon $T = 4$. Reject H_0.

23. The null hypothesis states that need for achievement has no effect on an individual's persistence. For the high nAch group $\Sigma R = 163.5$ and for the low nAch group $\Sigma R = 46.5$. $U = 10.5$. Reject H_0.

SOLUTIONS

CHAPTER 20 INTRODUCTION TO MINITAB

1.

```
MTB > HISTOGRAM C1


Histogram of C1    N = 30

Midpoint    Count
      10       7    *******
      20       3    ***
      30       4    ****
      40       2    **
      50       2    **
      60       5    *****
      70       4    ****
      80       3    ***

MTB > DOTPLOT C1


              .  ..: : ..  . : ..       .          .
          . ..: : ..  . : ..       .. .    . . . : .  .: ...
        +---------+---------+---------+---------+---------+-------C1
        0        15        30        45        60        75
```

3.

```
MTB > STEM-AND-LEAF C1

Stem-and-leaf of C1         N  = 30
Leaf Unit = 1.0


      3      0 579
      7      1 0134
      9      1 68
     10      2 3
     12      2 56
     14      3 01
     14      3
     (2)     4 23
     14      4 6
     13      5 2
     12      5 58
     10      6 122
      7      6 6
      6      7 234
      3      7 789
```

5.

```
MTB > TINTERVAL 90 C1

              N      MEAN    STDEV   SE MEAN    90.0 PERCENT C.I.
C1           30     41.27    25.43     4.64   (   33.38,    49.16)
```

7.

MTB > PLOT 'RT' 'BAC'

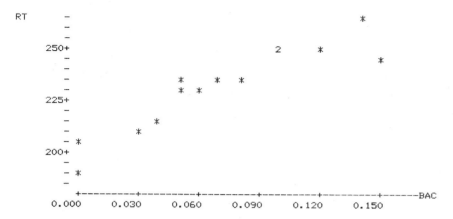

9.

MTB > REGRESS 'RT' 1 'BAC'

The regression equation is
RT = 203 + 395 BAC

Predictor	Coef	Stdev	t-ratio	p
Constant	203.245	4.183	48.59	0.000
BAC	394.51	49.77	7.93	0.000

s = 8.460   R-sq = 84.0%   R-sq(adj) = 82.6%

Analysis of Variance

SOURCE	DF	SS	MS	F	p
Regression	1	4496.9	4496.9	62.83	0.000
Error	12	858.8	71.6		
Total	13	5355.7			

Unusual Observations

Obs.	BAC	RT	Fit	Stdev.Fit	Residual	St.Resid
4	0.150	244.00	262.42	4.55	-18.42	-2.58R

R denotes an obs. with a large st. resid.

11.

MTB > DOTPLOT C1 C2

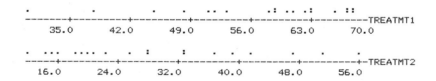

13.

MTB > MANN-WHITNEY C1 C2

Mann-Whitney Confidence Interval and Test

TREATMT1   N = 20   Median =   59.50
TREATMT2   N = 20   Median =   27.00
Point estimate for ETA1-ETA2 is   30.00
95.0 pct c.i. for ETA1-ETA2 is (21.00,38.00)
W = 588.5
Test of ETA1 = ETA2 vs. ETA1 n.e. ETA2 is significant at 0.0000
The test is significant at 0.0000 (adjusted for ties)

15.

```
MTB > DESCRIBE C1 C2
```

	N	MEAN	MEDIAN	TRMEAN	STDEV	SEMEAN
BEFORE	12	56.33	53.00	55.30	14.86	4.29
AFTER	12	73.17	76.00	74.90	14.73	4.25

	MIN	MAX	Q1	Q3
BEFORE	35.00	88.00	47.00	68.50
AFTER	39.00	90.00	64.25	84.25

17.

```
MTB > LET C3 = C2 - C1
MTB > TINTERVAL 80 C3
```

	N	MEAN	STDEV	SE MEAN	80.0 PERCENT C.I.
C3	12	16.83	17.13	4.94	(10.09, 23.58)

19.

```
MTB > DESCRIBE C1-C4
```

	N	MEAN	MEDIAN	TRMEAN	STDEV	SEMEAN
CONTROL	10	15.00	15.00	15.13	3.71	1.17
TRTMT A	10	21.40	23.00	21.75	6.65	2.10
TRTMT B	10	10.20	8.00	9.75	5.87	1.85
TRTMT C	10	26.80	28.00	26.87	8.28	2.62

	MIN	MAX	Q1	Q3
CONTROL	9.00	20.00	11.50	18.25
TRTMT A	10.00	30.00	14.75	26.50
TRTMT B	4.00	20.00	5.75	16.00
TRTMT C	15.00	38.00	19.25	34.00

21.

```
MTB > AOVONEWAY C1-C4
```

```
ANALYSIS OF VARIANCE
SOURCE    DF       SS      MS       F       p
FACTOR     3   1583.5   527.8   13.11   0.000
ERROR     36   1449.6    40.3
TOTAL     39   3033.1
                             INDIVIDUAL 95 PCT CI'S FOR MEAN
                             BASED ON POOLED STDEV
 LEVEL    N     MEAN    STDEV  --+---------+---------+---------+-----
CONTROL  10   15.000    3.712        (----*-----)
TRTMT A  10   21.400    6.653                (-----*----)
TRTMT B  10   10.200    5.865   (------*----)
TRTMT C  10   26.800    8.284                     (-----*-----)
                                --+---------+---------+---------+-----
POOLED STDEV =    6.346         7.0      14.0      21.0      28.0
```

23.

```
MTB > TABLE 'A' 'B';
SUBC> MEAN C3.
```

```
 ROWS: A     COLUMNS: B

            1        2      ALL

  1     4.833   10.667    7.750
  2     7.167    8.333    7.750
  3     9.833    3.333    6.583
  4    13.500    2.167    7.833
ALL    8.833    6.125    7.479

   CELL CONTENTS --
            C3:MEAN
```

25.

```
MTB > CHISQUARE C1-C3
```

Expected counts are printed below observed counts

	S	T	Y	Total
1	11	4	2	17
	7.08	4.25	5.67	
2	4	5	10	19
	7.92	4.75	6.33	
Total	15	9	12	36

```
ChiSq = 2.166 + 0.015 + 2.373 +
        1.938 + 0.013 + 2.123 = 8.627
df = 2
2 cells with expected counts less than 5.0
```

APPENDIX D   INTRODUCTION TO MYSTAT

MYSTAT is a data analysis program that allows you to enter data into the computer and perform a wide range of statistical computations. To use MYSTAT you first must type your data into the computer and save it in a computer "file." Once your data are saved in the computer, you may type in a variety of computer commands that will instruct MYSTAT to perform different statistical calculations and print out the results. This appendix will provide a basic set of instructions for using MYSTAT to perform most of the statistical procedures covered in this book. Please note that we will not attempt to describe all of the capabilities of MYSTAT; for more detailed instructions, please refer to the MYSTAT booklet that came with your program disk.

The information in this appendix is divided into four sections.

1. Getting started. This section outlines the procedure for starting the MYSTAT program on most PC compatible computers. The next two sections correspond to the two major components of the MYSTAT program.

2. The editor. One major portion of the MYSTAT program is dedicated to entering data into the computer. The Editor allows you to type in data, to edit data, and to use a set of Editor commands to modify or transform your data prior to analysis.

3. Statistical analysis. The second major portion of the MYSTAT program contains the set of commands that are used to perform the different statistical techniques that MYSTAT permits you to do.

4. Summary of MYSTAT commands. A complete summary of the MYSTAT commands is presented at the end of this appendix.

D.1 GETTING STARTED

The exact sequence of commands for starting MYSTAT will vary from one computer system to another. However, the following sequence of commands will start MYSTAT for most systems. Please note that we are assuming that the MYSTAT program is "installed" on your computer—that is, you have created a working copy of MYSTAT and a data disk for a floppy disk system or you have installed MYSTAT on your hard disk. If this is the very first time MYSTAT is being used on your computer, please refer to the INSTALLATION instructions in the MYSTAT booklet.

If you have a *floppy disk* system, insert a DOS boot disk and turn on the computer. At the A> prompt, remove the DOS disk, put in your working copy of

Figure D−1

The main command menu for
MYSTAT.

MYSTAT --- An Instructional Version of SYSTAT

DEMO HELP SYSTAT	EDIT USE SAVE PUT SUBMIT	MENU NAMES LIST FORMAT NOTE	PLOT BOX HISTOGRAM STEM TPLOT	STATS TABULATE TTEST PEARSON	MODEL CATEGORY ANOVA COVARIATE ESTIMATE
QUIT	OUTPUT	SORT RANK WEIGHT	CHARSET	SIGN WILCOXON FRIEDMAN	

>

MYSTAT, and type MYSTAT and press Return or Enter. When you see the
MYSTAT logo, press Enter and you will see the command menu which lists all of
the commands you can use (see Figure D−1).

If you have a *hard disk* system, turn on the computer and continue to press
Enter until you get the C> prompt. Then type

>CD\SYSTAT

>MYSTAT

pressing Enter after each command. When you see the MYSTAT logo, press Enter
and you will see the command menu which lists all of the MYSTAT commands
(see Figure D−1).

HELP   In the following sections we will introduce and describe most of the MYSTAT
commands. Before we start, however, we would like to call attention to the HELP
command. Whenever the command menu is on the screen, you can use the HELP
command to obtain more information about all of MYSTAT's commands. Type
HELP to obtain a brief description of each command. For more detailed
information about a specific command, type HELP followed by the command
name. For example, to obtain detailed information about the EDIT command,
simply type HELP EDIT.

D.2 THE EDITOR

When you first turn on the MYSTAT program you will find yourself looking at the
main command menu (see Figure D−1). This menu is the starting point for most
of MYSTAT's statistical analysis procedures. However, before you can perform
any statistical procedure, you must enter your data into the computer. To
accomplish this, you must leave the main command menu and enter The Editor
portion of the program where you can enter, edit, and modify data.

CREATING A DATA FILE   The first step in using the MYSTAT program is entering your data into the
computer. This is accomplished by using the following set of commands:

1. When the command menu is on the screen, type EDIT and press return.
   An empty data file will appear on the screen (see Figure D−2). Each row

Figure D–2

An empty data file for MYSTAT. Variable names are entered in the top row and the values for each variable are entered beneath the variable names in rows 1, 2, 3, etc. for each individual case.

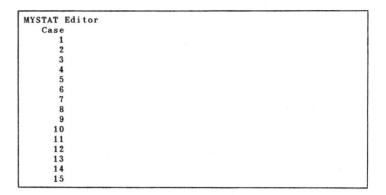

```
MYSTAT Editor
   Case
     1
     2
     3
     4
     5
     6
     7
     8
     9
    10
    11
    12
    13
    14
    15
```

of the data file represents an individual or a "case" and each column corresponds to a variable. For example, if you have measurements of Age, Sex, and IQ for a sample of $n = 8$ individuals, then you would enter each individual's Age in column #1, Sex in column #2, and IQ score in column #3.

2. Before you can start entering data, you first must enter names for the variables in the top row. The cursor is already positioned in the first cell in the top row so you are ready to type in your first variable name. The following rules apply to variable names:

a. Each name must be surrounded by single or double quotation marks.

b. Each name must start with a letter and can be no more than 8 characters long.

c. If the variable values consists of words or letters, the variable name must end with a dollar sign ($). For example, one of our variables is Sex and will consist of letter values (M for male and F for female).

For this example, our variables are Age, Sex, and IQ. To name these variables, type

'AGE'   (and press Enter)

'SEX$'   (and press Enter)

'IQ'   (and press Enter)

The cursor moves automatically to the next variable when you press the Enter key. Notice that when entering variable names, each name is surrounded by quotation marks. Also notice that we have used a dollar sign at the end of the Sex variable because the values for this variable will be letters (not numbers).

3. When you have named each variable, press the Home key to move the cursor to the first data cell. (For most computers, the Home key is 7 on the number keypad. If pressing this key types a 7 instead of moving the cursor, press the NumLock key and try again.) The following rules apply to entering data values:

a. If the value is a number, simply type the number and press return. If the number is very large or very small (more than 12 characters) you

MYSTAT

may use scientific notation. For example, the value 0.000000000023 would be entered as 2.3E-11.

b. If the value is a letter or a word, it must be surrounded by single or double quotation marks. For example, you must type 'M' if you are entering M for male. Press Enter after each value. Again, a value cannot be longer than 12 characters.

c. If you have missing data, enter a decimal (.) in place of the missing numeric value.

MYSTAT will move automatically to the next position in the data file when you press the Enter key.

EDITING DATA (CORRECTING MISTAKES)

You can use the arrow keys to move the cursor around in the data file. Also, the Home key will move to the first cell in the first row, the End key will move to the last cell in the last row, and the PgUp and PgDn keys will produce large moves if your data file is larger than the screen display.

To change a variable value or a variable name, move to the cell you want, type the new value, and press Enter.

USING EDITOR COMMANDS

When you have completed entering and editing your data, you exit the data file by pressing the ESC key. The cursor will move out of the data file to the bottom of the screen and present the command prompt (>). At this point you are ready to use other Editor commands.

If you want to return to the data file, press the Esc key again and the cursor will move back into the data file. Alternate presses of the Esc key will move you out of the data file or back into it.

ERASING ENTIRE ROWS OR COLUMNS

You can delete an entire row by typing DELETE and the row number. For example.

>DELETE 3   deletes the third row

>DELETE 5-10   deletes rows 5 through 10

You can erase a column by typing DROP and the variable name. For example,

>DROP SEX$ deletes the Sex variable (column)

NAMING AND SAVING YOUR DATA FILE

After you have completed entering and editing your data file, you must save the file so that it can be used for statistical analysis. This process is accomplished as follows:

1. Leave the data file by pressing the Esc key. The cursor will move to the bottom of the screen and present the command prompt (>).

2. Select a name for your data file. In order to save the data (and to call it back later) your file must have a name. File names can be up to 8 characters long and must begin with a letter.

3. To save the file, simply type SAVE followed by the file name you have selected. For example, if you want to name your data file EXAMPLE, then type

>SAVE EXAMPLE   (and press Enter)

Note: If you want to save your file on a work disk in the B drive, type SAVE B:EXAMPLE (and press Enter). To retrieve this file later for editing, you would type EDIT B:EXAMPLE.

EDITING AN EXISTING DATA FILE

If you have already created and saved a data file, you can retrieve it and edit it by typing EDIT followed by the name of the file. For example, if you have created and saved a data file named DATA, you can retrieve the file and have it available for editing (add new data or correct mistakes) by typing

EDIT DATA

Note: This command can be used only when the computer is displaying the main command menu (Figure D–1).

Note: If the file has been saved on a work disk on drive B, type EDIT B:DATA

EXAMPLES OF DATA FILES

For most statistical procedures, your data file will have one of the following three structures. These three types of data files correspond to the most common experimental designs and are appropriate for the most common statistical techniques.

1. A single set of scores For example, suppose you have a sample of $n = 15$ quiz scores and want to present them in a histogram, or compute the mean and standard deviation.

For this type of data, you create a data file consisting of only one column of scores. Use the EDIT command to enter a variable name, and then type in the individual scores. An example of this type of data file is shown in Table D–1. Note that we have named this file ONESAMPL and will use it later to help demonstrate other MYSTAT commands.

Table D–1

The ONESAMPL data file with $n = 15$ quiz scores.

		QUIZ
CASE	1	1.000
CASE	2	3.000
CASE	3	2.000
CASE	4	5.000
CASE	5	1.000
CASE	6	2.000
CASE	7	4.000
CASE	8	0.000
CASE	9	3.000
CASE	10	4.000
CASE	11	5.000
CASE	12	2.000
CASE	13	4.000
CASE	14	3.000
CASE	15	3.000

MYSTAT

Table D−2

The REPDATA data file showing Sex, Score1, Score2, and Difference score for each *n* = 12 individuals.

		SEX$	SCORE1	SCORE2	DIFF
CASE	1	M	14.000	18.000	4.000
CASE	2	M	12.000	19.000	7.000
CASE	3	F	17.000	15.000	-2.000
CASE	4	M	13.000	16.000	3.000
CASE	5	F	17.000	21.000	4.000
CASE	6	M	21.000	20.000	-1.000
CASE	7	F	16.000	17.000	1.000
CASE	8	F	16.000	22.000	6.000
CASE	9	F	13.000	13.000	0.000
CASE	10	F	15.000	26.000	11.000
CASE	11	M	11.000	14.000	3.000
CASE	12	F	17.000	19.000	2.000

2. A single set of individuals with several scores for each individual An example would be data from a repeated-measures experiment where you have obtained 2 (or more) scores for each subject. Other examples would be data for a correlation (*X* and *Y* scores for each individual) or data from a survey where each individual has answered a series of questions.

For this type of data, you create a data file where each individual corresponds to a row in the data file, and each variable corresponds to a column. Type in the variables names (column headings), and then type in the scores. Remember that you type in the row of scores for each individual, then the computer automatically moves to the next row where you enter the scores for the next individual. An example of this type of data file is shown in Table D−2. We have named this file REPDATA and we will use it later to help demonstrate other MYSTAT commands.

3. Separate sets of data from separate groups of individuals For example, you may have data from an independent-measures experiment with a separate sample for each treatment condition. Or, you may have data from two or more different populations (males vs females, 8-year-olds versus 10-year-olds, etc.). Usually these data would be used for an independent-measure *t* test, an analysis of variance, or a chi-square test for independence.

For this type of data, the file must contain at least one column that designates the group in which each individual belongs. Table D−3 shows an example of this type of data file. We have named this file INDEPDAT and we will use it later to demonstrate other MYSTAT commands. Notice that we have included two different grouping variables, one using numeric values and one using letters:

a) The first column identifies the treatment condition to which the subject has been assigned (Treatment 1 or Treatment 2). Notice that the treatments are identified by numeric values, 1 or 2.

b) The second column identifies the sex of the subject (M for male and F for female). Remember, when you are using letters or words for the variable values, you must enter the values surrounded by quotation marks and you must use a dollar sign ($) at the end of the variable name.

OTHER EDITOR COMMANDS   There are two other editor commands that are very useful for creating new variables out of the existing variables in your data file.

1. The LET command can be used to transform existing variables or to create new variables. The following format is used with the LET command:

Table D–3

The INDEPDAT data file for $n = 20$ individuals. The TREAT variable identifies one of two treatment conditions for each individual. The Sex and Score are recorded for each individual. The final two columns list the scores from Treatment 1 and Treatment 2 respectively.

		TREAT	SEX$	SCORE	X1	X2
CASE	1	1.000	M	20.000	20.000	.
CASE	2	1.000	M	16.000	16.000	.
CASE	3	1.000	F	21.000	21.000	.
CASE	4	1.000	F	13.000	13.000	.
CASE	5	1.000	F	15.000	15.000	.
CASE	6	1.000	M	17.000	17.000	.
CASE	7	1.000	F	22.000	22.000	.
CASE	8	1.000	M	19.000	19.000	.
CASE	9	1.000	F	20.000	20.000	.
CASE	10	1.000	M	16.000	16.000	.
CASE	11	2.000	F	23.000	.	23.000
CASE	12	2.000	M	19.000	.	19.000
CASE	13	2.000	M	24.000	.	24.000
CASE	14	2.000	F	22.000	.	22.000
CASE	15	2.000	F	24.000	.	24.000
CASE	16	2.000	M	20.000	.	20.000
CASE	17	2.000	F	24.000	.	24.000
CASE	18	2.000	F	26.000	.	26.000
CASE	19	2.000	M	21.000	.	21.000
CASE	20	2.000	M	18.000	.	18.000

> LET (newvariable) = (expression)

where "newvariable" is the variable you are creating (new column in the data file), and "expression" is the combination or transformation of old variables that you desire.

For example, suppose you have data from a repeated measures experiment consisting of two scores for each individual (see Table D–2). If the original scores are named SCORE1 and SCORE2, you can create a new column of *difference scores* by using the command

> \>LET DIFF = SCORE2 − SCORE1   (press Enter)

As soon as you execute this command, the computer will automatically add a new column named DIFF that contains the difference between the two original scores for each subject. This command was used to create the DIFF column in the REPDATA file shown in Table D–2.

Commonly used expressions and examples of how they can be used with the LET command are as follows:

+ addition	LET SUM = SCORE1+SCORE2
− subtraction	LET DIFF = SCORE2−SCORE1
* multiplication	LET PRODUCT = SCORE1*SCORE2
/ division	LET QUOTIENT = SCORE1/SCORE2
ˆ exponentation	LET SQUARE = SCORE1ˆ2

2. The IF-THEN command is used to create new variables in situations where you want to specify the conditions under which a new value is needed. For example, Table D–3 shows a data file where individuals are grouped into Treatment 1 and Treatment 2. You can use the IF-THEN command to create a column listing *only* the scores from Treatment 1. The command

> \>IF TREAT=1 THEN LET X1=SCORE

will create a column named X1 that lists only the scores for individuals for whom the TREAT variable is equal to 1. In the same way you can create a column containing only the scores from Treatment 2 by using the command

>IF TREAT=2 THEN LET X2=SCORE

These commands were used to create the final two columns (X1 and X2) in the INDEPDAT file shown in Table D−3. Notice that the missing values in the X1 and X2 columns are marked with decimals. Using this procedure to create separate columns for each individual treatment condition can be very useful because it allows you to compute statistics (mean, standard deviation, etc.) for each treatment condition separately.

QUITTING THE EDITOR AND PREPARING FOR DATA ANALYSIS

To leave the EDITOR, use the QUIT command at the command prompt:

>QUIT   (and press Enter)

Be sure that you have saved the final version of your data file before you quit. When you QUIT the EDITOR, you will be returned to the main command menu and you will have access to all the MYSTAT data analysis commands.

D.3 STATISTICAL ANALYSIS

Before you begin any data analysis procedures, there are two special commands you should know.

First, you *must* tell MYSTAT which data file you want to analyze. This is accomplished with the USE command. For example, if you want to examine or analyze the scores in the ONESAMPL file, you would type

>USE ONESAMPL

Note: If you have saved your data file on a work disk in the B drive, you would retrieve it by typing

>USE B:ONESAMPL

Remember, it is essential that you begin any analysis with the USE command. MYSTAT must know which file you are using before you can do any statistics.

The second useful command is LIST. The LIST command simply presents a complete listing of the data file you have selected. This provides you with an opportunity to view the data file and be sure it is the one you want before you start any statistical analysis.

PRINTING OUTPUT

The MYSTAT program will present the results of all analyses on the computer screen. To obtain printed copies of your results, you can direct MYSTAT to use the printer by typing

>OUTPUT@

After this command, all output will be sent to the printer and shown on the screen. To stop the printer and have output appear on the screen only, type

>OUTPUT *

After this command, all output will appear on the screen only.

DESCRIPTIVE STATISTICS

The STATS command provides basic descriptive statistics for all numerical variables in your data file: number of cases, maximum score, minimum score, mean, and standard deviation. For example to obtain statistics for the data in the ONESAMPL file (Table D−1), type

>USE ONESAMPL

>STATS

The resulting output appears as follows:

```
TOTAL OBSERVATIONS:     15

                        QUIZ

N OF CASES                15
MINIMUM                0.000
MAXIMUM                5.000
MEAN                   2.800
STANDARD DEV           1.474
```

If you want statistics for only one or two of the variables in your file, you can specify which variable(s) after the STATS command. For example, to obtain statistics for each of the two separate samples in the INDEPDAT file (Table D−3), type

>USE INDEPDAT

>STATS X1 X2

The resulting output appears as follows:

```
TOTAL OBSERVATIONS:     20

                        X1          X2

N OF CASES              10          10
MINIMUM             13.000      18.000
MAXIMUM             22.000      26.000
MEAN                17.900      22.100
STANDARD DEV         2.923       2.558
```

Note: The standard deviation computed by MYSTAT is the *sample* standard deviation using $n-1$ in the formula (see Chapter 4).

t TESTS

The TTEST command does either the independent-measures t test (Chapter 10) or the related-samples t test (Chapter 11).

To do an independent-measures test, you must designate which variable (column) contains the scores and you must designate which variable (column) identifies the different treatments or populations being compared. In the INDEPDAT file (Table D−3), for example, the actual scores are listed in the SCORE column, and the two treatment conditions are identified in the TREAT column. To perform the *t* test, type

>USE INDEPDAT   (and press Enter)

>TTEST SCORE*TREAT   (and press Enter)

The resulting output appears as follows:

```
INDEPENDENT SAMPLES T-TEST ON     SCORE      GROUPED BY      TREAT

        GROUP          N       MEAN           SD
        1.000          10      17.900         2.923
        2.000          10      22.100         2.558
   POOLED VARIANCES T =         3.419 DF =      18 PROB = .003
```

Most statistics programs, including MYSTAT, provide an exact probability for the test statistic rather than printing an alpha level. To determine whether or not a specific result is significant, you must compare the printed probability with your established alpha level. In this example, the probability of obtaining a *t* statistic as extreme as $t = 3.419$ is $p = 0.003$ (see printout). This probability value is less than .05 or .01 so the *t* statistic is significant at either $\alpha = .05$ or $\alpha = .01$.

Note: For the independent-measures *t* test, the first variable identified in the command statement must be the dependent variable (scores) and the second variable must be the independent variable with values that identify the two separate groups being compared.

Using the same data file (INDEPDAT), you can perform an independent-measures *t* test comparing the Males versus the Females by using the command

>TTEST SCORE*SEX$ (and press Enter)

The resulting output appears as follows:

```
INDEPENDENT SAMPLES T-TEST ON     SCORE      GROUPED BY      SEX$

        GROUP          N       MEAN           SD
M                      10      19.000         2.449
F                      10      21.000         4.082
   POOLED VARIANCES T =         1.328 DF =      18 PROB = .201
```

For a *related-samples* t test, your data file must have two scores for each individual. To perform a related-samples *t* test using the data in the REPDATA file (Table D−2), for example, you type

>USE REPDATA   (and press Enter)

>TTEST SCORE1 SCORE2   (and press Enter)

The resulting output appears as follows:

```
PAIRED SAMPLES T-TEST ON   SCORE1   VS   SCORE2   WITH   12 CASES

MEAN DIFFERENCE =      -3.167
SD DIFFERENCE =         3.639
T =      3.014 DF =      11 PROB = .012
```

ANALYSIS OF VARIANCE

To perform a single-factor, independent-measures ANOVA (Chapter 13), your data file must contain two variables. First, the file must contain an independent variable with values that identify the group or treatment condition for each individual. Second, the file must contain a column listing the dependent variable (score) for each individual. For example, the INDEPDAT file (Table D−3) contains a TREAT variable that specifies whether the individual is assigned to Treatment 1 or Treatment 2, and a SCORE variable that contains the score for each individual.

A series of three separate commands is used to perform the ANOVA:

1. The CATEGORY command is used to identify the independent variable and the number of levels (number of separate samples or k).

2. The ANOVA command is used to identify the dependent variable (scores).

3. The ESTIMATE command is used to start the analysis.

For example, to perform an ANOVA comparing Treatment 1 versus Treatment 2 for the INDEPDAT file (Table D−3), the complete sequence of commands would be

>USE INDEPDAT

>CATEGORY TREAT=2

>ANOVA SCORE

>ESTIMATE

The resulting output appears as follows:

```
DEP VAR:  SCORE    N:  20   MULTIPLE R:  .627   SQUARED MULTIPLE R:  .394
```

ANALYSIS OF VARIANCE

SOURCE	SUM-OF-SQUARES	DF	MEAN-SQUARE	F-RATIO	P
TREAT	88.200	1	88.200	11.691	0.003
ERROR	135.800	18	7.544		

Notice that the F-ratio in the ANOVA printout is related to the t value in the independent-measures t printout by the formula $F = t^2$. For the data in this example,

$$F = t^2$$

$$11.691 = (3.419)^2$$

MYSTAT

TWO-FACTOR ANALYSIS OF VARIANCE

A two-factor ANOVA (Chapter 15) requires a data file with three variables. First, the file must have a column listing the scores (dependent variable) for all of the subjects. The two other columns identify the levels of the first independent variable (factor A) and the second independent variable (factor B). For example, the INDEPDAT file in Table D–3 lists scores in the SCORE column and identifies the treatment condition (factor A) in the TREAT column and the subject's sex (factor B) in the SEX$ column. However, MYSTAT requires that the levels for the two factors be entered as integers (1, 2, 3, etc.). Before performing the analysis, the data in the INDEPDAT file would have to be modified. Specifically, the current values in the SEX$ column are alphabetical letters, not integers. The SEX factor would have to be recoded to integers (1 in place of M and 2 in place of F) before the analysis.

Once the three columns of data are entered correctly, a series of three commands is used to perform the two-factor ANOVA.

1. The CATEGORY command is used to identify the two independent variables and the number of levels for each.
2. The ANOVA command is used to identify the dependent variable (scores).
3. The ESTIMATE command is used to execute the analysis.

For example, to perform a two-factor ANOVA comparing Treatment 1 versus Treatment 2 (factor A) and Males versus Females (factor B) for the INDEPDAT file (Table D–3), the sequence of commands would be

> USE INDEPDAT

> CATEGORY TREAT=2, SEX=2

> ANOVA SCORE

> ESTIMATE

Note: This sequence of commands assumes that the SEX$ variable in the INDEPDAT file has been changed to a column named SEX that contains integer values 1 and 2 instead of the letters M and F.

The resulting output appears as follows:

DEP VAR: SCORE   N: 20   MULTIPLE R: .726   SQUARED MULTIPLE R: .527

ANALYSIS OF VARIANCE

SOURCE	SUM-OF-SQUARES	DF	MEAN-SQUARE	F-RATIO	P
TREAT	88.200	1	88.200	13.313	0.002
SEX	20.000	1	20.000	3.019	0.102
TREAT* SEX	9.800	1	9.800	1.479	0.242
ERROR	106.000	16	6.625		

If you compare the two-factor ANOVA printout with the single-factor printout, you will notice that the between-treatment sum of squares is the same for the two analyses (SS = 88.200). The F-ratios are different, however, because the two-factor analysis reduces the error variability by including sex as a second factor.

PEARSON CORRELATION AND REGRESSION

To compute a Pearson correlation (Chapter 16) your data file must contain at least two scores for each individual. The PEARSON command computes the Pearson correlation for all numeric variables in the data file. The results are presented in a correlation matrix.

For example, the REPDATA file (Table D–2) contains three variables (SCORE1, SCORE2, and DIFF). To compute all of the Pearson correlations for these variables, type

>USE REPDATA

>PEARSON

The resulting printout appears as follows:

```
PEARSON CORRELATION MATRIX
                    SCORE1       SCORE2       DIFF

        SCORE1       1.000
        SCORE2       0.389        1.000
          DIFF      -0.365        0.716       1.000

NUMBER OF OBSERVATIONS:    12
```

To find the correlation between any two variables, locate the first variable name across the top row of the matrix and the second variable name in the first column. The correlation between these two variables is found in the corresponding row and column position within the matrix. For example, the correlation between SCORE1 and SCORE2 is $r = 0.389$. Notice that the computer calculates *every possible* correlation including the self-correlations (for example, the correlation between SCORE1 and SCORE1 is $r = 1.00$). The self-correlations (all $r = 1$) appear across the diagonal of the matrix.

MYSTAT also can be used to compute the linear regression equation for predicting Y values from X values. Again, your data file must have at least two variables (two scores for each individual subject). The process of linear regression requires two MYSTAT commands. First, the MODEL command is used to identify the Y variable, the X variable, and the general form of the linear equation. Second, the ESTIMATE command is used to execute the regression program.

Using the data in the REPDATA file (Table D–2), the process for computing the regression equation for predicting SCORE2 (Y) from SCORE1 (X) would be as follows:

>USE REPDATA

>MODEL SCORE2 = CONSTANT + SCORE1

>ESTIMATE

The resulting printout appears as follows:

```
DEP VAR:  SCORE2      N:   12    MULTIPLE R:   .389    SQUARED MULTIPLE R:   .151
ADJUSTED  SQUARED MULTIPLE R:  .066        STANDARD ERROR OF ESTIMATE:      3.553


      VARIABLE    COEFFICIENT    STD ERROR    STD COEF  TOLERANCE      T    P(2 TAIL)
      CONSTANT        10.478        5.980       0.000      .          1.752   0.110
      SCORE1           0.518        0.388       0.389    .100E+01     1.333   0.212



                          ANALYSIS OF VARIANCE

      SOURCE     SUM-OF-SQUARES    DF   MEAN-SQUARE     F-RATIO       P

      REGRESSION      22.444        1      22.444        1.778      0.212
      RESIDUAL       126.223       10      12.622
```

Note: In this printout, the information relevant to the regression equation appears under the heading COEFFICIENT. The CONSTANT portion of the equation is 10.478 and the coefficient for the SCORE1 variable is 0.518. Thus, the regression equation is

$$SCORE2 = 0.518(SCORE1) + 10.478$$

CHI-SQUARE TEST FOR INDEPENDENCE

The TABULATE command can be used to construct the frequency matrix for two variables and to compute the chi-square value for the test for independence (Chapter 17). To use this chi-square test, each individual must be classified on two variables (two scores for each individual). Therefore, the data file must include two columns (variables) and each variable must have at least two different values. For example, the INDEPDAT file (Table D−3) has a TREAT variable and a SEX$ variable and each individual is classified into one of two treatments (1 or 2) and is identified as either M (male) or F (female). To construct the frequency distribution matrix for these two variables and to compute the chi-square value, type

>USE INDEPDAT

>TABULATE TREAT*SEX$

The resulting printout appears as follows:

```
TABLE OF     TREAT      (ROWS) BY      SEX$    (COLUMNS)
FREQUENCIES
                 F           M       TOTAL

     1.000       5           5        10

     2.000       5           5        10

   TOTAL        10          10        20
```

```
TEST STATISTIC                          VALUE      DF       PROB
    PEARSON CHI-SQUARE                   .000       1      1.000
    LIKELIHOOD RATIO CHI-SQUARE          .000       1      1.000
    MCNEMAR SYMMETRY CHI-SQUARE          .000       1      1.000
    YATES CORRECTED CHI-SQUARE           .000       1      1.000
    FISHER EXACT TEST (TWO-TAIL)                           1.000
```

(Note: Additional, irrelevant printout is not shown.)

Note: The relevant information concerning the chi-square statistic is contained in the row labeled PEARSON CHI-SQUARE. For these data the expected frequencies fit the observed frequencies exactly, so chi-square = 0 with $df = 1$ and a probability (alpha level) of $p = 1.000$.

SIGN TEST

To perform a sign test (Chapter 18) MYSTAT requires a data file with two scores for each individual. For example, the REPDATA file (Table D−2) lists SCORE1 and SCORE2 for each of twelve subjects. (Note: The same data file was used to demonstrate the related-samples t test.) The sign test is executed with the single command SIGN and identification of the two variables. To perform a sign test for the data in the REPDATA file, you type

> USE REPDATA

> SIGN SCORE1 SCORE2

The resulting printout appears as follows:

SIGN TEST RESULTS

COUNTS OF DIFFERENCES (ROW VARIABLE GREATER THAN COLUMN)

	SCORE1	SCORE2
SCORE1	0	2
SCORE2	9	0

TWO-SIDED PROBABILITIES FOR EACH PAIR OF VARIABLES

	SCORE1	SCORE2
SCORE1	1.000	
SCORE2	.065	1.000

Notice that MYSTAT does not report a z-score for the sign test. Instead, the printout shows a two-tailed probability, or alpha level, for the test. For this example, the probability of $p = .065$ is the probability of obtaining 9 or more out of 11 differences in one direction. Also, the MYSTAT program discards individuals with a zero difference score. For this example, the REPDATA file lists data for 12 individuals but MYSTAT uses $n = 11$ (discarding the zero difference for subject #9).

Caution: The probability displayed in the MYSTAT printout is the exact binomial probability which tends to be slightly larger than value you would obtain using a z-score computed by equations 18.1 or 18.2.

WILCOXON SIGNED-RANKS TEST

The Wilcoxon test is used with the same type of data file that is appropriate for either a related-samples t test or the sign test. The data file must contain two scores for each individual. MYSTAT computes the difference between scores for each individual, ranks the difference scores, and conducts the Wilcoxon test. For example, the REPDATA file (Table D−2) lists SCORE1 and SCORE2 for each of twelve subjects. The Wilcoxon test is executed with the single command WILCOXON followed by the names of the two variables. To perform a Wilcoxon test for the data in the REPDATA file, you type

>USE REPDATA

>WILCOXON SCORE1 SCORE2

The resulting printout appears as follows:

WILCOXON SIGNED RANKS TEST RESULTS

COUNTS OF DIFFERENCES (ROW VARIABLE GREATER THAN COLUMN)

	SCORE1	SCORE2
SCORE1	0	2
SCORE2	9	0

Z = (SUM OF SIGNED RANKS)/SQUARE ROOT(SUM OF SQUARED RANKS)

	SCORE1	SCORE2
SCORE1	.000	
SCORE2	2.494	.000

TWO-SIDED PROBABILITIES USING NORMAL APPROXIMATION

	SCORE1	SCORE2
SCORE1	1.000	
SCORE2	.013	1.000

Notice that MYSTAT computes a z-score and uses a normal-approximation technique for the Wilcoxon test. For the data in the REPDATA file, the z-score is $z = 2.494$ which is significant at the .05 level. (The probablity $p = .013$ is less than $\alpha = .05$.)

FREQUENCY DISTRIBUTIONS

MYSTAT can be used to construct either a frequency distribution histogram or a frequency distribution table. The HISTOGRAM command will construct a separate graph for each of the numeric variables in the data file. For example, the INDEPDAT file (Table D−3) contains five variables (TREAT, SEX$, SCORE, X1 and X2), and the HISTOGRAM command will construct four separate graphs (no graph for SEX$ because it is not a numeric variable).

If you want a histogram for a single variable, specify the variable after the HISTOGRAM command. For example, to produce a histogram showing the frequency distribution for the SCORE variable in the INDEPDAT file, type

>USE INDEPDAT

>HISTOGRAM SCORE

The resulting printout is shown in Figure D−3:

Figure D−3

Printout from HISTOGRAM command.

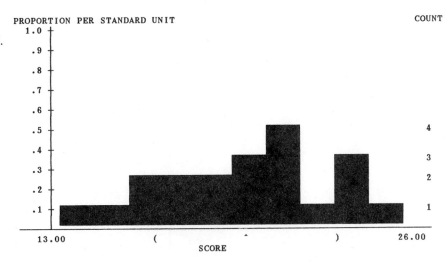

Note: The histograms generated by MYSTAT show the general shape of the frequency distribution. They do not list each individual score and show every frequency. Also, if your scores cover a wide range of values, the HISTOGRAM command will automatically group the scores into class intervals before constructing the histogram.

To obtain the exact frequency count for each individual score you can use the TABULATE command. This command will list each individual score and its frequency for all of the variables in your data file.

If you want a tabulated frequency distribution for only one variable, simple specify the variable name after the TABULATE command. For example, to obtain the frequency distribution for the SCORE variable in the INDEPDAT file (Table D−3), type

>USE INDEPDAT

>TABULATE SCORE

The resulting printout appears as follows:

TABLE OF VALUES FOR SCORE
FREQUENCIES

13.000	15.000	16.000	17.000	18.000	19.000
1	1	2	1	1	2

20.000	21.000	22.000	23.000	24.000	26.000	TOTAL
3	2	2	1	3	1	20

SCATTERPLOTS The PLOT command creates a scatterplot showing the relationship between two variables. Your data file must have at least two numeric variables.

For example, the REPDATA file (Table D−2) contains the variables SCORE1, SCORE2, and DIFF. To generate a scatterplot showing the relation between SCORE1 and SCORE2, type

>USE REPDATA

>PLOT SCORE1*SCORE2

The resulting printout is shown in Figure D−4:

Figure D−4

Printout from PLOT command showing the relation between SCORE1 and SCORE2.

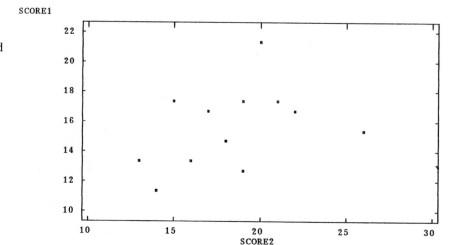

Note: The variable after the asterisk is plotted on the X-axis.

The PLOT command also can be used to show two different scatterplots in the same graph. For example, to show the relation between SCORE1 and SCORE2 along with the relationship between DIFF and SCORE2, type

>USE REPDATA

>PLOT SCORE1 DIFF*SCORE2/SYMBOL='1','2'

The resulting printout is shown in Figure D−5:

Figure D−5

Printout from PLOT command showing the relationship between SCORE1 and SCORE2 and the relation between DIFF and SCORE2 in one scatterplot.

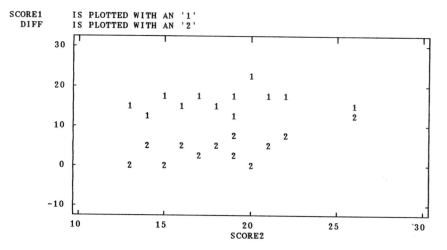

Note: The SCORE1 points will be shown as 1s in the graph and the DIFF points will be shown as 2s. Also note that you must use the same variable on the X-axis for both plots.

D.4 SUMMARY OF MYSTAT COMMANDS

EDITOR COMMANDS

1. EDIT moves you from the main command menu into the data file.
2. Within the data file, the arrow keys, Home, End, PgUp and PgUp move to a new cursor position.
3. Esc moves you out of the data file to the Editor command prompt (>). Pressing Esc again moves you back into the data file.
4. DELETE erases a row or rows of data.
5. DROP erases a column or columns of data.
6. LET creates a new variable by combining or transforming existing variables.
7. IF...THEN LET creates a new variable contingent on the specified conditions.
8. SAVE saves the data file.
9. QUIT moves you from the Editor back to the main command menu.

STATISTICAL ANALYSIS COMMANDS

1. USE selects the data file to be examined or analyzed.
2. LIST presents a complete copy of the data file.
3. EDIT moves you from the main command menu into an empty data file. EDIT FILENAME moves you into the file specified.
4. OUTPUT @ sends output to the printer and the screen.
5. OUTPUT * sends output to the screen only.
6. STATS presents basic descriptive statistics for the data file.
7. TTEST VARIABLE1*VARIABLE2 performs an independent-measures t test where VARIABLE1 contains the scores and VARIABLE2 identifies the two groups.
8. TTEST VARIABLE1 VARIABLE2 performs a related-samples t test.
9. CATEGORY, ANOVA, and ESTIMATE are used in sequence to perform an analysis of variance.
10. SIGN VARIABLE1 VARIABLE2 performs a sign test.
11. WILCOXON VARIABLE1 VARIABLE2 performs a Wilcoxon signed-ranks test.
12. TABULATE VARIABLE1*VARIABLE2 presents a frequency distribution matrix for the two variables and computes the chi-square test for independence.
13. PEARSON computes the Pearson correlation between all pairs of numeric variables in the data file.

14. MODEL Y=CONSTANT+X and ESTIMATE are used in sequence to compute a linear regression equation for predicting variable Y from variable X.

15. HISTOGRAM presents a frequency distribution histogram for all numeric variables in the data file.

16. TABULATE presents a frequency distribution for all variables in the data file.

17. PLOT VARIABLE1*VARIABLE2 presents a scatterplot showing the relation between the two variables with VARIABLE2 on the X-axis.

APPENDIX E

SPSS^X PRINTOUTS FOR SELECTED EXAMPLES

The following problems illustrate SPSS^X commands and printouts for selected examples. These examples have been noted in the text with the symbol, . Release 4.1 of SPSS^X was used.

From page 41.

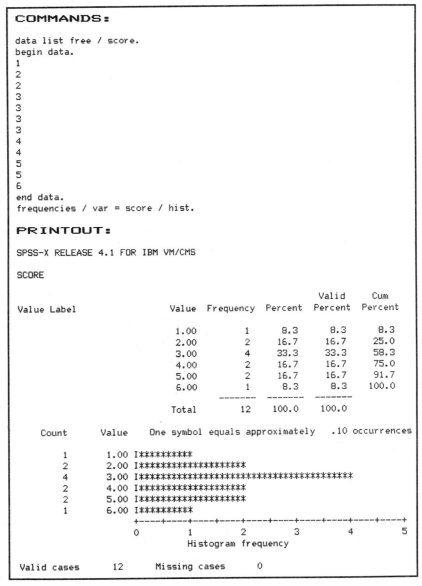

```
COMMANDS:

data list free / score.
begin data.
1
2
2
3
3
3
3
4
4
5
5
6
end data.
frequencies / var = score / hist.
```

```
PRINTOUT:

SPSS-X RELEASE 4.1 FOR IBM VM/CMS

SCORE
```

Value Label	Value	Frequency	Percent	Valid Percent	Cum Percent
	1.00	1	8.3	8.3	8.3
	2.00	2	16.7	16.7	25.0
	3.00	4	33.3	33.3	58.3
	4.00	2	16.7	16.7	75.0
	5.00	2	16.7	16.7	91.7
	6.00	1	8.3	8.3	100.0
	Total	12	100.0	100.0	

```
    Count    Value    One symbol equals approximately   .10 occurrences

       1     1.00  I**********
       2     2.00  I********************
       4     3.00  I******************************************
       2     4.00  I********************
       2     5.00  I********************
       1     6.00  I**********
                   +----+----+----+----+----+----+----+----+----+----+
                   0    1    2    3    4    5
                             Histogram frequency

Valid cases    12     Missing cases     0
```

From page 113.

```
COMMANDS:

data list free / scores.
begin data.
1
6
4
3
8
7
6
end data.
descriptives var = scores.

PRINTOUT:

SPSS-X RELEASE 4.1 FOR IBM VM/CMS

Number of valid observations (listwise) =        7.00


                                                 Valid
Variable    Mean     Std Dev   Minimum   Maximum    N    Label

SCORES      5.00      2.45      1.00      8.00       7
```

From page 275.

```
COMMANDS:

data list free / words image.
24 1
23 1
16 1
17 1
19 1
13 1
17 1
20 1
15 1
26 1
18 2
19 2
23 2
29 2
30 2
31 2
29 2
26 2
21 2
24 2
end data.
t-test groups = image / variables = words.
```

From page 275 *continued*.

```
PRINTOUT:

SPSS-X RELEASE 4.1 FOR IBM VM/CMS

t-tests for independent samples of  IMAGE

GROUP 1 - IMAGE  EQ     1.00
GROUP 2 - IMAGE  EQ     2.00

Variable          Number              Standard   Standard
                  of Cases     Mean   Deviation  Error
------------------------------------------------------------
WORDS
        GROUP 1     10      19.0000    4.216      1.333
        GROUP 2     10      25.0000    4.714      1.491

                   I Pooled Variance Estimate I Separate Variance Estimate
                   I                           I
      F    2-tail  I   t    Degrees of 2-tail I   t    Degrees of 2-tail
    Value  Prob.   I Value  Freedom    Prob.  I Value  Freedom    Prob.
------------------------------------------------------------------------------
    1.25   .745    I -3.00    18       .008   I -3.00   17.78      .008
```

From page 300.

```
COMMANDS:

data list free / before after.
begin data.
9 4
4 1
5 5
4 0
5 1
end data.
t-test pairs = before, after.

PRINTOUT:

SPSS-X RELEASE 4.1 FOR IBM VM/CMS

             - - - t-tests for paired samples - - -

Variable    Number              Standard   Standard
            of Cases     Mean   Deviation  Error
------------------------------------------------------------
BEFORE
              5        5.4000    2.074      .927
              5        2.2000    2.168      .970
AFTER

(Difference) Standard   Standard  I    2-tail I   t    Degrees of 2-tail
   Mean     Deviation   Error     I Corr. Prob. I Value  Freedom    Prob.
------------------------------------------------------------------------------
  3.2000     1.924      .860      I .589  .296  I 3.72     4        .020
```

From page 366.

```
COMMANDS:

data list free / time drug.
begin data.
0 1
0 1
3 1
0 2
1 2
2 2
3 3
4 3
5 3
8 4
5 4
5 4
end data.
anova variables = time by drug(1,4) / statistics = mean.

PRINTOUT:

SPSS-X RELEASE 4.1 FOR IBM VM/CMS

                        * * * C E L L   M E A N S * * *
                TIME
            BY DRUG

TOTAL POPULATION
     3.00
  (    12)

DRUG
        1          2          3          4
      1.00       1.00       4.00       6.00
  (     3) (      3) (      3) (      3)


                * * * A N A L Y S I S   O F   V A R I A N C E * * *

                TIME
            by  DRUG
                          Sum of                Mean              Sig
Source of Variation       Squares     DF       Square      F     of F
Main Effects              54.000       3       18.000    9.000   .006
   DRUG                   54.000       3       18.000    9.000   .006
Explained                54.000       3       18.000    9.000   .006
Residual                 16.000       8        2.000
Total                    70.000      11        6.364

12 cases were processed
0 cases (.0 pct) were missing.
```

From page 439.

```
COMMANDS:

data list free / X A B.
begin data.
1  1 1
6  1 1
1  1 1
1  1 1
1  1 1
7  1 2
7  1 2
11 1 2
4  1 2
6  1 2
3  1 3
1  1 3
1  1 3
6  1 3
4  1 3
0  2 1
3  2 1
7  2 1
5  2 1
5  2 1
0  2 2
0  2 2
0  2 2
5  2 2
0  2 2
0  2 3
2  2 3
0  2 3
0  2 3
3  2 3
end data.
anova X by A(1,2) B(1,3) / stat = means.

PRINTOUT:

SPSS-X RELEASE 4.1 FOR IBM VM/CMS

                            * * *  C E L L   M E A N S  * * *

                     X
                 BY  A
                     B

TOTAL POPULATION
      3.00
   (    30)

A
        1          2
      4.00       2.00
   (    15) (     15)

B
        1          2          3
      3.00       4.00       2.00
   (    10) (     10) (     10)


          B
                     1          2          3
A
          1        2.00       7.00       3.00
                (     5) (      5) (      5)

          2        4.00       1.00       1.00
                (     5) (      5) (      5)
```

From page 439 *continued.*

```
            *** ANALYSIS OF VARIANCE ***
                 X
          by     A
                 B
                        Sum of           Mean          Sig
Source of Variation     Squares    DF    Square      F   of F
Main Effects             50.000     3    16.667   3.333  .036
      A                  30.000     1    30.000   6.000  .022
      B                  20.000     2    10.000   2.000  .157
2-Way Interactions       80.000     2    40.000   8.000  .002
      A       B          80.000     2    40.000   8.000  .002
Explained               130.000     5    26.000   5.200  .002
Residual                120.000    24     5.000
Total                   250.000    29     8.621

30 cases were processed.
0 cases (.0 pct) were missing.
```

From page 494.

```
COMMANDS:

data list free / X Y.
begin data.
7 11
4 3
6 5
3 4
5 7
end data.
plot / format = regression / plot Y with X.

PRINTOUT:

SPSS-X RELEASE 4.1 FOR IBM VM/CMS

        5 cases plotted. Regression statistics of Y on X:
Correlation .80000 R Squared .64000 S.E. of Est    2.19089 Sig.   .1041
Intercept(S.E.)   -2.00000(  3.60000)  Slope(S.E.)   1.60000(   .69282)
```

From page 530.

```
COMMANDS:

data list free / RESP SIZE.
begin data.
1 1
1 1
1 1
1 1
1 1
1 1
1 1
1 1
1 1
1 1
1 1
1 2
1 2
1 2
1 2
1 2
1 2
1 2
1 2
1 2
1 2
1 2
1 2
1 2
1 2
1 2
1 2
1 3
1 3
1 3
1 3
2 1
2 1
2 2
2 2
2 2
2 2
2 2
2 2
2 2
2 2
2 2
2 2
2 3
2 3
2 3
2 3
2 3
2 3
2 3
2 3
2 3
end data.
crosstabs tables = RESP by SIZE / cells = count expected
                / stat = chisq.
```

From page 530 *continued.*

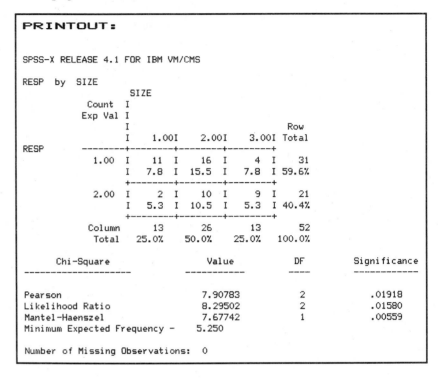

```
PRINTOUT:


SPSS-X RELEASE 4.1 FOR IBM VM/CMS

RESP  by  SIZE
                     SIZE
             Count  I
             Exp Val I
                     I                              Row
                     I    1.00I    2.00I    3.00I  Total
RESP        ---------+--------+--------+--------+
            1.00  I    11  I    16  I     4  I     31
                  I   7.8  I  15.5  I   7.8  I 59.6%
                  +--------+--------+--------+
            2.00  I     2  I    10  I     9  I     21
                  I   5.3  I  10.5  I   5.3  I 40.4%
                  +--------+--------+--------+
            Column       13       26       13       52
            Total     25.0%    50.0%    25.0%   100.0%

          Chi-Square              Value        DF      Significance
    --------------------       ----------      ----    ------------


    Pearson                     7.90783         2         .01918
    Likelihood Ratio            8.29502         2         .01580
    Mantel-Haenszel             7.67742         1         .00559
    Minimum Expected Frequency -    5.250

    Number of Missing Observations:  0
```

From page 570.

```
COMMANDS:

data list free / SCORE GROUP.
begin data.
23 2
18 2
29 2
42 2
21 2
37 1
56 1
39 1
34 1
26 1
104 1
48 1
25 1
end data.
npar tests / m-w = SCORE by GROUP(1,2).
```

From page 570 *continued*.

```
PRINTOUT:

SPSS-X RELEASE 4.1 FOR IBM VM/CMS

- - - - - Mann-Whitney U - Wilcoxon Rank Sum W Test

     SCORE
 by GROUP

   Mean Rank    Cases

      8.63         8    GROUP = 1.00
      4.40         5    GROUP = 2.00
                  --
                  13    Total

                                 Exact           Corrected for ties
           U            W       2-Tailed P       Z       2-Tailed P

          7.0         22.0        .0653        -1.9030      .0570
```

STATISTICS ORGANIZER

The following pages present an organized summary of the statistical procedures covered in this book. This organizer is divided into four sections, each of which groups together statistical techniques that serve a common purpose. You may notice that the four groups also correspond to major sections of the book. The four groups are:

I. Descriptive Statistics

II. Parametric Test for Means and Mean Differences

III. Nonparametric Tests

IV. Measures of Relationship between Two Variables

Each of the four sections begins with a general overview that discusses the purpose for the statistical techniques that follow and points out some common characteristics of the different techniques. Next, there is a decision map that leads you, step-by-step, through the task of deciding which statistical technique is appropriate for the data you wish to analyze. Finally, there is a brief description of each technique and the necessary formulas.

I DESCRIPTIVE STATISTICS

The purpose of descriptive statistics is to simplify and organize a set of scores. Scores may be organized in a table or graph, or the scores may be summarized by computing one or two values that describe the entire set. The most commonly used descriptive techniques are as follows:

A. Frequency Distribution Tables and Graphs
A frequency distribution is an organized tabulation of the number of individuals in each category on the scale of measurement. A frequency distribution can be presented either as a table or a graph. The advantage of a frequency distribution is that it presents the entire set of scores rather than condensing the scores into a single descriptive value. The disadvantage of a

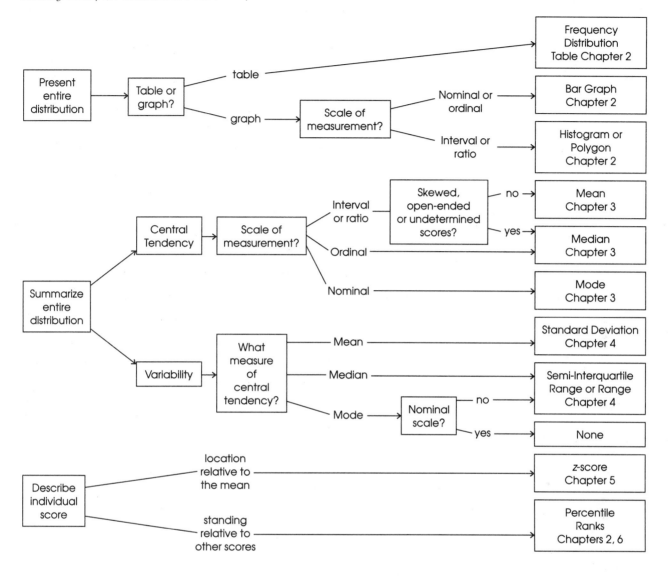

frequency distribution is that it can be somewhat complex, especially with large sets of data.

B. Measures of Central Tendency

The purpose of measuring central tendency is to identify a single score that represents an entire data set. The goal is to obtain a single value that is the best example of the average, or most typical score from the entire set.

Measures of central tendency are used to describe a single data set and they are the most commonly used measures for comparing two (or more) different sets of data.

C. Measures of Variability

Variability is used to provide a description of how spread out the scores are in a distribution. It also provides a measure of how accurately a single score selected from a distribution represents the entire set.

D. z-Scores

Most descriptive statistics are intended to provide a description of an entire set of scores. However, z-scores are used to describe individual scores within a distribution. The purpose of a z-score is to identify the precise location of an individual within a distribution by using a single number.

1. The Mean (Chapter 3) The mean is the most commonly used measure of central tendency. It is computed by finding the total (ΣX) for the set of scores, then dividing the total by the number of individuals. Conceptually, the mean is the amount each individual would receive if the total is divided equally.	Population: $\mu = \dfrac{\Sigma X}{N}$ Sample: $\bar{X} = \dfrac{\Sigma X}{n}$
2. The Median (Chapter 3) Exactly 50% of the scores in a data set have values less than or equal to the median. The median is the 50th percentile. The median usually is computed for data sets where the mean cannot be found (undetermined-scores, open-ended distribution) or in situations where the mean does not provide a good, representative value (ordinal scale, skewed distribution).	List the scores in order from smallest to largest. a. With an odd number of scores the median is the middle score. b. With an even number of scores the median is the average of the middle two scores. c. With several scores tied at the median, use interpolation to find the 50th percentile.
3. The Mode (Chapter 3) The mode is the score with the greatest frequency. The mode is used when the scores consist of measurements on a nominal scale.	No calculation. Simply count the frequency of occurrance for each different score.
4. The Range (Chapter 4) The range is the distance from the lowest to the highest score in a data set. The range is considered to be a relatively crude measure of variability.	Find the upper real limit for the largest score and the lower real limit for the smallest score. The range is the difference between these two real limits.
5. The Semi-Interquartile Range (Chapter 4) The semi-interquartile range is one-half of the range covered by the middle 50% of the distribution. The semi-interquartile range is often used to measure variability in situations where the median is used to report central tendency.	Find the first quartile (25th percentile) and the third quartile (75th percentile). The semi-interquartile range is one-half of the distance between the two quartiles.

6. **Standard Deviation** (Chapter 4) The standard deviation is a measure of the standard distance from the mean. Standard deviation is obtained by first computing SS (the sum of squared deviations) and variance (the mean squared deviation). Standard deviation is the square root of variance.	**Sum of Squares**	Definitional: $SS = \Sigma(X - \mu)^2$ Computational: $SS = \Sigma X^2 - \dfrac{(\Sigma X)^2}{N}$
	Variance	Population: $\sigma^2 = \dfrac{SS}{N}$ Sample: $s^2 = \dfrac{SS}{n-1}$
	Standard Deviation	Population: $\sigma = \sqrt{\dfrac{SS}{N}}$ Sample: $s = \sqrt{\dfrac{SS}{n-1}}$
7. **z-scores** (Chapter 5) The sign of a z-score indicates whether an individual is above (+) or below (−) the mean. The numerical value of the z-score indicates how many standard deviations there are between the score and the mean.		$z = \dfrac{X - \mu}{\sigma}$

II PARAMETRIC TESTS: INFERENCES ABOUT POPULATION MEANS OR MEAN DIFFERENCES

All of the hypothesis tests covered in this section use the means obtained from sample data as the basis for testing hypothesis about population means. Although there are a variety of tests, used in a variety of research situations, all use the same basic logic and all of the test statistics have the same basic structure. In each case, the test statistic (z, t, or F) involves computing a ratio with the following structure:

$$\text{test statistic} = \frac{\text{obtained difference between sample means}}{\text{mean difference expected by chance}}$$

The goal of each test is to determine whether the observed sample mean differences are larger than expected by chance. In general terms, a *significant result* means that the results obtained in a research study (sample differences) are more than would be expected by chance. In each case, a large value for the test statistic ratio indicates a significant result; that is, when the actual difference between sample means (numerator) is substantially larger than chance (denominator), you will obtain a large ratio which indicates that the sample difference is significant.

The actual calculations differ slightly from one test statistic to the next, but all involve the same basic computations.

1. A set of scores (sample) is obtained for each population or each treatment condition.

2. The mean is computed for each set of scores and some measure of variability (SS, standard deviation, or variance) is obtained for each individual set of scores.

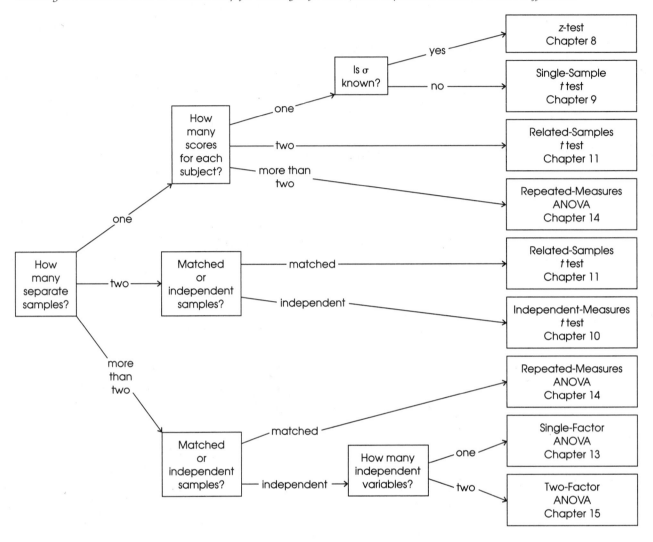

3. The differences between the sample means provide a measure of how much difference exists between treatment conditions. Because these mean differences may be caused by the treatment conditions, they are often called *systematic* or *predicted*. These differences are the numerator of the test statistic.

4. The variability within each set of scores provides a measure of unsystematic or unpredicted differences due to chance. Because the individuals within each treatment condition are treated exactly the same, there is nothing that should cause their scores to be different. Thus, any observed differences (variability) within treatments are assumed to be due to error or chance.

With these considerations in mind, each of the test statistic ratios can be described as follows:

$$\text{test statistic} = \frac{\text{differences (variability) between treatments}}{\text{differences (variability) within treatments}}$$

The hypothesis tests reviewed in this section apply to three basic research designs:

1. Single-Sample Designs. Data from a single sample are used to test a hypothesis about a single population.

2. Independent-Measures Designs. A separate sample is obtained to represent each individual population or treatment condition.

3. Related-Samples Designs. Related-sample designs include repeated-measures and matched-subjects designs. For a repeated-measures design, there is only one sample with each individual subject being measured in all of the different treatment conditions. In a matched-subjects design, every individual in one sample is matched with a subject in each of the other samples.

Finally, you should be aware that all parametric tests place stringent restrictions on the sample data and the population distributions being considered. First, these tests all require measurements on an interval or a ratio scale (numerical values that allow you to compute means and differences). Second, each test makes assumptions about population distributions and sampling techniques. Consult the appropriate section of this book to verify that the specific assumptions are satisfied before proceeding with any parametric test.

1. The z-score test (Chapter 8) The z-score test uses the data from a single sample to test a hypothesis about the population mean in situations where the population standard deviation (σ) is known. The null hypothesis states a specific value for the unknown population mean.	$z = \dfrac{\overline{X} - \mu}{\sigma_{\overline{X}}}$ where $\sigma_{\overline{X}} = \dfrac{\sigma}{\sqrt{n}}$
2. The single-sample t test (Chapter 9) This test uses the data from a single sample to test a hypothesis about a population mean in situations where the population standard deviation is unknown. The sample variability is used to estimate the unknown population standard deviation. The null hypothesis states a specific value for the unknown population mean.	$t = \dfrac{\overline{X} - \mu}{s_{\overline{X}}}$ where $s_{\overline{X}} = \dfrac{s}{\sqrt{n}}$ $df = n - 1$
3. The independent-measures t test (Chapter 10) The independent-measures t test uses data from two separate samples to test a hypothesis about the difference between two population means. The variability within the two samples is combined to obtain a single (pooled) estimate of population variance. The null hypothesis states that there is no difference between the two population means.	$t = \dfrac{(\overline{X}_1 - \overline{X}_2) - (\mu_1 - \mu_2)}{s_{\overline{X}-\overline{X}}}$ where $s_{\overline{X}-\overline{X}} = \sqrt{\dfrac{s_p^2}{n_1} + \dfrac{s_p^2}{n_2}}$ and $s_p^2 = \dfrac{SS_1 + SS_2}{df_1 + df_2}$ $df = df_1 + df_2 = (n_1 - 1) + (n_2 - 1)$

ORGANIZER

4. The related-samples *t* test (Chapter 11)
This test evaluates the mean difference between two treatment conditions using the data from a repeated-measures or a matched-subjects experiment. A difference score (D) is obtained for each subject (or each matched pair) by subtracting the score in treatment 1 from the score in treatment 2. The variability of the sample difference scores is used to estimate the population variability. The null hypothesis states that the population mean difference (μ_D) is zero.

$$t = \frac{\overline{D} - \mu_D}{s_{\overline{D}}} \qquad \text{where } s_{\overline{D}} = \frac{s}{\sqrt{n}}$$

$$df = n - 1$$

5. Single-factor, independent-measures analysis of variance (Chapter 13)
This test uses data from two or more separate samples to test for mean differences among two or more populations. The null hypothesis states that there are no differences among the population means. The test statistic is an F-ratio that uses the variability between treatment conditions (sample mean differences) in the numerator and variability within treatment conditions (error variability) as the denominator. With only two samples, this test is equivalent to the independent-measures t test.

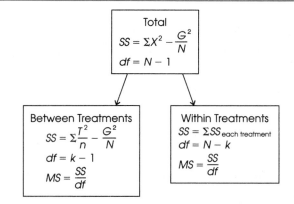

Total
$$SS = \Sigma X^2 - \frac{G^2}{N}$$
$$df = N - 1$$

Between Treatments
$$SS = \Sigma \frac{T^2}{n} - \frac{G^2}{N}$$
$$df = k - 1$$
$$MS = \frac{SS}{df}$$

Within Treatments
$$SS = \Sigma SS_{\text{each treatment}}$$
$$df = N - k$$
$$MS = \frac{SS}{df}$$

$$F\text{-ratio} = \frac{MS_{\text{between treatments}}}{MS_{\text{within treatments}}}$$

6. Single-factor, repeated-measures analysis of variance (Chapter 14)
This test is used to evaluate mean differences among two or more treatment conditions using sample data from a repeated-measures (or matched-subjects) experiment. The null hypothesis states that there are no differences among the population means. The test statistic is an F-ratio using variability between treatment conditions (mean differences) in the numerator exactly like the independent-measures ANOVA. The denominator of the F-ratio (error term) is obtained by measuring variability within treatments and then subtracting out the variability between subjects. The research design and the test statistic remove variability due to individual differences and thereby provide a more sensitive test for treatment differences than is possible with an independent-measures design.

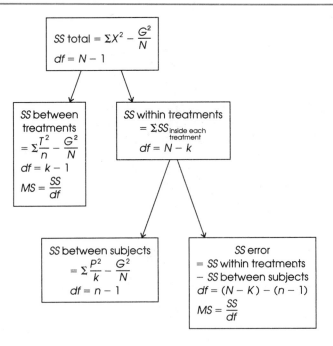

$$SS \text{ total} = \Sigma X^2 - \frac{G^2}{N}$$
$$df = N - 1$$

SS between treatments
$$= \Sigma \frac{T^2}{n} - \frac{G^2}{N}$$
$$df = k - 1$$
$$MS = \frac{SS}{df}$$

SS within treatments
$$= \Sigma SS_{\text{inside each treatment}}$$
$$df = N - k$$

SS between subjects
$$= \Sigma \frac{P^2}{k} - \frac{G^2}{N}$$
$$df = n - 1$$

SS error
$$= SS \text{ within treatments}$$
$$- SS \text{ between subjects}$$
$$df = (N - K) - (n - 1)$$
$$MS = \frac{SS}{df}$$

$$F = \frac{MS_{\text{between treatments}}}{MS_{\text{error}}}$$

7. Two-factor, independent-measures analysis of variance (Chapter 15)

This test is used to evaluate mean differences among populations or treatment conditions using sample data from research designs with two independent variables (factors). The two-factor ANOVA tests three separate hypotheses: mean differences among the levels of factor A (main effect for factor A), mean differences among the levels of factor B (main effect for factor B), and mean differences resulting from specific combinations of the two factors (interaction). The three separate null hypotheses each state that there are no population mean differences. Each of the three tests uses an *F*-ratio as the test statistic with the variability between samples (sample mean differences) in the numerator and the variability within samples (error variability) in the denominator.

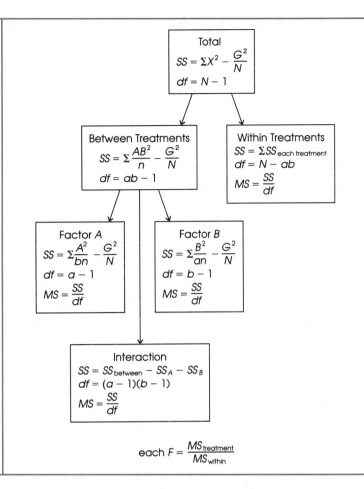

III NONPARAMETRIC TESTS: INFERENCES ABOUT POPULATIONS OR POPULATION DIFFERENCES

Although the parametric tests described in the previous section are the most commonly used inferential techniques, there are many research situations where parametric tests cannot or should not be used. These situations fall into two general categories:

1. The data involve measurements on nominal or ordinal scales. In these situations you cannot compute the means and variances that are an essential part of parametric tests.

2. The data do not satisfy the assumptions underlying parametric tests.

When a parametric test cannot be used there is usually a nonparametric alternative available. In general, parametric tests are more powerful than their nonparametric counterparts and they are preferred over the nonparametric alternatives. However, when a parametric test is not appropriate, the nonparametric tests provide researchers with a backup statistical technique for conducting an analysis and statistical interpretation of research results.

ORGANIZER

Choosing a Nonparametric Test: A Decision Map for Making Inferences about Populations or Population Differences

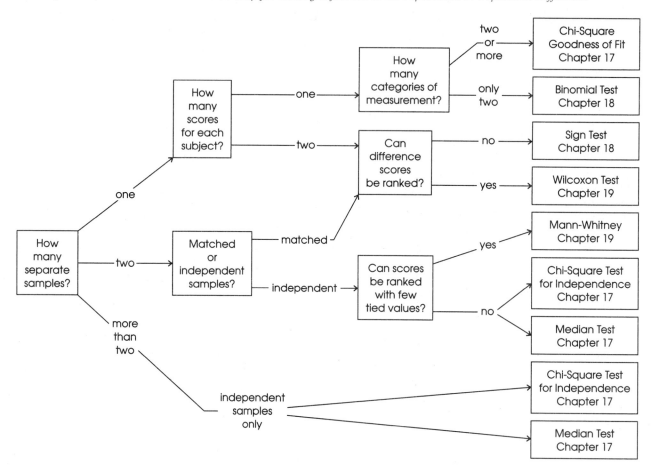

1. **The chi-square test for goodness of fit** (Chapter 17) This chi-square test is used in situations where the measurement procedure results in classifying individuals into distinct categories. The test uses frequency data from a single sample to test a hypothesis about the population distribution. The null hypothesis specifies the proportion or percentage of the population for each category on the scale of measurement.	$$\chi^2 = \Sigma \frac{(f_o - f_e)^2}{f_e}$$ where $f_e = pn$ $df = C - 1$
2. **The binomial test** (Chapter 18) When the individuals in a population can be classified into exactly two categories, the binomial test uses sample data to test a hypothesis about the proportion of the population in each category. The null hypothesis specifies the proportion of the population in each of the two categories.	$$z = \frac{X - pn}{\sqrt{npq}} \quad \text{or} \quad z = \frac{X/n - p}{\sqrt{\dfrac{pq}{n}}}$$

3. The chi-square test for independence
(Chapter 17)

This test serves as an alternative to the independent-measures t test (or ANOVA) in situations where the dependent variable involves classifying individuals into distinct categories. The sample data consist of frequency distributions (proportions across categories) for two or more separate samples. The null hypothesis states that the separate populations all have the same proportions (same shape). That is, the proportions across categories are independent of the different populations.

$$\chi^2 = \Sigma \frac{(f_o - f_e)^2}{f_e}$$

$$\text{where } f_e = \frac{(\text{row total})(\text{column total})}{n}$$

$$df = (R - 1)(C - 1)$$

4. The median test (Chapter 17)

The median test is a special application of the chi-square test for independence. This test is used to determine whether two or more populations share a common median. The test uses data from two or more separate samples and requires that each individual be classified as being above or below the median. The null hypothesis states that all of the separate populations share a common median.

Use the chi-square formula and df from the chi-square test for independence.

5. The Mann-Whitney U test (Chapter 19)

This test uses ordinal data (rank orders) from two separate samples to test a hypothesis about the difference between two populations or two treatment conditions. The Mann-Whitney test is used as an alternative to the independent-measures t test in situations where the data can be rank ordered but do not satisfy the more stringent requirements of the t test.

$$U_A = n_A n_B + \frac{n_A(n_A + 1)}{2} - \Sigma R_A$$

$$U_B = n_A n_B + \frac{n_B(n_B + 1)}{2} - \Sigma R_B$$

6. The Wilcoxon T test (Chapter 19)

The Wilcoxon test uses the data from a repeated-measures or matched-samples design to evaluate the difference between two treatment conditions. This test is used as an alternative to the related-samples t test in situations where the sample data (difference scores) can be rank ordered but do not satisfy the more stringent requirements of the t test.

Rank order the difference scores ignoring the signs (+ or −). Then compute the sum of the ranks for the positive differences and the negative differences. The Wilcoxon T is the smaller sum.

7. The sign test (Chapter 18)

This test evaluates the difference between two treatment conditions using data from a repeated-measures or matched-subjects research design. The null hypothesis states that there is no difference between the two treatment conditions.

The sign test is a special application of the binomial test and only requires that the difference between treatment 1 and treatment 2 for each subject be classified as an increase or a decrease. This test is used as an alternative to the related-samples t test or the Wilcoxon test in situations where the data do not satisfy the more stringent requirements of these two more powerful tests.

Count the number of positive differences (X) in the total sample (n). Then use the binomial test with $p = q = 1/2$.

IV MEASURES OF RELATIONSHIP BETWEEN TWO VARIABLES

As we noted in Chapter 1, a major purpose for scientific research is to investigate and establish orderly relationships between variables. The statistical techniques covered in this section all serve the purpose of measuring and describing relations. The data for these statistics involve two observations for each individual—one observation for each of the two variables being examined. The goal is to determine whether or not a consistent, predictable relationship exists and to describe the nature of the relationship.

Each of the different statistical methods described in this section is intended to be used with a specific type of data. To determine which method is appropriate, you must first examine your data and identify what type of variable is involved and what scale of measurement was used for recording the observations.

Choosing a Measure of Relationship Between Two Variables: A Decision Map

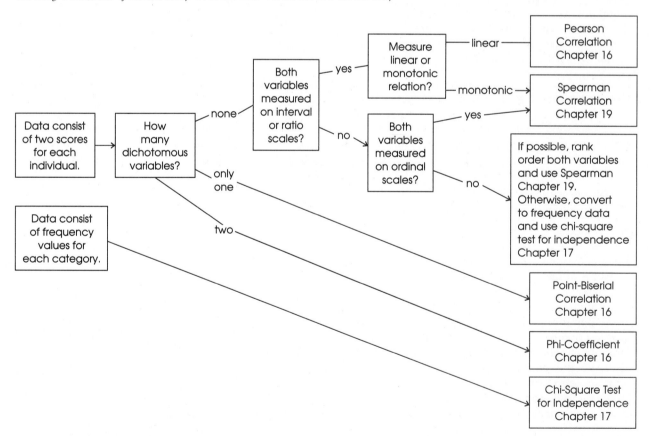

1. **Pearson Correlation** (Chapter 16)
   The Pearson correlation measures the degree of linear relation between two variables. The sign (+ or −) of the correlation indicates the direction of the relationship. The magnitude of the correlation (from 0 to 1) indicates the degree to which the data points fit on a straight line.

$$r = \frac{SP}{\sqrt{SS_X SS_Y}}$$

where $SP = \Sigma(X - \bar{X})(Y - \bar{Y}) = \Sigma XY - \frac{(\Sigma X)(\Sigma Y)}{n}$

2. **Linear Regression and Standard Error of Estimate** (Chapter 16)
   The purpose of linear regression is to find the equation for the best fitting straight line for predicting Y scores from X scores. The regression process determines the linear equation with the least squared error between the actual Y values and the predicted Y values on the line. The standard error of estimate provides a measure of the standard distance (or error) between the actual Y values and the predicted Y values.

$$\hat{Y} = bX + a \qquad \text{where } b = \frac{SP}{SS_X} \text{ and } a = \bar{Y} - b\bar{X}$$

$$\text{Standard error of estimate} = \sqrt{\frac{\Sigma(Y - \hat{Y})^2}{n - 2}} = \sqrt{\frac{(1 - r^2)SS_Y}{n - 2}}$$

3. **Spearman Correlation** (Chapter 19)
   The Spearman correlation measures the degree to which the relationship between two variables is one-directional or monotonic. The Spearman correlation is used when both variables, X and Y, are ranks (measured on an ordinal scale).

Use the Pearson formula on the ranked data or the special Spearman formula:

$$r_s = 1 - \frac{6\Sigma D^2}{n(n^2 - 1)}$$

4. **Point-Biserial Correlation** (Chapter 16)
   The point-biserial correlation is a special application of the Pearson correlation that is used when one variable is dichotomous (only two values) and the second variable is measured on an interval or ratio scale. The value of the correlation measures the strength of the relation between the two variables. The point-biserial correlation often is used as an alternative or a supplement to the independent-measures t hypothesis test.

Convert the two categories of the dichotomous variable to numerical values 0 and 1, then use the Pearson formula with the converted data.

5. **Phi-Coefficient** (Chapter 16)
   The phi-coefficient is a special application of the Pearson correlation that is used when both variables, X and Y, are dichotomous (only two values). The value of the correlation measures the strength of the relationship between the two variables. The phi-coefficient is often used as an alternative or a supplement to the chi-square test for independence.

For each variable, convert the two categories to numerical values 0 and 1, then use the Pearson formula with the converted data.

6. Chi-Square Test for Independence
(Chapter 17)

This test uses frequency data to determine whether or not there is a significant relationship between two variables. The null hypothesis states that the two variables are independent. The chi-square test for independence is used when the scale of measurement consists of relatively few categories for both variables, and can be used with nominal, ordinal, interval, or ratio scales.

$$\chi^2 = \Sigma \frac{(f_o - f_e)^2}{f_e}$$

$$\text{where } f_e = \frac{(\text{row total})(\text{column total})}{n}$$

$$df = (R - 1)(C - 1)$$

REFERENCES

Betz, B. J., and Thomas, C. B. (1979). Individual temperament as a predictor of health or premature disease. *The Johns Hopkins Medical Journal, 144,* 81–89.

Blest, A. D. (1957). The functions of eyespot patterns in the Lepidoptera. *Behaviour, 11,* 209–255.

Boker, J. R. (1974). Immediate and delayed retention effects of interspersing questions in written instructional passages. *Journal of Educational Psychology, 66,* 96–98.

Boyer, R., and Savageau, D. (eds.) (1989). *Places rated almanac.* Chicago: Rand McNally.

Bransford, J. D., and Johnson, M. K. (1972). Contextual prerequisites for understanding: Some investigations of comprehension and recall. *Journal of Verbal Learning and Verbal Behavior, 11,* 717–726.

Cook, M. (1977). Gaze and mutual gaze in social encounters. *American Scientist, 65,* 328–333.

Cowles, M., and Davis, C. (1982). On the origins of the .05 level of statistical significance. *American Psychologist, 37,* 553–558.

Craik, F. I. M., and Lockhart, R. S. (1972). Levels of processing: A framework for memory research. *Journal of Verbal Learning and Verbal Behavior, 11,* 671–684.

Darley, J. M., and Latané, B. (1968). Bystander intervention in emergencies: Diffusion of responsibility. *Journal of Personality and Social Psychology, 8,* 377–383.

Festinger, L., and Carlsmith, J. M. (1959). Cognitive consequences of forced compliance. *Journal of Abnormal and Social Psychology, 58,* 203–210.

Gibson, E. J., and Walk, R. D. (1960). The "visual cliff." *Scientific American, 202,* 64–71.

Gintzler, A. R. (1980). Endorphin-mediated increases in pain threshold during pregnancy. *Science, 210,* 193–195.

Hays, W. L. (1981). *Statistics* (3d ed.). New York: Holt, Rinehart and Winston.

Horn, J. L. (1978). The nature and development of intellectual abilities. In R. T. Osborne, C. E. Noble, & N. Weyl (eds.), *Human variation.* New York: Academic Press.

Katona, G. (1940). *Organizing and memorizing.* New York: Columbia University Press.

Keppel, G. (1973). *Design and analysis. A researcher's handbook.* Englewood Cliffs, N.J.: Prentice-Hall.

Levine, S. (1960). Stimulation in infancy. *Scientific American, 202,* 80–86.

McClelland, D. C. (1961). *The achieving society.* Princeton, N.J.: Van Nostrand.

Miller, N. E., and Dworkin, B. R. (1974). Visceral learning: Recent difficulties with curarized rats and significant problems for human research. In P. A. Obrist, A. H. Black, J. Brener, and L. V. DiCara (eds.), *Cardiovascular psychophysiology: Current issues in response mechanisms, biofeedback and methodology* (pp. 312–331). Chicago: Aldine.

Rogers, T. B., Kuiper, N. A., and Kirker, W. S. (1977). Self-reference and the encoding of personal information. *Journal of Personality and Social Psychology, 35,* 677–688.

Rosenthal, R. (1963). On the social psychology of the psychological experiment: The experimenter's hypothesis as unintended determinant of experimental results. *American Scientist, 51,* 268–283.

Rosenthal, R., and Fode, K. L. (1963). The effect of experimenter bias on the performance of the albino rat. *Behavioral Science, 8,* 183–189.

Sachs, J. (1967). Recognition memory for syntactic and semantic aspects of a connected discourse. *Perception and Psychophysics, 2,* 437–442.

Scaife, M. (1976). The response to eye-like shapes by birds. I. The effect of context: A predator and a strange bird. *Animal Behaviour, 24,* 195–199.

Schachter, S. (1968). Obesity and eating. *Science, 161,* 751–756.

Shrauger, J. S. (1972). Self-esteem and reactions to being observed by others. *Journal of Personality and Social Psychology, 23,* 192–200.

Snyder, S. H. (1977). Opiate receptors and internal opiates. *Scientific American, 236,* 44–56.

Tyron, R. C. (1940). Genetic differences in maze-learning ability in rats. *Yearbook of the National Society for the Study of Education, 39,* 111–119.

Tukey, J. W. (1977). *Exploratory data analysis.* Reading, Mass.: Addison-Wesley.

Tulving, E., and Osler, S. (1968). Effectiveness of retrieval cues in memory for words. *Journal of Experimental Psychology, 77,* 593–601.

Tversky, A., and Kahneman, D. (1973). Availability: A heuristic for judging frequency and probability. *Cognitive Psychology, 5,* 207–232.

Tversky, A., and Kahneman, D. (1974). Judgment under uncertainty: Heuristics and biases. *Science, 185,* 1124–1131.

Zigler, M. J. (1932). Pressure adaptation time: A function of intensity and extensity, *American Journal of Psychology, 44,* 709–720.

INDEX